THE CHANGING CONSTITUTION

Seventh Edition

EDITED BY

JEFFREY JOWELL

AND

DAWN OLIVER

OXFORD
UNIVERSITY PRESS

OXFORD
UNIVERSITY PRESS

Great Clarendon Street, Oxford OX2 6DP

Oxford University Press is a department of the University of Oxford.
It furthers the University's objective of excellence in research, scholarship,
and education by publishing worldwide in

Oxford New York

Auckland Cape Town Dar es Salaam Hong Kong Karachi
Kuala Lumpur Madrid Melbourne Mexico City Nairobi
New Delhi Shanghai Taipei Toronto

With offices in

Argentina Austria Brazil Chile Czech Republic France Greece
Guatemala Hungary Italy Japan Poland Portugal Singapore
South Korea Switzerland Thailand Turkey Ukraine Vietnam

Oxford is a registered trade mark of Oxford University Press
in the UK and in certain other countries

Published in the United States
by Oxford University Press Inc., New York

Fourth edition 2000
Fifth edition 2004
Sixth edition 2007

British Library Cataloguing in Publication Data
Data available

Library of Congress Cataloging in Publication Data
The changing constitution/edited by Jeffrey Jowell, Dawn Oliver.—7th ed.
p. cm.
Includes bibliographical references and index.
ISBN 978-0-19-957905-1 (pbk.)
1. Constitutional law—Great Britain. I. Jowell, Jeffrey. II. Oliver, Dawn.
KD3989.C52 2011
342.4102—dc23 2011023426

Typeset by Newgen Imaging Systems (P) Ltd, Chennai, India
Printed in Great Britain
on acid-free paper by
Ashford Colour Press Ltd, Gosport, Hampshire

ISBN 978-0-19-957905-1

1 3 5 7 9 10 8 6 4 2

PREFACE TO THE SEVENTH EDITION

In our introductory chapter in this edition, we reflect on the 25 years of constitutional change since this volume first appeared in 1985, and we venture the thought that the pace of change seems to be ever quickening. Empirical evidence for that proposition can be found in the ever-increasing changes in consecutive editions of this volume. This edition is no exception. All 13 of the authors who contributed to the previous edition have revised and updated their chapters to a much greater extent than has been necessary in any of the previous editions.

NEW TO THIS EDITION

Apart from our introductory chapter, three others are entirely new: Brigid Hadfield, who wrote the chapter on devolution to Wales and the implications of devolution for England in the previous edition, has written a single general chapter reflecting on devolution in the UK and the processes and mechanisms that have evolved to accommodate the pressures to which it gives rise. Richard Macrory's chapter draws on developments in environmental law and regulation to provide a case study of the connections between purely 'domestic' law, at the central, regional and local levels, and European and international law, and of the ways in which developments in environmental law and policy reflect the evolving constitutional settlement in the UK. Patrick Birkinshaw deals with the workings of the law on access to government information, considering the ways in which individuals are protected against abuse of personal information about them, and makes proposals for further reform.

We are grateful to all the authors for their considerable efforts and to Tom Young at Oxford University Press for his encouragement and assistance.

Jeffrey Jowell
Dawn Oliver
January 2011

Public Law Online Resources from Oxford

Visit **www.oxfordtextbooks.co.uk/orc/publiclaw/** for access to a wealth of resources that accompany this book and have been designed to support your study of public law. These resources will help you to keep up-to-date with what is happening in the law and politics, as well as introducing you to key debates and providing a host of links to further material to help you direct your online study.

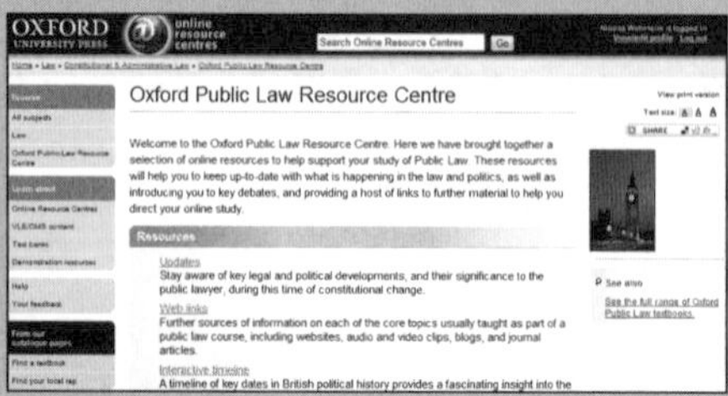

The following resources are all available on the site free of charge:

- **Regular updates** ensure that you are aware of key legal and political developments, and their significance to the public lawyer, during this time of constitutional change
- An extensive **'library' of web links** is an invaluable resource that directs you immediately to further sources of information on each of the core topics usually taught as part of a public law course, including websites, audio and video clips, blogs, and journal articles
- A **timeline of key dates** in British political history provides a fascinating insight into the events that have influenced the development of constitutional and administrative law in the UK
- **'Oxford NewsNow'** RSS feeds provide constantly refreshed links to the latest relevant news stories
- **Audio podcasts** from expert Oxford authors discuss some key issues in public law and introduce you to their textbooks

 **www.oxfordtextbooks.co.uk/orc/publiclaw/**

Scan this QR code image with your mobile device to instantly access this site.

QR Code is registered trademark of DENSO WAVE INCORPORATED

CONTENTS

TABLE OF CASES

TABLE OF LEGISLATION

UK AND SCOTTISH ACTS

EUROPEAN LEGISLATION

DIRECTIVES

FOREIGN LEGISLATION

AUSTRALIA

FRANCE

LIST OF ABBREVIATIONS

ACE	Agency Chief Executive
ACoBA	Advisory Committee on Business Appointments
ADR	Alternative Dispute Resolution
AJTC	Administrative Justice and Tribunals Council
C & AG	Comptroller and Auditor General
CA	Court of Appeal
CFI	Court of First Instance
CJEC	Court of Justice of the European Communities
CO	Compliance Officer
CPR	Civil Procedure Rules
CSPL	Committee on Standards in Public Life
CSR	Comprehensive Spending Review
DCA	Department for Constitutional Affairs
DPA 1998	Data Protection Act 1998
EC	European Community
ECA	European Communities Act
ECHR	European Convention on Human Rights
ECJ	European Court of Justice
ECSC	European Coal and Steel Community
ECtHR	European Court of Human Rights
EDC	European Defence Community
EEC	European Economic Community
EHRC	Equality and Human Rights Committee
EIR 2004	Environmental Information Regulations 2004
EOC	Equal Opportunities Commission
EP	European Parliament
EPC	European Political Community
EU	European Union
FOI	Freedom of Information
FOI 2000	Freedom of Information Act 2000
FSA	Financial Services Authority
GC	General Court
GCHQ	Government Communications Headquarters

GDP	Gross Domestic Product
GFAP	General Framework Agreement for Peace
GRECO	Council of Europe's Group of States against Corruption
HL	House of Lords
HoLAC	House of Lords Appointments Commission
HRA 1998	Human Rights Act 1998
IMF	International Monetary Fund
IPSA	Independent Parliamentary Standards Authority
IT	Information Technology
JCHR	Joint Select Committee on Human Rights
JCPC	Judicial Committee of the Privy Council
LCO	Legislative Competence Order
MP	Member of Parliament
MEP	Member of the European Parliament
MSP	Member of the Scottish Parliament
NAO	National Audit Office
NATO	North Atlantic Treaty Organization
NCND	Neither Confirm Nor Deny provision
NHS	National Health Service
NIHRC	Northern Ireland Human Rights Commission
NPM	New Public Management
OECD	Organisation for Economic Co-operation and Development
Ofcom	Office of Communications
Offer	Office of Electricity Regulation
Ofgas	Office of Gas Supply
Ofgem	Office of Gas and Electricity Markets
Ofsted	Office for Standards in Education, Children's Services and Skills
Oftel	Office of Telecommunications
Ofwat	Office of Water Services
OPSI	Office of Public Sector Information
ORR	Office of the Rail Regulator
PAC	Public Accounts Committee
PASC	Public Administration Select Committee
PCO	Protective Costs Order
PCS	Parliamentary Commissioner for Standards
PDR	Proportionate Dispute Resolution
PES	Public Expenditure Survey

PFI	Private Finance Initiative
Postcomm	Postal Services Commission
PPP	Public Private Partnership
PSA 2009	Parliamentary Standards Act 2009
RDA	Regional Development Agency
SADC	South African Development Community
SNP	Scottish National Party
SSRB	Senior Salaries Review Body
TME	Total Managed Expenditure
UNECE	United Nations Economic Commission for Europe
VFM	Value for Money

LIST OF CONTRIBUTORS

JEFFREY JOWELL, QC Director of the Bingham Centre for the Rule of Law and Emeritus Professor of Public Law, University College London

DAWN OLIVER, FBA Emeritus Professor of Constitutional Law, University College London

PATRICK BIRKINSHAW Professor of Public Law and Director Institute of European Public Law, University of Hull

ANTHONY BRADLEY Emeritus Professor of Constitutional Law, Edinburgh University; Research Fellow, Institute of European and Comparative Law, Oxford University

PAUL CRAIG, QC, FBA Professor of English Law, St John's College, Oxford

GAVIN DREWRY Emeritus Professor of Public Administration, University of London

DAVID FELDMAN, QC, FBA Rouse Ball Professor of English Law in the University of Cambridge, and Fellow of Downing College, Cambridge

BRIGID HADFIELD Professor of Constitutional Law, University of Essex

IAN LEIGH Professor of Law, University of Durham

PATRICIA LEOPOLD Emeritus Professor of Law, Reading University

LORD LESTER OF HERNE HILL, QC Honorary Professor of Public Law at University College London, Member of the Joint Parliamentary Committee on Human Rights

ANDREW LE SUEUR Professor of Public Law, Queen Mary, University of London

JOHN MCELDOWNEY Professor of Law, University of Warwick

RICHARD MACRORY, QC Professor of Environmental Law, University College London

TONY PROSSER Professor of Public Law, University of Bristol and Visiting Professor, the College of Europe, Bruges

EDITORS' INTRODUCTION

TWENTY-FIVE YEARS OF CONSTITUTIONAL CHANGE: RENEWAL BUT NOT PERFECTION

It is now 25 years since the first edition of this book appeared, 100 years after the publication of Dicey's *Law of the Constitution*. In our 1985 preface we noted how much the constitution had changed since Dicey's time, yet still felt it necessary to begin with his account of the constitution, 'since Dicey's word has in some respects become the only written constitution we have'.

We noted too that, in 1985, most courses in constitutional law devoted much time to areas 'that have only marginal relevance to the most pressing problems of the modern constitution'. We believed that an exploration of the tenets of our constitution required the joint efforts of the disciplines of law and politics, in the light 'not of what Dicey said, nor of what the courts might have said about what Dicey said, but of current governmental practice, where the true effect of constitutional theory can be observed'.

In that spirit we brought together chapters on traditional areas of constitutional law and practice, together with areas then not much considered, such as the role of political parties and techniques of accountability in respect of public expenditure. The last part of the book dealt with issues which we then thought ripe for reform, such as the electoral system, devolution to the nations and regions, freedom of information, a bill of rights and other matters put forward in Lester's 1985 chapter, most of which have since been reformed and thus incorporated in later chapters into the main corpus of the book.

The pace of constitutional change seems to be quickening, particularly since the reform programme of the first New Labour Government of 1997–2010. Hence this volume now includes chapters on the role of international law in domestic law to take account, as Feldman describes, of the increasing articulation of fundamental universal standards. Within Europe, as Craig shows, the principles of our association with the European Union have taken precedence over domestic law. Macrory's chapter – new to this edition – provides a case study of the interactions in our constitutional arrangements that need to be considered as a whole. He shows how the area of the environment is regulated partly by the European Union, partly by national law and administrative arrangements, partly by the devolved bodies in Scotland, Wales, and

Northern Ireland. Devolution is described more fully in Hadfield's chapter – new to this edition – and local authorities are addressed in Leigh's chapter.

Other fundamental changes since the first edition include the passing of the Human Rights Act 1998 incorporating provisions of the European Convention on Human Rights (ECHR) into domestic law (Lester's chapter); the separation of the top court (now the Supreme Court) from the House of Lords; and the ending of the powers of the Lord Chancellor to combine the roles of judge, politician, and appointer of judges (Le Sueur's chapter). Government secrecy has been reduced by means of a qualified right to receive information from official sources (discussed in a new chapter in this edition by Birkinshaw). Privatization has resulted in the regulation of formerly nationalized enterprises (Prosser's chapter); greater attention has been given to the attainment of standards of probity in public life (Leopold's chapter) and, recently, to strengthening the role of Members of Parliament in relation to the executive (McEldowney's and Oliver's chapters).

The impetus for constitutional change emanates not only from sources within the UK. There has been a net increase in 'constitutionalism' all over the world following the collapse of the Soviet Union and other (although by no means all) totalitarian regimes. Within Europe, there has been a significant convergence of constitutional standards which should not be underestimated. All 48 countries in the Council of Europe now engage with the ECHR as interpreted by the European Court of Human Rights in Strasbourg. Looking at the case law of the first year of our new Supreme Court we see intense analysis of the Strasbourg jurisprudence, and frequent reference to the interpretations of rights provisions by the courts of other countries, both in Europe and elsewhere. A comparative conversation is taking place between many liberal democracies, their courts and their politicians, about the minimum requirements of any democracy. The Council of Europe's Venice Commission collates experience across the continent and publishes documents setting common standards which have influenced practice not only in the new democracies but even in the oldest. A similar process is taking place in respect of the jurisprudence of the European Court of Justice.

DO WE REALLY HAVE A CONSTITUTION?

Even today, it is often said that the UK has no constitution beyond what Dicey allowed. That is wrong. Our constitutional foundations are deeply rooted and well-established, although it is right to say that they are not set out in any single document.[1] It is of course also not accurate to say that the British constitution is unwritten. It is not

[1] 'It has so often been said that Britain has no written constitution that we are in danger of believing it. Britain has an extremely elaborate constitution, almost all of which is written'. Jonathan Sumption, OBE, QC, 'The Constitutional Reform Act 2005', in *Judicial Appointments: Balancing Independence, Accountability and Legitimacy* (2010).

codified – with all the rules and principles set out in one document – but a great deal of its content is based on written sources, including many statutes and decided cases expressing the underlying values of our democratic arrangements, and in 'soft law' documents such as the newly drafted Cabinet Manual of 2011, resolutions on ministerial responsibility passed by each House of Parliament in 1996, and many others. Constitutional conventions, not necessarily written down in official documents, also form important parts of the system of government. The British constitution is therefore a patchwork constitution, but a constitution nonetheless.

Some authors believe that the British constitution is purely political, in the sense of reflecting only 'what happens', which is a result of the balance of political power at a particular time.[2] Others such as Vernon Bogdanor believe that our constitution is ultimately based on just one rule which can be summed up in eight words: '*What the Queen in Parliament enacts is law*'.[3] Bogdanor asserts that our constitution has recently undergone fundamental change but until the present century 'the fundamental, perhaps the only principle at the basis of our system of government, has been the sovereignty of Parliament...the idea that Parliament can legislate as it chooses and there can be no superior authority to Parliament.'[4]

For Bogdanor, parliamentary sovereignty under the pre-21st century ('old') constitution was mitigated only by 'informal' checks known as conventions which are determined not by law but by 'political vicissitudes'. Constitutional disputes were therefore confined to the questions about the limits of conventions and the balance of political power.

Bogdanor believes that the 'old' constitution gave way to a 'new' constitution after the passing of the Human Rights Act 1998, which provided the individual with a set of rights (in the form of the ECHR) against the state. Under the 'old' constitution, by contrast, rights were, as Dicey described them, 'mere inductions or generalisations from decisions made by the courts', protected by public opinion rather than law.[5]

The incorporation of the provisions of the ECHR through the Human Rights Act 1998 does indeed endorse and extend the place of those human rights within our constitution. However, we cannot agree with Bogdanor that parliamentary sovereignty has at any time in history been our sole constitutional rule, mitigated only by conventions which reflect the balance of power at a particular time. Our constitutional fabric is richer than that by far. It may be a patchwork, but it is not ephemeral and does not consist of only one legal rule or principle which affirms the superiority of just one branch of government and does not afford any particular status to the other branches, or guide the relations between them.

The historical evolution of the British constitutional system has given rise to a set of relatively 'thick' and deeply embedded normative values and principles which provide how state power should be exercised and constrained. Dicey accorded the status of

[2] J. A. G. Griffith, 'The Political Constitution' (1979) 42 *MLR* 1.

[3] V. Bogdanor, *The New British Constitution* (2009) 13.

[4] Ibid., p. 277.

[5] Ibid., p. 55.

'constitutional principle' to the sovereignty of Parliament, but balanced that by according the status of constitutional principle also to the Rule of Law, albeit that if the two principles clashed, the Rule of Law would have to give way. The chapters by Bradley (on sovereignty of Parliament) and Jowell (on the Rule of Law) show how the two principles have interacted over the years and how the Rule of Law seems to be gaining in status.

The rich texture of our constitutional norms can be observed through the thousands of challenges to official power in the courts, by means of judicial review. The judgments in these cases do not establish merely abstract notions of fairness, or lawfulness, or reasonableness. Each one of them probes a constitutional question: to what extent is this action, this decision, consistent with the kind of official behaviour permitted in a constitutional democracy? Thus the decision that a minister exercising so-called 'prerogative powers' could be judicially reviewed on the question of whether she ought to have consulted those affected by her decision[6] raises constitutional issues and articulates constitutional principle. The 'constitutional right' to access to justice (a central feature of the Rule of Law) has been recognized many times by the courts.[7] And the interpretative 'principle of legality' reconciles the sovereignty of Parliament with the Rule of Law and other constitutional imperatives such as free expression, or the presumption of liberty, by reading down discretionary power so as to accommodate these principles, unless the language of Parliament speaks clearly to the contrary.[8]

That is not to say that constitutional development only takes place through the judgments of the courts, nor that constitutional principle is only articulated there. Parliament itself passes legislation that expands (or indeed sometimes contracts) individual rights against the state, and which therefore has constitutional significance and creates new constitutional principles. Legislation expanding rights includes not only the Human Rights Act 1998 and devolution legislation of the 1990s, but also laws from the 1960s prohibiting discrimination, and providing fair hearings in tribunals or rights to public participation in planning. Legislation that has contracted rights includes permitting government departments almost arbitrarily to seize documents, or to detain suspected terrorists without trial.[9] Sometimes the constitutional principle persuades Members of Parliament to drop legislative proposals (such as the proposal to withdraw judicial review in asylum cases).[10]

Nor are constitutional conventions based only upon Bogdanor's 'political vicissitudes'. They too may embody principles necessary in a democratic society properly

[6] *Council of Civil Service Unions* v. *Minister for the Civil Service* [1985] AC 374.

[7] See e.g. *R.* v. *Secretary of State for the Home Department ex parte Leech (No. 2)* [1994] QB 198; *R.* v. *Lord Chancellor ex parte Witham* [1998] QB 575.

[8] *R.* v. *Secretary of State for the Home Department ex parte Simms* [2000] 2 AC 131.

[9] See e.g. Anti-terrorism Crime and Security Act 2001, s. 23, which provided for the indefinite detention of non-national terrorist suspects (held incompatible with Convention rights in *A* v. *Secretary of State for the Home Department* [2005] 2 AC 68).

[10] Described in Sir John Baker, *Our Unwritten Constitution*, Maccabean Lecture on Jurisprudence, British Academy, *Proceedings of the British Academy*, vol. 167 (2010) 91, 101ff.

so-called. The power of the monarch to refuse royal assent to parliamentary legislation is defunct in practice not only because for her to exercise that prerogative would provoke a political crisis, but because it would violate a fundamental principle of representative democracy. Whether or not the courts could (or would have the courage to) strike down the monarch's intervention in no way dilutes the force of that principle.

Our constitution certainly exists, and is no longer (if it ever was) a solely political constitution. At least those constitutional principles, rules, and expectations that are fundamental to a constitutional democracy are too embedded to be at the mercy of Bogdanor's mere 'political vicissitudes'.

The constitution includes a number of written sources, some having legal status and others less formal, such as a vast range of codes, concordats, guidance documents, manuals, memorandums of understanding, and other documents which regulate political behaviour. And it also includes unwritten sources, including settled expectations arising from conventional patterns of political behaviour which are in turn based upon democratic principles. These different strands – although not contained in any single overriding text – interweave to form a sturdy fabric of democratic constitutionalism. Like any codified constitution, we have the rules, principles, and conventions which *enable* government to operate; and which also provide a space in which governmental intervention is *disabled*, in the interest of individual rights and freedoms.

CONSTITUTIONAL CODIFICATION AND FURTHER REFORM?

One large issue not considered directly in this volume is whether the time has come to have a codified constitution. At the time of writing the issue does not seem to be on the agenda of any political party, but no account of our constitution should neglect it entirely. The obvious advantage of a written constitution is that it would provide an accessible single document setting out the scope and distribution of official power, and the principles by which it can (or cannot) be exercised. It would provide a guide to the citizens of their rights against the state. It would have symbolic as well as practical value, as it could also act as a statement of a country's political ideals. Its drafting would allow a holistic consideration of the constitution of the various rules, principles, and conventions now scattered across our constitutional landscape.[11]

On the other hand, there is a strong argument that a written constitution would inhibit the kind of evolution that we have seen in this country in response to changing circumstances, needs, and expectations. Nor might it be easy to agree on the content

[11] See e.g. R. Gordon, *Repairing British Politics: A blueprint for constitutional change* (2010); IPPR, *Written Constitution for the UK* (1991), also published as Robert Blackburn (ed.), *A Written Constitution for the UK* (1991); J. Cornford, 'On writing a constitution' (1991) 44 *Parliamentary Affairs* 558.

of a written constitution in a situation where there is no need to break abruptly with the past.[12]

Written constitution or no, there is still much that needs to be done with our well-worked (but perhaps not always so well-working) basic public institutions and procedures. All bodies making decisions about our lives (including Parliament itself) need to command legitimacy. They also need to be effective, to interact in a coherent way with each other, and be accountable to the public they serve.

Despite the constitutional change over the past 25 years, trust in our political and governmental institutions has probably never been lower.[13] Over the past two years the very integrity of our parliamentarians has been called in question by the so-called 'expenses scandal', outlined in Leopold's chapter. The legitimacy of our largely appointed House of Lords is similarly doubted, as Oliver's chapter points out. She also describes recent reforms in parliamentary procedure, but still there is insufficient monitoring by Parliament of the vast sea of legislation – about 15,000 pages every year. As a result of this bulk of legislation there is great uncertainty – even in such a fundamental area as the length of a convicted criminal's sentence,[14] contrary to the Rule of Law. Proposals for post-legislative scrutiny have gone unheeded.[15] Successive governments have resorted to Henry VIII clauses which permit the executive to alter legislation without resort to Parliament – without considering the dangers to the Rule of Law.[16] However, at the time of writing, Bills are going through Parliament to remedy some aspects of our constitutional framework that are seen as requiring correction, such as the proposal for fixed term elections and reform of the system of voting in Parliamentary elections.

The fact that the constitution is changing even as we prepare the 7th edition of this work indicates that even the most established democracy requires constant attention, renewal, and perfection.

Jeffrey Jowell
Dawn Oliver

[12] See e.g. N. Barber, 'Against a written constitution' [2008] *Public Law* 11; V. Bogdanor, 'Enacting a British Constitution. Some Problems' [2008] *Public Law* 38; R. Hazell, *Towards a New Constitutional Settlement* (June 2007; Constitution Unit website); R. Brazier, *Constitutional Reform* (2008), and 'How near is a written constitution?' (2001) 52 *NILQ* 1; D. Oliver, 'Written Constitutions. Principles and Problems' (1992) 45 *Parliamentary Affairs* 135.

[13] See 'A Crisis of Trust', *The Economist*, 1 January 2011.

[14] See e.g. *R. (no one)* v. *The Governor of HMP Drake Hall* [2010] UKSC 30, where Lord Judge, at [87] said that 'it is outrageous that so much intellectual effort, as well as public time and resources, have had to be expended in order to discover a route through the legislative morass to what should be, both for the prisoner herself, and for those responsible for her custody, the prison authorities, the simplest and most certain of questions – the prisoner's release date.'

[15] See the Law Commission's proposal, Law Com. No. 302 (2006), Cm. 6954; House of Lords Select Committee on the Constitution, *Fast Track Legislation*, para. 208.

[16] See Baker, above, n. 10, p. 104ff. See also Lord Judge's Speech at Dinner for Her Majesty's Judges, Mansion House, Tuesday, 13 July 2010. The latest attempt is the 2010 Public Bodies Bill which would authorise ministers to abolish 'quangos' created by Acts without the need for an Act of Parliament.

PART I

THE CONSTITUTIONAL FRAMEWORK

Editorial note

This book is divided into three parts. The chapters in this first part are concerned with the fundamental principles, theories, and factors that underpin the UK constitution. What Dicey in his *Introduction to the Law of the Constitution* referred to as the 'twin pillars' of the constitution, the Rule of Law and the sovereignty of the UK Parliament are dealt with in Chapters 1 and 2. The relationships between those two principles are among the issues explored in the following chapters in this part.

Chapter 3 deals with human rights, particularly the fundamental civil and political rights which are contained in the European Convention on Human Rights (ECHR) and incorporated into UK law by the Human Rights Act 1998.

The fact that the UK is a member of the European Union affects many aspects of government in the UK. These are discussed in Chapter 4. The European Union wields very great power over member states, and this raises issues about accountability arrangements and democracy within the Union as well as the approach of the UK courts to European legislation and the challenges that it poses to parliamentary sovereignty.

Chapter 5 focuses further on international influences on the UK constitution. It shows both the filters and defences in our arrangements which protect the legal system from unwanted outside influences, and how common standards and concepts from other legal systems influence domestic constitutional developments.

1

THE RULE OF LAW AND ITS UNDERLYING VALUES

Jeffrey Jowell

SUMMARY

Dicey believed that discretionary power offended the Rule of Law as it would inevitably lead to arbitrary decisions. His critics pointed out that in the modern state discretion is necessary to carry out a variety of welfare and regulatory tasks. Nevertheless, the Rule of Law contains a number of important values, including legality, certainty, accountability, efficiency, due process, and access to justice. These are not only formal values but also substantive. The Rule of Law is not a theory of law but a principle of institutional morality inherent in any constitutional democracy. In a country without a written constitution it constrains the way power is exercised. It is enforced and elaborated through judicial review but also serves as a critical focus for public debate. Although the Rule of Law is not the only requirement of a constitutional democracy, it is of great practical significance in promoting fair decisions and restraining the abuse of power.

INTRODUCTION

Professor Albert Venn Dicey told us, in 1885, that the two principles of our unwritten constitution were the sovereignty of Parliament and the Rule of Law.[1] Although he regarded parliamentary sovereignty as the primary principle – one that could override the Rule of Law – he recognized that, ideally, Parliament and all public officials should

[1] A. V. Dicey, *The Law of the Constitution* (1885) referred to here in its 10th edn, edited by E. C. S. Wade (reprinted 1960). For an account of Dicey's conception, see the articles on 'Dicey and the Constitution' in [1985] *Public Law* 583–724; I. Harden and N. Lewis, *The Noble Lie* (1986) ch. 2; P. Craig, *Public Law and Democracy in the United Kingdom and the United States of America* (1990) ch. 2; M. Loughlin, *Public Law and Political Theory* (1992); T. R. S. Allan, *Constitutional Justice: A Liberal Theory of the Rule of Law* (2001); A. Hutchinson and P. Monahan (eds) *The Rule of Law: Ideal or Ideology?* (1987). See also, Lord Bingham of Cornhill, 'Dicey Revisited' [2002] *PL* 39. See also D. Dyzenhaus, *The Constitution of Law* (2006).

respect the Rule of Law as a quality that distinguished a democratic from a despotic constitution.

What is meant by the Rule of Law and what is its value? Is it any more than a statement that individuals or officials should obey the law as it is? Or does it require positive legal authority for the acts of all public officials? Is it a guide to the justice of public decision-making – a framework that constrains the abuse of power? Or is it an assertion that law itself contains inherent moral qualities? Is its proper place not in the realm of constitutional legality but in the rhetoric of liberal–democratic values? Is it, as a distinguished legal historian has written, an 'unqualified human good'[2] or, as alleged by another, a device that 'enables the shrewd, the calculating, and the wealthy to manipulate its form to their own advantage'?[3] Is it 'an impossible ideal'?[4]

Despite the uncertainty attached to the precise definition of the Rule of Law it is, in the UK, accepted as never before as one of the fundamental principles of our uncodified democratic constitution. It is frequently invoked by the courts as a standard by which to judge whether power has been abused. It is engaged as a yardstick by which to assess the democratic validity of government proposals. One of the most senior and distinguished British judges very recently wrote a book extolling the virtues of the Rule of Law and elaborating its content.[5] It has even received statutory recognition in the Constitutional Reform Act 2005,[6] the first section of which states that that Act does not adversely affect 'the existing constitutional principle of the rule of law'. Most significantly, some of our judges have recently suggested that Dicey's hierarchy of principle, with the Rule of Law playing second-fiddle to the sovereignty of Parliament, might be changing, and that 'the rule of law enforced by the courts is the ultimate controlling factor on which our constitution is based'.[7]

DICEY'S RULE OF LAW: ITS CRITICS AND SUPPORTERS

Because its connotations have been developed so much by historical interpretation it is necessary, even today, to start with Dicey's interpretation of the Rule of Law, because of the immense authority he exercised for so long over the perception of our constitutional arrangements.[8]

[2] E. P. Thompson, *Whigs and Hunters: The Origin of the Black Act* (1975) 266.

[3] M. Horwitz, book review (1977) 86 *Yale LJ* 561, 566.

[4] M. Loughlin, *Foundations of Public Law* (2010) 337.

[5] Lord Bingham, *The Rule of Law* (2010).

[6] The Act seeks to further the principle of the separation of powers and independence of the judiciary. In particular, it removes the power of appointment of judges from the Lord Chancellor and places it in the hands of an independent Judicial Appointments Commission. It also precludes the Lord Chancellor from any judicial role and establishes a Supreme Court outside the House of Lords.

[7] Lord Hope, *obiter*, in *Jackson* v. *Her Majesty's Attorney General* [2005] UKHL 56 at [107].

[8] The conception of the Rule of Law has an older provenance than Dicey. For an account of its origins in the ancient world, see M. Loughlin, *Swords and Scales* (2000), ch. 5; B. Tamanaha, *On the Rule of Law: History, Politics and Theory* (2004), ch. 1.

For Dicey, the Rule of Law distinguished the British (or 'English', as he preferred to call it) from all other constitutions. He described how foreign observers of English manners (Voltaire and de Tocqueville in particular) visited England and were struck by the fact that here was a country distinguished above all by the fact of being under the Rule of Law:

> When Voltaire came to England – and Voltaire represented the feeling of his age – his predominant sentiment clearly was that he had passed out of the realm of despotism to a land where the laws might be harsh, but where men were ruled by law and not by caprice.[9]

That passage encapsulates Dicey's approach to the Rule of Law. By allowing for 'harsh' laws to coexist with the Rule of Law it is clear that he does not equate the Rule of Law with the notion of 'good' law. Nor does he contend that in order to qualify as 'law' a particular rule has to be fair, or reasonable, or just. So what did he mean by the Rule of Law?

According to Dicey, the Rule of Law has at least three meanings. The first is that individuals ought not to be subjected to the power of officials wielding wide discretionary powers. He wrote that no one 'is punishable or can be lawfully made to suffer in body or goods except for a distinct breach of law established before the ordinary courts of the land'. Fundamental to the Rule of Law, therefore, is the notion that all power needs to be authorized. But he took that notion further by contrasting the Rule of Law with a 'system of government based on the exercise by persons in authority of wide, arbitrary or discretionary powers of constraint'.[10] Here Dicey contends that to confer wide discretion upon officials is equivalent to granting them scope to exercise arbitrary powers, to which no one should be forced to submit. He writes that 'wherever there is discretion there is room for arbitrariness'[11] and therefore excludes discretionary powers from what he later calls 'regular law'.

Dicey's second meaning engages a notion of equality – what he calls the 'equal subjection' – of all classes to one law administered by the ordinary courts. He contrasts here what he saw as special exemptions for officials in continental countries such as France, where he considered that the French *droit administratif* operated a separate form of justice that treated ordinary citizens differently from the way it treated its public officials. 'With us', he wrote, 'every official, from the Prime Minister down to a constable or a collector of taxes, is under the same responsibility for every act done without legal justification as any other citizen.'[12]

Thirdly, Dicey saw the Rule of Law as expressing the fact that there was in England no separate written constitutional code, and that the constitutional law is 'the result of the judicial decisions determining the rights of private persons in particular cases brought before the courts'.[13] Like Bentham before him, he was against a basic document setting out a catalogue of human rights and saw our law and liberties as arising from decisions in the courts – the common law.

[9] Dicey, *Law of the Constitution*, 189. [10] Ibid., p. 188. [11] Ibid. [12] Ibid., p. 193.
[13] Ibid., p. 195.

One of the first attacks on Dicey's meanings of the Rule of Law came in 1928 when William Robson wrote his celebrated book *Justice and Administrative Law*, in which he roundly criticized Dicey for his misinterpretation of both the English and French systems on the question of whether officials were treated differently from others. He pointed out that there were, in England 'colossal distinctions'[14] between the rights and duties of private individuals and those of the administrative organs of government, even in Dicey's time. Public authorities possessed special rights and special exemptions and immunities, to the extent that the citizen was deprived of a remedy against the state 'in many cases where he most requires it'.[15] Robson also convincingly showed how Dicey had misinterpreted French law, where the *droit administratif* was not intended to exempt public officials from the rigour of private law, but to allow experts in public administration to work out the extent of official liability. Robson also noted the extent of Dicey's misrepresentation that disputes between officials and private individuals in Britain were dealt with by the ordinary courts. He pointed to the growth of special tribunals and inquiries that had grown up to decide these disputes outside the courts, and was in no doubt that a 'vast body of administrative law' existed in England.[16]

The attack on Dicey continued a few years later with Professor W. Ivor Jennings's *The Law and the Constitution*, which appeared in 1933. Repeating many of Robson's criticisms of Dicey's second and third meanings of the Rule of Law, Jennings also delivered a withering, and almost fatal, attack upon Dicey's first meaning – his claim that wide discretionary power had no place under the Rule of Law. It should be remembered here that Dicey was a trenchant critic of notions of 'collectivism'. An unreconstructed Whig, he had, throughout his life, believed in a *laissez-faire* economic system and had resisted the increasing regulatory role of the state.[17] He was supported by other constitutional theorists of his time,[18] and had an ally in the 1920s in Lord Hewart, who expressed similar views in his book *The New Despotism*.[19] Robson and Jennings were committed to the expansion of the state's role in providing welfare and other social services. Robson, George Bernard Shaw, Leonard Woolf, John Maynard Keynes, Harold Laski, and others worked together in the 1930s to promote these ideas.[20]

[14] W. A. Robson, *Justice and Administrative Law* (1928; 2nd edn, 1947) 343.

[15] Ibid., p. 345.

[16] Ibid. Robson approved of, and wished to develop, administrative law, but through a separate system outside of the 'ordinary courts'. See his 'Justice and Administrative Law reconsidered' (1979) *Current Legal Problems* 107. For an excellent critique and historic corrective of Dicey, see H. W. Arthurs, 'Rethinking Administrative Law: A Slightly Dicey Business' (1979) 17 *Osgoode Hall LJ*, Part I; and *Without the Law* (1985).

[17] See R. A. Cosgrove, *The Rule of Law: Albert Venn Dicey, Victorian Jurist* (1980), and the review by D. Sugarman (1983) *MLR* 102.

[18] Such as Maine and Bryce.

[19] Published in 1929.

[20] See e.g. Keynes's lecture published by Leonard and Virginia Woolf at The Hogarth Press in 1926, entitled *The End of Laissez-Faire*. See Victoria Glendinning, *Leonard Woolf* (2006).

Jennings felt that the Rule of Law implicitly promoted Dicey's political views. He equated Dicey's opposition to state regulation with that of the 'manufacturers who formed the backbone of the Whig Party', who:

> wanted nothing which interfered with profits, even if profits involved child labour, wholesale factory accidents, the pollution of rivers, of the air, and of the water supply, jerry-built houses, low wages, and other incidents of nineteenth-century industrialism.[21]

Jennings then turned his attention directly to Dicey, who:

> was more concerned with constitutional relations between Great Britain and Ireland than with relations between poverty and disease on the one hand, and the new industrial system on the other.[22]

Jennings concluded that if the Rule of Law:

> means that the state exercises only the functions of carrying out external relations and maintaining order, it is not true. If it means that the state ought to exercise these functions only, it is a rule of policy for Whigs (if there are any left).[23]

There were not too many Whigs or unreconstructed Diceyists left by the 1930s, when further legitimacy for the growth of official power was provided by the Donoughmore Committee, inquiring in 1933 into the question whether the growth of subordinate legislation (promulgated at the discretion of the executive) violated the Rule of Law.[24] Donoughmore found that it was inevitable, in an increasingly complex society, that Parliament delegate powers to ministers to act in the public interest. The Second World War then provided further compelling reasons to centralize power, an opportunity built upon by the Labour Government of 1945. As Robson wrote in the 2nd edition of his book in 1947, increasingly Parliament had given powers to resolve disputes between the citizen and the state not to the courts – to Dicey's 'ordinary law' – but to specialized organs of adjudication such as administrative tribunals and inquiries. This was not 'due to a fit of absentmindedness' but because these bodies would be speedier and cheaper, and would possess greater technical knowledge and have 'fewer prejudices against government' than the courts.[25] Here he may have been echoing the words of Aneurin Bevan, Minister of Health in the 1945 Labour Government and architect of the National Health Service, who caused a stir in the House of Commons by establishing tribunals in the Health Service, divorced from 'ordinary courts', because he greatly feared 'judicial sabotage' of socialist legislation.[26]

Despite this onslaught on Dicey's version of the Rule of Law, its epitaph refused to be written. Two particularly strong supporters wrote in its favour in the 1940s. F. A. Hayek's *The Road to Serfdom* in 1943 graphically described that road as being paved with governmental regulation. C. K. Allen, with less ideological fervour, pleaded

[21] Sir W. Ivor Jennings, *The Law and the Constitution* (1933) 309–10. [22] Ibid., p. 311.
[23] Ibid. [24] Report of the Committee on Ministers' Powers (1932) Cmd 4060.
[25] Robson, *Justice and Administrative Law* 347. [26] *Hansard*, HC col. 1983 (23 July 1946).

for the legal control of executive action.[27] Not much heed was paid to these pleas until the late 1950s when the Franks Committee[28] revived interest in Diceyan notions by proposing judicial protections over the multiplying tribunals and inquiries of the growing state. It was in the 1960s, however, that disparate groups once again started arguing in favour of legal values. Some of these groups were themselves committed to a strong governmental role in providing social welfare, but objected to the manner in which public services were carried out. Recipients of supplementary benefit, for example, objected to the fact that benefits were administered by officials in accordance with a secret code (known as the 'A Code') and asked instead for publication of a set of welfare 'rights'.[29] They also objected to the wide discretion allowed their case-workers to determine the level of their benefits. The heirs of Jennings and his followers, such as Professor Richard Titmuss, opposed this challenge to the free exercise of official discretion and objected strongly to a 'pathology of legalism' developing in this area.[30]

Another plea for the Rule of Law came at about the same time from individuals who were being displaced from their homes by programmes of urban redevelopment. While not asking for a catalogue of 'rights', their claim was for participation in decisions by which they were affected.[31] Their plea did not primarily concern the substance of the law. Just as the welfare recipients were not simply arguing for higher benefits, but for pre-determined rules and fair procedures to determine the benefits, citizens' groups directed their demands for the Rule of Law less at the content of the decisions ultimately taken than at the procedures by which they were reached. They were by no means adopting the undiluted Diceyan view that all discretionary power is bad. Nevertheless, they asked not to be condemned (in those cases, evicted from their communities) unheard.

THE VALUES UNDERLYING THE RULE OF LAW

Dicey's Rule of Law has been criticized, as we have seen, for the fact that it tendentiously seeks to promote an individualistic political theory and because of its inaccurate descriptions of the then-existing systems of governance – both in France and England. Yet it remains a compelling idea, although variously interpreted.[32] Some see the Rule of Law as embodying formal qualities in law (such as clarity, prospectivity,

[27] See C. K. Allen, *Law and Orders* (1945). See also F. A. Hayek, *The Constitution of Liberty* (1960), and *Law, legislation and liberty* (2 vols, 1976).

[28] Report of the Committee on Administrative Tribunals and Inquiries (1957) Cmnd 218.

[29] See e.g. T. Lynes, *Welfare Rights* (1969); and in the USA: C. Reich, 'The New Property' (1964) 73 *Yale CJ* 733.

[30] R. Titmuss, 'Law and Discretion' (1971) 42 *Polit Q* 113.

[31] N. A. Roberts, *The Reform of Planning Law* (1976); Patrick McAuslan, *The Ideologies of Planning Law* (1980) esp. chs 1 and 2.

[32] See P. Craig, 'Formal and Substantive Conceptions of the Rule of Law: An Analytical Framework' [1997] *Public Law* 467; N. Barber, 'Must Legalistic Conceptions of the Rule of Law Have a Social Dimension?' (2004) *Ratio Juris* 474.

stability, openness, and access to an impartial judiciary).[33] Others criticize that view. Ronald Dworkin has called it the 'rule-book conception' of the Rule of Law and prefers the 'rights conception', under which legal rules contain inherent moral content.[34] Dworkin's view must be seen in the context of his and others' opposition to the view of the positivist thinkers who contend that even extremely harsh and unjust laws, such as the discriminatory laws of Nazi Germany, must be regarded as law, despite their moral repugnance.[35] Dicey and Dworkin are aiming at different targets. Dworkin is seeking a general theory of law, and Dicey is seeking a general principle of how power should be deployed by government in a democracy.

In a recent book on the Rule of Law which has received much attention, the great British judge Tom Bingham defines the Rule of Law as follows:

> all persons and authorities within the state , whether public or private, should be bound by and entitled to the benefit of laws publicly made, taking effect (generally) in the future and publicly administered in the courts.[36]

This definition may at first reading sound rather too economical, but it encapsulates a number of features of a state grounded in the rule of law. Bingham expands that definition with eight features of the rule of law, including that the law must give protection to human rights. We shall discuss below the overlap between the rule of law and human rights, but meanwhile let us identify a number of *values* underlying the Rule of Law.[37]

Legality

At its most fundamental, the Rule of Law requires everyone to comply with the law. Legality in that sense contains two features. First, the law must be followed (Bingham's requirement that all persons must be 'bound by the law'). This requirement of the Rule of Law is often asserted by those who call for 'law and order' in the face of lax

[33] J. Raz, 'The Rule of Law and its Virtue' (1977) 93 *LQR* 195, and *The Authority of Law* (1979). Compare Lon Fuller's requirements of 'legality': generality, clarity, public promulgation, stability, consistency, fidelity to purpose and prohibition of the impossible. L. Fuller, *The Morality of Law* (1964) 153. See also R. Summers, 'The Principles of the Rule of Law' (1999) *Notre Dame LR* 1691; J. Waldron, 'Is the Rule of Law an Essentially Contested Concept?'(2002) *Law and Philosophy* 137.

[34] R. Dworkin, *A Matter of Principle* (1985) ch. 1, p. 11ff.

[35] See generally, H. L. A. Hart, *The Concept of Law* (1961).

[36] Tom Bingham, *The Rule of Law* (2010) 8. Compare the definition of the former Secretary General of the United Nations, Kofi Annan that the rule of law is a 'Principle of governance in which all persons, institutions and entities, public and private, including the State itself, are accountable to laws that are publicly promulgated, equally enforced and independently adjudicated, and which are consistent with international human rights norms and standards. It requires, as well, measures to ensure adherence to the principles of supremacy of law, equality before the law, accountability to law, fairness in the application of law, separation of powers, participation in decision-making, legal certainty, avoidance of arbitrariness and procedural and legal transparency'. *The Rule of Law and Transitional Justice in Conflict and Post Conflict Societies*, Report of the Secretary General, Doc.S/2004/616 23 August 2004, para. 6.

[37] Compare the eight *features* of the Rule of Law set out by Bingham, above: Accessibility of the Law; Law not Discretion; Equality before the Law; The Exercise of Power; Human Rights; Dispute Resolution; A Fair Trial; and the Rule of Law in the International Order.

enforcement of the law. It speaks both to the public (who are expected to obey the law) and to law-enforcement officials (who are expected to implement the law).

Secondly, in so far as legality addresses the actions of public officials, it requires that they act within the powers that have been conferred upon them. All decisions and acts of public officials must therefore be legally authorized. The modern view, as we shall discuss in a moment, is that discretionary power is not wholly inimical to the notion of legality, but that discretion must also be exercised within the scope of legality – in accordance with the purpose and objects of the power conferred on the decision-maker, fairly and not in a way that is capricious or arbitrary.

Certainty

The essence of Dicey's Rule of Law is that law should be certain and predictable. Both he, and his followers, Hewart and Hayek, mistrusted the grant of virtually any official discretion, and extolled the virtue of defined rules to govern the exercise of public power. We have seen that Dicey was less concerned that laws were 'harsh' than that they be known. Certainty, rather than substantive fairness, was the key value. Maitland wrote that 'Known general laws, however bad, interfere less with freedom than decisions based on no previously known rule.'[38] Hayek said:

> [I]t does not matter whether we all drive on the left or the right-hand side of the roads so long as we all do the same. The important thing is that the rule enables us to predict other people's behaviour correctly, and this requires that it should apply in all cases – even if in a particular instance we feel it to be unjust.[39]

An official possessed of discretion frequently has a choice about how it should be operated: whether to keep it open-textured, maintaining the option of a variety of responses to a given situation, or to confine it by a rule or standard – a process of legalization. For example, a local authority that provides grants for students could allocate them on a case-by-case basis, deciding each case on its merits. Or it could promulgate some rules, excluding grants for certain university courses, etc. Similarly, laws against pollution could be enforced by a variable standard whereby the official must be satisfied that the polluter is achieving the 'best practicable means' of abatement. Alternatively, levels of pollution could be specified in advance, based on the colour of smoke emission, or the precise quantities of sulphur dioxide. A policy of promoting safe driving could, similarly, be legalized by a rule specifying speeds of no more than 30 miles per hour on given streets.

Dicey and his followers prefer rules to discretion largely because rules allow affected persons to know what they are required to do – or not do – in advance of any sanction for breach of the rule. Certainty in that sense has an instrumental value in that it allows decisions to be planned in advance and people to know clearly where

[38] *Collected Papers*, vol. i (1911) 81. Maitland equated arbitrary power with power that was 'uncertain' or 'incalculable': ibid., p. 80.

[39] Hayek, *The Road to Serfdom* (1943) 60.

they stand. However, the value of legal certainty is also based in *substantive fairness*. It is unfair to penalize someone for an action that was lawful when it was carried out and it is unfair to punish someone for the breach of a law which they were not able to discover. And, as we shall see, when a person is encouraged by the decision-maker to believe that a particular course of action will take place, certainty will dictate that his 'legitimate expectation' shall not be disappointed.

Consistency

Related to the value of certainty is that of consistency, or *formal* equality. As Dicey says, the highest officers of state must be treated similarly to everyone else. And law enforcers must apply the law regardless of the status of any person or any threats or inducements to the decision-maker. The application of policy through rules promotes even-handed application of standards. Like cases can then be treated alike. In contrast, discretionary powers may be applied selectively. The extent to which *substantive* equality, as well as formal equality, is contained within the Rule of Law is considered further below.

Accountability

A fourth value of the Rule of Law is accountability. First, rules provide a published standard against which to measure the legality of official action. They thus allow individual redress against those officials who are not acting within the scope of their conferred powers. An announced level of resources to qualify for welfare assistance should allow a person who qualifies but is refused assistance to mount a legal challenge to the refusal. Secondly, the actual process of *making* rules and their publication generates public assessment of the content of the rule and whether it furthers the purposes of the governing law. Many statutes confer on the decision-maker broad discretionary powers to further the policy of the Act. The power may be to allocate housing, or to provide for the needs of children, or to diminish unacceptable pollution of the air or water. The process of devising a points system for housing allocation, benefit levels for the needy, and acceptable emission levels of pollution forces the official into producing a formal operational definition of purpose.

The legalization of policy does not simply allow officials to 'congratulate themselves – and await obedience'.[40] The process of making rules, as well as the rules themselves, may generate public scrutiny of the fidelity of the rules to the purpose of the governing scheme.

Efficiency

Although not considered in any detail by Dicey, rule-based action also provides the benefit of efficiency. Rules announce or clarify official policies to people who will be affected by them. A zoning system in planning or a list of features of 'substandard'

[40] P. Selznick, *Law, Society and Industrial Justice* (1969) 29.

housing, a list of required grades for university admission all allow people to comply themselves with the appropriate standard. Fruitless applications will be avoided. From the perspective of the decision-maker, rules allow decisions to be taken more quickly than a general standard that requires constant reappraisal of each case on its merits. Required grades for university admission can be routinely applied. Rules therefore reduce the anxiety and conserve the energy needed to reach decisions on a case-by-case basis. The portrayal by the sociologist Max Weber of his ideal-type bureaucrat applying rules '*sine ira et studio* – without hatred or passion, and hence without affection or enthusiasm'[41] – alludes to the neutral and non-affective approach to a legalized framework and the possibility of insulating the decision-maker from the pressure of constant reconsideration.

Due process and access to justice

Another of Dicey's features of the Rule of Law is that no person should be condemned unheard – that there should be no punishment without a trial. The requirement of 'due process' or 'natural justice' (these days called 'procedural fairness') furthers Bingham's requirement that people should be entitled to the 'benefit' of laws, and to ensure this by being able to challenge both the announced rule or the implementation of the rule by the official. In order to do this, the claimant will need access to the courts. So access to justice is another feature of the Rule of Law.

Once the claimant reaches the court, a further aspect of Rule of Law is engaged, namely the requirement that the decision-maker be unbiased, that is, both independent (in the sense of free of external pressure) and impartial (not apparently interested in the outcome of the case in favour of any one of the participants). Even if perfect impartiality on the part of the adjudicator is an unattainable goal (because we all have unconscious predilections and biases), the process of justification involved in adjudication does not easily permit predetermined or arbitrary decisions. Adjudication encourages 'purposive decisions',[42] by inviting the decision to be justified by reference to a general rule, standard, or principle. Due process is therefore also associated with Dicey's faith in legal certainty and prospectivity. The purpose of the trial is to judge whether the accused is guilty by existing legal standards. Due process also encourages decisions that are consistent, since like cases should be treated alike. In addition, due process is in itself a technique of accountability, especially when reasons are required, which then invite public scrutiny of those decisions.

Viewed in that light, due process is not a merely formal virtue. Its substantive dimension emerges when we consider that it endorses the notion that every person is entitled to be treated with due regard to the proper merits of their cause. Failure to provide that treatment diminishes a person's sense of individual worth and impairs their

[41] M. Weber, *The Theory of Social and Economic Organisation*, trans. A. Henderson and T. Parsons (eds) (1947) 340.

[42] P. Nonet, 'The Legitimation of Purposive Decisions' (1980) *Calif L Rev* 263.

dignity.[43] The right to due process goes further than forbidding actual punishment without a trial. It extends to a concern that individuals should not have decisions made about their vital interests without an opportunity to influence the outcome of those decisions. And it requires restrictions on rights, liberties, and interests to be properly *justified*. The culture of justification, rather than the culture of authority,[44] is another mark of the difference between democracy and despotism. Due process therefore provides 'formal and institutional expression to the influence of reasoned argument in human affairs'.[45] Overt reference to irrational or particularistic factors (such as the defendant's race or political views) will therefore be difficult to sustain. Because procedural fairness promotes full and fair consideration of the issues and evidence, as Lord Steyn has said, it plays 'an instrumental role in promoting just decisions'.[46]

Although Dicey favoured adjudication through the regular courts of law, adjudicative mechanisms of different kinds provide procedural checks on discretion in order to comply with the Rule of Law. Some are provided through appeals – for example, in planning, from local to central government by means of written representations or a public inquiry; or in immigration and asylum matters, from an adjudicator to an appeal tribunal. Special tribunals exist to permit appeals from the decisions of a variety of officials upon issues as diverse as the registration of a new variety of rose to compensation for the acquisition of land.

Some decisions decide not only rights between the individual and the public organization, but also questions of policy, such as whether a motorway should be built over a stretch of land. In those situations the decision may be structured by means of an inquiry or tribunal hearing, or may simply be made by an official within a government department. There has been a demand for public participation in those decisions. Even though those seeking participation have mere interests (rather than vested rights) in the decision's outcome, they ask for the right to participate in the process of making that decision. Neighbours want to be consulted about an application for planning permission on a local site, and people want to be consulted about the closure of hospitals, local railway lines or coal pits.[47] If the Rule of Law is concerned to protect individuals from being deprived of their rights without an opportunity to defend themselves, the concern is only narrowly stretched to protect group interests from being overridden without the opportunity to express views on the matter to be

[43] For a full account of the variety of justifications of procedural protections, see D. J. Galligan, *Due Process and Fair Procedures* (1996), and see G. Richardson, 'The Legal Regulation of Process', in G. Richardson and H. Genn (eds), *Administrative Law and Government Actions* (1994). The aspect of natural justice that requires the decision-maker to be unbiased also incorporates an aspect of the principle of separation of powers into the Rule of Law.

[44] Mureinik, 'A Bridge to Where? Introducing the Bill of Rights' (1994) 10 *SAJHR* 31.

[45] L. Fuller, 'Collective Bargaining and the Arbitrator' (1963) *Wisconsin L Rev* 1, 3. See also Rawls's view of natural justice as an element of the Rule of Law, in his *A Theory of Justice* (1972) 241–2.

[46] *Raji* v. *General Medical Council* [2003] UKPC 24.

[47] *R.* v. *British Coal Corpn and Secretary of State for Trade and Industry ex parte Vardy and others* [1993] ICR 720 (CA).

decided.[48] For example, a recent challenge to a government review which reversed the 'high policy' against nuclear power was struck down by the Administrative Court on the ground that the review was so deficient in content and form that its process was 'manifestly unfair'.[49]

THE LIMITS OF THE RULE OF LAW'S VALUES

The Rule of Law contains, as we have seen, the values of legality, certainty, consistency, accountability, efficiency, due process and access to justice. These values in themselves promote both formal and substantive qualities. However, they are not unqualified. Flip over the coin of the Rule of Law and we see some of the defects of rule and adjudication as techniques of governance.

The benefits of rules – their objective, even-handed features – are opposed to other administrative benefits, especially those of individual treatment, and responsiveness. The virtue of rules to the administrator (routine treatment and efficiency) may be a defect to the claimant with a special case (such as the brilliant applicant for a university place who failed to obtain the required grades because of a family upset or illness just before the examination). The administrator's shield may be seen as an unjustified protection from the claimant's sword. Officials themselves may consider that a task requires flexibility, or genuinely want to help a particular client, but feel unable to do so. Hence the classic bureaucratic response: 'I'd like to help you – but this is the rule.'

Our administrative law itself recognizes the limits of rule-governed conduct through the principle against the 'fettering' of discretion. Where an official has wide discretion – for example, to provide grants to industry or to students or to regulate safety standards for taxi drivers – a rule will often be introduced both to assist in the articulation of the standard and its even-handed application, and also to announce the standard to affected persons. The safety rules, for example, may require seat belts, and regular vehicle maintenance inspections. The courts do not object to the use of a rule in itself, but they do object to its rigid application without giving a person with something new or special to say about his case the opportunity to put his argument to the decision-maker. The principle against the fettering of discretion acknowledges how the rigid application of rules can militate against good and fair public administration.[50]

This balance of rule and discretion can be found etched into particular areas of public administration. In town and country planning, for example, permission is needed for development of land. By what criteria is that permission granted or refused? Some countries have adopted a system of zoning, by which the local map clearly marks

[48] For an account of 'the ideology of public participation', see Patrick McAuslan, *The Ideologies of Planning Law* (1980); Nonet, above, n. 42; J. Habermas, *Towards a Rational Society* (1971).

[49] *R. (Greenpeace Ltd.)* v. *Secretary of State for Trade and Industry* [2007] EWHC 311 (Admin).

[50] See D. Galligan, 'The Nature and Function of Policies within Discretionary Power' (1976) *Public Law* 332 and *Discretionary Powers* (1986); C. Hilson, 'Judicial Review, Politics and the Fettering of Discretion' [2002] *Public Law* 111.

out what can be done in each area. A would-be developer knows from the colour coding whether he can build a factory or change a shop to an office on a given site. In Britain this approach, whereby the zoning map in effect creates a series of rules about what can be done on the land, is greatly softened. Officials will take into account the formal plan for the area, but account may also be taken of 'other material considerations'.[51] So rule and discretion are mixed together, in an attempt to gain the benefits of each. Thus, an applicant for a craft centre in an area zoned as residential on the plan may nevertheless be granted permission because the centre fits in with the area, does not adversely affect its amenity, and generates local employment. These 'other material considerations' provide the flexibility to mitigate the rigours of a rule-bound plan.

We must note too that the existence of a rule does not automatically ensure its implementation. Nor is it always desirable that rules be enforced. Sometimes the prosecuting official will lack the resources to prosecute the law. This happened when the police withdrew full enforcement of the law against unlawful protesters against the shipping of live animals across the channel. The House of Lords accepted that the action was justified because it was stretching the chief constable's resources to the detriment of policing elsewhere in the county.[52] Full enforcement may also distort the purpose of the rule and require, for example, the prosecution of a doctor who narrowly exceeded the speed limit on a deserted street late at night while rushing to the scene of an accident. That prosecution makes no sense in furthering the goal of preventing unsafe driving.

In December 2006 the Director of the Serious Fraud Office (the Director) decided to abandon an investigation into allegations of bribery and corruption by BAE Systems Ltd (BAE), in relation to contracts for Al-Yamamah military aircraft with the Kingdom of Saudi Arabia. Threats had been made by Saudi officials that if the investigation were to continue the Saudi government would cancel a proposed order for Eurofighter Typhoon aircraft and withdraw security and intelligence co-operation with the UK.

Despite internal political pressure to drop the investigation, and just at the point when the trail of investigation was extended to Swiss bank accounts, the Director was persuaded to drop the case on the advice particularly of the British Ambassador to Saudi Arabia that national security ('British lives on British streets') would be imperilled if the threat were carried out. The Director's decision was challenged through judicial review and the Divisional Court held that the Director had not paid sufficient regard to the danger to the Rule of Law in submitting to the threat.[53] However, the House of Lords disagreed and held that the Director's decision was lawful and that courts should be 'very slow to interfere' in prosecutorial decisions outside of

[51] Town and Country Planning Act 1990, s. 54A.

[52] *R.* v. *Chief Constable of Sussex ex parte International Traders' Ferry Ltd.* [1999] 2 AC 418. But see also *R.* v. *Coventry City Council ex parte Phoenix Aviation* [1995] 3 All ER 37, where it was held that substantial non-enforcement of the law was in breach of the Rule of Law.

[53] *R. (on the application of Corner House)* v. *Director of the Serious Fraud Office* [2007] EWHC 311 (Admin).

'exceptional cases'.[54] This was because, first, respect should be accorded to the independence of the prosecutor. Secondly, it was said that prosecutorial decisions are not susceptible to judicial review because it is within neither the constitutional function nor the practical competence of the courts to assess matters concerning the public interest, especially when national security is in issue, as it was in this case.

It seems unfortunate in this case that the House of Lords considered itself powerless to prevent the caving in to threats to our system of justice, and thus to the Rule of Law. Had the threats in this case been made by a British citizen, he would be liable at least to prosecution for perverting the course of justice.

As with rules, adjudication is not appropriate in all situations. In the 19th century, writers such as Bentham[55] and his disciple Chadwick voiced strong opposition to the judicialization of administration. They agreed that to introduce such procedures would lead to mindless disputes upon 'such simple questions as to whether a cask of biscuits was good or bad'.[56] Due process may impede speed and despatch. Could we really allow a hearing as to whether the firefighters should douse a burning house with water? Or a pavement hearing before a police officer is able to tow away an illegally parked car? Should there be an appeal from a university lecturer's examination grade? Or from a decision to reject admission to a university? Sometimes parties who have to live with each other after the dispute prefer techniques of mediation to negotiate an acceptable solution.[57] These forms of resolving disputes differ from adjudication where the final decision is taken by the independent 'judge' and is imposed rather than agreed.

THE PRACTICAL IMPLEMENTATION OF THE RULE OF LAW

The Rule of Law is not a principle of moral law, yet it is a principle of institutional morality. As such it guides all forms both of law enforcement and of law making. In particular, it suggests that legal certainty and procedural protections are fundamental requirements of democratic constitutionalism. Nor are all its virtues simply formal. It encourages accountability, efficiency, fairness, and respect for human dignity.

In a country like the UK that does not have a codified constitution, the Rule of Law serves as a principle that constrains governmental power. We return now to Dicey's contention that the Rule of Law stands together with parliamentary sovereignty as a constitutional principle. Although many of Dicey's notions may have delayed the development in this country of a coherent public law, his genius was to recognize that our constitution does contain implied principles. The principle of parliamentary

[54] [2008] UKHL 6. [55] L. J. Hume, *Bentham and Bureaucracy* (1981) 82.

[56] H. Parris, *Constitutional Bureaucracy* (1969) 82.

[57] See V. Aubert, 'Competition and Dissensus: Two Types of Conflict and Conflict Resolution' (1963) *J Conflict Res* 26.

sovereignty, together with what he called conventions, *enables* powers to be exercised by government and specifies how it is to be exercised. The Rule of Law however *disables* government from abusing its power.

In countries with written constitutions the text itself provides the enabling features (such as who may vote and the composition of the executive and legislature). It also normally provides the disabling features through a Bill of Rights that constrains government, even elected Parliaments, from interfering with certain fundamental rights and freedoms (such as freedom of expression and association) which are considered necessary and integral to democracy. In Britain, the Rule of Law as an unwritten principle performs a similar disabling function, in the area where its values apply.

How does the Rule of Law operate in practice in the UK? Let us first note that our courts have not yet, outside directly effective EC law, felt themselves able to disapply primary legislation that offends the Rule of Law. However, since 1998 the Human Rights Act incorporates into domestic law most of the provisions of the ECHR, some of which contain values that inhere in the Rule of Law (such as the prohibition against retroactive laws, and the requirement of a fair trial). All decisions of public officials, including the courts, must now conform with Convention rights. Parliament's statutes may be reviewed by the courts for compatibility with Convention rights, but the courts may not, under the Act, strike down statutes that offend the ECHR; it may only declare them incompatible with Convention rights.

However, the absence of judicial authority to disapply primary legislation that is contrary to the Rule of Law does not mean that the Rule of Law has no influence on the content of legislation. As a constitutional principle, the Rule of Law serves as a basis for the evaluation of all laws and provides a critical focus for public debate. There have been a number of occasions in recent years where proposals to evade the Rule of Law (for example, by prohibiting judicial review of decisions about asylum or immigration) were abandoned, in the face of strong opposition on the ground that the proposals offended the Rule of Law's moral strictures.[58]

Even before the Human Rights Act 1998 came into force, the courts would seek to reconcile the principles of parliamentary sovereignty and the Rule of Law where possible. For example, in the case of *Pierson*,[59] it was held that, despite the fact that the Home Secretary had very broad discretionary power to set a prisoner's tariff (the minimum sentence prior to parole), the decision to increase the tariff retrospectively – contrary to an earlier indication that the lesser sentence would be imposed – offended the Rule of Law in its substantive sense. Lord Steyn in that case said:

> Parliament does not legislate in a vacuum. Parliament legislates for a European liberal democracy based upon the traditions of the common law...and...unless there is the

[58] See the account by R. Rawlings, 'Review. Revenge and Retreat' [2005] *MLR* 378; and A. le Sueur, 'Three Strikes and You're Out? The UK Government's Strategy to Oust Judicial Review from Immigration and Asylum' [2004] *Public Law* 225.

[59] *R.* v. *Secretary of State for the Home Department ex parte Pierson* [1998] AC 539.

clearest provision to the contrary, Parliament must be presumed not to legislate contrary to the Rule of Law.[60]

This presumption in favour of the Rule of Law (and other fundamental constitutional principles, such as freedom of expression) was referred to as 'principle of legality', described by Lord Hoffmann in a later case as follows:

> Parliamentary sovereignty means that Parliament can, if it chooses, legislate contrary to fundamental principles of human rights.... But the principle of legality means that Parliament must squarely confront what it is doing and accept the political cost. Fundamental rights cannot be overridden by general or ambiguous words. This is because there is too great a risk that the full implications of their unqualified meaning may have passed unnoticed in the democratic process. In the absence of express language or necessary implication to the contrary, the courts therefore presume that even the most general words were intended to be subject to the basic rights of the individual. In this way the courts of the United Kingdom, though acknowledging the sovereignty of Parliament, apply principles of constitutionality little different from those which exist in countries where the power of the legislature is expressly limited by a constitutional document.[61]

JUDICIAL REVIEW

The practical implementation of the Rule of Law has taken place primarily through judicial review of the actions of public officials. During the first half of the 20th century, a time of reaction to Dicey's Rule of Law, the courts rarely interfered with the exercise of discretionary powers.[62] From that time on, however, they began to require that power be exercised in accordance with three 'grounds' of judicial review, each of them resting in large part on the Rule of Law.

The first ground, 'legality', requires officials to act within the scope of their lawful powers. The courts ensure that the official decisions do not stray beyond the 'four corners' of a statute by failing to take into account 'relevant' considerations (that is, considerations that the law requires), or by taking into account 'irrelevant' considerations (that is, considerations outside the object and purpose that Parliament intended the statute to pursue).[63] This exercise is, as we have discussed, a clear instance of the implementation of the Rule of Law, whereby the courts act as guardians of Parliament's intent and purpose. The definition of the purpose of a given statute is no mere mechanical exercise, and is often complicated by the fact that the statute confers very wide discretionary powers on the decision-maker, for example to act 'as he sees fit'. For example, where a statute conferred broad powers upon a local authority to sell its own dwellings to their inhabitants, and where some local councillors decided to sell those dwellings

[60] Ibid., p. 575.

[61] *R.* v. *Secretary of State for the Home Department ex parte Simms* [2003] 2 AC 115, 131.

[62] For an account of this history, see J. Jowell, 'Administrative Law', and R. Stevens, 'Government and the Judiciary' in V. Bogdanor (ed.), *The British Constitution in the Twentieth Century* (2003).

[63] E.g. *Padfield* v. *Minister of Agriculture, Fisheries and Food* [1968] AC 997.

for the cynical purpose of securing electoral advantage for their party, the courts had to grapple with the question whether the councillors were entitled, as elected politicians, to assist their party to win the next election. The House of Lords held that statutory powers are conferred on trust, and not absolutely, and that the motive of the councillors – party gain – was extraneous to the purpose for which the powers were conferred.[64]

Although there are a number of administrative tasks that cannot be predetermined by any rule, the courts have reconciled Dicey's fear of any discretion with a view that no discretion is wholly unfettered. As was said in a leading case on the issue of 'legality', even if a discretion were expressly defined as 'unfettered':

> The use of that adjective, . . . can do nothing to unfetter the control which the judiciary have over the executive, namely that in exercising their powers the latter must act lawfully and that is a matter to be determined by looking at the Act and its scope and object in conferring a discretion upon the Minister rather than by the use of adjectives.[65]

The second ground of review, that of 'procedural propriety', requires decision-makers to be unbiased and to grant a fair hearing to claimants before depriving them of a right or significant interest (such as an interest in livelihood or reputation). We have seen that the right of due process – the right not to be condemned unheard – is a central value of the Rule of Law, which the courts presume Parliament to respect. The courts have affirmed the principle of procedural fairness, even where the statute conferring the power to decide was silent on the matter. In the 19th century the courts were not slow to allow the 'justice of the common law' to supplement the legislature's omission, looking back to the Garden of Eden as an example of a fair hearing being granted before Adam and Eve were deported from their green and pleasant land.[66] In the first half of the 20th century the courts were more reluctant to grant hearings, restricting them to matters where rights were in issue (rather than privileges). The case of *Ridge* v. *Baldwin*[67] then extended the hearing to the protections of more important interests, such as reputation or livelihood.

This kind of procedural protection, whether established by statute or the common law, is a concrete expression of the Rule of Law. Its content is variable, depending on the issue. However, as was said:

> The Rule of Law rightly requires that certain decisions, of which the paradigm examples are findings of breaches of the criminal law and adjudication as to private rights, should be entrusted to the judicial branch of government.[68]

Over the past few years, the courts have extended the requirement of a fair hearing even where the claimant does not possess a threatened criminal or private right or

[64] *Magill* v. *Porter* [2001] UKHL 67.

[65] *Per* Lord Upjohn in *Padfield* v. *Minister of Agriculture, Fisheries and Food* [1968] AC 997.

[66] *Cooper* v. *Wandsworth Board of Works* (1863) 14 CB (NS) 180.

[67] [1964] AC 40.

[68] *Alconbury Developments Ltd.* v. *Secretary of State for the Environment, Transport and the Regions* [2001] UKHL 23 at [42], *per* Lord Hoffmann. See also *Runa Begum* v. *Tower Hamlets LBC* [2003] UKHL 5 at [4].

even an important interest. A hearing will be required where a 'legitimate expectation' has been induced by the decision-maker.[69] In such a case the claimant has, expressly or impliedly, been promised either a hearing or the continuation of a benefit. The courts will not sanction the disappointment of such an expectation unless the claimant is permitted to make representations on the matter. The notion of the legitimate expectation is itself rooted in that aspect of the Rule of Law which requires legal certainty.

The third ground of judicial review, 'irrationality' or 'unreasonableness', also applies aspects of the Rule of Law. Suppose the police charge only bearded drivers, or drivers of a particular race, with traffic offences? Suppose an education authority chose to dismiss all teachers with red hair? Suppose a prison officer refused to permit a prisoner to communicate with his lawyer? Suppose a minister raised the minimum sentence of a prisoner, having earlier told him that the sentence would be set at a lower level? Would these decisions offend the Rule of Law? If so, the Rule of Law becomes a substantive doctrine and not merely formal or procedural. Our courts, through judicial review, tread warily in this area, interfering only if the decision was beyond the range of reasonable responses.[70] However, where the Rule of Law or other constitutional principles or fundamental rights are in issue, the courts scrutinize the decision with greater care[71] and also adopt the 'principle of legality' that we have seen above, which presumes that Parliament intends the Rule of Law to prevail.

In practice, many of the decisions held unreasonable are so held because they offend the values of the Rule of Law discussed above. The concept of 'unreasonableness', or 'irrationality', in itself imputes the arbitrariness that Dicey considered was the antithesis of the Rule of Law. Decisions based upon insufficient evidentiary basis,[72] or which are inconsistent,[73] fall foul of the Rule of Law's values. Where byelaws are not sufficiently clear they have been held unlawful for 'uncertainty'.[74] Dicey's abhorrence of arbitrary decisions is also endorsed when a decision is struck down because it is simply unreasonably harsh or oppressive.[75]

The practical implementation of the Rule of Law over the years makes it clear that its substantive aims underlie and endorse the striking down of a number of decisions, albeit often without mentioning its name. A local authority which withdrew the licence of a rugby club whose members had visited South Africa during the apartheid regime fell foul of the Rule of Law on the ground that there should be no punishment where there was no law (since sporting contacts with South Africa were

[69] Endorsed in the House of Lords in *Council of Civil Service Unions* v. *Minister of the Civil Service* [1985] AC 374.

[70] *Associated Provincial Picture Houses* v. *Wednesbury Corporation* [1948] 1 KB 223.

[71] Under the Human Rights Act 1998, applying the ECHR, the courts will adopt the even stricter scrutiny under the test of 'proportionality'. See Chapter 3 below.

[72] *E* v. *Secretary of State for the Home Department* [2004] EWCA Civ 49.

[73] See R. Clayton, 'Legitimate Expectations, Policy and the Principle of Consistency' [2003] *CLJ* 93. See *R (Rashid)* v. *Secretary of State for the Home Department* [2005] EWCA Civ 744.

[74] *Percy* v. *Hall* [1997] QB 924. And see *R (L)* v. *Secretary of State for the Home Department* [2003] EWCA Civ 25 ('Legal certainty is an aspect of the rule of law' at [25]).

[75] See e.g. *Wheeler* v. *Leicester City Council* [1985] AC 1054 (HL).

not then prohibited).[76] A minister's rules allowing a prison governor to prevent a prisoner corresponding with his lawyer, even when no litigation was contemplated, was held to violate the prisoner's 'constitutional right' of access to justice.[77] Access to Justice as a value of the Rule of Law (and considered a 'higher order' right) was again held to have been violated by the Lord Chancellor's imposition of substantial court fees which an impecunious litigant was unable to afford.[78] The inability of the remaining white farmers in Zimbabwe to challenge the proposed taking of their land, following a constitutional amendment, was held to violate the Rule of Law as a foundational principle of the Southern African Development Community (SADC).[79] And an order seeking to freeze the assets of known terrorists such as Usama Bin-Laden on a consolidated list was held by the Supreme Court to violate the Rule of Law because the person whose name is on the list had no right to challenge the listing before a court.[80]

The legitimate expectation, which began by grounding a procedural right to a fair hearing,[81] has since been extended to a substantive doctrine, grounding a right not merely to a fair hearing but to the promised benefit itself. For example, a local authority that promised the claimants a 'home for life' in an institution for the chronically ill, was not permitted to disappoint the resultant legitimate expectation.[82]

The remarkable elasticity of the Rule of Law, and the richness of its underlying values, was demonstrated in a case that concerned the legal effect of a decision that had not been communicated to the person affected. The relevant legislation permitted asylum seekers' right to income support to be terminated once their application for asylum had been refused by a 'determination' of the Home Secretary. The refusal in this case was recorded only in an internal file note in the Home Office and communicated to the Benefits Agency, which promptly denied the appellant future income support. The determination was not, however, communicated to the appellant.[83]

The appellant in this case could not easily invoke the normal requirements of the Rule of Law in her favour. The decision did not take effect retrospectively; ignorance of the law does not normally excuse its application. Nevertheless, the House of Lords, by majority, held that the decision violated 'the constitutional principle requiring the Rule of Law to be observed'.[84] Lord Steyn, with whom the majority of their Lordships concurred, based his argument both upon legal certainty ('surprise is the enemy of justice') and upon accountability: the individual must be informed of the outcome of her case so 'she can decide what to do' and 'be in a position to challenge the decision in the courts' (this being an aspect of the principle of the right of access to justice).[85] The House of Lords had no truck with the notion that the Home Secretary's determination

[76] Ibid. [77] *R.* v. *Secretary of State for the Home Department ex parte Leech* (*No. 2*) [1994] QB 198.

[78] *R.* v. *Lord Chancellor ex parte Witham* [1997] 1 WLR 104.

[79] *Campbell et al* v. *The Republic of Zimbabwe* [2007] SADC (T) Case no. 2.

[80] *Her Majesty's Treasury* v. *Ahmed and others* [2010] UKSC 2. [81] See above, n. 75.

[82] *R.* v. *North and East Devon Health Authority ex parte Coughlan* [2001] QB 213.

[83] *R.* (*on the application of Anufrijeva*) v. *Secretary of State for the Home Department* [2003] 3 WLR 252.

[84] Ibid., at [28], *per* Lord Steyn. [85] Ibid., at [26] and [31], *per* Lord Steyn.

had formally and strictly been made. This was 'legalism and conceptualism run riot', which is reminiscent of the state described by Kafka 'where the rights of an individual are overridden by hole in the corner decisions or knocks on the doors in the early hours'.[86]

The Rule of Law does, therefore, possess substantive content.[87] It always has. Its promotion of the core institutional values of legality, certainty, consistency, due process, and access to justice do not merely, as Jennings would have it, further the aims of free trade and the market economy. They also promote respect for the dignity of the individual and enhance democratic accountability. The Rule of Law thus advances substantive as well as formal goals.[88] As a principle rather than a specific rule, the Rule of Law is elaborated in the light of the practical reason of each generation and the developing imperatives of contemporary democracy.[89]

THE RULE OF LAW AND HUMAN RIGHTS

The scope of the Rule of Law is broad,[90] but not broad enough to serve as a principle upholding a number of other requirements of a democracy. Some of the features of the Rule of Law are incorporated in the rights set out in the ECHR – the right to a fair trial, for example, or against retrospective laws. However, the Rule of Law is not covered by other Convention rights (such as the right to privacy or sexual freedom).

Yet in other respects the Rule of Law goes further than Convention rights. The case of the asylum seeker whose welfare benefits were removed without her knowledge is a case in point. Another is a recent case where the Immigration Rules were held unlawful because they were changed by the minister after having been laid before Parliament.[91] Sedley LJ held that the practice abandoned a 'constitutional principle which for four centuries has stood as a pillar of the separation of powers in what is today a democracy under the rule of law'. He held that rules which differed from those approved by Parliament violated 'the certainty which rules must have if they are to

[86] Ibid., at [32] and [28], *per* Lord Steyn. See also *FP (Iran)* v. *Secretary of State for the Home Department*, where Arden LJ invoked the Rule of Law to safeguard access to a tribunal – a right which 'cannot be taken away before it has been communicated to the person entitled to it', at [61].

[87] This passage was cited with approval by Lord Steyn in *R.* v. *Secretary of State for the Home Department ex parte Pierson* [1998] AC 539 (HL).

[88] See Rawls, *A Theory of Justice* 235–43, and cf. Joseph Raz's view of the Rule of Law as a negative value in 'The Rule of Law and its Virtue' (1977) *LQR* 195–211. See also J. Raz, *Ethics in the Public Domain* (1994) ch. 16. See also J. Finnis, *Natural Law and Natural Rights* (1980) 270–6.

[89] See D. N. McCormick, 'Jurisprudence and the Constitution' (1983) *Current Legal Problems* 13. See also Allan, above, n. 1, and Craig, and Barber, above, n. 32.

[90] See e.g. Lord Steyn in *R.* v. *Home Secretary ex parte Venables* [1988] AC 407, 526, who states that it would be 'an abdication of the Rule of Law' for the Home Secretary, in sentencing the children, to have regard to views expressed in a campaign by a popular newspaper.

[91] *R (Paninka)* v. *Secretary of State for the Home Department* [2010] EWCA Civ 719. See also *Her Majesty's Treasury* v. *Ahmed and others* [2010] UKSC 2, discussed above, n. 80.

function as law'. Recently the Supreme Court pronounced in a case where the release date of a prisoner was not accurately calculated by the Home Office (due to a morass of legislation and further amending legislation). It was said that 'it is simply unacceptable in a society governed by the rule of law for it to be well nigh impossible to discern from statutory provisions what a sentence means in practice'.[92]

One lively question is the extent to which the Rule of Law contains the principle of equality. We have seen that Dicey considered that the Rule of Law required all officials, from the Prime Minister down to a constable or a collector of taxes, to be subject to the same responsibility for every act done without legal justification as any other citizen.[93] Dicey is here claiming for the Rule of Law formal equality, by which he meant that no person is exempt from the enforcement of the law; rich and poor, revenue official and individual taxpayer are all within the equal reach of the arm of law's implementation.

This type of equality, although sometimes derided,[94] is important. It is inherent in the very notion of law, and in the integrity of law's application that like cases be treated alike over time. Its reach however is limited because its primary concern is not with the content of the law but with its *enforcement* and *application* alone. So long as laws are applied equally, that is without irrational bias or distinction, then formal equality is complied with. Formal equality does not however prohibit *unequal laws*. It forbids, say, racially biased enforcement of the law, but does not forbid racially discriminatory laws from being enacted. For Dicey, the Rule of Law embraced only formal equality. This is because for him the role of equality in the Rule of Law was instrumental; to buttress the central value of certainty. It was not espoused as a virtue for its own sake. We have seen how Dicey's supporters freely acknowledged that it is more important that the law be certain than it be not 'harsh', 'bad', or 'unjust'.[95] Discriminatory or arbitrary enforcement of the law would violate legal certainty, but laws themselves that discriminated against certain groups or classes, but were uniformly enforced within the groups or class, would not violate legal certainty, or therefore the Rule of Law.

There are two opposing views as to whether substantive equality qualifies as a feature of the Rule of Law.[96] Those who believe that discriminatory laws are not 'law' would of course not permit them to qualify as fulfilling the Rule of Law.[97] On the other hand, as Lord Hoffmann has said, equality is in itself 'one of the building blocks of democracy'.[98] It is therefore not necessary to subsume substantive equality within

[92] *R (Noone)* v. *The Governor of HMP Drake Hall* [2010] UKSC 30.

[93] See Dicey, above, n. 1, p. 193.

[94] See Horwitz, above, n. 3.

[95] See Maitland, above, n. 38, and Hayek, above, n. 39.

[96] Raz, above, n. 33, thinks not. Bingham, above, n. 5, thinks it does.

[97] See Dworkin, above, n. 34.

[98] *Matadeen* v. *Pointu and Minister of Education and Science* [1999] AC 98 (PC). See also *Ghaidan* v. *Godin Mendoza* [2004] 2 AC 557 (same sex partner entitled to same inheritance rights as different sex partner): '[Unequal treatment] is the reverse of rational behaviour... Power must not be exercised arbitrarily' (*per* Lady Hale).

the Rule of Law in order to demonstrate that discriminatory laws violate one of the fundamental requirements of democratic constitutionalism.[99]

THE RULE OF LAW AND PARLIAMENTARY SOVEREIGNTY

What about the Rule of Law's status in relation to the sovereignty of Parliament? In the UK the principle of parliamentary sovereignty has always been able to override the Rule of Law; not on the authority of any written constitution, but on the authority of commentators such as Dicey and repeated assertions by the courts over time. In the absence of any formal constitutional source, is it theoretically open to the Rule of Law to replace the sovereignty of Parliament as our primary constitutional principle? This issue was raised in a most unlikely case involving a challenge to the Hunting Act 2004, which banned the hunting of most wild mammals with dogs.[100] The central issue in the case was the validity of the Parliament Acts 1911 and 1949, which were invoked to ensure the passage of the Bill without the approval of the House of Lords. The Parliament Acts were upheld, as was the Hunting Act 2004, but three significant *obiter dicta* questioned the relation of parliamentary sovereignty to the Rule of Law as had never been done before. Lord Steyn said that:

> in exceptional circumstances involving an attempt to abolish judicial review or the authority of the courts, [the courts] may have to consider whether this is a constitutional fundamental which even a complaisant House of Commons cannot abolish.

Lady Hale said:

> The Courts will treat with particular suspicion (and might even reject) any attempt to subvert the rule of law by removing governmental action affecting the rights of the individual from all judicial powers.

And Lord Hope, even more forthrightly, said that 'it is no longer right to say that [Parliament's] freedom to legislate admits of no qualification' and that 'the rule of law enforced by the courts is the controlling principle upon which our constitution is based'.

It may take some time, provocative legislation, and considerable judicial courage for the courts to assert the primacy of the Rule of Law over parliamentary sovereignty, but it is no longer self-evident that a legislature in a modern democracy should be able with impunity to violate the strictures of the Rule of Law.[101]

[99] I have expanded on this point in 'Is Equality a Constitutional Principle?' (1994) 47 *Current Legal Problems* (Part 2) 1. See also R. Singh, 'Equality: The Neglected Virtue' [2004] *EHRLR* 141. For a view that equality (both formal and substantive) is part of the Rule of Law, see Allan, above, n. 1.

[100] *Jackson* v. *Her Majesty's Attorney General* [2005] UKHL 56.

[101] See J. Jowell, 'Parliamentary Sovereignty under the New Constitutional Hypothesis' [2006] *PL* 562.

CONCLUSION

In 1938, the American jurist Felix Frankfurter wrote that:

> the persistence of the misdirection that Dicey has given to the development of administrative law strikingly proves the elder Huxley's observation that many a theory survives long after its brains are knocked out.[102]

Dicey's Rule of Law has indeed been damaged over the years by those who attacked it for failing to recognize that official discretion is necessary to perform the welfare and regulatory functions of modern government. Writing about American law from 1780 to 1860, Morton Horwitz describes the growth of legal power to bring about economic redistribution in favour of powerful groups who carefully disguised under a neutral façade the class bias inherent in the law.[103] Robert Unger distinguishes the Rule of Law, which exists in societies governed by formal rules and procedures, from one in which communal bonds and shared values leave no need for this formal legality.[104] Writing in 2010, Martin Loughlin still considers the Rule of Law's limitations to be evident:

> not least because, founded on eighteenth-century political convictions concerning limited government, it has little bearing on the contemporary world. Like rule by law, the doctrine of the rule of law presents itself as an impossible ideal.[105]

In his book *Whigs and Hunters*[106] on the origins of the Black Act of 1723, which led to a 'flood-tide of eighteenth-century retributive justice',[107] E. P. Thompson, the Marxist historian, concludes that 'the Rule of Law itself, the imposing of effective inhibitions upon power and the defence of the citizen from power's all-intrusive claims, seems to me to be an unqualified human good'.[108] In a critical review, Horwitz disagreed:

> I do not see how a man of the left can describe the Rule of Law as an 'unqualified human good'! It undoubtedly restrains power, but it also prevents power's benevolent exercise. It creates formal equality – a not inconsiderable virtue – but it *promotes* substantive inequality by creating a consciousness that radically separates law from politics, means from ends, processes from outcomes. By promoting procedural justice it enables the shrewd, the calculating, the wealthy to manipulate its forms to their own advantage. And it ratifies and legitimates an adversarial, competitive, and atomistic conception of human relations.[109]

[102] F. Frankfurter, Foreword to 'Discussion of Current Developments in Administrative Law' (1938) 47 *Yale LJ* 515, 517.

[103] M. Horwitz, *The Transformation of American Law 1780–1860* (1977).

[104] R. Unger, *Law in Modern Society* (1976).

[105] Martin Loughlin, *Foundations of Public Law* (2010) 337.

[106] E. P. Thompson, *Whigs and Hunters: The Origin of the Black Act* (1975).

[107] Ibid., p. 23.

[108] Ibid., p. 266.

[109] Horwitz, above, n. 3. Like Horwitz, Unger (above, n. 104) sees general rules as crystallizing and legitimizing the power of the ruling class, yet giving a false appearance of neutrality.

Horwitz's view of the Rule of Law is misleading. Law can, of course, be oppressive, but we must be careful about equating the Rule of Law with the substance of particular rules or with the substantive quality of the legal system. To claim that unjust laws and their rigorous enforcement demonstrate that the Rule of Law is an instrument of oppression is as misleading as the claim (often made in totalitarian countries) that the world described in Kafka's *The Trial*, with its maze of legal procedures, consistently yet heartlessly enforced, represents a state of perfect legality. Legality must be distinguished from legalism; rule *by* law is different from the Rule of Law.[110]

Surely Thompson is right that the Rule of Law does impose 'effective inhibitions upon power' and the defence of the citizen from power's 'all-intrusive claims'. The Rule of Law guides all forms both of law enforcement and of law making. Its values are fundamental requirements of democratic constitutionalism which rise, time and again, to defeat the designs of the executive and other officials who step outside their conferred powers or who act unreasonably or unfairly. It is a principle that requires feasible limits on official power so as to constrain abuses on the part of even the most well-intentioned and compassionate of governments.

FURTHER READING

Allan, T. R. S., *Constitutional Justice: A Liberal Theory of the Rule of Law* (2001).

Bingham, T., *The Rule of Law* (2010).

Craig, P., 'Formal and Substantive Conceptions of the Rule of Law: An Analytical Framework' [1997] *Public Law* 447.

Dworkin, R., 'Political Judges and the Rule of Law', in his *A Matter of Principle* (1985) ch. 1.

European Commission for Democracy through Law (The Venice Commission) *Report on the Rule of Law* (CDL_AD (2011)003-e-March 2011).

Raz, J., 'The Rule of Law and its Virtue' (1977) 93 *LQR* 195.

[110] This has been the Chinese government's understanding of the Rule of Law. See further, B. Tamanaha, *On the Rule of Law: History, Politics, Theory* (2004) 92.

2

THE SOVEREIGNTY OF PARLIAMENT – FORM OR SUBSTANCE?

Anthony Bradley

SUMMARY

As the primary forum for political debate and because of its law-making role, the Westminster Parliament occupies a central place in both the legal and the political constitutions. It is regarded as a fundamental constitutional rule that there are no legal limits upon Westminster's legislative powers, and that the courts may not question or review the validity of legislation. The authority of Parliament includes power to make constitutional changes by ordinary process of legislation, unlike the specific amendment procedures that apply to written constitutions. But does this authority extend to the rules governing the relationship between the courts and Parliament that lie at the heart of the unwritten constitution? It has long been asserted that Parliament may not 'bind its successors' and thus may not create limitations on its own powers. However, so long as the UK remains a member of the European Union, Westminster's authority is limited by European law and the courts must disapply UK legislation if it conflicts with EU law. Less fundamental questions are raised by the creation of the Scottish Parliament, which affects the political but not the legal authority of Westminster to legislate for Scotland. The Human Rights Act 1998 maintains legislative sovereignty as a matter of form, but it authorizes the superior courts to declare legislation by Parliament to be incompatible with the European Convention on Human Rights (ECHR). Against this background of constitutional change, it is asked whether the reasons for maintaining the 'sovereign' authority of Westminster go to the form rather than the substance of legislative power. A further question is whether the democratic process in the UK works so well as to justify the absence of any limit on the authority of Parliament to legislate.

INTRODUCTION

Analysis of 'the British constitution' is bound to be influenced by the perspective of the analyst. Within a democracy, the worlds of government, law, and politics necessarily coexist. A legal analysis will examine the extent to which rules of law penetrate government and politics and will emphasize the legal framework by which the state is organized. A political analysis will concentrate on the way in which political power is exercised, on how leaders emerge, on the organization of parties, on the conduct of elections, and on the way in which the people determine the choice of a government and influence the way in which government exercises its powers.[1]

Both legal and political analyses must deal with the role of Parliament in the modern state. From a political perspective, Parliament is the historic forum where between elections the inter-party contest is fought and public opinion is expressed, public policies are debated and approved, and the government called to account. From a legal perspective, Parliament underpins the entire legal system and machinery of justice (by authorizing and funding the existence of courts, tribunals and judiciary),[2] and meets the need for legislation that exists in every contemporary legal system. Politicians are interested in the process of legislation (for instance, in securing maximum advantage from supporting or opposing Bills as they go through Parliament), whereas lawyers must be concerned with the outcome of that process.

From both legal and political perspectives, Parliament has a central place amongst the institutions of the state, even if it often appears to have a merely instrumental role in giving effect to executive decisions taken outside Parliament – and despite the dramatic loss of respect that many Members of Parliament suffered through the expenses revelations in 2009 and 2010. The phrase 'sovereignty of Parliament' is often used loosely, but it does not mean the sovereignty of the House of Commons. From a political perspective, it is only to the House of Commons that elected representatives come from every part of the UK; and only that House has the power, by withdrawing its confidence from the government, to require there to be a new government or a general election. But, although the House of Commons is the dominant House in Parliament, in general rule new legislation must be approved by both the Commons and the House of Lords. Even though the House of Lords is not elected, the 'sovereignty of Parliament' is more attractive than the sovereignty of a monarch or of a state executive. Moreover, the authority of Parliament as the national legislature parallels the authority of the UK as a state in international law.[3]

[1] Neil MacCormick said that 'politics is essentially concerned with the power of decision making in human communities on matters of communal interest or importance, with competition for that power, and with its exercise. As for law, the essence is not power but normative order.... Law is about institutional normative relations between normatively recognized persons of all sorts', N. MacCormick, 'Beyond the Sovereign State' (1993) 56 *MLR* 1, 11.

[2] Thus the Constitutional Reform Act 2005 made extensive changes in the judicial system, creating the Supreme Court for the UK in place of the appellate jurisdiction of the House of Lords, providing new procedures for appointment of judges and placing new responsibilities on the Lord Chief Justice of England and Wales. And see Chapter 11.

[3] There is a compelling argument that legal and political analysis alike must consider whether political organization, at least in the European Union, has moved beyond the notion of the 'sovereign state': see MacCormick, above, n. 1, and C. M. G. Himsworth, 'In a State no longer: the End of Constitutionalism' [1996] *Public Law* 639.

THE LEGAL DOCTRINE OF LEGISLATIVE SOVEREIGNTY

From the perspective of law, the sovereignty or supremacy of Parliament forms one of the pillars that are vital to the legal system. It is often regarded as the single ultimate source of legal authority.

As Goldsworthy has observed:

> What is at stake is the location of ultimate decision-making authority – the right to the 'final word' – in a legal system.[4]

Other jurists have placed the constitution on a dual foundation, comprising Parliament and the courts. One judge, Lord Bridge, said in 1991:

> In our society the Rule of Law rests upon twin foundations: the sovereignty of the Queen in Parliament in making the law and the sovereignty of the Queen's courts in interpreting and applying the law.[5]

On this approach, the two 'sovereignties' exercise related but distinct functions: law making, on the one hand; on the other, interpreting and applying the law. Plainly both courts and legislature must coexist, whatever the dividing line between their respective functions. Sir Stephen Sedley, a senior English judge, has written of 'a new and still emerging constitutional paradigm,...of a bi-polar sovereignty of the Crown in Parliament and the Crown in its courts, to each of which the crown's ministers are answerable – politically to Parliament, legally to the courts'.[6] This insight inevitably raises questions as to the respective boundaries of legislature and courts, such as whether these two institutions neatly complement each other or whether there is competition or rivalry between them – and, if there is a disagreement between them, how may this be resolved.

Most legal systems observe a 'hierarchy of norms', since not all laws have equal authority: in case of conflict a law, or norm, that is superior in the hierarchy prevails over one with lesser authority. In UK law, the authority of laws made by Parliament serves in an important sense as the yardstick by which the validity of other laws are assessed. In general, a clear provision in an Act of Parliament prevails over rules contained in subordinate legislation, or over rules of the common law. When in 1968 Ungoed-Thomas J was asked to set aside a provision in income tax legislation on the ground that it was contrary to international law, he said:

> What the statute itself enacts cannot be unlawful, because what the statute says and provides is itself the law, and *the highest form of law that is known to this country*. It is the law which prevails over every other form of law.[7]

[4] J. Goldsworthy, *The Sovereignty of Parliament: History and Philosophy* (1999) 126, quoted by T. Bingham, *The Rule of Law* (2010) 167.

[5] *X* v. *Morgan-Grampian (Publishers) Ltd* [1991] 1 AC 1, 48. Lord Cooke of Thorndon, president of the New Zealand Court of Appeal, emphasized the complementary roles of a democratic legislature and independent courts: 'Fundamentals' (1988) *NZLJ* 158, 164.

[6] S. Sedley, 'Human Rights: a Twenty-First Century Agenda' [1995] *Public Law* 386, 389.

[7] *Cheney* v. *Conn* [1968] 1 All ER 779, 782 (emphasis supplied).

For several reasons, a statement about the authority of statute law in precisely these words would be unlikely today. One reason is the overriding effect that the courts now ascribe to EU law.[8] Another reason is the awareness of international human rights law that has developed since 1968.[9] As regards the judge's statement that 'what the statute says and provides *is itself the law*', it is fundamental in a legal system that the meaning of a statute and its application to particular facts are for the courts to determine.[10] Although the courts today, when a statutory provision is ambiguous, may look in *Hansard* at ministerial statements made in Parliament about the intended meaning,[11] an authoritative ruling on the intention of Parliament and the effect of a statute comes only from a judicial decision.

PARLIAMENTARY SOVEREIGNTY AS A LEGAL DOCTRINE

Not only since the publication in 1885 of A. V. Dicey's *The Law of the Constitution* but also long before this,[12] the sovereignty of Parliament has been one of the fundamental doctrines of constitutional law in the UK. In 1689, after the overthrow of James II but before the union of the English and Scottish Parliaments in 1707, the Earl of Shaftesbury wrote:

> The Parliament of England is that supreme and absolute power, which gives life and motion to the English Government.[13]

Despite the extensive political and social changes that have occurred since 1885, and despite criticism which his work received from constitutional lawyers such as Sir Ivor Jennings,[14] Dicey's statement of the doctrine has had a remarkable influence on both legal and political thinking about Parliament. Dicey summarized his views in this way:

> The principle of Parliamentary sovereignty means neither more nor less than this, namely, that Parliament [defined as the Queen, the House of Lords, and the House of Commons, acting together]...has, under the English constitution, the right to make or unmake any law whatever; and, further, that no person or body is recognised by the law as having a right to override or set aside the legislation of Parliament.[15]

[8] See below, and Chapter 4. [9] See below, and Chapters 3 and 5.

[10] On judicial interpretation of legislation, see (from different perspectives) A. Kavanagh, *Constitutional Review under the UK Human Rights Act* (2009) ch. 2, and J. Goldsworthy, *Parliamentary Sovereignty: Contemporary Debates* (2010) ch. 9.

[11] *Pepper* v. *Hart* [1993] AC 593. See also *R.* v. *Secretary of State for the Environment ex parte Spath Holme Ltd* [2001] 2 AC 349, and J. Steyn, 'Pepper v. Hart: a Re-examination' (2001) 21 *Ox J Legal Studies* 59.

[12] Goldsworthy, above, n. 4, argues with much illustrative material that Dicey's analysis of the sovereignty of Parliament was the restatement of a central theme in English legal history.

[13] *Some Observations Concerning the Regulating of Elections for Parliament* (1689), quoted in Goldsworthy, above, n. 4, p. 150.

[14] See I. Jennings, *The Law and the Constitution* (5th edn, 1959).

[15] A. V. Dicey, *The Law of the Constitution* (10th edn, 1959, edited by E. C. S. Wade) 39–40.

The principle, 'looked at from its positive side', ensures that any new statute will be obeyed by the courts. The same principle, 'looked at from its negative side', ensures that there is no person or body of persons who can make rules which override or derogate from an Act of Parliament or which, 'to express the same thing in other words',[16] will be enforced by the courts in contravention of an Act.

A further implication drawn from the principle is that a sovereign Parliament is not bound by the Acts of its predecessors: thus no Parliament can 'bind its successors'. This aspect of sovereignty has arisen because the courts, when faced with two conflicting statutes on the same subject, have applied the rule that the later Act prevails. By the doctrine of implied repeal, the later Act repeals the earlier Act to the extent that the later Act is inconsistent with provisions in the earlier Act.[17] This doctrine has been pressed into service to sustain the proposition that the one rule of the common law that Parliament may not change is the rule that the courts must always apply the latest Act of Parliament on a subject.[18] The validity of this over-broad proposition is examined below.

THE SOURCE OF LEGISLATIVE SOVEREIGNTY

Discussion of legislative sovereignty is bound to raise fundamental questions about the relationship between courts and Parliament.[19] It would be attractive if we could identify the legal source of the doctrine of sovereignty, but this is not an easy task. Could the source of the sovereignty of Parliament be found in an Act of Parliament itself? A well-known, but over-simple, answer to this question was given by the jurist, Sir John Salmond:

> No statute can confer this power on Parliament for this would be to assume and act on the very power that is to be conferred.[20]

But Parliament might be entitled to make such an assumption if over many years it had enacted a wide variety of statutes without its authority to legislate being questioned. Indeed, this leads directly to the next question, whether the legal source of authority for the doctrine of sovereignty may be found in decisions of the courts. Again, by similar logic, no decision of the court can confer ultimate authority to decide on the courts, for this would be to assume the very power to be conferred.[21] Yet decisions of the courts are authoritative in determining the common law. Thus the sovereignty of Parliament can be said to be based upon judicial decisions

[16] Ibid.

[17] See *Ellen Street Estates Ltd* v. *Minister of Health* [1934] 1 KB 590; and below, text at n. 74.

[18] H. W. R. Wade, 'The Basis of Legal Sovereignty' [1955] *Cambridge LJ* 172, 186–9.

[19] 'Traditionally, English lawyers have not worried about the problem of first causes; for them it is enough that authority can be found in Acts of Parliament *and* decisions of the courts': R. Q. Quentin-Baxter (1985) 15 *Victoria University of Wellington LR* 12, 13.

[20] Salmond, *Jurisprudence* (7th edn, 1924) 170; and see Wade, above, n. 18, p. 187.

[21] For a refutation of the 'myth of the common law constitution', see Goldsworthy, above, n. 10, ch. 2.

applying Acts of Parliament: if the courts when doing this say that they *must* do so because they are bound by *all* such Acts, then they are declaring a fundamental rule, namely that effect must be given to Acts of Parliament, whatever their content.

A third possibility, rather than attributing the source of legislative sovereignty to Parliament or to the courts acting separately, is to examine the past and present relationship between the courts, the legislature, and other stake-holders in the state, including the public at large, looking at what courts and legislature have done in relation to each other, and at the stance of other key actors in the political system (such as ministers of the Crown).[22] Since such an approach looks at past events, it may find that legislative sovereignty came about through a historical process, rather than from a 'big bang' creation of a fundamental rule. The pattern of past events may be assumed to continue, but has constitutional evolution in this area come to a full stop? Changes in the relationship between state institutions may occur over time, if only to reflect changes in the institutions themselves. Moreover, changes may happen more rapidly where the stimulus for change is created by a radical initiative taken by the legislature. In this situation the courts might respond to such an initiative in a manner for which there was no direct precedent, and in a way that the new legislation has not expressly stipulated.

'THE CONSTITUTION' AS THE SOURCE OF LEGISLATIVE SOVEREIGNTY?

In the passage quoted above, Dicey said that the Queen in Parliament 'has *under the English constitution* the right to make or unmake any law whatever'.[23] Where a state has a written constitution, this text may be regarded as the formal source from which all organs of the state, including legislature and courts, derive their powers. The United States Constitution of 1787 allocated the legislative, executive, and judicial powers of the new federal state respectively to Congress, the President, and the Supreme Court and other federal courts. Plainly the framers intended the Constitution to be binding on these bodies, but their text did not state whether an Act of Congress that was inconsistent with the Constitution must be applied by the Supreme Court, or whether the Court could declare the Act to be unconstitutional and thus unlawful. In the case of *Marbury* v. *Madison*, Marshall CJ said:

> The constitution is either a superior paramount law, unchallengeable by ordinary means, or it is on a level with ordinary legislative acts, and, like other acts, is alterable when the legislature shall be pleased to alter it. If the former part of the alternative is true, then a legislative act contrary to the constitution is not law; if the latter part be true, then written

[22] Cf. Goldsworthy, above, n. 4, ch. 10.

[23] Implications of the word 'English' in Dicey's usage are relevant to discussion of Scottish devolution below.

constitutions are absurd attempts, on the part of the people, to limit a power in its own nature illimitable.[24]

Upholding as it did the duty of the courts 'to say what the law is', *Marbury* v. *Madison* is one of the most influential decisions of English-speaking courts ever made. Today, judicial review of legislation on constitutional grounds is practised in many countries. Where such review occurs, the legislature is not sovereign but is limited by rules that are enforced by a supreme or constitutional court.

By contrast, since the UK has no written constitution, for Dicey to refer to 'the constitution' as the source of Parliament's authority is but to create difficulty. What *is* the constitution, in the absence of a written text? One political historian has written that the constitution is a historical process, 'an integrated expression of historical experience conferring a unified meaning on political existence'.[25] A senior judge, Sir John Laws, has said that the absence of a written constitution 'means that the legal distribution of public power consists ultimately in a dynamic settlement, acceptable to the people, between the different arms of government'.[26] Emphasis on a dynamic experience is important, since the 'constitution' of the UK is today experiencing a period of change, some of it resulting from deliberate political initiative, some of it resulting from evolving relationships within the state. Just as the UK's constitutional law changed during the 20th century to reflect the end of Empire,[27] so more recently it has adjusted to events that have taken the UK into the European Union. Since 1998, the reception into national law of the ECHR and the devolution of powers within the UK are political events to which the structure of constitutional law may need to adjust.

DEMOCRATIC BASIS FOR PARLIAMENTARY SOVEREIGNTY

Dicey's belief in the legislative power of Parliament was directly related to his view of the representative character of the legislature in the 1880s.[28] Thus he wrote:

as things now stand, the will of the electorate, and certainly of the electorate in combination with the Lords and the Crown, is sure ultimately to prevail on all subjects to be determined by the British government.... *The electors can in the long run always enforce their will.*[29]

For Dicey, this expression of democracy was linked with the sovereignty of the nation itself. However, there are many sovereign states without sovereign Parliaments, and there is no necessary connection between national sovereignty and the authority of

[24] Cranch 103, 177 (1803). [25] M. Foley, *The Silence of Constitutions* (1989) 87.

[26] J. Laws, 'Law and Democracy' [1995] *Public Law* 72, 81.

[27] P. C. Oliver, *The Constitution of Independence: the Development of Constitutional Theory in Australia, Canada and New Zealand* (2005), provides an illuminating study of parliamentary sovereignty, as well as its application in three common law countries.

[28] Dicey, above, n. 15, p. 68.

[29] Dicey, above, n. 15, p. 73, emphasis supplied. And cf. P. P. Craig, *Public Law and Democracy in the UK and the USA* (1990) ch. 2.

the national legislature. Legislative sovereignty in itself does not imply any particular degree of democracy in the structure of Parliament.[30] However, if the nature of the political system in 1885 was a vital influence on Dicey's analysis of sovereignty, events since then may call for sovereignty to be reassessed. The expansion of executive power, developments in the party system, changes in the electoral system, and the dominance of the government over the Commons mean that the government today can use the legislative process to carry out its policies, often without there being effective restraints or control. It would be wrong to assume that the electorate can always achieve its will, even supposing that it is possible to discover what the will of the electorate as an entity may be.

SOVEREIGNTY OF PARLIAMENT EXCLUDES JUDICIAL REVIEW

We have seen that under the sovereignty of Parliament, the courts may not review legislation with a view to deciding on its validity:

> In the courts there may be argument as to the correct interpretation of the enactment: there must be none as to whether it should be on the statute book at all.[31]

This position is thus very different from those countries where the courts may review legislation to see whether it conforms to the constitution. Is it possible that, in the absence of a written constitution, the judges could of their own initiative begin to review legislation by Parliament, based (say) on the need to respect fundamental human rights? The practice of British judges has long been to deny that they have any such role.[32] As the court said in 1872:

> There is no judicial body in the country by which the validity of an Act of Parliament can be questioned.[33]

Nevertheless, some judges have warned that 'some common law rights... lie so deep that even Parliament could not override them'.[34] In 1995, Lord Woolf argued that both Parliament and the courts were ultimately subject to the Rule of Law, so that if Parliament were to embark on the unthinkable by enacting legislation that undermined in a fundamental way the Rule of Law on which the unwritten constitution depends, the courts would not necessarily be required to uphold such legislation.[35] But in their decisions the courts continued to emphasize the power of Parliament to infringe even fundamental rights if it makes a sufficiently clear statement of its intention to do so. Thus, when Laws J struck down regulations made by the Lord Chancellor that prescribed fees that had to be paid to gain access to the court by every litigant

[30] Cf. Dicey, above, n. 15, pp. 70–85.

[31] *Pickin* v. *British Railways Board* [1974] AC 765, 789 (Lord Morris).

[32] Goldsworthy, above, n. 4, *passim*.

[33] *Ex parte Selwyn* (1872) 36 JP 54.

[34] *Taylor* v. *New Zealand Poultry Board* [1984] 1 NZLR 394, 398 (Sir Robin Cooke).

[35] Lord Woolf, 'Droit Public – English Style' [1995] *Public Law* 57, 67–9. See also Lord Woolf, 'Judicial Review – The Tensions Between the Executive and the Judiciary' (1998) 114 *LQR* 579; J. Laws, 'Law and Democracy' [1995] *Public Law* 72; and Sedley, above, n. 6.

(however poor), the basis of the decision was that Parliament had neither expressly nor by necessary implication authorized regulations that took away what the judge described as a 'common law constitutional right'.[36] Similarly, the House of Lords observed that there is a constitutional principle of legality in the light of which all legislation must be interpreted. Lord Hoffmann said that while Parliament 'can, if it chooses, legislate contrary to fundamental principles of human rights', the constraints on the exercise by Parliament of this power 'are ultimately political, not legal. But the principle of legality means that Parliament must squarely confront what it is doing and accept the political cost'.[37]

We examine below what the effect of the Human Rights Act 1998 on legislative supremacy has been. The fundamental question (whether a judge must in all circumstances give effect to legislation that affects fundamental rights in a manner that is morally repugnant) might need to be answered in the future should fears of 'unthinkable' legislation re-emerge despite the Human Rights Act 1998.

ONLY ACTS OF PARLIAMENT ARE SUPREME

The immunity of Acts of Parliament from judicial review does not extend to other documents or instruments that lack the same status. Measures that are in principle subject to judicial review include decisions taken by the Crown under prerogative power,[38] acts of devolved legislatures within the UK,[39] and subordinate instruments made by ministers of the Crown under delegated powers.[40] Nor is a resolution of the House of Commons effective to change the law.[41] Subject only to the Parliament Acts 1911 and 1949,[42] for a Bill to become law it must have been approved by both Houses of Parliament, and must have received the royal assent.[43] To decide whether these conditions are satisfied, and to avoid interfering with the internal proceedings of Parliament,[44] the courts have a limited function. As Lord Campbell said in 1842:

[36] *R.* v. *Lord Chancellor ex parte Witham* [1998] QB 575.

[37] *R* v. *Secretary of State for the Home Department ex parte Simms* [1999] 3 All ER 400, 412. Both common law principles and the Human Rights Act 1998 were applied in *R. (Daly)* v. *Secretary of State for the Home Department* [2001] UKHL 26, [2001] 2 AC 532.

[38] *CCSU* v. *Minister for the Civil Service* [1985] AC 374; *R. (Bancoult)* v. *Secretary of State for Foreign Affairs (No 2)* [2008] UKHL 61, [2009] 1 AC 453 (prerogative Order in Council).

[39] See e.g. *R. (Hume et al)* v. *Londonderry Justices* [1972] NILR 91; *Anderson et al.* v. *Scottish Ministers* [2001] UKPC D5, [2003] 2 AC 602.

[40] *Hoffmann-La Roche & Co.* v. *Secretary of State for Trade* [1975] AC 295, 365; *R.* v. *HM Treasury ex parte Smedley* [1985] QB 657. See also *R (Bancoult)* v. *Secretary of State for Foreign and Commonwealth Affairs* [2001] QB 1067.

[41] *Bowles* v. *Bank of England* [1913] 1 Ch 57.

[42] These are discussed below, text at nn. 51–55.

[43] *The Prince's case* (1606) 8 Co. Rep. 1a.

[44] And thus risk breaching the Bill of Rights 1689, Art. 9 (which protects 'proceedings in Parliament' from being impeached or questioned in any court or place out of Parliament). It does not breach Art. 9 for the courts to read *Hansard* for resolving an ambiguity in legislation: see above, n. 11.

> All that the Court of Justice can do is to look to the Parliament roll: if from that it should appear that a Bill has passed both Houses and received the Royal Assent, no Court of Justice can inquire into the mode in which it was introduced into Parliament, or into what was done previous to its introduction, or what passed in Parliament during its progress in its various stages through both Houses.[45]

This limited test, known as the 'enrolled Act' rule, leaves it to each House to regulate its internal procedures without interference from the courts.

THE QUESTION OF DEFINITION – WHAT IS AN ACT OF PARLIAMENT?

Disputes occasionally arose in the past as to whether a document before the court was an Act of Parliament.[46] It would be highly unusual today for an issue to arise as to whether a particular instrument is or is not an Act of Parliament.[47] Indeed, the reluctance of British courts to review the content of legislation extends to the process by which it has been enacted. Thus the courts decline to deal with questions of parliamentary procedure, taking the view that these are matters for Parliament itself.[48] A similar position exists in relation to Acts of the Scottish Parliament: by the Scotland Act 1998, s. 28(5), issues may not be raised as to whether the procedures of the Parliament were duly observed before the measures were enacted. But for this provision, the courts could have been asked to hold that a failure to follow the procedure for legislation meant that the outcome was invalid.[49] By contrast with this procedural protection for Acts of the Scottish Parliament, if the contents of such an Act are outside the powers of the Parliament, the provision will be held void.

As this illustration indicates, judicial review of legislation could be based on: (a) the procedure by which it has been enacted; and/or (b) the contents of the legislation. For the Westminster Parliament, the Dicey doctrine of legislative sovereignty does not make this distinction. However, the proposition that the courts ought not to review what the *contents* of legislation should be (since it must be open to the legislature for the time being to decide what laws to make) does not necessarily exclude the court from having jurisdiction to review whether the essential *procedures* of legislation have

[45] *Edinburgh and Dalkeith Railway* v. *Wauchope* (1842) 8 Cl. & F. 710, 725; and *Pickin* v. *British Railways Board* [1974] AC 765.

[46] See Goldsworthy, above, n. 4, p. 144, quoting Sir Orlando Bridgeman in 1660: 'it is no derogation to parliaments, that what is a statute should be adjudged by the common laws. We have often brought it into question, whether such and such a thing was an Act of Parliament, or not'. Howell, *State Trials*, v, 1066.

[47] But see *R. (Jackson)* v. *Attorney-General*, discussed below. Under the Human Rights Act 1998 problems may arise from the distinction between primary and subordinate legislation drawn by the Act: see below, n. 146.

[48] *Pickin* v. *British Railways Board*, above, n. 31. See also *Manuel* v. *Attorney-General* [1983] Ch 77 (Canada Act 1982 challenged unsuccessfully on the basis that the Indian people in Canada had not consented to it).

[49] And see *Whaley* v. *Lord Watson of Invergowrie* 2000 SC 125 (observation by Lord President Rodger that Scottish courts have no discretion not to enforce the law against the Scottish Parliament; and that Westminster, compared with many national legislatures, is unusual in its immunity from judicial review).

been observed. This distinction has been taken up by a number of constitutional lawyers in propounding what has been called the 'new view' of parliamentary sovereignty: on this view, the courts may consider whether the procedure of legislation adopted in a particular case has complied with the 'manner and form' that is in law required if legislation is to be validly enacted.[50] This position accepts that the Parliament has authority to legislate on any matter, but permits questions to arise as to whether it has followed the requisite procedure in doing so.

THE HUNTING ACT 2004 CASE

A rare instance of the UK courts having to decide on procedural grounds whether a document before them was in law a valid Act of Parliament arose in *R.* (*Jackson*) v. *Attorney General*.[51] We have seen that, under the 'enrolled Act' rule, for a Bill to be presented for the royal assent it must have been approved in each House: thus the House of Lords formerly had the power to veto legislation approved by the Commons. In 1911, the permanent Conservative majority in the Lords persistently blocked measures proposed by the Liberal government: the crisis was resolved only when the Parliament Act converted the Lords' power into a delaying power, thus enabling a Bill to become law after a period of delay (initially of two years, but reduced to one year in 1949) without the Lords having approved it.

The Hunting Bill, which aimed to abolish the ancient practice of hunting wild animals with hounds, had in two sessions of Parliament been blocked by the Lords, and the royal assent had been given to it under the Parliament Acts 1911 and 1949. The hunt supporters claimed that the Hunting Act 2004 was not law because its validity depended on the Parliament Act 1949 (reducing the delaying power of the Lords from two years to one year) which was itself invalid.

The foremost fact on which the claimants relied was that the 1949 Act had itself been passed under the 1911 Act, without the approval of the Lords. They argued that the authority delegated to the monarch and Commons in 1911 to legislate without consent of the Lords could not be used to amend the 1911 Act by reducing the delaying power of the Lords. The Law Lords, sitting as a court of nine judges, unanimously rejected this argument. Their speeches gave a wide variety of reasons for this conclusion.[52] One common theme was that in 1911 Parliament had authorized the Commons and monarch to legislate without the Lords, and the procedure was thus an alternative to the usual process of legislation. A measure passed under the 1911 Act was primary

[50] See e.g. R. F. V. Heuston, *Essays in Constitutional Law* (2nd edn, 1964) ch. 1; and G. Marshall, *Constitutional Theory* (1971) ch. 3.

[51] [2005] UKHL 56, [2006] 1 AC 262.

[52] For an analysis of the judgments, see 7th report of the House of Lords Committee on the Constitution, 'Constitutional aspects of the challenge to the Hunting Act 2004', HL Paper 141 (2005–06), App. 3 (A. W. Bradley). See also Lord Cooke of Thorndon, 'A Constitutional Retreat' (2006) 122 *LQR* 224, and M. Plaxton, 'The Concept of Legislation: *Jackson* v. *Attorney-General*' (2006) 69 *MLR* 249.

legislation, not delegated legislation, and the maxim *delegatus non potest delegare*[53] did not apply. The power to legislate without the Lords was not subject to implied limitations, only to the express limitations set out in the 1911 Act. The most important of these limitations was that the Act excluded from the procedure any power to prolong the life of Parliament beyond five years. It was not in dispute that a Bill that purported to prolong the life of Parliament beyond five years could not be enacted unless the Lords had approved it.

In *Jackson*, it was accepted by the Attorney General, arguing for the government, that the judges had jurisdiction to decide whether the Hunting Act 2004 was a valid statute. The Law Lords treated the question of validity as turning on a point of law (namely, the correct interpretation of the 1911 Act) and that the issue was one that judges were competent to decide. Although the Hunting Act 2004 was held to be an Act of Parliament, the judges did not hold that it was an Act of the sovereign Parliament – albeit that it was indirectly the outcome of a process authorized by the sovereign Parliament in 1911.[54] As the Parliament Act procedure was subject to express limitations contained in the 1911 Act (notably the exclusion from it of Bills to prolong the life of Parliament), we may conclude that Parliament consisting of the Commons and the monarch is not a sovereign legislature, since it does not have 'the right to make or unmake any law whatever'. Indeed, a majority of judges held *obiter* that the 1911 Act could not be used to force through an extension in the life of Parliament beyond five years, even if the exercise were to be attempted in two stages – first, in an Act to remove the limitation on the power, and secondly, only then to extend the life of Parliament.[55]

JUDICIAL INTERPRETATION AND APPLICATION OF LEGISLATION

We have already seen that the courts play a vital role in making authoritative decisions as to the meaning and effect of legislation. For Dicey, this role of the courts was an essential element in the Rule of Law:

> Powers [of the executive], however extraordinary, are never really unlimited, for they are confined by the words of the Act itself, and, what is more, by the interpretation put upon the statute by the judges. Parliament is supreme legislator, but from the moment Parliament has uttered its will as law giver, that will becomes subject to the interpretation put upon it by the judges ...[56]

[53] It was argued in *Jackson* that power to legislate had been delegated to the House of Commons and the monarch, and that the power could not be used to reduce limitations placed on the exercise of the power. And see A. McHarg, 'What is delegated legislation?' [2006] *Public Law* 539.

[54] See R. Ekins, 'Acts of Parliament and the Parliament Acts' (2007) 123 *LQR* 81.

[55] See the speeches of Lords Nicholls, Steyn, Hope, Carswell, and Lady Hale. Lord Bingham considered that a two-stage course of legislation to amend the 1911 Act would succeed.

[56] Dicey, above, n. 15, p. 413. The importance of judicial interpretation of legislation is examined by T. R. S. Allen, *Law, Liberty and Justice: the Legal Foundations of British Constitutionalism* (1993) 35–9 and ch. 4, and see above, n. 10.

One instance of this, important in administrative law, is the proposition that the executive's statutory powers are never 'unfettered'; even when a statutory discretion is phrased in absolute terms, the courts do not accept that the power is unlimited.[57] Statutory interpretation resembles judicial review of administrative action in being very far from a mechanical process; the courts need both to respond to social change[58] and to protect constitutional values.[59] Judicial interpretation of statute minimizes the risk of unintended constitutional changes being made through the use of general, and not express, words.[60] Presumptions of interpretation made by the courts include such matters as the presumption that property should not be taken without compensation, that those accused of criminal offences are to be presumed innocent until the contrary is proved,[61] that an individual's access to the courts should not be taken away,[62] and so on.

Such a presumption is 'a presumption of general application operating as a constitutional principle'.[63] Effect may be given to such presumptions when a statutory provision is ambiguous, or, more importantly, where general powers are conferred and the issue is whether the powers extend to encroaching upon human rights: Parliament can if it chooses legislate contrary to fundamental principles of human rights, but must do so explicitly. In dealing with the effect in national law of the ECHR before the Human Rights Act 1998, the House of Lords held that where an Act granted a general power to a minister to take action of a certain kind, the power was not ambiguous and its width could not be cut down by reference to the Convention.[64] The House of Lords subsequently stated its willingness to rely on a presumption in favour of the principle of legality even where there was no statutory ambiguity.[65]

Although these presumptions were judge-made, the practice of the courts in statutory interpretation can be altered by Act of Parliament.[66] One striking feature of the Human Rights Act 1998 is that it introduced a new rule of interpretation whereby all legislation must, 'so far as it is possible to do so', be interpreted so as to be consistent with the Convention rights protected by the Act.

[57] *Padfield* v. *Minister of Agriculture* [1968] AC 997.

[58] *Fitzpatrick* v. *Sterling Housing Association Ltd* [2001] 1 AC 271 (same sex partner of protected tenant may be member of tenant's family for purpose of succeeding to a statutory tenancy).

[59] See D. Feldman, 'Public Law Values in the House of Lords' (1990) 106 *LQR* 246, and cf. F. Bennion, *Statutory Interpretation* (5th edn, 2008) 1033–64.

[60] Cf. *Nairn* v. *University of St Andrews* [1909] AC 147.

[61] As to which, see *R.* v. *Lambert* [2001] UKHL 37, [2002] 2 AC 69.

[62] See above, n. 36.

[63] *R.* v. *Secretary of State for the Home Department ex parte Simms*, above, n. 37, p. 411 (Lord Steyn). And see R. Cross (eds J. Bell and G. Engle), *Statutory Interpretation* (1995) 166.

[64] *R.* v. *Secretary of State for the Home Department ex parte Brind* [1991] 1 AC 696.

[65] See cases cited above at n. 37.

[66] This is not to accept that the role of statutory interpretation could be taken away from the courts and substituted by executive decisions. This would be highly controversial in terms of the Rule of Law, and it would infringe the principle of legality protected by the ECHR, especially Art. 6(1).

PARLIAMENT MAY BY LEGISLATION MAKE CHANGES IN CONSTITUTIONAL LAW

In countries in which there is a written constitution that provides for its own amendment (for instance, by a process involving a referendum or a special majority in the legislature), the constitution can be lawfully amended only if that procedure is followed.[67] By contrast, the Westminster Parliament has authority to make changes in constitutional law, and no special procedure is needed even for novel courses of action (as for instance when Parliament in 1975 authorized a referendum on Britain's membership of the European Economic Community (EEC)). Since 1997, Parliament has created elected assemblies in Scotland and Wales to exercise devolved powers, has enacted the Human Rights Act 1998, has introduced the registration of political parties, and has excluded most hereditary peers from the House of Lords. Indeed, the exclusion of hereditary peers took effect at the end of the 1998–99 session of Parliament, even though the peers excluded had in May 1997 received writs of summons from the Queen to attend at Westminster for the life of the Parliament.[68]

The sovereignty of Parliament provides a remarkably flexible and efficient instrument for achieving constitutional reform. As the Royal Commission on reform of the House of Lords commented in 2000:

> There can be little question that the raft of constitutional legislation introduced by the current Government in its first two years of office.... would have been impossible under the laborious systems required to amend the written constitutions of many other countries.[69]

The powers of Parliament extend to reforming the composition and powers of its two Houses. As we have seen, the Parliament Acts 1911 and 1949 allow legislation to be enacted that has not been approved by the Lords. Although that procedure has seldom been used,[70] the availability of the procedure influences the relations between the two Houses, and the upper House is likely to give special attention to the constitutional implications of government Bills.

DOES PARLIAMENT'S POWER EXTEND TO LEGISLATING ON ALL FUNDAMENTAL CONSTITUTIONAL RULES?

While the Parliament of Commons, Lords, and monarch may change the composition of the two Houses, may reform the electoral system, and may create devolved governments, difficult questions arise about Parliament's power to legislate on certain

[67] See e.g. *Harris* v. *Minister of the Interior* 1952 (2) SA 428; *Independent Jamaica Council for Human Rights v Marshall-Burnett* [2005] UKPC 3, [2005] 2 AC 356.

[68] *Lord Mayhew of Twysden's Motion* [2002] 1 AC 109.

[69] *A House for the Future*, Cm. 4534 (2000) para. 5.2.

[70] Between 1911 and 2010, seven Acts were enacted under the Parliament Act procedure: the Government of Ireland Act 1914, the Welsh Church Act 1914, the Parliament Act 1949, the War Crimes Act 1991, the European Parliamentary Elections Act 1999, the Sexual Offences (Amendment) Act 2000, and the Hunting Act 2004.

constitutional matters. Two difficulties must be addressed. First, it is widely held that a sovereign Parliament is not bound by the Acts of its predecessors, and thus that no Parliament can 'bind its successors'. Secondly, on a related point, it is said that an Act of Parliament may change all rules of the common law except the rule whereby the courts recognize as law the Acts of Parliament.[71]

The rule that Parliament may not bind its successors has arisen in part because of the rule that when the courts are faced with two conflicting statutes on the same subject, they must apply the later Act of Parliament – the doctrine of implied repeal.[72] It must in general be possible for a future Parliament to legislate on a given subject, even if this means changing the law laid down by a former Parliament. There is, however, uncertainty as to the scope and effect of the doctrine of implied repeal.[73] In a well-known *obiter dictum*, Maugham LJ said in *Ellen Street Estates Ltd* v. *Minister of Health*:

> The legislature cannot, according to our constitution, bind itself as to the form of subsequent legislation, and it is impossible for Parliament to enact that in a subsequent statute dealing with the same subject-matter there can be no implied repeal.[74]

This proposition may be a means of resolving an awkward conflict between two Acts passed at different dates, but it goes very deeply into constitutional territory and it does not address the distinction drawn above between the procedure and the content of legislation. Its origin lies in Dicey's doctrine that a sovereign Parliament cannot bind its successors for the reason that the successor Parliament would not then itself be sovereign. Dicey said this:

> The logical reason why Parliament has failed in its endeavours to enact unchangeable enactments is that a sovereign power cannot, *while retaining its sovereign character*, restrict its own powers by any parliamentary enactment (original emphasis).

In a celebrated article, Sir William Wade justified the sovereignty of Parliament as a political fact that was fundamental to the legal system and could be changed only by the occurrence of events that constituted a revolutionary change in the ultimate basis of the legal system.[75] This argument challenged the views of critics of Dicey such as Jennings[76] and Latham,[77] who considered that Parliament's powers extended to legislating on the supremacy of Parliament itself. Herbert Hart, the legal philosopher, argued in *The Concept of Law* that the rules concerning the competence of the supreme legislature provided 'the ultimate rule of recognition' for the identification of law. Hart denied that it was a 'logical necessity' that the legislature should be sovereign in the sense that it should be free from any legal limitations, including those derived

[71] Wade, above, n. 18, pp. 186–9. [72] See above, text at n. 17.

[73] See A. Young, *Parliamentary Sovereignty and the Human Rights Act* (2009) ch. 2.

[74] [1934] 1 KB 590, 597. [75] Wade, above, n. 18.

[76] I. Jennings, *The Law and the Constitution* (5th edn, 1959). And M. Gordon, 'The Conceptual Foundations of Parliamentary Sovereignty: reconsidering Jennings and Wade' [2009] *Public Law* 519.

[77] R. T. E. Latham, *The Law and the Commonwealth* (1949).

from its own prior legislation. The reason why this was not a logical necessity, said Hart, was the ambiguity in the idea of legal omnipotence, since such omnipotence might logically be regarded either as *continuing* (restricted to all matters not affecting the competence of future parliaments) or as *self-embracing* (including matters that did affect that competence). In Hart's view, the prevailing constitutional view in the UK was one of continuing supremacy, but he added that the rule of continuing supremacy did not necessarily apply to all topics that might be the subject of future legislation.[78]

In any event, Parliament by legislation may determine the composition of Parliament: for example, by requiring the Commons to be elected by proportional representation and the Lords to be replaced by an appointed Senate. As so constituted, that Parliament would have the sole authority to decide whether further changes in the composition of Parliament should be made. So too, as shown by numerous statutes enacted at Westminster that have conferred independence on territories overseas, a sovereign Parliament may make an irreversible transfer of legislative authority in respect of particular territory.[79] Such a transfer does not require that a territory should itself acquire a sovereign legislature, as the competence of the territory's legislature would depend on the constitutional package that accompanied independence. In a similar way, a reconstruction of the Westminster Parliament might be accompanied by a statement of the legislative competence of the new structure (for instance, building in a requirement to observe certain fundamental rights). There is no logical or legal reason why the legislature in its new form should not be bound by these aspects of the new structure.

In his analysis of parliamentary sovereignty, Sir William Wade advanced the proposition that the only rule of the common law which Parliament may not change is the rule that courts recognize Acts of Parliament as law. Wade argued: 'If no statute can establish the rule that the courts obey Acts of Parliament, similarly no statute can alter or abolish the rule'.[80] But the argument at this point depends upon use of the word 'similarly' (consider the argument, 'No person can bring his or her own life into being; *similarly*, no person can bring his or her own life to an end'). In private correspondence with Wade in 1955, Herbert Hart made exactly this point.[81] It is certainly possible that although Parliament's power includes power to make constitutional changes affecting even Parliament itself, there are some indeterminate limits upon this power. Could, for instance, Parliament provide that it should not meet again for five years and that until then the Queen in Council should have unlimited power to make laws for the UK? Other less alarming scenarios can be imagined in which a proposed change would be met with intense opposition from the electorate. Even if the rule of

[78] H. L. A. Hart, *The Concept of Law* (1961) 144–50. Also R. Lakin, 'Debunking the Idea of Parliamentary Sovereignty' (2008) 28 *Ox J Legal Studies* 709.

[79] See e.g. the Canada Act 1982 and the Australia Act 1986. For a full analysis, see Oliver, above, n. 27.

[80] Wade, above, n. 18, p. 187.

[81] J. Beatson, 'Sir Henry William Rawson Wade 1918–2004', reprinted in H. W. R. Wade and C. F. Forsyth, *Administrative Law* (10th edn, 2009) 853, 856.

parliamentary sovereignty requires the courts to apply the later Act of Parliament in the event of a conflict between two Acts, does it follow that the legislature is unable to modify the rule by giving the courts greater power of decision?[82]

To justify the rule that a sovereign Parliament is not bound by legislation enacted by its predecessors, one must invoke the democratic principle that future representatives of the people should be free to make the laws that they consider are needed at that time. But this principle does not address the question: by what procedure may those representatives make the desired laws? Unless there is another authority with power to stipulate such requirements, it must be for Parliament to prescribe the 'manner and form' of future legislation – for example, by enacting a rule that a set period of notice should be given before Parliament may consider a Bill to abolish the Scottish Parliament, or that a referendum be held in Scotland before that Parliament is abolished.[83] Although the 'enrolled Act' rule respects the exclusive authority of each House over its own proceedings, there could be circumstances in which Parliament as a whole might wish to impose a measure of statutory procedure upon the legislative process.[84] Moreover, the need to maintain the ability of Parliament to repeal earlier legislation is stronger in relation to express repeal than it is to implied repeal. Maugham LJ's proposition that 'the legislature cannot, according to our constitution, bind itself as to the form of subsequent legislation' takes no account of the fact that some statutes are of great constitutional significance. In the case of the 'metric martyrs', *Thoburn* v. *Sunderland City Council*,[85] Laws LJ developed the argument that the European Communities Act 1972 is a 'constitutional statute', that is, a statute which:

> (a) conditions the legal relationship between citizen and state in some general, overarching manner, or (b) enlarges or diminishes the scope of what we would now regard as fundamental constitutional rights.

Whereas ordinary statutes may be impliedly repealed, 'constitutional statutes may not'; they can be repealed or amended in a significant respect only 'by unambiguous words on the face of the later statute'.[86] On this basis, the courts may respect the authority of Parliament to legislate on constitutional matters by holding that express words are needed before holding that an earlier provision is amended or repealed.[87] In some cases this is a matter to be inferred from the nature of the earlier Act, compared with the later Act. In other cases, notably that of the Human Rights Act 1998, Parliament

[82] Cf. T. R. S. Allan, 'Parliamentary Sovereignty: Law, Politics and Revolution' (1997) 113 *LQR* 443, 445, 448.

[83] And see Goldsworthy, above, n. 10, chs 6 and 7.

[84] Cf. the Parliamentary Standards Act 2009, placing on a statutory basis the scheme of MPs' expenses and allowances that had previously been a matter for self-regulation by the House.

[85] [2002] EWHC 195 (Admin), [2003] QB 151. And see J. Laws, 'Constitutional Guarantees' (2008) 29 *Statute Law Rev* 1.

[86] *Thoburn*, ibid., at [62]–[63].

[87] The judgment in *Thoburn*, above, n. 85, insists that the change in the doctrine of implied repeal is solely the work of the courts. But the 'constitutional Acts' which the judgment considers were, of course, the work of Parliament.

may use express words that minimize or eliminate scope for the courts to find that the Act has been impliedly amended or repealed. The effect will not be dissimilar from the manner in which the courts apply presumptions of legality in the interpretation of legislation that affect certain fundamental rights.[88] There is no reason to suppose that the emergence of a category of 'constitutional statutes' prejudices 'the sovereignty of the legislature' or 'the flexibility of our uncodified constitution'.[89]

Against this background, we now consider briefly the effects on parliamentary sovereignty of the European Communities Act 1972, the Scotland Act 1998, and the Human Rights Act 1998.[90]

PARLIAMENTARY SOVEREIGNTY AND THE EUROPEAN UNION[91]

Doctrines of constitutional law cannot ignore the reality of Britain's international relations. By virtue of the royal prerogative in foreign affairs, the government acting in name of the Crown may enter into treaties that bind the state in international law,[92] but may not alter the rights of individuals within the UK. If a treaty requires such rights to be changed, that can be done only by Act of Parliament. The UK would be in breach of its international obligations under such a treaty if Parliament failed to pass legislation that the treaty required.[93]

The conduct of foreign affairs may thus lead to a situation in which Parliament legislates under the constraint that otherwise the UK will be in breach of its treaty obligations. This constraint is not considered to infringe the sovereignty of Parliament. Conversely, an Act of Parliament is enforceable by British courts even if it breaches Britain's treaty obligations. However, in interpreting statutes that are enacted to give effect to such obligations, the courts if possible interpret the statute so as to conform with the treaty.[94]

These rules on the division of functions between treaty-making by the Crown and legislation by Parliament apply to the vast majority of treaties to which the UK

[88] See above, text at nn. 36–37. For discussion of implied repeal and related matters, see Goldsworthy, above, n. 10, pp. 137–40 and ch. 7, sections IV and VII.

[89] *Thoburn*, above, n. 85, at [64].

[90] On these current 'challenges' to the sovereignty of Parliament, see Goldsworthy, above, n. 10, ch. 10, section III.

[91] The literature includes T. C. Hartley, *The Foundations of European Community Law* (6th edn, 2007); P. Craig and G. de Búrca, *EU Law: Text, Cases and Materials* (4th edn, 2007); and S. Douglas-Scott, *Constitutional Law of the European Union* (2002). And see Chapter 4 below.

[92] Under the Constitutional Reform and Governance Act 2010, Part 2, treaties that must be ratified before they become binding will be laid in Parliament for at least 21 sitting days and if necessary may be debated. Certain treaties relating to the European Union must be approved by Act of Parliament before they are ratified: European Parliamentary Elections Act 2002, s. 12; European Union (Amendment) Act 2008, s. 5.

[93] *A-G for Canada* v. *A-G for Ontario* [1937] AC 326, 347–8.

[94] *Salomon* v. *Commissioners of Customs & Excise* [1967] 2 QB 116; *Garland* v. *British Rail Engineering Ltd* [1983] 2 AC 75 (below, text at n. 107). And see F. G. Jacobs and S. Roberts (eds), *The Effect of Treaties in Domestic Law* (1987).

is a party. But the European Union, the nature of which is outlined in Chapter 5, is a unique grouping of states. The UK acceded to the European Union's precursor, the EEC, by the Treaty of Brussels 1972, implemented in the UK by the European Communities Act 1972. What is distinctive about the Union is that broad executive, legislative, fiscal, and judicial powers are vested in the EU organs. The Court of Justice at Luxembourg (together with the General Court) exercises judicial powers in applying and enforcing EU law. Regulations made by the Council of Ministers are directly applicable in all member states as soon as they have been promulgated; Treaty provisions and other EC measures may have direct effect in member states.[95]

The Court has long emphasized that the binding force of the European Treaties and of measures taken under them must not differ from one state to another as a result of national measures.[96] As was said in 1964, EC law cannot be overridden by domestic legal provisions 'without being deprived of its character as Community law and without the legal basis of the Community being called into question'.[97]

The EU legal order is plainly inconsistent with the sovereignty of Parliament. Dicey declared that 'no person or body is recognised by the law of England as having a right to override or set aside the legislation of Parliament'.[98] But EU organs may make decisions and issue regulations which override legislation by Parliament. The supremacy or primacy of EU law within the economic or social areas with which it deals does not stand comfortably beside national structures of government. The UK is not the only member state to have experienced difficulties in adjusting constitutional law to take account of EU law. But the Court of Justice has repeatedly emphasized that the application of EU law may not be delayed by obstacles in national law, even where these arise from constitutional considerations, such as concern for the protection of fundamental rights.[99]

When Denmark, Ireland, and the UK acceded to the European Communities in 1973, each was obliged to accommodate EC law within the national legal system. In Denmark and Ireland, constitutional amendments were necessary. This course of action was not open to the UK, but it was essential that Parliament should authorize the reception of EC law – both the existing body of European law and also future rules.

Given this necessity, the sovereignty of Parliament was 'at once an advantage and a source of difficulty'.[100] The advantage was that it took only a few lines in an Act of Parliament to give effect to a massive body of EC law and to equip the British

[95] Chapter 4 below, pp. 122–7.

[96] Case 14/68, *Walt Wilhelm* v. *Bundeskartellamt* [1969] ECR 1, para. 6.

[97] Case 6/64, *Costa* v. *ENEL* [1964] CMLR 425, 455–6.

[98] Dicey, above, n. 15, p. 40.

[99] These concerns, particularly from Germany and Italy, influenced the Court of Justice in bringing fundamental rights within the principles of EC law: see e.g. Case 11/70, *Internationale Handelsgesellschaft* [1972] CMLR 255 and, for the German Constitutional Court's later position, *Wünsche Handelsgesellchaft* [1987] 3 CMLR 225. Also Case 106/77, *Amministrazione delle Finanze dello Stato* v. *Simmenthal SpA (No. 2)* [1978] 3 CMLR 263, 268; and J. E. K. Murkens, 'The Revival of National Sovereignty in the German Federal Constitutional Court's Decision on the Lisbon Treaty' [2010] *Public Law* 530.

[100] J. P. Warner, 'The Relationship between European Community Law and the National Laws of Member States' (1977) 93 *LQR* 349, 364.

government with additional powers to handle EC affairs. The difficulty came so far as the future was concerned: could a guarantee be given that Parliament would in the future neither legislate to leave the European Community nor legislate in a manner which conflicted with EC law?

The view of the government in 1972 was that no absolute undertaking by Parliament could be given, since a future Parliament could disregard such an undertaking. Instead, the European Communities Act 1972 went so far as was thought possible in instructing British courts how to apply EC law in the future.

The European Communities Act 1972, s. 2(1) gave effect in the UK to all rules of EC law (now EU law since the enactment of the Treaty of Lisbon) that had or might in future have direct application or direct effect within member states. By section 2(2), the government acquired very wide powers of making regulations to implement the UK's obligations and to give effect to rights arising under EC law. These powers include power to amend Acts of Parliament.[101]

By s. 2(4), 'any enactment passed or to be passed, other than one contained in this part of the Act, shall be construed and shall have effect subject to the foregoing provisions of this section' – subject, in other words, to the comprehensive reception of EC law made by s. 2(1). When these provisions were debated in Parliament, it was widely agreed that they did not exclude the possibility that Parliament might one day wish to repeal the Act and bring to an end the reception of EC law. The ultimate sovereignty of Westminster was thus not affected, which ministers admitted while refusing to allow a statement to this effect to be included in the Act.[102] But what would the position be in a less extreme situation, if an Act passed after 1972 contained a provision that was impossible to reconcile with a rule of EU law? In this situation, we have seen that the European Courts would insist that EU law must prevail. Should British courts adopt the same position, as ss 2 and 3 of the 1972 Act might indicate was their duty, or does the later Act of Parliament override those sections, to the extent of requiring the later Act to prevail? In 1972, since it was impossible to undertake that no such conflict would arise in future, the government accepted that a later Act might prevail over the 1972 Act to the extent of the conflict.[103]

The initial response of British judges to questions posed by the 1972 Act showed a preference for resolving clashes between UK and EC law by interpretation, and they were reluctant to reach the sovereignty question. Lord Denning MR said that the incoming tide of EC law could not be held back: 'Parliament has decreed that the Treaty is henceforward to be part of our law. It is equal in force to any statute'.[104] The crucial question, however, is not whether EU law has the same force as any statute, but

[101] On the effect of these 'Henry VIII' powers, see *Thoburn* v. *Sunderland City Council*, above, n. 85, discussed by Craig below, pp. 116–17; and see D. Campbell and J. Younger, 'The metric martyrs and the entrenchment jurisprudence of Lord Justice Laws' [2002] *Public Law* 399.

[102] *Hansard*, HC, cols 556–644 (5 July 1972).

[103] For Lord Diplock's advice on this point, see *Hansard*, HL, col. 1029 (8 August 1972).

[104] *H P Bulmer* v. *J Bollinger SA* [1974] Ch 410, 418. Cf. *Felixstowe Dock and Railway Co* v. *British Transport Docks Board* [1976] 2 *Lloyd's Law Reports* 656, 663.

whether it has greater force than a statute by prevailing over subsequent Acts which conflict with it. In a succession of difficult cases, UK law on sex discrimination and employment protection was called into question by European rules that required equal treatment of men and women as regards their pay and conditions of employment.[105]

Relying on s. 2(4) as a rule of construction, the courts took the view that where possible national legislation must be interpreted and applied so that it did not conflict with EC law.[106] In 1983, Lord Diplock stressed that in relation to all international treaties:

> the words of a statute passed after the treaty has been signed and dealing with the subject matter of the international obligation of the UK, are to be construed, if they are reasonably capable of bearing such a meaning, as intended to carry out the obligation and not to be inconsistent with it.[107]

That approach, said Lord Diplock, applied even more strongly to the European Treaties. As regards s. 2(4), he left open whether the courts would be justified in construing a future statute inconsistently with an EC obligation, except where the Act contained an express statement that the provision was intended to be made by Parliament in breach of an EC obligation.

The question of what the courts should do if Parliament legislated inconsistently with EC law eventually arose in *R.* v. *Secretary of State for Transport, ex parte Factortame Ltd*,[108] which concerned a claim by Spanish fishing-boat operators that provisions in the Merchant Shipping Act 1988 were in direct conflict with their rights under EC law. Since the litigation is fully discussed by Paul Craig in Chapter 5 below, it is sufficient here to state that, on the vital procedural point of whether the English courts must grant interim relief to the fishing-boat owners against the British government, the Court of Justice applied the principle that directly applicable rules of EC law 'must be fully and uniformly applied in all the member states from the date of their entry into force... in accordance with the principle of the precedence of Community law'.[109] This principle rendered 'automatically inapplicable' any conflicting provision of national law. The House of Lords duly granted an interim injunction that prevented the Secretary of State from removing the Spanish-owned ships from the register of British fishing vessels. On the constitutional question, Lord Bridge rejected the view that the decision of the Court of Justice was a novel or dangerous invasion upon the sovereignty of Parliament, saying that there was 'nothing in any way novel in according supremacy to rules of Community law in those areas to which they apply'. The insistence that, in the protection of rights under EC law, national courts must not

[105] See e.g. Case 152/84, *Marshall* v. *Southampton and South West Hampshire Health Authority* [1986] ECR 723, [1986] QB 401, and Case 222/84, *Johnston* v. *Chief Constable, RUC* [1986] ECR 1651, [1987] QB 129.

[106] *Macarthys Ltd* v. *Smith* [1979] 3 All ER 325 and [1981] QB 180.

[107] *Garland v British Rail Engineering Ltd* [1983] 2 AC 751, 771.

[108] [1990] 2 AC 85. Chapter 4, below, pp. 114–16.

[109] *R.* v. *Secretary of State for Transport ex parte Factortame Ltd (No. 2)* [1991] 1 AC 603, 643.

be inhibited by rules of national law from granting interim relief 'is no more than a logical recognition of that supremacy'.[110]

This judgment in *Factortame (No. 2)* is the plainest possible statement that so long as the UK remains in the European Union, laws made at Westminster must if necessary give way to the greater supremacy of EC law. In 1995, the House of Lords declared that conditions imposed by the Employment Protection (Consolidation) Act 1978 on the protection of part-time workers were discriminatory, since they were incompatible with the right of female workers under EC law to equal treatment with male workers.[111] And, in a later phase of the *Factortame* litigation, it was held that the British government was held liable to compensate the foreign fishing interests for the loss they suffered as a result of the Merchant Shipping Act 1988; liability arose in part because in 1988 the government had been advised by the European Commission in Brussels that the proposed Act infringed the right of establishment under EC law, but had ignored that advice.[112]

Thus the rule is now that British courts must not apply national legislation, whenever it was enacted, if to do so would conflict with EU law. The decision in *Factortame (No. 2)* was described as constituting a 'constitutional revolution',[113] but other explanations are possible.[114]

This profound change in the operation of parliamentary sovereignty is not necessarily permanent, because the duty of British courts to apply EU law would not exist as a matter of UK law but for the continued operation of the European Communities Act 1972. The constitutions of other EU states have also had to adjust to the development of European integration and to the impact that this has had on ideas of national sovereignty.[115] If in the future the situation in Europe changed to a point at which the UK decided to leave the European Union, the Westminster Parliament could exercise its ultimate authority to bring this about, a change that would involve repealing the 1972 Act. Short of such an extreme event, it is for many reasons highly unlikely that Westminster would expressly mandate the courts to disregard a specific EC obligation.

DEVOLUTION AND PARLIAMENTARY SOVEREIGNTY

In this section, we examine aspects of parliamentary sovereignty that arise in relation to the scheme of devolution in the Scotland Act 1998. We have seen that parliamentary sovereignty facilitated the process by which the UK joined the European Communities, but also that no binding undertaking was given that Parliament would in future

[110] Ibid.

[111] *R.* v. *Secretary of State for Employment ex parte Equal Opportunities Commission* [1995] 1 AC 1.

[112] *R.* v. *Secretary of State for Transport ex parte Factortame Ltd (No. 5)* [2000] 1 AC 524.

[113] H. W. R. Wade, 'Sovereignty: Revolution or Evolution?' (1996) 112 *LQR* 568.

[114] See Allan, above, n. 82; and below, pp. 119–21.

[115] Cf. I. Pernice, 'Multilevel Constitutionalism in the European Union' (2002) 27 *Euro L Rev* 511; and N. MacCormick, *Questioning Sovereignty: Law, State, and Nation in the European Commonwealth* (1999).

always respect the primacy of EC law. As regards devolution to Scotland, Wales, and Northern Ireland, the capacity of Westminster to devolve powers to elected bodies in those parts of the UK was not in dispute. However, as Chapter 9 below explains, each has been treated separately, and it is difficult to generalize about the three schemes of devolution.[116] This section will concentrate on Scotland, as broader legislative and executive powers have been devolved to Edinburgh than to Cardiff or Belfast.

So far as Wales is concerned, which has for several centuries had the same legal system as in England, Westminster is still the main legislature, notwithstanding some extra powers that were devolved in the Government of Wales Act 2006. Scotland, by contrast, has retained its own legal system since the Union with England in 1707, and the Scotland Act 1998 gives wide law-making powers to the Scottish Parliament. In relation to both Wales and Scotland, the orthodox doctrine of legislative sovereignty provides that what Westminster enacts may in law be varied or revoked by Westminster; and no court has power to protect the devolved institutions from being expressly overridden by the UK Parliament.[117]

In the case of *MacCormick* v. *Lord Advocate*, which concerned the legality of the numeral in Queen Elizabeth's title, Lord Cooper, Lord President of the Court of Session, famously remarked: '[t]he principle of the unlimited sovereignty of Parliament is a distinctively English principle which has no counterpart in Scottish constitutional law'.[118] Lord Cooper had in mind that the Treaty of Union of 1707, to which Acts of the Scottish and English Parliaments gave effect, contained guarantees for the Scottish legal system, the Church of Scotland, and other institutions that were declared to be fundamental to the Union. These guarantees have been argued to be binding on the Parliament at Westminster. In fact, the Scottish courts have not upheld such arguments.[119] Indeed, in expounding parliamentary sovereignty, Dicey cited the Acts confirming the Treaties of Union with Scotland and Ireland to show that the history of subsequent legislation in respect of those Acts 'affords the strongest proof of the

[116] See Chapter 8 below. See generally on devolution, V. Bogdanor, *The New British Constitution* (2009) ch. 4, and the series of books surveying the operation of devolution that have come from the Constitution Unit, University College of London. Also R. Hazell and R. W. Rawlings (eds), *Law Making, Devolution and the Constitution* (2005).

[117] On the approach to constitutional statutes taken by Laws LJ in *Thoburn v Sunderland City Council*, above, n. 85, the Scotland Act 1998 is such a statute, and it may therefore not be subject to being impliedly repealed.

[118] 1953 SC 396, 411. In *R. (Jackson)* v. *Attorney General*, above, n. 51, at [104], Lord Hope referred to 'the English principle of the absolute legislative sovereignty of Parliament'. For the argument that parliamentary sovereignty has long been recognized in Scotland, both as regards the pre-Union Parliament (see Goldsworthy, above, n. 10, pp. 270–2, citing J. Goodare, *The Government of Scotland 1560–1625* (2004)) and since the Treaty of Union (Goldsworthy, above, n. 4, pp. 165–73).

[119] *Gibson* v. *Lord Advocate* 1975 SC 136; *Pringle, Petitioner* 1991 SLT 330. And see D. N. MacCormick, 'Does the United Kingdom have a Constitution? Reflections on *MacCormick v Lord Advocate*' (1978) 29 *Northern Ireland LQ* 1; C. R. Munro, *Studies in Constitutional Law* (2nd edn, 1999) ch. 4; M. Upton, 'Marriage Vows of the Elephant: the Constitution of 1707' (1989) 105 *LQR* 79; C. M. G. Himsworth and N. C. Walker, 'The Poll Tax and Fundamental Law' (1991) *Juridical Review* 45; and E. Wicks, *The Evolution of a Constitution* (2006) ch 2.

futility inherent in every attempt of one sovereign legislature to restrain the action of another equally sovereign body'.[120] Within Scotland, there has long been considerable resentment of this 'English' view of sovereignty and a fear that the existence of a Scottish Parliament (as a subordinate legislature) would always be subject to threats of legislation from Westminster, or might even be closed down by it, as the former Northern Ireland Parliament was in 1972.

In 1995, an influential report, *Scotland's Parliament. Scotland's Right*, calling for a Scottish Parliament, was drawn up by the Scottish Constitutional Convention, that represented many bodies in Scotland, including the Labour and Liberal Democrat parties. Having outlined a scheme for the new Parliament, the framers of the report wished to ensure that it would not be at risk of legislative interference from Westminster.

> The Convention is adamant that the powers of Scotland's Parliament, once established, should not be altered without the consent of the Scottish Parliament representing the people of Scotland.[121]

The Convention had been advised by constitutional experts that 'in theory under Britain's unwritten constitution' an Act of the Westminster Parliament creating a Scottish Parliament 'can be repealed or amended without restriction'. The Convention, however, was firmly of the view that, if there was 'widespread recognition of the Scottish Parliament's legitimate authority, both within Scotland and internationally', no Westminster government would be willing to pay the political price of 'neutralising or destroying' a Parliament supported by the people of Scotland.[122] The Convention urged that the Westminster Parliament should make a solemn declaration of intent that the Act creating the Scottish Parliament 'should not be repealed, or amended in such a way as to threaten the existence of Scotland's Parliament, without the consent of the Scottish Parliament and of the people of Scotland, directly consulted through general election or referendum'.[123]

In July 1997, a white paper issued by the Labour Government set out the advantages of creating a Scottish Parliament with law-making powers. The government was plainly aware of the views of the Scottish Constitutional Convention and, on the other side, of fears from English critics that devolution might reopen debate on the desirability of the Union of 1707 itself. Trying to face both ways, the white paper explained that, while Westminster would be devolving wide legislative powers on the Scottish Parliament:

> Scotland will of course remain an integral part of the UK.... The UK Parliament is and will remain *sovereign in all matters*: but as part of the Government's resolve to modernise the British constitution Westminster will be choosing to exercise that sovereignty by devolving legislative responsibilities to a Scottish Parliament *without in any way diminishing its own powers*. The Government recognise that no UK Parliament can bind its successors. The Government however believe that the popular support for the Scottish Parliament, once established, will make sure that its future in the UK constitution will be secure.[124]

[120] Dicey, above, n. 15, p. 65. [121] *Scotland's Parliament. Scotland's Right* (1995) 18.
[122] Ibid. [123] Above, n. 121, p. 19.
[124] *Scotland's Parliament*, Cm. 3658 (1997) 12 (emphasis supplied).

Such support became evident in September 1997, when in a referendum a clear majority of the Scottish electorate favoured creation of a Parliament at Edinburgh.

The Scotland Act 1998 confers power on the Scottish Parliament to make laws on any matter except those matters that are declared by the Act to be outside its legislative competence.[125] Schedule 5 to the Act sets out a lengthy list of matters reserved to Westminster. The list includes: aspects of the constitution (including the Crown, the Union of England and Scotland and the Westminster Parliament), international relations, defence, the armed forces, and many detailed matters grouped under 11 subject heads (such as financial and economic matters, trade and industry, social security). Two important limitations on the general power to make laws for Scotland are that the Parliament may not legislate incompatibly with EC law, nor with rights secured by the ECHR. The power to make laws on all matters that are not reserved (such as education, local government, social services, criminal justice, the environment, and agriculture) necessarily includes power to amend or repeal existing Acts of the Westminster Parliament.

Several procedures were created by the Scotland Act 1998 to ensure that proposed legislation being considered by the Scottish Parliament does not go outside its competence.[126] Should it be claimed that the Parliament has enacted an Act that exceeds its competence, the matter may be raised in the courts as a 'devolution issue'.[127] Since the Scottish Parliament and Executive have no power to act incompatibly with rights under the ECHR, measures that it is claimed breach Convention rights also raise devolution issues. Devolution issues are decided by the superior courts and ultimately by the Supreme Court of the UK.[128]

Within this legal framework, or constitution, by which the domestic affairs of Scotland are now governed, Acts of the Scottish Parliament are not sovereign and may be set aside by the courts if they go outside the devolved powers. The Scottish Parliament may not enlarge its own competence, although this may be done at any time by the Westminster Parliament or in some cases by ministers of the Crown exercising delegated powers. Some guidance is given by the Act itself as to the way in which the courts should approach devolution issues. Thus, a provision of a Scottish Act which could be read in such a way as to be outside its competence, 'is to be read as narrowly as is required for it to be within competence, if such a reading is possible'.[129] No comparable interpretative duty applies to the Scotland Act 1998 nor to other Westminster Acts. Given the manner in which reserved matters are enumerated in the Act, it is left

[125] Scotland Act 1998, ss 28(1), 29(1).

[126] See generally C. M. G. Himsworth and C. M. O'Neill, *Scotland's Constitution: Law and Practice* (2nd edn, 2009).

[127] Scotland Act 1998, Sched. 6, Pt I. And see e.g. *Anderson et al* v. *Scottish Ministers* [2001] UKPC D5, [2003] 2 AC 602.

[128] Scotland Act 1998, Sched. 6, Pts II–V, amended by Constitutional Reform Act 2005, s. 40(4) and Sched. 9, Pt 2.

[129] Scotland Act 1998, s. 101.

to the courts to determine the approach that they must take in determining the width of the powers conferred.[130]

How does this limited constitution for Scotland affect the sovereignty of the Westminster Parliament? The Scotland Act 1998, s. 28, which provides that the Scottish Parliament may make laws for Scotland, includes a modestly phrased subsection: '(7) This section does not affect the power of the Parliament of the UK to make laws for Scotland'.[131] In one sense, this provision is legally unnecessary and exists only to assist readers of the Act unfamiliar with Dicey's view of parliamentary sovereignty. Scottish Members of Parliament continue to sit at Westminster, but their opportunity to raise in the House questions about the domestic affairs of Scotland is now much reduced. Possibly s. 28(7) serves a symbolic purpose, or is meant to guard against any legislative intervention by Westminster in Scottish affairs being regarded as 'unconstitutional' or in breach of a convention to the contrary. When the Scotland Bill was passing through Parliament, many considered that it would be a rare event in future for Westminster to legislate on matters which were devolved to Edinburgh. In the event, this has been a frequent occurrence, mainly to enable there to be changes in the law that relate to administrative schemes applying throughout Great Britain. However, both governments have observed a new convention (the 'Sewel convention') by which the Scottish Parliament by resolution grants its consent to the proposed legislation before it is enacted at Westminster.[132] While in law the Westminster Parliament could legislate on a devolved matter without the prior approval of the Scottish Parliament, such a breach of convention would be fiercely criticized in Scotland, especially while the Scottish National party holds office in the Scottish Executive.

To summarize the effects of the Scotland Act 1998 on Westminster's sovereignty, the following propositions may be advanced:

(a) as a matter of strict law, Westminster retains full capacity to amend or repeal the Scotland Act and may do so at any time, without any prior procedure such as a referendum of the Scottish electorate being legally necessary;

(b) Westminster retains full capacity to legislate on any aspect of Scotland's affairs, whether or not they are within Edinburgh's legislative competence, but as a matter of political obligation Westminster legislates on devolved matters only with the prior approval of the Scottish Parliament;

[130] See P. Craig and M. Walters, 'The Courts, Devolution and Judicial Review' [1999] *Public Law* 274; and S. Tierney, 'Constitutionalising the Role of the Judge: Scotland and the New Order' (2001) 5 *Edin L Rev* 49.

[131] Cf. the flamboyant formula in the Government of Ireland Act 1920, s. 75: 'the supreme authority of the Parliament of the UK shall remain unaffected and undiminished over all persons, matters and things in Ireland and every part thereof'. As to this and the Northern Ireland Act 1998, s. 5(6), see B. Hadfield, 'The Belfast Agreement, Sovereignty and the State of the Union' [1998] *Public Law* 599.

[132] See Himsworth and O'Neill, above, n. 126, pp. 140–3; *Memorandum of Understanding*, Cm. 4444 (1999) para. 13; A. Page and A. Batey, 'Scotland's Other Parliament: Westminster Legislation about Devolved Matters since Devolution' [2002] *Public Law* 501; and Hazell and Rawlings, above, n. 116, ch. 2 (B. Winetrobe).

(c) within its devolved powers, the Scottish Parliament may amend or repeal existing Acts of the Westminster Parliament and also future Acts enacted at Westminster that deal with matters within Edinburgh's competence, unless those later Acts show a clear intention to take a particular matter outside that competence by amending the Scotland Act 1998 so as to achieve this.[133]

This summary does not take into account the political reality. What will be more significant than the legal power that Westminster retains to legislate for Scotland on devolved matters is the strength of support in Scotland that attaches to the Scottish Parliament: this body may be seen as being more representative of the Scottish people than the Parliament at Westminster. Compared with the pre-1707 Scottish Parliament, the present Scottish Parliament has the marks of a subordinate legislature, but political opinion and national sentiment in Scotland rate it more highly than this.

THE SOVEREIGNTY OF PARLIAMENT AND THE HUMAN RIGHTS ACT 1998

As we have already seen, the doctrine of parliamentary sovereignty facilitates some but not all forms of constitutional change. In relation to the protection of human rights and liberties, the doctrine has often been seen as a massive obstacle in the way of any significant increase in the formal protection given to human rights in UK law. Where legislative supremacy reigns, there are no individual rights or freedoms that may not be curtailed or suspended by Act of Parliament. Dicey's concept of the Rule of Law assumed that Parliament would not use its legislative power to abrogate the liberties and freedoms which had emerged from the common law, and would not overturn such revered enactments as the Bill of Rights 1689 and the Habeas Corpus Acts (or, at least, not except in situations of acute and pressing emergency).

A strong argument for reform was put by Lord Scarman in 1974:

> It is the helplessness of the law in face of the legislative sovereignty of Parliament which makes it difficult for the legal system to accommodate the concept of fundamental and inviolable human rights. Means therefore have to be found whereby (1) there is incorporated into English law a declaration of such rights, (2) these rights are protected against all encroachments, including the power of the state, even when that power is exerted by a representative legislative institution such as Parliament.[134]

Britain's ratification of the ECHR in 1951 was an important first step on the way towards meeting the need for greater protection for human rights.[135] The Convention provided machinery at Strasbourg for judicial determination of claims brought against member states by other member states or by individuals claiming that their Convention

[133] See above, n. 117. [134] L. Scarman, *English Law: The New Dimension* (1974) 15.

[135] See A. Lester, D. Pannick and J. Herberg (eds), *Human Rights Law and Practice* (3rd edn, 2009) ch. 1; and Chapter 3 below.

rights have been infringed. The first decision of the European Court of Human Rights in a case against the UK was made in 1975;[136] the series of decisions that thereafter involved the UK[137] strengthened the argument for enabling such issues to be decided by judges in the UK.[138] Although it is for a state that is party to the ECHR to decide the means by which the Convention rights are protected within its jurisdiction,[139] the UK alone in Europe neither had a written constitution nor had incorporated the Convention into national law. During the 1980s and 1990s, pressure was placed on British courts to find ways and means of giving effect to the Convention even in the absence of incorporation.[140]

The turning point came with the election in 1997 of a Labour government that was committed, with Liberal Democrat support, to giving effect in UK law to the ECHR. Before we examine the implications of the Human Rights Act 1998 for the sovereignty of Parliament, two preliminary points may be made. First, a distinction must be drawn between: (a) strengthening the ability of the courts to protect human rights by means of statutory interpretation; and (b) empowering the courts to embark on judicial review of legislation with power to strike down invalid legislation. The former but not the latter is accepted as being compatible with parliamentary sovereignty.[141] Secondly, in giving greater power to the courts, a distinction may be drawn between: (i) existing Acts of Parliament; and (ii) future Acts. As we saw with regard to EU law, no sovereignty problems arise out of the former (since today's Parliament may modify the effect of all earlier Acts), but such problems arise if today's Parliament attempts to regulate or limit legislation to be enacted in the future. Taking account of these distinctions, discussion before 1998 of the manner in which the ECHR might be given legal effect in the UK envisaged three broad models.

Model 1: a new 'Interpretation Act', requiring the courts to take the ECHR into account in applying all legislation and, possibly, requiring the courts to give to that legislation a meaning consistent with the Convention, even if the disputed words are not ambiguous.[142] In terms of sovereignty, this model is uncontroversial since it does not affect the freedom of Parliament to legislate in the future.

Model 2: the courts to be empowered to apply the ECHR in respect of all earlier legislation, if necessary setting aside or quashing a statutory provision that conflicts

[136] *Golder* v. *United Kingdom* (1975) 1 EHRR 524.

[137] See A. W. Bradley, in W. Finnie, C. M. G. Himsworth and N. Walker (eds), *Edinburgh Essays in Public Law* (1991) 185–214.

[138] See Lord Browne-Wilkinson, 'The Infiltration of a Bill of Rights' [1992] *Public Law* 397; Sir John Laws, 'Is the High Court the Guardian of Fundamental Constitutional Rights?' [1993] *Public Law* 59; and Lord Bingham, 'The European Convention on Human Rights: time to incorporate' (1993) 109 *LQR* 390.

[139] *Swedish Engine-Drivers' Union* v. *Sweden* (1967) 1 EHRR 617, 631; *Republic of Ireland* v. *UK* (1978) 2 EHRR 25, 104.

[140] See *R.* v. *Secretary of State for the Home Department ex parte Brind* [1991] 1 AC 696; and M. Hunt, *Using Human Rights Law in English Courts* (1997).

[141] The stronger the rule of interpretation, the greater the possibility that matters of interpretation may merge into matters of review: see Allan, above, n. 82, p. 447.

[142] For an example of model 1, see the New Zealand Bill of Rights Act 1990.

with a Convention right; in respect of all subsequent legislation, the courts to apply the Convention in the form of an 'Interpretation Act' (on the lines of that in Model 1). Again, from a sovereignty standpoint, this model is uncontroversial, although it goes significantly further than the first model and gives the courts a totally new power to set aside existing legislation.[143]

Model 3: the courts to be empowered to apply the ECHR as against conflicting provisions in both existing and future Acts of Parliament (with a possible exception for future Acts in which Parliament had expressly stated that it its intention was to legislate inconsistently with Convention rights). From a sovereignty standpoint, this model is controversial in seeking to empower the courts to strike down future Acts of Parliament: on the orthodox Diceyan view, future parliaments cannot be bound by earlier Acts. Thus, in 1978 a House of Lords Select Committee on a Bill of Rights concluded:

> There is no way a Bill of Rights could protect itself from encroachment, whether express or implied, by later Acts. The most that such a Bill could do would be to include an interpretation provision which insured that... so far as a later Act could be construed in a way that was compatible with a Bill of Rights, such a construction would be preferred to one that was not.[144]

In effect, this was to say that any provision to protect human rights that went further than Model 2 would be nugatory in its effect on future legislation.

The scheme enacted by the Human Rights Act 1998 does not conform closely to any of these models. Its originality consisted of the following key elements:

(1) A new interpretative duty is applied to all legislation, whether primary or subordinate legislation, regardless of the date of the legislation; this duty must be observed by all persons who apply legislation, including courts and tribunals:

> So far as it is possible to do so, primary legislation and subordinate legislation must be read and given effect in a way which is compatible with Convention rights.[145]

(2) Where it is not possible to read and give effect to *subordinate* legislation in a way that is compatible with Convention rights, such legislation may be quashed or disapplied, except where the parent Act under which it was made prevents removal of the incompatibility.[146]

[143] For such a Bill of Rights, see the Hong Kong Bill of Rights Ordinance 1991; and J. Allan, 'A Bill of Rights for Hong Kong' [1991] *Public Law* 175.

[144] Report of the Select Committee on a Bill of Rights (1977–78) (HL Paper 176) 26.

[145] Human Rights Act 1998 (HRA), s. 3(1). The leading authority on s. 3(1) is *Ghaidan v Godin-Mendoza* [2004] UKHL 30, [2004] 2 AC 557. And see Kavanagh, above, n. 10, pts 1 and 2.

[146] HRA, s. 3(2) (by implication). For the novel demarcation between primary and subordinate legislation for this purpose, see HRA, s. 21(1). The definition given to 'primary' legislation by the Act goes considerably wider than measures of a sovereign Parliament: see P. Billings and B. Pontin, 'Prerogative powers and the Human Rights Act' [2001] *Public Law* 21. See also D. Squires, 'Challenging Subordinate Legislation under the Human Rights Act' [2000] EHRLR 116.

(3) Where it is not possible to read and give effect to *primary* legislation (a term which includes Acts of Parliament, but is not limited to them) in a way that is compatible with Convention rights, such legislation remains in force, but the High Court or other superior court may make a 'declaration of incompatibility'.[147] Such a declaration does not affect the validity or operation of the provision in question, but it enables the government by means of 'fast-track' delegated legislation to take remedial action where there are 'compelling reasons' for doing so; a remedial order may make such amendments to the primary legislation as the minister considers necessary to remove the incompatibility.[148]

(4) All public authorities, defined broadly to include all courts and tribunals and also private persons exercising public functions, are acting unlawfully if they act in a way which is incompatible with Convention rights, except when they are mandated by primary legislation to act in this way.[149]

(5) All courts and tribunals must take into account relevant decisions of the Strasbourg Court and other Convention authorities.[150]

(6) A minister in charge of a government Bill in Parliament must issue a statement to Parliament that either the Bill is compatible with the ECHR, or that the government wishes the Bill to proceed even though such a statement cannot be made.[151]

It will be apparent that the scheme does not distinguish between existing and future Acts. In the case of primary legislation (whenever enacted), the Act confers on the courts a two-part function comprising: (i) the duty of all courts and tribunals to interpret legislation compatibly with Convention rights, 'so far as it is possible to do so'; and (ii) where this is not possible, the power of superior courts to make a declaration of incompatibility. This approach does not give the courts power to strike down or disapply Acts of Parliament. As was said in the 1997 white paper, *Rights Brought Home: the Human Rights Bill*:

> The Government has reached the conclusion that courts should not have the power to set aside primary legislation, past or future, on the ground of incompatibility with the Convention. This conclusion arises from the importance which the government attaches to Parliamentary sovereignty.... In enacting legislation, Parliament is making decisions about important matters of public policy. The authority to make those decisions derives from a democratic mandate.... To make provision... for the courts to set aside Acts of Parliament would confer on the judiciary a general power over the decisions of Parliament which under our present constitutional arrangements they do not possess, and would be likely on occasions to draw the judiciary into serious conflict with Parliament. There is no evidence to suggest that they desire this power, nor that the public wish them to have it.[152]

[147] HRA, s. 4. [148] Ibid., s. 10 and Sched. 2.
[149] Ibid., s. 6(1) and for the related remedies, see ss 7–9. [150] Ibid., s. 2. [151] Ibid., s. 19.
[152] Cm. 3782 (1997) para. 2.14.

Some would argue that this policy does not make a sufficiently strong commitment to protecting human rights and relies on an outdated conception of the authority of Parliament; and the reliance on 'present constitutional arrangements' is not persuasive. But given that: (a) all courts and tribunals must apply the new rule of interpretation where it is possible to do so; and (b) if that is not sufficient to achieve an outcome that is compatible with Convention rights, the superior courts may make a 'declaration of incompatibility', the Act goes a very long way to enabling there to be judicial review of legislation in all but name.[153]

Although a declaration of incompatibility 'does not affect the validity, continuing operation or enforcement of the provision in respect of which it is given',[154] a court that makes such a declaration will have scrutinized the legislation closely against the Convention jurisprudence, and will explain the reasons for the incompatibility. The court will in effect have found that someone's Convention rights have been infringed because of the statutory provision in question. It would be surprising if that person did not immediately consider having recourse to the European Court of Human Rights.[155] Even if the Human Rights Act 1998 states that the offending legislation continues in force, in practice it may become inoperative, for the reason that every time it is applied, others affected by it may wish to have recourse to Strasbourg. As the Home Secretary stated in the House of Commons:

> One of the questions that will always be before Government, in practice, will be, 'Is it sensible to wait for a further challenge to Strasbourg, when the British courts have declared the provision to be outwith the Convention?'[156]

While therefore the courts have not acquired the power to strike down an Act of Parliament, the courts may under the Human Rights Act 1998 deliver a wound to Parliament's handiwork that is likely to prove fatal, even though life support for it must be switched off by the government or by Parliament, not by the courts.

Against this background, it is difficult to accept without qualification the many statements that judges and ministers have made asserting that the sovereignty of Parliament is not affected.[157] The fact that such assurances can be given, even though they tell only part of the story, certainly facilitated the passage of the Act. Lord Steyn

[153] See K. D. Ewing, 'The Human Rights Act and Parliamentary Democracy' (1999) 62 *MLR* 79, 92: 'As a matter of constitutional legality, Parliament may well be sovereign, but as a matter of constitutional practice it has transferred significant power to the judiciary'. See also Kavanagh, above, n. 10; and Goldsworthy, above, n. 4, pp. 299–304.

[154] HRA, s. 4(6)(a).

[155] That Court is not, of course, required to take the same view of the legislation as that taken by the British courts and could hold that the applicant's Convention rights had not been breached.

[156] *Hansard*, HC, col. 773 (16 February 1998).

[157] See e.g. *R.* v. *Lambert* [2001] UKHL 37, [2002] 2 AC 545, at [79] (Lord Hope); *Re S (Minors) (Care Order: Implementation of Care Plan)* [2002] UKHL 10, [2002] 2 AC 291, at [39] (Lord Nicholls); and *Wilson* v. *First County Trust Ltd* [2003] UKHL 40, [2004] 1 AC 816, at [127] (Lord Hobhouse). Cf. 32nd Report of the Joint Committee on Human Rights (2005–06) (HL Paper 278, HC 1716): *The Human Rights Act: the DCA and Home Office Reviews.*

has declared, 'It is crystal clear that the carefully and subtly drafted Human Rights Act preserves the principle of parliamentary sovereignty'.[158] But in 'preserving the principle', the Act made a significant change in the legal status of legislation that affects Convention rights. Indeed, Lord Steyn also stated that 'a new legal order' would come into existence when the Human Rights Act 1998 came into effect.[159] In this legal order, parliamentary sovereignty has been reasserted and continues as a matter of form. But the substance of legislative power is now subject to a significant measure of judicial control[160] that both places a new duty of interpretation upon the judges and makes necessary a reconsideration of the doctrine of implied repeal.[161] For a future Act to be guarded against the new powers of the courts, it would need to include a provision that expressed a plain intention to exclude operation of the Human Rights Act 1998.[162]

CONCLUSIONS

Each of the main instances of constitutional legislation considered in this chapter has affected the sovereignty of Parliament in a different way. The Parliament Acts 1911 and 1949 provide an illustration of legislation that affects the political dynamic of the legislative process and raises questions for the courts to resolve that cannot simply be answered in the well-worn terms of Diceyan orthodoxy. The European Communities Act 1972 goes furthest, enabling the courts to decide whether an Act of Parliament complies with EU law and, if it does not, to disapply it. The Human Rights Act 1998 has created a new and movable point of constitutional balance, located somewhere between the opposing poles of parliamentary and judicial supremacy. In the Scotland Act 1998, Parliament devolved legislative powers to a subordinate assembly that may in future acquire a political authority that could rival that of Westminster in respect of law and government in Scotland. These instances all illustrate the undoubted power of Parliament to legislate on constitutional matters, including its own relationship with the courts. The response of the courts to such legislation needs to be known before we can be certain of the extent of the constitutional changes that Parliament has initiated.

Discussion of parliamentary sovereignty is liable to become enmeshed in legal technicalities, and to give too little attention to the political significance of the relationship between the courts and Parliament. There is a defence to be made of legislative

[158] *R.* v. *DPP ex parte Kebilene* [2000] 2 AC 326, 367.

[159] 'The Role of the Bar, the Judge and the Jury: Winds of Change'[1999] *Public Law* 51, 55.

[160] The numerous articles include P. Craig, 'The Courts, the Human Rights Act and Judicial Review' (2001) 117 *LQR* 589; M. Elliott, 'Parliamentary sovereignty and the new constitutional order' (2002) 22 *Legal Studies* 340; A. L. Young, 'Judicial Sovereignty and the Human Rights Act' (2002) 61 *Camb L J* 53; and D. Bonner, H. Fenwick and S. Harris-Short, 'Judicial Approaches to the Human Rights Act' (2003) 52 *Int & Comp Law Quarterly* 549.

[161] See above, text at nn. 73–75, 85–89.

[162] See *Thoburn* v. *Sunderland City Council*, above, n. 85.

sovereignty on democratic grounds. Professor Ewing has referred to parliamentary sovereignty as 'a constitutional principle acquired before the advent of democracy yet one which might be said to be the most democratic of all constitutional principles'. The reason is that 'in the democratic era, parliamentary sovereignty is the legal and constitutional device which best gives effect to the principle of popular sovereignty, whereby the people in a self-governing community are empowered – without restraint – to make the rules by which they are to be governed through the medium of elected, representative and accountable officials'.[163]

This makes a point of great importance, but does any political system today work in such a perfect way as to justify the removal of all restraint upon the making of laws by a popular assembly? How much restraint, of what kind, and what checks and balances there should be on electoral power – these are issues that must be addressed in every democracy.[164] And it is essential to consider as a matter of social justice what the outcomes may be, in terms of gainers and losers, from new layers of government at supranational level (as in the European Union) or within the state (as with the Scottish Parliament), or from new forms of protection for the individual (as under the Human Rights Act 1998).[165]

Decisions about future constitutional developments should be made on the authority of Parliament, not by the judiciary. But in the case of *Jackson* (the Hunting Act 2004 case) several of the Law Lords made comments on the sovereignty of Parliament that were not directly called for by issues in the case. These passages suggest that some senior judges have deep reservations as to the power of the majority in the Commons to legislate on matters of constitutional principle (for example, by encroaching on essential functions of the courts). Lord Steyn, dealing with an argument by the Attorney General (Lord Goldsmith) based on the supremacy of Parliament, said: 'We do not have in the United Kingdom an uncontrolled constitution as the Attorney General implausibly submits'. Further, said Lord Steyn, Dicey's account of 'the supremacy of Parliament, pure and absolute as it was, can now be seen to be out of place in the modern United Kingdom'. While that supremacy 'is still the *general* principle of the constitution, [it] is a construct of the common law', and it was not 'unthinkable that circumstances could arise where the courts may have to qualify a principle established *on a different hypothesis of constitutionalism*'.[166]

Lord Hope began his speech in *Jackson* robustly: 'Our constitution is dominated by the sovereignty of Parliament. But parliamentary sovereignty is no longer, if it ever was, absolute'.[167] Remarking that '[the] rule of law enforced by the courts is the ultimate controlling factor on which our constitution is based', Lord Hope stressed that the

163 K. D. Ewing, '*Just Words* and Social Justice' (1999) 5 *Review of Constitutional Studies* 53, 55.

164 See S. Kentridge, 'Parliamentary Supremacy: Some Lessons from the Commonwealth' [1997] *Public Law* 96.

165 And see Sedley, above, n. 6.

166 Above, n. 51, at [102]. The first emphasis is Lord Steyn's – the second emphasis has been supplied. And see J. Jowell, 'Parliamentary Sovereignty under the New Constitutional Hypothesis' [2006] *Public Law* 562.

167 Above, n. 51, at [104].

ultimate rule by which people are prepared to recognize the existence of law 'depends upon the legislature maintaining the trust of the electorate'.[168] Lady Hale considered that, in addition to limitations on parliamentary sovereignty that have arisen from the European Communities Act 1972 and the Human Rights Act 1998, '[it] is possible that other qualifications may emerge in due course'.[169]

Statements of this kind are consonant with the approach that this chapter takes in questioning in both descriptive and normative senses the absolutist position associated with Dicey. It must not be assumed from these statements in *Jackson* that today's judges are anxiously waiting to impose judicial supremacism upon the UK, but they indicate a willingness not merely to address the content of parliamentary sovereignty, but also to examine the link between that doctrine, the principle of democracy, and the Rule of Law.

If there are serious concerns in a democracy about ways in which the political process, the conduct of government, and the law's contribution to social order can be improved, they deserve to be debated in a mature and rational manner. Such a debate will be stunted if it proceeds from the starting point that 'Parliament is unable to bind its successors' or if it assumes that the 19th- or mid-20th-century relationship between Parliament and the courts was preordained by a beneficent power and is unalterable. The place of the doctrine of parliamentary sovereignty in the UK is neither static nor immutable. It may be, as with the Human Rights Act 1998 and the Scotland Act 1998, that ways can be found of retaining the form (or appearance) of parliamentary sovereignty: an emphasis on form may be expedient in facilitating the changes in substance that in reality are being made. Professor Allan has advocated open debate based on constitutional principles: 'When constitutional debate is opened up to ordinary legal reasoning, based on fundamental principles, we shall discover that the notion of unlimited parliamentary sovereignty no longer makes any legal or constitutional sense'.[170] Others will disagree, but we can be certain that future constitutional developments will not be restricted by what may be no more than an outdated straitjacket, and that past decisions cannot be determinative of all issues that may arise in a changing world.

FURTHER READING

Foley, M., *The Silence of Constitutions* (1989).

Goldsworthy, J., *The Sovereignty of Parliament: History and Philosophy* (1999); and *Parliamentary Sovereignty: Contemporary Debates* (2010).

Hickman, T., *Public Law after the Human Rights Act* (2010).

Kavanagh, A., *Constitutional Review under the UK Human Rights Act* (2009).

MacCormick, N., *Questioning Sovereignty: Law, State and Nation in the European Commonwealth* (1999).

[168] Above, n. 51, at [126]. [169] Above, n. 51, at [159]. [170] Allan, above n. 82, p. 449.

Oliver, P.C., *The Constitution of Independence: the Development of Constitutional Theory in Australia, Canada, and New Zealand* (2005).

Wade, H. W. R., 'The basis of legal sovereignty' [1955] *Camb L J* 172.

Among the leading legal journals, the quarterly *Public Law* regularly includes informative articles and lively analysis relating to issues discussed in this chapter.

USEFUL WEBSITES

Supreme Court of the UK: **www.supremecourt.gov.uk**
The website of the Supreme Court contains decisions of the Court.

UK Parliament: **www.parliament.uk**
The website of the UK Parliament is a rich storehouse of information about the recent and current work of Parliament, and it includes judgments of the House of Lords made until the Supreme Court for the UK began its work in October 2009.

3

HUMAN RIGHTS AND THE BRITISH CONSTITUTION

Anthony Lester[1]

SUMMARY

The European Convention on Human Rights (ECHR) was drafted in the aftermath of the Second World War to confer enforceable rights upon individuals against sovereign states. It provides for an individual right of petition to the European Court of Human Rights. The UK ratified the ECHR in 1951 and accepted the individual right of petition in 1966. Many significant cases have been taken successfully by individuals against the UK to the Court, resulting in Parliament making major alterations to UK law. British courts were not prepared to give full domestic effect to the ECHR in the absence of legislation incorporating it into domestic law, but they developed the common law to protect civil and political rights. With the passage of the Human Rights Act 1998, which came into force for the UK as a whole in October 2000, the ECHR can be relied upon directly in domestic courts.

The Act reconciles the sovereignty of Parliament with the effective protection of Convention rights by requiring the courts where possible to read and to give effect to legislation in a way compatible with Convention rights and also by requiring public authorities, other than Parliament - including the courts - to respect and uphold these rights. The courts now develop both public and private law in line with the ECHR. Where legislation cannot possibly be interpreted in a way compatible with Convention rights, the courts are unable to grant an effective remedy, but may grant a declaration of incompatibility stating that the legislation in question violates Convention rights. The Joint Select Committee on Human Rights (JCHR) scrutinizes government measures for their compatibility with Convention rights, and since 2007, the Equality and Human Rights Commission (EHRC) has had broad powers and duties in relation to the promotion and protection of human rights, as well as tackling unlawful discrimination, now under the Equality Act 2010.

[1] The author is grateful to Emily Gray and Caroline Baker, parliamentary legal and research officers of The Odysseus Trust, for their assistance in revising this chapter.

The Human Rights Act 1998 exerts a magnetic force over the entire political and legal system, and is a measure of fundamental constitutional importance, supplemented by the devolution legislation for Scotland, Northern Ireland and Wales, and the Equality Act 2010. This legislative scheme has created effective domestic remedies for many violations of human rights.

It is unlikely that the Human Rights Act 1998 will be repealed, but there may be political movement in favour of a Great Charter of Rights and Freedoms by 2015 – the 800th anniversary of Magna Carta.

PARLIAMENTARY SUPREMACY VERSUS FUNDAMENTAL RIGHTS

Since the Second World War the universality of human rights has been recognised by the United Nations as inherent in the very nature of human beings, an essential part of their common humanity. For religious thinkers, human rights are considered to be fundamental because they derive from divine revelation or natural law. Secular thinkers treat human rights as fundamental in the sense that they are grounded in ethical principles, and have a special claim to protection because they are rooted in democratic concepts of popular sovereignty and government by consent, combined with equal rights and freedoms of the citizen and legal protection against the abuse of power and what John Stuart Mill termed 'the tyranny of the majority'.

There are important British intellectual sources of the concept of fundamental rights, in particular, the writings of Locke, Paine, and Mill. However, for most of the past two centuries, the prevailing British constitutional ideology, influenced by the works of constitutional writers as different as Blackstone, Burke, Bentham, Dicey, and Sir Ivor Jennings, treated British citizens as 'subjects of the Crown', without the benefit of fundamental constitutional rights giving legal protection to the individual against the state and its agents. According to those writers, what are known as the 'liberties of the subject' are residual and negative in their nature; the individual has the freedom to do what he or she likes, unless forbidden to do so by the common law or by statute. The notion of special constitutional protection of human rights, based upon a higher legal order than ordinary law, was regarded as incompatible with parliamentary supremacy.[2]

The earlier concepts of 'fundamental rights', and of a 'fundamental' constitutional law taking precedence over ordinary laws, became eclipsed at the end of the 17th century by the concept of absolute parliamentary sovereignty. In the early part of the century, the judges had struggled not only for independence from undue executive interference but also for the right to withhold effect from laws that they regarded as unconscionable or as contrary to a higher, fundamental natural law. The judges

[2] See Lester, Pannick and Herberg (eds), *Human Rights Law and Practice* (3rd edn, 2009) ch. 1.

won the struggle for independence against the Crown's claim to rule by prerogative, but the price paid by the common lawyers for their alliance with Parliament against the divine right of kings was that the common law could be changed by Parliament as it pleased. The 'glorious bloodless' revolution of 1688 was won by Parliament, and although the Bill of Rights of 1688–89 and the Act of Settlement of 1700 recognized some important personal rights and liberties, the terms of the constitutional settlement were mainly concerned with the rights and liberties of Parliament. The alliance of Parliament and the common lawyers ensured that the supremacy of the law would mean the supremacy of Parliament; more realistically, it came to mean, between general elections, the supremacy of the government in Parliament. The doctrine of the supremacy of Parliament, described by Lord Hailsham of St Marylebone as operating in practice as an 'elected dictatorship', became the keystone of the British constitution.

According to the traditional English political and legal theory that prevailed until the late twentieth century, as Parliament is sovereign (acting in place of the monarch who could do no wrong) the subjects of the Crown could not possess fundamental rights as against Parliament (which can also do no wrong), such as are guaranteed by the many foreign and Commonwealth constitutions containing fundamental and paramount law. There were no rights that were 'fundamental' in the sense that they enjoy special constitutional protection against interference by Parliament. All Acts of Parliament are equal; a constitutional measure, such as Magna Carta, or the Petition of Right, or the Act of Union with Scotland, has no greater legal importance than, say, a statute to regulate the practice of dentistry. According to this tradition of legal positivism, the liberties of the subject are derived from two principles. The first principle is that we may say or do what we please, provided we do not transgress the substantive law, or infringe the rights of others. The second principle is that public authorities (including the Crown) may do only what they are authorized to do by some rule (including the royal prerogative) or by statute.

Again according to traditional English theory, the role of the independent judiciary is essential to maintaining the common law principles of the rule of law, but the courts are subordinate to Parliament. The task of law making is the exclusive province of Parliament, and it would be undemocratic for the non-elected judiciary to act as law-makers. The judges' constitutional task is faithfully and strictly to interpret the will of Parliament, expressed in detailed legislation, to be read according to its so-called 'plain meaning', and to declare common law principles when the law is incomplete or obscure. In accordance with this constitutional orthodoxy, if either the textual analysis of the words of a statute or the courts' interpretation of the common law has undesirable consequences, the matter must be corrected by the legislature and not by the courts.

The surest and most effective safeguards, in the opinion of thinkers such as Sir Ivor Jennings, are not the rigid legalism and paper guarantees of written constitutions and Bills of Rights, but the benevolent exercise of administrative discretion by public officials, acting as Platonic guardians of the public interest, accountable through their political masters to the legislature and the people. Until recently, the effective safeguards against the misuse of public powers were regarded as being not legally enforceable safeguards but malleable constitutional conventions: the sense of fair play of ministers and the professional integrity of civil servants in using their broad delegated powers; the vigilance of the opposition and of individual members of Parliament in calling the government to account; the influence of a free and vigorous press and a well-informed and active citizenry; and the periodic opportunity to change the government through free and secret elections. It was this state of mind, as well as political convenience, that underpinned the refusal by successive governments to introduce a constitutional Bill of Rights or to make Convention rights directly enforceable in British courts.

THE SPREAD OF FUNDAMENTAL CONSTITUTIONAL LAW AND RIGHTS

Although the ideology of fundamental rights was rejected by successive generations of British governments and constitutional thinkers on the political left and right, it has been a potent force across the wider world. American and French concepts of fundamental human rights and judicial review shaped systems of government subject to binding constitutional codes in Europe and beyond. The conquests of Napoleon's armies spread through the European continent not only the Code Civil but also the public philosophy and public law of the USA and France. These ideas and systems were also spread to other continents. Today, the many countries whose legal systems are based upon the civil law have legally binding constitutional guarantees of fundamental human rights derived from 17th-century England and the 18th-century European Enlightenment. In the common law world, as the colonies of the British Empire gained independence, Bills of Rights were introduced giving constitutional protection to human rights in the Commonwealth.

The human rights-based philosophy also became profoundly influential in creating a new international legal order in the wake of the horrors of the Second World War. In December 1948, the UN General Assembly adopted the Universal Declaration of Human Rights,[3] recognizing certain rights as basic human entitlements: free speech as much as freedom from torture. In 1966, two International Covenants were opened for signature, a Covenant on Civil and Political Rights, and a Covenant on Economic, Social and Cultural Rights. The two Covenants came into force in 1976, and are reinforced by several UN human rights conventions, for example, against torture, race and sex discrimination, and protecting the rights of the child.[4]

[3] See Lord Steyn, 'Human Rights: The Legacy of Mrs Roosevelt' [2002] *Public Law* 473.

[4] Lester, Pannick and Herberg, above, n. 2, ch. 9.

THE EUROPEAN CONVENTION ON HUMAN RIGHTS

Meanwhile, in Western Europe, a second terrible war in half a century and the barbarous atrocities of the Nazi Holocaust convinced European politicians and jurists of the need to forge a new European legal order. The need to guard against the rise of new dictatorships, to avoid the risk of relapse into another disastrous European war, and to provide a beacon of hope for the peoples of Central and Eastern Europe living under Soviet totalitarian regimes, inspired the foundation, in 1949, of the Council of Europe. Members of the Council of Europe are obliged to accept the principles of the European rule of law and the enjoyment by everyone within their jurisdiction of human rights and fundamental freedoms.

One of the Council of Europe's first tasks was to draft a human rights convention for Europe, conferring enforceable rights upon individuals against sovereign states. The inventors of the Convention were determined never again to permit state sovereignty to shield from international liability the perpetrators of crimes against humanity, never again to allow governments to shelter behind the traditional argument that what a state does to its own citizens or to the stateless is within its exclusive jurisdiction and beyond the reach of the international community. So they resolved to create a binding international code of human rights with effective legal safeguards for all victims of violations by contracting states.

For the first time, individuals would be able to exercise personally enforceable rights under international law, before an independent and impartial judicial tribunal – the European Court of Human Rights – against the public authorities of their own states. No matter whether the violation occurred because of an administrative decision by a minister or civil servant, or because of the judgment of a national supreme court, or because of legislation enacted by a national Parliament; there would be no privilege or immunity enabling state authorities automatically to shield themselves against supranational European judicial scrutiny.

The birth pangs of the ECHR were not easy. In the UK, the Attlee government was particularly keen to preserve strong ministerial powers from judicial review by an international court of unknown worth.[5] It decided only very reluctantly to ratify the ECHR, and only on the basis that it would not accept the right of individual petition to the European Commission and European Court of Human Rights.[6]

[5] Lester, Pannick and Herberg, above, n. 2, ch. 1.

[6] The ECHR guarantees fundamental civil and political rights to everyone within the jurisdiction of the contracting states: the right to life (Art. 2); the prohibition of torture and inhuman or degrading treatment or punishment (Art. 3); the prohibition of slavery and forced labour (Art. 4); the right to liberty (Art. 5); the right to a fair trial (Art. 6); no punishment without law (Art. 7); respect for private and family life (Art. 8); freedom of thought, conscience, and religion (Art. 9); freedom of expression (Art. 10); freedom of assembly and association (Art. 11); the right to marry and found a family (Art. 12); the right to an effective national remedy (Art. 13); and non-discrimination in the enjoyment of Convention rights (Art. 14).

In December 1965, the first Wilson government decided to accept the right of individual petition and the jurisdiction of the European Court of Human Rights to rule on cases brought by individuals against the UK. It was to prove to be a momentous decision, for it meant that, in fact if not in a formal sense, political (if not legal) sovereignty was henceforth to be shared with the European institutions created by the ECHR. In spite of the importance of the decision and its controversial implications in making Acts of Parliament subject to judicial review, the matter was not discussed in Cabinet or in a Cabinet Committee.[7] Unlike the decision to join the European Community and make EC law directly effective in our courts, Parliament was not asked to legislate to give effect to the consequences of acceptance of the right of petition; there was no public consultation by means of a green or white paper.[8]

BRITISH CASES BEFORE THE EUROPEAN COURT OF HUMAN RIGHTS

Judgments of the European Court of Human Rights are binding in international law upon the state concerned,[9] and the Committee of Ministers of the Council of Europe supervises their execution. Compliance may require the passing of legislation to amend or repeal an offending statute or to overrule a judgment of the country's highest court.[10]

Acceptance of the right of petition gave British lawyers an important opportunity to obtain effective redress for their clients under the ECHR, for want of effective remedies within the UK. In the *East African Asians* case,[11] the Commission decided that Parliament itself had breached the ECHR in enacting the Commonwealth Immigrants Act 1968, which subjected British Asian passport-holders to inherently degrading treatment by excluding them on racial grounds from their country of citizenship.

The first case where the European Court found a breach by the UK was *Golder*, which held[12] that the Home Secretary had infringed a prisoner's right of access to the English courts and his right to respect for his correspondence. The first case in which the Court

The UK ratified the First Protocol to the ECHR on 3 November 1952, which added the right to the protection of property (Art. 1); the right to education (Art. 2); and the right to free elections (Art. 3). The UK ratified the Sixth Protocol to the ECHR on 27 January 1999, abolishing the death penalty. On 1 February 2004, the UK ratified the Thirteenth Protocol to the ECHR, which abolishes the death penalty completely, including in time of war or imminent threat of war. The Equality Act 2010 amended domestic law so as to enable the UK to ratify the Seventh Protocol to the ECHR. However, at the time of writing, the coalition government has not done so.

[7] A. Lester, 'Fundamental Rights: The UK Isolated?' [1984] *Public Law* 46, 58–61, and 'UK Acceptance of the Strasbourg Jurisdiction: What Went on in Whitehall in 1965' [1998] *Public Law* 237.

[8] Cf. *The United Kingdom and the European Communities*, Cmnd 4715 (1971).

[9] ECHR, Art. 46(1).

[10] The JCHR reviews the implementation of the Court's judgments in UK cases, see, for example, Fifteenth Report of Session 2009–10, *Enhancing Parliament's role in relation to human rights judgments*, HL 85/HC 455 (26 March 2010).

[11] *East African Asians* v. *United Kingdom* [1981] 3 EHRR 76. Commission's admissibility decision of 14 December 1973 (published only in 1981 after it had been 'leaked').

[12] *Golder* v. *United Kingdom* (1975) 1 EHRR 524.

held that the House of Lords had breached the ECHR arose from an injunction restraining *The Sunday Times* from publishing an article about the 'thalidomide' tragedy because it was prejudicial to pending civil proceedings. By a narrow majority, the Court held[13] the Law Lords' decision to have interfered unnecessarily with the right to free expression.

There have been more than 270 judgments of the European Court finding breaches by the UK, many of them politically controversial and far-reaching.[14] They include: the inhuman treatment of suspected terrorists in Northern Ireland; inadequate safeguards against telephone tapping by the police; unfair discrimination against British wives of foreign husbands under immigration rules; unjust administrative restrictions upon prisoners' correspondence and visits; corporal punishment in schools; excessive corporal punishment by a parent; the criminalization of private homosexual conduct; the exclusion of homosexuals from the armed services; the lack of legal recognition of transsexuals; ineffective judicial protection for detained mental patients, or would-be immigrants, or individuals facing extradition to countries where they risk being exposed to torture or inhuman treatment, or homosexuals whose private life is infringed; the dismissal of workers because of the oppressive operation of the closed shop; interference with free speech by unnecessarily maintaining injunctions restraining breaches of confidence, or because of a jury's award of excessive damages for libel, or by punishing a journalist for refusing to disclose his confidential source; the absence of a right to have a detention order under the Mental Health Act judicially reviewed; denial of parental access to children; access to child care records; inadequate review of the continuing detention of those serving discretionary and mandatory life sentences; the blanket exclusion of the right of prisoners to vote in elections; lack of effective remedy for violations of personal privacy; lack of access to legal advice for fine and debt defaulters; unfair court martial procedures; lack of availability of legal aid in some criminal cases; the unnecessary retention of DNA samples in violation of the right to personal privacy; and lack of access to civil justice.

USE OF THE CONVENTION IN BRITISH COURTS

The landmark judgments of the European Court of Human Rights against the UK had a profound impact upon senior British judges. The Strasbourg jurisprudence made them more sensitive to the fault-line in the British legal system that had resulted in repeated failures to give sufficient legal protection to individual rights. It caused them to take Convention law more seriously than had been the case in the 1970s and 1980s; and, eventually, to support moves to make Convention rights directly enforceable in British courts.

The ECHR was invoked in proceedings before English courts, even before Convention rights became directly enforceable.[15] The courts became willing to have

[13] *Sunday Times* v. *United Kingdom* (1979) 2 EHRR 245.

[14] European Court of Human Rights website, United Kingdom Country Information. Number of judgments current as of 1 January 2010. See www.echr.coe.int/50/en/#countries-infos (accessed 17 September 2010).

[15] M. Hunt, *Using International Human Rights Law in English Courts* (1997). Appendix 1 to that work contains a chronological table of English cases in which judicial reference has been made to unincorporated international human rights law. See also Michael J. Beloff, QC and Helen Mountfield 'Unconventional Behaviour? Judicial Uses of the European Convention in England and Wales [1996] *EHRLR* 467. The proposition that the

regard to the unincorporated ECHR and its case law as sources of principles or standards of public policy. They did so when common law or statutory law was ambiguous, or where the common law was undeveloped or uncertain, or in determining the manner in which judicial (as distinct from administrative) discretion should be exercised.[16] In *Brind*,[17] however, the Law Lords decided that they would be usurping the functions of Parliament by incorporating Convention rights through the back door, if they were to interpret broad statutory powers as being limited by or subject to the ECHR.

Nevertheless, the European Court's judgments influenced British courts in declaring, as a matter of common law, that there are fundamental constitutional rights, notably, the right to free expression,[18] the right of access to the courts and lawyers,[19]

ECHR, as an international Treaty, is not part of English domestic law 'has been in no way altered or amended by the 1998 Act. Although people sometimes speak of the Convention having been incorporated into domestic law, that is a misleading metaphor. What the Act has done is to create domestic rights expressed in the same terms as those contained in the Convention. But they are domestic rights, not international rights. Their source is the statute, not the Convention. They are available against specific public authorities, not the United Kingdom as a state. And their meaning and application is a matter for domestic courts, not the court in Strasbourg', *In Re McKerr* [2004] UKHL 12, [2004] 1 WLR 807 (HL) at [63], *per* Lord Hoffmann.

[16] *R* v. *Secretary of State for the Home Department ex parte Brind* [1991] 1 AC 696 (HL), 747H–8A, *per* Lord Bridge, with whom Lord Roskill agreed, and 760D–G, *per* Lord Ackner, with whom Lord Lowry agreed. The interpretative principle was applied in relation to the Convention for the Elimination of All Forms of Discrimination Against Women in the decision of the Hong Kong Special Administrative Region Court of First Instance in *Equal Opportunities Commission for Hong Kong* v. *Director of Education* [2001] HKCFI 880 at [89]–[91] and [109]–[110], *per* Hartmann J.

[17] *R.* v. *Secretary of State for the Home Department ex parte Brind* [1991] 1 AC 696 (HL). The author was leading counsel for the unsuccessful appellants.

[18] See e.g. *Reynolds* v. *Times Newspapers* [2001] AC 127 (HL) at [206], *per* Lord Steyn, and at [190], *per* Lord Nicholls of Birkenhead; *Derbyshire County Council* v. *Times Newspapers* [1993] AC 534, (HL). See also *McCartan Turkington Breen* v. *Times Newspapers Limited* [2001] 2 AC 227 (HL), 297H, *per* Lord Steyn, that even before the coming into force of the Human Rights Act 1998, 'the principle of freedom of expression [had] attained the status of a constitutional right with high attendant normative force'. However, when one considers the examples of the development of the protection of the right to privacy based on equitable principles of confidence, and the recognition of the limits on the law concerning contractual duties of confidence when it is necessary to promote discussion on matters of public interest (*London Regional Transport* v. *Mayor of London* [2001] EWCA Civ 1491, [2003] EMLR 4 (CA) at [46]–[49], *per* Robert Walker LJ, and [55]–[58], *per* Sedley LJ), there is little doubt that the Human Rights Act 1998 has exercised a significant influence on the judicial approach to limitations on free speech. The change of judicial approach necessitated by the Human Rights Act 1998 is seen at work principally in the application of the concept of proportionality when used in scrutinizing the legality of interferences with freedom of speech (see Sedley LJ in *London Regional Transport* v. *Mayor of London*, above at [57]). The application of that concept has heralded the necessity for a new approach which promotes freedom of expression to a much higher protected status than that which it enjoyed in both public and private law prior to the Human Rights Act 1998. As expressed by Lord Nicholls in *Reynolds* v. *Times Newspapers* [2001] 2 AC 127 (HL), 200F–G, the ECHR requires any curtailment of freedom of expression to be 'convincingly established by a compelling countervailing consideration, and the means employed must be proportionate to the end sought to be achieved'. See also *R* v. *BBC ex parte ProLife Alliance* [2003] UKHL 23, [2004] 1 AC 185 (HL), and *R (Animal Defenders International)* v. *Secretary of State for Culture, Media and Sport* [2008] UKHL 15, [2008] 1 AC 1312 (HL). See also *R. (on the application of JF (by his litigation friend OF) and another)* v. *Secretary of State for the Home Department* [2010] UKSC 17, [2010] 2 WLR 992 (SC).

[19] See e.g. *R.* v. *Secretary of State for the Home Department ex parte Leech (No. 2)* [1994] QB 198 (CA), 210A, *per* Steyn LJ; *R.* v. *Lord Chancellor ex parte Witham* [1998] QB 575, 585G–6G, *per* Laws LJ; *R* v. *Lord Chancellor ex parte Lightfoot* [2000] QB 597 (CA); *R. (Wright)* v. *Secretary of State for Health* [2009] UKHL 3, [2009] 1 AC 739 (HL).

and the right to equal treatment without unfair discrimination.[20] Recently the courts have begun to recognize the right to personal privacy, founded on the existing legal doctrine of breach of confidence.[21] Although *Brind* was a narrowly restrictive decision, the Law Lords recognized that stricter scrutiny of administrative decisions was called for where fundamental human rights were at stake. The Court of Appeal also decided[22] that the more substantial the interference with human rights, the more the court would require by way of justification before it was satisfied that the decision was reasonable. However, the European Court of Human Rights held that this approach was insufficient to satisfy the requirement for an effective domestic remedy under ECHR, Art. 13.

Brind revealed a serious gap in the effective legal protection of human rights in the UK. English courts, influenced by the development of a modern system of public law and by the requirement to give effect to the supremacy of EC law, did their best to give effect to Convention rights, without statutory incorporation, but it was deference to parliamentary sovereignty which made the Law Lords draw back from complete judicial incorporation. The gap could only be filled by legislation to make Convention rights directly enforceable in British courts.

[20] *Arthur J S Hall & Co.* v *Melvyn Keith Simons* [2002] 1 AC 615 (HL), *per* Lord Hoffmann. See also *R. (Association of British Civilian Internees Far East Region)* v. *Secretary of State for Defence* [2003] EWCA Civ 473, [2003] QB 1397 (CA); *A* v. *Secretary of State for the Home Department* [2002] EWCA Civ 1502, [2004] QB 335 (CA). See also *European Roma Rights Centre* v. *Immigration Officer at Prague Airport (United Nations High Commissioner for Refugees intervening)* [2004] UKHL 55, [2005] 2 AC 1 (HL); *R. (on the application of E) v. Governing Body of JFS and others (Secretary of State for Children, School and Families and others, interested parties) (United Synagogue intervening); R. (on the application of E)* v. *Office of the Schools Adjudicator (Governing Body of JFS and others, interested parties) (British Humanist Association and another intervening)* [2009] UKSC 1, [2009] 1 WLR 2353 (SC).

[21] *Douglas, Zeta-Jones, Northern Shell plc* v. *Hello! Ltd* [2005] EWCA Civ 595, [2006] QB 125 (CA); *Campbell* v. *MGN* [2005] UKHL 61, [2005] 1 WLR 3394 (HL); *McKennitt v. Ash* [2006] EWCA Civ 1714, [2008] QB 73 (CA); *His Royal Highness the Prince of Wales* v. *Associated Newspapers Ltd* [2006] EWCA Civ 1776, [2008] Ch 57 (CA). But for limits to the right in English law see *Re S (A child) (Identification: Restrictions on Publication)* [2005] 1 AC 593 (HL). See also *A* v. *B plc* [2002] EWCA Civ 337, [2003] QB 195 (CA) at [4], *per* Lord Woolf CJ, where he described ECHR, Arts 8 and 10 as providing 'new parameters' within which the court will decide, in an action for breach of confidence, whether a person is entitled to have his privacy protected by the court or whether the restriction of freedom of expression which such protection involves cannot be justified. See also J. Morgan, 'Privacy in the House of Lords, again' (2004) 120 *LQR* 563; Rachael Mulheron, 'A potential framework for privacy? A reply to Hello!' (2006) *MLR* 679; David Mead, 'It's a funny old game – privacy, football and the public interest' [2006] *EHRLR* 541; Rabinder Singh, QC and James Strachan, 'The Right to Privacy in English Law' [2002] *EHRLR* 129. See also *Douglas* v. *Hello! Ltd and others (No 3)* [2007] UKHL 21, [2008] 1 AC 1 (HL); *Mosley* v. *News Group Newspapers Limited* [2008] EWHC 1777 (QB); *Lord Browne of Madingley* v. *Associated Newspapers Limited* [2007] EWCA Civ 295, [2008] QB 103 (CA); *Napier* v. *Pressdram Ltd.* [2009] EWCA Civ 443, [2010] 1 WLR 934 (CA); *Murray* v. *Big Pictures (UK) Ltd.* [2008] EWCA Civ 446, [2009] Ch 481 (CA). See also D. Leigh, 'Media groups lobby Strasbourg over "threat to freedom"', *Guardian*, 31 March 2010, www.guardian.co.uk/media/2010/mar/31/max-mosley-press-freedom.

[22] *R.* v. *Ministry of Defence ex parte Smith* [1996] QB 517 (CA), 554E–G, *per* Sir Thomas Bingham MR for the Court of Appeal. Approved by Lord Woolf MR in *R* v. *Secretary of State for the Home Department ex parte Canbolat* [1997] 1 WLR 1569 (CA). See also *R* v. *Lord Saville of Newdigate ex parte A* [2000] 1 WLR 1855 (CA).

The 30 year campaign which resulted in the enactment of the Human Rights Act 1998 is summarized in the previous edition.

THE HUMAN RIGHTS ACT 1998

INTRODUCTION

The Human Rights Act 1998[23] reconciles formal adherence to the doctrine of parliamentary sovereignty[24] with the need to enable the courts to provide effective legal remedies for breaches of Convention rights. It is a constitutionally holistic measure, in the sense that each branch of government – the legislature and executive, as well as the judiciary – is called upon to use its public powers compatibly with Convention rights. Apart from Parliament itself,[25] the Act creates a duty upon all public authorities, including the Crown and the courts, to do so.

So far as Parliament is concerned, the JCHR enables systematic parliamentary scrutiny of government measures for their compatibility with Convention rights and the other human rights conventions to which the UK is party. Parliament, like every public authority, is bound in international law to comply with international human rights law. It is essential for each House to have the necessary information and expertise to be able to understand the implications for the protection of human rights of the enactment of primary and delegated legislation.[26] Parliament needs to be well informed where the government takes remedial action[27] to amend a statutory provision declared by a UK court[28] to be incompatible with Convention rights. The JCHR also plays a key role in scrutinizing government action in response to declarations of

[23] 1998 Cap 42. See Lester, Pannick and Herberg, above, n. 2, ch. 2.

[24] See *R.* v. *Secretary of State for the Home Department ex parte Simms* [1999] UKHL 33, [2000] 2 AC 115 (HL); *R. (on the application of Morgan Grenfell & Co. Limited)* v. *Special Commissioner of Income Tax* [2002] UKHL 21, [2003] 1 AC 563 (HL). See further Lord Irvine of Lairg QC, 'The Impact of the Human Rights Act: Parliament, the Courts and the Executive' [2003] *Public Law* 308; N. Bamforth, 'Parliamentary Sovereignty and the Human Rights Act 1998' [1998] *Public Law* 572. See also *A* v. *B (Investigatory Powers Tribunal: jurisdiction)* [2009] UKSC 12, [2010] 2 WLR 1 (SC).

[25] The broad definition of 'public authority' in s. 6 does not include either House of Parliament or a person exercising functions in connection with proceedings in Parliament: see s. 6(3). However, it includes the House of Lords in its judicial capacity: see s. 6(4).

[26] In addition to the scrutiny work of the JCHR, other parliamentary select committees perform important scrutiny functions. In the House of Lords, the Constitution Committee examines the constitutional implications of all public Bills coming before the House and keeps under review the operation of the constitution. The House of Lords Select Committee on Delegated Powers and Regulatory Reform is required to report whether the provisions of any Bill inappropriately delegate legislative power, or whether they subject the exercise of legislative power to an inappropriate degree of parliamentary scrutiny; that Committee also scrutinizes Regulatory Reform Orders introduced under the Regulatory Reform Act 2001. The Select Committee on the European Union scrutinizes EU measures for their compatibility with human rights. The Joint Committee on Statutory Instruments has regard to the human rights implications of delegated legislation although the remit is limited to an assessment of whether the legislation is *vires* the enabling legislation. See also David Feldman, 'Parliamentary Scrutiny of Legislation and Human Rights' [2002] *Public Law* 323.

[27] Under s. 10 and Sched. 2.

[28] Under s. 4.

incompatibility[29] and to findings by the European Court of Human Rights that the UK has violated the ECHR.[30]

CONVENTION RIGHTS

Convention rights are legally enforceable civil and political rights and, as such, are regarded as appropriate to be interpreted and applied by the independent judiciary.

The Act does not empower the judiciary to strike down legislation that cannot possibly be read in a way compatible with Convention rights. To that extent, the Act gives a weaker legal status to Convention law than is given to directly effective EC law under European Communities Act 1972, s. 2. The Act is also weaker than the written constitutions of other Commonwealth countries under which the courts are empowered and required to strike down unconstitutional legislation.[31] However, it endows the UK judiciary with strong interpretative powers which are intended to be used robustly.

DUTY TO AVOID INCOMPATIBILITY BETWEEN DOMESTIC LEGISLATION AND THE CONVENTION

Section 3 of the Act is pivotal. It imposes a duty on courts and tribunals to strive to avoid incompatibility between domestic legislation and the ECHR. Existing and future legislation must, so far as is possible, be read and given effect in a way which is compatible with Convention rights.[32] The crucial words in relation to this interpretative obligation are 'possible' and 'must'. As Lord Steyn has pointed out, Parliament specifically rejected the legislative model of requiring a 'reasonable' interpretation, which is to be found in the New Zealand Bill of Rights Act.[33] As the white paper explained:[34]

> This goes beyond the present rule which enables the courts to take the Convention into account in resolving any ambiguity in a legislative provision. The courts will be required to

[29] See Lester, Pannick and Herberg, above, n. 2, ch. 8.

[30] Information about the process is contained in the Fifteenth Report of Session 2009–10, above, n. 10. See also for a wider European perspective the Report of the Council of Europe Parliamentary Assembly Committee of Legal Affairs and Human Rights, *Implementation of judgments of the European Court of Human Rights*, Doc. 11020 (18 September 2006). The government's response to the JCHR's report was published on 28 July 2010, Ministry of Justice, *Responding to Human Rights Judgments: Government Response to the JCHR*, Cm. 7892 (28 July 2010).

[31] Apart from New Zealand. In Australia the courts are empowered to strike down unconstitutional legislation, but the Federal Constitution does not contain a full Bill of Rights.

[32] 'Convention rights' are defined in Human Rights Act 1998, s. 1(1). They are the rights guaranteed under ECHR, Arts 2–12 and 14, Arts 1–3 of the First Protocol to the ECHR, and Art. 1 of the Thirteenth Protocol to the ECHR. ECHR, Art. 13 – which provides that everyone whose rights and freedoms are violated shall have 'an effective remedy before a national authority' – is not included. That is because the Human Rights Act 1998 itself gives effect to Art. 13 by establishing a scheme under which Convention rights can be raised before our domestic courts: *R. (on the application of K)* v. *Camden and Islington Health Authority* [2001] EWCA Civ 240, [2002] QB 198 (CA), 233G–H, *per* Sedley LJ.

[33] *Ghaidan* v. *Godin-Mendoza* [2004] UKHL 30, [2004] 2 AC 557 (HL), 574F–G, *per* Lord Steyn.

[34] *Rights Brought Home*, Cm. 3782 (1997) para. 2.7.

> interpret legislation so as to uphold the Convention rights unless the legislation itself is so clearly incompatible with the Convention that it is impossible to do so.

This duty applies to primary and secondary legislation. It requires courts and tribunals, using techniques developed by Commonwealth and US courts, to construe constitutional Bills of Rights, to 'read down' (that is, to interpret delegated public powers to be exercised only subject to Convention rights), and to read into legislation necessary procedural safeguards of Convention rights.[35] In the words of the Lord Chancellor, 'in 99% of the cases that will arise, there will be no need for judicial declarations of incompatibility'.[36] However, as the Lord Chancellor also observed,[37] the Act:

> does not allow the courts to set aside or ignore Acts of Parliament. [Section] 3 preserves the effect of primary legislation which is incompatible with the Convention. It does the same for secondary legislation where it is inevitably incompatible because of the terms of the parent statute.

Case law on s. 3 has established fundamental principles to be applied when construing legislation to make it compatible with Convention rights. In *Re S (Care Order: Implementation of Care Plan)*,[38] Lord Nicholls of Birkenhead stated that s. 3 is 'a powerful tool whose use is obligatory. It is not an optional canon of construction. Nor is its use dependent on the existence of ambiguity'. Lord Bingham of Cornhill approved *Re S* in *R. (Anderson)* v. *Secretary of State for the Home Department*[39] but warned that s. 3 allowed for judicial interpretation but not 'judicial vandalism' so as to give the statutory provision 'an effect quite different from that which Parliament intended'. Lord Steyn examined the interpretative obligation of s. 3 in the rape shield case, *R.* v. *A (No. 2)*,[40] and concluded that:

> in accordance with the will of Parliament as reflected in section 3 it will sometimes be necessary to adopt an interpretation which linguistically may appear strained. The techniques to be used will not only involve the reading down of express language in a statute but also the implication of provisions. A declaration of incompatibility is a measure of last resort. It must be avoided unless it is plainly impossible to do so. If a *clear* limitation on Convention rights is stated *in terms*, such an impossibility will arise.[41]

In *Ghaidan* v. *Godin-Mendoza*[42] Lord Nicholls of Birkenhead observed that s. 3 'is one of the primary means by which Convention rights are brought into the law of this country'. He stated that:

> Parliament, however, cannot have intended that in the discharge of this extended interpretative function the courts should adopt a meaning inconsistent with a fundamental

[35] See Lord Lester of Herne Hill, QC, 'The Art of the Possible: Interpreting Statutes under the Human Rights Act' [1998] *EHRLR* 665.

[36] Lord Irvine of Lairg, 585 HL Official Report, col. 840 (5 February 1998).

[37] Lord Irvine of Lairg, 583 HL Official Report, cols 1230–1 (3 November 1997).

[38] [2002] UKHL 10, [2002] 2 AC 291 (HL).

[39] [2002] UKHL 46, [2003] 1 AC 837 (HL), 882G–883D.

[40] [2002] 1 AC 45 (HL), 68.

[41] See *R.* v. *Secretary of State for the Home Department ex parte Simms* [1999] UKHL 33, [2000] 2 AC 115 (HL), 132A–B, *per* Lord Hoffmann; *R.* v. *Lambert* [2001] UKHL 37, [2002] 2 AC 545 (HL), *per* Lord Hope of Craighead.

[42] *Ghaidan* v. *Godin-Mendoza* [2004] UKHL 30, [2004] 2 AC 557 (HL).

> feature of legislation. That would be to cross the constitutional boundary section 3 seeks to demarcate and preserve. Parliament has retained the right to enact legislation in terms which are not Convention-compliant.[43]

Section 19 requires a minister in charge of a Bill to issue a statement that it is compatible with Convention rights. The compatibility statement is published on the face of the Bill. The JCHR has sought fuller explanations for government views on the compatibility of Bills with the Act, with limited success.[44] Where the minister has expressed the official view that a Bill's provisions are compatible with Convention rights, the courts will readily conclude that nothing in the Bill was intended to override such rights. However, s. 19 statements do not bind the court to conclude that the relevant legislation is compatible with Convention rights, nor do they have persuasive authority.[45]

The JCHR[46] has recommended that ministers should provide the Committee with a redacted version of the human rights memorandum circulated within the government when a Bill is introduced, as the Department of the Environment, Food and Rural Affairs did with the Marine and Coastal Access Bill and the Government Equalities Office with the Equality Bill. The JCHR recommended that government guidance on the introduction of legislation should be amended to give effect to this proposal in time for the first session of the new Parliament.

However, regrettably, the Brown administration refused[47] to change the Cabinet Office guidance, arguing that the principal purpose of the Memorandum is to provide legal advice to the Legislation Committee when Bills and Draft Bills are considered for introduction, and that it may contain advice from Law Officers which is privileged legal information.

IMPLIED REPEAL

The deliberate omission from the Human Rights Act 1998 of the equivalent of New Zealand Bill of Rights Act 1990, s. 4[48] is significant. Such a provision would have

[43] Ibid., p. 572B, *per* Lord Nicholls of Birkenhead.

[44] *The Work of the Committee in 2007 and the State of Human Rights in the UK*, HL 38/HC 270 (2007–08) para. 28.

[45] *R.* v. *A (No. 2)* [2002] 1 AC 45 (HL), 75E, *per* Lord Hope of Craighead. Where a Bill is enacted in substantially the same form as it was in when the statement of compatibility was made, it should in principle be more difficult to argue that altering the meaning of its provisions to make them Convention-compliant constitutes impermissible 'legislation' rather than permissible 'interpretation' under s 3: see Beatson et al, *Human Rights: Judicial Protection in the United Kingdom* (2008) paras 5-28 and 5-121.

[46] Second Report of Session 2009–10, *Work of the Committee in 2008–09*, HL 20/HC 185 (15 January 2010).

[47] Cm. 7892 (28 July 2010).

[48] 'No court shall, in relation to any enactment (whether passed or made before or after the commencement of this Bill of Rights) (a) find any provision of the enactment to be impliedly repealed or revoked, or to be in any way invalid or ineffective, or (b) decline to apply any provision of the enactment by reason only that the provision is inconsistent with a provision of the Bill of Rights'.

required the courts to apply the doctrine of implied repeal to the interpretation of the Act,[49] with the result that a future Parliament would have been deemed to have intended, by implication, to depart from Convention rights in a later statute. Such an approach would have seriously weakened the effectiveness of the Act in securing compatibility between future legislation and Convention rights. The significance of the deliberate omission of the traditional doctrine of implied repeal is that the courts will require *express* provision in a later statute before deciding that a Convention right has been abridged.[50] As Lord Steyn has explained:

> What is the significance of classifying a right as constitutional? It is meaningful. It is a powerful indication that added value is attached to the protection of the right. It strengthens the normative force of such rights. It virtually rules out arguments that such rights can be impliedly repealed by subsequent legislation. Generally only an express repeal will suffice.[51]

The first question the courts must answer is whether the legislation interferes with a Convention right. At that stage, the purpose or intent of the legislation will play a secondary role, for it will be seldom, if ever, that Parliament will have intended to legislate in breach of Convention rights. It is at the second stage, when the government or other public authority is seeking to justify the interference with a Convention right, under one of the exception clauses, that legislative purpose or intent becomes relevant. It is at that stage that the principle of proportionality will apply.

[49] According to the doctrine of implied repeal, if a later Act makes contrary provision to an earlier Act, Parliament (though it has not expressly said so) is taken to intend the earlier Act to be repealed. The same applies where a statutory provision is contrary to a common law rule: see e.g. F. A. R. Bennion, *Statutory Interpretation* (5th edn, 2008) s. 87.

[50] In *R.* v. *Lord Chancellor ex parte Witham* [1998] QB 575, 585G Laws J stated that the common law had given special weight to the citizen's constitutional right of access to the courts which could not be abrogated except by express statutory words. This proposition has been doubted: see *Pierson* v. *Secretary of State for the Home Department* [1998] AC 539 (HL), 575, *per* Lord Browne-Wilkinson. However, it is submitted that such a proposition must inform the interpretation of future legislation under Human Rights Act 1998, s. 3, especially since the implied repeal doctrine has been deliberately rejected by government and Parliament. Sovereignty belongs to the Parliament of the day, but it must use express words before it will be taken to have decided to use its legislative powers in a way which is incompatible with Convention rights: *pace* Sir William Wade, 'Sovereignty: Revolution or Evolution?' (1996) 112 *LQR* 568 (in relation to the decision of the House of Lords in *R.* v. *Secretary of State for Transport ex parte Factortame (No. 1)* [1990] 2 AC 85 (HL), 240, *per* Lord Bridge of Harwich, interpreting European Communities Act 1972, s. 2(4)).

[51] The Rt Hon. Lord Steyn, 'The Intractable Problem of the Interpretation of Legal Texts' (2003) 25(1) *Sydney Law Review* 5. See also *Thoburn and Others* v. *Sunderland City Council and Others* [2002] EWHC 195 (Admin), [2003] QB 151 (DC). See also *R. (on the application of Junttan Oy)* v. *Bristol Magistrates' Court* [2003] UKHL 55; *A and others* v. *Secretary of State for the Home Department* [2004] UKHL 56, [2005] 2 AC 68 (HL); *Percy* v. *Board of National Mission of the Church of Scotland* [2005] UKHL 73, [2006] 2 AC 28 (HL); *Watkins* v. *Secretary of State for the Home Department* [2006] UKHL 17, [2006] 2 AC 395 (HL); *Oxfordshire County Council* v. *Oxford City Council and another* [2006] UKHL 25, [2006] 2 AC 674 (HL); *Deutsche Morgan Grenfell Group plc* v. *Inland Revenue Commissioners and another* [2006] UKHL 49, [2007] 1 AC 558 (HL).

PROPORTIONALITY

In applying the principle of proportionality, the court needs to ask itself[52] whether: (i) the legislative objective is sufficiently important to justify limiting a Convention right; (ii) the means used to impair the Convention right are rationally connected to it;[53] and (iii) the means used to impair the Convention right are no more than is necessary to accomplish that objective.[54]

British courts already had the task of deciding, in areas where EU law governs, whether a statutory rule is necessary and proportionate to the legislative aim. This involved the judicial review of Acts of Parliament against European legal standards, requiring the courts to evaluate the measure's impact in the light of its aims, having regard to evidence about its policy and the social and economic context in which it operates.[55] That is also what is required in interpreting legislation to be compatible with Convention rights.[56]

Although the courts have adopted new interpretive techniques, they cannot usurp the legislative powers of Parliament by adopting a construction which it could not be supposed that Parliament had intended by enacting the Human Rights Act 1998 and by previously or subsequently enacting the impugned statutory provision. Where only a fanciful or perverse construction is possible to make the statute compatible with Convention rights, or where the problem created by the apparent mismatch between

[52] See *de Freitas* v. *Permanent Secretary of Ministry of Agriculture, Fisheries, Lands and Housing* [1999] 1 AC 69 (PC), 80C–H, *per* Lord Clyde, approved by Lord Steyn in *R.* v. *Secretary of State for the Home Department ex parte Daly* [2001] UKHL 26, [2001] 2 AC 532 (HL), 547A–8B. See also *Huang* v. *Secretary of State for the Home Department* [2007] UKHL 11, [2007] 2 AC 167 (HL) at [19], *per* Lord Bingham.

[53] See Lord Bingham in *R* v. *Secretary of State for the Environment, Transport and the Regions ex parte Spath Holme Ltd.* [2001] 2 AC 349 (HL), 395E–6B; *Wilson* v. *First County Trust Ltd (No. 2)* [2003] UKHL 40, [2004] 1 AC 816 (HL); *R (Pretty)* v. *DPP (Secretary of State for the Home Department intervening)* [2001] UKHL 61, [2002] 1 AC 800 (HL); *R. (Carson)* v. *Secretary of State for Work and Pensions* [2005] UKHL 37, [2006] 1 AC 173 (HL); *R. (Animal Defenders International)* v. *Secretary of State for Culture, Media and Sport* [2008] UKHL 15, [2008] 1 AC 1312 (HL); *Re P (A Child) (Adoption: Unmarried Couples)* [2008] UKHL 38, [2009] 1 AC 173 (HL).

[54] See Lester, Pannick and Herberg, above, n. 2, para. 3.10. See also e.g. *R. (Farrakhan)* v. *Secretary of State for the Home Department* [2002] EWCA Civ 606, [2002] QB 1391 (CA), 1418H: a factor of considerable relevance to the test of proportionality is the extent to which the right (there the right to freedom of expression) is restricted. See also the observations of Baroness Hale in *Miss Behavin' Ltd* v. *Belfast City Council* [2007] UKHL 19, [2007] 1 WLR 1420 (HL); *E* v. *Chief Constable of the Royal Ulster Constabulary* [2008] UKHL 66, [2009] AC 536 (HL).

[55] See e.g. *R.* v. *Employment Secretary ex parte Equal Opportunities Commission* [1995] 1 AC 1 (HL).

[56] The principle of proportionality 'does not mean that there has been a shift to merits review', *R.* v. *Secretary of State for the Home Department ex parte Daly* [2001] UKHL 26, [2001] 2 AC 532 (HL), 548B–C, *per* Lord Steyn. But, as Lord Steyn there stated, 'the differences in approach between the traditional grounds of review and the proportionality approach may therefore sometimes yield different results'. In particular, 'the doctrine of proportionality may require the reviewing court to assess the balance which the decision-maker has struck, not merely whether it is within the range of rational or reasonable decisions'. Also proportionality 'may require attention to be directed to the relative weight accorded to interests and considerations'. See also *R. (on the application of Alconbury Developments Ltd)* v. *Secretary of State for the Environment, Transport and the Regions* [2001] UKHL 23, [2003] 2 AC 295 (HL).

the statute and Convention rights requires extensive redrafting and choice among different legislative options, the courts can make a declaration of incompatibility. By doing so, they will be marking the boundary between the powers of the judiciary, the legislature, and the executive in deciding how the constitutional principles contained in the Act are to be applied. As Lord Steyn has commented, the Act has strengthened the rule of law and separation of powers in the UK, and has made Britain (in effect) a 'constitutional state'.[57]

In *R. (Anderson)* v. *Secretary of State for the Home Department*,[58] Lord Hutton stated that Parliament has made it clear that:

> it remains supreme and that if a statute cannot be read so as to be compatible with the Convention, a court has no power to override or set aside the statute. All that the court may do, pursuant to s 4 of the 1998 Act, is to declare that the statute is incompatible with the Convention. It will then be for Parliament itself to decide whether it will amend the statute so that it will be compatible with the Convention. Therefore if a court declares that an Act is incompatible with the Convention, there is no question of the court being in conflict with Parliament or of seeking or purporting to override the will of Parliament. The court is doing what Parliament has instructed it to do in s. 4 of the 1998 Act.

JUDICIAL INTERPRETATION AND DECLARATIONS OF INCOMPATIBILITY

In deciding to what extent to defer to the opinion of the legislature, and the area of discretion given to the executive or other relevant public authority, the courts take account of the nature of the Convention right involved.[59] Some rights are absolute, for example, the prohibition of torture and inhuman or degrading treatment or punishment.[60] Many Convention rights require a fair balance to be struck between competing rights and interests.[61] There are cases in the social, economic, and political spheres where the legislature must reconcile competing interests in choosing one policy among several which might be acceptable.

The extent to which the decision maker has expertise is also a relevant factor. As Lord Bingham of Cornhill observed in *R.* v. *Secretary of State for the Environment*,

[57] Lord Steyn, 'Democracy, the Rule of Law and the Role of Judges' [2006] *EHRLR* 243, 250.

[58] [2002] UKHL 46, [2003] 1 AC 837 (HL), 895G–H.

[59] In *R.* v. *Secretary of State for the Home Department ex parte Daly* [2001] UKHL 26, [2001] 2 AC 532 (HL) Lord Steyn commented at 548C that Laws LJ was correct in *Mahmood* v. *Secretary of State for the Home Department* [2001] 1 WLR 840 (CA) to point out that 'the intensity of review in a public law case will depend on the subject matter in hand'. Lord Steyn added: 'That is so even in cases involving Convention rights. In law context is everything'.

[60] ECHR, Art. 3.

[61] E.g. ECHR, Arts 8–11, and Arts 1, 2, and 3 of the First Protocol.

Transport and the Regions ex parte Spath Holme Ltd, 'the allocation of public resources is a matter for ministers, not courts'.[62]

The courts will take into account the extent to which they have special expertise, as they have, for example, in deciding what constitutes a fair civil or criminal trial.[63] Where the rights claimed are of particular importance, 'a high degree of constitutional protection' will be appropriate.[64] The European Court of Human Rights has recognized as being of especial importance the rights to freedom of expression, to access to the courts, and to the protection of intimate aspects of private life. In such contexts, judicial deference is far less appropriate, and the courts will carry out particularly strict scrutiny.

In view of the constitutional importance of a declaration of incompatibility, only specified higher courts may make such a declaration,[65] and the Crown must be notified where a court is considering making such a declaration.[66] The declaration of incompatibility is expressed as a discretionary power, but the courts will usually exercise the power if it is impossible to interpret legislation compatibly with Convention rights, unless the government indicates its willingness to resolve the issue without the need for a remedial legislative order. A declaration is not binding on the parties involved. This leaves open the possibility for the government to argue before the European Court that the measure concerned is compatible with Convention rights.

The declaration of incompatibility brings the problem to the attention of the executive and the legislature, and acts as trigger for amending legislation by means of a remedial order. Despite its incompatibility with Convention rights, the offending legislation remains valid and effective, unless and until legislative amendments are made.[67] Parliamentary sovereignty is maintained and Parliament's legislative powers remain intact in deciding whether to remove the incompatibility. However, failure to make such amendment to remedy the domestic court's declaration of incompatibility could lead to a complaint to the European Court of Human Rights in Strasbourg, with a high probability that the European Court would come to a similar conclusion. This is a powerful incentive to the government to introduce, and for Parliament to approve, the necessary remedial order.

[62] [2001] 2 AC 349 (HL), 395. See also *Secretary of State for the Home Department* v. *Rehman* [2001] UKHL 47, [2003] 1 AC 153 (HL), 187 and 195 (in relation to national security); *R. (Farrakhan)* v. *Secretary of State for the Home Department* [2002] EWCA Civ 606, [2002] QB 1391 (CA), 1418B–D (in relation to public order and immigration matters).

[63] *R.* v. *DPP ex parte Kebeline* [2000] 2 AC 326 (HL), 381.

[64] *Libman* v. *A-G of Quebec* (1996) 3 BHRC 269 (Supreme Court of Canada), 289–90; also *R.* v. *DPP ex parte Kebeline* [2000] 2 AC 326 (HL), 381.

[65] Section 4(5) – the Supreme Court; the Judicial Committee of the Privy Council; the Court Martial Appeal Court; in Scotland, the High Court of Justiciary sitting otherwise than as a trial court or the Court of Session; in England and Wales or Northern Ireland, the High Court or the Court of Appeal; the Court of Protection, in any matter being dealt with by the President of the Family Division, the Vice-Chancellor or a puisne judge of the High Court.

[66] Section 5.

[67] Section 4(6); s. 10 provides for remedial action to amend the relevant provision.

Twenty-six declarations of incompatibility have been made since the Human Rights Act 1998 came into force. Of these, 18 have become final (in whole or in part) and eight have been overturned on appeal.[68] In each case the incompatibility has been remedied by primary or secondary legislation, or is under review with a view to being remedied. The Human Rights Act 1998 contains a specific mechanism for making swift remedial orders[69] to remedy incompatibility.[70] In *International Transport Roth GmbH* v. *Secretary of State for the Home Department*,[71] the Court of Appeal held that the scheme under the Immigration and Asylum Act 1999 which imposed automatic penalties on those responsible for bringing clandestine entrants into the UK, even if they had done so without their knowledge, was incompatible with Art. 6(2). In response to this finding, a clause was inserted into the Nationality, Immigration and Asylum Act 2002. In *A* v. *Secretary of State for the Home Department*,[72] the House of Lords held that the indefinite detention of terrorist suspects under Anti-Terrorism, Crime and Security Act, Pt IV[73] was incompatible with ECHR, Arts 5 and 14. In response, the relevant provisions were repealed and a system of control orders was contained in the Prevention of Terrorism Act

[68] For a full list see Ministry of Justice, *Responding to Human Rights Judgments: Government Response to the JCHR*, above, n. 30, Annex A: Declarations of Incompatibility.

[69] Remedial Orders are secondary legislation made under the Human Rights Act 1998 (s. 10, Sched. 2) to remove an incompatibility with Convention rights in primary legislation identified by either our domestic courts or the European Court of Human Rights. The government can then remove the relevant breach of the ECHR through the fast-track Remedial Order process. The Minister must consider that there are 'compelling reasons' to use the remedial order process and can choose to use either an 'urgent' or a 'non-urgent' Remedial Order. (For more details about the procedure see Lester, Pannick and Herberg, above, n. 2, ch. 8, and see the Appendix to 'Enhancing Parliament's Role in relation to human rights judgments', Fifteenth Report of Session 2009–10, above, n. 10.) There have only been five Remedial Orders since the introduction of the Human Rights Act 1998: four by the non-urgent procedure (Mental Health Act 1983 (Remedial) Order 2001, Naval Discipline Act 1957 (Remedial) Order 2004, Marriage Act 1949 (Remedial) Order 2006, and Asylum and Immigration (Treatment of Claimants, etc) Act 2004 (Remedial) Order 2011) and one by the urgent procedure (Terrorism Act 2000 (Remedial) Order 2011) which relates to section 44 stop and search powers. The JCHR has encouraged greater use of remedial orders to ensure speedy action to remove identified breaches of Convention rights in the UK and published 'Guidance for Departments on Responding to Court Judgments on Human Rights', which includes guidance on when a remedial order should be used and what considerations should be taken into account when deciding whether to make the order by the urgent or non-urgent procedure. (Appendix to 'Enhancing Parliament's Role in relation to human rights judgments', Fifteenth Report of Session 2009–10 above, n. 10, and Sixteenth Report of 2006–07, *Monitoring the Government's Response to Court Judgments Finding Breaches of Human Rights*, HL 128/HC 728, para. 119.)

[70] Section 10. See further Seventh Report of Session 2001–02, *The Making of Remedial Orders*, HL 58/HC 473 (17 December 2001); Annex 5 to 'The Work of the Committee in the 2001–2005 Parliament', HL 112/HC 552 (26 May 2005). See also Fifteenth Report of Session 2009–10, above, n. 10 (Annex: Guidance for Departments on Responding to Court Judgments on Human Rights).

[71] [2002] EWCA Civ 158, [2003] QB 728 (CA).

[72] [2004] UKHL 56, [2005] 2 AC 68 (HL).

[73] 2001 Cap 24.

2005;[74] that system has also been held to be incompatible with the Human Rights Act 1998 .[75]

In *Wright* v. *Secretary of State for Health*,[76] the House of Lords made a declaration of incompatibility in relation to the scheme for placing care workers employed to look after vulnerable adults on a list of people considered unsuitable to work with such adults. In July 2010, the government stated in a report in response to human rights judgments of the European Court of Human Rights that 'the Government has announced the remodelling of the Vetting and Barring Scheme, and relevant human rights issues will be considered as part of this process'.[77]

In *Baiai* v. *Secretary of State for the Home Department*[78] the House of Lords held that legislation which provided that any marriage outside the Church of England involving a person subject to immigration control had to be subject to a Certificate of Approval issued by the Secretary of State, was incompatible with the right to enjoy respect for religion and belief without discrimination (as guaranteed by ECHR, Arts 9 and 14).[79]

[74] 2005 Cap 2. In *Al-Ghabra (Her Majesty's Treasury (Respondents)* v. *Mohammed al-Ghabra (FC) (Appellant)* [2010] UKSC 2, [2010] WLR 378 (SC), the Supreme Court quashed as *ultra vires* the Terrorism (United Nations Measures) Order 2006 (SI 2006/2657) and provisions in the Al-Qaida and Taliban (United Nations Measures) Order 2006 (SI 2006/2952). The judgment established that the UK's international obligations under the UN resolution extend only to those involved in terrorism; that, because the relevant orders purport to go much further and to apply to those in respect of whom there are only reasonable grounds for suspecting their involvement in terrorism, those orders were not validly made under the United Nations Act 1946; and that the destructive effect of these orders on the lives of those affected and the consequent need for considerable care and attention in ensuring the legality of any such order. As a consequence, the government introduced emergency legislation (Terrorist Asset Freezing (Temporary Provisions) Act 2010) to keep the assets of suspected terrorists frozen and the government had to get an agreement from the banks not to release the fund whilst the Bill was being passed. As it was emergency legislation it meant that matters of constitutional importance were not properly debated and the provisions of the Bill not properly scrutinized. Consequently, following a consultation on the government's approach to terrorist asset freezing and its proposals to provide a durable legal basis for the UK to freeze the assets of suspected terrorists in fulfilment of our international obligation, the Terrorist Asset Freezing etc Bill was introduced in the House of Lords on 15 July 2010, and is pending.

[75] *Secretary of State for the Home Department* v. *MB* [2007] UKHL 46, [2008] 1 AC 440 (HL); *Secretary of State for the Home Department* v. *JJ* [2007] UKHL 45, [2008] 1 AC 385 (HL). See also *Secretary of State for the Home Department* v. *AF* [2007] UKHL 46, [2008] 1 AC 440 (HL); *Secretary of State for the Home Department* v. *E* [2007] UKHL 47, [2008] AC 499 (HL); *Secretary of State for the Home Department* v. *AP* [2010] UKSC 24, [2010] 3 WLR 51 (SC).

[76] *R (Wright)* v. *Secretary of State for Health and another* [2009] UKHL 3, [2009] 1 AC 739 (HL). It declared Care Standards Act 2000, s. 82(4)(b) to be incompatible with the right to a fair trial (Art. 6) and to respect for private life (Art. 8).

[77] Ministry of Justice, *Responding to Human Rights Judgments: Government Response to the JCHR*, above, n. 30, p. 27.

[78] *R (Baiai)* v. *Secretary of State for the Home Department* [2008] UKHL 53, [2009] AC 287 (HL).

[79] Fifteenth Report of Session 2009–10, above, n. 10, para. 145.

EFFECT ON POWERS AND DUTIES OF PUBLIC AUTHORITIES

The Human Rights Act 1998 radically affects the scope of the powers conferred and duties imposed upon public authorities. Section 6 created a new constitutional or public law tort, committed whenever a public authority acts in a way which is incompatible with Convention rights, with a potential liability to pay damages for breach of the new statutory duty. A person who claims that a public authority has acted or proposes to act in a way made unlawful by s. 6(1) of the Act is able, if he or she is a victim, to bring proceedings against the authority,[80] or rely on the Convention right or rights concerned in any legal proceedings.[81] In relation to any act (or proposed act) of a public authority, which the court finds is (or would be) unlawful, it is able to grant such relief or remedy, or make such order, within its powers as it considers just and appropriate.[82]

A public authority is expansively defined to include courts and tribunals and 'any person certain of whose functions are functions of a public nature'.[83] This is intended to ensure that a private body must act compatibly with Convention rights where, for example, it administers a prison, or runs a railway, or deals as a regulatory body with complaints against the press. In *Aston Cantlow Parochial Church Council* v. *Wallbank*,[84] Lord Nicholls of Birkenhead explained the purpose of s. 6:

> those bodies for whose acts the state is answerable before the European Court of Human Rights shall in future be subject to a domestic law obligation not to act incompatibly with Convention rights. If they act in breach of this legal obligation victims may henceforth obtain redress from the courts of this country. In future victims should not need to travel to Strasbourg.

But the courts have adopted a restrictive and narrow interpretation of the meaning of public authority, and are at risk of failing to give effect to the intention of Parliament in passing the Act to give full effect to the obligations imposed by the ECHR.[85] The JCHR has published thorough, critical reports on the subject;[86] and during the passage of

[80] Section 7(1)(a). [81] Section 7(1)(b).

[82] Section 8(1). No award of damages may be made unless, taking into account all of the circumstances of the case, including any other relief or remedy granted in relation to the act in question, and the consequences of any decision in respect of that act, the court is satisfied that an award is necessary to afford just satisfaction to the person in whose favour it is made: see s. 8(3). The award of damages is therefore a discretionary matter, not an entitlement: see *R. (KB)* v. *Mental Health Review Tribunal* [2003] EWHC 193 (Admin), [2004] QB 936, and *R. (N)* v. *Secretary of State for the Home Department* [2003] EWHC 207 (Admin) [2003] HRLR 20 at [196], *per* Silber J. See also *R. (Greenfield)* v. *Secretary of State for the Home Department* [2005] UKHL 14, [2005] 1 WLR 673 (HL).

[83] Section 6(3). [84] [2003] UKHL 37, [2004] 1 AC 546 (HL), 553H–4A.

[85] See *R. (on the application of Heather)* v. *Leonard Cheshire Foundation* [2002] 2 EWCA Civ 366, [2002] HRLR 30 (CA). The House of Lords gave a more expansive interpretation in *Aston Cantlow* but did not refer to the *Leonard Cheshire* or *Poplar Housing* decisions, leaving the law in an uncertain state.

[86] Seventh Report of Session 2003–04, *The Meaning of Public Authority under the Human Rights Act*, HL 39/HC 3 (3 March 2004). See also JCHR, Report of Session 2006–07, *The Meaning of Public Authority under the Human Rights Act*, HL 77/HC 210 (28 March 2007).

the Equality Act 2006 the government undertook to intervene in a suitable test case to clarify the scope of 'public authority' in the Act, so far without success.[87] It is vital that this issue is resolved, so that the UK is not at risk of breaching its international obligations to protect the rights of everyone within its jurisdiction and to provide effective legal redress where those rights are breached.

In *YL* v. *Birmingham City Council*,[88] the Law Lords, by a majority of three to two, gave a narrowly restrictive interpretation of the phrase 'functions of a public nature', and stated the law in a way which creates a mismatch between the Human Rights Act 1998 and the obligations imposed upon the UK by the ECHR. As a result of such a narrow interpretation, the JCHR recommended that there is 'a strong case for a separate, supplementary and interpretative statute, specifically directed to clarifying the interpretation of "functions of a public nature" in s. 6(3)(b) Human Rights Act'.[89] However, this has not met with a positive response.

The fact that courts and tribunals have a duty to act compatibly with the ECHR is significant because of the Act's potential 'horizontal effect' upon the common law and equity, and statutory interpretation.[90] The courts have a duty to act compatibly with the ECHR, not only in cases involving other public authorities, but also in developing the common law and equitable principles, and construing legislation, when deciding cases between private persons. This is especially the case where the ECHR imposes positive obligations on the state to protect individuals against breaches of their rights.[91] In *X* v. *Y*,[92] the Court of Appeal held that employment tribunals had, so far as it was

[87] Equality Bill, Second Reading Debate, 672 HL Official Report, col. 1303 (15 June 2005). The government intervened in the case *R. (on the application of Johnson and others)* v. *London Borough of Havering* [2007] EWCA Civ 26, [2008] QB 1 (CA), but the Court of Appeal upheld the narrow approach in *R. (on the application of Heather)* v. *Leonard Cheshire Foundation* [2002] 2 EWCA Civ 366, [2002] HRLR 30 (CA). The then Lord Chancellor indicated that the government would seek out another suitable test case if necessary. See JCHR, Thirty-Second Report of Session 2005–06, *The Human Rights Act: the DCA and Home Office Reviews*, HL 278, para. 88.

[88] [2007] UKHL 27, [2008] 1 AC 95 (HL).

[89] Report of Session 2006–07, above, n. 86, para. 150.

[90] See further M. Hunt, 'The "Horizontal Effect" of the Human Rights Act' [1998] *Public Law* 423; A. Lester and D. Pannick, 'The Impact of the Human Rights Act on Private Law: The Knight's Move' (2000) 116 *LQR* 380; I. Hare, 'Vertically challenged: Private Parties, Privacy and the Human Rights Act' [2001] 5 *EHRLR* 526; S. Pattinson and D. Beyleveld, 'Horizontal applicability and horizontal effect' (2002) 118 *LQR* 623; T. Bennett, 'Horizontality's new horizons – re-examining horizontal effect: privacy, defamation and the Human Rights Act: parts 1 and 2' [2010] *Entertainment Law Review* 96, 145; M. Du Plessis and J. Ford, 'Developing the common law progressively –horizontality, the Human Rights Act and the South African experience' [2004] *EHRLR* 286. See also the cases on privacy listed above, n. 21.

[91] In *Costello-Roberts* v. *United Kingdom* (1993) 19 EHRR 112, 132, paras 26–7 the European Court of Human Rights recalled that it has 'consistently held that the responsibility of a state is engaged if a violation of one of the rights and freedoms defined in the ECHR is the result of non-observance by that state of its obligation under art. 1 to secure those rights and freedoms in its domestic law to everyone within its jurisdiction.... [T]he state cannot absolve itself from responsibility by delegating its obligation to private bodies or individuals'. See also Application No. 25599/94, *A* v. *United Kingdom* (human rights: punishment of child) (1998) 27 EHRR 611 (ECtHR), para. 22; *Veznedaroglu* v. *Turkey* (2001) 33 EHRR 1412 (ECtHR), para. 32; *Pretty* v. *United Kingdom* (2002) 35 EHRR 1, para. 50.

[92] (2004) ICR 1634.

possible, to read and give effect to employment legislation in a way that was compatible with the ECHR, albeit the Human Rights Act 1998 did not give an applicant any cause of action against a respondent that was not a public authority.

RELATIONSHIP WITH THE COMMON LAW

The Human Rights Act 1998 weaves Convention rights into the warp and woof of the common law and statute law. Convention rights have effect not as free-standing rights; they are given effect through and not around UK statute law and common law, by interpreting, declaring, and giving effect to written and unwritten law compatibly with Convention rights.[93] The courts must, so far as possible, declare the common law in a way compatible with Convention rights, just as they must, so far as is possible, interpret and give effect to legislation in that way.[94] Before the coming into force of the Act, the courts had already redrawn the contours of defamation law[95] and of the law protecting confidential information[96] to give greater weight to what they began to recognize as a positive right to free speech. Over the last decade, a right of personal privacy has developed out of existing principles of law and equity, having regard to the Convention right to respect for one's private life, home and correspondence.[97]

Wisely, the Act does not require the courts to interpret and apply Convention rights by treating the Strasbourg case law as binding precedent. The courts must have regard to the Strasbourg jurisprudence,[98] but are not bound to follow it. The

[93] See s. 11: a person's reliance on a Convention right does not restrict any other right or freedom conferred on him or her by or under any law having effect in any part of the UK, or his or her right to make any claim or bring any proceedings which he or she could make or bring apart from ss 7–9.

[94] For an example of judicial consideration of whether a common law offence is compatible with Convention rights, see *R.* v. *Rimmington* [2005] UKHL 63, [2006] 1 AC 459 (HL). See also *Norris* v. *Government of the United States of America* [2008] UKHL 16, [2008] 1 AC 920 (HL).

[95] See e.g. *Reynolds* v. *Times Newspapers* [2001] AC 127 (HL); and *Derbyshire County Council* v. *Times Newspapers* [1993] AC 534 (HL); *AG* v. *Guardian and Times Newspapers* [1990] 1 AC 109 (HL). See also Lord Lester QC's Private Member's Defamation Bill (www.publications.parliament.uk/pa/ld201011/ldbills/003/11003.i-ii.html) and the coalition government's commitment to introduce its own Bill to reform defamation law in 2012 (see Lord McNally, *Hansard*, HL, col. 475 (9 July 2010)).

[96] See e.g. A. Lester, 'English Judges as Law Makers' [1993] *Public Law* 269, 284–6. T. Aplin, 'The development of the action for breach of confidence in a post-HRA era' [2007] *IPQ* 19.

[97] See above, n. 21, and A. Lester, 'English Judges as Law Makers' [1993] *Public Law* 269, 284–6; Dawn Oliver, *Common Values and the Public/Private Divide* (1999); M. Arden, 'Human rights and civil wrongs: tort law under the spotlight' [2002] *PL* 140; J. Strachan and R. Singh, 'The right to privacy in English law' [2002] *EHRLR* 129; R. Singh and J. Strachan, 'Privacy postponed?' [2003] *EHRLR* 12. Lester, Pannick and Herberg, above, n. 2, ch. 4.8 (Thomas de la Mare, Brian Kennelly and Catherine Donnelly).

[98] Section 2. Domestic courts should normally follow the decisions of the European Court of Human Rights: *R. (Alconbury Developments Ltd)* v. *Secretary of State for the Environment, Transport and the Regions* [2001] UKHL 23, [2003] 2 AC 295 (HL), 313C, *per* Lord Slynn of Hadley; and *R. (Anderson)* v. *Secretary of State for the Home Department* [2002] UKHL 46, [2003] 1 AC 837 (HL), 879H–80C, *per* Lord Bingham. See also Lord Bingham in *R. (Ullah)* v. *Special Adjudicator* [2004] UKHL 26, [2004] 2 AC 323 (HL) at [20]; *N* v. *Secretary of State for the Home Department* [2005] UKHL 31, [2005] 2 AC 296 (HL) at [24], *per* Lord Hope; *Lambeth London Borough Council* v. *Kay* [2006] UKHL 10, [2006] 2 AC 465 (HL) at [87], *per* Lord Hope; *Secretary of State for Work and Pensions* v. *M* [2006] UKHL 11, [2006] 2 AC 91 (HL) at [129], *per* Lord Mance;

European Court has recognized[99] that 'By reason of their direct and continuous contact with the vital forces of their countries, the national authorities are in principle better placed than an international court to evaluate local needs and conditions'. In *Lambeth London Borough Council* v. *Kay*,[100] the Law Lords held that, although domestic courts were not strictly required to follow the rulings of the European Court, they were obliged to give practical recognition to the principles it laid down. However, UK judges must follow binding domestic precedent rather than a subsequent, inconsistent Strasbourg authority in the interests of adhering to the rules of precedent, even in the Convention context.[101]

The elastic and elusive Strasbourg doctrine of the 'margin of appreciation'[102] is applied by the European Court on the basis of ad hoc pragmatic judgments, sometimes lacking in clear and consistent principles. There has been some uncertainty about whether domestic courts should use the ECHR as a floor or a ceiling in relation to interpreting the rights protected under the Human Rights Act 1998 . In *R. (Ullah)* v. *Special Adjudicator* Lord Bingham commented:[103]

> It is of course open to member states to provide for rights more generous than those guaranteed by the Convention, but such provision should not be the product of interpretation of the Convention by national courts, since the meaning of the Convention should be uniform throughout the states party to it. The duty of national courts is to keep pace with the Strasbourg jurisprudence as it evolves over time: *no more, but certainly no less.*

Lord Bingham also observed that the purpose of the Human Rights Act 1998 'was not to enlarge the rights or remedies of those in the UK whose Convention rights have been violated but to enable those rights and remedies to be asserted and enforced by

R. (Al Skeini) v. *Secretary of State for Defence* [2007] UKHL 26, [2008] 1 AC 153 (HL) at [90], *per* Baroness Hale, and [105], *per* Lord Brown; *Huang* v. *Secretary of State for the Home Department* [2007] UKHL 11, [2007] 2 AC 167 (HL) at [18], *per* Lord Bingham for the Committee; *Secretary of State for the Home Department* v. *JJ* [2007] UKHL 45, [2008] 1 AC 385 (HL) at [83], *per* Lord Carswell, and [106], *per* Lord Brown; *Whaley* v. *Lord Advocate* [2007] UKHL 53, 2008 SC 107 (HL) at [18], *per* Lord Hope; *R. (Animal Defenders International)* v. *Secretary of State for Culture, Media and Sport* [2008] UKHL 15, [2008] 1 AC 1312 (HL) at [37], *per* Lord Bingham, and [53], *per* Baroness Hale; *R. (Gentle)* v. *Prime Minister* [2008] UKHL 20, [2008] 1 AC 1356 (HL), *per* Baroness Hale; *Re P (A Child) (Adoption: Unmarried Couples)* [2008] UKHL 38, [2009] 1 AC 173 (HL) at [30], *per* Lord Hoffmann, [50], *per* Lord Hope, [79], *per* Lord Walker, [120], *per* Baroness Hale, and [127], *per* Lord Mance. But it may be appropriate for the domestic court to depart from a decision of the European Court of Human Rights if the reasoning is unpersuasive. See *R* v. *Spear and others* [2002] UKHL 31, [2003] 1 AC 734 (HL), 750D–1B, *per* Lord Bingham, and at 774G–5F, *per* Lord Rodger of Earlsferry. See also *R.* v. *Lyons and others* [2002] UKHL 44, [2003] 1 AC 976 (HL), 996H–7F, *per* Lord Hoffmann.

[99] *Buckley* v. *United Kingdom* (1996) 23 EHRR 101, 129.

[100] *Lambeth London Borough Council* v. *Kay* [2006] UKHL 10, [2006] 2 AC 465 (HL).

[101] In *Kay* the allegedly inconsistent decisions were the House of Lords' decision in *Harrow London Borough Council* v. *Qazi* [2003] UKHL 43, [2004] 1 AC 983 (HL) and the subsequent European Court of Human Rights' decision in *Connors* v. *United Kingdom* [2004] 40 EHRR 189.

[102] See Application No. 20348/92, *Buckley* v. *United Kingdom* (1996) 23 EHRR 101 (ECtHR), para. 75; Application No. 36022/97, *Hatton* v. *United Kingdom* (2003) 37 EHRR 611, paras 97–103 and 123.

[103] [2004] UKHL 26, [2004] 2 AC 323 (HL), 350C, emphasis added.

the domestic courts of this country and not only by recourse to Strasbourg'.[104] While this was certainly an object of the Human Rights Act 1998 , it is to be hoped that our judges will not regard the Convention jurisprudence as a cage or ceiling on human rights protection in the UK.[105] If they continue to do so, it will strengthen the case for a British Bill of Rights and Freedoms.

In the previous version of this chapter it was remarked that the developing principles contained in the constitutional case law of courts in other common law countries – such as the Constitutional Court of South Africa, the Supreme Courts of the USA, Canada, and India, the High Court of Australia, and the Court of Appeal of New Zealand – were likely to be at least as persuasive as the Strasbourg case law. There have been several references to international and comparative jurisprudence in cases under the Human Rights Act 1998,[106] but also some reservation expressed about its use. In *R. (Gillan)* v. *Commissioner of Police of Metropolis* Lord Bingham remarked that:[107]

> The Strasbourg jurisprudence is closely focused on the facts of particular cases, and this makes it perilous to transpose the outcome of one case to another where the facts are different. Still more perilous is it, in my opinion, to seek to transpose the outcome of Canadian cases decided under a significantly different legislative regime.

Courts have also continued to decide cases involving important principles of human rights on the basis of the common law, in addition to the ECHR. For example, in *A v. Secretary of State for the Home Department*,[108] which concerned the use of evidence obtained by torture, the House of Lords relied on principles of the common law, together with the ECHR and the UN Convention Against Torture, to hold that evidence obtained by torture should be excluded as unreliable, unfair, offensive to ordinary standards of humanity and decency and incompatible with the principles on which courts should administer justice. In the *Binyam Mohamed* case, the Court of Appeal ruled that the unprecedented attempt by the security and intelligence agencies, backed by the Attorney General and senior Whitehall officials, to suppress evidence in a civil trial undermined deep-seated principles of common law and open justice.[109]

[104] *R. (SB)* v. *Denbigh High School* [2006] UKHL 15, [2007] 1 AC 100 at [29], *per* Lord Bingham.

[105] See Roger Masterman, 'Taking the Strasbourg jurisprudence into account: Developing a "municipal law of human rights" under the Human Rights Act' [2005] ICLQ 907.

[106] See e.g. *R. (Ullah)* v. *Special Adjudicator* [2004] UKHL 26, [2004] 2 AC 323 (HL), 351B–2A, *per* Lord Bingham; *R.* v. *A (No 2)* [2001] UKHL 25, [2002] 1 AC 45 (HL) at [100]–[102], *per* Lord Hope of Craighead; *R.* v. *Lambert* [2001] UKHL 37, [2002] 2 AC 545 at [34]–[35], *per* Lord Steyn.

[107] [2006] UKHL 12, [2006] 2 AC 307 (HL), 342E. See also *Brown* v. *Stott* [2003] 1 AC 681 (PC), 724, *per* Lord Hope of Craighead.

[108] [2005] UKHL 71, [2006] 2 AC 221 (HL).

[109] *R. (Mohamed)* v. *Secretary of State for Foreign and Commonwealth Affairs* [2010] EWCA Civ 65, [2010] 3 WLR 554.

NON-IMPLEMENTATION OF CASES OF THE EUROPEAN COURT OF HUMAN RIGHTS IN THE UK

According to the JCHR, the rulings in some important cases from the European Court of Human Rights have not been properly implemented by the UK. In 2009, the Court delivered 18 judgments in cases brought against the UK, in 14 of which it found at least one violation of the ECHR. Seven of these cases involved the prohibition on discrimination in ECHR, Art. 14, three involved the right to liberty (Art. 5); two involved the length of proceedings (Art. 6); two involved the right to respect for private life (Art. 8); and one involved the right to freedom of expression (Art. 10).[110]

Although these cases represented only one per cent of the violations found by the court in 2009, the UK has a high proportion of cases which have remained unimplemented for more than five years.[111] Some of the most significant cases that remain unimplemented deal with the detention of foreign terrorism suspects;[112] the retention of DNA samples;[113] and the blanket exclusion of prisoners' voting rights.[114]

REMEDIES FOR BREACH

Where a court finds a breach of Convention rights, it may grant such remedy as is just and appropriate, provided that the remedy is within its powers.[115]

When all effective domestic remedies have been exhausted, applicants may apply to the European Court of Human Rights. Since the Human Rights Act 1998 came into force, there have been over 100 judgments of the European Court finding violations of the ECHR by the UK. Several Human Rights Act 1998 cases have been considered by the Strasbourg Court, and the Court has continued to find violations of the ECHR despite the protection offered by the Human Rights Act 1998.[116]

[110] Fifteenth Report of Session 2009–10, above, n. 10, para. 34, p. 15.

[111] A. Wagner, 'Many European Human Rights decisions left unimplemented for years', UK Human Rights Blog, 9 August 2010.

[112] Application No. 3455/05, *A* v. *United Kingdom* (2009) 49 EHRR 625.

[113] Application No. 30562/04, *S and Marper* v. *United Kingdom* (2008) ECHR 1581.

[114] Application No. 74025/01, *Hirst* v. *United Kingdom (No. 2)* (2005) 42 EHRR 849.

[115] Section 8. The Act is intended to give effect to ECHR, Art. 13 by creating effective domestic remedies for breaches of Convention rights. Under s. 1(1), Art. 13 is not included in the list of Convention rights directly secured by the Act, because the Act gives effect to Art. 13 by establishing a scheme under which Convention rights can be raised before our domestic courts: see *R. (on the application of K)* v. *Camden and Islington Health Authority* [2001] EWCA Civ 240, [2002] QB 198 (CA), 233G–H, *per* Sedley LJ; *In Re S (Minors)* [2002] UKHL 10, [2002] 2 AC 291 (HL), 318E, *per* Lord Nicholls of Birkenhead. See also *R.* v. *Secretary of State for the Home Department ex parte Brind* [1991] 1 AC 696 (HL); *Rantzen* v. *Mirror Group Newspapers* [1994] QB 670 (CA); *R.* v. *Khan* [1997] AC 558 (HL).

[116] See e.g. Application No. 12350/04, *Wainwright* v. *United Kingdom* (2007) 44 EHRR 809, and Application No. 74025/01, *Hirst* v. *United Kingdom (No. 2)* (2005) 42 EHRR 849, where the Strasbourg court found a violation of the ECHR where domestic courts had not. By contrast, in Application No. 2346/02, *Pretty* v. *United Kingdom* (2002) 35 EHRR 1 and Application No. 6339/05, *Evans* v. *United Kingdom* (2006) 43 EHRR 21, the Strasbourg court confirmed domestic decisions that there was no breach of Convention rights.

Treasury concern about public expenditure persuaded the government to require the courts to have regard to Convention law where domestic law provides well-developed and more appropriate standards.[117] The Act adopts[118] the ECHR 'victim' test[119] as the requirement for standing to bring a direct action against public authorities for breaches of Convention rights; and, in an attempt to restrict liability in damages, the courts must have regard[120] to the European Court's case law[121] on what constitutes 'just satisfaction', when awarding damages for such breaches.

After some early indications that UK courts would apply domestic scales of damages, along the lines of awards in tort cases, and that awards of damages should not be on the low side as compared with tort case awards,[122] the House of Lords has indicated that our courts should not aim to be significantly more or less generous than the European Court, though they are not inflexibly bound by awards given in Strasbourg.[123] In *R. (Greenfield)* v. *Home Secretary*, Lord Bingham emphasized that a finding of violation will be an important part of the remedy and an important vindication of the right asserted, and further that damages need not ordinarily be awarded to encourage high standards of compliance by member states.[124] Our courts' restraint is in part attributable to the lack of clarity in Strasbourg case law about the principles of just satisfaction, which has frequently been remarked upon by UK courts and others.[125] But UK judges have also displayed a more general reluctance to award damages in human rights cases, which cannot be attributed solely to the limited utility of Strasbourg jurisprudence.[126]

[117] A similar concern probably explains the inclusion of s. 7(1)(a) which requires proceedings against a public authority by a victim of an unlawful act to be brought within one year from the date on which the act complained of took place, or such longer period as the court considers equitable. The framers of Commonwealth constitutional guarantees of human rights have not found it necessary to include such a limitation.

[118] Section 7(3), (4) and (7).

[119] Under ECHR, Art. 34, dealing with the standing to bring individual applications.

[120] Section 8(4). [121] Under ECHR, Art. 41.

[122] *R. (Bernard)* v. *Enfield London Borough Council* [2002] EWHC 2282 (Admin), [2003] HRLR 4; *R. (KB)* v. *Mental Health Review Tribunal* [2003] EWHC 193 (Admin), [2004] QB 936. See also *Anufrijeva* v. *Southwark London Borough Council* [2003] EWCA Civ 1406, [2004] QB 1124 (CA), 1160, where the Court of Appeal stated that the suggestion that damages should be on the low side in comparison to those awarded for torts 'should in future be ignored'.

[123] *R. (Greenfield)* v. *Secretary of State for the Home Department* [2005] UKHL 14, [2005] 1 WLR 673 (HL).

[124] Ibid., p. 684B–C, *per* Lord Bingham of Cornhill.

[125] See e.g. the Law Commission and Scottish Law Commission Report, *Damages Under the Human Rights Act 1998: Report on a Reference under Section 3(1)(e) of the Law Commissions Act 1965*, LC266, Cm. 4853 (October 2000).

[126] See Application No. 12742/87, *Pine Valley Development Ltd* v. *Ireland* (1993) 16 EHRR 370 (ECtHR); Application Nos 7601/76, 7806/77, *Young, James and Webster* v. *United Kingdom* (1982) 5 EHRR 201 (ECtHR); *R. (KB)* v. *Mental Health Review Tribunal* [2003] EWHC 193 (Admin), [2004] QB 936. '[T]here is very little guidance from Strasbourg as to the quantification of non-pecuniary loss in human rights cases, and the Courts in the UK are only slowly building up sufficient precedent to enable advisers to make informed decisions about likely compensation', B. Collins, 'Just Satisfaction – But Only Just? The award of damages under the Human Rights Act', 1 Crown Office Row, May 2009. See www.1cor.com/1155/records/1213/BC%20public%20law%20talk.pdf.

Whether the approach of UK courts to remedies under the Human Rights Act 1998 will withstand scrutiny in Strasbourg remains to be seen. In *Wainwright v. UK*,[127] the European Court of Human Rights found a violation of ECHR, Art 13 (the right to an effective remedy) where the applicants had been subjected to a negligent strip search in violation of Art. 8. One of the applicants had been awarded damages for battery, but the House of Lords held that they could not secure redress for the alleged breach of Art. 8. While the European Court did not comment specifically on whether Human Rights Act 1998, s. 8 could afford an effective remedy for the purposes of the ECHR, it may be that the restrictive approach of our domestic courts will be revised in future.[128]

EXTRA-TERRITORIAL AND RETROSPECTIVE EFFECT

The territorial reach of the Human Rights Act 1998 has been tested in a number of cases, with some issues still to be resolved by the House of Lords. The approach of the UK courts has been to hold that the territorial ambit of the Act is coextensive with that of ECHR, Art 1, thereby importing the Convention case-law on the ambit of Art. 1.[129]

The Human Rights Act 1998 offers no protection for acts committed prior to 2 October 2000, when the Act came into force, even though the UK was bound by the ECHR before that date.[130] In *R. (Hurst)* v. *Commissioner of Police of the Metropolis*,[131] the House of Lords rejected the prospect of a limited retrospective application for s. 3 of the Act, on the basis that courts were not obliged to give effect to the UK's international obligations to respect the Convention rights which predated the coming into force of the Human Rights Act 1998.

[127] Application No. 12350/04, *Wainwright* v. *United Kingdom* (2007) 44 EHRR 40. See also *Jain* v. *Trent Strategic Health Authority* [2009] UKHL 4, [2009] 1 AC 853 (HL).

[128] See R. Clayton, 'Damage limitation: the courts and Human Rights Act damages' [2005] *Public Law* 429; R. Clayton, 'Human Rights Act Damages after *Greenfield*: Where Are We Now?' [2006] *JR* 213.

[129] In *R. (on the application of Al-Skeini)* v. *Secretary of State for Defence* [2007] UKHL 26, [2008] 1 AC 153 (HL), the House of Lords ruled on the territorial scope of the Human Rights Act 1998 in relation to the deaths of six Iraqi civilians who were killed by UK troops in southern Iraq in 2003. Five of the civilians were innocent bystanders who were caught up in the fire when British troops thought they were under attack. The sixth, Baha Mousa, however, died after mistreatment in custody in a UK military detention centre in Iraq. The House of Lords ruled that the UK had obligations under the ECHR only to Baha Mousa, as the UK military detention unit was akin to an embassy, and being under UK control. See also Ralph Wilde, 'The Extraterritorial Application of the Human Rights Act' (2005) 58 *Current Legal Problems* 47–82.

[130] *Re McKerr* [2004] UKHL 12, [2004] 1 WLR 807 (HL); *R.* v. *Lambert* [2001] UKHL 37, [2002] 2 AC 545 (HL); *R.* v. *Kansal (No. 2)* [2001] UKHL 62, [2002] 2 AC 69 (HL); *Wilson* v. *Secretary of State for Trade and Industry* [2003] UKHL 40, [2004] 1 AC 816 (HL).

[131] [2007] UKHL 13, [2007] 2 AC 189 (HL). On the retrospective effect of s. 3, see also *Wilson* v. *Secretary of State for Trade and Industry* [2003] UKHL 40, [2004] 1 AC 816 (HL).

THE EQUALITY ACTS AND THE EQUALITY AND HUMAN RIGHTS COMMISSION

The Equality Act 2010 largely replaced the 2006 Act.[132] It gives new protection to the fundamental right to equality before the law and the equal protection of the law, anchored in ECHR, Art 14 and EU equality legislation. It adopts an integrated approach, harmonizing, clarifying and extending the concepts of discrimination, harassment and victimization and applying them across nine protected characteristics. It also extends positive duties to public authorities to have due regard to the need to eliminate discrimination, advance equality of opportunity, and foster good relations between different groups. It clarifies and broadens the circumstances in which positive action may be taken voluntarily to further these aims, and replaces nine major earlier pieces of legislation covering gender, race, disability, religion or belief, sexual orientation, and implements the EU equality directives.[133]

The Equality Act 2010, together with the Human Rights Act 1998, should be treated as a matter of legal public policy as constitutional measures containing values inherent in our common humanity, and giving effect to international human rights law by encouraging good practice, and providing effective legal protection and redress.

THE HUMAN RIGHTS ACT AND BEYOND

The Human Rights Act 1998 was introduced by the Blair government to give effect to a Labour–Liberal Democrat agreement on constitutional reform,[134] and was the most significant British constitutional reform of the 20th century. But it receives a bare mention in the Rt Hon. Tony Blair MP's political autobiography,[135] and was attacked by him and other senior ministers in his administration,[136] as well as by the Rt Hon. David Cameron MP when Leader of the Opposition.[137] The Brown administration toyed with the idea of introducing a so-called British Bill of Rights and Responsibilities, not to strengthen the Human Rights Act 1998 but to stand alongside the Act, without adding new enforceable rights or obligations.[138] The object was political – to make the

[132] The Equality Act 2006 remains in force (as amended by the 2010 Act) so far as it relates to the constitution and operation of the EHRC.

[133] See generally, Sir Robert Hepple QC, *Equality: The New Legal Framework* (2011).

[134] The Cook-Maclennan Agreement on Constitutional Reform of 1997. In October 1996 the two parties established a Joint Consultative Committee. Their Report outlines the conclusions. The Cook-Maclennan agreement laid the foundations for the reshaping of the British constitution and led to legislation for major reforms including Scottish and Welsh devolution, the Human Rights Act 1998, and removing the majority of hereditary peers from the House of Lords.

[135] Tony Blair, *A Journey* (2010) 26.

[136] 'Blair leads the attack on his own human rights laws', *The Times*, 16 May 2006.

[137] 'Balancing freedom and security – a modern British Bill of Rights', speech at the Centre for Policy Studies, 26 June 2006.

[138] Green paper, Ministry of Justice, *Rights and Responsibilities: developing our constitutional framework*, Cm. 7577 (March 2009).

Human Rights Act 1998 more popular with the media and the public by emphasizing 'responsibilities'. The Prime Minister, the Rt Hon. Gordon Brown MP indicated his wish to move towards a written constitution, a view reflected in his party's election manifesto.[139] The Conservative opposition threatened to repeal the Human Rights Act 1998, and to replace it with its own UK Bill of Rights, without specifying what was intended.[140] The Liberal Democrats viewed the issue through the prism of wider constitutional reform, including the need for a written constitution for the UK. Their election manifesto promised to introduce a written constitution and to determine this constitution in a citizens' convention, and to protect the Human Rights Act 1998.[141]

Meanwhile, in Northern Ireland,[142] there were demands for a separate Bill of Rights going beyond the Human Rights Act 1998 and the devolution legislation. The difficulty of meeting this demand within the incomplete 'federal' framework of the UK as a whole was not directly confronted, and, shortly before the May General Election, the Labour government effectively rejected the recommendations by the Northern Ireland Human Rights Commission, developed for some eight years after the Good Friday Agreement of 1998 had promised a Bill of Rights for Northern Ireland 'to reflect the particular circumstances of Northern Ireland drawing as appropriate on international instruments and experience'.

In the aftermath of the General Election, the Coalition Programme for Government[143] undertook to establish a Commission:

> to investigate the creation of a British Bill of Rights that incorporates and builds on our obligations under the European Convention on Human Rights, ensures that these rights continue to be enshrined in British law, and protects and extends British liberties. We will seek to promote a better understanding of the true scope of these obligations and liberties.

At the time of writing, no moves have been made to set up this Commission, but it seems likely that the Human Rights Act 1998 will remain intact, and that there will

[139] Labour Manifesto 2010, 9:3 'Democratic reform: the challenge for Britain'.

[140] Conservative Manifesto 2010, An Invitation to join the Government of Britain – Restore Our Civil Liberties, p. 79.

[141] Liberal Democrat Manifesto 2010, pp. 88 and 94.

[142] Northern Ireland Affairs Committee, Sixth Report of Session 2009–10, *A Bill of Rights for Northern Ireland: an interim statement*, HC 236 (24 March 2010). A Bill of Rights Forum was created after the St Andrews Agreement of 2006 and its recommendations, made in March 2008, were considered by the Northern Ireland Human Rights Commission (NIHRC). The NIHRC produced its Advice to the Secretary of State for Northern Ireland in December 2008 which contained 78 recommendations relating to the substantive rights additional to the rights contained in the ECHR and included recommendations on how a Bill of Rights could be implemented and enforced. The NIHRC had expected that the Northern Ireland Office would launch its own 12-week consultation on the advice in the spring of 2009 and the Commission had hoped for a Bill to be presented at Westminster before the 2010 General Election. However, the Northern Ireland Office did not respond to the Advice until 30 November 2009 and launched its own consultation on the NIHRC's proposals seeking responses by 1 March 2010. This was later extended for a further four weeks so there was then no prospect of a Bill of Rights for Northern Ireland being presented or enacted in the 2009–2010 Session of Parliament.

[143] May 2010, p. 11.

not be a constitutional Bill of Rights to replace it during the lifetime of the coalition government.

Whatever happens to the Human Rights Act 1998, the UK will remain bound by ECHR, Art. 1 to secure Convention rights to everyone within its jurisdiction,[144] and by Art. 13 to provide effective domestic remedies for violation of Convention rights.[145] There is no doubt of the success of the legislation in securing effective domestic remedies and relieving the overburdened European Court of British cases successfully resolved at national level. The fact that our courts have strong interpretative obligations to ensure that British statute and case law is compatible with the Convention rights, has meant that the British judiciary and legal profession analyze the Strasbourg jurisprudence more closely than do the courts of other European States whose written constitutions are given precedence. And, as Lord Hope of Craighead has observed,[146] were the Human Rights Act 1998 to be repealed:

> all that [Strasbourg] jurisprudence is there...And the right of individual petition will be there. And we will still have to recognise that if we take a decision which is contrary to the human rights convention, somebody is going to complain to Strasbourg and that may cause trouble for the UK. So it's very difficult to see how simply wiping out the Human Rights Act is really going to change anything until we withdraw from the convention – which, personally, I don't think is conceivable.

The arguments in favour of a Great Charter of Rights and Freedoms remain powerful. Such a constitutional measure, enacted with popular as well as parliamentary consent, would enhance the political legitimacy of fundamental human rights, and would no longer depend on mimicking the ECHR. A Great Charter could go further than the ECHR and draw upon the more open-textured language of the International Covenant on Civil and Political Rights and of the Bills of Rights of other Commonwealth democracies, such as South Africa. It would locate the British system within the wider framework of Europe in which the other 46 states parties to the ECHR all have written constitutional Bills of Rights, with the EU Charter of Fundamental Rights protecting Europe's citizens against the misuse of public powers.

CONCLUSION

Unless the present and future administrations recognize the Human Rights Act 1998 as no ordinary law, but a constitutional measure that, except in highly exceptional circumstances, takes precedence over ordinary legislation, there will be a powerful case to entrench human rights by means of a new constitutional settlement. It is unlikely

[144] See Lester, Pannick and Herberg, above, n. 2, paras 4.1.1–4.1.10.

[145] Ibid. paras 4.13.1–4.13.17.

[146] Lord Hope reported in J. Rozenberg, 'Are Supreme Court Justices more assertive than they were as Law Lords?', *The Law Society Gazette*, 5 August 2010.

to happen during the lifetime of the present government. However, it remains altogether possible that there will be political advance towards a Great Charter before we celebrate the 900th anniversary of Magna Carta in 2015.

FURTHER READING

ANDENAS, M. and FAIRGRIEVE, D., *Tom Bingham and the Transformation of the Law: A Liber Amicorum* (2009).

BEATSON, J., GROSZ, S., HICKMAN, T., SINGH, R. and PALMER, S., *Human Rights Protection in the United Kingdom* (2008).

BINGHAM, T., *The Rule of Law* (2010).

BOGDANOR, V., *The New British Constitution* (2009).

BRAZIER, R., *Constitutional Reform: Reshaping the British Political System* (2008).

CLAYTON, R. and TOMLINSON, H., *The Law of Human Rights* (2009).

FELDMAN, D., *Civil Liberties and Human Rights in England and Wales* (2nd edn, 2002).

GEARTY, C., *Can Human Rights Survive?* (The Hamlyn Lectures 2005).

HEPPLE, R., *Equality: The New Legal Framework* (2011).

HOFFMAN, D. and ROWE, J., *Human Rights in the UK* (3rd edn, 2009).

Institute for Public Policy Research, *A British Bill of Rights* (2nd edn, 1996).

KAVANAGH, A., *Constitutional Review under the Human Rights Act* (2009).

KING, A., *The British Constitution* (2007).

LAUTERPACHT, H., *International Law and Human Rights* (1950).

LESTER, PANNICK and HERBERG (EDS), *Human Rights Law and Practice* (3rd edn, 2009).

OVEY, C. and WHITE, R. C. A. (eds), Jacobs & White, *European Convention on Human Rights* (3rd edn, 2002).

REID, KAREN, *A Pratitioner's Guide to the European Convention on Human Rights* (2nd edn, 2004).

STARMER, K., *European Human Rights Law* (1999).

WADHAM, J., MOUNTFIELD, H., EDMUNDSON, A. and GALLAGHER, C., *Blackstone's Guide to the Human Rights Act 1998* (4th edn, 2007).

YOUNG, A., *Parliamentary Sovereignty and the Human Rights Act* (2008).

USEFUL WEBSITES

Amnesty International: **www.amnesty.org.uk**
Bill of Rights in Northern Ireland: **www.borini.info**
British Institute of Human Rights: **www.bihr.org.uk**
Equality and Human Rights Commission: **www.equalityhumanrights.com**
Government, citizens and rights – human rights: **www.direct.gov.uk/en/citizensandrights/Yourrightsandresponsibilities/DG_4002951**
Liberty: **www.liberty-human-rights.org.uk/index.php**
Northern Ireland Human Rights Commission **www.nihrc.org**

Supreme Court of the UK: **www.supremecourt.gov.uk**
The Odysseus Trust: **www.odysseustrust.org**
UCL Constitution Unit: **www.ucl.ac.uk/constitution-unit**
UK Human Rights Blog: **http://ukhumanrightsblog.com**
UK Parliament Joint Select Committee on Human Rights: **www.parliament.uk/business/committees/committees-archive/joint-committee-on-human-rights**

4

BRITAIN IN THE EUROPEAN UNION

Paul Craig

SUMMARY

Membership of the European Union raises a number of important issues in domestic constitutional law. In political terms, the fact that an increasing amount of legislation emanates from the European Union means that we should be concerned about the method by which this legislation is made at EU level, and the way in which it is scrutinized in Parliament. In legal terms, EU law raises issues about sovereignty and how our membership of the European Union has affected traditional conceptions of parliamentary supremacy. Treaty articles and norms made thereunder often give rise to rights which individuals can use in their own name in national courts. The EU Charter of Rights is now binding and will have legal implications for national law. Membership of the European Union has also had important constitutional implications for the judiciary, since national courts also function as EU courts.

INTRODUCTION

All aspects of national law have been affected to varying degrees by our membership of the European Union. Constitutional law is no exception. Indeed it is arguable that the effects of EU law on constitutional law have been particularly far reaching. This chapter will describe and evaluate this impact. The discussion will begin by considering the effect of the European Union on the political order. There will be an analysis of the European Union's legislative process, and the ways in which the Westminster Parliament has sought to accommodate this legislation. The focus will then shift to the effect of the European Union on the constitutional legal order. There will be discussion of sovereignty, the constitutional importance of direct effect, the relevance of EU concepts of fundamental rights, and the changed role of national courts.

THE EUROPEAN UNION AND THE NATION STATE

The idea of national identity played a powerful part in forging modern nation states out of principalities in both Germany and Italy in the second half of the nineteenth century. The nation state was lauded in literature, philosophy, and music. The horrors of the Second World War were however believed by many to be the result of excessive nationalism. It was felt that the states within Europe should be organized so as to reduce the likelihood of further conflict.[1] This practical ideal lay behind the European Coal and Steel Community (ECSC) which was signed 1951. Coal and steel were the primary materials used in warfare. If production and distribution could be controlled by a centralized authority it would be less possible for any country to develop a war machine which could be used against its neighbours. The success of the ECSC led pro-Europeanists to believe that more complete economic and political integration was feasible. Plans were drawn up for a European Defence Community (EDC). This was felt to require some form of wider European Political Community (EPC), which would coordinate foreign policy, as well as provide for economic and political integration.[2] Germany would be allowed a limited rearmament within the framework of the EDC. These plans proved to be too ambitious. The French left and right wings both objected, albeit for different reasons, to the idea of German rearmament, even within the EDC. The collapse of the EDC led also to the abandonment of ideas for the EPC.

This setback convinced advocates of European integration that a less overtly political step would be more likely to gain agreement. This was the rationale behind the European Economic Community (EEC) in 1957, the Treaty of Rome. The focus was primarily on economic integration, bringing down trade barriers and ensuring free movement of economic factors of production. The architects of the original Treaty were however fully cognisant of the relationship between economics and politics. They realized that closer economic integration would bring closer coordination on social policy, as well as matters which had a more direct political impact.

There were important amendments to the Treaty of Rome. The Single European Act 1986 had the principal objective of facilitating the completion of the single market. The Treaty on European Union, the Maastricht Treaty, which entered into force in 1993, was more far-reaching. It introduced the three pillar structure. The First Pillar embraced the Community Treaties, and was supranational in nature. A number of important institutional and substantive changes were made, including an increase in the powers of the European Parliament, and the setting of a detailed timetable

[1] J. Pinder, *European Community: The Building of a Union* (3rd edn, 1998); D. Urwin, *The Community of Europe: A History of European Integration since 1945* (2nd edn, 1995); M. Holland, *European Integration from Community to Union* (1993).

[2] The proposal for an EDC was made by France in 1950 and the EDC Treaty was signed, but not ratified, in 1952 by the six states of the ECSC. The French National Assembly refused to ratify the EDC Treaty. Plans for both defence and political union were then shelved.

for economic and monetary union. The Second Pillar was concerned with Common Foreign and Security Policy, and the Third Pillar with Justice and Home Affairs. What distinguished the Second and Third Pillars was that decision-making remained much more intergovernmental in nature, as compared to that which operates in the First Pillar. The member states dominated decision making under the Second and Third Pillars, largely to the exclusion of the Commission and the European Parliament, with the European Court of Justice excluded from the Second Pillar and given only a limited role under the Third Pillar. Notwithstanding this fact, it should not be forgotten that the Maastricht Treaty overall increased the powers of the European Union and the European Community. Decision-making under the Second and Third Pillars may well have been more intergovernmental than under the First Pillar, but the reality was nonetheless that the sphere over which the European Union had competence increased, and there was now an institutionalized forum within which to discuss important matters such as foreign policy, asylum, cross-border crime and the like. The Treaty of Amsterdam, which entered into force in 1999, brought further changes. The line between decision making within the Second and Third Pillars, and that within the First Pillar, was blurred. While the former remained intergovernmental in nature, they were infused with more supranational tenor than hitherto, and some of the subject matter previously dealt with under the Third Pillar was transferred to the First Pillar. The Treaty of Nice 2000 dealt primarily with the institutional consequences of enlargement. The Treaty provisions dealing with institutional issues had remained largely unchanged since the inception of the EEC. The expansion of the European Community to include 15 member states, with the prospect of further significant enlargement eastwards, was the catalyst for addressing some of the basic issues concerning institutional structure, such as the size of the European Parliament, the voting rules in the Council and whether each member state should continue to have one Commissioner.

The new millennium saw attempts at more comprehensive treaty reform, the origins of which are to be found in the Nice Treaty, which left open four issues for future deliberation: the 'delimitation of powers' between the European Union and the member states, the status of the Charter of Fundamental Rights, simplification of the Treaties, and the role of the national Parliaments. The Laeken European Council in 2001 issued a Declaration that considerably broadened the range of matters that should be discussed concerning the future of Europe. No longer were there four 'discrete' issues. The Laeken Declaration placed just about every issue of importance concerning the future of Europe on the agenda for discussion, including major issues concerning the inter-institutional disposition of power within the European Union. It led to the establishment of the Convention on the Future of Europe, headed by the ex-French President, Giscard d'Estaing. It was not preordained that it would produce a Constitutional Treaty, but it did so.[3] The Constitutional Treaty was, after some

[3] Treaty Establishing a Constitution for Europe [2004] OJ C310/1.

hesitation and amendment, accepted by the member states. It then had to be accepted by all of the member states in accord with their constitutional traditions for Treaty ratification. After the negative votes in the French and Dutch referenda the ratification process was however put on hold.

The process of treaty reform was revived in 2007, and this led to the Treaty of Lisbon,[4] which was finally ratified by all member states in 2009.[5] The Treaty of Lisbon amends the previous treaties. The European Union is henceforth to be founded on the Treaty on European Union (TEU), and the Treaty on the Functioning of the European Union (TFEU), and the two Treaties have the same legal value.[6] The European Union is to replace and succeed the European Community.[7] The TEU contains some but not all of the constitutional principles that govern the European Union. The TFEU contains the provisions as amended that were previously to be found in the EC Treaty. The Treaty of Lisbon has removed the formal three pillar structure. The provisions of the Third Pillar have been incorporated into the TFEU and are subject to the ordinary Treaty regime. There are however still distinct rules relating to the Common Foreign and Security Policy that are found in the TEU. In terms of overall content the Treaty of Lisbon drew heavily on the Constitutional Treaty.

There are now seven formal EU institutions.[8] The Assembly was originally an indirectly elected body representing the people. It is now called the European Parliament and is composed of directly elected representatives from the member states. The European Council consists of the heads of state, the President of the European Council, and the President of the Commission. The Council of Ministers is composed of representatives from the member states. The members of the Commission are appointed from the states, but they are independent of their own country and represent the EU interest. The fifth official EU institution is the Court of Justice of the European Union, and the remaining two are the European Central Bank, and the Court of Auditors. The powers accorded to the different institutions, and the way in which they interact, have changed markedly over time.

THE LEGISLATIVE AND DECISION-MAKING PROCESS

For the first 30 years of the Community's existence decision-making was dominated by the Council and Commission. The Assembly had limited formal powers in the EEC Treaty. Its role in the legislative process was restricted: it only had a right to be consulted where a specific treaty article stipulated that this should be so. The confined nature of the Assembly's powers was explicable in part because few if any international

[4] P. Craig, *The Lisbon Treaty, Law, Politics and Treaty Reform* (2010).

[5] Consolidated Versions of the Treaty on European Union and the Treaty on the Functioning of the European Union [2010] OJ C83/1.

[6] TEU, Art. 1, para. 3. [7] Ibid, Art. 1 para. 3. [8] Ibid, Art. 13.

organizations had any democratically elected legislature which possessed real power at the international level. The explanation was also in part a reflection of the view of the Community held by its prime architects. Monnet, one of the principal founders, adopted a strategy of what has been termed elite-led gradualism.[9] It was hoped that popular consent would follow this lead, but the need to engage powerful business and labour organizations was accorded a much higher priority than the 'direct involvement of as yet uninformed publics'.[10] While Monnet was broadly in favour of a democratic Community 'he saw the emergence of loyalties to the Community institutions developing as a *consequence* of elite agreements for the functional organization of Europe, not as an essential *prerequisite* to that organization'.[11] Moreover, the legitimacy of the Community was to be secured through outcomes: peace and prosperity.

It was the Commission and the Council that dominated decision-making during this 30-year period. The Commission was given a plethora of powers of a legislative, administrative, executive, and judicial nature.[12] Its legislative powers were of particular importance. The Commission has the right of legislative initiative, which means that it has a major influence over the development of the Community's legislative agenda. This, and its other powers, served to place the Commission at the heart of the Community.

Notwithstanding this array of formal powers, the Council exerted increasing control over the Commission during this period. This was largely through institutional developments that were initially outside the strict letter of the Treaty, all of which served to increase the Council's influence over Community legislation. The Luxembourg Accords ensured that decisions which affected important interests of a particular member state would not be taken unless that state agreed, even where the Treaty stipulated that voting was to be by qualified majority. Decision-making was thus carried forward under the 'shadow of the veto' even when it was not formally invoked. The Committee of Permanent Representatives, the organ providing institutional support for the Council, developed its own working parties which enabled it to engage in a dialogue with the Commission over the details of legislative proposals. Management and regulatory committees emerged as the vehicle through which member state input could be ensured when decision-making had been delegated to the Commission. Finally, the European Council, meetings of the heads of state, became an institutionalized forum through which member states could influence the overall direction of the Community at the highest level.

The Assembly, formally renamed the European Parliament (EP) by the Maastricht Treaty, pressed for greater powers in the legislative process, bolstered by the fact that it had been directly elected since 1979. In the early 1980s it put forward radical proposals for a revision of the entire Treaty, which would have placed it in the centre of the

[9] W. Wallace and J. Smith, 'Democracy or Technocracy? European Integration and the Problem of Popular Consent', in J. Hayward (ed.), *The Crisis of Representation in Europe* (1995) 140.

[10] Ibid., p. 140.

[11] M. Holland, above, n. 1, p. 16. Original emphasis.

[12] P. Craig and G. de Búrca, *EU Law, Text, Cases and Materials* (5th edn, 2011) ch. 2.

legislative process. These proposals fell largely on stony ground. However, the Single European Act 1986 did afford the EP a real role in the legislative process for the first time. The co-operation procedure gave the EP power in the enactment of legislation, and made it necessary for the Commission, when drafting legislation, to take account of the EP's views.[13] The years since 1986 saw the powers of the EP increase still further. The Maastricht Treaty[14] introduced the co-decision procedure, which gave more power to the EP than the co-operation procedure. The Treaty of Amsterdam[15] further strengthened the EP's position under the co-decision procedure and extended its sphere of application. The Treaty of Lisbon has continued this development. The co-decision procedure has been re-labelled the ordinary legislative procedure, its sphere of application has been further extended, with the consequence that the Council and EP are said to exercise legislative functions jointly.[16]

The details of the procedure are complex.[17] A proposal is sent by the Commission to the Council and the EP. The EP can if it wishes propose amendments at its first reading of the measure. If the Council approves these then the proposed act can be adopted at that stage. The Council may however not agree with the EP's amendments, in which case the Council adopts its position, which is communicated to the EP. The EP then has three months to respond. It can at this Second Reading of the measure agree to the Council's position, or not take a decision. The act will then be deemed to have been adopted in accordance with the Council's position. The EP may alternatively reject the Council's position in which case the act will not be adopted. It may however suggest further amendments. It is open to the Council to accept the EP's Second Reading amendments, in which case the act becomes law in the form of the Council's position as amended. If the Council does not approve of all the amendments then a meeting of the Conciliation Committee is convened. The Conciliation Committee has an equal number of representatives from the Council and the EP. Its task is to reach agreement on a joint text. If it is able to do, then this must be approved by the EP and the Council.

Although the ordinary legislative procedure is complex it accommodates the differing institutional interests of those concerned with the passage of EU legislation. The Commission will consult with the EP and the Council about the overall legislative programme for the coming year. It will also consult with the Council, or more accurately the Committee of Permanent Representatives, and the EP, or the relevant committee thereof, about a draft measure before it begins to go through the TFEU, Art. 294 procedure. The formal powers given to the EP by Art. 294 enable it to propose changes at an early stage which, if accepted by the Council, can then be embodied in the measure which becomes law at that stage. The EP is then given further power if the Council does not accept all the EP's first reading suggestions. The EP can accept, reject, or

[13] M. Westlake, *The Commission and the Parliament: Partners and Rivals in the European Policy-Making Process* (1994), and *A Modern Guide to the European Parliament* (1994).

[14] The Maastricht Treaty entered into force in 1993.

[15] The Treaty entered into force in 1999.

[16] Treaty of Lisbon, TEU, Arts 14(1) and 16(1).

[17] Ibid., TFEU, Art. 294.

propose further amendments to the Council's position at the Second Reading stage. The bottom line is that an act will not be passed unless both the EP and the Council agree.

THE NATURE OF THE EUROPEAN UNION

It is important not to view the European Union as if it were a nation state, nor should one necessarily expect the form of institutional ordering to conform to that commonly found at the domestic level. Conceptions of the separation of powers, which play a marked role in the allocation of functions within domestic constitutions, do not have the same centrality within the European Union. The legislative process is divided between the Council, the EP, and the Commission. This has a real impact on the relationship between the EP and the Council. The latter, for all its power, cannot dominate the former in the way that the executive dominates the legislature at Westminster. The EP will be run by the largest party, or a coalition, which will have its own agenda, albeit being mindful of what will be acceptable to the Council and the Commission. Responsibilities of an executive nature are exercised by the Commission, the Council, and the European Council. Administrative responsibility for the implementation of EU policy lies principally with the Commission, but it will often work through and with national bureaucracies. The EP does moreover have oversight powers through which it can call the Commission to account for the way in which EU policy is administered. It was the exercise of these powers that led to the appointment of the Committee of Independent Experts, whose report prompted the resignation of the Santer Commission in 1999.

Judicial power resides principally with the European Court of Justice (ECJ) and the General Court (GC), which is the new name for the Court of First Instance (CFI). The Commission also has powers of a judicial nature. It will be the body that brings member states to court under TFEU, Art. 258 if they are in breach of the Treaty. The Commission will give the initial judicial decision on important issues such as competition law and state aids. The ECJ and the GC have far-reaching powers of judicial review, which can be used to ensure that EU institutions do not exceed their power. The ECJ will adjudicate on important inter-institutional disputes between the principal EU organs. The ECJ has read into the Treaty general principles of law which are used to judge the legality of EU action. These principles include proportionality, legitimate expectations, principles of procedural legality and fundamental rights. It is the ECJ which will also adjudicate on disputes concerning subsidiarity, whereby member states will challenge the competence of the European Union to act, arguing that the subject matter should have been left for resolution at state level.[18]

[18] Case C-84/94, *United Kingdom* v. *Council* [1996] ECR I-5755; Case C-233/94, *Germany* v. *European Parliament and the Council* [1997] ECR I-2405.

The theme which appears repeatedly in papers emanating from the European Union is that of institutional balance, rather than separation of powers.[19] This refers to the desirability of preserving a proper balance of power between the Council, as representing the interests of the member states, the EP as representing the people, and the Commission as guardian of the overall aims of the treaty. While classical ideas of the separation of powers are not therefore central to the institutional ordering within the European Union, another constitutional principle, the Rule of Law, is of prime importance. TEU, Art. 2 declares that the European Union is founded on the respect for human dignity, freedom, democracy, equality, human rights and the Rule of Law. Respect for these principles is made a condition of membership of the European Union.[20]

THE UK PARLIAMENT AND LEGISLATIVE SCRUTINY

EU membership has significant implications for the Westminster Parliament, and also for the Welsh Assembly and the Scottish Parliament. We shall begin by considering the machinery introduced to deal with EU legislation, and then consider the subsidiarity controls that reside with national parliaments.

In terms of machinery,[21] Committees of the House of Commons have been established to consider whether delegated legislation is necessary in order to implement, for example, an EU directive, and also to scrutinize proposals that emerge from the European Union, in order to provide Parliament with information about impending European legislation. The system works in the following way. The European Scrutiny Committee examines EU documents, such as draft proposals for legislation, and reports on the 'legal and political importance' of each document. The scrutiny is conducted in the light of the Explanatory Memorandum produced by the relevant government department on the EU documents. The Committee considers approximately 1,000 documents each year, half of which are deemed to be of legal or political importance, such that the Scrutiny Committee reports substantively on them. It recommends approximately 40 such documents per year for further consideration by one of the European Standing Committees, and approximately three per year for debate on the floor of the House. The latter only occurs if the House decides that they should be considered in this way. There are three European Standing Committees[22]

[19] P. Craig, 'Democracy and Rulemaking within the EC: An Empirical and Normative Assessment' (1997) 3 *ELJ* 105.

[20] Treaty of Lisbon, TEU, Art. 49.

[21] T. St J. N. Bates, 'European Community Legislation before the House of Commons' (1991) 12 *Stat LR* 109; E. Denza, 'Parliamentary Scrutiny of Community Legislation' (1993) 14 *Stat LR* 56; *The European Scrutiny System in the House of Commons* (2010), available at www.parliament.uk/documents/commons-committees/european-scrutiny/ESC%20Guide%20Revised%202010.pdf.

[22] Committee A: Energy and Climate Change; Environment, Food and Rural Affairs; Transport; Communities and Local Government; Forestry Commission. Committee B: HM Treasury; Work and

and the relevant committee will consider the merits of the issues. The reports of the European Scrutiny Committee are clearly and succinctly presented.[23] They show an awareness of the legal and political importance of issues that are often complex. The committee's evaluation will sometimes support that of the relevant government minister, and will sometimes take a differing line. The very fact that there is a body within the UK looking at such issues, other than the relevant department of state, is undoubtedly beneficial. The European Scrutiny committee will also liaise where necessary with departmental select committees. The new regime has undoubtedly had a positive impact.[24]

It has in the past been hampered by the brevity of time left for discussion before the EU legislation is considered by the Council. The Treaty of Lisbon is designed to alleviate this problem. Documents such as green and white papers are sent to national Parliaments as soon as they are published, and draft legislative acts are transmitted to them at the same time as they are sent to the Council and Commission.[25] The general rule is that an eight-week period must elapse between transmission of a draft legislative act to national Parliaments, and its being placed on a provisional agenda for the Council for its adoption or for adoption of a position under a legislative procedure.[26] The national Parliaments also receive the agendas and outcomes of Council meetings at the same time as national governments.[27]

There is in addition a House of Lords' Select Committee on the European Union. It is chaired by a salaried officer of the House[28] and considers any EU proposal that it believes should be drawn to the attention of the House. The Committee functions through a number of subcommittees which are subject-matter based.[29] These subcommittees will co-opt other members of the House of Lords for the investigation of particular issues. The House of Lords' Select Committee is therefore different from that in the House of Commons. The latter will sift through EU legislation and refer matters on to the standing committee where this is warranted.

Pensions; Foreign and Commonwealth Office; International Development; Home Office; Justice; and matters not otherwise allocated. Committee C: Business, Innovation and Skills; Children Schools and Families; Innovation, Culture, Media and Sport; and Health.

[23] See e.g. Twenty-Seventh Report of the Select Committee on European Scrutiny, HC 34-xxvii (1999), dealing with diverse matters such as the extension to third-country nationals of social security rights, the decommissioning of nuclear research facilities, and the revision of Community competition law; Third Report of the European Union Scrutiny Committee, *The European Union's Annual Policy Strategy 2006*, HC 34-iii (2005); Fourteenth Report of the European Union Scrutiny Committee, *Aspects of the EU's Constitutional Treaty*, HC 38-xiv-1 (2005); Fourteenth Report of the European Union Scrutiny Committee, 2008–09, *Free Movement of Workers in the EU*, HC 324 (2009).

[24] *The European Scrutiny System in the House*, above, n. 21.

[25] TEU, Art. 12; Protocol (No. 1) On the Role of National Parliaments in the European Union, Art. 1.

[26] Protocol (No. 1), Art. 4. [27] Ibid., Art. 5.

[28] The chairman will decide which issues are of sufficient importance to warrant scrutiny by one of the subcommittees.

[29] There are seven such subcommittees which deal with: economic and financial affairs, and international trade; internal market, energy, and transport; foreign affairs, defence and development policy; agriculture, fisheries and environment; justice and institutions; home affairs; social policies and consumer protection.

The House of Lords' committee will produce its own valuable, detailed reports on particular issues.[30]

The role of national Parliaments in the scrutiny of draft EU legislation has been strengthened by the Treaty of Lisbon provisions on subsidiarity. The basic idea behind subsidiarity is that action should only be undertaken at EU level where because of the scale or effects of the action it can be better achieved through EU action rather than national action.[31] The detailed scheme is contained in the Protocol on the Application of the Principles of Subsidiarity and Proportionality.[32] It imposes an obligation to consult widely before proposing legislative acts.[33] The Commission must provide a detailed statement concerning proposed legislation so that compliance with subsidiarity can be appraised.[34] The Commission must submit an annual report on the application of subsidiarity to the European Council, the EP, the Council, and to national Parliaments.[35] The ECJ has jurisdiction to consider infringement of subsidiarity under TFEU, Art. 263, brought by the member state, or 'notified by them in accordance with their legal order on behalf of their national Parliament or a chamber of it'.[36]

The most important innovation in the Protocol on Subsidiarity is the enhanced role accorded to national Parliaments.[37] The Commission must send all legislative proposals to the national Parliaments at the same time as to the EU institutions.[38] A national Parliament or Chamber thereof, may, within eight weeks, send the Presidents of the Commission, EP, and Council a reasoned opinion as to why it considers that the proposal does not comply with subsidiarity.[39] The EP, Council and Commission must take this opinion into account.[40] Each national Parliament has two votes[41] and where non-compliance with subsidiarity is expressed by national Parliaments that represent one third of all the votes allocated to them, the Commission must review its proposal.[42] The Commission, after such review, may decide to maintain, amend or

[30] See e.g. Third Report of the Select Committee on the European Communities, HL 23 (1999), dealing with reforms to Comitology procedures; Nineteenth Report of the Select Committee on the European Communities, HL 101 (1999), dealing with the then forthcoming European Council meeting which was the first such meeting to deal with justice and home affairs; Tenth Report of the European Union Committee, *The Future Regulation of Derivatives Markets: Is the EU on the Right Track?*, HL 93 (2010).

[31] TEU, Art. 5(3).

[32] Protocol (No. 2), On the Application of the Principles of Subsidiarity and Proportionality.

[33] Ibid., Art. 2. [34] Ibid., Art. 5. [35] Ibid., Art. 9. [36] Ibid., Art. 8.

[37] J-V. Louis, 'National Parliaments and the Principle of Subsidiarity – Legal Options and Practical Limits', in I. Pernice and E. Tanchev (eds), *Ceci n'est pas une Constitution – Constitutionalization without a Constitution?* (2009) 131–54; G. Bermann, 'National Parliaments and Subsidiarity: An Outsider's View', ibid., 155–61; J. Peters, 'National Parliaments and Subsidiarity: Think Twice' (2005) *European Constitutional L Rev* 68.

[38] Subsidiarity and Proportionality, above, n. 32, Art. 4.

[39] Ibid., Art. 6.

[40] Ibid., Art. 7(1).

[41] Ibid.

[42] Ibid., Art. 7(2). This threshold is lowered to one quarter in certain cases concerning the area of freedom, justice and security.

withdraw the proposal, giving reasons for the decision.[43] Where a measure is made in accord with the ordinary legislative procedure, and at least a simple majority of votes given to national parliaments signal non-compliance with subsidiarity, then the proposal must once again be reviewed and although the Commission can decide not to amend it, the Commission must provide a reasoned opinion on the matter and this can, in effect, be overridden by the EP or the Council.[44]

It remains to be seen how subsidiarity operates in practice. It is clear that there will continue to be many areas in which the comparative efficiency calculus in TFEU, Art. 5(3) favours EU action, more especially in an enlarged European Union. Time will tell how far the new provisions in the Protocol according greater power to national Parliaments affect the incidence and nature of EU legislation. Much will depend on the willingness of national Parliaments to devote the requisite time and energy to the matter. The national Parliament has to submit a reasoned opinion as to why it believes that the measure infringes subsidiarity. It will have to present reasoned argument as to why the Commission's comparative efficiency calculus is defective. This may not be easy. It will be even more difficult for the requisite number of national Parliaments to present reasoned opinions in relation to the same EU measure so as to compel the Commission to review the proposal. The Commission is nonetheless likely to take seriously any such reasoned opinion, particularly if it emanates from the Parliament of a larger member state.

SOVEREIGNTY

THE TRADITIONAL DEBATE

A detailed analysis of sovereignty is provided by Anthony Bradley in this volume.[45] The present discussion will focus on sovereignty and the European Union. It is however necessary to mention, albeit briefly, some of the background to the general sovereignty debate.

The debate over sovereignty has been characterized as a contest between the traditionalists, represented by Dicey[46] and Wade,[47] and upholders of the New View, represented by Jennings,[48] Heuston,[49] and Marshall.[50] The form of argument used by Sir William Wade is in fact different from that advanced by Dicey, and therefore it is the views of Wade that will be considered here. No attempt will be made to consider the

[43] Subsidiarity and Proportionality, above, n. 32, Art. 7(2).

[44] Subsidiarity and Proportionality, above, n. 32, Art. 7(3).

[45] Chapter 2 above.

[46] A. Dicey, *An Introduction to the Study of the Law of the Constitution* (10th edn, 1967).

[47] H. W. R. Wade, 'The Basis of Legal Sovereignty' [1955] *CLJ* 172.

[48] Sir I. Jennings, *The Law and the Constitution* (5th edn, 1959) ch. 4.

[49] R. F. V. Heuston, *Essays in Constitutional Law* (2nd edn, 1964) ch. 1.

[50] G. Marshall, *Constitutional Theory* (1971) ch. 3.

detail of the debate between Wade and the advocates of the New View.[51] The view of sovereignty advanced by Sir William Wade is captured in the following quotation:[52]

> An orthodox English lawyer, brought up consciously or unconsciously on the doctrine of parliamentary sovereignty stated by Coke and Blackstone, and enlarged on by Dicey, could explain it in simple terms. He would say that it meant merely that no Act of the sovereign legislature (composed of the Queen, Lords and Commons) could be invalid in the eyes of the courts; that it was always open to the legislature, so constituted, to repeal any previous legislation whatever; that therefore no Parliament could bind its successors...He would probably add that it is an invariable rule that in case of conflict between two Acts of Parliament, the later repeals the earlier. If he were then asked whether it would be possible for the United Kingdom to 'entrench' legislation—for example, if it should wish to adopt a Bill of Rights which would be repealable only by some specially safeguarded process—he would answer that under English law this is a legal impossibility: it is easy enough to pass such legislation, but since that legislation, like all other legislation, would be repealable by any ordinary Act of Parliament the special safeguards would be legally futile. This is merely an illustration of the rule that one Parliament cannot bind its successors. It follows therefore that there is one, and only one, limit to Parliament's legal power: it cannot detract from its own continuing sovereignty.

This thesis has been vigorously challenged by the proponents of the New View, who argued that 'manner and form' provisions enacted in a particular statute would be binding, in the sense that a later statute dealing with the same subject matter could only alter the earlier statute if passed in accordance with the provisions of that earlier statute.[53]

THE JUDICIAL RESPONSE PRIOR TO *FACTORTAME*

On the traditional view of sovereignty as represented by Sir William Wade the latest will of Parliament must predominate. If there is a clash between a later and an earlier norm, then the latter is taken to be impliedly repealed or disapplied by the former. This view of sovereignty meant that there could be tensions between UK and EU law. The primacy of EU law over national law[54] was asserted by the ECJ early in its developing jurisprudence,[55] and extended by later case law.[56]

Prior to *Factortame* there were three differing strands within the UK jurisprudence. In some cases courts spoke in terms of the traditional orthodoxy on sovereignty.[57] The second, and dominant, line of cases sought to blunt the edge of any conflict between the two systems by using strong principles of construction: UK law

[51] P. Craig, 'Parliamentary Sovereignty of the United Kingdom Parliament After Factortame' (1991) 11 *YBEL* 221.

[52] Wade, above, n. 47, p. 174.

[53] Above, nn. 48, 49 and 50.

[54] Craig and de Búrca, above, n. 12, ch. 10.

[55] Case 6/64, *Costa* v. *ENEL* [1964] ECR 585, 593.

[56] Case 106/77, *Amministrazione delle Finanze dello Stato* v. *Simmenthal Spa* [1978] ECR 629.

[57] *Felixstowe Docks Railway Co.* v. *British Transport Docks Board* [1976] 2 CMLR 655, 664.

would, whenever possible, be read so as to be compatible with EU law.[58] In the third type of case the courts accepted, in principle, the idea of purposive construction, but felt unable to read the UK legislation to be in conformity with the relevant EU norm.[59]

FACTORTAME, *EOC*, AND *THOBURN*

The leading decision is now *R.* v. *Secretary of State for Transport ex parte Factortame Ltd.*[60] The applicants were companies which were incorporated under UK law, but the majority of the directors and shareholders were Spanish. The companies were in the business of sea fishing and their vessels were registered as British under the Merchant Shipping Act 1894. The statutory regime governing sea fishing was altered by the Merchant Shipping Act 1988. Vessels that had been registered under the 1894 Act had to register under the new legislation. Ninety-five vessels failed to meet the new criteria and the applicants argued that the relevant parts of the 1988 Act were incompatible with, *inter alia*, EC Treaty, Arts 52, 58 and 221.[61]

Whether the 1988 statute was in breach of EC law was clearly a contentious question. All the UK courts involved in the case agreed that a reference should be made to the ECJ under EC Treaty, Art. 177 (now TFEU, Art. 267). The issue in the first *Factortame* case concerned the status of the 1988 Act pending the ECJ's decision on the substance of the case. If the applicants could not fish in this intervening period they might well go out of business. The applicants sought therefore either for the 1988 Act to be 'disapplied' (i.e. not enforced) pending the decision of the ECJ; or, if the court did grant an interim injunction to the government to prevent the applicants from fishing, that the government should have to give a cross-undertaking to pay damages if it should lose in the main action before the ECJ. Their Lordships held that, as a matter of domestic law, interim relief against the Crown was not available.[62] The House of Lords then sought a preliminary ruling as to whether the absence of any interim relief against the Crown was itself a violation of EC law. The ECJ was therefore being asked to rule on whether a 'gap' in the availability of administrative law remedies in UK law constituted a breach of EC law.

The ECJ decided in favour of the applicants.[63] It reasoned from the *Simmenthal* case[64] where it had held that provisions of EC law rendered 'automatically inapplicable' any conflicting provision of national law. The *Simmenthal* decision gave a broad construction to the idea of a 'conflicting provision' of national law, interpreting it to cover any legislative, administrative, or judicial practice that might impair

[58] *Litster* v. *Forth Dry Dock* [1990] 1 AC 546.

[59] *Duke* v. *GEC Reliance* [1988] AC 618.

[60] [1990] 2 AC 85.

[61] TFEU, Arts 49, 54 and 55, after the Treaty of Lisbon.

[62] Such relief is now available: *M* v. *Home Office* [1994] 1 AC 377.

[63] Case C-213/89, *R.* v. *Secretary of State for Transport, ex parte Factortame Ltd* [1990] ECR I-2433.

[64] Above, n. 56.

the effectiveness of EC law.[65] With this foundation the ECJ in the *Factortame* case concluded that:[66]

> [T]he full effectiveness of Community law would be just as much impaired if a rule of national law could prevent a court seised of a dispute governed by Community law from granting interim relief in order to ensure the full effectiveness of the judgment to be given on the existence of the rights claimed under Community law. It follows that a court which in those circumstances would grant interim relief, if it were not for a rule of national law, is obliged to set aside that rule.

The case then returned to the House of Lords to be reconsidered in the light of the preliminary ruling given by the ECJ, *R. v. Secretary of State for Transport ex parte Factortame Ltd (No. 2)*.[67] Their Lordships accepted that, at least in the area covered by EC law, such relief would be available against the Crown. *Factortame (No. 2)* also contains *dicta* by their Lordships on the more general issue of sovereignty. The final decision on the substance of the case involved a clash between Articles of the EC Treaty, and a later Act of the UK Parliament, the Merchant Shipping Act 1988. The traditional idea of sovereignty in the UK is, as we have seen, that if there is a clash between a later statutory norm and an earlier legal provision the later statute takes precedence. The ECJ has repeatedly held that EC law must take precedence in the event of a clash with national law. Moreover, the conflict in this instance was between national law and Articles of the Treaty itself. The ECJ has made it clear that in the event of such a clash EC law trumps national law. The duty of the national court was not therefore confined to seeing whether national law might be construed to be in conformity with EC law, as is the case in actions between individuals based on directives. The dicta of the House of Lords in *Factortame (No. 2)* are therefore clearly of importance. Lord Bridge had this to say:[68]

> Some public comments on the decision of the Court of Justice, affirming the jurisdiction of the courts of the member states to override national legislation if necessary to enable interim relief to be granted in protection of rights under Community law, have suggested that this was a novel and dangerous invasion by a Community institution of the sovereignty of the United Kingdom Parliament. But such comments are based on a misconception. If the supremacy within the European Community of Community law over the national law of member states was not always inherent in the EEC Treaty it was certainly well established in the jurisprudence of the Court of Justice long before the United Kingdom joined the Community. Thus, whatever limitation of its sovereignty Parliament accepted when it enacted the European Communities Act 1972 was entirely voluntary. Under the terms of the 1972 Act it has always been clear that it was the duty of a United Kingdom court, when delivering final judgment, to override any rule of national law found to be in conflict with any directly enforceable rule of Community law. Similarly, when decisions of the Court of Justice have exposed areas of United Kingdom statute law which failed to implement Council directives, Parliament has always loyally accepted the obligation to make

[65] Above, n. 56, paras 22 and 23.
[66] Above, n. 63, para. 21.
[67] [1991] 1 AC 603.
[68] Ibid., pp. 658–9.

> appropriate and prompt amendments. Thus there is nothing in any way novel in according supremacy to rules of Community law in areas to which they apply and to insist that, in the protection of rights under Community law, national courts must not be prohibited by rules of national law from granting interim relief in appropriate cases is no more than a logical recognition of that supremacy.

Three aspects of this reasoning should be distinguished. One was essentially *contractarian*: the UK knew when it joined the European Community that priority should be accorded to EC law, and it must be taken to have contracted on those terms. If, therefore, 'blame' was to be cast for a loss of sovereignty then this should be laid at the door of Parliament and not the courts. The second facet of Lord Bridge's reasoning was *a priori* and *functional*: it was always inherent in a regime such as the European Community that it could only function adequately if EC law could take precedence in the event of a clash with domestic legal norms. The third factor at play was the existence of the European Communities Act 1972 (ECA 1972), which was said to impose a duty on national courts to override national law in the event of a clash with directly enforceable EC law.

The impact of *Factortame* was made clear in the *Equal Opportunities Commission* case,[69] which was concerned with the compatibility of UK legislation on unfair dismissal and redundancy pay with EC law. Under UK law[70] entitlement to these protections and benefits operated differentially depending upon whether the person was in full-time or part-time employment. Full-time workers were eligible after two years; part-time workers only after five. The majority of part-time workers were women and the Equal Opportunities Commission (EOC) took the view that the legislation discriminated against them, contrary to Art. 119.[71] The EOC sought a declaration that the relevant provisions of the UK legislation were in breach of EC law. The House of Lords held that the national legislation was in breach of Art. 119 and the directives. The *Factortame* case was regarded as authority for the proposition that it was open to a national court to declare provisions of a primary statute to be incompatible with norms of EC law.[72] The House of Lords also made it clear that this power to review primary legislation resided in all national *courts*, not just the UK's top court.

The impact of the European Union on traditional concepts of sovereignty was also considered in *Thoburn*.[73] Certain street traders were prosecuted for continuing to use imperial measures, rather than metric, when selling their goods. The obligation to use metric measures as the primary form of measurement derived from EC directives, and the UK government had complied with this obligation through the enactment of a series of regulations, some of which were based on ECA 1972, s. 2(2). The defendants argued, *inter alia*, that in this context the power to make such regulations through s. 2(2) had been impliedly repealed by provisions contained in the Weights

[69] *R.* v. *Secretary of State for Employment ex parte Equal Opportunities Commission* [1995] 1 AC 1.

[70] Employment Protection (Consolidation) Act 1978.

[71] Now TFEU Art. 157.

[72] [1995] 1 AC 1, 27.

[73] *Thoburn* v. *Sunderland City Council* [2003] QB 151.

and Measures Act 1985. Laws LJ held that there was no inconsistency between ECA 1972, s. 2(2) and the Weights and Measures Act 1985, and therefore that no issue of implied repeal arose in the case. He held more generally that the constitutional relationship between the UK and the European Union was not to be decided by the ECJ's jurisprudence: that case law could not itself entrench EU law within national law.[74] The constitutional relationship between the European Union and the UK, including the impact of membership of the European Union on sovereignty, was to be decided by the common law in the light of any statutes that Parliament had enacted.[75] The common law had, said Laws LJ, modified the traditional concept of sovereignty, in the sense that it had created exceptions to the doctrine of implied repeal. Ordinary statutes were subject to the doctrine of implied repeal. What Laws LJ referred to as 'constitutional statutes', which conditioned the legal relationship between citizen and state in some overarching manner, or which dealt with fundamental constitutional rights, were not subject to the doctrine of implied repeal.[76] The repeal of such a statute, or its disapplication in a particular instance, could only occur if there were some 'express words in the later statute, or by words so specific that the inference of an actual determination to effect the result contended for was irresistible'.[77] The ECA 1972 was regarded as just such a constitutional statute. It contained provisions that ensured the supremacy of substantive EU law in the event of a clash with national law, and was not subject to implied repeal.

SUPREMACY AFTER *FACTORTAME*, *EOC*, AND *THOBURN*: THE SUBSTANTIVE IMPACT OF THE DECISIONS

The decisions considered above generated much academic comment.[78] Space precludes a detailed analysis of the differing views. It is nonetheless clear that there are two issues of central importance. One concerns the substantive impact of these decisions on the previous orthodoxy concerning sovereignty. The other is as to the best way of conceptualizing what has occurred. The former will be considered here, the latter in the section that follows. The substantive impact of *Factortame*, *Equal Opportunities Commission*, and *Thoburn* may be described as follows.

First, in doctrinal terms these decisions mean that the concept of *implied repeal*, or *implied disapplication*, under which inconsistencies between later and earlier norms were resolved in favour of the later norms, will, subject to what is said below, no longer apply to clashes concerning EU and national law. This proposition is sound in terms of principle, whether viewed simply in terms of membership of the European Union, or as part of a broader category of constitutional statutes that are not subject to implied repeal. There are good normative arguments for requiring the legislature to state expressly its intent to repeal or derogate from statutes of constitutional importance,

[74] Ibid., paras 57–8. [75] Ibid., para. 59. [76] Ibid., para. 62. [77] Ibid., para. 63.

[78] Craig, above, n. 51; Sir William Wade, 'Sovereignty – Revolution or Evolution?' (1996) 112 *LQR* 568; T. R. S. Allan, 'Parliamentary Sovereignty: Law, Politics and Revolution' (1997) 113 *LQR* 443.

and this is so notwithstanding the fact that there may be room for disagreement as to which statutes come within this category.

Secondly, if Parliament ever does wish to derogate from its EU obligations then it will have to do so *expressly and unequivocally*. The reaction of our national courts to such an unlikely eventuality remains to be seen. In principle, two options would be open to the national judiciary. Either they could follow the latest will of Parliament, thereby preserving some remnant of traditional orthodoxy on sovereignty. Or they could argue that it is not open to our legislature to pick and choose which obligations to subscribe to while still remaining within the European Union. Which of these options our courts would choose will be dependent, in part, on the issues addressed in the next section.

Thirdly, the supremacy of EU law over national law *operates in areas where EU law is applicable*, as is made clear from the dictum of Lord Bridge set out above. This may well be a statement of the obvious, but the point is more complex than might initially have been thought.[79] The problem addressed here is often referred to as *Kompetenz-Kompetenz*: who has the ultimate authority to decide whether a matter is within the competence of the European Union? The ECJ may well believe that it is the ultimate decider of this issue. However, national courts may not always be content with this arrogation of authority. This is particularly so given that the ECJ has, as is well known, often reasoned 'teleologically'[80] and expanded the boundaries of EU competence in a manner which has caused disquiet in some national legal systems. The German Federal Constitutional Court held that it will not inevitably accept EU decisions, including those of the ECJ, which it regards as crossing the line between legitimate Treaty interpretation and de facto Treaty amendment.[81] The general tenor of Laws LJ's judgment in *Thoburn* is also inclined to the conclusion that the ultimate competence to decide on the scope of EU competence resides with the national court. While he does not address the point directly his reasoning to the effect that the fundamental legal basis of the UK's relationship with the European Union rests with domestic, not European, law lends support to that conclusion. This is reinforced by his statement that if the European Union were to enact a measure repugnant to a constitutional right guaranteed by UK law, it would be for the national courts to decide whether the general words of the ECA 1972 were sufficient to give it overriding effect in domestic law.[82]

[79] P. Craig, 'Report on the United Kingdom', in A.-M. Slaughter, A. Stone Sweet and J. Weiler (eds), *The European Courts and National Courts, Doctrine and Jurisprudence* (1998) ch. 7.

[80] Teleological judicial reasoning connotes the idea that a court will reason in order to attain the end which it believes that the particular Treaty article was intended to serve.

[81] *Brunner* v. *The European Union Treaty* [1994] 1 CMLR 57, paras 49 and 99; *Treaty of Lisbon Consitutionality Case*, BVerfG, 2 BvE 2/08, 30 June 2009, available at www.bverfg.de/entscheidungen/es20090630_2bve000208.html; English translation available at www.bundesverfassungsgericht.de/entscheidungen/es20090630_2bve000208en.html.

[82] *Thoburn*, above, n. 73, para. 69.

SUPREMACY *AFTER FACTORTAME, EOC*, AND *THOBURN*: THE CONCEPTUAL BASIS OF THE DECISIONS

Commentators have been divided as to how best to conceptualize the impact of the courts' jurisprudence.[83] The issues here are complex, but the main features of the debate can be presented as follows.

It is possible to rationalize what the courts have done as a species of *statutory construction*. All would agree that if a statute can be reconciled with an EU norm through construing the statutory words without unduly distorting them then this should be done, more especially when the statute was passed to effectuate a directive. However the species of statutory construction being considered here is more far-reaching. On this view accommodation between national law and EU law is attained through a rule of construction to the effect that inconsistencies *will* be resolved in favour of EU law *unless* Parliament has indicated clearly and unambiguously that it intends to derogate from EU law. The degree of linguistic inconsistency between the statute and the EU norm is not the essential point of the inquiry. Provided that there is no unequivocal derogation from EU law then it will apply, rather than any conflicting domestic statute. Counsel for the applicants framed their argument in this manner in the first *Factortame* case.[84] This view was posited by Lord Bridge in the same case where he stated that the effect of ECA 1972, s. 2(4) was that the Merchant Shipping Act 1988 should take effect as if a section were incorporated that its provisions would be without prejudice to directly enforceable Community rights.[85] We have already seen that Lord Bridge relied on ECA 1972 in his argument in the second *Factortame* case.[86] A similar argument has been made judicially by Laws LJ in *Thoburn*.[87] Laws LJ voiced the same views extra-judicially,[88] as did Lord Hoffmann.[89] The construction view is said to leave the essential core of the traditional view of legal sovereignty intact, in the sense that it is always open to a later Parliament to make it unequivocally clear that it wishes to derogate from EU law. In the absence of such an explicit derogation, s. 2(4) serves to render EU law dominant in the event of a conflict with national law. The attractions of this approach are self-evident. Clashes between EU law and national law can be reconciled while preserving the formal veneer of legal sovereignty. There are nonetheless a number of points to note about the construction approach:

(1) The doctrine of implied repeal or implied disapplication of an earlier statute was itself part of the traditional view of legal sovereignty, and in this sense the construction approach constitutes a modification of traditional doctrine. This

[83] Limits of space preclude coverage of all views on this issue. The sophisticated argument presented by Neil MacCormick can be found in *Questioning Sovereignty, Law, State and Nation in the European Commonwealth* (1999) ch. 6.

[84] [1990] 2 AC 85, 96.

[85] Ibid., 140. [86] [1991] 1 AC 603, 658–9. [87] Above, n. 73.

[88] 'Law and Democracy' [1995] *Public Law* 72, 89.

[89] Lord Hoffmann, 'Europe and the Question of Sovereignty', the Second Lord Neill Lecture, 15 October 1999.

is so even if one adopts Laws LJ's view that implied repeal should not generally apply to constitutional statutes.[90]

(2) The wording of s. 2(4) is notoriously difficult to disentangle. The section is framed in terms of 'any enactment passed or to be passed... shall be construed and have effect' subject to Community rights. The very word 'construed' conveys the sense that the later statute must be capable of being read so as to be compatible with EU law without thereby unduly distorting its meaning or rewriting it. This may well not be possible. A statute might be seriously at odds with EU law, even where Parliament has not, through any express wording, manifested its intent to derogate from the EU norm. It is doubtful whether s. 2(4) was intended to cure all such absences of fit.

(3) Sir William Wade has argued forcefully that Lord Bridge's reasoning entails more than an exercise of construction as we normally understand that phrase. He contends that putatively incorporating s. 2(4) of the 1972 Act into a later statute, such as that of 1988, 'is merely another way of saying that the Parliament of 1972 has imposed a restriction upon the Parliament of 1988', which is what 'the classical doctrine of sovereignty will not permit'.[91] Nor can this be countered simply by saying that the later Parliament could defeat the exercise of construction by expressly providing that the later statute is to prevail over any conflicting EU law. It is by no means clear that an express provision of the kind being postulated here would work, *given* the very reasoning of Lord Bridge. Such a statutory provision would itself be held to be contrary to EU law by the ECJ. This holding would be part of the 'Community law to which by the Act of 1972 the Act of 1988 is held to be subject'.[92] In order to overcome this argument the later statute would have to contain an express provision that it was to prevail over any conflicting EU law and also a provision rendering the relevant provisions of the ECA 1972 inapplicable to the subject matter covered by the later statute.

A second way to conceptualize what the courts have done is to regard it as a *technical legal revolution*. This is the preferred explanation of Sir William Wade who sees the courts' decisions as modifying the ultimate legal principle or rule of recognition on which the legal system is based.[93] On this view the 'rule of recognition is itself a political fact which the judges themselves are able to change when they are confronted with a new situation which so demands'.[94] Such choices are made by the judiciary at the point where the law 'stops'.[95]

There is however a third way in which to regard the courts' jurisprudence. This is to regard decisions about supremacy as being based on *normative arguments of legal principle the content of which can and will vary across time*. This is my own preferred

[90] *Thoburn*, above, n. 73. [91] Wade, above, n. 78, p. 570. [92] Wade, above, n. 78.
[93] H. L. A. Hart, *The Concept of Law* (1961) ch. 6. [94] Wade, above, n. 78, p. 574.
[95] Wade, above, n. 47, pp. 191–2.

view[96] and a similar argument has been advanced by Allan.[97] On this view there is no *a priori* inexorable reason why Parliament, merely because of its very existence, must be regarded as legally omnipotent. The existence of such power, like all power, must be justified by arguments of principle that are normatively convincing. Possible constraints on Parliamentary omnipotence must similarly be reasoned through and defended on normative grounds. This approach fits well with the reasoning of Lord Bridge in the second *Factortame* case. His Lordship did not approach the matter as if the courts were making an unconstrained political choice at the point where the law stopped. His reasoning is more accurately represented as being based on *principle*, in the sense of working through the principled consequences of the UK's membership of the European Union. The contractarian and functional arguments used by Lord Bridge exemplify this style of judicial discourse. They provide sound normative arguments as to why the UK should be bound by EU law while it remains within the European Union. These arguments would moreover be convincing and have force even if s. 2(4) had never been included in the 1972 Act. It may be that those who disagree with the courts' decisions in *Factortame* and *Equal Opportunities Commission* believe that they can counter the normative arguments presented by Lord Bridge.[98] They should then present such arguments since the discourse must be conducted at this level. Debates on such issues are of value.

SUPREMACY AFTER THE TREATY OF LISBON

The Constitutional Treaty contained a supremacy clause in Art. I-6, which provided that the 'Constitution, and law adopted by the Union's institutions in exercising competences conferred on it, shall have primacy over the law of the member states'. There were, however, problems surrounding the interpretation of this provision. It was, for example, unclear whether it was intended to assert the supremacy of EU law over all national law, including national constitutions. If this was indeed the case then it was doubtful whether it would have proven to be constitutionally acceptable to the member states.[99] The Treaty of Lisbon dropped the primacy clause, and replaced it with Declaration 17 which states that the 'Conference recalls that, in accordance with well settled case law of the Court of Justice of the European Union, the Treaties and the law adopted by the Union on the basis of the Treaties have primacy over the law of Member States, under the conditions laid down by the said case law'. This Declaration suffers from the same ambiguity as the primacy clause in the Constitutional Treaty, and it is

[96] Craig, above, nn. 51 and 79, and P. Craig, 'Public Law, Political Theory and Legal Theory' [2000] *Public Law* 211.

[97] Allan, above, n. 78.

[98] It might, for example, be possible to argue that on normative grounds priority should be accorded to an Act of the domestic legislature which expressly derogates from an EU norm, even where the state remains within the European Union. The nature of this argument would however have to be explicated clearly and it is by no means self-evidently correct.

[99] Craig, above, n. 4, ch. 4.

very unlikely that national courts will be persuaded to forget their previous concerns, and accept that EU law prevails over national constitutions, based on a Declaration appended to the Treaties.[100]

DIRECT EFFECT

The doctrine of the supremacy of EU law has been one of the notable achievements of the ECJ. It has been a cornerstone in the building of an EU legal order. The ECJ's other principal contribution has been the doctrine of direct effect. Detailed analysis can be found elsewhere.[101] It is nonetheless important to understand the basic tenets of direct effect in order that its constitutional significance can be appreciated.

DIRECT EFFECT: AN OUTLINE

The meaning of direct effect is not free from ambiguity. It most commonly connotes the idea that individuals can bring actions in national courts in order to vindicate rights secured to them by the Treaty, or legislation made thereunder. It is in this sense a species of private enforcement of EU law. The Treaty makes explicit provision for public enforcement of EU law in TFEU, Art. 258: the Commission can bring an action before the ECJ if member states fail to comply with the Treaty or EU legislation.[102] Whether the framers of the original Treaty intended for there to be direct effect is doubtful. It is, however, clear that private enforcement through direct effect provided a welcome supplement to public enforcement through the Commission, enabling EU law to be applied on a scale and in a manner that would not otherwise have been possible.[103] Moreover, the very fact that individuals were given rights that they could enforce in their own name transformed the very nature of the Treaty. It could no longer be viewed solely as the business of nation states in the manner of many other international Treaties. It was to be a form of social ordering in which individuals were involved in their own capacity. They were no longer to be passive receptors, who had to await action taken on their behalf by others. They were now accorded rights that they could enforce in their own name.

The seminal case in the development of direct effect was *Van Gend en Loos*.[104] Dutch importers challenged the rate of duty imposed on a chemical imported from Germany. They argued that a reclassification of the product under a different heading of the Dutch tariff legislation had led to an increase in the duty and that this was

[100] See the *Treaty of Lisbon Consitutionality Case*, above, n. 81.

[101] Craig and de Búrca, above, n. 12, ch. 7.

[102] It is also possible for a member state to initiate an action against another member state under TFEU, Art. 259, but this rarely happens.

[103] J. Weiler, 'The Community System: The Dual Character of Supranationalism' (1981) 1 *YBEL* 267; P. Craig, 'Once upon a Time in the West: Direct Effect and the Federalization of EEC Law' (1992) 12 *OJLS* 453.

[104] Case 26/62, *Van Gend en Loos* v. *Nederlandse Administratie der Belastingen* [1963] ECR 1.

prohibited under EEC Treaty, Art. 12 (now TFEU, Art. 30), which prohibits the imposition of any new customs duties on imports and also precludes any increase in existing rates. The Dutch court asked the ECJ whether Art. 12 gave rise to rights that could be invoked by individuals before their national courts. The member states argued that the Treaty was simply a compact between states, to be policed in the manner dictated by the Treaty, through public enforcement at the hands of the Commission. They believed that direct effect would alter the nature of the obligations accepted by the signatories.

The ECJ disagreed. It held that the EEC Treaty was not simply to be viewed as a compact between nations. The 'interested parties' included the people. This was affirmed by the preamble and by the existence of institutions charged with the duty of making provisions for those individuals. It was this crucial conceptual starting point which laid the foundation for the now famous passage from the judgment, depicting the European Community as a new legal order for the benefit of which states have limited their sovereign rights, with the consequence that individuals have rights and can be regarded as subjects of the Community. The ECJ emphasized that Art. 12 was a natural candidate for enforcement by individuals through national courts. It stressed the negative nature of the obligation, the fact that it was unconditional, and that its implementation was not dependent on any further measures before being effective under national law.

The years immediately following *Van Gend en Loos* witnessed the application of the concept to a growing range of Treaty articles. The Court was keen to expand the concept given the advantages it possessed. In applying direct effect to other treaty articles the ECJ relaxed the conditions for its application. Direct effect was applied in circumstances where it could not be said that the treaty article in question created a negative obligation which was legally perfect, in the sense that no further action was required by the Community or the member states, and no real residue of discretion existed. The concept was applied to articles of the Treaty dealing with broad areas of regulatory policy, which were as much social as economic.[105] The general test now is that a Treaty article will have direct effect provided that it is intended to confer rights on individuals and that it is sufficiently clear, precise and unconditional.

It was inevitable that the ECJ should be asked whether EC legislation passed pursuant to the Treaty could also have direct effect. There are various types of such legislation. Regulations are defined in TFEU, Art. 288 as having general application. They are binding in their entirety and directly applicable in all member states. The ECJ had no reluctance in concluding that regulations were capable of having direct effect, provided that they were sufficiently certain and precise, which was normally the case.[106]

There has been more difficulty over directives. These are, according to TFEU, Art 288, binding as to the result to be achieved while leaving the choice of form and

[105] Case 2/74, *Reyners* v. *Belgian State* [1974] ECR 631; Case 43/75, *Defrenne* v. *Sabena* [1976] ECR 455.

[106] Case 93/71, *Leonosio* v. *Italian Ministry of Agriculture and Forestry* [1973] CMLR 343; Case 50/76, *Amsterdam Bulb* v. *Produktschap voor Siergewassen* [1977] ECR 137.

methods to the states to which they are addressed. Moreover, while regulations are binding on all states, directives are only binding on the specific states to which they are addressed. Directives have proved to be a particularly useful device for legislating in an enlarged European Union. Many areas of EU policy concern complex topics ranging from product liability to the environment, and from the harmonization of company law to the free movement of capital. If legislation could only be enacted in the form of regulations then it might be difficult to draft a measure with sufficient precision that it could be immediately applicable within the territories of all the member states. The directive enables the European Union to specify the ends to be attained, often in great detail, while leaving a choice of form and methods of implementation to the individual member states.

However, the very nature of directives seemed to indicate that they could not have direct effect: they clearly require further action on the part of the member states, and they leave them with discretion as to methods of implementation. The ECJ nonetheless concluded that directives are capable of having direct effect. It held that it would be inconsistent with the binding effect of directives to exclude the possibility that they can confer rights.[107] The ECJ also drew on TFEU, Art. 267, which allows questions concerning the interpretation and validity of EU law to be referred by national courts to the ECJ. From the generality of this provision the Court concluded that questions relating to directives can be raised by individuals before national courts.[108] A further reason for according direct effect to directives is the estoppel argument: a member state that has not implemented the directive 'may not rely, as against individuals, on its own failure to perform the obligations which the directive entails'.[109] Provided, therefore, that the directive is sufficiently precise, that the basic obligation is unconditional, and that the period for implementation has passed, an individual can derive enforceable rights from a directive.

While the ECJ has been willing to give direct effect to directives it has, however, also held that they only have vertical as opposed to horizontal direct effect. Treaty articles and regulations give individuals rights that can be used both against the state, vertical direct effect, and against private parties, horizontal direct effect. Directives only have vertical direct effect. Thus, in the *Marshall* case[110] the ECJ held that Directive (EEC) 76/207 on equal treatment could not impose obligations on individuals, but only on the state, either *qua* state or *qua* employer. The reason proffered by the court for this limitation was the wording of Art. 288: the binding nature of the directive existed only in relation to 'each Member State to which it is addressed'. The correctness of this ruling and the rationale for this limitation of direct effect are by no means

[107] Case 41/74, *Van Duyn* v. *Home Office* [1974] ECR 1337, para. 12. [108] Ibid., para. 12.

[109] Case 148/78, *Pubblico Ministero* v. *Ratti* [1979] ECR 1629, para. 22.

[110] Case 152/84, *Marshall* v. *Southampton & South West Hampshire Area Health Authority (Teaching)* [1986] ECR 723; Case C-91/92, *Faccini Dori* v. *Recreb Srl* [1994] ECR I-3325.

self-evident.[111] The existence of this limitation has however generated a very complex case law.

This is in part because the ruling that directives only have vertical and not horizontal direct effect requires some definition of the state for these purposes.[112] The complexity of the case law in this area is in part the result of the doctrine of indirect effect. The doctrine is associated with the decision in *Von Colson*.[113] The applicants relied upon the provision of a directive in order to argue that the quantum of relief provided by German law in cases of discrimination was too small. The ECJ held that the provisions were not sufficiently precise to have direct effect. It held, however, that national courts had an obligation to interpret national law to be in conformity with the directive. The purpose of the directive was to provide an effective remedy in cases of discrimination, and if states chose to fulfil this aim through the provision of compensation then this should be adequate in relation to the damage suffered. National courts should, therefore, construe their own national law with this in mind. In *Marleasing*[114] the ECJ held that in applying national law, whether passed before or after the directive, a national court was required to interpret national law in every way possible so as to be in conformity with the directive.

While therefore an individual cannot, in a literal sense, derive rights from a directive in an action against another individual, it is possible to plead the directive in such an action. Once the directive has been placed before the national court, then the obligation to interpret national law in conformity with the directive where possible comes into operation. Where the directive encapsulates precise obligations, and where the national court is minded to interpret national law in the required fashion, this 'indirect' species of enforcement of a directive as between individuals will have much the same results as if the directive had been accorded horizontal direct effect.

The interpretative obligation does however create problems for courts and litigants alike.[115] It places national courts in some difficulty in deciding how far they can go in reconciling national legislation with directives while still remaining within the realm of interpreting, as opposed to rewriting or overruling, national norms. It places litigants in a difficult position since they will have to guess how far their national courts might feel able to go in reconciling national law with differently worded EU legislation. If directives had horizontal direct effect then at least the individual would know that in the event of any inconsistency between the two norms EU law would trump national law.

[111] W. van Gerven, 'The Horizontal Direct Effect of Directive Provisions Revisited: The Reality of Catchwords', in T. Heukels and D. Curtin (eds), *Institutional Dynamics of European Integration, Liber Amicorum for Henry Schermers* (1994); P. Craig, 'The Legal Effect of Directives: Policy, Rules and Exceptions' (2009) 34 *ELR* 349.

[112] Case C-188/89, *Foster* v. *British Gas* [1990] ECR I-3133; D. Curtin, 'The Province of Government: Delimiting the Direct Effect of Directives in the Common Law Context' (1990) 15 *ELR* 195.

[113] Case 14/83, *Von Colson and Kamann* v. *Land Nordrhein-Westfalen* [1984] ECR 1891.

[114] Case C-106/89, *Marleasing SA* v. *La Commercial International De Alimentacion SA* [1990] ECR 4135.

[115] G. de Búrca, 'Giving Effect to European Community Directives' (1992) 55 *MLR* 215.

The jurisprudence in this area has become even more complex as a result of case law in which the ECJ has been willing to accord some measure of 'incidental horizontal direct effect' to a directive in actions between private individuals,[116] and because the ECJ has held that general principles of EU law can have horizontal direct effect, even where they cover the same terrain as a directive which would not have such effect between private parties.[117]

DIRECT EFFECT: CONSTITUTIONAL IMPLICATIONS

There are two ways in which direct effect is of constitutional relevance, one of which is obvious, the other less so.

First, direct effect enables individuals to derive rights that are enforceable in their own national courts from an international treaty and legislation made thereunder. The general position in public international law is that individuals do not derive such rights, and this is so even where they are the beneficiaries of the norms laid down in an international treaty.[118] There are instances where individuals have been held to have such rights, but they are exceptional and there has been nothing on the scale of the direct effect doctrine as developed by the ECJ. Indeed this was one of the reasons why the ECJ sought to distance EC law from general public international law in the *Van Gend* case. It wished to buttress the argument that because the EEC Treaty was distinct from other international treaties, therefore it should not be thought strange that an individual derived rights from the former, even though he normally did not do so from the latter. There was clearly an element of circularity in this argument. The very decision as to whether direct effect did or did not exist was of crucial importance in deciding whether the EEC Treaty really could be regarded as distinct from other international treaties. Major constitutional developments are not infrequently characterized by such reasoning. Be that as it may, direct effect is a central feature of EU law, and recognized as such by all the member states. In terms of national constitutional significance this means that law derived from sources other than Parliament and the common law will avail individuals before their own national courts in a way which has not been so on this scale hitherto.

The second reason why direct effect is of constitutional significance resides in the connection between this concept and the supremacy of EU law. The essence of this connection is that direct effect allows the supremacy doctrine to be applied at national level, and thereby makes it far more potent than it would otherwise

[116] Case C-194/94, *CIA Security International SA* v. *Signalson SA and Securitel SPRL* [1996] ECR I-2201; Case C-129/94, *Criminal Proceedings against Rafael Ruiz Bernaldez* [1996] ECR I-1829; Case C-441/93, *Panagis Pafitis* v. *Trapeza Kentrikis Ellados AE* [1996] ECR I-1347; Case C-443/98, *Unilever Italia SpA* v. *Central Foods SpA* [2000] ECR I-7535. For discussion, J. Coppel, 'Horizontal Direct Effect of Directives' (1997) 28 *ILJ* 69; S. Weatherill, 'Breach of Directives and Breach of Contract' (2001) 26 *ELRev* 177; M. Dougan, 'The Disguised Vertical Direct effect of Directives' [2000] *CLJ* 586; Craig, above, n. 111.

[117] Case C-144/04, *Mangold v Helm* [2005] ECR I-9981.

[118] I. Brownlie, *Principles of Public International Law* (5th edn, 1998) ch. 24.

have been. It would in theory be perfectly possible for the ECJ to have developed its supremacy doctrine even if it had never created direct effect. EU law would have been held to be supreme, and judicially enforceable through actions brought by the Commission under Art. 258. The supremacy doctrine applies to such actions. Direct effect however enables the supremacy of EU law to be enforced by individuals through their own national courts. This renders such supremacy more effective for a number of reasons. Member states might be more inclined to listen to their own national courts than to the ECJ. The national courts become EU courts in their own right, being able to pass judgment on national primary legislation in the context of an action brought by an individual. Direct effect spreads the workload of enforcing EU law, and its supremacy, across all the individuals and the national courts of the European Union.

FUNDAMENTAL RIGHTS

There is little doubt that most claims to protect rights will now be brought under the Human Rights Act 1998 (HRA 1998).[119] It will, however, be open to claimants to use rights-based arguments derived from EU law.

The European Union promulgated a Charter of Fundamental Rights in 2000. The ECJ had, however, developed a fundamental rights' jurisprudence prior to this. The original EEC Treaty contained no list of traditional fundamental rights. The catalyst for the creation of such rights was the threat of revolt by some national courts. Individuals who were dissatisfied with an EC regulation argued before their national court that it was inconsistent with rights in their national constitutions. The ECJ denied that EC norms could be challenged in this manner. However, in order to stem any national rebellion it also declared that fundamental rights were part of the general principles of EC law, and that the compatibility of an EC norm with such rights would be tested by the ECJ.[120] It became clear that national norms could also be challenged for compliance with fundamental rights. This was so where member states were applying provisions of EC law based on the protection of human rights;[121] where they were enforcing EC rules on behalf of the European Community or interpreting EC rules;[122] or where member states were seeking to derogate from a requirement of EC law.[123] The supremacy doctrine applied with the consequence that national norms, including primary legislation, which were inconsistent with EC law could be declared inapplicable

[119] See Chapter 3 above.

[120] Case 11/70, *Internationale Handelsgesellschaft* v. *Einfuhr- und Vorratstelle für Getreide und Futtermittel* [1970] ECR 1125, 1134.

[121] Case 222/84, *Johnston* v. *Chief Constable of the Royal Ulster Constabulary* [1986] ECR 1651.

[122] Case 5/88, *Wachauf* v. *Germany* [1989] ECR 2609; Case 63/83, *R.* v. *Kent Kirk* [1984] ECR 2689.

[123] Case C-260/89, *Elliniki Radiophonia Tileorassi AE* v. *Dimotki Etairia Pliroforissis and Sotirios Kouvelas* [1991] ECR I-2925; Case C-159/90, *Society for the Protection of Unborn Children Ireland Ltd* v. *Grogan* [1991] ECR I-4685.

in the instant case. This is by way of contrast with the HRA 1998 where the courts are limited, in cases involving primary legislation, to making a declaration of incompatibility under s. 4.

The European Union Charter of Fundamental Rights of the European Union was promulgated in 2000.[124] The direct catalyst for this development came from the European Council. In June 1999 the Cologne European Council[125] decided that there should be a Charter of Fundamental Rights to consolidate the fundamental rights applicable at EU level and to make their importance and relevance more visible to the citizens of the European Union. It was made clear that the document should include economic and social rights, as well as traditional civil and political rights. A Convention was established to produce the Charter, which consisted of representatives of the member states, a member of the Commission, members of the EP, and representatives from national Parliaments. The Charter was accepted by the member states, but its legal status was left undecided by the Nice Treaty.

This issue has now been addressed by the Treaty of Lisbon. The Charter is legally binding and has the same legal value as the TEU and the TFEU.[126] The Charter itself is not therefore incorporated in the Treaty of Lisbon, but it is accorded the same legal value as the Treaties. The Treaty of Lisbon is premised on the version of the Charter as amended in 2004, and this version has been reissued in the *Official Journal*.[127] The Treaty of Lisbon also stipulates that the European Union shall accede to the European Convention on Human Rights.[128] The Member States are bound by the Charter only when they are implementing EU law.[129] Commentators disagree as to whether the term 'implement' means that Charter rights can only be used against member states in a narrower range of cases than was possible under the ECJ's previous fundamental rights' jurisprudence.[130] The better view is however that member states are bound by the Charter whenever they act within the scope of EU law,[131] and this view is supported by the explanatory memorandum, which must be given due regard when interpreting Charter rights.[132] The UK and Poland negotiated a Protocol designed to limit the application of the Charter in certain respects.[133] Space precludes detailed interpretation of this Protocol here. Suffice it to say for the present that it does not wholly

[124] Charter of Fundamental Rights of the European Union [2000] OJ C364/1.

[125] 3–4 June 1999.

[126] TEU, Art. 6(1).

[127] Charter of Fundamental Rights of the European Union [2007] OJ C303/1; Explanations Relating to the Charter of Fundamental Rights [2007] OJ C303/17. The Charter has been reissued with the Treaty of Lisbon [2010] OJ C83/2.

[128] TEU Art. 6(2).

[129] Charter, Art. 51(1).

[130] Compare L. Besselink, 'The Member States, the National Constitutions and the Scope of the Charter' (2001) 8 *MJ* 68, and R. Alonso Garcia, 'The General Provisions of the Charter of Fundamental Rights' (2002) 8 *ELJ* 492.

[131] Craig, above, n. 4, ch. 6.

[132] TEU, Art. 6(1).

[133] Protocol (No. 30) on the Application of the Charter of Fundamental Rights of the European Union to Poland and to the United Kingdom.

exclude the application of the Charter in the UK, but merely limits the application of certain Charter provisions.[134]

NATIONAL COURTS AS EU COURTS

Those who are not familiar with EU law are accustomed to think that there are only two EU courts: the ECJ and the GC. This belies reality. National courts have general jurisdiction over matters of EU law. This is a matter worthy of constitutional note. The explanation for this role played by national courts is to be found in a conjunction of two factors.

The first is the very concept of direct effect considered above. The fact that individuals are able to enforce their EU rights through national courts means that it will be the national judiciaries that frequently apply EU law doctrine.

This first factor has been reinforced by a second. The ECJ made it clear that national courts should apply existing case law of the ECJ and the GC. They should therefore only refer a case to the ECJ pursuant to TFEU, Art. 267 where the question before the national court had not already been adequately answered in a previous ruling given by the ECJ. This became clear from the seminal decision in the *Da Costa* case.[135] The facts in the case were materially identical to those in *Van Gend en Loos*,[136] as were the questions posed by the national court. The ECJ acknowledged that a national court of final resort was bound to refer a question to the ECJ, but then qualified this by stating that 'the authority of an interpretation under Article 177 already given by the Court may deprive the obligation of its purpose and thus empty it of its substance'.[137] This would especially be the case where the question raised was 'materially identical with a question which has already been the subject of a preliminary ruling in a similar case'.[138] The ECJ made it clear that the national court could refer the issue again if it had new questions to ask. It made it equally clear that if this was not so, then it would simply repeat the ruling given in the original case from which the legal point arose. The *Da Costa* case, therefore, initiated what is in effect a system of precedent, whereby national courts would apply the prior rulings of the ECJ. The ECJ extended this idea in *CILFIT*[139] where it held that the obligation to refer contained in Art. 267(3) could also be qualified 'where previous decisions of the Court have already dealt with the point of law in question, irrespective of the nature of the proceedings which led to those decisions, even though the questions at issue are not strictly identical'. Provided that the point of law had already been determined by the ECJ, this should be relied on by a national court in a later case, thereby obviating the need for a reference. The

[134] Craig, above, n. 4, ch. 6.

[135] Cases 28–30/62, *Da Costa en Schaake NV, Jacob Meijer NV and Hoechst-Holland NV* v. *Nederlandse Belastingadministratie* [1963] ECR 31.

[136] Above, n. 104.

[137] Above, n. 135, p. 38. [138] Above, n. 135.

[139] Case 283/81, *Srl CILFIT and Lanificio di Gavardo SpA* v. *Ministry of Health* [1982] ECR 3415, para. 14.

application of precedent by national courts has enhanced the enforcement of EU law, and eased the workload on the ECJ and the GC. The EU system of adjudication could not have functioned as it has if the national courts had not been accorded this role.

The *Equal Opportunities Commission* case[140] considered earlier provides a good example of this process at work. Not only did the House of Lords make a declaration that provisions of a statute were incompatible with EU law, but it did so without making a reference to the ECJ, having satisfied itself that the existing ECJ precedents meant that the national statute was indirectly discriminatory.

CONCLUSION

The EEC has, since its inception, had an impact on national constitutional law. The significance of this impact has become greater over time, in part through the ECJ's jurisprudence and in part through subsequent Treaty amendments. The Treaty of Lisbon has brought further changes that are relevant legally and politically in the ways explicated in this chapter.

The most significant constitutional change on the immediate horizon in our relations with the European Union is the 2011 European Union Bill, which provides for a regime of referendum and statutory locks. The obligation to hold a referendum and/or for there to be an Act of Parliament is determined primarily by cl. 4, which is very broad. It covers all forms of treaty amendments that accord new competence to the European Union or increase existing competence, subject to the caveat that the Bill in effect excludes new treaty accessions from the need for a referendum. The Bill raises a wide range of legal and political issues, and there are question marks over the compatibility of parts of the Bill with EU law.

FURTHER READING

Anthony, G., *UK Public Law & European Law, The Dynamics of Legal Integration* (2002).

Birkinshaw, P., *European Public Law* (2003).

Craig, P., *The Lisbon Treaty, Law, Politics and Treaty Reform* (2010).

Craig, P. and de Búrca, G., *EU Law, Text, Cases and Materials* (5th edn, 2011).

Ladeur, K.-H. (ed.), *Europeanisation of Administrative Law: Transforming National Decision-Making Procedures* (2001).

MacCormick, N., *Questioning Sovereignty* (1999).

Nicol, D., *EC Membership and the Judicialization of British Politics* (2001).

Pinder, J., *The Building of the European Union* (3rd edn, 1998).

Slaughter, A.-M., Stone Sweet, A. and Weiler, J. H. H. (eds), *The European Court of Justice and National Courts: Doctrine and Jurisprudence* (1998).

[140] Above, n. 69.

Urwin, D., *The Community of Europe: A History of European Integration since 1945* (2nd edn, 1995).
de Witte, B., 'Direct Effect, Primacy and the Nature of the Legal Order', in Craig, P. and de Búrca, G. (eds), *The Evolution of EU Law* (2nd edn, 2011) ch. 12.

USEFUL WEBSITE

European Union: **http://europa.eu**

5

THE INTERNATIONALIZATION OF PUBLIC LAW AND ITS IMPACT ON THE UK

David Feldman[1]

SUMMARY

Municipal public law is always influenced by foreign developments. The existence of a state depends at least partly on its recognition by other states. Political theories and legal ideas have always flowed across and between regions of the world. Yet any state has good reasons for controlling the introduction of foreign legal and constitutional norms to its own legal order. National interests and a commitment to the Rule of Law, human rights, and democratic accountability demand national controls over foreign influences. This chapter considers the nature and legitimacy of the channels and filters, particularly as they apply in the UK, in the light of general public law standards.

INTRODUCTION

As in other countries, public law in the UK is affected by international law, and influenced by external and international considerations. Developments outside a territory have always influenced its internal organization and external affairs. States surrender part of their autonomy in exchange for the benefits of co-operation, allowing them to pursue objectives unattainable without coordination. International organizations can help to maintain peace, bolster social or economic stability, and foster free trade and open markets. At the same time, co-operation has significant costs for states. They must

[1] I am grateful to Professor John Bell, His Honour Ian Campbell, Professor Constance Grewe, Professor Jeffrey Jowell, Professor Didier Maus, Professor Nicolas Maziau, Professor Dawn Oliver, Judge Tudor Pantiru, Professor Cheryl Saunders, Anna-Lena Sjolund, Christian Steiner, and Dr Rebecca Williams for valuable discussions of the subject-matter of this chapter and helpful comments on drafts. Remaining errors and idiosyncrasies are, of course, entirely my responsibility.

take account of internationally agreed objectives and values in their internal decision-making. Sometimes they must subordinate their own interests to those of other states. This may compromise systems of accountability for the exercise of public power which are traditionally based on the political and legal processes operating within states. Traditional criteria for the legitimacy of state action, such as democracy, compliance with Rule of Law standards, or respect for fundamental rights, may be hard to apply when decision-making processes are shaped by international agreements or institutions which do not contain equivalent systems for control and accountability of the exercise of power. This leads some people to argue that a 'democratic deficit' in the European Union leads to a crisis of legitimacy which the Treaty of Lisbon has only partly addressed.[2]

This has consequences for UK public law. The structures of important state institutions are potentially challenged by such organizations as the Group of States against Corruption (GRECO), operating under the aegis of the Council of Europe,[3] and the European Charter of Local Self-Government,[4] which the UK ratified with effect from 1 August 1998. This chapter attempts to draw out three characteristics of the relationship between national systems of public law and international developments. The first is the importance of international influence over the very existence and fundamental structures of states. No state is an island (although some islands are states). Secondly, the channels between national and international planes normally permit influence to be exerted in both directions, and are usually subject to filters allowing states to preserve an element of autonomy, although the nature and effectiveness of the filters depends on national traditions and interests. Thirdly, the mechanisms by which states allow foreign influences to affect their systems of public law reflect their constitutional traditions and patterns of social interaction, and their legitimacy depends at least in part on their compatibility with those traditions and patterns.

[2] See Chapter 4 above.

[3] GRECO, *First Evaluation Report on the United Kingdom* (2001), criticized the UK Parliament's handling of complaints against members, because (e.g.) the Parliamentary Commissioner for Standards, who dealt with the House of Commons, had not been put on a statutory basis, and there was no independent system for dealing with complaints against members of the House of Lords. See A. Doig, 'Sleaze fatigue: an inauspicious year for democracy' (2002) *Parliamentary Affairs* 389; GRECO RC-I (2003) 8E, *Compliance Report on the United Kingdom*, 7–11 July 2003, paras 27–31; GRECO RC-I (2003) 8E Addendum, 1 July 2005, paras 9–13. The position changed in 2009 after it was revealed that some members of both Houses had made highly questionable use of their entitlement to claim reimbursement of expenses. The House of Commons is now subject to the statutory Independent Parliamentary Standards Authority: see Parliamentary Standards Act 2009, as amended by the Constitutional Reform and Governance Act 2010. The House of Lords is still self-regulating, but members are now required to sign and comply with a new Code of Conduct (www.publications.parliament.uk/pa/ld/ldcond/code.pdf) from the start of the new Parliament after the general election in May 2010. Complaints are investigated by an independent House of Lords Commissioner for Standards, who reports to the Lords' Conduct Sub-Committee of the Committee on Privileges and Conduct. Members may appeal to the Committee against a recommendation of the Commissioner or Sub-Committee.

[4] European Treaty Series No. 122 (1985).

THE IMPORTANCE OF FOREIGN INFLUENCES TO THE FOUNDATIONS OF PUBLIC LAW

An entity or group of entities may seek the status of statehood in a variety of circumstances: for example, following the break-up of an existing state, the attempted secession of part of a state, a merger of existing states, or an exercise of foreign control over a state. In such situations, the reaction of other states is of great consequence when deciding whether the entity has the necessary characteristics of statehood. International lawyers agree that recognition by other states is important, although they disagree about its strictly legal significance. Some hold that recognition by other states is legally constitutive of the new state as a body with full personality in international law (the 'constitutive theory'). Others argue that recognition is politically and evidentially rather than legally important: it does not constitute the new state, but is a sign that other states accept that the new state already has that status in international law (the 'declaratory theory'). Whichever view is correct (and the balance of opinion currently tends towards the declaratory theory),[5] lack of recognition is at least persuasive evidence that an entity is not a state,[6] and international recognition may be crucial, as when the United Nations agreed to the establishment of the state of Israel in 1948. Sometimes, as in the case of Cyprus, the international community may intervene in the process of developing statehood, and effectively control the form and content of the new state's first constitution. If the international community uses armed force to end a conflict and secure a state's continued existence, it may impose a new constitution designed to protect the interests of the various parties to the conflict in order to give effect to the agreement which brings it to a close, as in Bosnia and Herzegovina in 1995.[7]

But there are no internationally accepted criteria for recognition. Individual states must decide on what grounds to recognize other entities as states. Most states look for an organized governmental authority exercising effective control over a permanent population and a defined territory, together with an ability to carry on external relations independently of other states and give effect to international obligations.[8] Other relevant factors may include: respect for the UN Charter, human rights, and established international frontiers; a commitment to peaceful resolution of international disputes; and respect for the rights of minorities.[9] None of these factors is necessarily decisive. For example, when the constituent parts of the former Yugoslavia broke

[5] See the discussions in James Crawford, *The Creation of States in International Law* (2nd edn, 2006) ch. 1, esp. 26–8; Ian Brownlie, *Principles of International Law* (6th edn, 2003) 86–8; Malcolm Shaw, *International Law* (6th edn, 2008) 197–208.

[6] Shaw, *International Law*, ibid., pp. 207–8.

[7] For an illuminating analysis of the kinds and consequences of international intervention in the formation of states and their constitutions, see Nicolas Maziau, 'L'internationalisation du pouvoir constituant' 2002 (3) *Revue Générale de Droit International Public* 549–79.

[8] See e.g. Montevideo Convention on the Rights and Duties of States 1933, Art. 1; American Law Institute, *Restatement of the Foreign Relations Law of the United States*, 3rd edn, 1987, § 201.

[9] See Shaw, above, n. 5, pp. 374–5.

up from 1992, the government of one of the republics claiming the status of a new state, Bosnia and Herzegovina, controlled only about half its territory when it was recognized by (among others) the UK. The remainder was under the control of anti-secessionist military groups. The integrity of the new state was secured only when military action by the North Atlantic Treaty Organization (NATO) ended three years of war, and the Dayton–Paris Accord of 1995 imposed a General Framework Agreement for Peace (GFAP) on the warring parties. Among other things, this set in stone an internationally agreed constitution, and put in place continuing international control through an international Peace Implementation Council and a High Representative with extensive powers. It has been argued that this external control makes it hard to accept that Bosnia and Herzegovina is an independent sovereign state.[10]

It is some time since the UK has faced that level of external intervention in its affairs, but ideas from abroad have shaped its structure for centuries. Medieval feudalism was imported from western Europe,[11] and overlay the pre-Norman structures to produce a system of government which made possible the growing central authority of the monarchy and the standardization of law across the country. Similarly, between the 10th and 12th centuries, Scotland:

> was regulated by a complex patchwork combining a typically western European feudal framework with Celtic custom, which can be traced in many of its details to Irish law tracts of the seventh or eighth centuries. The result was what has been called a 'hybrid kingdom', and one of its marks was the emergence of a composite common law of Scotland by the end of the twelfth century.[12]

Public law and political theory in England and Scotland were essentially modelled on those of western European at that period. In the 13th century, the model was extended to Wales by military conquest. As elsewhere in Europe, there was a tension between the gradual centralization of law and bureaucracy and the vigorous desire of the nobility and a developing class of free men for an increased role in decision-making.[13] The tension remained, but the structures of the constitution developed so as to accommodate both central and local authority and recognize the interests of a wider variety of free people than previously within the 'community of the realm',[14] encapsulated in such instruments as the Magna Carta of 1215 and the Statute of Marlborough 1267, which provided that writs should be issued freely against those who were alleged to have committed breaches of the Magna Carta, putting the Charter of 1215 (or at least those parts of it which were capable of judicial enforcement) on the same footing as a statute.

[10] For an analysis of efforts to end the war and the Dayton Agreement, see Christine Bell, *Peace Agreements and Human Rights* (2000) esp. pp. 91–117. On whether post-Dayton Bosnia and Herzegovina is a state, see Gerald Knaus and Felix Martin, 'Lessons from Bosnia and Herzegovina: Travails of the European Raj' (2003) 14(3) *Journal of Democracy* 60–74; Crawford, above, n. 5, pp. 398–401; Shaw, above, n. 5, p. 201.

[11] See R. C. van Caenegem, *An Historical Introduction to Western Constitutional Law* (1995) ch. 4.

[12] Michael Lynch, *Scotland: A New History* (1992) 53 (footnotes omitted).

[13] van Caenegem, above, n. 11, ch. 5.

[14] See Sir Maurice Powicke, *The Thirteenth Century 1216–1307* (2nd edn, 1962) 131–50, 216–18.

By the 16th century, British public lawyers and administrators travelling to Avignon, Paris, Pavia, and other European universities to study Roman law and Greco-Roman political theory at the fountainhead of the Renaissance brought their learning home.[15] In the 17th century, the English state was effectively re-founded three times (in 1649 after the Civil War and the execution of King Charles I, at the end of the Protectorate in 1660, and after the flight of King James II in December 1688). The royalists in the lead-up to the Civil War relied on ideas derived from the law of nations (*ius gentium*) or natural law to bolster their claim to the divine right of kings,[16] and political philosophers, including Thomas Hobbes on the side of absolute monarchy and John Locke for constitutional monarchy, were part of major western European philosophical traditions.[17]

In 1706–07, the Treaty of Union between England and Scotland led to the foundation of the United Kingdom of Great Britain. It was an instrument of international law, negotiated between the representatives of two sovereign nations and given effect in national law by a combination of Acts of their respective Parliaments and action taken by the monarch of each state (who happened by coincidence to be the same person).[18] Events on the international plane continue in the 21st century to help shape the UK's constitution through international human rights and other Treaties, and participation in international organizations such as the United Nations, the Council of Europe, NATO, and the European Union. For example, the devolution legislation allows the UK government in Westminster to prevent the devolved authorities legislating in a manner incompatible with the UK's international obligations or EU law.[19] International law is woven into the fabric of public law.

INTERNATIONALIZATION AND PROTECTION FOR NATIONAL INTERESTS: INFLUENCES, CONTROLS, AND FILTERS

National authorities do not usually allow ideas from elsewhere to permeate national institutions unless two conditions are met. First, the state must have something to

[15] W. Gordon Zeefeld, *Foundations of Tudor Policy* (1969) chs I–VI, esp. pp. 20–2, 50–1, 79–80, 129–31; David Ibbetson and Andrew Lewis, 'The Roman Law tradition', in A. D. E. Lewis and D. J. Ibbetson (eds), *The Roman Law Tradition* (1994) 1–14.

[16] See e.g. J. W. Gough, *Fundamental Law in English Constitutional History* (1955) 12–174. The parliamentarians looked more to the pre-Norman period of English constitutional history: see Christopher Hill, 'Sir Edward Coke – Myth-Maker', in Christopher Hill, *Intellectual Origins of the English Revolution* (1972) 225–65.

[17] On the western European roots of the idea of public law as developed in the UK, see Martin Loughlin, *Foundations of Public Law* (2010) Introduction and Pt I; John Allison, *The English Historical Constitution: Continuity, Change and European Effects* (2007).

[18] For discussion of the implications of this, see Elizabeth Wicks, 'A new constitution for a new state? The 1707 Union of England and Scotland' (2001) 117 *LQR* 109–26, and Elizabeth Wicks, *The Evolution of a Constitution: Eight Key Moments in British Constitutional History* (2006) ch. 2.

[19] Northern Ireland Act 1998, ss 6, 14(5) and 26; Scotland Act 1998, ss 29(2), 35(1) and 58; Government of Wales Act 2006, ss 80, 81 and 82.

gain from accepting the ideas, either in terms of rationalizing or guaranteeing its own organization and security (as in the case of Bosnia and Herzegovina in 1995) or because of a promise of reciprocal benefits from other states. Secondly, unless the state faces irresistible armed force or economic sanctions it will insist on being able to influence the development and application of the ideas which it agrees to accept. Internationalization is thus a two-way street. Benefits must flow inwards to the nation, and the state must have the benefit of being able to influence or export as well as import ideas.

International law reflects this in that a Treaty does not bind a state unless it has accepted the obligations arising under it. Internally, state constitutions usually impose filters to ensure that the state's legislative organs maintain control of the impact on municipal law of international Treaties (binding agreements between two or more states), customary international law (those state practices internationally accepted as obligatory by most states),[20] and general principles of law.[21] Constitutions usually adopt a position lying somewhere between two poles, commonly known as 'monism' and 'dualism'. A 'monist' approach draws no clear division between national and international law, allowing both customary international law and treaties[22] to produce effects in national law without the need for national legislation to give effect to them. In civil law systems, the influence of classical Roman law ensured that *ius gentium*, which by the time of Justinian had come to be seen as founded on human reason assumed to be common to Roman citizens and foreigners alike,[23] encouraged the adoption of constitutions which made at least some international obligations directly part of municipal law, treating national and international law as parts of a single, continuous fabric of law, rather than two entirely separate systems. This makes it easier to allow standards of civilized behaviour which form part of international law, including respect for human rights and prohibitions on genocide, torture, and other crimes against humanity, to take effect within states without the need for legislation, and to some extent to control inconsistent national laws.[24] Furthermore, if the existence of a state and its legal system depend on that state being recognized as meeting criteria for statehood set by international law (the 'constitutive theory' mentioned earlier), there can logically be no separation between national and international law.[25] Constitutions in civil law countries, and some common law countries like the USA which rebelled against British control, usually adopt some form of monism.

But there are sound reasons for having filters at national level to control the way in which the obligations affect national law- and policy-making. The principled reason is the desire to uphold constitutional guarantees, including the Rule of Law, and keep

[20] Shaw, above, n. 5, pp. 68–88. [21] Shaw, above, n. 5, 92–103. [22] Shaw, above, n. 5, 88–92.

[23] See Barry Nicholas, *An Introduction to Roman Law* (1962) 54–9; Wolfgang Kunkel, *An Introduction to Roman Legal and Constitutional History*, trans. J. M. Kelly (2nd edn, 1973) 100.

[24] See e.g. Hersh Lauterpacht, *International Law: Collected Papers*, vol. I (1970).

[25] Hans Kelsen, *General Theory of Law and State* (1946) 363–80; Hans Kelsen, *The Pure Theory of Law*, trans. Max Knight (1967) 328–47.

in the hands of the nations the democratic control of and accountability for national law and policy, in order to maintain the legitimacy of politics and public law in the state. The pragmatic reason is that international obligations may be contrary to the national interest and may derail important national objectives. 'Dualism' provides such a filter by treating national and international law as two separate systems. This prevents international law from directly affecting national law. The UK has traditionally adopted a broadly dualist approach.

However, there is no sharp distinction between monist and dualist approaches. The principled and pragmatic considerations mentioned earlier ensure that few monist states are without controls over the incorporation of international law, while in dualist states the separation between municipal and international law has never been total. Monist states typically maintain essential national interests in the face of international pressure by providing that treaty obligations become enforceable through national law without national legislation only under strict conditions: they must be reciprocal obligations, binding on all the states parties to the treaty; and they must be compatible with the national constitution, which remains hierarchically superior to treaties as a matter of national constitutional law. For example, *Grundgesetz* (Basic Law) of the Federal Republic of Germany, Art. 25 makes the 'general rules of public international law' integral to federal law, creating rights and duties directly for inhabitants of the federal territory and taking precedence over national laws. This is an understandable reaction to the disregard, during the Third Reich, of the norms of public international law. On the other hand, under Art. 59.2 treaties which regulate the political relations of the Federation or relate to matters of federal legislation must have the consent or participation, in the form of a federal statute, of the bodies which are competent to make such federal legislation, and Treaties affecting federal administration must have the consent or participation of the competent bodies for federal administration. Even then the treaty has the status of a federal statute, it is of no effect if it is incompatible with a provision of the Basic Law, including those protecting state sovereignty, democracy, and fundamental rights.[26]

Furthermore, the constitutional structures of monist states normally allow the legislature to control the exercise of treaty-making power by state institutions authorized by the constitution to exercise that power. For example, the US Constitution provides that treaty obligations, together with the Constitution and federal laws made in pursuance of it, are the supreme law of the land,[27] but the President may make treaties only with the concurrence of two-thirds of the members of the Senate who

[26] *Internationale Handelsgesellschaft mbH* v. *Einfuhr- und Vorratstelle für Getreide und Futtermittel* [1974] 2 CMLR 540 (BvfG); *Re the Application of Wünsche Handelsgesellschaft* [1987] 3 CMLR 225 (BvfG); *Unification Treaty Constitutionality Case* (1991) 94 ILR 42 (BvfG); *Lisbon Treaty Constitutionality Case*, BVerfG, 2 BvE 2/08, 30 June 2009, available at www.bverfg.de/entscheidungen/es20090630_2bve000208.html; English translation available at www.bundesverfassungsgericht.de/entscheidungen/es20090630_2bve000208en.html. On which see Jo Erik Khushal Murkens, '"We want our constitution back" – the revival of national sovereignty in the German Federal Constitutional Court's decision on the Lisbon Treaty' [2010] *PL* 530–50.

[27] US Constitution, Art. VI *bis*.

are present.[28] The legislative arm has a veto – at least in theory – over the USA's treaty obligations, and so over the state of federal law, although executive agreements, such as those recognizing foreign states, do not require Congressional approval, and may allow federal authorities to enforce obligations arising from them despite the Tenth Amendment, which reserves to the states all powers not conferred by the Constitution on federal authorities.[29] In France, Constitution of the Fifth Republic (1958), Art. 52 provides that the President of the Republic negotiates and usually also ratifies treaties, and under Art. 55 once ratified or approved they prevail over legislation if the other state party reciprocally gives similar effect to the treaty obligations in its own law. But Art. 53 preserves parliamentary control by providing that certain kinds of treaties may be ratified or approved only under an enactment, and take effect only after ratification or enactment.[30] What is more, no cession, exchange or annexation of territory is valid without the consent of the population of the territory.[31]

By the same token, in the UK dualism is only partial. Courts have long accepted that 'customary international law', the part of international law consisting of standards accepted by states by common consent without the need for multinational treaties or resolutions of international organizations, forms part of municipal law automatically, by incorporation, without the need for legislation, if sufficiently clear.[32] However, this is subject to the operation of certain filters. First, customary international law is incorporated only so far as it is compatible with national statutes and binding case law. For example, in *Al-Adsani* v. *Government of Kuwait* the Court of Appeal held that torture was contrary to customary international law, but that the plaintiff, who claimed to have been tortured by Kuwaiti officials in Kuwait, could not sue the Government of Kuwait in English courts because by clear words the State Immunity Act 1978 established that the defendant could still rely on state immunity notwithstanding any violation of customary international law.[33] State immunity remains an important principle of international law.[34] It has been restricted by the Convention against Torture and other Cruel, Inhuman or Degrading Treatment or Punishment 1984 (the Torture

[28] Ibid., Art. II.2 *bis*.

[29] See *United States* v. *Belmont* 301 US 324 (1937) on the recognition by the USA of the USSR. See also *Breard* v. *Commonwealth* 248 Va. 68, 445 S.E. 2d 670 (1994), cert. denied 513 US 971 (1994).

[30] The types of Treaty are: 'peace treaties, trade treaties, treaties or agreements concerning international organizations, those which commit national resources, those which modify provisions of a legislative character, those concerning personal status, and those involving the cession, exchange, or annexation or territory', Art. 53, trans. in S. E. Finer, Vernon Bogdanor and Bernard Rudden, *Comparing Constitutions* (1995) 229.

[31] For further examples, see Shaw, above, n. 5, pp. 151–62.

[32] See Shaw, above, n. 5, pp. 141–8; *Trendtex Banking Corporation* v. *Central Bank of Nigeria* [1977] QB 529 (CA); *J. H. Rayner (Mincing Lane) Ltd* v. *Department of Trade and Industry* [1990] 2 AC 418 (HL).

[33] (1996) 107 ILR 536 (CA). This was held not to violate the right to be free of torture or the right to a fair hearing under ECHR, Arts 3 and 6.1: Application No. 35763/97, *Al-Adsani v. United Kingdom*, judgment of 21 November 2001, RJD 2001-XI.

[34] *Jones* v. *Ministry of the Interior of the Kingdom of Saudi Arabia and another (Secretary of State for Constitutional Affairs and others intervening)* [2006] UKHL 26, [2007] 1 AC 270 (HL); Shaw, above, n. 5, pp. 715–8.

Convention) to allow criminal proceedings against state agents, but it has not been limited so as to allow civil proceedings against representatives of states for torture.

Secondly, crimes in customary international law do not automatically become crimes justiciable before domestic courts in England and Wales. The common law is no longer capable of generating new crimes, and there are good constitutional reasons for requiring parliamentary authorization for new crimes and extensions to the criminal jurisdiction of domestic courts.[35] The requirement preserves parliamentary sovereignty and the integrity of municipal common law, and protects people against uncontrolled creation of criminal liabilities. The value of filters protecting a state's constitution and law from being changed without national authorization explains the decision in *R.* v. *Jones (Margaret)*[36] that the crime of aggression in international law was not part of English criminal law, so people who used force to try to prevent the UK's preparations for the attack on Iraq in 2003 could not rely on the defence under Criminal Law Act 1967, s. 3 of having used reasonable force to prevent an unlawful act. Nevertheless, it points up the moral argument for a more monistic approach in order to uphold international criminal law.

The interplay of customary international law, international Treaty obligations, and UK statute is illustrated by *R.* v. *Bow Street Metropolitan Stipendiary Magistrate and others ex parte Pinochet Ugarte (No. 3)*.[37] The applicant was a former President of Chile who was alleged to have authorized acts of torture and murder during his period in power, including some against Spanish citizens. A Spanish judge had issued an international arrest warrant seeking his extradition to Spain to face trial. The applicant had been arrested in England while on a visit to receive medical treatment. The question was whether he could be extradited. An exceptional seven-judge appellate committee of the House of Lords held:

(a) unanimously, that a head of state would normally be entitled to claim immunity from legal process in the UK by virtue of a combination of customary international law and UK statutes dealing with state immunity and diplomatic immunity;[38]

(b) by a majority of four to three,[39] that torture (unlike murder) is an international crime against humanity by virtue of customary international law, and a peremptory norm of general international law (sometimes called *jus cogens*), defined in Vienna Convention on the Law of Treaties 1969, Art. 53 as 'a norm accepted and recognized by the international community of States as a whole

[35] Roger O'Keefe, 'Customary international crimes in English courts' [2001] *BYIL* 293, 335.

[36] [2006] UKHL 16, [2007] 1 AC 136 (HL). [37] [2000] 1 AC 147 (HL).

[38] See State Immunity Act 1978, s. 20(1) read together with Diplomatic Privileges Act 1964, Sched. 1, para. 39 (giving effect to the Vienna Convention on Diplomatic Relations).

[39] Lords Browne-Wilkinson, Hope of Craighead, Hutton, and Saville of Newdigate. Lords Millett and Phillips of Worth Matravers dissented on the ground that conspiracy to murder in Spain was also an international crime for which no immunity would be available. Lord Goff dissented on the ground that the statutory immunity applied even in relation to torture.

as a norm from which no derogation is permitted and which can be modified only by a subsequent norm of general international law having the same character', so that it overrides incompatible rules in customary international law or treaties;

(c) unanimously, that the Extradition Act 1989 in the UK prevented extradition for a crime which was not a crime in the UK (as well as in the state which has requested extradition of the suspect) at the time when it was committed (known as the 'double criminality rule');

(d) by a majority of four to three,[40] that torture committed outside the UK did not become a criminal offence in the UK until two conditions were met. First, there had to be legislation to make it a criminal offence. This was done by the Criminal Justice Act 1988, which came into force on 29 September 1988. Secondly, all the relevant states (Spain, Chile, and the UK) had to have ratified the International Convention against Torture and other Cruel, Inhuman or Degrading Treatment or Punishment 1984, which required states to recognize and provide in their own law for universal jurisdiction over offences of torture. In other words, every state party to the Convention was then obliged in international law both to accept jurisdiction over such cases in its own courts (wherever the torture was alleged to have been committed) and to recognize that other states' courts had similar jurisdiction. That happened on 8 December 1988; and

(e) by a majority of six to one, that after 8 December 1988 torture committed abroad was a criminal offence in the UK and so was an extradition crime.

This makes three constitutional principles clear. First, the UK operates a dualist filter not only in respect of treaties, but even in respect of a peremptory norm of general international law which establishes a crime against humanity. Only a legislature can authorize courts in the UK to impose criminal liability. Secondly, even when legislation is in place, English law[41] may recognize a treaty binding on the states involved in a case as an additional necessary step in establishing that there is international jurisdiction. In other words, English courts do not give effect to treaties as such, but may require a treaty before accepting that there is jurisdiction to extradite someone for an international crime against humanity, even when that crime has been shown to exist under statute and customary international law. Thirdly, so far as UK statutes dealing with state and diplomatic immunity are designed to give effect to international

[40] Lords Browne-Wilkinson, Goff, Hope of Craighead, and Saville of Newdigate. Lord Hutton argued that it became an offence in the UK from the 29 September 1988 when Criminal Justice Act 1988, s. 134 came into force. Lords Millett and Phillips of Worth Matravers argued that it had been an international crime under customary international law before that, so there could be no immunity.

[41] This is probably also the position in Northern Ireland. Nothing is said here about the applicability of the *Pinochet Ugarte (No. 3)* decision in Scotland.

treaties, they will be interpreted in the light of those treaties, which themselves may be subject to a peremptory norm of general international law.

A further constitutional filter is the territorial principle. The scope of UK legislation is generally limited to the territory of the UK, even when giving effect to international obligations, although the legislation will be read in the light of those obligations, which may require courts to give limited extra-territorial effect to the legislation. For example, the Human Rights Act 1998 gives domestic effect to rights under European Convention on Human Rights (ECHR), Art. 1 of which requires the high contracting parties to secure the rights to everyone within their jurisdictions. The European Court of Human Rights has interpreted this as imposing obligations towards people in areas outside a state's territory if the state has actual control there or, perhaps, exercises factual or *de jure* authority over the victim of the alleged violation. The House of Lords and the Supreme Court have held that it should follow the Strasbourg Court's recognition of extra-territorial effect for the ECHR, but only so far as a clear line of case law in the Strasbourg Court requires. As a majority of the Supreme Court currently regards the Strasbourg jurisprudence on this matter as ambiguous as to extensions beyond areas directly and effectively controlled by the UK's armed forces, the 1998 Act currently applies only where agents of the UK have effective control over the area where people claim to have suffered a violation of rights.[42]

Where international law operates as a source of domestic law, the courts have regard to the whole of public international law when establishing the scope of any right or obligation that is to have effect in domestic law. Elements cannot be examined in isolation. We have already seen one example of this: tort liability for torture is limited by the international law of state immunity unless it has been restricted by a treaty or *jus cogens*.[43] Other international law rules capable of limiting human rights obligations in international and domestic law include those concerning diplomatic immunity[44] and the overriding effect of decisions in UN Security Council Resolutions to preserve international peace and security by virtue of UN Charter, Art. 103.[45]

Thus dualism operates in the UK, but the division between municipal and public international law should be seen as a semi-permeable membrane, which allows rules to pass through it in different directions for different purposes. The matter is further complicated by two decisions going in different directions. In one, the Strasbourg Court held that acts of a country's armed forces operating abroad under the authority

[42] *R. (Al-Skeini)* v. *Secretary of State for Defence (The Redress Trust and another intervening)* [2007] UKHL 26, [2008] AC 153 (HL); *R. (Smith)* v. *Oxfordshire Assistant Deputy Coroner (Equality and Human Rights Commission intervening)* [2010] UKSC 29, [2010] 3 WLR 223 (SC). The Grand Chamber of the European Court of Human Rights is currently deliberating on an application in *Al-Skeini* v. *United Kingdom*. The judgment when it comes may resolve any ambiguity.

[43] *Jones* v. *Ministry of the Interior of the Kingdom of Saudi Arabia and another (Secretary of State for Constitutional Affairs and others intervening)* [2006] UKHL 26, [2007] 1 AC 270 (HL).

[44] *R. (B.)* v. *Secretary of State for Foreign and Commonwealth Affairs* [2004] EWCA Civ 1344, [2005] QB 643 (CA).

[45] *R. (Al-Jedda)* v. *Secretary of State for Defence (JUSTICE intervening)* [2007] UKHL 58, [2008] AC 332 (HL), also currently the subject of an application to the European Court of Human Rights.

of a UN Security Council resolution made under UN Charter, Chapter VII were attributable to the United Nations rather than the state concerned, which was accordingly not liable for any violation of the ECHR.[46] In the other, the European Court of Justice held that the European Union is an autonomous legal order independent of international law, so that its fundamental rights are not affected by developments such as UN Security Council Chapter VII resolutions.[47] This will have effect in the UK in relation to EU norms and acts, including those carried out by UK authorities on behalf of the European Union's organs.

The UK's dualist filter has been most fully applied in respect of treaties and action of international organizations established under treaties. Usually, rights and obligations arising under treaties do not take effect in municipal legal systems with a dualist principle unless legislation has been passed to give effect to them. For example, rights under the ECHR, as a multilateral treaty, could not be directly litigated before courts in the UK until the Human Rights Act 1998 had made them effective in municipal law.[48] This has two effects. First, it prevents the Crown (in reality the government of the day, which conducts foreign affairs under the royal prerogative), from exercising its treaty-making prerogative in ways which change the law in the UK without parliamentary approval. In the absence of a statutory requirement, there is no need to obtain parliamentary approval before negotiating, signing, or ratifying a treaty.[49] The main statutory exceptions relate to EU Treaties. European Parliamentary Elections Act 2002, s. 12 prevents the Crown from ratifying any Treaty to increase the powers of the European Parliament unless approved by an Act of the UK Parliament; and the same applies to treaties amending the treaty on European Union and the Treaty on the Functioning of the European Union under European Union (Amendment) Act 2008, s. 5.

In other cases, to compensate for the loss of democratic control, dualism prevents the treaty-making prerogative being used to extend the power of the executive, and protects the legislative supremacy of Parliament against attrition. It also protects both the government and Parliament against the direct imposition of the will of other states, contrary to the UK's national interests, through international treaties and the resolutions of international organizations. The UK Parliament can refuse to give effect to treaty obligations in municipal law. It, and the government of the day, can also refuse to accept that a treaty imposes any binding obligation. For example, the previous (Labour) government's view of economic and social rights arising under the International Covenant on Economic, Social and Cultural Rights and the Convention

[46] Application No. 71412/01, *Behrami* v. *France*, admissibility decision of 2 May 2007 (GC).

[47] Joined Cases C-402/05P and C-415/05P, *Kadi* v. *Council of the European Union* [2008] ECR I-6351, [2009] AC 1225 (CJEC). See also *A.* v. *HM Treasury* [2010] UKSC 2, [2010] 2 WLR 378 (SC).

[48] See e.g. *Malone* v. *Metropolitan Police Commissioner (No. 2)* [1979] Ch 344; *R.* v. *Secretary of State for the Home Department ex parte Brind* [1991] 1 AC 696 (HL); *R.* v. *Ministry of Defence ex parte Smith* [1996] QB 517 (CA).

[49] See *JH Rayner (Mincing Lane) Ltd.* v. *Department of Trade and Industry* [1990] 2 AC 418 (HL), 500, *per* Lord Oliver of Aylmerton. Statutory requirements for parliamentary approval are rare.

on the Rights of the Child was that the obligations were aspirational rather than immediate, and did not require the state to guarantee an ascertainable level of protection at any one time.[50] Refusing to recognize or comply with treaty obligations might lead to sanctions for breach of international law if any are available, but it leaves the UK's legislatures ultimately in control of their own legal systems.

This protection for state autonomy can be attenuated. The European Communities Act 1972 provides for some EU rights and obligations to be enforced directly in courts and tribunals in the UK.[51] This allows ministers to change the law in the UK by agreement in Brussels without parliamentary approval. There are some safeguards for national interests. When the supremacy of EC law was established by the Court of Justice of the European Communities (CJEC), the Council needed to agree unanimously in order to legislate. This has since changed. The range of decisions requiring unanimity has steadily narrowed, most recently in the Treaty of Lisbon, and there is no legal protection for parliamentary sovereignty, although some procedural safeguards have been put in place. These include the 'scrutiny reserve' which usually prevents the UK government from agreeing to measures being adopted in Brussels until they have been scrutinized by the Houses of Parliament, a task performed with distinction by committees in both Houses.[52]

In relation to treaties which do not directly alter municipal law, Parliament's position is weak, despite (or because of) dualism. At present, the two Houses normally have no right to be consulted before the text of a treaty is concluded, much less a veto over its signing or ratification. The government makes treaties, and is usually accountable to Parliament only afterwards. There is a constitutional convention (the 'Ponsonby rule') that treaties will not be ratified until they have been laid before both Houses of Parliament. This originated in a statement to the House of Commons on 1 April 1924 by Arthur Ponsonby, then Under Secretary of State for Foreign Affairs in Ramsay MacDonald's Labour administration. The government, he said, wished Parliament to have 'an opportunity for the examination, consideration and if need be discussion of all treaties before they reach the final stage of ratification'. They would be laid before each House for 21 days before the government ratified them. If a treaty did not require ratification, and was merely technical,[53] it would not be laid before Parliament. But 'the government shall inform the House of all agreements,

[50] For the government's position on the Convention on the Rights of the Child and criticism of it, see Joint Committee on Human Rights, Tenth Report of 2002–03, *The UN Convention on the Rights of the Child*, HL 117/HC 81 (2003) paras 21–23.

[51] European Communities Act 1972, s. 2, discussed further below.

[52] See the resolutions of the two Houses at *Hansard*, HC, col. 778ff. (17 November 1998), and *Hansard*, HL, col. 1019ff. (6 December 1999); K. M. Newman, 'The impact of national parliaments on the development of Community law', in F. Capotorti (ed.), *Du Droit International au Droit de l'Integration: Liber Amicorum Pierre Pescatore* (1987) 481–97; T. St. John Bates, 'European Community legislation before the House of Commons' (1991) 12 *Stat. LR* 109–24.

[53] 'Technical' is not a technical term. It is capable of covering Treaties establishing procedures for giving effect to already existing substantive obligations, and perhaps Treaties concerned with the way states deal with fields in which their jurisdictions overlap, for instance in relation to double-taxation agreements.

commitments and undertakings which may in any way bind the nation to specific action in certain circumstances'.[54] However, the Ponsonby rule, which governments still accept today, gives Parliament no more than a right to receive information about the government's Treaty-making activities. The rule has now been enshrined in statute, with certain adjustments which serve to limit its impact on governmental freedom, by Constitutional Reform and Governance Act 2010, Pt 2 (ss 20–25). This came into force on 11 November 2010, so Parliament no longer relies on the Ponsonby rule.

Treaties by which the UK becomes a member of supranational or international organizations whose institutions have law-making powers especially call for filters to protect the municipal legal systems against adverse effects, but also make it more difficult to secure that protection. The value of filters in such a system depends on the power of the state to influence the content of obligations imposed on it by treaty bodies. When the UK became part of the European Economic Community (EEC) in 1973 it was an association of a small group of western European nations designed to remove national barriers to economic development and to turn the member states into a single market (the 'Common Market') in goods and services. At that stage, national interests were strongly protected by equal state representation on the main law-making body and (as noted earlier) a requirement for unanimity to make law. The veto power of each member state gave reasonable protection for the UK's national interests, making possible the UK's acceptance of the direct effect of some Community legislation and of the doctrine of the supremacy of Community law. Over time, however, the number of member states and the diversity of their interests increased, and the law-making activities of the institution grew in range and complexity. The EEC turned into the European Community and later the European Union, dedicated to harmonizing a growing range of economic and social policies, including the regulation of police and judicial cooperation and other fields of common concern. As qualified majority voting was introduced, the safeguards for vital national interests, which had originally justified relaxing the national filters by accepting the direct effect of EC law, became progressively weaker, and the Treaty of Lisbon in 2007 (which came into force on 1 December 2009) continued that trend.

Some international organizations never demand unanimity in decision making. From its establishment in 1946, the United Nations had such a large membership that unanimity was never a practical option. Each member state has a seat in the General Assembly, but that body's recommendations do not bind states in public international law except in relation to the internal governance of the United Nations[55] (although resolutions may be evidence of the emergence of binding rules of customary international law if they reflect state practice). The main power to impose obligations binding states in international law is conferred on the Security Council, which forms the

[54] *Hansard*, HC (5th series), vol. 171, col. 2001 (1 April 1924).

[55] UN Charter, Art. 17.

executive group of the United Nations with special responsibility for preserving international peace and security.[56] Decisions of the Council (but not mere recommendations) bind all member states.[57] Only 15 states are members of the Security Council. Five of them, the 'great powers' of the period following the Second World War (China, France, Russia, the UK, and the USA), are permanent members. The other nine members are elected for a period of two years from among the remaining members of the General Assembly, as laid down by UN Charter, Art. 23.2. Security Council Resolutions must be approved by an affirmative vote of at least nine members, but any of the permanent members may veto any proposed resolution, except in relation to procedural matters (such as the agenda for sessions, or the states which should be given the opportunity to address the Council in matters affecting them), where there is no veto.[58] This offers asymmetric protection to national interests. Those of the five permanent members are well protected by their veto. Those of the non-permanent members can be subordinated to the interests of nine concurring members, although they may benefit from overlapping the vital interests of one of the permanent members. States without a seat on the Security Council are even less well protected. As members of the United Nations they can use diplomatic techniques in defence of their interests, but their success will depend significantly on the balance of power and the interests of the 'great powers'.

For historical reasons, the UK is a permanent member of the UN Security Council, so it has a measure of control over the most important decisions. In other international organizations, it has influence rather than control, and the extent of its influence depends on the arguments and pressure it can apply. By contrast, the USA, the former USSR, and today China, as world superpowers in terms of their military or economic might, can exercise great influence by offers of aid with strings attached, or by explicit or implicit threats of trade sanctions, withdrawal of aid, or in extreme cases invasion. Such influence does not depend on the quality of the superpower's arguments or the morality of its stance. It extends beyond organizations of which the superpowers are members, although even a superpower must sometimes take account of other states' points of view, as the aftermath of the second Gulf War in 2003 has shown.

MECHANISMS FOR INTERNATIONALIZATION, CONSTITUTIONAL STRUCTURES, AND LEGITIMACY

Those international influences to which states are inevitably subject must be channelled into municipal law and made to fit within the state's constitutional law and traditions. How is this done?[59]

The most direct form of international (or at least supranational) influence arises when rules made by another state or states, or accepted at inter-state level, are

[56] Ibid., Arts 23, 24, 25 and 28. [57] Ibid., Art. 25. [58] Ibid., Art. 27.

[59] David Feldman, 'Modalities of internationalisation in international law' (2006) 18 *ERPL* 131.

automatically incorporated into the municipal legal system, without the need for any prior or subsequent legislative action. In the UK, the most straightforward example of this is the automatic incorporation of rules of customary international law subject to legislation and the doctrine of *stare decisis*, as mentioned in the previous section.

Marginally less direct, but more powerful, is the process whereby certain rules of EU law become part of the municipal legal system. European Communities Act 1972, s 2(1) creates what is in effect a statutory rule of automatic incorporation of what it calls 'enforceable Community rights'. Because of the doctrine of the supremacy of EC law over national law, this form of incorporation has a greater impact than the incorporation of customary international law. Enforceable Community rights need not be compatible with previous or subsequent parliamentary legislation. Instead, inconsistent parliamentary legislation must be disapplied to the extent that it is inconsistent with enforceable Community rights.[60]

In addition, s. 2(2) of the Act allows Her Majesty in Council or designated ministers and departments to give effect to or implement other EC obligations or rights (including those arising under directives which do not have direct effect) in municipal law by way of statutory instruments, a form of subordinate legislation. These are usually subject only to the negative resolution procedure: they take effect unless either House passes a resolution annulling them.[61] Statutory instruments under s. 2(2) can make any provision that could be made by Act of Parliament. They can even amend or repeal Acts of Parliament; and any provision of primary legislation is to be construed and to have effect subject to the provisions of the statutory instrument.[62] A subsequent Act of Parliament could revoke the statutory instrument, as long as that would not be incompatible with the enforcement of enforceable Community rights. Nevertheless, the filters protecting parliamentary control over the implementation of EU law are limited: the negative resolution procedure is hardly a strong form of scrutiny or protection, and the best filter is the pre-adoption scrutiny of EU measures by the House of Commons EU Scrutiny Committee and the House of Lords EU Select Committee and its subcommittees.[63] What is more, in some fields the member states have delegated power to the European Commission to negotiate Treaties on their behalf with non-member states, including agreements on tariffs and trade and arrangements for extradition. The impact of such agreements on the rights and obligations of member states is as yet uncertain.[64]

Following the establishment of the United Nations in 1946, Parliament conferred power on the government to implement certain decisions of the UN Security Council by way of subordinate legislation, with limited or non-existent parliamentary oversight. When the Security Council, acting to preserve international peace and security under UN Charter, Chapter VII, calls on the government to apply any measures to

[60] See Chapter 4 above. [61] European Communities Act 1972, Sched. 2, para. 2(2).

[62] Ibid., s. 2(4). [63] See discussion in Chapter 4 above.

[64] See Vienna Convention on the Law of Treaties between States and International Organisations and between International Organisations 1986; Shaw, above, n. 5, pp. 953–5.

give effect to any decision of the Council under UN Charter, Art. 41 (that is, decisions not involving the use of armed force), United Nations Act 1946, s. 1(1) allows Her Majesty by Order in Council to make 'such provision as appears to Her to be necessary or expedient for enabling the measures to be effectively applied'. The Order must be laid before Parliament forthwith after it is made, and, if it relates to a matter within the legislative competence of the Scottish Parliament, before that Parliament as well,[65] but neither Parliament can annul the Order save by means of an Act. Still less do such Orders require the approval of either House. The only control available is through judicial review. An Order can be quashed if it is outside the scope of the power conferred by the Act or is incompatible with a Community right (such as the right to be free of quantitative restrictions on free movement of goods)[66] or a Convention right under the Human Rights Act 1998. But if it acts compatibly with EC law and Convention rights the government has a very wide discretion as to the terms of the Order and the Treasury has a very wide discretion as to the manner of its implementation.[67]

The scope of the power is enormous, and Orders can directly affect individuals. For example, after the terrorist attack on the World Trade Center on 9 September 2001 the UN Security Council passed Resolution 1373 of 28 September 2001, calling on the governments of member states to apply measures to give effect to decisions of the Council to combat terrorist activities. It required steps to be taken to freeze terrorist assets. In the UK, the government implemented this by Orders in Council making it a criminal offence to make funds or financial services available to or for the benefit of people participating in acts of terrorism or to fail to report suspicions that people are intending to use funds for such a purpose, and allowing the Treasury to freeze the funds of such people whom the Treasury has reasonable grounds for suspecting may be holding funds for the purpose of committing, facilitating, or participating in acts of terrorism.[68] These Orders were subject to no parliamentary control or scrutiny either before or after they were made. In reliance on them, the Treasury froze the assets of several dozen people, and announced its action in press releases.[69] The Security Council resolution thus authorized a direct attack by the British government on individuals' property, with very limited safeguards and filters within the jurisdiction for Rule of Law requirements and the democratic process.

However, the Supreme Court reasserted respect for fundamental rights, holding that several of these orders were *ultra vires* United Nations Act 1946, s. 1, partly because they infringed fundamental rights without a fair hearing and subordinate

[65] European Communities Act 1972, s. 1(4), as amended by the Scotland Act 1998.

[66] See *R.* v. *HM Treasury ex parte Centro-Com Srl* [1997] QB 863 (CJEC).

[67] See *R.* v. *HM Treasury ex parte Centro-Com Srl*, *The Independent*, 3 June 1994 (CA), affirming (in relation to municipal law) [1994] 1 CMLR 109. On the implications of EC law, see the decision of the Court of Justice on the reference from the Court of Appeal: [1997] QB 683 (CJEC).

[68] Terrorism (United Nations Measures) (Channel Islands) Order 2001 (SI 2001/3363); Terrorism (United Nations Measures) (Isle of Man) Order 2001 (SI 2001/3364); Terrorism (United Nations Measures) Order 2001 (SI 2001/3365).

[69] See e.g. Treasury Press Release 110/01, 12 October 2001, which includes a list of names.

legislation could not validly do that unless an Act of Parliament had expressly conferred a power to do so, and partly because the orders were drafted more broadly than was justified by the Security Council resolutions. The government introduced an emergency Bill to preserve the orders until new legislation could be passed to define the asset-freezing power more closely and provide for appeal to or review by courts of Treasury decisions.[70]

Today, a provision in a Bill allowing the government to introduce international obligations to municipal law by delegated legislation would be likely to face more intensive parliamentary scrutiny than in 1946. In particular, the House of Lords Select Committee on Delegated Powers and Regulatory Reform, which scrutinizes all provisions in Bills before Parliament which confer power to make delegated legislation, would seek to insist on including sufficient safeguards in the Bill by way of a requirement for adequate parliamentary scrutiny of proposed subordinate legislation to protect the Rule of Law and human rights. Where the proposed power could affect human rights or constitutional principles, the Joint Select Committee on Human Rights and the House of Lords Select Committee on the Constitution provide additional pressure. It is noteworthy that the powers included in the Anti-terrorism, Crime and Security Act 2001 to permit EU initiatives on police and judicial co-operation in criminal matters to be given effect in the UK by way of subordinate legislation included far more safeguards than are found in the United Nations Act 1946.[71] Even then the government agreed that legislation to implement the Framework Decision on the European Arrest Warrant would be introduced by way of a Bill (now Extradition Act 2003, Pt 1) rather than by using the power to make subordinate legislation under the 2001 Act.[72]

Similar caution about authorizing subordinate legislation can be seen in the Human Rights Act 1998 and the devolution legislation to making rights under the ECHR ('the Convention rights') effective in municipal law in the UK.[73] Human Rights Act 1998, s. 1, applied in the devolution legislation,[74] appears to import the rights bodily from international law (the ECHR) to national law. However, the transplant is complicated by two factors. First, the rights in international law bind states, whereas in municipal law they bind public authorities within the state. This necessitated adjustments designed, among other things, to adapt the rights for municipal application

[70] *Ahmed and others.* v. *HM Treasury (JUSTICE intervening) (Nos. 1 and 2)* [2010] UKSC 2, [2010] 2 WLR 378 (SC); Terrorist Asset-Freezing (Temporary Provisions) Act 2010; Terrorist Asset-Freezing etc. Act 2010, Pt 1, in force 17 Dec 2010.

[71] See Anti-terrorism, Crime and Security Act 2001, ss 111 and 112. For further primary legislation on cross-border co-operation, see Crime (International Co-operation) Act 2003. The same point was made by Lord Hope of Craighead DPSC in *Ahmed* v. *HM Treasury* [2010] UKSC 2, [2010] 2 WLR 378 (SC) at [48]–[53], arguing that the government should have used either primary legislation or the procedure under the 2001 Act to give effect to the Security Council resolutions.

[72] See Joint Committee on Human Rights, Second Report, 2001–02, *Anti-terrorism, Crime and Security Bill*, HL 37/HC 372, para. 13.

[73] See Chapter 4 above, and Chapter 9 below.

[74] See Scotland Act 1998, ss 29(2), 54(2) and 126(1); Northern Ireland Act 1998, ss 6(2), 24(1) and 98(1); Government of Wales Act 2006, ss 81(5) and 158(1).

and maintain consistency with constitutional principles such as parliamentary sovereignty and parliamentary privilege.[75] Secondly, there is a difference between formulating a right and understanding what it means when applied in practice. Both the scope of the Convention rights and the circumstances (if any) in which it is justifiable to interfere with them in international law depend on the extensive case law of the European Commission and the European Court of Human Rights. Parts of it, such as the notion of the 'margin of appreciation', arise from the position of international tribunals *vis-à-vis* national authorities and cannot be transferred to municipal law. Even if a particular line of case law can be transferred to the municipal sphere, there may be good reasons for limiting its impact. Human Rights Act 1998, s. 2 therefore provides that courts and tribunals in the UK must take into account the case law of the Strasbourg organs when interpreting the Convention rights, but does not make it binding. Courts in the UK have on occasions declined to follow judgments of the European Court of Human Rights.[76] For example, the House of Lords has held that normal rules of precedent generally require a lower court in England and Wales to follow an earlier decision of a higher domestic court on the application of Convention rights in preference to a later, inconsistent decision of the European Court of Human Rights, unless it is clear that the policy justification for the earlier English decision no longer applies.[77] This introduces a filter into the channel by which the Convention rights enter municipal law: courts and tribunals in the UK are not required to follow decisions of international tribunals if they seem inappropriate to the structure of the domestic legal order or plainly wrong.

The Act also empowers ministers to make statutory instruments for various purposes, providing further channels for bringing municipal law into line with the ECHR. With relatively few preconditions or procedural filters a Secretary of State can make a statutory instrument adding an extra right to the list of Convention rights which became part of municipal law by virtue of s. 1 of the Act. With equally little formal constraint, a Secretary of State can add a reservation to the newly recognized right to the list of reservations in s. 1 of, and Pt 1 of Sched. 3 to, the Act, or add a derogation from a Convention right to those recognized in s. 1 of, and Pt 2 of Sched. 3 to, the Act. Any UK court or tribunal interpreting a Convention right must then read it subject to the reservation or derogation in question. There have been two changes to the derogations recognized in the Act, both in relation to terrorism: the original derogation was

[75] See e.g. the partial delimitation of the term 'public authority' in Human Rights Act 1998, s. 6.

[76] On the circumstances in which courts in the UK should follow Strasbourg judgments, see e.g. *R. (Alconbury Developments Ltd)* v. *Secretary of State for the Environment, Transport and the Regions* [2001] UKHL 23, [2003] 2 AC 295 (HL) at [26], *per* Lord Slynn of Hadley; *R. (Anderson)* v. *Secretary of State for the Home Department* [2002] UKHL 46, [2003] 1 AC 837 (HL) at [18], *per* Lord Bingham of Cornhill; *R. (Ullah)* v. *Special Adjudicator* [2004] UKHL 26, [2004] 2 AC 323 at [20], *per* Lord Bingham of Cornhill; *Secretary of State for the Home Department* v. *AF (No. 3)* [2009] UKHL 28, [2009] 3 WLR 74 (HL); *R. v. Horncastle* [2009] UKSC 14, [2010] 2 WLR 47 (SC); *Manchester City Council* v. *Pinnock* [2010] SC 45 at [48]–[49]; David Feldman (ed.), *English Public Law* (2nd edn, 2009) paras 7.29–7.30.

[77] *Kay* v. *Lambeth LBC; Leeds City Council v. Price* [2006] UKHL 10, [2006] 2 AC 465 (HL) (not overruled on this point in *Manchester City Council v. Pinnock*, n. 76 above.).

repealed, and later a new one was inserted; but the derogation order adding the new derogation was subsequently held to be *ultra vires* because the measures concerned were not strictly required by the exigencies of the terrorist threat and consistent with the UK's other international obligations so as to meet the requirements of Article 15 of the ECHR, so at present (as of April 2011) there is no designated derogation.[78]

If the Strasbourg Court or a UK court decides that UK legislation is incompatible with a Convention right, Human Rights Act 1998, s. 10 empowers the appropriate Secretary of State to make an Order in Council amending or repealing the incompatible provision, which is usually in an Act of Parliament. When the Human Rights Bill was before the House of Lords in 1997, the Select Committee on Delegated Powers and Deregulation[79] recommended that this 'Henry VIII' power should be hedged about with preconditions and procedural requirements, now contained in s. 10 of, and Sched. 2 to, the Act, even though the purpose is to protect and extend, rather than to interfere with, human rights. This has the odd result that it is easier to make a statutory instrument which restricts rights by requiring courts in the UK to interpret Convention rights in the light of a reservation or new derogation than to extend rights by way of a statutory instrument (a remedial order) amending previously incompatible legislation.

Even where there is no express legislative authority for allowing international standards and Treaties to influence municipal law, both Treaties and the judgments of international and foreign tribunals can influence parliamentary and judicial decision making in the UK. Parliament and government departments are increasingly aware of the UK's obligations as a result of the work of the government's legal advisers, and select committees and individual members in Parliament. This is affecting both the content of legislation and the way in which scrutiny of government is conducted.[80] If it cannot yet be said that the influence is pervasive, it is at least significant and growing.

[78] See Human Rights Act 1998 (Amendment) Order 2001 (SI 2001/1216), removing a derogation made to remove the derogation from ECHR, Art. 5 in relation to detaining terrorist suspects without charge for up to seven days before being brought before a judicial officer; Human Rights Act 1998 (Designated Derogation) Order 2001 (SI 2001/3644), introducing a new derogation from Art. 5 to allow indefinite detention without trial of suspected international terrorists who were not UK nationals if they could not be removed abroad for legal or practical reasons under the Anti-terrorism, Crime and Security Act 2001; Human Rights Act 1998 (Amendment) Order 2004 (SI 2004/1574), replacing Protocol 6 with Protocol 13 in the list of Convention rights; and Human Rights Act 1998 (Amendment) Order 2005 (SI 2005/1071), removing the derogation from Art. 5 after the House of Lords had held it to be invalid in *A* v. *Secretary of State for the Home Department* [2004] UKHL 56, [2005] 2 AC 68 (HL). Lord Scott of Foscote expressed doubt as to the applicability of Art. 15, as it was not one of the provisions made part of the legal systems of the UK by Human Rights Act 1998, s. 1, but the Home Secretary had conceded its relevance.

[79] The forerunner of the Select Committee on Delegated Powers and Regulatory Reform.

[80] See e.g. Lord Lester of Herne Hill, QC, 'Parliamentary scrutiny of legislation under the Human Rights Act 1998' [2002] *EHRLRev* 432; David Feldman, 'The impact of human rights on the legislative process' (2004) 25 *Stat. L. Rev.* 91; Janet Hiebert, 'Parliamentary review of terrorism measures' (2005) 58 *MLR* 676; Janet Hiebert, 'Interpreting a Bill of Rights: the importance of legislative rights review' [2005] *BJPS* 235; Carolyn Evans and Simon Evans, 'Legislative scrutiny committees and parliamentary conceptions of human rights' [2006] *PL* 785.

The main constraint is the government's unwillingness to accept that economic, social, and cultural rights can impose immediate, binding, and justiciable obligations on the UK,[81] but this may change over time. This use of international standards is fully consistent with parliamentary democracy.

The judiciary too is a channel for allowing foreign influences into national public law systems. Judges in many countries round the world have a keen interest in foreign and international public law standards, including but not limited to human rights. In many common law jurisdictions they consider and draw illumination from public law judgments of courts elsewhere in the world. Judges do not simply adopt solutions or interpretations which have found favour elsewhere. The differences between constitutional and political structures in different countries make that undesirable: there may be no certainty that the solutions would fit a local context. Instead, they find it helpful to see how courts in different constitutional traditions have conceptualized and analysed the conflicting interests relevant to public law problems. This can help to crystallize issues and suggest approaches without dictating an outcome. Courts in the UK regularly use comparative law as a source of ideas for developing the common law and interpreting human rights.[82] Senior British judges have long been familiar with different constitutional and human rights arrangements through sitting regularly as members of the Judicial Committee of the Privy Council on public law appeals.

Interaction with academics also encourages judges to take an interest in comparative law. Judges regularly participate in academic seminars and conferences concerning international and comparative public law. The Judicial Studies Board increasingly involves academics in judicial discussions and seminars. A growing number of senior judges had previous experience as legal academics.

Senior judges in different jurisdictions communicate extensively with each other, building up personal friendships and professional links through judicial colloquia and email. The internet offers access to a huge archive of legal materials from many jurisdictions.[83] The Law Commission and other bodies entrusted with the task of law reform now routinely undertake comparative research on the areas of law under review. English judges have also become far readier than before to make use of international legal materials in their judgments, including opinions, recommendations and resolutions of experts and inter-national bodies that do not bind states in public international law. This 'soft law' influences outcomes by establishing a normative framework which tends to favour one outcome of the 'hard law' dispute over another. In England and Wales, judges sometimes assume that its appropriateness is self-evident, but may in many cases be able to justify it on the ground that it represents customary international law. Where that is so, it is tenable to argue that treaty obligations should

[81] See above, n. 51.

[82] For a critical analysis of the uses made of comparative law, see Mads Andenas and Duncan Fairgrieve, '"There is a world elsewhere" – Lord Bingham and comparative law', in Mads Andenas and Duncan Fairgrieve (eds), *Tom Bingham and the Transformation of the Law: A Liber Amicorum* (2009) 831–66.

[83] See A.-M. Slaughter, 'A global community of courts' (2003) 44 *Harvard International Law Journal* 191.

be interpreted in the light of the matrix of international obligations within which they operate, and 'if, and to the extent that, development of the common law is called for, such development should ordinarily be in harmony with the UK's international obligations and not antithetical to them'.[84] This open intellectual atmosphere, influenced by judges' growing familiarity with international and comparative methods through their work with the Human Rights Act 1998, various commercial law conventions and other sources, is likely to grow stronger. Judges will be keen to compare techniques of constitutional reasoning and hear how courts elsewhere approach such matters as the interpretation of legislation so as to make it compatible with human rights.

This approach offers benefits, but it can be taken too far if, without constitutional authority, one makes comparative legal methods a judicial duty rather than an optional aid. For example, in *Lange* v. *Atkinson and Australian Consolidated Press NZ Ltd*[85] David Lange, a former Prime Minister of New Zealand, sued for libel in both New Zealand and Australia in respect of a magazine article criticizing his performance as a politician and suggesting that he suffered from selective memory loss. The defendants pleaded, among other defences, that the article was 'political expression' and, as such, entitled to privilege against liability. They also pleaded qualified privilege (which protects people from liability for libel if they act pursuant to a duty to bring the matters to the attention of the intended recipients, and do not act maliciously). In the Australian proceedings, the High Court of Australia decided that common law qualified privilege protected communications to the public of information, opinions, and arguments relating to governmental and political matters, as long as the publishers proved that they had acted reasonably.[86] In the New Zealand proceedings, however, the Court of Appeal held that the publications attracted qualified privilege, but, unlike the High Court of Australia, held that at common law in New Zealand, only malice could deprive the publishers of the privilege, so the reasonableness of the publishers' conduct was irrelevant.[87]

Mr Lange appealed to the Privy Council against the decision of the Court of Appeal. Before the Privy Council could deliver its judgment, the House of Lords ruled on the same issue in *Reynolds* v. *Times Newspapers Ltd*, an unrelated but similar libel action. The House held that at common law in England and Wales a publication was not privileged merely because it was about governmental or political matters. The publisher had to show that there was a duty to publish the material to its intended recipients (or, to put it another way, that publication was in the public interest).[88]

[84] *A* v. *Secretary of State for the Home Department (No. 2)* [2005] UKHL 71, [2006] 2 AC 221 (HL) at [27], *per* Lord Bingham of Cornhill; see also [28]–[29]. See further, e.g. cases on the implications for law in the UK of allegations of torture abroad: *Jones* v. *Ministry of the Interior of the Kingdom of Saudi Arabia (Secretary of State for Constitutional Affairs and others intervening)* [2006] UKHL 26, [2007] 1 AC 270 (HL).

[85] [2000] 1 NZLR 257 (PC).

[86] *Lange* v. *Australian Broadcasting Corporation* (1997) 189 CLR 520 (HC of Australia).

[87] *Lange* v. *Atkinson and Australian Consolidated Press NZ Ltd* [1998] 3 NZLR 424 (CA of New Zealand).

[88] [2001] 2 AC 127 (HL). On the meaning of a duty to publish, see now *Jameel (Mohammed)* v. *Wall Street Journal Europe Sprl* [2006] UKHL 44, [2007] 1 AC 359 (HL).

Giving judgment subsequently on Mr Lange's appeal, the Privy Council noted the differences between the Australian, New Zealand, and English approaches, and accepted that 'striking a balance between freedom of expression and protection of reputation calls for a value judgment which depends upon local political and social conditions'. Furthermore, 'there is a high content of judicial policy in the solution of the issue raised by this appeal;...different solutions may be reached in different jurisdictions without any faulty reasoning or misconception...; and...within a particular jurisdiction the necessary value judgment may best be made by the local courts'. Nevertheless, the Privy Council sent the case back for a further hearing in New Zealand because the Court of Appeal had not had the opportunity to consider the Law Lords' decision in *Reynolds* before making its decision.[89]

This comes close to imposing a duty on top common-law courts to have regard to (though not to follow) each other's leading decisions. Yet the decision does not explain the legitimate basis for having regard to foreign authorities as guides to developing one's own public law, let alone justify allowing an appeal in order to force another court to do so.

On constitutional grounds, the decision is hard to justify. Unstructured picking and choosing between sources can undermine or evade the filters which, for good constitutional reasons, constrain foreign influences on domestic legal systems. There has been heated disagreement in the USA about the propriety of taking account of either international law standards which do not form part of municipal law in the USA or decisions of courts in other common law countries. American judges are comfortable with comparative law techniques, as federal law must take account of dozens of state legal systems and constitutions, but some have challenged the legitimacy of relying on international developments when taking US constitutional jurisprudence in a new direction. In *Atkins* v. *Virginia*[90] the US Supreme Court, in a footnote to the majority judgment of Stevens J, adverted in passing to the fact that 'within the world community, the imposition of the death penalty for crimes committed by mentally retarded offenders is overwhelmingly disapproved' as evidence for an evolving standard of decency making such punishment cruel and unusual, and so contrary to the Eighth Amendment to the US Constitution.[91] The dissent by Rehnquist CJ (in which Scalia and Thomas JJ joined) argued that only standards within the USA, evidenced by federal and state legislation and decisions of juries, were relevant when deciding whether a punishment is cruel and unusual for constitutional purposes. It would be illegitimate to decide US constitutional law by reference to foreign standards.

[89] *Lange* v. *Atkinson and Australian Consolidated Press NZ Ltd* [2000] 1 NZLR 257 (PC). For the further proceedings in the Court of Appeal of New Zealand, see [2000] 3 NZLR 385.

[90] 536 US 304 (2002).

[91] Ibid., n. 21 of the judgment, referring to the Brief for the European Union as *Amicus Curiae* in *McCarver* v. *North Carolina*, O.T. 2001, No. 00–1727, p. 4.

This does not mean that the dissentients are unaware of developments elsewhere. In *Lawrence* v. *Texas*,[92] the majority of the US Supreme Court held that there was no rational basis for a state law criminalizing homosexual sodomy. Scalia J's dissent (in which Rehnquist CJ and Thomas J joined) referred to a Canadian decision[93] as part of a 'slippery slope' argument, suggesting that judicially striking down laws which discriminate against homosexuals could lead to the judicial imposition on the legislature of homosexual marriage, which would be unacceptable under the US Constitution. Where the national constitution does not authorize courts to draw on foreign decisions, it may (as Rehnquist CJ pointed out in *Atkins* v. *Virginia*) be difficult to justify being guided from elsewhere in interpreting one's own constitution. As aids to articulating issues and becoming aware of possible approaches, not to mention a state's international obligations, comparative and international studies are hard to better, but in the USA, unlike most other jurisdictions, the matter is being approached as one of constitutional principle.[94]

It is rare for a codified constitution either to authorize or to prohibit courts taking account of international legal standards or judgments of foreign or international tribunals when deciding municipal public law cases, but the 1996 Constitution of the Republic of South Africa is an exception. The Constitution is an outward-looking document. The formulation of the Constitution's Bill of Rights was heavily influenced by the examples of Canada, Ireland, India, and Nigeria, but the formulation of the rights and their constitutional status was a response to the particular needs of post-apartheid society. Section 39(1) of the 1996 Constitution provides that a court, tribunal or forum, when interpreting the Bill of Rights:

a. must promote the values that underlie an open and democratic society based on human dignity, equality and freedom;
b. must consider international law; and
c. may consider foreign law.

As a result, the judgments of the Constitutional Court of South Africa are a valuable repository of learning on international and comparative human rights law, and their constitutional legitimacy is beyond question.

Courts in the UK are not required to be as systematic as those in South Africa in their use of international and foreign law, but UK judges have regularly used both international and comparative law.[95] Treaties can be used to interpret legislation, on the

[92] 539 US 558 (2003), overruling *Bowers* v. *Hardwick* 478 US 186 (1986).

[93] *Halpern* v. *Toronto* 2003 WL 34950 (Ontario CA).

[94] See, e.g. *Printz* v. *United States*, 521 US 898 (1997); *Foster* v. *Florida*, 537 US 990 (2002); *Roper* v. *Simmons*, 125 S Ct 1183 (2005); Norman Dawson, 'The relevance of foreign legal materials in US constitutional cases: a conversation between Justice Antonin Scalia and Justice Stephen Breyer' (2005) 3 *Int. J. Const. Law* 519, available at www.wcl.american.edu; Ruth Bader Ginsburg, '"A decent respect to the opinions of [human] kind": the value of a comparative perspective in constitutional adjudication' (2005) 64 *CLJ* 575.

[95] Historically, Roman law (including the notion of *ius gentium*) had an influence on parts of the common law: see Andrew Lewis, '"What Marcellus says is against you": Roman law and common law', in Lewis and Ibbetson, above, n 15, ch. 12; Daan Asser, '*Audi et alteram partem*: a limit to judicial activity', in Lewis

assumption that Parliament does not intend to violate the UK's international obligations unless an intention to do so appears clearly.[96] Where a statute is designed to give effect to international obligations, the assumption is that Parliament intended to achieve that and nothing else.[97] A treaty may give rise to a legitimate expectation, enforceable in administrative law, that the government will act in accordance with the UK's international obligations, although this has been criticised as a 'constitutional solecism' amounting 'to a means of incorporating the substance of obligations undertaken on the international plane into our domestic law without the authority of Parliament'.[98] Treaties may provide a guide to the requirements of public policy,[99] and can guide courts when exercising discretion in relation to such matters as levels of damages.[100] Where an administrative act or decision infringes a human right in international law, courts will anxiously scrutinize it, giving more attention than usual to the evidence, though not necessarily applying a higher than usual intensity of review, when deciding whether it is 'unreasonable'.[101]

However, UK courts retain a certain reserve in the face of treaties. Unless a treaty has been transformed into municipal law by legislation, like parts of the ECHR, they do not usually consider that they are under any obligation to take account of them:[102] for the UK lawyer, the dualism of the constitution means that treaties generally still exist as part of a different system of law. In cases reported in 11 leading series of law reports for England and Wales in 2001 and 2002, only two international conventions apart from the ECHR were considered, in a total of six public law cases: the Convention and Protocol relating to the Status of Refugees, and the Convention on International Trade in Endangered Species of Wild Fauna and Flora.[103] UK courts clearly felt no obligation to delve into a wide range of treaties such as is imposed on the South African judiciary in cases on constitutional rights. In the first seven months of 2010, a broadly similar pattern emerged: apart from the ECHR, the Refugee Convention and its Protocol were

and Ibbetson, above, n 15, ch. 13. Courts have also had regard to treaties, although only relatively recently in Scotland: see *T., Petitioner* 1997 SLT 734 (Court of Session (Inner House)), and above, text at n. 39ff.

96 See e.g. *Waddington* v. *Miah* [1974] 1 WLR 683 (HL).

97 See e.g. *R. (on the application of Mullen)* v. *Secretary of State for the Home Department* [2004] UKHL 14, [2005] 1 AC 1 (HL), where the problem was to decide how the international Treaty should be interpreted.

98 For the origin of the application of the doctrine to human rights treaties, see *Minister for Immigration and Ethnic Affairs* v. *Teoh* (1995) 183 CLR 273 (HC of Australia); *R.* v. *Secretary of State for the Home Department ex parte Ahmed and Patel* [1998] INLR 570; *R.* v. *Uxbridge Magistrates' Court ex parte Adimi* [2001] QB 667 (DC), esp. at 686, *per* Simon Brown LJ. For the criticism, see *Behluli* v. *Secretary of State for the Home Department* [1998] Imm AR 407, 415, *per* Beldam LJ; *R. (European Roma Rights Centre)* v. *Immigration Officer at Prague Airport (United Nations High Commissioner for Refugees intervening)* [2003] EWCA Civ 666, [2004] QB 211 (CA) at [99] and [101], *per* Laws LJ, and see also Simon Brown LJ at [51]. On appeal in the *Roma Rights* case, the House of Lords did not consider the issue.

99 See e.g. *Blathwayt* v. *Baron Cawley* [1976] AC 397 (HL).

100 See e.g. *John* v. *MGN Ltd.* [1997] QB 586 (CA).

101 See e.g. *Bugdaycay* v. *Secretary of State for the Home Department* [1987] AC 514 (HL), and Chapter 4 above.

102 See e.g. *R.* v. *Secretary of State for the Home Department, ex part Brind* [1991] 1 AC 696 (HL).

103 *The Consolidated Index 2001–2002 to Leading Law Reports* (2002) 347.

considered in three cases, and in one of them the court also considered the Statute of the International Criminal Court.[104]

Direct application of foreign judgments in public law cases is also limited, though they may have persuasive authority. One must leave aside decisions which have to be considered as a matter of law, such as foreign judgments in certain cases in the Privy Council, decisions of the Court of Justice of the European Communities and the Court of First Instance, and those of the European Court of Human Rights. In purely domestic cases reported in 2001 and, the editors of *The Consolidated Index*[105] identified only 13 foreign public law cases which received substantial consideration, in a total of 17 English public law cases. All but one of the foreign cases were decided by the Privy Council (which could almost count as a UK court), the sole exception being a decision of the Supreme Court of Canada.[106] The editors took the view that foreign decisions had been applied in six English cases,[107] considered in another four,[108] and distinguished in a further three.[109] Foreign *dicta* were applied in four English cases,[110] and considered in another one.[111]

[104] *Law Reports Cumulative Index August 2010* (2010) 144.

[105] *The Consolidated Index 2001–2002 to Leading Law Reports* (2002) 241–313.

[106] *Proprietary Articles Trade Association* v. *Attorney General for Canada* [1931] AC 310 (PC), from which *dicta* of Lord Atkin at 324 were applied in *R. (McCann)* v. *Crown Court at Manchester* [2002] UKHL 39, [2003] 1 AC 787 (HL).

[107] *Attorney General of Hong Kong* v. *Nai-Keung* [1987] 1 WLR 1339 (PC), applied in *In re Celtic Extraction Ltd* [2001] Ch 475 (CA); *Calvin* v. *Carr* [1980] AC 574 (PC), applied in *Modahl* v. *British Athletic Federation Ltd* [2002] 1 WLR 1192 (CA); *Darmalingum* v. *The State* [2000] 1 WLR 2303 (PC), applied in *Porter* v. *Magill* [2002] 2 AC 357 (HL); *De Freitas* v. *Permanent Secretary of Ministry of Agriculture, Fisheries, Lands and Housing* [1999] 1 AC 69 (PC), applied in *R.* v. *Benjafield* [2002] UKHL 2, [2003] 1 AC 1099 (HL); *Kemper Reinsurance Co.* v. *Minister of Finance* [2000] 1 AC 1 (PC), applied in *R. (on the application of Burkett)* v. *Hammersmith and Fulham London Borough Council* [2002] 1 WLR 1593 (HL); and *Liyanage* v. *The Queen* [1967] 1 AC 259 (PC), applied in *R. (on the application of Bancoult)* v. *Secretary of State for Foreign and Commonwealth Affairs* [2001] QB 1067 (DC).

[108] *Attorney General of Hong Kong* v. *Lee Kwong-Kut* [1993] AC 951 (PC), considered in *International Transport Roth GmbH* v. *Secretary of State for the Home Department* [2002] EWCA Civ 158, [2003] QB 728 (CA); *Darmalingum* v. *The State* [2000] 1 WLR 2303 (PC), considered in *Dyer* v. *Watson* [2002] UKPC D1, [2004] 1 AC 379 (PC) (a devolution case); *Prebble* v. *Television New Zealand Ltd* [1995] 1 AC 321 (PC), considered in *R. (on the application of Asif Javed)* v. *Secretary of State for the Home Department* [2001] EWCA Civ 789, [2002] QB 129 (CA); and *Winfat Enterprise (HK) Co. Ltd* v. *Attorney General for Hong Kong* [1985] AC 733 (PC), considered in *R. (on the application of Bancoult)* v. *Secretary of State for Foreign and Commonwealth Affairs* [2001] QB 1067 (DC).

[109] *Attorney General of Hong Kong* v. *Ng Yuen Shiu* [1983] 2 AC 629 (PC), distinguished in *R.* v. *Falmouth and Truro Port Health Authority, ex parte South West Water Ltd* [2001] QB 445 (CA); and *Darmalingum* v. *The State* [2000] 1 WLR 2303 (PC), distinguished in (1) *Attorney General's Reference (No. 2 of 2001)* [2001] 1 WLR 1869 (CA), and (2) *Mills* v. *HM Advocate* [2002] UKPC D2, [2004] 1 AC 441 (PC) (a devolution case).

[110] *Dictum* of Lord Diplock in *Baker* v. *The Queen* [1975] AC 774 (PC), 788 applied in *R. (on the application of Kadhim)* v. *Brent London Borough Council Housing Benefit Review Board* [2001] QB 955 (CA); *dicta* of Lord Clyde in *De Freitas* v. *Permanent Secretary of Ministry of Agriculture, Fisheries, Lands and Housing* [1999] 1 AC 69 (PC), 80 applied in *Gough* v. *Chief Constable of Derbyshire Constabulary* [2002] QB 1213 (CA); *dictum* of Lord Atkin in *Eshugbayi Eleko* v. *Officer Administering the Government of Nigeria* [1931] AC 662 (PC), 670 applied in *R.* v. *Governor of Brockhill Prison, ex parte Evans (No. 2)* [2001] 2 AC 19 (HL); and *dicta* of Lord Atkin in *Proprietary Articles Trade Association* v. *Attorney General for Canada* [1931] AC 310 (PC), 324 applied in *R. (on the application of McCann)* v. *Crown Court at Manchester* [2002] UKHL 39, [2003] 1 AC 787 (HL).

[111] *Dicta* of Wilson J in *Perka* v. *The Queen* (1984) 13 DLR (4th) 1 (SC of Canada), 36 considered in *In re A (Children) (Conjoined Twins: Surgical Separation)* [2001] Fam 147 (CA).

The same pattern emerges from a survey of an index of 13 leading series of law reports published in the first seven months of 2010.[112] Three Privy Council decisions and one decision of the High Court of Australia were considered or applied in four public law cases (broadly defined to include criminal law).[113]

That is not to say that foreign decisions have a minimal impact. Many more have been cited to and by courts, and might have influenced their thinking, without being expressly analysed, followed, or distinguished in judgments. Some public law principles have been shaped, at least partly, by foreign influences. The rule against anyone being a judge in his own cause derives from Roman law,[114] as does much else in the common law. Coercive interim remedies against the Crown entered English law after they came to be available to protect Community rights in EU law.[115] The principle of proportionality is significant in national law because of its importance in EU and ECHR law, and there has been some support for applying it in preference to *Wednesbury* unreasonableness, even in cases not involving EC law or Convention rights.[116] In *R. (Association of British Civilian Internees: Far East Region)* v. *Secretary of State for Defence*, the Court of Appeal had 'difficulty in seeing what justification there now is for retaining the *Wednesbury* test', but considered that, since it had been applied on several occasions by the House of Lords, the Court of Appeal could not 'perform its burial rites'.[117] However, on this point the potential for extending proportionality seems to be limited. It is hard to see how it would apply to a case in which no infringement of a right is alleged. The structure of a proportionality assessment presupposes that the challenged act, rule or decision is presumptively unlawful because it infringes a right, and so needs to be justified. A proportionality test then places the burden on the defendant to justify the infringement. By contrast, a test of unreasonableness presupposes that the act, etc. is prima facie lawful, casting the burden of establishing unlawful unreasonableness on the claimant. Proportionality as deployed in EU and ECHR law therefore cannot easily be transposed into review of acts, etc. which do not infringe rights.

[112] *Law Reports Cumulative Index August 2010* (2010) 99–128.

[113] *Appellant S395/2002* v. *Minister for Immigration and Multicultural Affairs* (2003) 216 CLR 473 (HC of Australia), applied in *HJ (Iran) v. Secretary of State for the Home Department* [2010] 3 WLR 386 (SC); *Bowe* v. *R.* [2001] UKPC 19 (PC): dictum of Lord Bingham of Cornhill applied in *R.* v. *Bell* [2010] 1 Cr App R 407 (CA); *Brannigan* v. *Davison* [1997] AC 238 (PC), considered in *Rottmann v. Brittain* [2010] 1 WLR 67 (CA); *Walton* v. *R.* [1978] AC 788, applied in *R.* v. *Khan (Dawood)* [2010] 1 Cr App R 74 (CA).

[114] See Asser, above, n. 95.

[115] *R.* v. *Secretary of State for Trade and Industry ex parte Factortame (No. 2)* (Case C-213/89) [1991] 1 AC 603 (CJEC and HL); see now e.g. *R.* v. *Secretary of State for Health, ex parte Imperial Tobacco Ltd* [2002] QB 161 (CA).

[116] See e.g. *R. (Daly)* v. *Secretary of State for the Home Department* [2001] 2 AC 532, 548–9, *per* Lord Cooke of Thorndon; *R. (Alconbury Developments Ltd)* v. *Secretary of State for the Environment, Transport and the Regions* [2001] UKHL 23, [2003] 2 AC 295 at [51], *per* Lord Slynn of Hadley.

[117] [2002] EWCA Civ 473, [2003] QB 1397 at [34]–[37].

CONCLUSION

The internationalization of public law in the UK is a process of long standing and is continuing. It has benefits, but there are also risks. These are, first, that a borrowed solution will not be workable in a constitution with the special balance of power and democratic accountability found within the state, and, secondly, that reasoning relying on foreign thinking will not be regarded as a legitimate way of deciding public law cases under the constitution. The latter concern is evident in the Chief Justice's dissenting opinion in the US Supreme Court in *Atkins* v. *Virginia*, mentioned earlier. Where in the UK's constitutional rules are judges authorized to look for emerging standards abroad to guide UK public law? Statutes can authorize or require courts to look abroad, as the European Communities Act 1972 and the Human Rights Act 1998 show. But in the absence of such express provisions, there is a danger to the perceived constitutional legitimacy of judicial decisions if courts resort to foreign guidance without a legal basis in national law.

For these reasons, international influences must be treated with caution in developing the structures of an established state and constitutional arrangements. Filters are needed. If the relationship between national and international legal planes is not defined in a constitutional document (such as South Africa's 1996 Constitution) or statute, a case-by-case approach can lead to distinct oddities. We can conclude with two questions about the UK to illustrate this. First, how well are the fundamental values of representative democracy, executive accountability to Parliament, and parliamentary sovereignty protected against the inappropriate introduction to municipal law (either by the executive or by judges) of obligations derived from international law or EU law? Secondly, why do UK judges seem more receptive to foreign judicial developments than to international treaties? One could argue that treaty obligations binding the UK in international law impose standards which should be respected by all organs of the state, including courts, and that there can be no justification in terms of UK constitutional law for having regard to judgments of foreign courts in jurisdictions which have no current constitutional link to the UK. This distinction is recognized by the Constitution of South Africa: there is a duty to consider treaties, but no duty to consider foreign judgments, in cases on constitutional rights. It will be interesting to see whether the influence of the ECHR and the European Court of Human Rights under Human Rights Act 1998, ss 1 and 2, bringing with it other treaties which the European Court of Human Rights uses to interpret the ECHR, will gradually lead UK courts to give greater weight to a range of treaties than they presently feel able to do.

FURTHER READING

Allison, John W. F., 'Transplantation and cross-fertilisation in European public law', in Jack Beatson and Takis Tridimas (eds), *New Directions in European Public Law* (1998) ch. 12.

Bell, J., 'Mechanisms for cross-fertilisation of administrative law in Europe', in Jack Beatson and Takis Tridimas (eds), *New Directions in European Public Law* (1998) ch. 11.

Brewer-Carrías, A. R., 'Constitutional implications of regional economic integration', in John Bridge (ed.), *Comparative Law facing the 21st Century* (2001) 675–752, on the way in which integration of markets between states depends on and in turn influences national constitutional structures and rules.

Chigara, B., 'Pinochet and the administration of international criminal justice', in Diana Woodhouse (ed.), *The Pinochet Case: A Legal and Constitutional Analysis* (2000) ch. 7, on the interaction of Treaties, peremptory norms of customary international law, and the criminal law.

Dupré, C., *Importing the Law in Post-Communist Transitions: The Hungarian Constitutional Court and the Right to Human Dignity* (2003) esp. ch. 2 on the importation by nascent or re-nascent states of constitutional law and constitutional values from other systems.

Ellis, E. (ed.), *The Principle of Proportionality in the Laws of Europe* (1999), for essays on the use of a single public law principle in a variety of legal systems.

European Review of Public Law (2006) 18 (1) (Spring) 25–653 contains papers derived from a valuable colloquium of the European Group of Public Law in 2005 on the internationalization of public law, including general surveys and studies of particular European jurisdictions.

Fatima, S., *Using International Law in Domestic Courts* (2005), for full consideration of the various ways in which municipal legal systems can take account of different kinds of public international law.

Feldman, D., 'The Role of Constitutional Principles in protecting International Peace and Security through International, Supranational and National Legal Institutions', in Claudia Geiringer and Dean R. Knight (eds), *Seeing the World Whole: Essays in Honour of Sir Kenneth Keith* (2008) 17–47, examines the relationship between UN Security Council resolutions under UN Charter, Chapter VII and national constitutional law. (A slightly earlier version can be found at (2008) 6(1) *New Zealand Journal of Public International Law* 1–33.)

Henkin, L., Pugh, R. C., Schachter, O. and Smit, H., *International Law: Cases and Materials* (3rd edn, 1993) ch. 3, on the relationship between public international law and municipal law.

Smith, E., 'Give and take: cross-fertilisation of concepts in constitutional law', in Jack Beatson and Takis Tridimas (eds), *New Directions in European Public Law* (1998) ch. 8.

Zines, L., *Constitutional Change in the Commonwealth* (1991) ch. 1, on the development of the constitutional orders of Australia, Canada, and New Zealand towards autonomy from the UK.

USEFUL WEBSITES

Foreign and Commonwealth Office: **www.fco.gov.uk**

The website of the Foreign and Commonwealth Office includes a link to an Official Documents page, which allows further links to useful information, including an explanation of UK Treaty practice and procedure, a Treaty Enquiry Service giving access to a searchable database of Treaties to which the UK is a party, and the texts of the Treaties.

United Nations: **www.un.org**

The United Nations website provides (among much other information and material) the text of the UN Charter, information about the working of the institutions of the United Nations including the General Assembly and the Security Council, the texts of many international Treaties, and information about international tribunals.

Venice Commission: **www.venice.coe.int**

This website, maintained by the European Commission for Democracy through Law (the 'Venice Commission') under the auspices of the Council of Europe, offers a wealth of material, including reports, recommendations and amicus curiae *opinions, together with summaries of significant decisions of, and links to, constitutional courts and other courts with similar jurisdictions in Europe and elsewhere.*

Virtual Institute of the Max Planck Institute for Comparative Public Law and International Law: **www.mpil.de/ww/en/pub/news.cfm**

This website offers both valuable documentation and links to many other useful sources.

World Legal Information Institute: **www.worldlii.org**

The website of the World Legal Information Institute provides links to web-based sources on international and national law throughout the world. It includes decisions of international tribunals as well as constitutional texts and decisions of national courts.

Yale University Law School's Comparative Administrative Law Blog: **http://blogs.law.yale.edu/blogs/compadlaw**

This is an interesting website with information about developments in many jurisdictions.

PART II

THE INSTITUTIONAL CONTEXT

Editorial note

The chapters in this part of the book are concerned with institutional matters.

Chapters 6 and 7 focus on institutional reform at UK level. Parliament itself has been going through a period of reform, particularly of the procedures and working practices in the House of Commons. Some of these have facilitated the processing of government business. The extent to which these reforms strengthened the capacity of the House of Commons to hold government to account is debatable: since 2010 the powers of backbenchers in the House of Commons in relation to their party whips and to the government have been increased by reforms to the arrangements for select committees, and control of the agenda for backbench business. But it remains to be seen what effects these changes will have on the ability of the House of Commons to impose effective accountability on the government.

The membership and committee structure in the House of Lords have also been going through changes. The composition of the House, the question of whether any of its members should be elected, and how any appointments should be made, have proved highly controversial, partly because of conflicting perceptions of the role and character of the second chamber. These issues in parliamentary reform are the subjects of Chapter 6. As this book goes to press new proposals for further reform of the House of Lords are anticipated.

The conduct of government itself has been affected by a range of theories about management, some imported from the private sector. These have resulted in institutional changes in the form of the creation of executive agencies within government departments. These have in turn altered relationships between ministers and civil servants, and between ministers and Parliament, and thus accountability arrangements. These changes have also produced an increased emphasis on effectiveness – on outputs and outcomes rather than inputs and procedures in government – and on the citizen as the 'consumer' of services. These are discussed in Chapter 7.

Other institutional reforms include devolution in Scotland, Northern Ireland, and Wales, and implications of these for England and for the UK as a whole. These form the subject of Chapter 8. The arrangements for each country in the UK differ in response to the different needs of and pressures from Scotland, Northern Ireland, and Wales. In each of those three countries there are elected institutions – the Scottish Parliament, the Northern Ireland Assembly, and the Assembly for Wales, with executives possessing extensive powers. Each of the devolution arrangements preserves the formal legislative sovereignty of the UK Parliament, discussed in Part I. But each changes the political climate in which the UK Parliament and government operate: referendums have been held before devolution takes place; conventions of consultation and consent before changes of government policy in relation to devolution have developed. These constrain the exercise of parliamentary sovereignty.

Local government too has been undergoing a period of change, which goes back many years. Chapter 9 is concerned with the most recent reforms, intended to reinvigorate local democracy by institutional arrangements such as the use of cabinets instead of committees and, in some places, elected mayors, and by relaxing central control over local authorities which meet government-set criteria. Recent reforms have also sought to enable local authorities to fulfill a mission as 'community leaders', which may fit in with the coalition government's 'Big Society' agenda. The Localism Bill 2010 proposes a general power of competence that would free local authorities from much central government control. Attempts by the government to introduce elected regional tiers of government where local opinion was in favour came to an end after a referendum on the matter in the North East in 2004 failed to produce sufficient support.

Finally in this Part of the book, Chapter 10 discusses administrative justice, including judicial review, tribunals, ombudsmen and more informal methods of 'alternative dispute resolution'. In these mechanisms principles of constitutionalism and informality may come into conflict with one another. Administrative justice should be recognized as a constitutional principle, which informal dispute-settlement should not be permitted to marginalize.

6

REFORMING THE UNITED KINGDOM PARLIAMENT

Dawn Oliver

SUMMARY

The two Houses of Parliament are supposed to hold the executive accountable for its conduct of government. In practice for many decades the government has controlled the House of Commons, and the House of Lords, lacking legitimacy because of its unelected membership, has exercised restraint in challenging governments. Efforts by Members of Parliament (MPs) to redress the balance between government and Parliament have met with resistance. However, since 2010 the House of Commons has asserted greater autonomy in its relations with the government. And it is having to adjust to a coalition government, which affects the working of many of the conventions of the constitution.

As far as the House of Lords is concerned, despite its reluctance to confront government where legitimacy issues arise there is general support for the ways in which the Lords perform their functions of acting as constitutional watchdogs, scrutinizing Bills and draft Bills, holding government to account, and providing a forum for the examination of matters of public interest. The composition of the House of Lords is however controversial and problematic. The patronage that the current arrangements creates is not subject to any legal regulation. It has proved impossible to achieve support for an independent merit-based appointment system. The coalition government has committed itself to legislation for a wholly or substantially elected second chamber. Whether such a house will continue to accept conventions as to the primacy of the House of Commons and not blocking manifesto Bills is uncertain. It is also uncertain whether elected members would perform the scrutiny functions well.

INTRODUCTION

One of the recurring concerns in debates about the UK constitution for at least 40 years has been about the capacity, even the willingness, of the two Houses of Parliament to discharge their constitutional functions of holding government to account and giving or withholding consent to legislation. Given that normally, as a result of the workings of the first past the post electoral system, one party commands a majority in the House of Commons and that party forms the government, and given the strong party discipline exercised by party whips on behalf of the Prime Minister and the leaders of opposition parties, governments have been able to resist both opposition to their policies and attempts to reform the workings and procedures of the House so as to increase its capacity to hold government to account effectively. The position was reached in 1976 that Lord Hailsham, Lord Chancellor in waiting at the time, coined the phrase 'elective dictatorship' to describe the system.[1]

But is the common assumption that Parliament should hold government to account and that it should be reformed in order to enable it to perform that function well founded in contemporary politics? Or is the House of Commons' real constitutional function rather to provide and support the government of the day? The answer depends whether these questions are asked from the point of view of independent parliamentarians or government.

A prevalent assumption is that Parliament is, and rightly so, at the heart or apex[2] of the political and governing processes in the UK. The emphases in constitutional orthodoxy on parliamentary sovereignty, parliamentary privilege, parliamentary self-regulation, the parliamentary executive, and ministerial responsibility to Parliament as being fundamental to the system imply this centrality.[3] Yet it became increasingly obvious in the 1990s and 2000s that Parliament's centrality was declining for a number of reasons. British membership of the European Union means that the freedom of action of national legislatures and executives are necessarily limited by EU policies (though the functions of national legislatures in relation to EU measures have been enhanced under the Treaty of Lisbon[4]). The devolution of power to the Scottish Parliament, the Welsh Assembly, and the Northern Ireland Assembly has removed both legal and political power from Westminster and Whitehall and created new bodies in those parts of the UK that are, in effect, operating under law-based, written constitutions. The UK Parliament and executive now have to share power with, defer to, or compromise with other bodies with political power and legitimacy.[5] Enactment of the Human Rights Act 1998 reduced reliance on the two Houses to provide political protection against abuses of power by the executive, and increased legal, judicial protections against such abuses.[6]

The growing focus on law-based constitutionalism[7] – the law being a combination of Acts of Parliament and common law doctrines[8] – in preference to 'the political

[1] *Elective Dictatorship*, the Richard Dimbleby lecture, 1976, published by the BBC. See also Hailsham, *The Dilemma of Democracy*, 1979.

[2] See Report of the Hansard Society Commission on Parliamentary Scrutiny, *The Challenge for Parliament: Making Government Accountable* (2001).

[3] See e.g. *Strengthening Parliament*, the report of the Conservative Party's Committee to Strengthen Parliament chaired by Lord Norton of Louth (2000).

[4] See Chapter 4 above. [5] See Chapter 8 below. [6] See Chapter 3 above.

[7] See D. Oliver, *Constitutional Reform in the UK* (2003). [8] See Chapter 1 above.

constitution'[9] as a result of devolution, the Human Rights Act 1998, and membership of the European Union has meant that Parliament operates increasingly within legal and political constraints. The UK constitution has had to adapt to these new constitutional realities.[10] But constitutional adaptation has not taken the form of extra-parliamentary, US-style judicial review of legislation and executive action by a Supreme Court, or continental-style, pre-legislative constitutional or administrative scrutiny such as operates in France. Instead adaptations have been largely intra-parliamentary.

PARLIAMENT'S RELATIONS WITH GOVERNMENT

The relationships between the two Houses and the government are largely regulated by a combination of conventions, standing orders, and Acts of Parliament. As far as conventions are concerned, it is a fairly settled tenet of the system that the government is entitled to get its business through the House of Commons, and to have it considered in the Lords. It has been the position that the government was entitled to have measures that were promised in its election manifesto given a fair wind in the House of Lords (the Salisbury convention[11]). However, under a coalition government such as was formed in 2010 the agreement of the coalition partners about policies cannot reflect the manifesto promises of all coalition partners, or indeed of the coalition as a whole. Thus it is no longer clear what obligation the House of Lords has as regards manifesto promises. It used to be accepted that it is the sole prerogative of the Commons as the elected House and the chamber in which the Prime Minister sits, to withdraw confidence from the government so that a general election or resignation of the government followed by appointment of a new Prime Minister charged with producing a new administration should take place. The Fixed Term Parliaments Bill that was introduced into the Commons in the summer of 2010 will, if passed, change this by making it difficult or impossible for an early election to be called if, for instance, the government lost the confidence of the House. This will place considerable responsibility on the parties in the House of Commons when a government, particularly a coalition government, has only a small, or no, majority.

Turning to the House of Lords' relations with government, the chamber generally accepts that its role is secondary, in recognition of the fact that the government and the Commons have democratic legitimacy flowing from election which the Lords have not been able to claim.[12] On the other hand, the fact that the House of Lords Act 1999 removed most of the hereditary peers but left other aspects of the House unaltered

[9] See J. A. G. Griffith, 'The Political Constitution' (1979) 42 *MLR* 1.

[10] See M. Elliott, 'Parliamentary sovereignty and the new constitutional order: legislative freedom, political reality and convention' (2002) 22 *Legal Studies* 340.

[11] According to this convention, a 'manifesto' Bill, foreshadowed in the governing party's most recent election manifesto and passed by the House of Commons, should not be opposed by the second chamber on second or third reading.

[12] The composition of the House of Lords is discussed below.

has been taken to legitimate their exercise of their ancient powers. And it has come to be accepted that the Lords have important functions in the revision of legislation, especially on technical or drafting points; functions in delaying legislation in order for the Commons or the government to reconsider a proposal where there are serious concerns, in the House of Lords or elsewhere, about its wisdom; a constitutional and human rights watchdog function; functions in the scrutiny of, for instance, the grant of delegated powers, of deregulation orders, and of European legislation; and generally functions in debating matters of public importance. The very fact that the Lords are not elected and are relatively independent of party, and that the House contains members with particular skills, expertise, and interests in these kinds of activity would serve to legitimate much of their activity if it took place outside somewhere called 'Parliament', such as a constitutional council or a council of state. But difficulties are undeniably caused by the fact that this is a 'House of Parliament' whose members are not elected: it is understandable that governments will object to opposition from that quarter. We shall consider these difficulties in due course.

The House of Lords is supposed to complement, rather than compete with or duplicate, the House of Commons. Since it is not elected, it cannot be part of its role to give or refuse consent to legislation on behalf of the electorate – or of any other body. It is not a body of 'representatives', though to an extent it is a body of 'voices' – a 'civic forum' – in the sense of a body of people who can contribute particular and significant perspectives to debate. Although its consent is required to legislation other than money Bills (unless the Parliament Acts 1911 and 1949 apply to facilitate the giving of royal assent to legislation without the consent of the Lords, normally after a year's delay) the Lords' power to withhold consent to legislation is in practice a mechanism for securing that the House of Commons (and the government) take seriously and respond to concerns, often of a non-party political nature, expressed in the second chamber.

We need to bear in mind at this point that giving (or refusing) consent to government policy and legislation are not the only checking functions that need to be performed in a democracy which accepts – as the UK seems to do – that majoritarianism can pose a threat to the principles which underlie most democratic arrangements. Uninhibited majoritarianism can undermine respect for minorities' interests and human rights and the operation of effective, often non-political, mechanisms for imposing accountability on government, such as constitutional review. The question then is, where and how and by what criteria are such checking functions performed in the UK?

In most other democracies a written constitution provides the criteria for checking government. The legislature – often primarily the second or upper chamber or senate – and constitutional courts or councils or councils of state perform checking functions. The UK lacks such external, independent institutions. My suggestion is that the House of Lords has come to fill this gap and to compensate for the fact that other non-parliamentary checking institutions commonly provided for in written constitutions do not exist in the UK.

With these background considerations in mind let us turn to examine the roles and functions of the two Houses of Parliament.

THE HOUSE OF COMMONS

The role and functions of the House of Commons are relatively well settled, in theory at least. They are:

- to provide the government of the day (all ministers must by convention be members of one or other of the two Houses, and the Prime Minister and the Chancellor of the Exchequer must be members of the Commons);
- to sustain the government in power by passing its legislation;
- to give – or refuse – consent to taxation;
- to authorize and control public expenditure;
- to secure redress of constituents' grievances; and
- generally to hold the executive to account for its policies and the conduct of government.

A major problem has been that executive dominance of all aspects of House of Commons activities has made it virtually impossible, until recently, for the Commons to act as a body collectively committed to holding the government to account, as opposed to blocks or tribes of party politicians. This has been partly due to the strongly party and partisan culture in the House which subordinates consideration of the general public interest to party interests.

In the run-up to the 1997 general election the Joint (Labour Party–Liberal Democrat) Consultative Committee on Constitutional Reform committed the two parties to 'renewing Parliament' as a key to wider modernization of the UK's constitutional arrangements.[13] This signaled the possibility of what, since the formation of the coalition in 2010, has come to be known as 'new politics'. But despite the pre-election commitment of Labour and the Liberal Democrats, modernization of the House proved very difficult to achieve in the Parliaments of 1997 to 2010. This was due in large part to the conservative ethos of both main political parties, lack of commitment to reform on the part of Leaders of the House, a lack of trust in the government on the part of the opposition parties, and suspicion of its possibly ulterior motives in responding to modernization proposals. The fact of the matter was that the House of Commons was incapable of taking initiatives to modernize itself and depended on the approval of the government if any reforms were to be implemented.[14]

After the 2001 election the former Foreign Secretary, Robin Cook, was appointed Leader of the House and he pushed the modernization programme forward with some success – and some failures. He resigned in April 2003 in protest at the government's policy on Iraq. The pace of reform of the Commons then slackened. However, in

[13] Joint Consultative Committee Report (1997) para. 64.

[14] See A. Kennon, *The Commons: Reform or Modernisation* (2000).

the summer of 2009 reform of the House of Commons entered a new phase, which resulted in what have come to be known as the 'Wright Reforms' in which the House decided to act more autonomously in its relations with government. These reforms are discussed below.

INDIVIDUAL MINISTERIAL RESPONSIBILITY: GOVERNMENT'S DUTY TO PARLIAMENT

A major challenge has been, and remains, to give teeth to the convention of individual ministerial responsibility to Parliament.[15] The classic version of the doctrine is that ministers are responsible to Parliament for all that happens in their departments, though they will only be regarded as culpable in respect of their own decisions or failures. They must give an account to Parliament, and they are expected to make amends if something has gone wrong.[16] The effectiveness, and content, of this convention had become a high-profile issue over a number of decades[17] but it crystallized in the Arms to Iraq Affair in the early 1990s. Certain defendants had been prosecuted for breach of the rules relating to the export of arms to Iraq, but it emerged during the trial that members of the government had known about the exports and had, in effect, allowed the prosecution to proceed in the knowledge that the defendants were at risk of wrongful convictions. The trial judge stopped the trial. Sir Richard Scott, then Vice Chancellor (Head of the Chancery Division of the High Court), was asked to report on the matter. His Report[18] made severe criticisms of ministers. These were debated in Parliament, ministers rejected the criticisms, and no ministers resigned. However, concerns about the basis and weaknesses of the conventions of ministerial responsibility that emerged from that affair were accepted as valid by the John Major government, and the requirement that ministers be accountable to Parliament was reaffirmed by both Houses and formalized through the resolutions on ministerial accountability passed by each House just before the 1997 general election.[19]

After the general election of 1997 and the change of government, these obligations were incorporated into the Ministerial Code by the new Prime Minister, Tony Blair, who accepted that the Prime Minister is responsible to Parliament for enforcing these rules. The Ministerial Code is revised after each election: the resolution has been retained in the code ever since. The Prime Minister also agreed to meet members of the House of Commons Liaison Committee (consisting of the chairs of select committees) twice a year. These concessions were only made, however, after sustained pressure

[15] See Chapter 7 below for further discussion of the convention.

[16] See G. Marshall, *Ministerial Responsibility* (1989); D. Woodhouse, *Ministers and Parliament: Accountability in Theory and Practice* (1994); S. E. Finer, 'The Individual Responsibility of Ministers' (1956) 34 *Public Administration* 377; Hansard Society Commission on Parliamentary Scrutiny, above, n. 2.

[17] See for instance Lord Hailsham, *Elective Dictatorship* (1976); and *The Dilemma of Democracy* (1978).

[18] See *Report on the Export of Dual-Use Goods to Iraq*, HC 115 (1995–6) (the Scott Report); A. Tomkins, *The Constitution After Scott* (1998).

[19] See discussion of these resolutions on ministerial responsibility in Chapter 7 below.

from select committees in the House of Commons and expressions of press and public concern about the weak accountability of ministers to Parliament. And they did not by any means solve the problem of weak ministerial responsibility. Subsequent reforms have, however, strengthened the House of Commons' influence over ministers and its independence from government, and these will be outlined in what follows.

In the last 20 years or so a number of independent agencies have been created with responsibility for holding government to account for matters which previously were for Parliament alone, but which the House of Commons lacked the resources, expertise and independence from government to undertake. Examples of recently formed bodies include the Monetary Policy Committee of the Bank of England, created in 1997 and the Independent Office for Budget Responsibility, created in summer 2010.[20] These bodies are required to report to Parliament. Implicit in these arrangements is the principle that the accountability of the executive should be depoliticised in the sense of being conducted outside party politics in some areas. This raises one of the uncertainties of the role of Parliament, the extent to which it and its members are expected to act free of mandates, whipping, and politicking as if they were independent experts searching for the public interest, as opposed to loyally following their political leaders.

THE SCRUTINY OF LEGISLATION

A major problem over the scrutiny of legislation on the floor of the House of Commons or in its Standing or Public Bill Committees is that it is not conducted according to any particular criteria, but at large. Scrutiny tends to be highly politically partisan, aimed only partly towards improving the Bill and largely towards drawing attention to weaknesses in the Bill and opposing and harassing ministers.[21] As Feldman has pointed out, scrutiny should include the examination of measures against certain standards that are independent of the terms or subject matter of the measure itself.[22] These standards should include matters such as clarity of drafting, compatibility with international obligations and the Human Rights Act 1998, and respect for various constitutional principles such as the independence of the judiciary, legal certainty, non-retroactivity, proportionality of penalty, and so on. This kind of scrutiny is not done well by the House of Commons,[23] dominated as it is by party.

A number of measures were taken in the early 2000s to improve House of Commons scrutiny of legislation and to facilitate the passage of government legislation. The two objectives are commonly in tension with one another. The scrutiny of legislation has been improved by publication of explanatory notes with Bills, and the introduction of pre-legislative scrutiny of some draft Bills. 'Public Bill Committees'

[20] On which see Chapter 13 below.

[21] See Second Report of the Select Committee on Procedure, *Public Bill Procedure*, HC 49 (1984–5) para. 30.

[22] See D. Feldman, 'Parliamentary scrutiny of legislation and human rights' [2002] *Public Law* 323.

[23] But note the discussion of the Joint Committee on Human Rights, below and in Chapter 3 above.

have been introduced to take expert evidence in the course of scrutiny of bills. Acceptance of the carry-over of some Bills from one session to the next[24] takes the time pressure off scrutiny and thus enables it to be done thoroughly if the will to do so exists among backbenchers. However, the norm remains for scrutiny to be completed to enable Bills to receive royal assent before the end of the session. The establishment in 2002 of a Joint Committee on Human Rights[25] (on an initiative from the House of Lords) with the specific responsibility for scrutiny of legislation for compatibility with the Human Rights Act 1998 and the European Convention on Human Rights and for other human rights implications has produced focused, expert, and independent scrutiny of bills.

THE SELECT COMMITTEES

Important reforms have been designed to increase the influence and powers of the House of Commons' select committees and thus the effectiveness of individual ministerial responsibility. The departmental and other investigative select committees have the function of monitoring the expenditure, administration, and policy of government and its departments. These committees now have an agreed, explicit set of core objectives, extending beyond the long established role of imposing direct ministerial responsibility to tasks such as monitoring performance against targets in public service agreements, taking evidence from independent regulators and inspectorates, considering the reports of Executive Agencies,[26] considering major appointments made by ministers[27], and examining treaties within their subject areas.[28]

The government accepts that it has an obligation to respond to select committee reports within two months of their publication. Government responses are published by the House of Commons. In some cases proposals from select committees have first been rejected outright and then ultimately, after a long campaign, been accepted: the Prime Minister's agreement in 2000 to meet the Liaison Committee twice a year is an example of a concession won only after determined persistence on the part of that Committee.

The ways in which departmental select committees were composed attracted criticism over the years. By convention each committee has a majority of government party members, and – until 2010 – each party's whips decided which of their own

[24] See *Hansard*, HC, cols 688–828 (29 October 2002). Normally if a Bill does not complete its parliamentary passage by the end of the parliamentary session each year it is 'lost'. The government will have to reintroduce the Bill in the following session and start the parliamentary process over again. 'Carry over' enables the Bill to continue its parliamentary passage from one session to the next.

[25] See Chapter 3 above. [26] See Chapter 7 below.

[27] Note that the House of Commons Children, Schools and Families Select Committee found the candidate selected by the Minister to be unsuitable: *Appointment of the Children's Commissioner for England*, Eighth Report, HC 998 (2008–09). The minister nevertheless confirmed the appointment.

[28] See Modernisation Committee, First Report, *Select Committees*, HC 221 (2001–02); Liaison Committee, Second Report, *Select Committees: Modernisation Proposals*, HC 692 (2001–02); approved *Hansard*, HC, cols 648–730 (14 May 2002).

party members shall be nominated to each committee. The chairs are shared between the political parties in rough proportion to the balance in the House and – until 2010 – they were in effect appointed by the whips. By convention certain committees are chaired by opposition backbenchers.

In October 2003 the House of Commons resolved that the chairs of the investigative committees should receive additional salaries of £12,500 per annum in recognition of the extra workload they carry, and with a view to providing an alternative career path for backbenchers who might otherwise seek or accept government appointment. But it was also agreed that committee chairs would serve for only two Parliaments. A difficulty here was that the chairs' reliance on the whips for their reappointment to committees after an election, and thus the additional salary, undermined their independence. The extent of the patronage of the whips was increased by this provision.

In the summer of 2010 things changed, though we shall not know for a while how much. In the wake of the scandal over MPs' expenses claims of the summer of 2009[29] both government and Parliament realised that the status of MPs needed to be enhanced.[30] A Select Committee on the Reform of the House of Commons was established in July 2009 and was required to report by November 2009.[31] The 'Wright Report' (named after the chair of the Committee) recommended the election of Select Committee chairs by the whole House in a secret ballot utilizing the alternative vote system, and election of Committee members by secret ballot within the parties. These recommendations were agreed in a series of votes in the House of Commons on 4 March 2010, before the general election, and implemented in the new Parliament in June and July 2010. By then, it will be recalled, a new, Conservative–Liberal Democrat coalition government had been formed: parties who have been in opposition for lengthy periods commonly see things from the opposition's point of view rather than the government's. The control of the House of Commons by the executive was, from that point of view, contrary to the spirit of parliamentary government;[32] political reform was one of the longstanding ambitions of the Liberal Democrat partners in the coalition. Hence the willingness of the new government, and the House of Commons, to implement the reforms. The Wright Report also recommended the formation of a Backbench Business Committee, with responsibility for scheduling debates for 35 days in the current session. This was created under a new House of Commons Standing Order 14 agreed on 15 June 2010.[33]

[29] See Chapter 15 below.

[30] The Parliamentary Standards Act 2009 was rushed through Parliament. It transferred responsibility for a scheme for the reimbursement of MPs' expenses to a new Independent Parliamentary Standards Authority, thus reducing the scope of the House's 'exclusive cognisance' of its own proceedings. See Chapter 15 below.

[31] See 'Rebuilding the House', HC 1117 (2008–09), and 'Rebuilding the House – Implementation', HC 372 (2009–10).

[32] Many reforms to parliamentary procedure have been introduced when a party takes power after a long interval in the wilderness – the reforms to select committees in 1979 were introduced against that background.

[33] See new House of Commons Standing Order 14, 122B, 122D, 152 and 152J. The Committee issued a consultation paper on its method of working in July 2010 (HC 334).

Debates on at least 27 of these days will be in the main chamber. The chairs of select committees and their members were duly elected soon after the new Parliament met. The government has, at last, relaxed its grip over the House of Commons agenda and its select committees.[34] This is part of the 'new politics'.

THE HOUSE OF COMMONS AND ROYAL PREROGATIVE POWERS[35]

Soon after he became Prime Minister in 2007 Gordon Brown and his government embarked on a public consultation[36] about possible constitutional reforms, many of them designed to modernize the arrangements for government's accountability for the exercise of prerogative powers.[37] The upshot was the passage of the Constitutional Reform and Governance Act 2010. This Act, among other things, subjects the prerogative Treaty making power to a requirement that Treaties be laid before Parliament for 21 days (thereby placing what had been known as 'the Ponsonby rule' on a statutory footing) before they can be ratified, and gives the House of Commons a power to veto their ratification.[38]

The 2007 consultation paper had asked whether the prerogative power to send British troops into armed combat – the war power – should be placed on a statutory basis.[39] A number of select committees in each House considered the matter and a consensus emerged that a better approach would be for the two Houses to pass resolutions that would require the Prime Minister to provide information to Parliament as to a proposed deployment in advance of the deployment (where appropriate), and for a deployment to be subject to authorization by the Commons. It would become a convention of the constitution that the Prime Minister would comply with the resolutions.[40] To date however (April 2011) no such resolutions have been passed, though the Prime Minister gave Parliament this information on a debate about Libya on 21 March 2011 and deployment was approved.

ASSESSMENT OF HOUSE OF COMMONS REFORM AND FUTURE PROSPECTS

On the face of it there was a great deal of reform of the House of Commons between 1997 and 2009. But unless and until the culture, the ethos and the politics of the House

[34] See *Constitution Unit Report on the Effectiveness of Select Committees* [forthcoming, 2011].

[35] See also discussion of the royal prerogative in Chapter 7 below.

[36] *The Governance of Britain*, Cm. 7170 (July 2007). See also Joint Committee on the Draft Constitutional Renewal Bill, HL 166/HC 551 (2007–08).

[37] These include, for instance, the dissolution of Parliament, Treaty making, defence, war, the running of the civil service, pardons, and honours.

[38] See Chapter 7 below for discussion of other reforms to the royal prerogative under the Constitutional Reform and Governance Act 2010.

[39] *The Governance of Britain – War Powers and Treaties: Limiting Executive Powers*, Cm. 7239, October 2007.

[40] HL 166/HC 551, above, n. 36.

of Commons and its members changed, reform was likely to add up to little more than tinkering. Robin Cook, former Leader of the House, noted that the House was highly tribal, and that the parties which make up the tribal groupings, though they are rivals and competitive with one another, were attached to and defensive of the tribal system itself.[41] And that system required loyalty to the government on the part of its front- and backbenchers. There was no real sense that the House of Commons was or ought to be autonomous in its relations with government or independent of the parties that operate in the House:[42] the House deliberately rejected an opportunity to increase independence by reforming the process for appointment of members of select committees in 2002.

After around 2009, however, the ethos and politics changed and reform has entered a new phase. This has been reinforced by the formation of a coalition government. On forming a government David Cameron made a point of stating that:

> Today we are not just announcing a new government and new ministers. We are announcing a new politics. A new politics where the national interest is more important than party interest, where co-operation wins out over confrontation, where compromise, give and take, reasonable, civilised, grown-up behaviour is not a sign of weakness but of strength.[43]

The point of relevance for the moment in this quotation is that Cameron was signaling a weakening of tribalism in the House. Opinion polls over the following months indicated that the public was broadly happy with a coalition. But it is too early to know whether politics has really changed in this way.

AND THE FUTURE?

Not only have backbenchers taken control of the election of chairs and members of select committees and of the backbench business agenda, but further reforms that will affect the House of Commons are envisaged in the coalition agreement as part of a commitment to the new politics.[44] The Fixed Term Parliaments Bill, if enacted, will remove the power of the Prime Minister to call an election at the time most favourable to his party – the timing of elections will be depoliticized. The right to recall an MP, if enacted, would increase the influence of voters as against parties over MPs and provide additional incentives for MPs to perform their duties conscientiously.[45] The introduction of the Alternative Vote for elections to the House of Commons,[46] if supported in the 2011 referendum, while it would not secure proportionality between the parties according

[41] *Parliament and the People: Modernisation of the House of Commons*, Hansard Society (2002).

[42] See B. Winetrobe, 'The Autonomy of Parliament', in D. Oliver and G. Drewry (eds), *The Law and Parliament* (1998).

[43] Reported in *The Guardian*, available at www.guardian.co.uk/politics/2010/may/12/coalition-government-seven-page-pact. It is usual for newly appointed Prime Ministers to assert their commitment to the service of the whole country.

[44] www.Cabinetoffice.gov.uk/media/409088/pfg_coalition.pdf.

[45] See Chapter 15 below.

[46] 2010 Parliamentary Voting System and Constituencies Bill.

to their share of the vote (it is a preferential voting, not a proportional representation, system) would, if enacted, produce a House whose members had received a majority of the votes in their constituencies, even if as the second or third choices of voters. The electorate itself would enjoy more power over the composition of the House. Backbenchers, it is envisaged, will then have more authority as representatives of their constituents as against the government than the many MPs who are currently elected on the votes of a minority of their electorate under the first past the post system.

THE HOUSE OF LORDS

The House of Lords is undoubtedly a constitutional anachronism. The membership consists of hereditary peers and life peers, and archbishops and bishops of the Church of England (who are not peers and serve until retirement). The Prime Minister decides how many new members should be appointed to the House, how many new members each party should have and consequently the party balance, and how many new cross-benchers (members who do not take a party whip) there should be. There is no statutory or other formal regulation of this power, which is an exercise of the royal prerogative. As a matter of practice when appointing peers from other parties, the Prime Minister accepts the nominations of the leader of that party. These party nominees are expected to take their party whip. An understanding has grown up that some party nominees will be 'working peers' who will be expected to attend regularly and participate actively in the work of the House; others, though taking a party whip, are there as an honour and reward for past service. There is no regulation of the ways in which the parties select these members, although there is a general understanding, not always observed, that award of a peerage should normally only be granted to people who have achieved distinction in their lives. Nor are there any other formal criteria (for example the needs of the House of Lords for particular experience or expertise in its membership, or a gender or ethnic balance) for these appointments.

Before nominees are appointed they are subject to scrutiny, for propriety only, by a non-statutory Appointments Commission that was established in 2000.[47] In 2006 concerns were raised that persons who had made loans to parties before the 2005 general election had been nominated for peerages as rewards for the financial support – 'cash for peerages'.[48] The concerns were raised by the Appointments Commission, partly because the making of loans had not been disclosed to them. There was also public concern that criminal offences may have been committed in the offer of peerages. After investigating the matter the Director of Public Prosecutions decided that there was not the evidence to justify prosecutions. The Appointments Commission has no veto on appointments even if it is not satisfied as to propriety. This experience increased skepticism about the system of appointing, rather than electing, members of the second chamber.

[47] See House of Lords Appointments Commission website, www.lordsappointments.gov.uk.

[48] See Chapter 15 below.

The Appointments Commission is also charged with nominating independent members for appointment to the House of Lords. The Prime Minister however reserves the right to make some independent appointments, for instance of immediate past holders of public positions including the Speaker of the House of Commons, the Cabinet Secretary, the Chief of the Defence Staff, the Queen's Principal Private Secretary, and the Archbishops of Canterbury and York.

The practice in recent years has been for the Prime Minister to seek approximate proportionality among the party aligned members of the House of Lords according to the vote each party received in the most recent election. There is no cap on the number of members of the House, and there is no possibility of retirement. After the general election in 2010 the number of members of the House was increased greatly as the outgoing Prime Minister rewarded outgoing members of the House of Commons with 'dissolution' peerages, and the new Prime Minister sought to build up the numbers in the coalition parties towards proportionality.

As of 1 April 2011 the membership of the House of Lords was as follows: 92 hereditary peers; up to 26 archbishops and bishops of the Church of England; 700 life peers, appointed by the Queen on the advice of the Prime Minister, to be members of the House for life.

The life peers included:[49]

- Members taking the Labour whip 239
- Members taking the Conservative whip 170
- Members taking the Liberal Democrat whip 89
- Retired Lords of Appeal in Ordinary /Justices of the Supreme Court 23
- Other cross-benchers who take no party whip 130
- Others 29

The presence of hereditary peers and archbishops and bishops of the Church of England requires explanation. Until 1999 membership included some 750 hereditary peers. The House of Lords Act 1999 removed all hereditary peers from membership of the House, save for 75, who were elected by the body of hereditary peers in proportion to the then party allegiance or cross-bench membership of all hereditary peers, two hereditary Great Officers of State, and a further 15, elected to membership by all the then members of the House to serve as office holders, for example as deputy speakers. When one of the 75 hereditary members elected by hereditary peers dies, runners-up from the 1999 election take their place. When one of the 15 holders of office dies (as happened in 2003) the whole House elects a replacement from among the hereditary peers who wish to stand for election. The Clerk of the Parliaments (a permanent official of the House) maintains a register of those peers.[50]

---

[49] See www.parliament.uk/directories/house_of_lords_information_office.

[50] Lord Weatherill introduced the House of Lords (Amendment) Bill (HL 32) in the House of Lords in February 2003, which if enacted would have ended the system of replacing hereditary peers by election. The number of hereditary peers in the House of Lords would thus, over time, diminish, although the party

Up to 26 archbishops and bishops of the Church of England become members of the House of Lords by seniority of appointment as bishops, and they serve until retirement, normally at 70. They are not life peers, though some are awarded peerages after their retirement. They sit on the Bishops' Benches as Lords Spiritual.

The overall allegiance of members of the House of Lords (including hereditary peers) as of 1 April 2011 was as follows:[51]

- Conservative 218
- Labour 243
- Liberal Democrat 93
- Crossbench 184
- Bishops 25
- Others 29

Party affiliation is not proportionate to the level of support for the parties in the 2010 election; nor indeed is it rationally or explicitly related to any other measure. These arrangements are extraordinarily anomalous.

After the House of Lords Act 1999 removed most of the hereditary peers, these arrangements meant that the neither one party nor the government had a majority in the House of Lords. This has generally been regarded as a positive feature of the House, since in order to win a vote the government has to persuade the cross-bench members as well as its own supporters. But majorities in votes depend upon who attends, and many members of the House attend only sporadically or not at all. The unexpected position in late 2010 was that the Conservatives and Liberal Democrat peers, if they voted together and in support of the coalition, could normally expect to constitute a majority in the House on any given vote.

Despite these anomalies the House of Lords is in many respects a highly regarded and effective chamber in much of what it does. It is one of the busiest parliamentary chambers in the world.[52] Although its members are part-time it is a full-time house. Increasingly its best work is done in committees and is of a non-partisan, technical, expert, or constitutional kind.

CONCEPTUALIZING THE ROLE AND FUNCTIONS OF A SECOND CHAMBER

It is not easy to reconcile the facts that the House of Lords' members are for the most part party aligned and are not elected, and yet that it is an effective chamber, with

balance would change since most hereditary peers are Conservative. This would mean that new life peers would be created to maintain the desired party balance.

[51] See www.parliament.uk/directories/house_of_lords_information_office.

[52] See for instance its Annual Report, e.g. HL 41 (2004–05). See also Annual Report, HL 20 (2009–10), available at www.publications.plt.uk/pa/ld200910/ldbrief/20/20.pdf.

democratic principles. At root the problem is how we conceptualize institutions called 'chambers of Parliament', and how we conceptualize the House of Lords in particular. Generally, chambers of Parliament are bodies through which consent is given on behalf of the electorate or, in the case of second chambers in federal systems, on behalf of the members of the federation, to legislation proposed by the government and to the granting of supply. Consent to legislation and supply is in practice given or refused conditionally upon the government maintaining the confidence of the chamber through discharge of its duties to give an account of its conduct of government and its policies. Chambers of Parliament are elected for the very reason that, in a democracy, only the people through their elected representatives have the right to give consent to legislation. The House of Lords does not fit this model at all.

This is not however a full picture of the consent-giving – or perhaps more appropriately, consent-refusing – processes in democracies operating under the Rule of Law. In many countries other bodies besides the Parliament have the right to delay or refuse consent to legislation or to set aside legislation passed by the Parliament. For instance, supreme courts may have the power to strike down or disapply legislation on grounds of unconstitutionality.[53] Constitutional councils or councils of state pronounce, before legislation is passed, on matters such as the constitutionality or workability of legislation or draft legislation and this may affect the eventual validity of laws. Arrangements of this kind exist even in countries with elected second chambers, such as France,[54] suggesting perhaps that elected bodies are not suited to the performance of these functions and so additional institutions should play a part in the legislative process. Consent-refusing activity carried out by such independent, unelected, expert bodies is a central part of the democratic arrangements in those countries: democracy there is not taken to mean that elected legislators in the Parliament are entitled to pass, on bare majorities of those present and voting, any law they wish, regardless of its compatibility with the constitution, human rights, or international obligations. Such consent-refusing activity by external institutions is not possible in relation to primary legislation passed by the UK Parliament because of the almost uniquely British doctrine of parliamentary sovereignty.[55]

Second chambers in countries with federal systems normally have special functions in representing the regions, states or provinces and concerning themselves principally with federal matters. In a non-federal state like the UK, whose devolution arrangements are asymmetrical and evolving,[56] the potential role of a second

[53] As in the USA and Germany.

[54] See e.g in relation to France, M. Hunter-Henin, 'Constitutional Developments and Human Rights in France: One Step Forwards, Two Steps Back' (2011) 60 *International Comparative Law Quarterly* 1–22; J. Bell, *French Constitutional Law* (1992); J. Massot, 'Legislative drafting in France: The Role of the Conseil d'Etat' (2001) 22 *Statute Law Review* 96–107; J. Bell, S. Boyron and S. Whittaker, *Principles of French Law* (2nd edn, 2008); S. Boyron, *The French Constitution* (2011, forthcoming).

[55] See Chapter 2 above. The exception to the doctrine of parliamentary sovereignty is that European law prevails over inconsistent UK legislation: see Chapter 5 above.

[56] See Chapter 8 below.

chamber in representing and protecting the interests of the nations and regions is less clear than in federal states. In most bicameral states, all of which have written constitutions, second chambers also have functions as constitutional watchdogs, their consent being required to constitutional amendments and other constitutional measures, often with a requirement for a special majority in each House.[57] Given the fact that the UK, almost uniquely, has no written constitution and a sovereign Parliament (in the special sense that its legislation on any subject matter will be given effect to by the courts, unless it is incompatible with EC law),[58] it would not be possible for the UK's second chamber to perform the same kind of watchdog role as can second chambers in states with written constitutions. Nonetheless it is natural that the House of Lords, being less political than the House of Commons, should have come to be looked to as a kind of constitutional watchdog. This is strongly reflected in its committee work. And given the operation of the electoral and party systems, which, as has been noted, mean that almost invariably the government – even a coalition government – has a safe majority in the House of Commons, the House of Lords is accepted as having a role in making the government and the House of Commons think again about controversial legislation and about the quality of legislation – drafting, workability, and so on.

The capacity of the House of Lords to perform its relatively apolitical functions has been incrementally increased in important ways in recent years. This is because the party-aligned members are relatively free from party pressures, being there for life; they have their careers behind them and thus normally have no ambitions for a future career in politics and thus no reason to seek to please their party leadership. The presence of members mostly of distinction and with experience and expertise in matters coming before the House has enabled its debates to be authoritative and well informed. Cross-benchers hold the balance in the House, and this means that the parties seeking the support of cross-benchers, as will often be the case since no one party has a reliable[59] majority in the House (and nor have the coalition parties as of 2010), have to argue the issues on the merits rather than appeal to party loyalty.

THE HOUSE OF LORDS IN ACTION

The House of Lords has established important and influential select committees to perform some watchdog functions. We have already noted the role of the Joint Committee on Human Rights, established in February 2001, in scrutinizing Bills and draft Bills for human rights implications and generally commenting on human rights issues.[60] The House of Lords Constitution Committee was formed in 2001 in response

[57] For comparative studies of second chambers see M. Russell, *Reforming the House of Lords: Lessons from Overseas* (2000); S. C. Patterson and A. Mughan, *Senates: Bicameralism in the Contemporary World* (1999).

[58] See discussion in Chapters 2, 3, and 4 above.

[59] The coalition does not have a majority of all the seats in the House of Lords, but in practice it may win votes because of non attendance by many members. This is a new position for a government since 2010.

[60] See also discussion in Chapter 3 above.

to the recommendation of the Royal Commission on the Reform of the House of Lords that the role of the second chamber as a constitutional 'longstop' should be increased, not by increasing the formal powers of the House to delay or veto legislation but through the establishment of a Constitutional Affairs Committee which would monitor legislation for constitutional issues and generally keep a watching brief on the constitution.[61]

The House of Lords' European Union Committee undertakes in-depth scrutiny of selected items of EU business, through its six subcommittees. The reports are widely regarded in Europe as being of extremely high quality and are capable of having a significant influence on European policy development. The Delegated Powers and Regulatory Reform Committee scrutinizes proposals in Bills for the delegation of powers and reports to the House whether the provisions of any Bill inappropriately delegate legislative power, or whether they subject the exercise of legislative power to an inappropriate degree of parliamentary scrutiny. (There is no parallel in the House of Commons with the scrutiny of delegated powers functions of the Lords, so this is a function, essentially constitutional in nature, performed uniquely by the Lords.) The Committee's functions were extended into the scrutiny of deregulation orders under the Deregulation and Contracting Out Act 1994, the Regulatory Reform Act and the Legislative and Regulatory Reform Act 2006. The Merits Committee reports on the merits of Statutory Instruments.

What has been happening in the UK, then, is that functions performed pre-legislatively by councils of state or constitutional councils or post-legislatively by supreme or constitutional courts in other countries are being institutionalized and internalized in the second chamber. They are intra-, not extra-parliamentary. But the ability of the chamber to perform those functions, and the legitimacy of its doing so, depend upon its composition and in particular the degree of party political penetration of its intrinsically apolitical, constitutional, functions.

Self-restraint on the part of the politicians in the House is necessary to counter the predictable allegations of illegitimacy that will be made where government bills are opposed by unelected members on party political rather than constitutional or other non-partisan grounds.[62] Ultimately, under the Parliament Acts 1911 and 1949 a Bill may receive the royal assent without the consent of the House of Lords.[63]

The Royal Commission on the Reform of the House of Lords, which reported in 2000, considered whether further conventions might be elaborated to give effect to a principle that the second chamber should be cautious about challenging the clearly expressed views of the House of Commons on any public policy issue, whether or not contained in the election manifesto of the governing party. But it felt that it was

[61] Royal Commission on the Reform of the House of Lords, *A House for the Future*, Cm. 4534 (2000).

[62] A degree of self-restraint has been observed under the Salisbury convention, noted earlier. But since the formation of the coalition and the consequent absence of a winning manifesto the Salisbury convention cannot operate.

[63] See e.g. *Jackson* v. *Attorney-General* [2006] 1 AC 262.

not possible to reduce this principle to a simple formula, and proposed that the second chamber should pragmatically work out a new convention reflecting the principles.[64] If necessary a new conciliation mechanism should be developed through a joint committee. Neither of these proposals has been implemented.

PROPOSALS FOR REFORM OF THE COMPOSITION OF THE SECOND CHAMBER

The Royal Commission on the Reform of the House of Lords (of which I was a member) recommended in 2000 that the hereditary members should be removed, and the Prime Minister should no longer have the right to appoint to the second chamber. The Church of England's representation should be reduced to 16. An independent statutory Appointments Commission should be established with responsibility for appointments. Membership should include up to 35 per cent elected people, 20 per cent independents and the rest appointed party aligned members. Overall the party membership should reflect the proportion of the vote won by parties at the most recent general election. The Appointments Commission should move towards a gender and ethnic balance, secure that a range of 'voices' were in the second chamber, and use ten places for members of Christian denominations other than the Church of England and of other faiths.[65] These proposals did not find favour with the press, the parties or the public on a number of grounds. The parties did not want 'their' nominees to be subject to the Appointments Commission. And public opinion favoured election (while at the same time not wanting partisan party politics in the second chamber).

Since the Royal Commission reported the composition of the House of Lords has been the subject of a number of parliamentary debates and government and other proposals.[66] Broadly, the House of Commons tends to favour a wholly or substantially elected second chamber and the House of Lords tends to prefer a wholly appointed one. The coalition agreement of summer 2010 commits the government to legislation for a wholly or mainly elected House. An all party committee chaired by Nick Clegg, the Deputy Prime Minister and leader of the Liberal Democrats, was established in the summer of 2010 with a view to publishing a draft bill in due course which would be scrutinized by a joint committee of the two Houses. As of 14 April 2011 no draft has been published.

Overall, the possible reforms of the composition of the House of Lords will have important repercussions for the UK's 'political constitution'. If the second chamber is to be wholly or substantially elected by a system of proportional representation, it will be more political. It may have greater legitimacy than the House of Commons and feel confident in challenging it and the government. The Salisbury convention, according to which the second chamber should not oppose manifesto Bills on first or second

[64] Royal Commission, above, n. 61, pp. 40–1.

[65] Ibid., Chapter 12.

[66] For instance the white paper, *The House of Lords: Reform*, Cm. 7027 (2007).

reading, will be yet further undermined. The primacy of the House of Commons may be challenged.

If, further, the ability of the House of Lords to perform its functions of independent, expert scrutiny of bills is undermined by an elected and therefore more politically partisan, less expert or experienced membership, then inevitably a need will arise, and be argued for, for the scrutiny function to be entrusted to external bodies of the kinds that exist in France (the Conseil d'état and the Conseil constitutionnel), for instance. It might even be suggested that such a body should replace the second chamber. That argument has already begun to be made.[67] Indeed, if a reformed House of Lords were less able to perform its legislative scrutiny work it is not unthinkable that the courts might feel justified in dealing with provisions that they consider to be contrary to fundamental constitutional principles[68] by either declaring them to be unconstitutional (though valid) or refusing to give effect to them.[69] That would not be the best way of dealing with constitutionality in the absence of a written constitution, but it might be better than leaving matters to a Parliament that lacks the capacity and commitment to prevent such laws being passed.

My own view is that members of the second chamber should all be appointed, in stages, on merit for a single term of, say, 12 years, by an independent, statutory Appointments Commission. The members would be part time, and paid a *per diem* allowance for participation. The Commission should be under duties to secure that no party or coalition of parties has a majority in the chamber (indicating therefore some 25 per cent of independent members), that the balance between the parties reflects the distribution of the votes between parties in the most recent general election, that there is a gender and ethnic balance, that 'voices' that are not heard in the Commons are heard there (for example disabled people) and that the members include individuals with the expertise the House needs to enable it to perform its functions of scrutiny of legislation and inquiry into matters of public interest (for instance as to as to human rights, constitutional matters, treaties, foreign affairs, European law, culture, sport, industry, commerce, finance, economics, and so on). Its special responsibilities would include, as now, human rights, the constitution, delegated powers, European law and treaties. There would need to be transitional provisions to phase out the present members of the House, for example by not replacing the hereditary peers as they die and by permitting retirement (taking permanent leave of absence), and to reduce the overall number of numbers.[70]

Such an arrangement would secure that the good work currently performed by the second chamber can continue to be done, and that the legitimacy problems stemming from the exercise of unregulated political patronage in making appointments are resolved.

[67] See Lord Bingham of Cornhill 'The House of Lords: its Future?' [2010] *Public Law* 261.

[68] See Chapters 1, 2 and 3 above.

[69] See *Jackson* v. *Attorney-General* [2006] 1 AC 262.

[70] The 2010–11 House of Lords Reform Bill, introduced into the House of Lord by Lord Steel of Aikwood proposes reforms along similar lines, though in less detail and with less regulation of party nominations.

CONCLUSIONS

The long standing problem of executive domination of the House of Commons, having been half-heartedly tinkered with between 1997 and 2009, has been tackled more vigorously since then by provisions for the independent election of members of select committees and a Backbench Business Committee. The reality of coalition government is changing the politics of the House to what might be a less competitive and more co-operative one. But MPs are likely to continue to be limited in their ability to scrutinize Bills against criteria such as constitutionality, legal certainty, and workability because of their own party loyalties and the commitments they have to their constituents and to other Commons business.

The chamber that does include members willing and able to perform this important scrutiny function is the House of Lords. But if the House of Lords were to become substantially politicized through elections, there would be a major new lacuna in our constitutional checks and balances: provisions for the proper scrutiny of bills and for the government to take notice of such scrutiny because of a delaying power would be missing. In my view the case for moving, perhaps bit by bit, to a written constitution with a supreme court with power to strike down unconstitutional legislation, and a constitutional council or council of state with powers of pre-legislative scrutiny of draft Bills for workability and compatibility with important constitutional principles, would then become overwhelming. This would reduce the freedom of action of the House of Commons and the government. In other words, the trend from a political to a law-based constitution would be accelerated by politicization of the House of Lords. An independently appointed second chamber would be preferable.

FURTHER READING

Blackburn, R. and Kennon, A. (eds), with Wheeler-Booth, Sir Michael, *Griffith and Ryle on Parliament. Functions, Practice and Procedures* (2nd edn, 2003).

Hansard Society Commission on the Legislative Process, *The Challenge for Parliament. Making Government Accountable* (2001).

HM Government, *The House of Lords: Reform*, Cm. 7027 (2007).

Limon, D. W. and McKay, W. R. (eds), *Erskine May: Parliamentary Practice* (22nd edn, 1997).

Report of the Royal Commission on the Reform of the House of Lords, *A House for the Future*, Cm. 4534 (January 2000).

Rogers, R. and Walters, R., *How Parliament Works* (6th edn, 2006).

Russell, M., *Reforming the House of Lords. Lessons from Overseas* (2000).

USEFUL WEBSITES

Cabinet Office: **www.cabinetoffice.gov.uk**
UK Parliament: **www.parliament.uk**

7

THE EXECUTIVE: TOWARDS ACCOUNTABLE GOVERNMENT AND EFFECTIVE GOVERNANCE?

Gavin Drewry

SUMMARY

We sometimes talk about modern constitutions as if there is a clear-cut distinction between 'executive', 'legislative', and 'judicial' functions. This way of thinking originated in the notion of separation of powers, formulated by Montesquieu in the 18th century. But, today, even in the USA, the tripartite division of 'powers' is far from watertight. The UK constitution is based upon a fusion between executive and legislative powers, in which ministers are also members of the legislature.

The traditional British view of the executive needs to be revised in line with new models of decision making based on sectoral policy networks and policy communities. How much of the 18th-century concept of an 'executive' has survived the growth of complex bureaucracies, in which the boundary between the respective functions of ministers and civil servants has become increasingly blurred?

Locating the latter boundary has become more difficult in the wake of a New Public Management (NPM) revolution that has transformed the public services of many developed countries, including the UK. Governments, influenced by free market economic theories, have, on the one hand, sought to diminish the scale of state intervention and, on the other, have increasingly questioned the efficiency of traditional bureaucracy and have come to prefer more market-orientated, performance-driven, and 'business-like' modes of public service delivery. In the UK there has been a long series of important public sector reforms, including privatization, contracting out and the Citizen's Charter, subsequently incorporated into a wider agenda of public service modernization. One of the UK's most significant NPM reforms was the Next Steps programme, launched in 1988, which transferred many of the functions of central government departments to semi-independent agencies, headed by chief executives employed on short-term contracts - many of them recruited from outside the civil service.

Cumulatively, all these reforms – and many others that have taken place more recently – have had very important implications for ministerial responsibility, for parliamentary scrutiny of government, and for the structure of the civil service itself. After much procrastination, in the last days of the 2005–10 Parliament, the Labour government enacted the Constitutional Reform and Governance Act 2010, which includes provisions that create a statutory basis for the civil service and for its management by ministers. It also creates a statutory opportunity for Parliament to consider Treaties, made under the royal prerogative, prior to ratification.

INTRODUCTION

The familiar word 'executive' which features in the title of this chapter is more problematical than might at first be supposed. Much constitutional discourse still revolves around traditional 'separation of powers' distinctions between executives, legislatures, and judiciaries. But, as this chapter shows, in an age in which traditional notions of 'government' have given way to the broader and more flexible concept of 'governance', and as policy making is seen as a complex and evolving process, conducted in an array of specialized policy networks with varied and shifting memberships, it has become unfashionable to depict the modern executive function as being confined merely to presidents, prime ministers, and cabinets and (by extension) their civil servants.

This shift in the terminology is linked to the growing complexity of the relationship between political and bureaucratic office-holders – ministers and civil servants. The comfortingly democratic idea that the 'policy' decisions that matter are taken by ministers, accountable to citizens via the ballot box (and in the UK, to Parliament), while civil servants merely play a subordinate 'administrative' role has long been recognized as a myth. The constitutional doctrine of ministerial responsibility suggests that ministers should account to Parliament for all the actions of their officials, but in an era of 'big government' in which ministries are large, fragmented, and decentralized, this too is largely a mythical aspiration. This gap between fact and fiction has, as we shall see, been exacerbated (or at least consolidated) in recent years by NPM developments, such as the Next Steps agency programme in the 1980s and by subsequent moves by the Labour government to modernize the machinery of government and the public services. The arrival of a Conservative–Liberal Democrat coalition government after the 2010 general election has given rise to yet more challenges to established constitutional theory and practice.

So today – for reasons that this chapter seeks to explain – the meaning of the term 'executive', and the constitutional character of the executive function, have become afflicted by much doubt and confusion. And this ambiguity poses particular difficulty when we seek to determine who is responsible for what, and who is to be held accountable, and by what means, for the deeds and misdeeds of a government.

THE EXECUTIVE AND SEPARATION OF POWERS – THE HISTORY OF AN IDEAL

Everyday usage of the term executive often refers to a mechanism or an office-holder *in charge* of an organization or a process, responsible for making sure that things run efficiently and that goals are met. Thus, we encounter various species of executive officers, chief executives, and executive committees, running bodies of various types – private companies, hospitals, and local authorities; and most UK civil servants now work in Next Steps executive agencies (discussed later in this chapter), responsible for the delivery of major central government services and headed by agency chief executives. The word is also associated with the function of 'execution', particularly in legal contexts: for instance, the execution of a warrant or of a death sentence, or being the executor of a will. But this meaning is quite different from being 'in charge'; on the contrary, it has much more to do with carrying out the instructions of a higher authority.

The meaning of the term executive and the nature and the boundaries of executive office and of the executive function become even more complex and elusive when applied to national governments and considered in the context of a 'changing constitution'. Those familiar with the doctrine of separation of powers – associated originally with the writings of the 18th-century French philosopher, Montesquieu, and then enshrined in the US Constitution – have probably become accustomed to structuring their thinking about governmental arrangements around the ostensibly simple tripartite array of 'legislatures', 'executives', and 'judiciaries'. But even 250 years ago, when Montesquieu wrote his famous work, *The Spirit of the Laws*, this constitutional model begged a lot of questions.

The modern usage of the term began with the founding and early development of the US Constitution – and with discussions among the founding fathers about 'separation of powers' and ways of safeguarding liberty under the law. But there is an important *pre-history* of that debate wherein the meaning of the term executive became entangled with the early intermixing of 'executive' and 'judicial' (and indeed 'legislative') functions in the absolute monarchies of feudal Europe.

The doctrine of separation of powers may in fact be traced back to the ancient Greek and Roman belief in 'mixed government': ordered in such a way as to ensure the accommodation of different social orders and interests – foreshadowing the more modern constitutional notion of checks and balances enshrined in the US Constitution. Centuries later, medieval writers began to refer to a distinction between *making* law and *putting it into effect*: but in those days the latter was usually taken to refer to the role of the courts in applying the law (we must remember in this context that English absolute monarchs used to dispense justice in their high court of Parliament).

This interpretation of executive power in judicial terms survived in the work of John Locke, writing in context of the 17th-century English conflicts between Parliament and monarchy. His *Second Treatise on Government* (1690) moved on from the Greek notion of mixed government, by advocating a two-way institutional/

functional separation between legislative and executive powers (though the latter was still essentially seen in the 'judicial' sense, just described).

Institutional developments in the aftermath of the 17th-century Cromwellian interregnum paved the way for a more developed notion of executive power in the modern sense of applying the law by *administrative* rather than judicial means. This was the sense in which Montesquieu used the term in *The Spirit of the Laws*, first published in 1748:

> Where the legislative and executive powers are united in the same person or body there can be no liberty, because apprehensions may arise lest the same monarch or senate should enact tyrannical laws to execute them in a tyrannical manner.

This argument was taken up by James Madison in one of *The Federalist Papers*[1] which argued the case for ratification of the US Constitution. Madison had to concede that in England the legislative, executive, and judicial branches were far from being as separate and as distinct from one another as Montesquieu had claimed, but he argued (somewhat tendentiously) that Montesquieu clearly can only have meant:

> No more than this, that when the *whole* power of one department is exercised by the same hands which possess the *whole* power of another department, the fundamental principles of a free constitution are subverted.

Madison went on to show that none of the existing constitutions of the then American States, working to formulate and agree the new federal constitution, while they might pay lip-service to separation of powers, displayed in fact a complete functional separation. And he went on to develop the notion of checks and balances between the constituent branches, summed up in one of the earlier Federalist essays,[2] which begins:

> To what expedient, then, shall we finally resort, for maintaining in practice the necessary partition of power among the several departments, as laid down in the Constitution? The only answer that can be given is, that as all these exterior provisions [such as setting out functional boundaries in the Constitution, and hoping everyone abides by them] are found to be inadequate, the defect must be supplied, *by so contriving the interior structure of the government as that its several constituent parts may, by their mutual relations, be the means of keeping each other in their proper places.* (emphasis added)

The founding fathers linked their perception of the need to avoid combining the legislative and executive functions to their concerns about preserving the Rule of Law. If the same institution/ruler both makes the laws and interprets/applies them, then those laws can be redefined according to the whim and caprice of that ruler, and no citizen can be certain about the limits of lawful conduct. And this poses a fundamental threat to liberty – the right of the individual to do whatever is not prohibited by law.

[1] The generic title of the 85 essays, written by Alexander Hamilton, John Jay, and James Madison, that were published in New York newspapers between autumn 1787 and spring 1788. The one referred to here is essay XLVII, February 1788.

[2] Federalist essay LI.

SEPARATION OF POWERS IN THE UK?

But of course the constitutional picture was and is very different in England (unsurprisingly so, given that the American founding fathers wanted to create a republican constitutional order that would be an improvement on that to which they had been subjected under the English monarchy prior to the War of Independence). In his classic work, *The English Constitution*, published in 1867, Walter Bagehot rejected traditional 18th-century accounts of British politics, deploying his famous distinction between the 'dignified' and the 'efficient' parts of the constitution. The former (the monarch and the House of Lords) merely 'impressed the many' and secured popular support for the system. But behind this dignified façade lay the 'efficient secret' of the English Constitution, 'the close union, the nearly complete fusion, of the executive and legislative powers'. The key to this fusion was a hitherto largely unrecognized assemblage of Her Majesty's ministers, the cabinet. This arrangement is of course the very antithesis of American-style separation of powers, which prohibits officers of the executive branch, headed by the President, from sitting in Congress; in Britain, ministerial members of the executive must (by constitutional convention) be selected either from the elected House of Commons or from the non-elected House of Lords – and nowadays, on democratic grounds, mainly from the former. Bagehot attached particular importance to the constitutional position of the House of Commons, which had what he called the 'elective' function of making and unmaking cabinets.

A lot has happened to the constitutional structure since 1867, and some of it happened quite soon after Bagehot's commentary was published. Written in an age of small-scale government, his analysis predated the development of a large, complex, and decentralized civil service. In the 1860s the functions of government were very largely to do with war, peace, diplomacy, trade, and the running of the Empire: government was not concerned with the provision of public services like education, health care, pensions, or urban planning. Local government existed then only in a very rudimentary form.

And the growth of the electorate in the second half of the 19th century led to the rise of party machines to compete for the popular vote. In the same period, following the industrial revolution, governments were becoming more interventionist with regard to issues like public health, factory safety, and policing. Party labels became much more important to candidates standing for election to Parliament, and MPs became increasingly subject to party discipline in the House of Commons as governments sought to mobilize their majorities to enact ever larger and more ambitious programmes of legislation. The position of the Prime Minister as party leader and the party's chief media spokesman, as the selector of his (or, in Mrs Thatcher's case, her) ministerial team and as chair of cabinet became ever more dominant. In an introduction to a new edition of Bagehot's *The English Constitution*, Richard Crossman argued that cabinet government had been superseded by prime ministerial government.[3] The

[3] R. H. S. Crossman, 'Introduction', to Walter Bagehot, *The English Constitution* (1963) 1–57.

growing role of prime ministers as big players on the international stage has further encouraged this view. Experience of the administrations of, in particular, Margaret Thatcher (1979–90) and Tony Blair (1997–2008) has fuelled debates about whether we now have, in essence if not in strict constitutional form, a 'British Presidency'.[4]

This issue has become, at least for the time being (after the 2010 general election), a bit more complicated in circumstances of coalition government, where the prime ministerial leader of the largest party in the House of Commons is constrained by the necessity of sharing power with the leader of the party with which he is in coalition and by having to award some ministerial positions to leading members of that party. Were a system of proportional representation to be introduced for Westminster elections then this exceptional situation – though it is quite normal in other Western European countries – would probably become the norm and the 'prime ministerial government thesis' would have further to be re-examined.

FROM GOVERNMENT TO GOVERNANCE

Nowadays, the old tripartite distinction between the different 'powers' looks crude and out of date, though it is still an important part of the vocabulary of constitutional discourse. It has in any case become increasingly fashionable to try to break free of traditional constitutional and institutional categories by thinking in more flexible and wide-ranging terms about what institutions are (the 'new institutionalism'[5] has become an important concept in political science) and by employing the concept of 'governance' alongside that of 'government'. In the mid-1990s a working group of the International Institute of Administrative Sciences came up with the following working definition of governance:

- Governance refers to the process whereby elements in society wield power and authority, and influence and enact policies and decisions concerning public life, and economic and social development.
- Governance is a broader notion than government, whose principal elements include the constitution, legislature, executive, and judiciary. Governance involves interaction between these formal institutions and those of civil society.
- Governance has no automatic normative connotation. However, typical criteria for assessing governance in a particular context might include the degree of legitimacy, representativeness, popular accountability, and efficiency with which public affairs are conducted.

[4] The arguments are extensively and cogently reviewed in Michael Foley, *The British Presidency* (2000).

[5] See B. G. Peters, 'Political Institutions, Old and New', in R. E. Goodin and H.-D. Klingemann, *A New Handbook of Political Science* (1996) 205–20.

Nowadays, the word governance is commonly used, not only by academic political scientists but also by politicians and international aid agencies (as in the phrase, 'good governance', widely used by aid agencies, such as the World Bank). It also features in the title of the Constitutional Reform and Governance Act 2010, discussed later in this chapter. At the same time, the processes of government and governance, including policy decision making, have come to be seen as crossing traditional institutional boundaries and involving wider communities and networks of actors both from inside government and from outside, whose composition varies from one policy sector to another. There is no place in this chapter to explore the interesting ramification of the extensive policy networks/communities literature, but the following passage captures some of the flavour:

> A policy network (or policy community) is a systematic set of relationships between political actors who share a common interest or general orientation in a particular area. These relationships typically cut across formal institutional arrangements and the divide between government and non-governmental bodies. A policy network may therefore embrace government officials, key legislators, well-placed lobbyists, sympathetic academics, leading journalists and others. The recognition of the existence of policy networks highlights the importance of informal processes and relationships in policy making and particularly in policy initiation.[6]

THE CORE EXECUTIVE

The debates about 'prime ministerial' versus 'cabinet' government and about the possible emergence of a 'British presidency' still attract scholarly interest, but – in similar vein to the movement from government towards governance – some political science commentators began, towards the end of the 20th century, to move away from traditional notions of a British 'executive' comprising Prime Minister and cabinet by employing the broader and more flexible term, *core executive*. Thus, Professor Rod Rhodes has written as follows:

> In fact, what constitutes the executive varies from policy area to policy area. Departments take important policy decisions with little or no reference to the cabinet and Prime Minister. Equally, central co-ordination, for example the Treasury's role in economic policy making, is not a function solely of Prime Minister and cabinet. The term 'executive' is used here to refer to the centres of political authority which take policy decisions. In other words, the executive institutions are not limited to Prime Minister and cabinet but also include ministers in their departments. The term 'core executive' refers to all those organisations and procedures which coordinate central government policies, and act as final arbiters of conflict between different parts of the government machine. In brief, the 'core executive' is the heart of the machine, covering the complex web of institutions, networks and practices surrounding the Prime Minister, cabinet, cabinet committees and their official counterparts,

[6] A. Heywood, *Politics* (3rd edn, 2007) 432.

less formalised ministerial 'clubs' or meetings, bilateral negotiations and interdepartmental committees.[7]

One feature of this approach is that it both implicitly ('all those organisations and procedures') and explicitly ('and their official counterparts') draws civil servants into the ambit of the core executive, alongside ministers. Traditional UK constitutional analysis draws a clear demarcation line between the role and the status of *elected* ministerial members of the political executive, both members of and answerable to Parliament, and the *non-elected* civil servants who advise them. That line was relatively easy to identify in the first half of the 19th century when the government and its agendas, and the bureaucracy that supported it, were very small. But it became ever more blurred and more permeable as we moved into the complexities of the 20th-century interventionist state. And the blurring has become more noticeable with the NPM programmes that began after Mrs Thatcher's first election victory in 1979 and continued under her successors.

It is to these matters that we now turn our attention.

FROM EXECUTIVE POWER TO THE ADMINISTRATIVE STATE

Discussion of executive functions has been complicated by the rise of modern, economically and politically developed administrative states, with large and complex bureaucracies. The 'executive' functions of presidents, prime ministers, and cabinets have come to be shared with salaried administrators – and the boundaries of the executive function have expanded and become blurred. One by-product of this is the endless debate in public administration about the 'policy'/'administration' dichotomy, and about the division of responsibility for 'policy' and 'operational' matters.

Many early writers on the phenomenon of bureaucracy depicted it as an unqualified evil, at odds with democratic government. But others (notably the German scholar Max Weber)[8] came to recognize bureaucracy as a ubiquitous and effective organizational model, essential to developed social systems underpinned by rational-legal forms of authority. Decades before Weber, the English philosopher John Stuart Mill's classic essay on representative government, published in 1861, had acknowledged the need for trained officials, so long as the ultimate control lies with representative institutions:

[7] R. A. W. Rhodes, 'From Prime Ministerial Power to Core Executive', in R. A. W. Rhodes and P. Dunleavy (eds), *Prime Minister, Cabinet and Core Executive* (1995) 12. See also C. Hay and D. Richards , 'The Tangled Webs of Westminster and Whitehall: The Discourse, Strategy and Practice of Networking Within the British Core Executive' (2000) 78 *Public Administration* 1–28.

[8] See in particular M. Weber, *The Theory of Social and Economic Organisation*, trans. A. M. Henderson and T. Parsons (eds) (1947). For more general discussion of the development of the concept of bureaucracy, see M. Albrow, *Bureaucracy* (1970); A. Dunsire, *Administration: The Word and the Science* (1973).

> Government by trained officials cannot do, for a country, the things which can be done by a free government; but it might be supposed capable of doing some things which free government, of itself, cannot do... There could not be a moment's hesitation between representative government among a people in any degree ripe for it, and the most perfect imaginable bureaucracy. But it is, at the same time, one of the most important ends of political institutions, to attain as many of the qualities of the one as are consistent with the other; to secure as far as they can be made compatible, the great advantage of the conduct of affairs by skilled persons bred to it as an intellectual profession, along with that of a general control vested in, and seriously exercised by, bodies representative of the entire people.[9]

But Mill was, of course, writing in an age of 'small government', when the nominal size of the civil service (in 1851) was around 39,000.[10] Central government ministries were very small, and the great majority of civil servants were copy clerks and messengers who have no modern counterparts in an age of word processing, photocopiers, telephones, emails, and twitter. Nearly all government offices were centrally located in and around Whitehall. Ministers were able, and were expected, to be personally involved in all the key decisions in their ministries – and to shoulder the responsibility in Parliament, if things went wrong (although, even then, they often managed to side-step parliamentary criticism). A century later the size of the civil service had swelled tenfold; the functions of government had expanded far beyond the grasp of day-to-day ministerial control; senior civil servants, not directly accountable to Parliament, not subject, as ministers are, to periodic re-election, and operating largely out of the public eye, had – both by default and by deliberate delegation – acquired a great deal of power in their own right.

Though the role of some senior civil servants involves working closely with ministers on matters of policy, the great majority of civil servants are involved in delivering public services – paying welfare benefits, issuing passports, licensing road vehicles, collecting taxes, etc. But whatever their role, it is a firm principle that all civil servants are politically neutral. They give loyal service to the government of the day, of whatever party. Serving civil servants, particularly senior ones, are required to refrain from active involvement in party politics – campaigning or standing as candidates for elected office. And the spectacle that occurs in Washington, DC whenever there is a change of presidency, of thousands of political advisers moving out and being replaced by the appointees of the new incumbent, has, notwithstanding the use of a few 'special advisers' on temporary contracts,[11] no parallel in the UK when there is a change of Prime Minister.

Civil service neutrality means serving ministers of any government currently in office with non-partisan loyalty. Thus, when a Labour government came to power in May 1997, under the premiership of Tony Blair, civil servants who, for 18 years, had served Conservative administrations, headed first by Margaret Thatcher and then

[9] J. S. Mill, *Considerations on Representative Government*, R. B. McCallum (ed.) (1948) 180.

[10] See G. Drewry and T. Butcher, *The Civil Service Today* (2nd edn, 1991) 48.

[11] Defined in Constitutional Reform and Governance Act 2010, s. 15, see below.

by John Major, stayed in post following the transition (apart from ones who would have moved jobs anyway). Some temporary special advisers replaced the advisers who had been serving the outgoing government, but their numbers were small. Much the same thing occurred after the general election of 2010, when a Conservative–Liberal Democrat coalition replaced Labour governments that had been in office for 13 years.

The problem of ensuring that public bureaucracy serves rather than usurps democratic government, and gives good and cost-effective service to the taxpayer (who funds it) and to the consumer of public services (who is in most cases also a taxpayer), acquires new urgency in an age of large-scale, interventionist government. And since the 1980s, concern about the 'bigness' of government and the scope and cost of its activities has become a key item on the agenda of political debate – increasingly so in the recent circumstances of economic crisis that have led to drastic public sector cutbacks.

MODERNIZING GOVERNMENT: FROM PUBLIC ADMINISTRATION TO PUBLIC MANAGEMENT

The election of the Thatcher government in 1979 marked the beginning of a period of rapid and radical change in UK public administration. The process continued under Margaret Thatcher's Conservative successor, John Major – and was further developed and repackaged by Tony Blair's Labour government. Public administration was displaced – at least in part – by NPM, which rejected traditional bureaucratic methods and structures in favour of market-based and business-like regimes of public service.[12] The radical nature and extent of the NPM phenomenon has been summarized by the Australian academic, Owen Hughes:

> Since the mid-1980s there has been a transformation in the management of the public sectors of advanced countries. The rigid, hierarchical, bureaucratic form of public administration, which has predominated for most of the twentieth century, is changing to a flexible, market-based form of public management. This is not simply a matter of reform or a minor change in management style, but a change in the role of government in society and the relationship between government and citizenry.[13]

As Hughes observed, variations on the NPM theme can be found in the recent administrative histories of many developed countries. He went on to characterize this as 'a new paradigm in the public sector', though whether it is sufficiently universal to amount – as is sometimes suggested – to a new '*global* paradigm', seems much more

[12] There is a very large literature on the nature and development of NPM. See, in particular, Owen Hughes, *Public Management and Administration* (3rd edn, 2003); N. Flynn, *Public Sector Management* (5th edn, 2007); K. McLaughlin, S. P. Osborne and E. Ferlie (eds) *New Public Management: Current Trends and Future Prospects* (2002) – all of which contain good bibliographies.

[13] Hughes, ibid., p. 1.

questionable.[14] Privatisation of major public utilities has certainly been a feature of recent administrative history in many countries around the world, including Europe. But in some other Western European countries (for example France) the impact of NPM has been less than in the UK and traditional Weberian bureaucracy, based on strong principles of administrative law and formal organizational hierarchies, remains the core paradigm. Indeed, even in the UK, the phenomenon of NPM has lost some of its 'newness' and the terminology itself has now become a bit dated – though many of its key characteristics have remained firmly embedded in the administrative culture.

NPM has seen the growth of new relationships between the public sector and the private and voluntary sectors. Public bodies have striven for managerial accolades of quality, like Chartermark (more recently updated to 'Customer Service Excellence'), Investors in People, and the Business Excellence Model. A new public service vocabulary has been invented: privatization, contracting out, market testing, internal markets, public–private partnerships – and, in the late 1990s, 'joined-up government'. So far as the civil service is concerned, the beginning of the 1980s was marked by tough new managerial policies. Substantial cuts in manpower were announced by the Thatcher government: in 1979 there were 732,000 civil servants; ten years later the figure stood at 570,000; by the beginning of the new millennium it was around 450,000. Following the reports of two efficiency reviews, chaired, respectively, by Sir Peter Gershon[15] and Sir Michael Lyons,[16] the Blair government adopted an ambitious programme to cut public service manpower and to move a lot of government jobs out of London and the South East of England. Since 2010, the coalition government has embarked upon a radical programme of cutbacks across the entire public sector.

The early Thatcher years saw a substantial squeeze on civil service pay, and subsequently there have been moves in many parts of the public sector away from traditional, more or less automatic incremental pay increases towards more performance-related pay regimes. Pay and conditions of service in the civil service, below the small number of top grade posts in the senior civil service, have since been decentralized to departments and agencies. Unprecedented friction between the Thatcher government and its civil service reached a climax in the litigious confrontation between the Prime Minister and the civil service unions in the Government Communications Headquarters (GCHQ) case[17] – a *cause célèbre* of modern judicial review.[18]

During the Thatcher years there were also – as we shall see later – important changes in the management and organizational culture of the civil service. Ministers

[14] See Christopher Hood, 'Contemporary Public Management: a New Global Paradigm?' (1995) 10(2) *Public Policy and Administration* 104–17.

[15] The Treasury, *Releasing resources to the front line*, July 2004

[16] The Treasury, *Well Placed to Deliver? – Shaping the Pattern of Government Service*, March 2004.

[17] *Council of Civil Service Unions* v. *Minister for the Civil Service* [1985] AC 374. The Prime Minister, as Minister for the Civil Service, had removed union membership rights from civil servants working at GCHQ. The unions' challenge to the decision failed in the Appellate Committee of the House of Lords, having succeeded at first instance.

[18] The Blair government largely restored trade union rights at GCHQ.

were attracted to ideas, and management nostrums imported from the private sector, designed mainly to improve cost effectiveness and value for money. The transformative process culminated, in 1988, in the launch of the radical Next Steps initiative, a development aptly described by the Commons Treasury and Civil Service Committee as 'the most far-reaching since the Northcote–Trevelyan reforms in the nineteenth century'.[19] The Next Steps initiative effected a transformation of the structure and culture of the civil service, and has had a massive impact upon the organizational arrangements of government departments.[20] It is only one aspect of the much wider NPM agenda, but we pay particular attention to it in this chapter, not least because of the important questions it has raised about the principles and mechanisms of public accountability.

Subsequently, in 1991, came the launch of the Citizen's Charter, with its promise of improved services and enhanced consumer sensitivity throughout the public service; and a big market-testing initiative in central government[21] – and then a re-launch of the Charter initiative by the Blair government, in 1998, under the new title, 'Service First'. This was followed by a white paper on *Modernising Government*, that appeared in May 1999.[22]

It might of course be argued that the arrangements for delivering public services – such as welfare, education, and health – are not a 'constitutional' matter at all, being concerned with administrative superstructure rather than with those fundamental principles of government that are the essence of a constitution. The Next Steps white paper, for instance, was not itself regarded as, or presented as, a 'constitutional' document, neither was the Blair government's *Modernising Government* white paper. However, both these documents – particularly the former – have important implications for 'the changing constitution'. Although the Thatcher government insisted from the outset that existing constitutional principles (particularly those relating to ministerial responsibility) would remain undisturbed, the Next Steps programme had a significant impact on the relationships between civil servants and ministers and between ministers and Parliament – and indeed on the shape and functions of the civil service itself.

The *Modernising Government* proposals consolidated and developed changing ideas about the relationship between the citizen, as consumer of public services, and the state as a service provider (or, in many contexts, a facilitator of service provision through contractual and quasi-contractual partnerships with the private and voluntary sectors). And of course the Blair–Brown government's wider programme featured

[19] Eighth Report from the Treasury and Civil Service Committee, *Civil Service Management Reform: The Next Steps*, HC 494 (1987–88) vol. I, para. 1. The Northcote-Trevelyan Report of 1854 was a landmark in the process of establishing a modern and independent civil service, recruited by merit rather than by ministerial patronage.

[20] See P. Dunleavy, 'The Architecture of the British Central State' (1989) 67 (3) *Public Administration* 249–75, and (1989) 67 (4) *Public Administration* 391–417.

[21] *Competing for Quality: Buying Better Public Services*, Cm. 1730 (1991).

[22] *Modernising Government*, Cm. 4310 (1999).

major items of constitutional reform that have both formed a backcloth to and have fed into the micro-agenda of public service and public management reform: devolution, for instance, has added extra layers and varieties of bureaucracy to what was already there, and has implications both for local government and for the traditional unity of the UK civil service; the Freedom of Information Act 2000 (see below) added some extra 'teeth' to the transparency promised by the Citizen's Charter and Service First.

Let us now look in more detail at some important features of the NPM reforms and at some of their implications for the position of civil servants in a broadly defined core executive.

THE 'NEXT STEPS' PROGRAMME

In November 1986 the Cabinet Office Efficiency Unit embarked upon a service-wide scrutiny exercise, to take stock of the progress already made in managerial reform of the civil service under the Thatcher government (in particular, the Financial Management Initiative) and to report on what further measures should be taken. The outcome of this review was a prospectus for radical changes in the structure and culture of the civil service, published in February 1988, under the title, *Improving Management in Government: the Next Steps*.[23] The outcome of this review, which was immediately accepted by the Thatcher Government, was the launch of the Next Steps agency programme – which can be seen, at least in hindsight, as the flagship initiative of the NPM era and, in some respects, as the last gasp of the fiction that ministers can and should be held 'responsible' for everything that happens in their departments.

A key paragraph of the Efficiency Unit's report read as follows:

> The aim should be to establish a quite different way of conducting the business of government. The central Civil Service should consist of a relatively small core engaged in the function of servicing ministers and managing departments, who will be the 'sponsors' of particular government policies and services. Responding to these departments will be a range of agencies employing their own staff, who may or may not have the status of Crown servants, and concentrating on the delivery of their particular service, with clearly defined responsibilities between the Secretary of State and the Permanent Secretary on the one hand and the Chairmen or Chief Executives of the agencies on the other. Both departments and their agencies should have a more open and simplified structure.[24]

At the heart of the report was a formula for institutionalizing that crucial, though in practice elusive, distinction between the functions of 'administration' and 'policy making' in government. It distinguished between ministerial support and policy functions (performed by about 20,000 civil servants, working closely with ministers) and executive, or service delivery functions. The latter would progressively be transferred to semi-autonomous executive agencies. These agencies, headed by chief executives,

[23] Published by the Cabinet Office. [24] Ibid., para. 44.

would be managed, within an agreed policy framework (which would normally be published), operating at arm's length from day-to-day ministerial control.

On the day of publication, the Prime Minister made a House of Commons statement endorsing the recommendations.[25] She said that the new agencies would 'generally be within the Civil Service, and their staff will continue to be civil servants'. Mrs Thatcher made clear that the convention of ministerial responsibility (discussed below) would still apply to agencies, which would remain within the purview of parliamentary select committees, the National Audit Office, and the Parliamentary Ombudsman.

The early history of the agency programme (nowadays, more than two decades after the launch of the programme, the term 'Next Steps agency' is seldom used other than historically) was outlined in this writer's chapter in the previous edition of this book.[26] Today, nearly 80 per cent of all civil servants work either in executive agencies or in parts of government (such as HM Inland Revenue and Customs) that are organized 'on agency lines'. There are more than 100 agencies, some (like Job Centres Plus) employing tens of thousands of civil servants, others (like various government laboratories) employing fewer than 100 people. The administration of justice has seen an interesting proliferation of agencies: the Prison Service, the Courts Service, and (more recently) the Tribunals Service are all executive agencies of the Ministry of Justice.

AGENCY CHIEF EXECUTIVES

Recalling our earlier discussion of the meanings of 'executive', one interesting aspect of the executive agency programme is the basis upon which agency chief executives (ACEs) have been appointed. In the upper echelons of many parts of the public sector there has, since the 1980s, been a steady movement away from permanent career appointments, automatic salary increments, and internal promotions, towards filling higher-level posts by open competition, performance-related pay, and short-term service contracts whose renewal depends upon proven capacity to achieve stipulated targets. The performance targets of executive agencies are included in published 'framework agreements'.

The UK higher civil service used to be a world of lifetime tenure, annual incremental salary rises, and steady progression up the promotion ladder for those who have passed through the tough graduate recruitment programme (usually in their early twenties) and found their perch on the bottom rung. This culture has been changing for some time, and the Next Steps programme markedly accelerated the process of change.

ACEs have been appointed on three- to five-year contracts; most have been recruited by open competition, and many of the latter have come from outside the

[25] *Hansard*, HC, cols 1149–56 (18 February 1988).

[26] *The Changing Constitution* (6th edn, 2007) 195–201.

civil service. Historically, open competition and security of tenure have substantial constitutional significance, in signalling the neutrality and the independence of a minister's senior official advisers, and rejection of a US-type 'spoils' system based on political patronage (there have been separate concerns about the role and status of politically appointed 'special advisers', which we will return to later). Of course running an agency (the service delivery end of civil service activity) is different – no less important, but generally less politically sensitive – from being a top ministerial adviser. But in practice the distinction is far from absolute: the powerful chief executive of a large agency may be expected to have lines of direct communication with ministers, and the latter may turn to ACEs for 'advice'. And ACEs have had to become accustomed to operating, from time to time, in the very public glare of media and select committee scrutiny.

NEW PUBLIC MANAGEMENT, AGENCIES, AND MINISTERIAL RESPONSIBILITY

In an essay on ministerial responsibility, contributed to an earlier edition of this book, Colin Turpin wrote that, while ministerial responsibility is an 'essential' feature of the constitution, it 'is something malleable and precarious in practice, depending as it does upon procedure and custom, upon intangible understandings and traditions, and upon political circumstances'.[27] This malleability has proved particularly significant – conducive both to useful adaptiveness to change and to problematical uncertainties about who is responsible for what – in the context of NPM reforms. Turpin noted elsewhere in his essay that hiving off and privatizing public services, key items in the NPM agenda, 'entails a further truncation of ministerial responsibility as governmental activities are transferred to the private sector'.[28]

Executive agencies – although remaining embedded within government – have provided some particularly vivid and interesting illustrations of the malleability and precariousness of these constitutional principles. From the outset, questions have been raised as to whether the Next Steps agency programme really was compatible with the traditional principles and mechanisms of ministerial responsibility that Margaret Thatcher, in 1988, insisted would remain intact.

The logic of the programme, strengthening and making more explicit the existing division between the functions of and responsibility for 'policy making' and 'administration', seemed tacitly to recognize a point made earlier in this chapter – that the practical workings of ministerial responsibility are divorced from the theory. And can ministers resist the temptation to interfere in 'operational' matters in circumstances where agency performance that is perceived (by the media and/or

[27] C. Turpin, 'Ministerial Responsibility', in *The Changing Constitution* (3rd edn, 1994) 150.
[28] Ibid., p. 145.

Parliament) to be substandard, or the misconduct or maladministration of agency staff, threatens to cause them political embarrassment? The chequered history of the former nationalized industries – most of them subsequently privatized during the Thatcher–Major years – supposedly operating at arm's length from ministerial control but in practice subject to frequent interference, reinforced some of these concerns.[29]

Meanwhile, Parliament – the forum in which constitutional theories about ministerial responsibility are supposed to be translated into action – has had to adapt to the arrival of these executive agencies. The House of Commons Select Committee on Procedure noted in its 1990 report on the select committee system that, 'as their numbers and scope grow, scrutiny of executive agencies, and of their relationships with their parent Departments, ought to play an increasingly important part in the work of select committees',[30] and a glance at the lists of past reports of committees, published on the web pages of the House of Commons confirms that they have done so. MPs were from the outset encouraged to establish direct contact with agency chief executives on operational matters and, following some persistent lobbying by MPs, letters from ACEs replying to MPs' written questions have, since October 1992, been included in *Hansard*.

The National Audit Office (NAO) has also investigated agencies,[31] and early in the life of the Next Steps initiative it was decided (following a recommendation by the former House of Commons Treasury and Civil Service Committee) that ACEs could appear before the Public Accounts Committee (PAC) as agency accounting officers.[32] Early in 1992 the NAO published its first report on a Next Steps Agency, the Vehicle Inspectorate; and in May that year the Chief Executive of the Agency gave evidence to the PAC, sitting alongside the Permanent Secretary of the Department of Transport. The accountability of ACEs is particularly problematical. According to the Cabinet Office's guidelines for civil servants entitled *Departmental Responses and Evidence to Select Committees* (the so-called Osmotherly Rules):

> Where a Select Committee wishes to take evidence on matters assigned to an Agency in its Framework Document, ministers will normally wish to nominate the Chief Executive as being the official best placed to represent them. While Agency Chief Executives have managerial authority to the extent set out in their Framework Documents, like other officials they give evidence on behalf of the minister to whom they are accountable and are subject to that minister's instruction.[33]

The Commons Treasury and Civil Service Committee objected to this approach from the very beginning of the Next Steps programme and recommended that Chief

[29] See National Economic Development Office, *A Study of UK Nationalised Industries* (1976).

[30] HC 19 (1989–90) paras 42 and 44.

[31] *The Next Steps Initiative*, Cm. 410 (June 1989).

[32] The Treasury, *The Financing and Accountability of Next Steps Agencies*, Cm. 914 (1989) ch. 5.

[33] At para. 50, available at www.cabinetoffice.gov.uk/media/cabinetoffice/propriety_and_ethics/assets/osmotherly_rules.pdf. The most recent edition of this document was published in July 2005.

Executives should be made *directly* responsible to select committees.[34] Six years later, the same committee repeated its earlier recommendation:

> We do not believe that ministerial power to intervene in the actions and decision of Agencies justifies the retention of ministerial accountability for the actions and decisions of Agencies for which the Chief Executives are responsible... The delegation of responsibility should be accompanied by a commensurate delegation of accountability. We recommend that Agency Chief Executives should be directly and personally accountable to Select Committees in relation to their annual performance agreements. Ministers should remain accountable for the framework documents and for their part in negotiating the annual performance agreement, as well as for all instructions given to Agency Chief Executives by them subsequent to the annual performance agreement.[35]

Rejecting this proposal, the government argued:

> a minister is 'accountable' to Parliament for everything which goes on within his Department, in the sense that Parliament can call the minister to account for it. The minister is responsible for the policies of the Department, for the framework through which those policies are delivered, for the resources allocated, for such implementation decisions as the Framework Document may require to be referred or agreed with him and for his response to major failures or expressions of Parliamentary or public concern. But a minister cannot sensibly be held responsible for everything which goes on in his Department in the sense of having personal knowledge and control of every action taken and being personally blameworthy when delegated tasks are carried out incompetently, or when mistakes or errors of judgement are made at operation level.[36]

In recent years, governments have sought to address the tricky problem of how to maintain some credibility for the classical doctrine of ministerial responsibility in an age of 'big government' by claiming – as in the passage just cited – that there is a clear distinction between *responsibility* (the job one is charged with doing) and *accountability* (the duty to explain, or render an account of what has or has not been done). Thus, in the present context, ACEs are *responsible* for the operational performance of their agencies (and liable to shoulder the blame when things go wrong); ministers are *responsible* for the policy framework within which agencies operate and – in accordance with the rules of ministerial responsibility – *account* to Parliament and the electorate both for that policy and for matters that fall within the responsibility of the ACE.

This anxiety of ministers to steer clear of blame for operational failure by distinguishing between responsibility and accountability was vividly exhibited in the row over the escape of prisoners from Parkhurst prison in January 1995. The then Home Secretary, Michael Howard, maintained that he was not responsible for operational

[34] Eighth Report from the Treasury and Civil Service Committee, *Civil Service Management Reform: The Next Steps*, HC 494 (1987–88) para. 46.

[35] Fifth Report from the Treasury and Civil Service Committee, *The Role of the Civil Service*, HC 27 (1993–94) para. 171.

[36] *Taking forward Continuity and Change*, Cm. 2748 (1995) 28.

matters such as ensuring that prisons were secure. In his statement to the House of Commons he claimed that:

> With regard to operational responsibility, there has always been a division between policy matters and operational matters. That has existed not only since the introduction of agencies – it has been recognised for years, and indeed for generations.[37]

He was responsible for matters of policy regarding prison security, funding, and so on, but as there was no criticism of those matters he could not be held to blame – and therefore had no duty to resign. His accountability meant that he was required to ascertain the relevant facts, to explain them to Parliament – and to ensure that security was improved.

The next episode in the saga came with the publication in October 1995 of the Report of the Learmont Inquiry into prison security, which concluded bleakly that the Parkhurst escapes 'revealed a chapter of errors at every level and a naivety that defies belief'.[38] In a House of Commons statement, the Home Secretary noted that Learmont had not found that any decision of his had, directly or indirectly caused the escape, and he then announced that the Director General of the Service, Derek Lewis, had 'ceased to hold his post with effect from today'.[39]

Derek Lewis – a man with a private sector background, and refreshingly uninhibited by the polite mandarin reticence of more traditional senior civil servants – did not take this lying down. He and other critics were quick to point out that Learmont had also found that the Director General had been regularly distracted from his operational responsibilities by constant ministerial demands for information and advice: the Report called for an in-depth study of the relationship between the Home Office and the Prison Service Agency 'with a view to giving the Prison Service the greater operational independence that Agency status was meant to confer'.[40] Questions were also raised about the recent transfer of the Governor of Parkhurst, it being alleged that the Home Secretary had put pressure on the Director General to take this 'operational' decision. An opposition motion in the Commons, deploring the Home Secretary's unwillingness 'to accept responsibility for serious operational failures', was comfortably defeated.[41] But this did little to dispel unease, in Parliament and elsewhere, about the artificiality of the policy/operational distinction, particularly in an area of high political sensitivity in which the Home Secretary had staked his political reputation on a hard-line penal policy.

In the 1995–96 parliamentary session the former Commons Public Service Committee launched an inquiry into Next Steps agencies, with particular reference

[37] *Hansard*, HC, col. 40 (10 January 1995).

[38] The Learmont Report, *Review of Prison Service Security in England and Wales and the Escape from Parkhurst Prison on Tuesday 3rd January 1995*, Cm. 3020 (1995) para. 2.257.

[39] *Hansard*, HC, cols 31–3 (16 October 1995).

[40] Learmont Report, para. 3.87.

[41] *Hansard*, HC, cols 502–50 (19 October 1995).

to the relationship between ministers and chief executives, and the controversy surrounding the Lewis case. Following publication of and debate on the Scott Report on Arms Sales to Iraq early in 1996, the Committee widened the scope of its inquiry to cover broader issues of ministerial accountability to Parliament. In January 1997, the Committee produced a further report on the same subject, following the government's response to the earlier report.[42] The two reports were debated in the Commons a few weeks before the 1997 general election, and both Houses of Parliament passed resolutions on ministerial responsibility.[43] The House of Commons resolution read as follows:

> That, in the opinion of this House, the following principles should govern the conduct of ministers of the Crown in relation to Parliament:
>
> (1) Ministers have a duty to Parliament to account, and be held to account, for the policies, decisions, and actions of their Departments and Next Steps Agencies.
>
> (2) It is of paramount importance that ministers give accurate and truthful information to Parliament, correcting any inadvertent error at the earliest opportunity. Ministers who knowingly mislead Parliament will be expected to offer their resignation to the Prime Minister.
>
> (3) Ministers should be as open as possible with Parliament, refusing to provide information only when disclosure would not be in the public interest, which should be decided in accordance with relevant statute and the Government's *Code of Practice on Access to Government Information* (second edition, January 1997).
>
> (4) Similarly, ministers should require civil servants who give evidence before Parliamentary Committees on their behalf and under their directions to be as helpful as possible in providing accurate, truthful and full information in accordance with the duties and responsibilities of civil servants as set out in the *Civil Service Code (January 1996).*

Soon after the 1997 election the new Home Secretary, Jack Straw, told the Commons that, in his judgement, his predecessor's reputation had been 'deeply damaged by his refusal to accept proper responsibility for the Prison Service, and his arcane and unconvincing attempts to distinguish between policy and operations'.[44] He said that, in future, 'as a first step towards restoring proper ministerial responsibility' all parliamentary questions about the Prison Service would be answered by ministers, and not by the Director General, adding that, 'I regard it as essential that ministers should answer personally to the House for what is done in our prisons and not leave the matter to their civil servants'.

[42] HC 234 (1996–97). [43] *Hansard*, HC, cols 273–93 (12 February 1997).

[44] *Hansard*, HC, col. 396 (19 May 1997).

NEW LABOUR, THE CIVIL SERVICE, AND NEW PUBLIC MANAGEMENT

The election of the Labour Government in May 1997 marked the end of 18 years of Conservative government, during which time public service reform, rather than being seen as a *means* to enabling government to realize its key objectives with the minimum of cost and difficulty, had been an *end* in its own right – at the very top of the government's substantive policy agenda. This writer has argued elsewhere that the civil service inherited by Tony Blair and his colleagues in 1997 'was in a transitional state, between old and new – caught between "continuity and change"'[45] – the latter being the interestingly evocative title of two white papers published during the John Major years.

Labour, certainly in the later years of its long stint in opposition, had not, by and large, contested the main elements of the NPM reform programme in principle – and once in office it showed no inclination to reverse them. Indeed, given the decision to adhere to the previous government's public spending targets, unravelling reforms that emphasized performance measurement and greater financial discipline would have made no sense.

The Blair government, a very different animal from its Old Labour ancestors, eschewed the 1960s and 1970s device of reformist royal commissions and committees of inquiry into aspects of the public service. But, although by 1997 most of the principles underlying the NPM agenda had become matters of consensus politics, the new government did have its own substantial reform programme – focusing upon decentralization (including devolution and local government reform),[46] the further improvement of public service standards, and 'joined-up' government. These were summarized in a white paper on *Modernising Government*, published in March 1999,[47] which stated three main aims:

- Ensuring that policy making is more joined up and strategic.
- Making sure that public service users, not providers, are the focus, by matching services more closely to people's lives.
- Delivering public services that are high quality and efficient.

Much of the Blair agenda for public service reform and modernization could trace its ancestry to the 'new right' politics of the Thatcher years, though this rather embarrassing lineage was camouflaged by the New Labour rhetoric of a 'third way'. And, since the replacement of the Labour government in 2010 by a coalition whose main

[45] Gavin Drewry, 'The Civil Service', in R. Blackburn and R. Plant (eds), *Constitutional Reform: The Labour Government's Constitutional Reform Agenda* (1999) 154–72, 162.

[46] See the white paper, *Modern Local Government: In Touch with the People*, Cm. 4014 (1998), the Local Government Act 2000, and Chapters 9, 10 and 11 below.

[47] Above, n. 22.

initial priority was to try to resolve the budgetary crisis by making drastic cuts in public services, the political commitment to 'modernization' seems to have all but disappeared.

So where do things now stand in that complex, and sometimes ambiguous, relationship between ministers and their civil servants, discussed earlier in this chapter?

MINISTERS AND CIVIL SERVANTS: THE CONSTITUTIONAL REFORM AND GOVERNANCE ACT 2010[48]

Unlike the civil services of most other countries, the position and status of the UK civil service has been largely non-statutory. The Northcote–Trevelyan Report of 1854 said that the newly reformed civil service should be put on to a statutory footing, but that never happened – until recently. Much of the detailed regulatory framework relating to civil service conduct and ethics (as well as the conduct of special advisers and ministers) has been set out in various orders in council and in an assortment of non statutory codes – the current versions of which can be accessed on the Cabinet Office website.[49]

But are non-statutory codes good enough – particularly given the immense cumulative impact of NPM reforms, such as Next Steps, which have exacerbated ambiguities in the role of civil servants *vis-à-vis* ministers? As one commentator has aptly put it:

> Parliament should assert its primary authority on the regulation of the civil service. Parliament should legislate to demarcate a new, clearer constitutional function for the civil service. The cloak of the crown, so convenient to the government, should be stripped away, and the civil service should be clothed in a new parliamentary garb.[50]

It is true that orders in council do have statutory status, but they are issued under the royal prerogative and are not subject to parliamentary scrutiny: the Committee on Standards in Public life has described their use in this context as 'inherently unsatisfactory'.[51] Episodes like the Derek Lewis/Michael Howard row (see above), the 'arms to Iraq' saga in the 1990s,[52] and more recently the suicide, in July 2003, of the civil servant and senior government weapons inspector, Dr David Kelly[53] have raised real concerns about the adequacy of the present framework. The waters have been

[48] The arguments for and against enacting a Civil Service Act are usefully summarized on the website, 'How to be a Civil Servant', www.civilservant.org.uk/csact.shtml, and the links to be found therein.

[49] www.cabinetoffice.gov.uk/conduct-ethics.aspx.

[50] Adam Tomkins, *The Constitution After Scott* (1998) 94.

[51] 9th Report of the Committee on Standards in Public Life, Cm. 5775 (April 2003) para. 10.7.

[52] There is a good overview of many of the issues discussed here, written in the wake of the Scott Report on Arms to Iraq, in Tomkins, above, n. 50, ch. 2.

[53] David Kelly, an official in the Ministry of Defence, was publicly identified as one of the sources used by a BBC journalist who claimed that the government had put improper pressure on the Joint Intelligence Committees to 'sex up' their assessment of Iraq's military capabilities in the run-up to the 2003 invasion. The

muddied further, and the perceived need for clarification intensified, by the continuing proliferation of special advisers in government departments.[54]

The Labour and Liberal Democrat parties went into the 1997 general election with a joint commitment to enacting a Civil Service Act, and that ostensibly remained the formal position of the Blair government. In 2000, the Committee on Standards in Public Life called for a timetable to implement this commitment.[55] The same committee revisited the issue in 2003 and took extensive evidence. Some of that evidence was negative. The Labour peer, Lord Donoughue, said that he was:

> not clear what the problem is: what is the need for legislation? I can see all the disadvantages…For a start a Civil Service Act would be constitutionally significant…The Civil Service traditionally works for the Crown… You have a big statutory Act and they are actually under Parliament.[56]

Other witnesses warned about the inflexibility that would accompany a new Act. The then Head of the Civil Service, Sir Andrew Turnbull, seemed to be in favour, though his tone was rather lukewarm:

> I do not know that it would make a huge difference. I think it is seeking the reassurance that the long-standing kind of values and structure cannot be changed by stealth. In the actual day-to-day practice, I do not think there would be a great deal changed… But an Act would underpin [the Civil Service Code]… it would give reassurance that, over 10 or 20 years, you will not suddenly wake up and find you have got a world that you did not like and you do not quite know how you got there.[57]

But the balance of the evidence was positive. Baroness Prashar, the then First Civil Service Commissioner,[58] suggested that an Act:

> will disentangle what I call the constitutional position of the Civil Service from what I call the organisation development and the reform of the Civil Service. So, it will free that up and I do not see the Act in any way interfering with the development and the reform of the Civil Service.…I think the disadvantage at the moment is the minute you talk about reform… people start talking about the values.[59]

The Wicks Committee Report (noted previously) reported concern in some quarters that the government appeared to have been dragging its feet on the issue of a Civil Service Act, and it reiterated its previous call for a consultative timetable, 'the Government should begin an early process of public consultation on the contents of a

report of an inquiry into his death, by Lord Hutton (HC 247 (2003–04)) did little to dampen the speculation and controversy that surrounded this episode.

[54] The role of special advisers lies beyond the scope of this chapter, but there is a good discussion of some of the issues in the 9th Report of the Committee on Standards in Public Life, above, n. 51, ch. 7.

[55] 6th Report, ch. 5. [56] 9th Report, para. 10.8. [57] Ibid., para. 10.10.

[58] The Civil Service Commissioners are responsible for maintaining the principle of civil service recruitment by merit through open competition and for upholding core civil service values. Details can be found on their website, www.civilservicecommissioners.gov.uk.

[59] 9th Report, para. 10.12.

draft Bill. The Bill should receive pre-legislative scrutiny by a Joint Committee of both Houses of Parliament'.

In its response to the Report, the government confirmed that it still accepted the case in principle for legislation, but said that 'any legislation has to compete for its place alongside many other priorities'. Meanwhile, the House of Commons Public Administration Select Committee had renewed its call for legislation,[60] and it later published its own draft Bill[61] which, *inter alia*, would put the Civil Service Code onto a proper statutory footing, give new powers to the Civil Service Commissioners and clarify the role of special advisers. On 15 November 2004 the government published its own draft Bill, accompanied by a consultation document.[62] Its version was along similar lines to that of the Select Committee, though without the extended powers for the Civil Service Commissioners. Referring to the consultation exercise, the newly-appointed Cabinet Secretary and Head of the Civil Service, Sir Gus O'Donnell, told the Public Administration Committee in October 2005 that he was 'in favour of anything which entrenched the traditional [civil service] values of honesty, objectivity and impartiality' – but that the Government had 'more important' legislative priorities.[63]

At last, however, there was a breakthrough when, in March 2008, the Lord Chancellor announced the introduction of a rather grandiosely titled Constitutional Renewal Bill which would include provisions to put the civil service onto a statutory footing, incorporating into law its core values of impartiality, integrity, honesty, and objectivity, along with the principle of appointment on merit through open competition. It would also include provisions relating to special advisers (making clear that they cannot authorize public expenditure or exercise managerial functions) and the role and status of the Civil Service Commission. The Minister for the Civil Service would be required to publish codes of conduct for civil servants and for special advisers. The Bill (preceded by a consultation exercise) did not complete its parliamentary passage in the 2008–09 session, but was eventually enacted, just before the 2010 general election, as part of the Constitutional Reform and Governance Act 2010.

This hardly amounts to a revolution in UK public administration, but undertaking the seemingly straightforward task of putting the management of the civil service onto a proper statutory footing – something that most other countries take for granted – has taken far too long. The old saying, 'better late than never' comes very much to mind in this context.

PARLIAMENTARY SCRUTINY OF PREROGATIVE POWERS

Many important government functions are exercised by ministers without statutory authority, under the royal prerogative – a hangover from the distant days of absolute

[60] 8th Report, 2001–02, published on 19 July 2002. [61] Published on 5 January 2004.
[62] Cm. 6373 (2004). [63] HC 513-I (2005–06), Q. 120.

monarchy. The use of such prerogative powers is particularly prevalent in the fields of foreign policy and diplomacy, defence (including the declaration of war and the deployment of the armed forces), and national security. The dissolution of Parliament prior to the holding of a general election is through the use of one of the monarch's very few remaining personal prerogative powers, albeit exercised in modern times on the advice of her prime minister. The machinery of government itself – for example changes to the names and functions of government departments – is shaped largely by the Prime Minister's use of inherited prerogative powers: the development of the Next Steps agency programme, discussed earlier in this chapter, was achieved mainly through use of the prerogative, with very little recourse to statute.

Because prerogative powers are non-statutory, they offer only limited opportunity for parliamentary scrutiny, though they are sometimes the subject of parliamentary questions and of intermittent enquiries conducted by select committees. There are also the so-called 'Ponsonby Rules', dating back to 1924, which (by convention) require treaties to be laid before Parliament for a period of 21 sitting days before the UK ratifies, accepts, approves or accedes to them. And any treaty that alters UK law requires express parliamentary approval through the enactment of a statute: the passing of the European Communities Act 1972 to give effect to the Treaty of Rome is one important example of this.

Over the years there has been growing concern about this lacuna in parliamentary scrutiny of government, and this concern was particularly evident in the context of the Blair government's decision in 2003 to deploy troops in the invasion of Iraq. Although the government allowed a parliamentary vote on the issue it was by no means clear that this might constitute a precedent – and perhaps be the starting point for a new convention. In any case, a mere convention, covering such an important area of government activity, was felt by many critics to be too elastic and insufficiently binding.

In 2006, the House of Lords Select Committee on the Constitution produced a report on the subject, which concluded that the use of the prerogative to deploy armed forces overseas 'is outdated' and that Parliament's ability to challenge the executive in this context 'must be protected and strengthened'.[64] In its *Governance of Britain*, green paper[65] the following year, the government suggested putting the Ponsonby Rules (see above) onto a statutory footing and this was followed by a consultation document.[66] Constitutional Reform and Governance Act 2010, Pt 2 (already discussed with reference to the statutory basis of the civil service) provides that a Treaty that is subject to ratification must be published and laid before Parliament for a period of 21 sitting days, during which both Houses are given the opportunity to resolve that the

[64] *Waging War: Parliament's Role and Responsibility*, 15th Report, HL 236 (2005–06) para. 103. see also discussion of war powers in Chapter 6 above.

[65] Cm. 7170 (2007).

[66] *The Governance of Britain – War Powers and Treaties: Limiting Executive Powers*, Cm. 7239 (2007).

Treaty should not be ratified. This change is welcome – and long overdue, but its effects have yet to be tested.

ACCOUNTABILITY, TRANSPARENCY, AND FREEDOM OF INFORMATION

The biggest single obstacle to effective public accountability is lack of transparency. It is quite impossible for Parliament, the public and, for that matter, the media, to hold public authorities to account if their actions are shrouded in secrecy. Some other countries – notably the USA, New Zealand and Sweden – have strong freedom of information legislation that opens up wide categories of official information to public scrutiny. Campaigns to introduce similar legislation in the UK always foundered on the official objection that it would undermine the confidential relationship between ministers and their civil service advisers which is dependent on plain-speaking and mutual trust. Eventually, however, the Blair government bit the bullet and introduced the Bill that became the Freedom of Information Act 2000.

The provisions and significance of this legislation are fully and critically discussed in Chapter 15 below. Suffice it to say here that, while the Freedom of Information Act 2000 may be seen as a useful additional weapon in enhancing the transparency and thereby the accountability of public authorities, some critics have argued strongly that it does not go nearly far enough and has far too many loopholes and exemptions. Conversely, however, at least one prominent proponent of the original legislation, apparently feels, with hindsight, that the Act goes too far and has not fulfilled its democratic purpose. In his controversial memoirs, ex-Prime Minister, Tony Blair, says that he regards the enactment of the Freedom of Information Act 2010 as one of the great 'blunders' of his time in office, the gist of his regret being that the Act has been used mainly by journalists as a stick with which to beat the government, rather than by ordinary citizens in pursuit of democratic accountability.[67]

CONCLUSIONS

Not all of the issues discussed in this chapter are particularly new in themselves. Narrow definitions of the 'executive' function, founded on 18th-century constitutional theory, have long been recognized as providing, at best, an incomplete basis for understanding the complexities of modern government and governance. And the largely fictional character of ministerial responsibility in an era of large-scale government and huge public bureaucracies has been increasingly apparent since the latter part of the 19th century – even though a lot of the fiction has been preserved, largely

[67] Tony Blair, *A Journey* (2010) 516–17.

for the convenience of ministers who are only too happy to accept the credit for successful initiatives (even if they are quick to pass the buck to their officials when things go wrong).

What is new is that recent reform agendas – NPM and 'modernization' programmes – have thrown some of these longstanding issues and concerns into much sharper relief. The NPM reforms have blurred the line between 'public' and 'private' services, and heavily compromised the traditional Weberian model of public bureaucracy. Next Steps executive agencies have spawned a new species of public service hybrid – the agency chief executive – whose accountability, and whose relationship to ministers, has sometimes appeared ambiguous. This chapter has noted the recent decision to put the civil service on to a firmer, statutory footing. But, welcome though this overdue step may be, it must be conceded that statute law operates only at the margins of a public service. The practicalities of achieving an appropriate balance between 'efficiency, effectiveness and economy' (watchwords of NPM) and democratic accountability, and the transparency that must underpin it, are to be found much more in the evolutionary and incremental development of a organizational culture and in the fine-tuning of constitutional conventions than in the imposition of formal legal norms.

FURTHER READING

Burnham, J. and Pyper, R., *Britain's Modernised Civil Service* (2008).

Flynn, N., *Public Sector Management* (4th edn, 2002).

Foley, M., *The British Presidency* (2000).

Heywood, A., *Politics* (3rd edn, 2007).

Hughes, O., *Public Management and Administration* (3rd edn, 2003).

Kavanagh, D., Richards, D., Smith, M., and Geddes, A., *British Politics* (5th edn, 2006) chs 10–13.

Newman, J., *Modernising Governance, New Labour, Policy and Society* (2001).

Rhodes, R. A. W. and Dunleavy, P. (eds), *Prime Minister, Cabinet and Core Executive* (1995).

Tomkins, A., *The Constitution After Scott* (1998).

USEFUL WEBSITES

Cabinet Office: **www.cabinetoffice.gov.uk**

How to be a Civil Servant: **www.civilservant.org.uk/csact.shtml**

Public Administration Select Committee: **www.parliament.uk/business/committees/committees-a-z/commons-select/public-administration-select-committee**

8

DEVOLUTION: A NATIONAL CONVERSATION?

Brigid Hadfield

SUMMARY

It is customary to speak of the devolution 'settlement' but devolution itself evolves. This chapter explains the key differences between the three systems of devolution within the UK and reviews the perimeters within which they are evolving. Recommendations for the expansion of Scottish devolution and for a referendum on the enhancement of the law-making powers of the Welsh Assembly have both been proposed. There has been a debate within Scotland about the possibility of the holding of a referendum to address the question of its independence outside the union. After a period of suspension lasting over four years, devolution to Northern Ireland resumed in 2007 and has expanded with the devolution of justice and policing powers.

This chapter explores the nature of devolution and its capacity for expansion, focusing particularly on the processes and mechanisms through which such constitutional change may be recommended and implemented. The UK coalition government has a wide agenda for constitutional change for the UK. This programme includes the establishment of a commission to consider the English dimensions within the devolved UK. There are also other key elements in their programme for constitutional reform and it is suggested that there are lessons to be learnt from the experience of the devolved nations.

INTRODUCTION

A consideration of the devolved UK constitution may be placed within the perspective of the UK as a unitary state; that is, one in which popular power flows to and political power flows from the centrally located Parliament and government in London. Devolution then is viewed as a means of the granting or 'delegation' of power from the centre to new regional institutions which then exercise whatever power is devolved for as long as it is devolved. Alternatively, a wider political and historical perspective would emphasise the centuries' old formation of the UK through the various Acts of

Union involving England, Wales, Scotland and (Northern) Ireland and their terms and conditions. Devolution then is viewed as an (incomplete) reversion to a status quo *ante* or, better, a dynamic renewal of an '*ancien regime*'. One value of the latter perspective is to accentuate the different histories, legal systems, educational and local government structures, cultures and traditions within the component parts of the UK and to negate an apparently dominant perspective of a constitutional and historico-political monolith composed mainly of the sovereign Westminster Parliament and central government based on support (at least until the 2010 general election) for one of only two nationally based political parties.[1] Elements of both perspectives may be seen in the introduction and evolution of devolution since New Labour's key legislation of 1998.

Thus there is more than one model of devolution and more than one set of principles to be served by it. Devolution for Scotland and Wales, for example, was presented by the Labour government of the late 1990s as a way of strengthening the Union through decentralization and subsidiarity and consequently of weakening any separatist tendencies. By contrast, devolution for Northern Ireland was part of both a peace and a political process accommodating internal cross-community and all-Ireland dimensions, the principle of parity of esteem across a wide range of factors, and with statutory provision made for the termination of the Union under certain specified conditions.

If it is accurate to state that devolution may serve a variety of constitutional and political purposes, whatever the similarities of the delivered statutory models, it is equally accurate to state that the founding principles cannot constrain its development. The actual introduction of devolution itself creates the probability of alternative political conceptions of its evolution which may run counter to its original design. These alternative conceptions may emerge from either the devolved institutions themselves or from the electorate. A central aspect of all the devolution packages was the requirement that the relevant nation's electorate should endorse the government's proposals before their enactment in legislation, thus adding the third element of popular sovereignty to the 'equation for change', alongside the Westminster Parliament and the devolved authorities. It is a possible, if not probable, hypothesis, that the development of devolution in real terms, as opposed to the formal conferment of powers, will be more influenced by the devolved authorities and their electorate than by Westminster.

This chapter reviews the key elements of the devolved systems in Scotland, Wales, and Northern Ireland and the processes of their evolution, before highlighting some of the impact devolution has had, or should have had, on the UK constitution as a whole. In terms of this impact, the processes for initiating constitutional change are the main

[1] See Neil McCormick, 'Is there a Constitutional Path to Scottish Independence' [2000] 53 *Parliamentary Affairs* 721, 727: 'There is no doubt that we have a single state, but it is at least possible that we have two interpretations, two conceptions, two understandings of the constitution of that state'. To avoid any terminological debate, the term 'nation' will be used in this chapter for the four components of the UK.

focus of this chapter. The formation of the Conservative–Liberal Democrat coalition government as based on the terms set out in their Coalition Negotiations Agreement of May 2010 led to the publication in July 2010 of two Bills containing major constitutional change, namely the Parliamentary Voting System and Constituencies Bill and the Fixed-Term Parliaments Bill. Also, the section in the Coalition Negotiations Agreement on 'political reform'[2] contained a promise to implement in full the 2009 recommendations of a House of Commons Committee,[3] specifically on the creation of a Backbench Business Select Committee to give the House of Commons itself greater powers over the scheduling of its business. Also, as already agreed by the House of Commons before the 2010 general election, recommendations on the method of appointment of Select Committee chairpersons and members were carried forward after the general election.

The Coalition Negotiations Agreement also contained promises to implement proposals from the Calman Commission regarding changes to devolution to Scotland,[4] to offer a referendum on further Welsh devolution and to establish a Commission to consider the 'English Question'. In light of these actual or projected changes it seemed appropriate to focus in this chapter on the substance of these changes and on the processes of change, against the background of the systems of devolution as they were originally introduced and as they had evolved prior to the election of the new government in May 2010.

Other aspects of devolution will, therefore, not be considered.[5] These matters include the impact of devolution upon the devolved nations themselves, both in terms of policy formulation and policy delivery; the impact of devolution upon policy formulation in Whitehall and the operation of inter-governmental relations in the devolved UK; the EU dimensions; the financing of devolution;[6] the role of the judges in determining devolved *vires* questions, particularly *vires* questions arising out of the

[2] See www.cabinetoffice.gov.uk/media/409088/pfg_coalition.pdf.

[3] See Chapter 7 above.

[4] The Commission on Scottish Devolution was established after a vote by the Scottish Parliament in December 2007. Sir Kenneth Calman was appointed the chairman in March 2008, it began its work in April 2008 and it produced two reports: *The Future of Scottish Devolution within the Union* was published in December 2008 (the first report), and *Serving Scotland Better: Scotland and the United Kingdom in the 21st Century* was published in June 2009 (the final report).

[5] See more broadly the Report of the House of Commons' Justice Select Committee, *Devolution: A Decade On*, HC 529-1, 2008–09 (May 2009).

[6] The debate concerning the continuation or replacement of the 'Barnett Formula', which has become a shorthand phrase for referring to (part of) the mechanisms for determining the overall funding for the devolved nations, would constitute a separate chapter on its own. Most of the pertinent arguments are covered in the House of Commons Research Paper 07/91 of December 2007; it updates the earlier Research Paper 01/108. See also the Report of the House of Lords' Select Committee on the Barnett Formula, HL 139, 2008–09 (July 2009), and the (then) government's response to the report, Cm. 7772 (December 2009). See also the Report of the Independent Commission on Funding and Finance for Wales, *Fairness and Accountability: a new funding settlement for Wales* (July 2010); House of Commons' Justice Select Committee, n. 5, ch. 6 and related evidence, the Calman Commission, first report, above, n. 4, ch. 6 and Annexe C, the Northern Ireland Assembly Research Paper 12/01 of September 2001, 'A Background Paper on the Barnett Formula', and Northern Ireland Assembly Research and Library Services, HCS 104/09 of February 2009, Head of the NI Civil Service Evidence to the House of Lords' Select Committee on the Barnett Formula.

human rights provisions of the devolution Acts, and whether the jurisprudence of the Supreme Court, as from 1 October 2009, will be different in devolution cases from that of the Judicial Committee of the Privy Council (JCPC).[7] All are worthy constitutional topics in their own right but, for the above reasons, they are not considered here.

SCOTLAND AND DEVO-MAX?

INTRODUCTION

The Scotland Act 1998 established the 129 member Scottish Parliament; its members – Members of the Scottish Parliament (MSPs) – are elected by a mixture of the first-past-the-post electoral system for the 73 constituency MSPs, and, to ensure greater proportionality in the outcome, by the additional member system for the 56 regional list MSPs, eight regions returning seven members each. From the Parliament are chosen the Scottish ministers: the First Minister (nominally appointed by the Queen) and (as appointed by the First Minister) the other members of the Scottish Executive.

The emphasis in the Scotland Act 1998 on alternative principles of representation, and hence the chosen electoral system, is a factor of increasingly current significance: coalition politics were *ab initio* regarded not as a failure of political, or public, will but as an acceptable alternative way of delivering policies. In 1999 the elections to the Scottish Parliament led to a coalition between the first and third most successful parties in the election: Labour and the Liberal Democrats. This coalition continued after the 2003 elections. In 2007 a minority Scottish National Party (SNP) government[8] was formed.

The Scotland Act 1998 withheld or reserved certain legislative powers to Westminster. These reserved powers, which are listed in Scheds 4 and 5, include both general reservations such as the Crown, foreign affairs, defence and all macro-economic policy, and specific reservations across a wide range of central government department responsibilities including social security, immigration and nationality, misuse of drugs, aspects of energy regulation, and employment. All other non-reserved legislative power, both primary and subordinate, was devolved to the Parliament subject to its lack of competence to legislate contrary to EU Law, the European Convention on Human Rights (ECHR), and with extra-territorial effect. The extent of devolved legislative power is, therefore, considerable and includes agriculture and fisheries, the

[7] See *Martin* v. *Her Majesty's Advocate (Respondent) (Scotland)*; *Miller* v. *Her Majesty's Advocate (Respondent) (Scotland)* [2010] UKSC 10 on whether the Criminal Proceedings etc (Reform) (Scotland) 2007 Act, s 45 was within the legislative competence of the Scottish Parliament. Cf. e.g. *DS* v. *Her Majesty's Advocate (Appeal No 12 of 2006)* [2007] UKPC D1. The other JCPC Scottish devolution cases mainly concerned the compatibility of aspects of Scottish criminal law with the ECHR, especially Art. 6.

[8] The formal term of the devolved government remains the 'Scottish Executive', but the more popular title for some time, certainly within Scotland, is government, and in September 2007, the SNP government decided to use the title Scottish government on, e.g. all official documents and government buildings.

arts, education, the environment, health, home affairs, housing, law and justice, local government, planning, the police service, social work, sport and most aspects of internal transport. The 1998 Act also includes mechanisms for the expansion of devolved responsibilities: under s. 30(2) changes can be made to the list of general and specific reservations under Scheds 4 and 5. This power has in fact been only very rarely used although expansion of the responsibilities of Scottish ministers under s. 63 has been more frequent.

The Scottish Parliament lacks the competence to legislate in relation to reserved matters. By contrast, as stated in s. 28(7), the UK Parliament retains the power to legislate on all matters whether or not devolved. The formal legal position is, however, modified by constitutional convention. Legislation by Westminster on devolved matters is covered by the Sewel Convention, technically a Legislative Consent Motion;[9] its substance is contained in the Memorandum of Understanding between the UK government and, *inter alia*, the Scottish Executive. This provides that the UK government will not normally legislate on a devolved matter, or in a way that affects devolved responsibilities, without the consent of the Scottish Parliament. There have been of the order of 100 Legislative Consent Motions since 1999, considerably more than was originally forecast. Their use reflects a variety of factors including factors of legal or administrative convenience or complexity, and the maximization of the time available to the Scottish Parliament. The general election of May 2010 with the formation of a coalition government marks the first time since the institution of devolution that there has been a change in the political complexion of UK government. It is not clear whether this will engender any real changes in the relationships between the Scottish and UK governments but at the time of writing this seems to be unlikely. Much, of course, also depends on the political complexion of the devolved government formed after the May 2011 elections to the Scottish Parliament.

POPULAR SOVEREIGNTY

The establishment of the Scottish Parliament and Executive in 1999 under the terms of the Scotland Act 1998 was preceded by two key events. The first was the establishment of the Scottish Constitutional Convention in 1989, a non-official coalition of representatives of most of the political parties, churches, trade unions and civil society in Scotland although not supported by the Conservative Party and (eventually also) not

[9] See (the latest and revised version of) Ministry of Justice, *Devolution. Memorandum of Understanding and Supplementary Agreements Between the United Kingdom Government, the Scottish Ministers, the Welsh Ministers and the Northern Ireland Executive Committee*, Cm. 7864 (March 2010), para. 14, and Devolution Guidance Note 10, 'Post-Devolution Primary Legislation affecting Scotland'. Both refer to the undertaking given in the House of Lords on 21 July 1998 by Lord Sewel, on behalf of the government, in the context of Scottish devolution. The Calman Commission, final report, above, n. 4, paras 4.129–4.149 has recommended that the Sewel Convention should be 'entrenched' through its inclusion in the Standing Orders of both Houses of Parliament. The term 'Sewel Motion' tends to be used in Scotland and 'Legislative Consent Motion' in Wales and Northern Ireland. See NI Assembly Research Paper 23/09 of February 2009.

by the SNP. Its report entitled *Scotland's Parliament, Scotland's Right* was published on 30 November 1995 and is generally credited with forming the principles on which devolution would later be based. The significance of this is the context it provides for the autochthonous nature of devolution to Scotland.

The second key event was the referendum held in Scotland on 11 September 1997 under the terms of the Referendums (Scotland and Wales) Act 1997 as introduced by the new Labour government elected to power in May of that year. In the referendum the opinions of the electorate living in Scotland were invited as to whether a Scottish Parliament should be established and if it should have tax-varying powers.[10] The referendum was preceded by a government white paper in which the key devolution principles were contained.[11] All this was before the publication of the devolution Bill. Consequently, both through the Convention and in the referendum, the wishes of the electorate may be seen as authorizing the institution of devolution and its fundamental terms; hence popular consent, in one form or another, becomes a prerequisite for any subsequent fundamental change to the devolution 'settlement'. This is the case even if the formal source of devolution and its powers lies with an Act of the Westminster Parliament. There is thus built into the foundations of Scottish devolution a principle of necessary popular consent which runs counter to the traditional doctrine of the Sovereignty of Parliament: that is, the idea that devolution is the unilateral gift of the Westminster Parliament and that its formative principles can be unilaterally amended by it.

Lurking behind, and indeed reinforcing, these factors too is the experience of a non-event: the non-implementation of the system of devolution contained in the Scotland Act 1978. That Act was never implemented because the results of the *post-enactment* referendum, held in March 1979,[12] failed to meet the particular statutory requirements of the 1978 Act.[13] The significance of the debate which that legislation engendered, however, should not be overlooked. The fact that the referendum came after the enactment of the 1978 Act and blocked its coming into force may mean that the Act is regarded as an immense waste of Parliamentary time. In a longer view, it can equally illustrate the value of preparing the ground. It showed that devolution was possible. Had the referendum majority requirement in 1979 been a simple majority of those voting (rather than the support of 40 per cent of the electorate) the yes vote

[10] 74.3 per cent voted for establishment and 25.7 per cent against; and 63.5 per cent voted for tax-varying powers and 36.5 per cent against, on a turnout of 60.4 per cent of the electorate.

[11] See *Scotland's Parliament*, Cm. 3658 (July 1997).

[12] To the question whether the provisions of the Act should be put into effect, on a 63.8 per cent turnout, 51.6 per cent of those voting voted 'yes' and 48.4 per cent voted 'no'. This meant that only some 33 per cent of the electorate was in favour of devolution.

[13] Scotland Act 1978, s. 85(2) required 40 per cent of the electorate to vote in favour of devolution. The requirement to hold a referendum was announced by the Labour government (which by then had lost its majority) at the end of the second reading of the Bill in the House of Commons and inserted at its behest at the committee stage. The clause was amended against its wishes to include the 40 per cent requirement at this stage and the government was not able to reverse it during the report stage. See *Current Law Statutes Annotated* on the Scotland Act 1978.

would have carried the day with more than 51 per cent of the vote (a larger percentage than carried the vote for devolution in Wales in 1997).

The Parliamentary and also public debates on devolution to Scotland indeed pre-dated the 1978 Act itself. The Royal Commission on the Constitution,[14] the government's (combined and eventually withdrawn) Scotland and Wales Bill of November 1976 and the Scotland Act 1978 together generated a wide-ranging debate about the nature of the constitution, a debate sometimes overlooked in all the rhetoric on the new constitutional vision of New Labour. The 1997 referendum and the 1998 Act, therefore, did not arrive in a constitutional vacuum. Much ground-breaking work had been done well before the late 1990s.

DEVOLUTION AND ITS EVOLUTION: FLEXIBILITY AND INITIATIVE

The flexibility in devolution is most acutely tested with regard to its capacity, or lack of it, to evolve into independence. Although its flexibility is much more likely to be manifest in the more 'mundane' issue of expansion in the devolved powers, the extent to which, if at all, devolution may be regarded as a staging post towards independence is a real question. Before considering the issue regarding Scotland it must be remembered that the Northern Ireland Act 1998 contains an express mechanism for the termination of the Union between Great Britain and Northern Ireland.[15]

At the time of writing, the Scottish government consists of a Party (the SNP) fully committed to the independence of Scotland. Almost immediately after its formation after the May 2007 Scottish elections, the government, following on from a manifesto commitment, (and while also seeking through its policies and performance to show that it could be, and is, a party fit for government) commenced what it termed 'the national conversation' with the aim of exploring with the people living in Scotland the desirability of various different options for constitutional change. The conversation began with the launch of a white paper entitled *Choosing Scotland's Future*[16] which listed various options including maintenance of the devolved status quo, the expansion of (particularly non-constitutional) devolved powers, and independence. The last option is not a devolved matter under the Scotland Act 1998; the Union between England and Scotland is expressly reserved.[17]

Termination of the Union, however, while being the policy of the SNP government finds no political favour with the majority of the parties represented in the Scottish Parliament. The Labour, the Conservative and the Liberal Democrat parties (whose

[14] Under the chairmanship of first Lord Crowther and then Lord Kilbrandon, the Royal Commission was set up in 1969 and reported in 1973 in favour of devolution to Scotland and Wales: Cmnd. 5460. It received an extensive amount of evidence running to several volumes.

[15] Northern Ireland Act 1998, s. 1 and Sched. 1.

[16] *Choosing Scotland's Future* (August 2007).

[17] Scotland Act 1998, Sched. 5, Pt 1, para. 1 (b); hence technically any referendum organised by a Scottish government needs to focus on the question whether the powers of the Scottish Parliament should be enlarged so as to enable independence to be achieved.

seats total 78 as against the 47 held by the SNP[18]), in the face of ineffective opposition from the Scottish government but with the support of the UK government, resolved in December 2007 to establish a Commission on Scottish Devolution, chaired by Sir Kenneth Calman, with a remit that expressly excluded the possibility of independence. Its remit was to:

> review the provisions of the Scotland Act 1998 in the light of experience and to recommend any changes to the present constitutional arrangements that would enable the Scottish Parliament to serve the people of Scotland better, improve the financial accountability of the Scottish Parliament, and continue to secure the position of Scotland within the United Kingdom.[19]

Thus there have been two virtually parallel processes operating within Scotland, one sponsored or favoured by the Scottish government and one by the Scottish Parliament, not a likely scenario in the Westminster model of governance. It is at least a moot point as to which is the healthier or more democratic model of engaging in constitutional reform.

The amount of public engagement with the Scottish government's national conversation was detailed in a Scottish government white paper published on St Andrew's day, 30 November 2009, and entitled *Your Scotland, Your Voice*:

> The National Conversation began in August 2007... Over 5,300 people have attended more than 50 National Conversation events throughout Scotland. Some 500,000 have viewed the website, which provides video and audio records of meetings, access to documents, Ministerial blogs and an opportunity to comment...[20]

No amount of public consultation, however, can mask the political opposition to independence for Scotland in both the Scottish and UK Parliaments. The manifest political limits on what may be achieved by a minority devolved government seeking such fundamental constitutional change in the face of opposition from parties well represented in the Scottish Parliament and in power at Westminster are seen here. A draft Referendum (Scotland) Bill with an accompanying consultation paper was published by the Scottish government in February 2010,[21] the consultation period closing at the end of April 2010. The Scottish government, however, announced in September 2010 that its legislative proposals on the independence referendum would be shelved and

[18] There are 46 Labour MSPs; the Conservatives and Liberal-Democrats have 16 MSPs each; there are four 'Others'.

[19] Calman Commission, first report, above, n. 4, para. 1.1; the remit was agreed by the Scottish Parliament on 6 December 2007. The vote to establish the Commission was carried by 76 votes to 46, with three abstentions. The (then) UK government indicated its support for the Commission in January 2008 and pledged to provide resources to the Commission in March 2008: see ibid., paras 1.2–1.4.

[20] *Your Scotland, Your Voice*, para. 1.11. This is not to state, however, that all who engaged in the debate supported independence for Scotland; see further M. Harvey and P. Lynch, 'From National Conversation to Independence Referendum?', Spring 2010, available at www.psa.ac.uk/journals/pdf/5/2010/1041_870.pdf.

[21] *Scotland's Future* (February 2010).

it would, instead, make the issue a central part of its campaign during the May 2011 elections to the Scottish Parliament.

The consultation paper on the draft Bill did, however, address the possibility of a multi-option referendum, incorporating constitutional options additional to that of the acquisition of powers to facilitate a move to independence.[22] This was because the parallel process wrought by the Calman Commission (and indeed the national conversation) has engendered a series of proposals concerning the expansion of devolution, proposals which the UK government has implemented in the 2010–11 Scotland Bill, which began its parliamentary stages in January 2011.[23] There is no suggestion that a referendum will be held (other than under the Scottish government's Bill) on the implementation of the Calman recommendations, almost certainly because they are regarded as constituting incremental and not fundamental change to the devolution 'settlement'.[24] This would appear to be justified by a brief consideration of Calman. The Commission's 'incremental' recommendations[25] certainly do not constitute what is called full devolution or 'devo-max'; this is a shorthand phrase for a form of devolution which falls just short of independence. It essentially means devolution of everything but defence, foreign affairs, and the currency and major economic policy. The Calman Commission, by way of contrast, focused on improving the financial accountability of the Scottish Parliament and government; it also sought to strengthen the operation of devolution as contained in the Scotland Act 1998 by recommending amendments to its division of responsibilities, either by addition or deletion, in those areas where 'there appear to be problems or pressures for change'.[26] These included the recommendations that the administration of Scottish elections, the regulation of airguns, of the drink-driving limits, and of the national speed limit, for example, should all be devolved. Conversely, the Commission recommended that the regulation of all health professionals, and aspects of charity and insolvency law be returned to Westminster.

[22] Four possible models were explored in *Your Scotland, Your Voice*, ch. 2: the status quo, implementation of the Calman proposals, full devolution or independence. See further the text below.

[23] Statement by the Secretary of State for Scotland, Mr Michael Moore, published in the *Scottish Daily Express*, 5 July 2010, available at www.scotlandoffice.gov.uk. The Conservative, Liberal Democrat and Labour Parties' manifestos for the 2010 general election all contained a promise to implement or carry forward the Calman proposals.

[24] See *Your Scotland, Your Voice*, above, text to n. 20, paras 10.14–10.20, and *The Times*, 14 June 2009, which, on the publication of the Calman Commission's final report, provides statements from spokespersons from the three 'main' parties as regarding the proposals falling short of fundamental change or as anyway (it was hoped) as receiving any necessary mandate at the then forthcoming general election.

[25] For the extent of the public consultation carried out by the Calman Commission, see its final report, above, n. 4, para. 4: 'We distributed 150,000 copies of an information leaflet about the Commission's work across Scotland. Over 900 people filled in our questionnaire. We held 12 local engagement events throughout Scotland... We have received over 300 written submissions. We have held over 50 public evidence sessions and 27 private sessions, and published transcripts or notes of each'.

[26] Calman Commission, final report, above, n. 4, Pt 5. Other topics not covered here include strengthening the co-operation between the governments and Parliaments, and certain reforms to the operation of the Scottish Parliament.

Their recommendations on finance related to the funding of the Scottish budget, and, in order to enhance accountability, were aimed at increasing the amount of the Scottish budget raised within Scotland. The Scottish variable tax rate (of plus or minus three pence in the pound on the *basic* income tax rate), devolution of which power was approved at the referendum in September 1997, has never been introduced and the Commission recommended its abolition. In its place, or building on this principle, as it were, it recommended that *all* existing UK income tax rates applying in Scotland should be reduced by ten pence in the pound; this would then be accompanied by a 'reduction in the [block] grant to the Scottish Parliament by an equivalent amount'.[27] This would mean that the decisions of the Scottish Parliament to maintain the UK tax rates, or to raise or to lower them, would have consequences for which the Scottish government and Parliament would be responsible. The remainder of the block grant to Scotland would continue to be based on the primarily population- and not needs-based requirements of the Barnett Formula.[28]

At least until after the results of the May 2011 elections are known, if not in the much longer term, any changes to devolution to Scotland now lie well and truly with the implementation of the Calman proposals as contained in the Scotland Bill currently being debated by the Westminster Parliament.

WALES, 'DEVO-MIN', AND 'CATCH-UP' DEVOLUTION

INTRODUCTION

The considerable interlocking of the English and Welsh legal systems, the importance of the cultural and linguistic history of Wales, and possibly internal differences within the Labour Party, led in 1998 to a much more limited form of devolution for Wales as compared with Scotland (and Northern Ireland); the Welsh model was much closer to local government decentralization. The system of devolution introduced under the Government of Wales Act 1998 was originally, and somewhat unhelpfully, labelled 'executive' devolution. The reason for this label was that, in brief, the statutory delegated powers, which before the 1998 Act were exercised in relation to Wales by UK government ministers, usually the Secretary of State for Wales, were 'devolved' to a 60-member National Assembly for Wales, elected under the same electoral system

[27] Calman Commission, final report, above, n. 4, 'An Executive Summary of the Final Report', para. 33. National insurance contributions, corporation tax and value added tax are not to be devolved. Stamp duty on property transactions, air passenger duty, and landfill tax could be devolved. For an accessible summary of the Report and the debates that the Calman Commission has engendered, see House of Commons Standard Note SN/PC/04744 (June 2010).

[28] See above, n. 6. The coalition government is not expected to re-visit the Barnett Formula in the short term, although when the Calman changes are implemented in Scotland, a reassessment may become more compelling.

as used for Scotland. There were 40 constituency members and 20 members for the regional seats (four members for each of the five regions). There, however, the current similarities between Wales and Scotland end.

The transfer or devolution of (executive) functions was wrought by Orders in Council, made under Government of Wales Act 1998, s. 22. The first such major Order was the National Assembly for Wales (Transfer of Functions) Order 1999,[29] which, in its lengthy first Schedule, listed in chronological order some 330 public and general statutes (in whole or in part), ten local and private Acts, and 50 statutory instruments under which functions had previously been exercised by a minister of the Crown, and which functions were thereby transferred to the Welsh Assembly.

Further, unlike the Scottish model of devolution, under which all matters were devolved except those listed as reserved, there was for Wales no overall clarity or cohesion in the devolved areas. The listed transferred functions fell within, but did not by any means fully encompass, the 18 fields listed in Government of Wales Act 1998, Sched. 2, as expanded and reorganized eventually to 20 fields under Government of Wales Act 2006, Sched. 5:[30] agriculture, fisheries, forestry and rural development; ancient monuments and historic buildings; culture; economic development; education and training; environment; fire and rescue services and the promotion of fire safety; food; health and health services; highways and transport; housing; local government; aspects of the National Assembly for Wales; public administration; social welfare; sport and recreation; tourism; town and country planning; water and flood defence; and the Welsh language.

Under the 1998 Act the Assembly had delegated legislative powers over matters specified within these fields but no primary powers at all. It was also possible for additional powers to be conferred upon the Assembly under a new Act of the UK Parliament, and in the making of such, and other pertinent, legislation the Secretary of State for Wales was, and remains, under a statutory duty[31] to consult the Assembly, but the dependence of the Assembly upon the laws and policies of the UK Parliament and upon the breadth or narrowness of the wording of the statutory delegation was manifest. Consequently, the Assembly's capacity for developing its own laws and policies was at best seriously restricted. This fact, coupled with the 'enhanced accountability' to the people of Wales that both justified the existence of the Assembly and was furthered by it, created inevitable tensions. Heightened expectations of real power and the reality of fettered power constitute an unhelpful mix.

A further complicating factor was that the Welsh Assembly was, under the 1998 Act, a unitary or single corporate body; that is, there was no distinction made between the Assembly and the executive which was formed from it. From this unpromising beginning, certainly as compared with both Scotland and Northern Ireland, there

[29] SI 1999/672. The extent of the power devolved varied from field to field.

[30] The other changes wrought by the 2006 Act will be considered further below. The 2006 Act as well as reordering the devolved responsibilities largely added as devolved matters fire and rescue services, food and industry. The 2006 Act came into force after the May 2007 Assembly elections.

[31] 1998 Act, s. 31, 2006 Act, s. 33.

has emerged a far fuller, more extensive system of devolution primarily because of the efforts of the Welsh Assembly.

POPULAR SOVEREIGNTY

There are three key differences between Wales and Scotland in this regard. First, the March 1979 referendum on the provisions for very limited devolution contained in the Wales Act 1978 was overwhelmingly lost, nearly 80 per cent of those voting being against the proposals.[32] Secondly, there was no Welsh Constitutional Convention, such as the Scottish one from 1989 to 1995 and, therefore, devolution, when it did commence in Wales under the terms of the 1998 Act, was growing in less fertile soil. Thirdly, the referendum on New Labour's white paper[33] proposals held on 18 September 1997[34] came very close to a rejection[35] in spite of being held a week after the Scottish referendum on the principle of '*encourager les autres*'. The swing in favour of devolution, however, between the 1979 and 1997 Welsh referendums was considerable, and larger than the comparable swing in Scotland.

There was, further, within the New Labour government in 1997 no grand constitutional or political design for Welsh devolution. As in 1978–79, it was rather a coattails approach caught up with the demand for Scottish devolution but coupled with the intention that it should not be the same. The 1997 referendum result was, however, enough to carry the day and to lead to the establishment of devolved institutions with, legally, very limited powers but crucially with the power both to deliver policies formulated (at least in part) in Wales and to facilitate debate about the further evolution of devolution. One matter notably lacking in the Westminster model of governance is the power of significant initiative outside the government. With the honourable exception of the Select Committees generally, and (possibly) specifically with the establishment of the Backbench Business Committee, the opportunity or power within Parliament to instigate debate such as to influence, change or alter national policy and its delivery is very limited. Once the devolved institutions had been established in Wales, however, the dynamics of political and constitutional engagement changed. Alternative voices had the mandate and opportunity to speak for the people of Wales, with at least the same authority as the UK Parliament and government. The electoral system for the Assembly has also given experience in government, as it has in Scotland, to a wider number of political parties.[36] The 1999 Welsh Assembly elections led first to the formation of a minority Labour executive, followed (from 2000) by a Labour–Liberal

[32] The figures were 20.26 per cent (yes) and 79.74 per cent (against) on a 58.3 per cent turnout. This constituted support for devolution of only some 12 per cent of the Welsh electorate.

[33] *A Voice for Wales*, Cm. 3718 (July 1997).

[34] Under the terms of the Referendums (Scotland and Wales) Act 1997.

[35] On a 50.1 per cent turnout, 50.3 per cent voted 'yes' and 49.7 per cent voted 'no'. In numerical terms, the difference in the votes was 6,721.

[36] With the exception of the Conservative Party, all the larger parties within both Scotland and Wales have been a part of the devolved governments.

Democrat coalition; between 2003–07 there was a single party Labour government, and this was followed in 2007 (eventually[37]) by a Labour–Plaid Cymru coalition.

DEVOLUTION AND ITS EVOLUTION: FLEXIBILITY AND INITIATIVE

Simply to list the key developments up to and beyond the Government of Wales Act 2006 is to show a very extensive and intense programme of reform. Between 1999 and 2003 there developed a de facto separation of the executive from the Assembly itself, and this was reflected in the accompanying terminology. The Welsh Assembly government, as it became known from 2002 (and formally so under s. 45 of the 2006 Act), crystallised into a distinct identity as a policy and law initiator, as a key player in the Assembly legislative processes and as consulted by the UK government. The Assembly First Secretary for Wales (the statutory term until the 2006 Act) transmuted de facto into the First Minister for Wales and Assembly secretaries into ministers as early as 2000, forming a cabinet rather than an executive committee of the National Assembly.[38]

Crucially, in terms of the dynamics for more substantive change, the then coalition government in July 2002 established a Commission, under the chairmanship of Lord (Ivor) Richard, to consider the breadth and depth of the Assembly's powers.[39] This, it should be noted, was within only three years of the start of devolution. The Commission published its extensive report in Spring 2004, by which time the House of Lords' Select Committee on the Constitution had reported on *Inter-Institutional Relations in the Devolved United Kingdom*[40] and, more significantly here, the Select Committee on Welsh Affairs had produced its report into the *Primary Legislative Process as it affects Wales.*[41]

The amount of public engagement carried out by the Richard Commission was extensive. The Commission reported that: 'Between October 2002 and September 2003 we held 115 evidence sessions, 3 seminars, and issued 2 consultation papers. We received over 300 written submissions. We held 9 public meetings...'.[42] The major recommendations of the report were geared primarily to enhancing the legislative powers of the Assembly beyond those formally conferred by the 1998 Act (recommendations which were significantly modified by the UK government's own subsequent proposals) and also to abolishing the Assembly as single corporate body and replacing it with two distinct bodies, a legislature and an executive. There were also

[37] Between May and July 2007, various attempts were made to form a differently composed coalition government, namely a 'rainbow coalition' formed from the Conservative, Liberal Democrat, and Plaid Cymru Parties.

[38] See the Report of the Assembly Review of Procedure, instigated by the First Minister, in July 2000; it reported in 2002.

[39] Commission on the Powers and Electoral Arrangements of the National Assembly for Wales. See its Final Report, Introduction (Spring 2004), para. 4.

[40] HL 28, 2002–03 (January 2003).

[41] HC 79, 2002–03 (March 2003).

[42] Above, n. 39, para. 16 (their footnotes omitted) and ch. 3.

subsidiary recommendations (not implemented) concerning an increase in the size of the Assembly to 80 members and a change in the electoral system to the highly proportionate single-transferable-vote system. The UK Labour government responded with its own proposals in a July 2005 white paper entitled *Better Governance for Wales*,[43] which was itself considered by an ad hoc Committee of the Welsh Assembly[44] and by the House of Commons' Select Committee on Welsh Affairs.[45] The substance of what became the 2006 Act, therefore, had been the subject of intense discussions within Wales and by the UK Parliament.

The Government of Wales Act 2006, by s. 1, created the legally new National Assembly for Wales and, by s. 45, the Welsh Assembly government consisting of the First Minister and the other Welsh ministers (to a maximum number of 12) and repealed, *inter alia*, s. 1 of the 1998 Act which had established the National Assembly for Wales as a single body corporate. The other key changes came in the form of the legislative competence of the Assembly.[46] The 2006 Act conferred on the Assembly, as from the 2007 Welsh Assembly elections, a new power to make Assembly Measures. Under s. 93, the Assembly now has the power to make laws, known as Assembly Measures, on its own initiative on specified matters (often written with a capital 'M') within the 20 devolved fields listed in Sched. 5 to the 2006 Act and mentioned above. A Measure has the same effect as an Act of Parliament and is enacted by being passed by the Assembly and approved by the Queen in Council. Such Measures are closer to primary law[47] than the 1998 Act's executive devolution model, in the sense that they are not simply implementing the substance of a law enacted by the UK Parliament but contain policy formulated by the Assembly itself.

A Matter may become specified under Sched. 5 and hence capable of being legislated on by Assembly Measure in one of two ways: either through provision made by a 'Framework' or Measure-Making Act of the UK Parliament, or by a Legislative Competence Order (LCO) made under s. 95 of the 2006 Act.[48] An LCO is made in the form of a UK Order in Council and it may add to (or indeed vary or remove) the powers of the Assembly to pass a Measure on any Matter within any of the 20 devolved

[43] *Better Governance for Wales*, Cm. 6582 (July 2005).

[44] The Committee's Report of 16 September 2005 was debated by the Assembly on 21 September 2005.

[45] See 2005–06, HC 551, and the government's Response to the Report, 2005–06, HC 839.

[46] The commitment on the part of the government to use more framework legislation did not need legislation to be implemented. See Devolution Guidance Note 9, which also addresses the operation of the legislative consent convention for Wales. On the formal legislative supremacy of the UK Parliament, see ss 93(5) and 107(5).

[47] They are technically subordinate legislation.

[48] See 2006 Act, s. 95. The Report of the All-Wales Convention (November 2009) paras 3.3.2 and 3.3.3, states that as of July 2009, 28 Matters had been added to Sched. 5, 12 by LCOs and 16 through Framework Bills. The National Assembly for Wales has a website dedicated to Assembly Powers Tracking Notes which provides an 'updated log of amendments' to Sched. 5. It currently (August 2010) lists some 80 Matters. Six of these were on the face of Sched. 5 and 11 were added through conversion into Matters of certain Assembly powers pre-dating the 2006 Act: see the Report of the All-Wales Convention, ibid., para 3.3.2. The remainder have been added subsequently.

fields.[49] An LCO may be initiated by the Welsh Assembly government, an Assembly Committee or by one of the Assembly Members and must be scrutinized and approved by the Assembly. It is then transmitted by the First Minister to the Secretary of State for Wales who, within 60 days, must either lay the draft LCO before both Houses of Parliament for their approval,[50] or, for reasons given, refuse to do so. The LCO or the Framework Act does not as such change the substance of the law in Wales; this becomes a matter for the Assembly.[51]

From 2008 until the time of writing (autumn 2010) there have been 11 Assembly Measures and, from 2007, some 14 LCOs, perhaps the most notable of which is the LCO on housing and local government, which took some three years to be made. It concerned issues of homelessness, social housing, and tenants' rights and therefore, involved, *inter alia*, the location of the responsibility for council houses and of the 'right to buy'. After a number of disagreements with first the Labour and then (after May 2010) the coalition UK governments, all the powers sought by the Assembly have now been transferred into its legislative competence.[52]

The 2006 Act also facilitates the future devolution of a more significant power, namely the power to pass Acts on any of the matters on which the 'executive' functions have already been devolved,[53] that is, in effect with regard to the 20 devolved fields. This would be moving closer to the powers already possessed by the Scottish Parliament.[54] This part of the Act can only be implemented, however, after a referendum in Wales and after an Order in Council has been approved by both Houses of the UK Parliament and by a vote of the Welsh Assembly on a majority representing at least two-thirds of the Assembly seats.[55] The conferment of such a power is regarded as a fundamental change to devolution and that is why, in order for this to happen, there has to be a referendum. Under s. 104 of the 2006 Act, the process for calling a referendum is begun at the instigation of a resolution put to the Assembly by the First Minister or a Welsh minister and carried by at least two-thirds of the total number

[49] Under subs (1)(b), but subject to subs (2), an LCO may also add a new field to Sched. 5.

[50] The Select Committee on Welsh Affairs has an important role to play at Westminster in the scrutiny of draft LCOs.

[51] The 2006 Act is not exactly a model of clarity on this topic. For useful and clear summaries, see Devolution Guidance Note 16 and the Report of the All-Wales Convention, above, n. 48, chs 2 and 3. On the All-Wales Convention, see further below.

[52] The National Assembly for Wales (Legislative Competence) (Housing and Local Government) Order 2010 (SI 2010/1838).

[53] 2006 Act, Sched. 7 (as updated by post-2006 devolution changes) lists those subjects on which the Assembly may be given this primary legislative power. The headings in Sched. 7 are the same as those in Sched. 5. Unlike Scotland, therefore, for Wales the *devolved* matters are listed, rather than the reserved matters listed. This is primarily to prevent the English and Welsh legal systems from becoming separate systems and no doubt has consequences too for the 'English Question'. See the submission to the Welsh Affairs' Select Committee by the Secretary of State for Wales and the First Minister, HC 551, above, n. 45, as reprinted in the Explanatory Notes to the Government of Wales Bill, para. 374.

[54] Such Acts of the Assembly would, under s. 108, fall outside its legislative competence if, e.g. incompatible with EU law or the ECHR. Section 94(6)(c) makes identical provision for Measures.

[55] 2006 Act, s. 103.

of Assembly seats. The request for a referendum then goes, as soon as is reasonably practicable, via the First Minister to the Secretary of State for Wales. Within 120 days beginning from the receipt of the request, he or she[56] must either lay a draft Order in Council before each House of Parliament for their approval or give the First Minister notice in writing of the reasons for the refusal to do so. There is thus a statutory reinforcement of the (established) convention that any major change to devolution must be endorsed by the electorate as well as by the Assembly and the UK Parliament.

The Assembly triggered the process for the holding of the referendum on 9 February 2010 by a unanimous vote of 53 Assembly Members in favour, with three abstentions.[57] The Assembly vote took place against the background of the preparatory work carried out by the All-Wales Convention established by the Welsh coalition government. That government's 'One Wales' agenda included the full utilization of the provisions in the 2006 Act, and a 'successful outcome of a referendum for full law-making powers'.[58] To that latter end, in October 2007, an All-Wales Convention was established with its remit, in brief, to assess public views on all aspects of the law-making powers of the Assembly.[59] It reported in November 2009. Specifically on the referendum issue, the findings of the Convention were that 72 per cent of the population supported the present system or enhanced devolution, with declared voting intentions in a referendum for increased law-making powers showing 47 per cent in favour and 37 per cent against. The Convention concluded (allowing for varying factors) that a 'yes' vote was obtainable but not certain.[60] 2011 may indeed see considerable change in Wales; the referendum took place on 3 March 2011, with 63.5 per cent voting 'yes' and 36.5 per cent voting 'no' on a 35.4 per cent turnout.

NORTHERN IRELAND: TOWARDS 'SUPER-DEVO'?

CONSTITUTIONAL STATUS AND DEVOLUTION HISTORY

The situation with regard to devolution to Northern Ireland is very different in key respects from that pertaining in Scotland and Wales, and an overall picture in this

[56] Mrs Cheryl Gillan replaced Mr Peter Hain after the 2010 general election.

[57] The Secretary of State for Wales announced, on 15 June 2010, the general time scale for the referendum which will take place before the Assembly elections in May 2011. The inability to lay the requisite draft Order before Parliament within the 120-day period was attributed to 'circumstances... inherited from the previous administration', a factor they contest. See www.walesoffice.gov.uk. The Welsh Assembly and both Houses of Parliament approved the draft of the requisite Order in Council in November 2010 and it was made on 15 December 2010: the National Assembly for Wales Referendum (Assembly Act Provisions) (Referendum Question, Date of Referendum Etc) Order 2010 (SI 2010/2837). There are also related Orders on expenses and on the amendment to 2006 Act, Sched. 7.

[58] An agreement between the Labour and Plaid Cymru Groups of the National Assembly, 27 June 2007, Part 2, A Strong and Confident Nation, para. 6.

[59] The work of the All-Wales Convention can only be briefly mentioned here, but its Report, above, n. 48, merits full consideration.

[60] Report of the All-Wales Convention, above, n. 48, pp. 99–100, specifically paras 6.2.9 and 6.2.16.

context must be highly selective. The focus of this chapter overall is on the 1998 devolution statutes, here the Northern Ireland Act 1998, and the subsequent evolution of devolution. With regard to Northern Ireland, however, history cannot be overlooked.

There are at least two key differences here in terms of the prelude to the 1998 statute. First, the history of devolution to Northern Ireland is tied into the very existence of Northern Ireland itself as a constitutional, or it may be argued non-constitutional, entity. A prior, and very different, system of devolution existed in Northern Ireland, under the Government of Ireland Act 1920, until 1972. Under s. 1(2) of the 1920 Act, Northern Ireland was actually defined in such a way as to create the largest geographic unit with the largest Unionist majority. There was (then) a high convergence of religious belief and political opinion in Ireland. The Unionists (usually simply labelled as Protestants and who supported the Union between Great Britain and Northern Ireland) were concentrated within the North-east part of Ireland. Of the ancient nine-county Province of Ulster, the north-eastern Province, four counties had a clear Protestant majority and two had a narrow Roman Catholic majority (who on the 'convergence basis' were Nationalists who supported a united Ireland). In spite of the latter point, all these six counties together constituted Northern Ireland. The remaining three counties, all with clear Roman Catholic majorities, were 'excluded' from Northern Ireland as their populations would have given the Unionists an overall majority of around 56 per cent rather than the 66 per cent which the six county unit established. These Unionist preferences prevailed and the six counties were divided or partitioned from the rest of Ireland.[61] These facts, coupled with the change in the electoral system from 1929, from a highly proportional one to first-past-the-post (and with hindsight at least this was a strange matter to devolve[62]), led to a single-party Unionist government, with effectively no opposition in Parliament and with no likelihood at all of it losing power. This marched with increasingly powerful arguments made by the Nationalists about abuse of power on the part of the Unionists: arguments on gerrymandering, discrimination in housing and employment (including in the police, the judiciary and other public sector employment), and police over-reaction to the civil rights marches of the mid to late 1960s. Consequently, the 1998 Act had to address constitutional status and the divisive experience of an earlier system of devolution, with, consequently, the need for an autochthonous constitution to be created and 'owned' by all parties within Northern Ireland.

The second key difference between Northern Ireland, on the one hand and Scotland and Wales on the other, is that from March 1972, when the 1920 system of devolution was suspended and later abolished,[63] to January 1974 and from July 1974[64] until the implementation of the 1998 Act, a period of 'direct rule', in which all laws were

[61] In the 2001 census, the figures are (approximately) 46 per cent Protestant; 40 per cent Roman Catholic; and 14 per cent of no identified religion.

[62] 1920 Act, s. 14.

[63] See the Northern Ireland (Temporary Provisions) Act 1972, and Northern Ireland Constitution Act 1973, s. 31 which abolished the Northern Ireland Parliament.

[64] For the first five months of 1974 a system of power-sharing devolution operated under the 1973 Act.

made at and by the Westminster Parliament and government with minimal input from Northern Ireland's MPs. operated during a time of considerable civil unrest, commonly referred to as 'The Troubles'. This system of direct rule was regarded as a 'temporary' expedient pending the introduction of a new form of power-sharing devolution but the duration of 'The Troubles', in which over 3,500 lives were lost, meant that direct rule lasted eventually for well over 25 years. The extensive deployment of British troops from August 1969 for 'peace-keeping purposes', the introduction of curfews and internment, or detention without trial, the events of Bloody Sunday in January 1972,[65] the rise of both republican and loyalist paramilitary groups, all connected to a bloody and conflictual foreground[66] of direct rule which became the background to the 1998 devolution agreement. The prime but not sole factor behind the violence related to the constitutional status of Northern Ireland. Thus alongside the political processes leading to the 1998 Act, there was also an inextricably linked peace process.[67] Like many if not all places where there has been violent conflict, Northern Ireland's present cannot be understood without reference to its past.

During this time also there was a steady process of bridge-building between the governments of the UK and Ireland, leading to joint decision making for Northern Ireland. These relationships for several decades have not been dependent upon the existence of any devolved government in Northern Ireland itself. This was most clearly seen in the Anglo–Irish Agreement of 1985 and in the processes leading to the Belfast Agreement of 1998, which involved representatives of both the British and Irish governments and of all Northern Ireland political parties.[68]

THE 1998 ACT, POPULAR SOVEREIGNTY, AND POWER-SHARING

The Northern Ireland Act 1998 is the statutory fruit of the Belfast Agreement 1998,[69] which was two agreements, that between the political parties and that between the British and Irish governments, each being the Annexe to the other. The provisions of the Belfast Agreement were submitted in May 1998 to the electorates of both Northern Ireland and (on constitutional status) of the Republic of Ireland. Support in the latter jurisdiction for the changes was nearly 95 per cent of those voting; in the former, nearly 72 per cent. A referendum in Northern Ireland is not as such noteworthy, however;

[65] See the 10-volume Report of the Inquiry into Bloody Sunday chaired by Lord Saville. Established in January 1998, it reported in June 2010.

[66] D. McKitterick *et al.*, *Lost Lives* (1999).

[67] See C. McCrudden, 'Northern Ireland and the British Constitution since the Belfast Agreement', in J. Jowell and D. Oliver, *The Changing Constitution* (6th edn, 2007) ch. 10. See specifically, and for example, the issues relating to the changes from the Royal Ulster Constabulary to the Police Service of Northern Ireland, the decommissioning of paramilitary weapons, the early release of paramilitary prisoners, the demilitarisation of Northern Ireland and the withdrawal of British troops, the search for the bodies of the 'disappeared', the Commission for Victims and Survivors, the Human Rights and Equality Commissions, and the fair employment and treatment legislation.

[68] See specifically now the British–Irish Intergovernmental Conference.

[69] Cm. 3883 (April 1998).

virtually every election held there (at least up to the Belfast Agreement) has involved its constitutional status as a key question.

The 1998 Act, by s. 1 and Sched. 1, makes provision for a border poll, the outcome of which on a simple majority of those voting would terminate the union between Great Britain and Northern Ireland and lead to the creation of a united Ireland.[70] The all-Ireland dimensions of the 1998 Agreement and Act, as well as being important in and of themselves, also provide a platform towards such a possible change. Within the context of devolution, there is an all-Ireland North South Ministerial Council which oversees cross-border implementation bodies and co-operation across a range of specified matters.

Under the 1998 Act, the Northern Ireland political parties themselves are both empowered and required, with very little preparation[71] (because the constitutional and cognate issues had dominated virtually all political debate in Northern Ireland for decades) to share power in a unionist–nationalist/republican coalition. That is, there is no devolution without power-sharing.[72]

The Northern Ireland Assembly consists of 108 members, and is elected by the single- transferable-vote system, with six members representing each of the 18 constituencies. Comparing the populations of Scotland, Wales, and Northern Ireland and the size of their legislatures, this is a large Assembly.[73] To the Assembly has been transferred, or devolved, legislative powers over a wide range of matters, similar but not identical to the position in Scotland.[74] Acts of the Assembly may not be incompatible with EU law or the ECHR. The devolved matters are agriculture, sea fisheries, forestry and rural development; culture, arts and leisure, including language diversity; education (primarily schools); employment and learning, including higher and further education; enterprise, trade and investment; the environment, including planning, pollution and local government; health, social services and public safety, including

[70] Similar provisions have been in previous legislation and, e.g. the Anglo–Irish Agreement of 1985 but here the sole alternative to the Union with Great Britain, a united Ireland, is expressly articulated.

[71] During direct rule, all major local government decision making, particularly housing and education, had been in the hands of nominated and not elected bodies, leaving the political parties to address together only refuse collection, burials, and leisure centres.

[72] Hence the suspensions of devolution in Northern Ireland which took place primarily from February to May 2000, and October 2002 to May 2007, with two technical but important brief suspensions in August and September 2001. The sole purpose behind the suspensions and the ensuing negotiations was to ensure that the set purposes of the devolved settlement were maintained or adjusted so as to secure its continuation. See the Northern Ireland Act 2000, the Northern Ireland (Elections and Periods of Suspension) Act 2003, the Northern Ireland Act 2006, and the Northern Ireland (St Andrews Agreement) Act 2006.

[73] The 2010 Parliamentary Voting System and Constituencies Bill, by cl. 9 seeks to reduce the number of MPs in the House of Commons from 650 to 600. The population of the UK as a whole is (approximate figures) 62 million, that of Scotland 5.1 million, Wales 3 million and Northern Ireland 1.8 million.

[74] Because of the earlier devolved systems in Northern Ireland, there is a different terminology as well as an additional category of power: devolved powers are transferred matters in Northern Ireland, reserved matters are called excepted matters and the (additional) category of power, unhelpfully called the reserved powers, relate to a category of power which may become devolved in the future. Justice and policing matters which are now devolved are one such illustration: see Northern Ireland Act 1998, Sched. 3.

child protection, mental health and hospital services; regional development including transport and transportation strategies; and social development, including housing programmes and urban regeneration. To this was (eventually) added in April 2010 the transfer of justice and policing powers.[75] Matters of national concern are withheld to the UK Parliament. The UK Parliament retains the power to legislate on any devolved matter but will not do so without the consent of the Assembly.[76]

The creation of the offices of First and Deputy First Prime Ministers, who, in spite of their titles, possess joint and equal powers, indicates clearly the depth of the requirement of power-sharing at all levels: they are in effect the political heads of the two largest 'traditions' in Northern Ireland. The departmental ministries and the chairs of the statutory shadowing Committees[77] are shared on a strictly proportionate basis; at the time of writing there is an executive, consisting of twelve departments, including the Office of First and Deputy First Ministers; five different political parties are represented in the executive.

Little assessment can be made of devolution to Northern Ireland which commenced in December 1999 because it has been suspended for much of its existence until the last three years or so. What is clear is that the end result of devolution is not closed as it currently is with Scotland; devolution does not *per se* preclude a change of constitutional status although clearly further legislation would be needed. Secondly, the ability of the Northern Ireland executive to enter into relations with the government of a sovereign state (Ireland) indicates the potential extent of powers that may be devolved within the framework of devolution. It may of course be argued that Northern Ireland remains *sui generis*. The point being made here concerns the flexibility of devolution as a constitutional model. Both factors take the Northern Ireland model beyond even Devo-Max, although fiscal autonomy is not at all present in Northern Ireland. This issue is, however, likely to become more pressing during and after the next Assembly elections scheduled for May 2011.

MIND THE DEVO-GAP: THE ENGLISH QUESTION

The Conservative–Liberal Democrat Coalition Negotiations Agreement, following the UK general election in May 2010, contained the following commitment under the heading of 'political reform': 'We have agreed to establish a commission to consider the "West Lothian question"'. As at February 2011, the Commission had not been established.[78] The failure to deal adequately heretofore with the English Question, by which is meant here the formulating of policies and the making of laws for England

[75] See the Northern Ireland Act 2009, and the Department of Justice Act (Northern Ireland) 2010.

[76] Northern Ireland Act 1998, s. 5(6), and Devolution Guidance Note 8.

[77] The chairpersons must come from another party from that represented by the minister being 'shadowed'.

[78] See HC Parliamentary Question, 14 July 2010, 799W and Hc Deb. 31 January 2011, c549W. See too 'The West Lothian Question', SN/PC/02586, March 2011.

within the devolved UK, is thus to be addressed shortly but to rectified, if at all, at an unknown date.

The issue impacts first upon the political complexion of those who enact laws which apply to England on matters that are (or may become) devolved throughout the rest of the UK. Had Labour and the Liberal Democrats formed a coalition government after the May general election, and such a possibility was, albeit briefly, considered, the democratic deficit for England would have been considerable.[79] Arguments on the lack of representation of the Conservatives at Westminster from Scotland and Wales are now, given devolution, far less serious. If the primary law provisions of the Government of Wales Act 2006 are brought into force after the May 2011 Assembly election (the necessary legislation being passed by the UK and Welsh legislatures) then the need properly to address the ways in which laws for England are enacted and policies formulated, and by whom, will be compelling.[80]

CONCLUSIONS

POPULAR SOVEREIGNTY AND CONSTITUTIONAL REFORM

There are two major points to be made concerning the UK's 'Changing Constitution' and devolution. First, devolution marks a clear movement from the formal doctrine of parliamentary sovereignty standing alone (which ultimately concerns nothing other than the status in law of an Act of Parliament) to its combination with a process, already a constitutional convention, whereby the holding of a referendum on any fundamental change to devolution (itself based on the 'will of the people') is not a matter of a concession or a (central government) convenience (for resolving internal disputes) but a nascent right. Devolution is not simply a gift from the Westminster Parliament but a reflection of an autochthonous movement which continues to develop.

To this convention on a fundamental terms referendum, should be added the legislative consent or Sewel convention under which the UK Parliament will not legislate on a devolved matter without the consent of the devolved legislature. This convention may be seen as standing against the formal legal position in the three devolution statutes but as it is virtually contemporaneous with them, it should be viewed in a particular light. A created convention, such as this convention is, has arguably greater force than one which emerges over time; it is established for a deliberate (even if flexible)

[79] In England, the Conservatives won 296 seats, Labour 191, and the Liberal Democrats 43, with two 'Others'. On votes cast, the latter two parties combined would have been in a clear majority but in the absence of voting reform, that is no more relevant than the fact that at the 2005 general election 65,000 more people in England voted Conservative than Labour.

[80] See also above, n. 53. A crystallization of the English dimension within the UK constitution might also breathe much needed new constitutional value into certain bodies, some of which are rooted in the Belfast Agreement, whose remit is to enhance inter-institutional relationships, such as the UK's Joint Ministerial Committee, the British–Irish Council, and the British–Irish Inter Parliamentary Assembly.

purpose and the political relationships in which it is forged and which it reflects should be understood as moderating the formal doctrine of legislative supremacy. That is, the convention is a response to, or for that matter the creation of, the political realities of devolution to which legal theory should yield.

Paradoxically the same point may be made with regard to Northern Ireland. The suspension of the devolved Assembly by and under an Act of the UK Parliament may be viewed as a clear example of Westminster's sovereign powers. It confers devolution and it removes it, *pro tempore* or for a longer period. This is, however, to view the suspensory legislation from too narrow a perspective. The sole purpose behind the suspensions and the ensuing negotiations was to ensure that the set purposes of the devolved settlement were maintained or adjusted so as to secure its continuation. Any idea that the sovereignty of Westminster may here be regarded as the unilateral assertion of the UK Parliament's legal powers does not fit the political reality. The embedded relationship between the governments of the UK and Ireland, and the requirements of the 1998 model of devolution, agreed by the Northern Ireland parties and confirmed by the electorate in both Northern Ireland and the Irish Republic, regarding the fullest expression within Northern Ireland of both the British and Irish dimensions indicate the parameters of the UK Parliament's supremacy. Even during the suspensions of the Northern Ireland devolved institutions between 2000 and 2007, legislative power, often nominally exercised through UK statutory instruments alone, reflected the cross community and inter-governmental principles.

The first lesson thus involves the uniting of the legal powers of the UK Parliament with the holding of referendums or, more generally, the ownership of the constitution and constitutional change. The second concerns the sapping of the political powers of the UK government and Parliament. This is first and obviously through the creation of the devolved institutions. The political landscape has changed and new configurations of power and new parties possessing elected power within a national law-making context, such as the SNP in government alone, and Plaid Cymru in coalition in Wales, cannot be discounted as merely a blip on the traditional landscape. New constitutions have created new politics.

In addition, these new political institutions, with an authority to govern within the devolved jurisdiction which is politically or democratically at least equal to that of the UK institutions, have revitalized popular politics beyond referendums. They have engendered a much wider engagement with the public than that ever achieved by the pre-devolved UK; and this is *pace* the now seemingly dated resort to Royal Commissions or (fractionally still more fashionable) Tribunals of Inquiry. Simply to list those bodies which have engaged with the issues surrounding the evolution of devolution to Scotland and Wales and the extensive multi-party talks on the peace and political processes for Northern Ireland is enough to indicate the extent of the difference between the ways in which such issues have been considered there, compared with England or the UK as a whole. The focal points for change have moved away from the government and legislature alone.

By way of brief contrast, consider the two Bills on constitutional reform, published in July 2010 by the UK coalition government, and the extent of public engagement with them. These Bills, namely, the Parliamentary Voting System and Constituencies Bill and the Fixed-Term Parliaments Bill, both began their parliamentary stages in September 2010. Whether or not they are passed by Parliament is not the point here. Failure to do that would relate to the relationship between a coalition government and (particularly) the House of Commons or the increasing assertiveness of Parliament. The point being made here relates to the mechanisms of constitutional change. In the case of these two Bills (and their significance is obvious from their short titles alone), there has been nothing comparable at all to the commissions or inquiries which have operated in Scotland and Wales on matters of arguably less constitutional importance. This point is ameliorated somewhat by cl. 1 of the Parliamentary Voting Bill which provides for a referendum to be held on the issue of replacing the first-past-the-post electoral system with the alternative vote system[81] but even there the amount of public engagement with the issues and the possible range of alternative electoral systems has been much more limited.[82]

House of Commons Temporary Standing Orders established in June 2010 a Select Committee on Political and Constitutional Reform, with its membership appointed on 10 July 2010 but already by August 2010 it was complaining that it did not have 'adequate opportunity to conduct [the] scrutiny'[83] required for such major legislation.

There needs to be a national conversation for both the UK constitution and that of England. Revitalization of the UK Parliament is important and the devolved legislatures may well give significant leads on both procedure and, for example, public petitions, but the debate on matters of constitutional importance is over-concentrated within Parliament and this is unhealthy when compared with the devolved nations. Constitutional reform is not solely for the political elites and devolution has shown the better way forward.

FURTHER READING

Hadfield, Brigid, 'Devolution, Westminster and the English Question' (2005) *Public Law* 286.

Hadfield, Brigid, 'The United Kingdom as a Territorial State' in V. Bogdanor (ed.), *The British Constitution in the Twentieth Century* (2003).

Rawlings, Richard and Hazell, Robert, *Devolution, Law Making and the Constitution* (2005).

Trench, Alan, *Devolution and Power in the United Kingdom* (2007).

[81] To be held on 5 May 2011. It would appear from cl. 6(1)(a) of the Bill that the outcome of the referendum is binding on the government.

[82] See, for the most recent government–public engagement with this issue, the Report of the Independent Commission on the Voting System (the Jenkins' Report), Cm. 4090-1 (1998). It received over 1,500 written submissions and letters (p. v).

[83] HC 422, 2010–11 (2 August 2010), p. 3, para. 2. The House of Lords' Select Committee on the Constitution has yet to consider the Bills.

USEFUL WEBSITES

Ministry of Justice: **www.justice.gov.uk**

The devolution guidance notes and other devolution material can be found on this website because this Ministry is responsible 'for the overall management of relations between the UK government and the devolved administrations in Scotland, Wales and Northern Ireland'.

National Assembly for Wales: **www.assemblywales.org**

Northern Ireland Assembly: **www.niassembly.gov.uk**

Northern Ireland Executive: **www.northernireland.gov.uk**

The Scottish Parliament: **www.scottish.parliament.uk**

The Scottish Government: **www.scotland.gov.uk**

Welsh Assembly Government: **www.wales.gov.uk**

9

THE CHANGING NATURE OF LOCAL AND REGIONAL DEMOCRACY

Ian Leigh

SUMMARY

This chapter evaluates the programme of reform aimed at reinvigorating local democracy begun by the Blair and Brown governments and continued under the coalition government. Successive governments have sought to reverse the decline in interest in local democracy by the electorate that has followed decades of central-local conflict and dwindling local powers. The chapter discusses the various interlocking strands in the reform programme: the relaxation of the *ultra vires* rule to enable councils to fulfil their new mission as 'community leaders' and the proposal for a new general power of competence; the introduction of strong Leaders and cabinets and scrutiny committees, which radically alter the role of councillors; the creation of new offices of directly elected mayors, especially in London; and the rise and decline of regional government. Finally it considers the future of local government within the coalition government's 'Big Society' agenda.

THE NATURE OF LOCAL GOVERNMENT

In the absence of a written constitution in the UK local government enjoys no formal constitutional status or protection. There is no legal restraint on central government enlisting Parliament to abolish local government altogether, still less reforming its essential characteristics. From an international perspective this is anomalous: references to local government abound in written constitutions the world over.[1] They do so because the idea has been found useful and important.

[1] See e.g. Constitution of the Fifth Republic 1958, Art. 72 (France); Basic Law of the Federal Republic of Germany, Art. 28.

This idea is no less important in the UK, although for clues to the constitutional significance of local government one must look to different sources. Two can be cited: a little-noticed Treaty ratified in 1998 and official reports.

The Treaty is the European Charter of Local Self-Government 1985. It defines the constitutional status to be given to local government by the signatory states.[2] The Charter contains some important principles, if broadly expressed. These include 'subsidiarity', a democratic principle stipulating that decisions should be taken at the nearest feasible level to those who are affected by them. For example, Art. 4, paras 3–5 state:

3. Public responsibilities shall generally be exercised, in preference, by those authorities which are closest to the citizen. Allocation of responsibility to another authority should weigh up the extent and nature of the task and the requirements of economy and efficiency.
4. Powers given to local authorities should normally be full and exclusive. They may not be undermined or limited by another, central or regional, authority except as provided for by the law.
5. Where powers are delegated to them by central or regional authority, local authorities shall, insofar as possible, be allowed discretion in adapting their exercise to local conditions.

In addition, Art. 9 guarantees the freedom to determine expenditure priorities and to raise adequate resources. The UK government's decision to ratify this Treaty in 1998 is of greater symbolic than legal significance. The Charter is binding between member states only (local authorities cannot invoke it on the international stage) and is only of tangential domestic legal significance: it is open to a court to refer to it in order to help resolve statutory ambiguity.

So far as official domestic recognition of the importance of local government is concerned, the following statement – from the report in 1986 of the Committee on the Conduct of Local Authority Business (the Widdicombe Committee) – is hard to improve upon as a summary of constitutional values:

[T]he value of local government stems from its three attributes of:

(a) pluralism, through which it contributes to the national political system;
(b) participation, through which it contributes to local democracy;
(c) responsiveness, through which it contributes to the provision of local needs through the delivery of services.[3]

[2] C. Crawford, 'European Influence on Local Self-Government' (1992) 18(1) *Local Government Studies* 69.

[3] *The Conduct of Local Authority Business, Report of the Committee of Inquiry Into the Conduct of Local Authority Business*, Cmnd 9797 (1986) para. 3.11.

Several characteristics are usually said to distinguish British local government: that it is elected, that councils have a measure of statutory discretion and financial autonomy, and that they have multiple local functions. In recent decades each of these features has come under some strain, so much so that at times central government (especially during the Conservative administrations from 1979 to 1997) has been accused of acting unconstitutionally in rebalancing them. It is worth briefly considering these further before moving on to discuss the reforms that have been introduced in recent years in an attempt to reinvigorate local democracy.

Local authorities have been elected since the 1880s, with the introduction under the Local Government Act 1888 of elected county councils (earlier legislation gave a right for householders only to vote). The changes since then have been not so much to the democratic character of local government as a regular process of adjusting its structures. The most prominent examples were reforms in the Local Government Act 1972, establishing a two-tier system of elected counties and districts over much of the country, but with variations in the split of functions between the tiers in the metropolitan areas,[4] and the creation in 1963 of the Greater London Council (abolished in 1986). Since a further reorganization of local government in 1992–96 most of England and all of Scotland and Wales now have a single tier of elected local authorities. In places these are district, borough, or city councils and in others county councils. In parts of rural England, however, the two tiers of counties and districts introduced in the Local Government Act 1972 survive, with functions divided between them.[5] In London, borough councils exercise most of the functions of unitary councils but a new elected strategic body, the Greater London Authority, came into operation in 2000.

The independent electoral approval that local councillors enjoy underlines the claim that this is local *government*, rather than local administration. The latter would suggest local implementation of centrally determined policies for merely practical reasons. The former implies that locally elected politicians have some degree of democratic legitimacy and discretion and control over how local functions are performed. Without such discretion local elections would be meaningless exercises. The elected nature of local authorities inevitably imports into their business party political conflict (although it is still common to find some independent councillors in a council). It also creates the possibility of conflict between the politics of the council and of central government, with each claiming their own electoral mandate.

Significantly, less than a decade after the introduction of popularly elected local authorities the courts could be seen deferring to the new bodies in a case in which a local byelaw was unsuccessfully challenged, on the grounds that it was made by councillors who had been elected as local representatives and who must be presumed to

[4] Metropolitan county councils were subsequently abolished, however, by the Local Government Act 1985.

[5] The coalition government acted rapidly to halt the further introduction of unitary authorities by compulsion: a Local Government Bill to reverse changes in train to require the restructuring of local government in Norfolk, Suffolk, and Devon, was introduced in May 2010.

have knowledge of local conditions.[6] In modern times, however, judges have been generally less deferential to local democracy. In a 1995 judgment declaring unlawful the decision of Somerset County Council to prevent deer hunting on land controlled by it, Laws J specifically rejected the council's argument that its statutory powers to manage land should be given a wider interpretation because elected council members were entitled to reflect local feelings on the issue.[7] Nor have councillors been allowed to use popular endorsement of their local manifesto policies by electoral success as cover for otherwise unlawful decisions:[8] to do so would in effect allow them to enlarge their own powers by making reckless electoral promises. On the other hand, the courts have been sensitive to local democracy in preventing councils from suing for defamation on the grounds that to do so would inhibit free discussion and public accountability.[9] Taken together these decisions tend to show the judiciary recognizing the value of local democracy as a mechanism for accountability to local people but, somewhat paradoxically, restricting the powers that elected councillors can wield.

It would be misleading, however, to suggest that local authorities are models of representative democracy. Electoral apathy is a serious and longstanding concern. Local elections have rarely produced turnouts of more than 40 per cent for decades, unless coinciding with a general election, but when, during the 1990s, voting dropped to around 10 per cent in some parts of the country the legitimacy of local democracy was seriously called into question.

The powers of local authorities and their democratic legitimacy are inextricably linked. Why bother to vote in local elections if councils are powerless to change anything? Equally, however, why should bodies that are ignored by the electorate be trusted with new powers by Parliament or deferred to by the courts? This conundrum explains why recent governments have attempted to reform simultaneously the powers of local government and their democratic governance. We will examine the reforms to local powers and executive structures in turn, paying less attention to the electoral reforms.

POWERS

Much of an individual's daily contact with the state and its officials is with local authorities. Councils are responsible for services such as education, social services, roads, swimming pools and leisure centres, libraries and planning, not to mention mundane but nonetheless vital matters like refuse collection and disposal.

[6] *Kruse* v. *Johnson* [1898] 2 QB 91, 98–9 (Lord Russell), and 104 (Sir F. H. Jeune), Mathew J dissenting.

[7] *R.* v. *Somerset CC ex parte Fewings* [1995] 1 All ER 513, 529; the Court of Appeal affirmed the decision on slightly different grounds: [1995] 3 All ER 20.

[8] *Bromley* v. *GLC* [1983] 1 AC 768, esp. Lord Wilberforce at 814; cf. *Secretary of State for Education and Science* v. *Tameside MBC* [1977] AC 1014, holding that the council's manifesto commitment (to retain grammar schools) was relevant to the reasonableness of the minister's intervention.

[9] *Derbyshire CC* v. *Times Newspapers* [1993] AC 534.

In recent decades, however, there has been a shift from councils acting as the primary providers of local services to coordinating and leading a range of public, private, and voluntary bodies. To some extent this had been foreshadowed in the fashionable notion of the 1980s – the 'enabling council' (i.e. enabling rather than doing) – although that was associated with an ideological bias in favour of contracting out the delivery of council services. A broader, communitarian, vision involving 'partnership' between councils, other local agencies, voluntary bodies, and the private sector was first articulated by Professor John Stewart in 1995.[10] It influenced an important report by a House of Lords Select Committee, *Rebuilding Trust*, the work of the self-styled Commission for Local Democracy, and the Labour government that took office in 1997.[11] The 1998 white paper *Modern Local Government* endorsed this vision of local authorities as 'community leaders' describing them as 'uniquely placed' among public institutions to play this role. The 2007 Lyons report continued in the same vein but used different terminology – speaking of the council's role in 'Place-Shaping'. This was described 'the creative use of powers and influence to promote the general well-being of a community and its citizens'.[12] 'Place-shaping' has several dimensions: including, representing the local community in discussions with government and business, working with other bodies locally (such the police, health authorities and voluntary sector), understanding and responding to the needs and preferences of local people (rather than simply following national standards for services), and working to make the local economy more successful.

The legal regime was felt to be inadequate for this new role in being merely a collection of diverse statutory functions, powers, and duties with no indication of what the sum of the parts amounted to. Moreover, the *ultra vires* rule created some artificial barriers to partnership working between local authorities and other bodies. Since it prevented the unlawful delegation of power from a council to another body, the rule inhibited cooperative working with other agencies in the public, voluntary, and private sectors and the establishment of free-standing, arm's-length, enterprises (such as companies) for such joint work. All co-operative enterprises of this kind were under the shadow that the courts might find them to be unlawful if they exercised powers entrusted by Parliament to the local authority or if the council was unable to point to explicit legal authority for its participation in them.

The *ultra vires* rule had come to be seen as increasingly rigid. It had developed lineally from 19th-century legal doctrines concerning the powers of corporations, whether public or private (such as companies). Whereas in relation to companies it was applied increasingly liberally in the early 20th century and was finally abolished

[10] E.g. J. Stewart and G. Stoker (eds), *Local Government in the 1990s* (1995) ch. 14.

[11] See *Report of the House of Lords Select Committee on Relations Between Central and Local Government 'Rebuilding Trust'*, HL 97 (1995–96); Commission for Local Democracy, *Taking Charge: the Rebirth of Local Democracy* (1995); Labour Party, *Renewing Democracy, Rebuilding Communities* (1995).

[12] Lyons Inquiry into Local Government, *Place-Shaping a Shared Ambition for the Future of Local Government* (March 2007), para. 2.43, available at www.lyonsinquiry.org.uk/index8a20.html.

by legislation, for public corporations it became an increasingly potent method of judicial control.[13]

As Laws LJ put it in the *Fewings* decision:

> any action to be taken must be justified by positive law. A public body has no heritage of legal rights which it enjoys for its own sake; at every turn all of its dealings constitute the fulfilment of duties which it owes to others; indeed it exists for no other purpose.... It is in this sense that it has no rights of its own, no axe to grind beyond its public responsibility: a responsibility which defines its purpose and justifies its existence. In law this is true of every public body. The rule is necessary in order to protect the people from arbitrary interference by those set in power over them.[14]

Central government can influence the parliamentary process to obtain wide grants of discretionary power and is only rarely subjected to detailed duties. This is not the case with local government. The legacy, then, for local authorities is that each action and decision, however minor, must be shown to rest on explicit statutory authority.[15] The courts, moreover, have compounded the situation by often interpreting narrowly even apparently widely drafted statutory powers when the actions of the council could adversely affect local taxpayers by imposing financial liability for an unsuccessful transaction[16] or where private rights or interests would be affected.[17] A particularly controversial judicial construct is the fiduciary principle, by which the courts have treated a local authority as a type of trustee of money received from local taxpayers.[18] Under the guise of this dubious doctrine some decisions involving council expenditure have been held to be unlawful in giving too little weight to taxpayers' interests.[19]

Recent attempts at statutory reform are an attempt to undo some of these negative implications of *ultra vires*. They have taken three main forms.[20]

[13] The turning point came in *Ashbury Railway Carriage Co.* v. *Riche* (1875) LR 7, HL 653 when the House of Lords rejected the argument that statutory corporations should be regarded as having the legal attributes of a natural person except to the extent that the statute expressly or impliedly restricted them. See M. Stokes, 'Company Law and Legal Theory', in W. Twining (ed.), *Legal Theory and Common Law* (1986); H. Rajak, 'Judicial Control: Corporations and The Decline of Ultra Vires', (1995) 26 *Cambrian Law Review* 9.

[14] *R.* v. *Somerset CC ex parte Fewings* [1995] 1 All ER 513, 524.

[15] All local authorities now enjoy their powers solely under statute: Local Government Act 1972, ss 2(3), 14(2) and 21(2). The Act extinguished the claim that boroughs created under royal charter possessed the powers of an ordinary person and so were not subject to *ultra vires*; and see *Hazell* v. *Hammersmith LBC* [1992] 2 AC 1, 39–43 *per* Lord Templeman.

[16] As in *Hazell*, ibid., and *Credit Suisse* v. *Allerdale BC* [1996] 4 All ER 129, CA.

[17] E.g. *Fewings*, above, n. 14.

[18] M. Loughlin, *Legality and Locality: the Role of Law in Central-Local Relations* (1996) ch. 4; I. Leigh, *Law, Politics and Local Democracy* (2000) 131–9.

[19] *Roberts* v. *Hopwood* [1925] AC 578; *Prescott* v. *Birmingham Corp.* [1955] Ch 210; *Bromley LBC* v. *Greater London Council* [1983] AC 768.

[20] A fourth measure, the Local Government (Contracts) Act 1997, aimed to remedy some of the disadvantages where a contract involving a local authority was held void because it was *ultra vires* (as in the *Hazzell* and *Allerdale* cases), is less important here.

First, expanded discretionary powers to enter into partnership arrangements with other local bodies or agencies have been introduced by the Local Government Act 2000, ss 2(4) and 4.[21] These were intended to remove the uncertainty over the legality of some of these co-operative ventures. In the spirit of 'joined-up' government various programmes have been introduced to stimulate local authorities to work in partnership, both with other public authorities and with the voluntary and private sectors. Local Area Agreements are three-year agreements setting out the priorities for a local area made between central government (through the relevant regional office), the lead local authority and other key partners.[22] Strategic Service-delivery Partnerships are similar collaborative agreements aimed at improving the delivery of services in the locality. Local authorities play a leading role in Local Strategic Partnerships – forums to bring together the public sector as well as the private, business, community and voluntary sectors at a local level, so that initiatives and services support each other and work together.

Secondly, a power of 'community initiative' was introduced in 2000 by the Labour government. This was hailed as enshrining in law the role of the council as 'the elected leader of their local community'.[23] This was intended as an 'over-arching' or under-pinning duty, with a linked power of community initiative – a type of quasi-constitutional mission statement which would give structure and purpose to the many specific powers and duties of councils.[24]

In the form in which they were ultimately introduced these proposals were diluted, however. The legal power is supplementary, rather than fundamental, and the duty was omitted. All local authorities now have power to do anything which they consider is likely to promote or improve the economic, social, or environmental well-being of their area.[25] When exercising the power (or considering whether to do so) an authority must consider the effect on the achievement of sustainable development in the UK.[26] Linked to the power is a specific duty to 'prepare a strategy for promoting or improving the economic, social and environmental well-being' of the authority's area (s. 4(1)). The strategic plan is intended to provide focus for the leadership and coordinating aspects of the community leadership role. Apart from a specific power to incur expenditure, detailed powers to enter partnerships also feature prominently.[27] Although the power of community initiative is undoubtedly useful there are various limitations: the power cannot be used by a council to override restrictions in other

[21] The community initiative power includes specific ability to give financial assistance, to enter into arrangements or agreements, to co-operate with, or facilitate, or coordinate the activities of any person, to exercise on behalf of any person any functions of that person, and to provide staff, goods, services, or accommodation to any person: Local Government Act 2000, s. 2(4).

[22] Local Government Association, *Leading Localities: Local Area Agreements* (2005).

[23] *Modern Local Government: In Touch With the People*, Cm. 4014 (1998), para. 8.9.

[24] See the green paper, Department of the Environment, Transport and the Regions, *Modernising Local Government: Local Democracy and Community Leadership* (February 1998) ch. 8, and the earlier Labour Party policy document, *Renewing Democracy, Rebuilding Communities*, above, n. 11.

[25] Local Government Act 2000, s. 2(1). [26] Ibid., s. 2(3). [27] Ibid., s. 2(6).

more detailed legislation,[28] and ministers have a wide power to exclude activities by delegated legislation.[29]

The third strand of reform of powers involves relaxation by ministers of legal and ministerial controls over local authorities, for example, where existing legal provisions prevented councils from delivering 'best value' or from exercising their community well-being power.[30]

The coalition government programme promised to go further than these reforms and to introduce a general power of competence for local government.[31] Although this idea is something of a holy grail (similar proposals have been made for more than 80 years[32]), interest in it has been revived in recent years by local government reforms in Scandinavia[33] and in the Republic of Ireland.[34] In its purest form a general power of competence takes the direct obverse form to the *ultra vires* principle: the actions of the council are presumptively lawful if they are (in its view) for the benefit of the local area, provided they do not otherwise constitute a crime, tort or involve a breach of contract.[35] This would radically alter the nature of legal accountability, so much so that the Widdicombe Committee argued in 1986 that such a power would be fundamentally incompatible with the current regime of statutory grants to local authorities of specific functional powers.[36]

Prior to the election a Conservative policy document described the contours of the proposed new power:

> an explicit freedom to act in the best interests of their voters, unhindered by the absence of specific legislation supporting their actions

It continued, however:

> No action – except raising taxes, which requires specific parliamentary approval – will any longer be 'beyond the powers' of local government in England, unless the local authority is prevented from taking that action by the common law, specific legislation or statutory guidance.[37]

Inevitably, much will depend, however, on the attitude of the courts to the new power. Although the proposal refers to the power as one of 'first resort' it is likely that in

[28] Anything subject to a 'prohibition, restriction or limitation on their powers which is contained in any enactment' is specifically excluded under s. 3(1). This applies to existing and future legislation ('whenever passed or made') and to subordinate legislation also (subs. 3(6)).

[29] Local Government Act 2000, s. 3(3).

[30] Under ibid., s. 5.

[31] *The Coalition: our programme for government* (2010) 12.

[32] Leigh, above, n. 18, pp. 53–56.

[33] See discussions of the 'Free Local Government' initiatives: H. Kitchin, 'A Power of General Competence for Local Government', in L. Pratchett and D. Wilson, *Local Democracy and Local Governnment* (1996); L. Rose, 'Nordic Free-Commune Experiments: Increased Local Autonomy or Continued Central Control?', in D. King and J. Pierre (eds), *Challenges to Local Government* (1990).

[34] Local Government Act 1991 (Republic of Ireland).

[35] As proposed by the *Royal Commission on Local Government in England*, Cmnd. 4040 (1969) ch. 8, para. 323.

[36] The *Report of the Committee of Inquiry into the Conduct of Local Authority Business*, 9797 (1986) paras 8.23ff.

[37] Conservative Party, *Control Shift: Return Power to Local Communities* (2009).

the great majority of cases councils will continue to act under specific, detailed, and limited statutory powers. The question then will be how these specific powers and the new general competence power fit together. Attempts in the past to liberalize *ultra vires* by giving broad powers to local authorities have foundered at this stage.[38] The experience with community initiative power under the Local Government Act 2000 has been similarly mixed. Some judges have given the provision a wide and generous interpretation.[39] On the other hand, where a consortium of local authorities formed a mutual insurance company with which one of them entered into a contract of insurance (leading to an estimated 15 per cent saving in costs) the Court of Appeal found that this was *ultra vires*.[40] The well-being power could not be used since the economic benefit of the scheme was too generalised. Lord Justice Moore-Bick found that:

> section 2 gives a local authority power to take steps that have as their object, direct or indirect, some reasonably well defined outcome which it considers will promote or improve the well-being of its area.[41]

However, these steps had to directly affect the well-being of the area, whereas the scheme in question was merely designed to reduce general costs and did 'not have as its object the use of the money saved for an identified purpose'.[42]

The proposals in the 2010–11 Localism Bill are indeed far-reaching. If enacted they would confer a power 'to do anything that individuals generally may do' even if it is unlike anything that the authority or other public authorities may otherwise do.[43] The general power includes the means to execute it 'in any way whatever' without territorial restrictions, whether as a commercial purpose or not and 'for *or otherwise* than for the benefit of the authority its area or persons resident in its area' (emphasis added). This formulation seems broad enough to override most of the arguments that have prevailed in the courts against earlier apparently general powers. The only significant limitation is that the new power will not be take priority over express limitations in specific overlapping statutory powers.[44]

The potentially thorny question of restrictions imposed in legislation coming after the enactment of the general competence power is dealt with by a provision that seems to require an express parliamentary statement of intention to override the

[38] See especially decisions in relation to Local Government Act 1972, s. 111, which allows a council to do anything 'which is calculated to facilitate, or is conducive or incidental to, the discharge of any of their functions'. As examples of restrictive interpretations of s. 111: *Hazell* v. *Hammersmith and Fulham LBC* [1991] 1 All ER 545; *McCarthy and Stone* v. *Richmond upon Thames LBC* [1991] 4 All ER 897; *Credit Suisse* v. *Allerdale BC* [1996] 4 All ER 129; *Credit Suisse* v. *Waltham Forest LBC* [1996] 4 All ER 176; *Morgan Grenfell* v. *Sutton LBC* (1996) 95 LGR 574; *Allsop* v. *North Tyneside MBC* (1992) 90 LGR 462.

[39] *R. (J)* v. *Enfield LBC* [2002] EWHC 432 (Admin), [2002] LGR 390 (potential use to give financial assistance towards rental to an asylum seeker who was specifically barred under other legislation from being offered accommodation); and see *R. (Khan)* v. *Oxfordshire County Council* [2004] EWCA Civ 309, [2004] LGR 257.

[40] *Brent LBC v Risk Management Partners Limited* [2009] EWCA Civ 490.

[41] Ibid., para. 180. [42] Ibid., para. 180.

[43] 2010–11 Localism Bill, cl. 1. All references are to the text of the Bill published on 13 December 2010.

[44] Ibid., cl. 2(1).

general power.[45] The coalition government apparently intends the courts to follow the examples of the European Communities Act 1972 and the Human Rights Act 1998 and treat this as a de facto suspension of the implied repeal rule.[46] If carried through in this form the power of general competence will be a constitutionally significance measure marking a significant departure from more than a century of local government legislation and judical practice.

From reform of powers we turn now to the reform of local government executive structures.

NEW FORMS OF DEMOCRATIC GOVERNANCE

THE PROBLEM

The elected nature of local government inevitably gives rise to the influence of party politics: in most local authorities there are caucuses of councillors grouped according to party affiliation in imitation of the arrangements at Westminster. This is a long-standing feature of local government, although it appears that party politics at the local level became more intense during the 1970s and 1980s.[47]

Traditionally, councils have organized themselves quite differently, however, from the central state. Legally speaking, the whole council (all the councillors of whatever political affiliation) was responsible for the authority's decisions. In practice, most decisions were delegated to committees of elected members with smaller areas of responsibility or, in the case of purely administrative matters, to council employees, the officers. The officers, however, served the council as a whole, rather than the majority group of councillors.

The mismatch between these two features – the political nature of local government and the legal responsibility of the whole council – became acute in a number of local authorities during the 1980s. The Widdicombe Committee found in 1986 that 85 per cent of local authorities were organized on political lines with party groups meeting outside the council's structure to determine political strategy.[48] These party groups, however, had no formal place within the decision-making process. Attempts to regularize the position by giving the majority party group an official decision-making power were held to be unlawful in depriving opposition councillors of access to information.[49] On the other hand, unless they were guaranteed a secure environment in

[45] Ibid., cl. 2(2)(a).

[46] See *Explanatory Notes to Localism Bill 2010–11*, para. 51: 'Restrictions in post-commencement legislation will only apply to the general power where if they are expressed to do so'.

[47] J. Gyford, S. Leach and C. Game, *The Changing Politics of Local Government* (1989); K. Young, 'Party Politics in Local Government: an Historical Perspective', in *Aspects of Local Democracy, Research Volume IV, Report of the Committee of Inquiry into the Conduct of Local Authority Business* (1986) 81–105.

[48] *The Conduct of Local Authority Business*, Cmnd 9797 (1986) paras 2.37–2.40. See also the follow-up study: K. Young and M. Davies, *The Politics of Local Government Since Widdicombe* (1990).

[49] *R. v. Sheffield City Council ex parte Chadwick* (1985) 84 LGR 563.

which to reach policy decisions there was no incentive for a controlling majority of councillors to bring policy formulation out of closed party group meetings and into the council as such.

Consequently, the legal constitution of local government was founded on a bizarre and unhealthy silence about its most visible attribute – party politics. Decisions would be reached behind closed doors in the group meeting of the majority party, to be rubber-stamped in public council meetings.[50] Furthermore, the legal framework still clung doggedly to the fiction that all councillors were of equal importance, regardless of political affiliations. In many local authorities, however, the chairmen of committees had assumed a role that paralleled at the local level the function of a Secretary of State, with political direction and control of an area of the council's work. This too was of dubious legality.[51]

An obvious solution to these problems would have been to acknowledge the political realities by allowing for the legal creation of a political executive with effective balancing mechanisms. Instead, in its Local Government and Housing Act 1989, the Conservative government focused on outlawing political abuses – a duty that all council committees must reflect the political balance of the parties was introduced.[52]

REFORM

More radical proposals for reform came about because of dissatisfaction with the system of decision making by committees that operated in local authorities and because of the need to reinvigorate local politics in the light of dwindling participation rates in local elections. These have taken three main forms: experiments in the use of 'direct' or 'deliberative' (rather than 'representative') democratic devices such as local referendums, citizens' juries, service user panels, questionnaires, and focus groups; minor reforms to electoral procedure; and changes to the democratic governance of councils.

The 2010–11 Localism Bill, published in December 2010, *inter alia* contains several initiatives to promote direct democracy under the coalition's 'Big Society' agenda. Residents of a local authority area will have the power to instigate local referendums on any local issue (subject to collecting signatures from 5 per cent of the electorate in a six-month period), to be held at the same time as other elections, and be given the

[50] In *R.* v. *Amber Valley DC ex parte Jackson* [1984] 3 All ER 501 it was held that the mere fact that a planning application had been discussed in a prior party group meeting of the majority group did not mean that the council could not later determine it fairly. In *R.* v. *Waltham Forest Borough Council ex parte Baxter* [1988] 2 WLR 257 there was an unsuccessful attack on a decision reached after councillors, who had voted against the policy in closed group meeting but lost, later followed the party whip and supported it in a council meeting; on the facts the Court of Appeal found that their discretion not been fettered.

[51] The Local Government Act 1972 did not permit a council to delegate functions to an individual councillor, and where an officer acted under the instruction of a committee chairman this might be held unlawful: *R.* v. *Port Talbot BC ex parte Jones* [1988] 2 All ER 207.

[52] Local Government and Housing Act 1989, s. 15; the Local Government (Committees and Political Groups) Regulations 1990 (SI 1553/1990).

power to veto council tax increases seen as excessive.[53] Local referendums are not entirely new and some local authorities have been experimenting with them as an exercise in direct democracy for more than a decade. Earlier legislation introduced referendums for local authorities about the adoption of directly elected mayors[54] and in Scotland and Wales older legislation allowed for local polls on Sunday opening of shops and public houses.[55] Under the Local Government Act 2003 councils have a general power to conduct a local poll on a wide range of matters.[56] These proposals are different, however, in that the initiative will lie with local residents rather than the council.

Details of the proposed referendum power over council tax increases were published in a consultation document in July 2010.[57] Under these proposals any council that set its council tax increase above a set ceiling, approved annually by Parliament, would trigger an automatic referendum of all registered electors in their area.[58] The referendum would give a choice between the council's proposed council tax rise and a shadow budget, which the council would be required to prepare within the defined limit. The referendum will be determined by a simple majority of those voting, with no minimum requirement for voter turnout. In the event of a ' no' vote in the referendum the council would be required to refund council taxpayers or to give a tax credit at the end of the year.

This proposal is linked to the proposed abolition of central government powers of capping of council tax rates,[59] and has considerable democratic advantages.[60] A long-standing objection to capping,[61] which was first introduced during the bitter central–local disputes of the 1980s,[62] is that it amounts to the over-ruling by central government of budgetary decisions taken by locally elected and accountable politicians. Under the referendum proposal the power of veto will be returned to the local

[53] 2010–11 Localism Bill, Pt 4, ch. 1.

[54] The Local Authorities (Conduct of Referendums) (England) Regulations 2007 (SI 2007/2089).

[55] Under the Licensing (Scotland) Act 1959 and Licensing Act 1961 (provisions now repealed) respectively.

[56] A local authority may conduct a poll to ascertain the views of those polled about any matter relating to services provided in pursuance of the authority's functions, the authority's expenditure on such services, or any other matter relating to the authority's power to promote well-being of its area. It is for the local authority concerned to decide who is to be polled, and how the poll is to be conducted: Local Government Act 2003, s. 116.

[57] Department of Communities and Local Government, *Local Referendums to Veto Excessive Council Tax Increases Consultation* (July 2010), available at www.communities.gov.uk/documents/localgovernment/pdf/1657699.pdf. See also House of Commons Library briefing, *Council Tax: Local Referendums* (2010), available at www.parliament.uk/briefingpapers/commons/lib/research/briefings/snpc-05682.pdf.

[58] 2010–11 Localism Bill, ch. 4, Pt 2 and Sched. 5.

[59] Ibid., cl. 56 and Sched. 6.

[60] Some critics have argued, however, that local referendums should not supplant local elections: G. Jones and J. Stewart, 'Council tax referendums are damaging', *Local Government Chronicle*, 5 August 2010, p. 9.

[61] Introduced by the Rates Act 1984. Capping involves imposing a legal limit on the rate of council tax that can be set by a local authority.

[62] For example, *Nottinghamshire CC* v. *Secretary of State for the Environment* [1986] AC 240; *Hammersmith and Fulham* v. *Secretary of State for the Environment* [1990] 3 All ER 589. See generally Loughlin, above, n. 18.

electorate, thus restoring the direct link between local residents and the spending decisions of the local authorities to whom they pay their council tax.

Apart from these moves towards direct democracy, experimental attempts have also been introduced to tackle low levels of voter turnout more directly. Legislation permits councils to apply for permission to use alternative electoral arrangements to the traditional single day voting in person at polling station.[63] These schemes have included the use of postal ballots, rather than polling stations, electronic voting, and the use of non-conventional polling stations such as supermarkets and doctors' surgeries. At the same time many councils have moved to a cycle of more frequent elections – a third of councillors stand for re-election in three years out of a four-year cycle in an attempt to make councils more responsive to the local electorate. More radical reform, such as the introduction of proportional representation for local elections, has been rejected – for England and Wales. In Scotland, however, following the report of the MacIntosh Committee,[64] proportional representation was introduced in local government by the Local Government (Scotland) Act 2004.

So far as the system of decision making is concerned, the problem with the traditional local government model was its lack of separation of policy formulation, implementation, and scrutiny – the council as a whole was responsible for all of these functions. Consequently, the decision-making processes were confusing and lacked transparency. Instead of focusing on their representation and scrutiny roles councillors were involved in close management of tasks better left to officers.[65]

A consultation paper from the Department of Environment, published in 1993, argued for recognition of political executives on several grounds, 'they provide clear political direction for the authority; make clear where accountability lies; provide a more efficient, quicker and coordinated decision-making process; and provide a confidential forum for the ruling group to test the range of policy options with its official advisers'.[66] Moreover, the change would enable councillors who were not members of the executive to take on stronger scrutiny and constituency roles. The proposal that the government should allow experimentation with different forms of political executive did not appeal to the ministers at that time. However, the concept of a political executive became an accepted feature of later reform models[67] and, ultimately, part of the Labour government's programme in the Local Government Act 2000.

Initially, the legislation required councils to review their administrative arrangements and to adopt one of three forms (the *status quo* was not a permitted option): a leader and cabinet system, an elected mayor and cabinet, or an elected mayor and

[63] Representation of the People Act 2000, s. 10.

[64] The Final Report of the Commission on Local Government and the Scottish Parliament, *Moving Forward Local Government and the Scottish Parliament* (June 1999).

[65] E.g. Commission For Local Democracy, *Taking Charge: The Rebirth of Local Democracy* (1995) chs 3 and 4.

[66] *Community Leadership and Representation: Unlocking the Potential* (1993) para. 5.22.

[67] *Modernising Local Government: Local Democracy and Community Leadership* (1998) ch. 5; *Modern Local Government*, above, n. 23, ch. 3.

council manager (a powerful officer). Not surprisingly, most councils opted for the leader and cabinet, since it represented 'the formalisation of already existing group-dominated political processes'.[68] A much smaller number adopted the elected mayor and cabinet model. In 2007 these models were narrowed and refined by enhancing the position of the leader (compelling those councils that took this route to follow the so-called 'strong leader' model) and eliminating the (little used) mayor and council manager option. All councils were required to consult the public on a choice between a strong leader and cabinet model and a directly elected mayor and cabinet.[69] In its programme the coalition government stated that councils will in future be given the freedom to return to the committee system where they consider this to be preferable.[70]

Under the leader and cabinet model[71] the leader is chosen by councillors[72] and is removable by them without reference to the electorate. Except in 'hung' authorities (those where no party has overall control), where the election of the leader may become a semi-transparent process, normally the leadership and membership of the cabinet will be decided in the group meeting of the majority party and then presented to the Council meeting for endorsement. The leader decides on the size and responsibilities of the cabinet and has power to dismiss other members of the cabinet. The leader is elected for a four-year fixed term but can be removed by a vote of councillors.

The political executive is balanced by overview and scrutiny committees.[73] The purpose of these committees is, first, to scrutinize the discharge of executive functions and, secondly, to provide a policy role in reporting and making recommendations to the authority or the executive about the discharge of their functions and on matters which affect the authority's area or inhabitants.[74]

Overview and scrutiny committees have the power to require members of the executive and officers to attend and answer questions (and there will be a corresponding duty on them to do so) and to invite other people.[75]

The division between executive and scrutiny councillors is based on a parliamentary select committee model. Separation from the executive is enforced by a provision preventing oversight and scrutiny committees from including members of the executive.[76] However, as with parliamentary select committees, there is a majority of councillors who are from the same party as the executive. Critics argued that unless the reforms addressed the hidden influence of the party group they would prove ineffective.[77] Studies suggested that there may be a reluctance among councillors on scrutiny

[68] C. Copus, 'The Party Group: A Barrier to Democratic Renewal' (1999) 25(4) *Local Govt Studs* 76, 89–90.

[69] Local Government and Public Involvement in Health Act 2007, Pt 3; and see the white paper, *Strong and Prosperous Communities* (2006) ch. 3.

[70] Proposals to this effect are contained in the 2010–11 Localism Bill, ch. 3.

[71] S. Leach, 'Introducing Cabinets into British Local Government' (1999) 52(1) *Parl. Affs.* 77.

[72] Local Government Act 2000, s. 10(3)(a).

[73] A council opting for a mayor and cabinet model (below) is required to have overview and scrutiny arrangements also.

[74] Local Government Act 2000, s. 15(1). [75] Ibid., s. 15(3) and (4). [76] Ibid., s. 15(2).

[77] Copus, above, n. 68, pp. 76, 88–9.

committees to criticize party colleagues[78] and that it might have been preferable to require scrutiny committees to be chaired by an opposition councillor, an omission from the legislation. There are indications that in some councils 'backbench' councillors have struggled since these reforms to find a worthwhile role, since they have been formally excluded from the policy process.[79] In an attempt to counteract this trend the possibility of single member constituencies was introduced in 2007, allowing for an enhanced role for individual backbench councillors (so-called 'Democratic Champions').[80] At the same time powers of oversight and scrutiny committees were strengthened by requiring councils to consider and publicly respond to their recommendations and by giving them powers to question and influence other public service providers in the locality.[81]

ELECTED MAYORS

The more innovative model is the directly elected mayor. This is an imported office: mayors are common in local government overseas, especially in the cities of the USA, France, Italy, and Germany.[82]

In the UK the idea was first championed by Michael Heseltine as Secretary of State for the Environment, and then taken up by the Campaign for Local Democracy in 1995.[83] It was first officially proposed as an option for the proposed new London Authority.[84] The idea was approved in a referendum held in Greater London in May 1998 and the Greater London Authority Act 1999 gave effect to these proposals, with the first elected mayor, Ken Livingstone, returned in May 2000.

In the case of councils outside London, a 1999 white paper proposed that councils should be placed under a duty to consult local people about the form of government they wished to see, with an elected mayor as one of the options. Fearing resistance from councillors to the idea, the government proposed that there would be a possibility of a referendum being triggered to put the elected mayor option to the electorate, even where this was not the council's preferred choice.[85]

[78] M. Cole, 'Local Government Modernisation: the Executive and Scrutiny Model' (2001) 72(2) *Pol Q* 239; R. Ashworth, 'Toothless Tiger? Councillor Perceptions of the New Scrutiny Arrangements in Welsh Local Government' (2003) 29 *Local Govt Studs* 1.

[79] Cole, ibid., pp. 241–2.

[80] Local Government and Public Involvement in Health Act 2007, s. 55: see *Strong and Prosperous Communities*, above, n. 69, ch. 3.

[81] Local Government and Public Involvement in Health Act 2007, ss 119–28.

[82] See H. Elcock, 'Leading People: Some Issues of Local Government Leadership in Britain and America' (1995) 21(4) *Local Govt Studs* 546; G. Stoker, 'The Reform of the Institutions of Local Representative Democracy: Is there a role for the mayor-council model?', CLD Research Report No. 18 (1996); G. Stoker and H. Wolman, 'Drawing Lessons from US Experience: An Elected Mayor For British Local Government' (1992) 70(2) *Public Admin.* 241.

[83] Commission for Local Democracy, *Taking Charge: the Rebirth of Local Democracy* (1995) ch. 4.

[84] *A Mayor and Assembly for London*, Cm. 3897 (1998).

[85] *Local Leadership, Local Choice*, Cm. 4298 (1999) ch. 2.

Advocates of the idea of a directly elected mayor hoped that it would bring about functional separation in the council between the executive (comprising a directly elected mayor or leader and the council's staff) and the elected assembly of councillors. Moreover, with an elected mayor, instead of the political leadership of council being determined by the party group, it is a matter directly for the electorate. The idea was to bring about a working tension which might increase public knowledge about local government and weaken party dominance. This has been partially successful: several of the mayors elected to date are independent and in other cases the mayorship and the majority on the council are in the hands of different parties.

Low turnout rates however (typically between 11 and 42 per cent of the electorate) suggest that generally the experiment has failed to revive significant public interest in local democracy The significant exceptions have been the campaigns to elect a mayor for London in 2000, 2004, and 2008 which have attracted extensive press attention and the entry of candidates with a high public profile from Westminster politics. Apart from the Greater London Authority there are currently 12 councils where the elected mayor and cabinet system has been adopted and one area (Stoke on Trent) where a referendum approved a change back from the model.[86] By late 2010 only only 37 referendums had been held; in 13 instances the result was in favour of an elected mayor.[87] After a flurry of interest in 2001 and 2002, only a handful of referendums has been held. The failure of other major cities to follow London's lead is disappointing, especially since one aspiration was that elected mayors would be figureheads who would represent their communities nationally and in Europe.

Despite this low uptake, the coalition government appears as enthusiastic as its predecessor about potential of elected mayors. At the 2010 general election the Conservative party argued that mayors would provide strong, conspicuous, individual leadership of councils and boost democratic engagement.[88] The coalition policy is to introduce elected mayors into the 12 biggest English cities in May 2013, subject to approval in local referendums.[89]

LONDON

The creation of a mayor and a new strategic authority for London in the Greater London Authority Act 1999[90] can be counted a success in raising the profile of issues

[86] Bedford, Doncaster, Hartlepool, Mansfield, Middlesbrough, North Tyneside, Torbay, and Watford, and in the London Boroughs of Hackney, Lewisham, Newham, and Tower Hamlets. See also N. Rao, 'Options for Change: Mayors, Cabinets or Status Quo?' (2003) *Local Govt Studs* 1.

[87] See further Electoral Commission, *Factsheet: Directly Elected Mayors* (October 2010).

[88] *Control Shift*, above, n. 37, para. 3.1.

[89] Birmingham, Leeds, Sheffield, Bradford, Manchester, Liverpool, Bristol, Wakefield, Coventry, Leicester, Nottingham, and Newcastle-upon-Tyne. 2010–11 Localism Bill, Pt 1, ch. 3.

[90] M. Supperstone and T. Pitt-Payne, 'The Greater London Authority Bill' [1999] *Public Law* 581; B. Pimlott and N. Rao, *Governing London* (2002). Some enhanced powers were added by the Greater London Authority Act 2007.

affecting London as a whole. The Authority comprises two elected institutions with complementary roles, the mayor and the London Assembly. Elections are held for both simultaneously every four years.[91] The mayor is elected under the supplementary vote system. This, if there are three or more candidates, allows voters to express a first and second preference among the candidates. At the counting stage unsuccessful candidates are eliminated and second preferences are redistributed if no candidate achieves more than 50 per cent of first preferences. (If there are fewer than three candidates, the 'first past the post' voting system is applied.) Ken Livingstone, who served as the first mayor, following his election in May 2000, as an Independent, and his re-election as a Labour candidate in 2004, and Boris Johnson, his Conservative successor since 2008, became recognisable figure-heads for the metropolis both nationally and internationally.

There are 25 Assembly members, chosen by a mix of electoral methods: 14 represent constituencies and 11 are chosen for London-wide seats, according to the Additional Member system reflecting the electoral strengths of the respective political parties.

The mayor is the most visible face of the new Authority and is the main source of initiatives in policy affecting London as a whole, as well as being responsible for coordinating other agencies and bodies across the capital. As well as running new transport and economic development bodies, the mayor works closely with (and makes appointments to) the new Metropolitan Police Authority and London Fire and Emergency Planning Authority, and is responsible for setting the overall framework for the development of London, within which borough councils deal with planning and housing strategy. He also has a coordinating role to improve the environment and air quality in London, in other environmental issues such as waste and noise, and encouraging local initiatives. The mayor prepares a series of strategies to deal with various matters: transport, economic development and regeneration, spatial development, biodiversity, municipal waste management, air quality, ambient noise, climate change mitigation, and culture.

The mayor and the Assembly operate clearly within the pattern of English local government and in that respect they perhaps compare unfavourably with their counterparts in major cities elsewhere in the world. Finance, for example, is derived from council tax and central grant: there is no power to raise money by local income tax. Although accountability for policing in the metropolis has been removed from the Home Secretary and a new Metropolitan Police Authority established,[92] the mayor's power is indirect and in keeping with arrangements for police authorities elsewhere in the UK,[93] compared, for example, to the more interventionist powers of a US mayor.

The mayor's most high-profile contribution to date has come in the field of transport.[94] In 2003, London became the first major conurbation in the world to introduce

[91] Greater London Authority Act 2007, ss 1 and 2 and Sched. 1.

[92] Ibid., Pt VI. [93] Police Act 1996, Pt 1. [94] Pimlott and Rao, above, n. 90, ch. 7.

a system of congestion charging on the capital's roads. This is the type of bold policy initiative that perhaps could only be taken forward by a powerful mayor operating at a strategic level. Undoubtedly, also the successful bid for the 2012 Olympics to come to London owed much to collaborative efforts of the mayor and national government.

The Assembly comprises paid, full-time politicians, with a scrutiny and policy remit. The Assembly keeps the mayor's exercise of statutory functions under review[95] and has power to investigate, and prepare reports about, any actions and decisions of the mayor or any of the Authority's staff, and matters in relation to which statutory functions are exercisable by the mayor. It may also investigate matters relating to the principal purposes of the Authority or any other matters which the Assembly considers to be of importance to Greater London. The Assembly may submit proposals to the mayor, to which he is required to make a formal response.[96] It can amend the mayor's overall budget and plans, although it requires a two-thirds majority to do so. It also exercises oversight over the performance of the functional bodies, for transport and economic development, the police and fire authorities. It also has power to consider any other issues that it believes are important to Londoners.

The mayor is accountable to the Assembly through several mechanisms. A written report must be given by the mayor to the Assembly at least three clear working days prior to each of its monthly meetings, dealing with the significant decisions taken, with reasons, and responses to any formal proposals made by the Assembly.[97] The mayor attends the Assembly's meetings to answer questions but is not be obliged to disclose advice received from the staff of the Authority or from functional bodies or their staff.[98] The Assembly has powers to summon such people, but, in the same way, they are not obliged to disclose advice given to the mayor. This is a move towards treating such officers more in the mould of civil servants than has been customary with local government officers (similar restrictions apply to civil service evidence to parliamentary select committees) and follows, perhaps inevitably, from the formal recognition of a distinct political executive. The Assembly meetings, the mayor's reports, the text of questions and answers, and the minutes of the meetings are open or available to the public.[99] The mayor is required to prepare an Annual Report assessing progress on implementing strategies, including the achievement of any targets and giving any information which the Assembly has asked to be included before the beginning relevant year. The report is followed by an annual State of London debate.[100] In addition, a 'People's Question Time' must be held twice yearly.[101] A more radical proposal for accountability – that the Assembly be able to impeach the mayor – was, however, rejected.

95 Greater London Authority Act 2007, s. 59. 96 Ibid., s. 60. 97 Ibid., s. 45.

98 See ibid., ss 61–5 for the attendance of witnesses at Assembly meetings and production of documents to it.

99 Subject to the exceptions for confidential and other exempt material set out in Local Government Act 1972, Pt VA.

100 Greater London Authority Act 2007, s. 47. 101 Ibid., s. 48.

The overall scheme of the Act carries through the objective of creating a strong mayor's office – most power vests in the mayor and there are few formal restraints. Nevertheless, co-operation between the mayor and the Assembly is necessary since the Assembly has strong powers to review the work of the mayor. Its powers to block initiatives or policies are weak: the necessary two-thirds veto by the Assembly is unlikely to be obtainable in practice, especially within an Assembly elected at the same time as the mayor. The mayor, therefore, is clearly in the stronger position.

As we have seen the success of the arrangements in London has stimulated interest in strong leadership models for other cities. It also raises the question of whether regional government exercising strategic powers might be appropriate for other parts of England.

THE RISE AND DECLINE OF REGIONAL GOVERNMENT

Unlike many other countries in England there is no tradition of government (as opposed to administration) at the regional (rather than the local) level. During the Blair government regionalism briefly came into vogue and it seemed for a time that it could develop to challenge the position of local government. This section describes how regional government became a fashionable policy option and its subsequent decline.

The main pressures for the introduction of regional government stemmed from dissatisfaction with central, rather than local, government. The principal arguments were that regional government would allow for a sense of political identity to be recognised even where the central government at Westminster failed to reflect the political mood of the regions. Regional government might therefore counteract a feeling of political disenfranchisement. A further argument related to the lack of regional democratic accountability for central government offices dispersed regionally and regional quangos. Oversight of such bodies featured prominently in the proposals for regional government from the Constitution Unit, for example.[102] However, the subsidiary arguments for regional government related more strongly to issues about local government functions and focused on the need for strategic planning in such areas as land use and transportation and the need for coordination at the regional level of economic development and bids for and implementation of EU funding.

The Regional Development Agencies Act 1998 established agencies for London and eight regions[103] responsible for regional economic development. These were business-led and dominated boards, although the membership also contains local

[102] Constitution Unit, *Regional Government in England* (1996). For earlier proposals, see the minority dissenting memorandum to the report of the Role Commission on the Constitution, suggesting that the House of Lords be amended to include a strong provincial presence, which would give it an indirectly elected character by being drawn from regional assemblies: *Report of the Royal Commission on the Constitution 1969/73*, volume ii: Memorandum of Dissent, Cmnd. 5460-i (1973).

[103] Regional Development Agencies Act 1998, s. 1 and Sched. 1. The regions were the East Midlands, Eastern, North East, North West South, East South West, West Midlands, and Yorkshire and Humberside.

authority members and representatives of other regional interests, such as the education and voluntary sectors. The government intended that one third of members should be drawn from local councillors in the region which the agency serves, to reflect the size of local authorities, the geographical spread, and political balance. The Regional Development Agencies (RDAs) replaced a number of existing quangos and became the lead agencies in coordinating bids for funding for regional EU funding.

To address the democratic deficit in these arrangements this legislation provided for discretionary ministerial designation of Regional Chambers where the Secretary of State was satisfied that a suitable representative body existed.[104] Where a Regional Chamber was designated the RDA was under a duty to consult it. The Labour government recognised eight regional assemblies.[105] These, however, were *indirectly* elected consultative assemblies drawn mainly from members of the local authorities in the region: about two-thirds of members of the regional assemblies are councillors (some also included MPs and Members of the European Parliament). The remaining members were from local business, voluntary, charitable, educational and religious organizations.

In comparison with the directly elected chambers in other parts of the UK, the RDAs and regional assemblies were poor relations, being subject to ministerial powers and patronage and lacking any powers over central government regional offices. The Labour government was prepared to consider *elected* regional government in parts of England which could a demonstrate demand for it[106] – this would have produced an asymmetric form of regionalism in practice.

However, the policy ran aground following the first regional referendum, held in November 2004 in which the electorate in North East England voted, by a majority of more than 3 to 1 of those voting, against an elected assembly. Since the government had anticipated that, if anywhere, demand was strongest in the North East because of proximity to Scotland, distance from London, and a strongly regional identity, effectively the outcome killed the prospects of further regional campaigns. In the aftermath, critics were divided over whether the voters were disinterested because the proposals for an assembly had been too expensive and unnecessary or because it lacked sufficient powers to be worth establishing as an elected body – it lacked law-making powers or the range of executive functions of the National Assembly for Wales, for instance.

Following the referendum outcome in North East England, reflecting voter disinterest in elected regional assemblies, the existing regional chambers were left in the position of appointed and co-opted quangos, with no direct electoral accountability. Prior to the 2010 election the Conservatives argued that regional government was distant and remote ('unelected, unaccountable and unloved') and pledged to dismantle it

[104] Regional Development Agencies Act 1998, s 8(1).

[105] East of England Regional Assembly; East Midlands Regional Assembly, North East Assembly, North West Regional Assembly, South East England Regional Assembly, South West Regional Assembly, West Midlands Regional Assembly and Yorkshire and Humber Assembly.

[106] See the white paper, *Your Region, Your Choice*, Cm. 5551 (May 2002).

and return power to local government. It was claimed that this would bring considerable administrative savings.[107]

A first step – implemented in July 2010 – was the revocation of the policy guidance for regional planning pending the abolition of the regional powers over land use planning (Regional Spatial Strategies).[108] The coalition government also announced its intention to abolish the RDAs and ended funding for the Regional Leaders' Boards (the successors to the regional assemblies). The Government Office for London was closed and the government decided in principle to disband the nine other government regional offices.[109] The 2010 Public Bodies Bill gives power to complete the abolition of RDAs. They will be replaced with Local Enterprise Partnerships – joint business–local authority bodies to promote local economic development. Local Enterprise Partnerships will be business-led and reflect the 'natural' economies of cities and regions rather than mapping the jurisdiction of the regional government offices.[110]

It would seem that the time for the possible emergence of regional government with a democratic base to rival local government has now passed.

CONCLUSION: THE 'BIG SOCIETY' AND LOCAL GOVERNMENT

The self-proclaimed visionary idea of the Cameron government is the 'Big Society'. This is built around the strands of social action, public sector reform, and community empowerment and is to be achieved, *inter alia*, by decentralisation, direct government financial assistance to charities and voluntary groups by-passing public bodies and removing the obstacles currently preventing implementation of local initiatives.[111] The government's view as to the place of local government within the 'Big Society' agenda is ambivalent: it appears to be both part of the solution and part of the problem.

On the one hand the 'Big Society' can be seen as a development and continuation of the thinking of earlier administrations under which local government's task was to enable the delivery of local services (but not necessarily to deliver them itself) and to be a community leader in partnership with other public, private and voluntary bodies in 'place shaping'.[112] Thus, for example, the coalition government's promise to enact a general power of competence can be portrayed as freeing local authorities to be more

[107] *Control Shift*, above, n. 37, p. 6.

[108] The Secretary of State for Communities and Local Government announced the revocation of all existing regional strategies on 6 July 2010, using powers under Local Democracy Economic Development and Construction Act 2009, s. 79(6), available at www.communities.gov.uk/statements/newsroom/regionalstrategies.

[109] Ibid.

[110] Vince Cable and Eric Pickles, 'Economy needs local remedies not regional prescription', *Financial Times*, 6 September 2010.

[111] Rt Hon. David Cameron, 'Big Society Speech', Liverpool, 19 July 2010, available at www.number10.gov.uk/news/speeches-and-transcripts/2010/07/big-society-speech-53572.

[112] Lyons Inquiry, above, n. 12, para. 2.43.

innovative, responsive to local wishes, and removing obstacles to councils working in partnership with non-governmental bodies. On the other hand, a strong theme of the 'Big Society' is the emphasis on the empowerment of local community groups by liberating them from bureaucracy to find more participatory ways of delivery services in response to local needs. The implication of this alternative theme is that public bodies (including elected local authorities) are insufficiently responsive and that alternatives to services run by conventional representative democratic structures need to be found. The coalition government's undertaking to enable local communities to take over local services currently run by councils and threatened with closure, such as libraries and parks, is an illustration.[113]

One prominent example of diversion of control and funding away from local government is in the field of education with the rise of academies and free schools. The Academies Act 2010 extends the availability of academy status (schools funded directly by central government rather than under local education authority control) so that for the first time all local authority schools are able to apply to be designated academies. If approved by the Secretary of State for Education both secondary and primary schools can become academies.[114] They then have increased freedom to control use of their budget, curriculum, school year, and teachers' pay and conditions. The legislation was controversial because it was perceived by critics as an attack on local education authorities. In the event the initial take-up by council maintained schools was small (96 academies opened in September 2010) but this may also reflect the rushed nature of the legislation, which became law in July 2010, less than two months before the start of 2010–11 school year. The coalition government further intends to make it easier to establish new schools with academy status in response to parental demand in its projected 'Free Schools' programme which is to come into operation from September 2011.[115] This will simplify the process by which charities, universities, businesses, educational groups, teachers and groups of parents can obtain permission start new state-funded schools free of local authority control. Whether these moves in education signal a more general trend remains to be seen.

The ambivalence in the coalition government's policies – simultaneously empowering local authorities and by-passing them – encapsulates the dilemma of modern local government. Despite all recent attempts at reform it remains a necessary but imperfectly functioning democratic institution.

FURTHER READING

Arden, A., Manning, J. and Collins, S., *Local Government Constitutional and Administrative Law* (1999).

Bailey, S., *Cross on Principles of Local Government Law* (3rd edn, 2004).

[113] 2011–11 Localism Bill, Pt 4, ch. 3.

[114] www.education.gov.uk/academies.

[115] www.education.gov.uk/freeschools; *The Coalition: our programme for government* (2010) 29–30.

Commission for Local Democracy, *Taking Charge: The Rebirth of Local Democracy* (1995).
Copus, C., *Leading the Localities: Executive Mayors in English Local Governance* (2006).
Copus, C., *Party Politics and Local Government* (2004).
Leigh, I., *Law, Politics and Local Democracy* (2000).
Loughlin, M., *Legality and Locality: the Role of Law in Central-Local Relations* (1996).
Pimlott, B. and Rao, N., *Governing London* (2002).
Pratchett, K. and Wilson, D. (eds), *Local Democracy and Local Government* (1996).
Stewart, J. and Stoker, G. (eds), *Local Government in the 1990s* (1995).

USEFUL WEBSITES

Commission for Local Administration (Local Government Ombudsmen): **www.lgo.org.uk**
Department for Communities and Local Government: **www.communities.gov.uk**
Greater London Authority (the Mayor of London and London Assembly): **www.london.gov.uk**
INLOGOV (The Institute of Local Government Studies, University of Birmingham): **www inlogov.bham.ac.uk**
(Local Government) Improvement and Development Agency: **www.idea.gov.uk**
Local Government Information Unit: **www.lgiu.org.uk**
Local Government Association: **www.lga.gov.uk**
Lyons Inquiry into Local Government: **www.lyonsinquiry.org.uk**

10

ADMINISTRATIVE JUSTICE AND THE RESOLUTION OF DISPUTES

Andrew Le Sueur

SUMMARY

An important aspect of the principle of administrative justice is that citizens can challenge the decisions of public authorities. The concept and practice of administrative justice is undergoing far-reaching reform. Two sets of values - associated with constitutionalism and informality - underpin the reforms. These values express laudable aims, but they also give rise to tensions and contradictions. Where this happens, the values of constitutionalism ought to prevail. Administrative justice should be recognized as a constitutional principle.

INTRODUCTION

> A council has been criticized [by the Local Government Ombudsman] after it cancelled a travel scheme enabling elderly and disabled people access to cheap or free public transport.
>
> Greenpeace is taking the government to court [in a claim for judicial review] to try to stop new UK deep-sea drilling licences being issued until the causes of the BP oil spill in the Gulf of Mexico are fully established.
>
> US rap star Snoop Dogg has won the latest round in a long-running fight [in the Asylum and Immigration Tribunal] with UK border authorities over his right to enter the country.

As these headlines show,[1] in a constitutional democracy, it is important that people can challenge the wrongful decisions, actions and omissions of public authorities.

[1] Taken from reports during 2010 on the BBC News website, http://news.bbc.co.uk.

There are various ways of seeking to get things put right. Most commonly, and away from the gaze of journalists, citizens manage to do this by themselves by simply asking the public authority to think again. In relation to some functions, public authorities have been required or encouraged to set up complaints systems and internal appeal mechanisms to facilitate this.[2] Elected representatives – MPs and councillors – often get involved in disputes through their constituency casework.[3] Some agencies and their sponsor departments have created 'independent' complaints handling agencies to receive and seek to resolve complaints (such as the Independent Case Examiners' Office dealing with child support and the Adjudicator's Office dealing with tax).[4] Beyond these avenues of redress are three types of external mechanism for challenge – courts (especially through claims for judicial review), appeals to the First-tier Tribunal under various Acts of Parliament, and the work of the public sector ombudsmen.[5]

Together, these avenues of challenge form a major part of the administrative justice system (a term that is examined in the next section). In recent years, the administrative justice system has undergone far-reaching reform. This chapter is about the two sets of values – constitutionalism and informality – which have underpinned the reform agenda.

One set of values – implemented for example by the Constitutional Reform Act 2005 and the Tribunals, Courts and Enforcement Act 2007 – seeks to promote the values associated with constitutionalism.[6] The aim here is to put the governance of courts and tribunals on a new statutory footing, with a greater independence from government and more transparency in their organizational structures. Thus, relatively informal ways of working (such as the 'tap on the shoulder' judicial appointments system based on 'secret soundings') have been replaced by more formal, transparent, and accountable institutional structures and processes (for example the Judicial Appointments Commission of England and Wales using a competence-based approach in open competitions and the appointments of ombudsmen being made subject to advisory hearings by House of Commons select committees). The values of constitutionalism include the idea that citizens are holders of legally

[2] See D. Cowan and S. Halliday, *The Appeal of Internal Review: Law, Administrative Justice and the (non-emergence) of disputes* (2003).

[3] As well as helping constituents by writing letters to public authorities, MPs also (controversially) continue to control access to the Parliamentary Ombudsman, who is able to investigate complaints of maladministration by central government bodies only if a case is referred by an MP.

[4] See Table 10.1 below.

[5] In quantitative terms, the tribunal system is by far the most significant arena for citizen–state dispute resolution, handling almost 800,000 cases a year (of which the biggest categories are social security, immigration and asylum, tax and VAT, and mental health). The two main ombudsmen – the Parliamentary and Health Service Ombudsman (dealing with central government bodies and the National Health Service (NHS)) and the Local Government Ombudsman – together receive over 40,000 inquiries relating to alleged injustice caused by maladministration each year. About 9,000 people a year seek permission to bring a judicial review claim in the Administrative Court, though the court ends up giving a full hearing to fewer than 500.

[6] This is not the place to examine the scope and meaning of constitutionalism in detail, see further A. Le Sueur, M. Sunkin and J. Murkens, *Public Law: Text, Cases, and Materials* (2010) ch. 3.

enforceable rights and entitlements. It is part of the constitutional paradigm that disputes – especially between the state and the citizen – should be adjudicated upon by independent and impartial judges (not civil servants); and it follows that access to justice is to be improved by better quality and better funded legal services. There is understood to be a public – not merely a private – interest in calling public authorities to account for their errors and omissions. The citizen's 'day in court' (or a tribunal) is celebrated as an opportunity for open and impartial justice. Many facets of these values are, as discussed below, expressed or implied by European Convention on Human Rights (ECHR), Art. 6.

The other set of values within the reforms seeks to promote informality (resolving disputes other than through formal institutions and processes) and the 'user perspective' in the handling of grievances against public bodies.[7] Internal dispute resolution inside public authorities is seen as a major way of dealing with disputes. Where this fails, the values of informality encourage, perhaps even insist upon, a range of alternative dispute resolution (ADR) techniques,[8] such as mediation, in place of formal adjudication before judges (in the case of courts and tribunals) and formal investigations and reports (in the case of the ombudsmen). These reforms – in and of themselves and in the way they are being introduced – will result in a more informal, less public, and more discretionary dispute resolution system. The values associated with informality and the user perspective reject a one-size-fits-all approach to resolving disputes; flexibility and innovation in dispute resolution are to be encouraged, as these will help ensure that there is greater practical access to justice. Administrative justice is conceived of as a service to be delivered to the public, effectively and efficiently. The figure of an independent judge is not seen as either a necessary or sufficient part of the equation needed to achieve justice; indeed, a day in court (or the tribunal) far from being a matter of pride, is portrayed as a stressful experience that most citizens wish to avoid, or perhaps cannot even cope with.[9] Public accountability – revealing what has gone wrong – is not seen as important an aspect of the dispute resolution process as other mechanisms (such as audits and inspections) are better attuned to that task.

ADMINISTRATIVE JUSTICE

Before looking at the currents and cross-currents of reform, something needs to be said about the concept and practice of administrative justice. This chapter focuses on

[7] On the user perspective as a strategy to enhance legitimacy, see further A. Le Sueur, 'People as "Users" and "Citizens": the Quest for Legitimacy in British Public Administration', in M. Ruffert (ed.), *Legitimacy in European Administrative Law: Reform and Reconstruction* (2011) ch. 3.

[8] ADR techniques are not *necessarily* informal in character (some involve highly structured decision taking); for the purposes of this essay, what is notable about ADR is that it takes place outside formal institutions and procedures governed by constitutional norms.

[9] See Department for Constitutional Affairs, *Transforming Public Services; Complaints, Redress and Tribunals*, Cm. 6243 (July 2004) paras 2.7, 6.20 and 6.23.

one part of administrative justice: the redress of grievances against public authorities. It needs to be acknowledged, however, that administrative justice has a much wider reach, covering internal decision making by public authorities and the need to prevent disputes arising in the first place.[10]

One problem in understanding administrative justice in the sense of redress of grievances has been the lack of any overarching concept, reflected in the haphazard development of a myriad of avenues of complaint and challenge and criteria for assessing the wrongfulness of administrative action. Writing in 1994, Martin Partington lamented that despite all the changes from the 1960s onwards – with the creation of public sector ombudsmen, the expansion of the tribunal system, and the development of judicial review – 'there has been no official inquiry or review into the structure of administrative justice as a whole to see how the various constituent parts are or are not hanging together'.[11]

A major contributory factor to this fragmented approach is that no one single official organization has overall leadership responsibility for the administrative justice 'system' (if it can be called that). Within central government, the Ministry of Justice (the successor to the former Department for Constitutional Affairs),[12] the Cabinet Office,[13] and the Department for Communities and Local Government[14] all have general responsibilities for aspects of administrative justice. Other departments have responsibility for the development of the grievance redress mechanisms that relate to their areas of administration. At arm's length from government, the Law Commission for England and Wales[15] and the Administrative Justice and Tribunals Council (AJTC)[16] have both contributed to the reform agenda. The National Audit Office (the body responsible for ensuring value for money across central government) has in recent years taken particular interest in grievance resolution and how systems might

[10] DCA, ibid., para. 1.6 (administrative justice 'embraces not just courts and tribunals but the millions of decisions taken by thousands of civil servants and other officials').

[11] 'Rethinking the structure of administrative justice in Britain', in O. Mendelsohn and L. Maher (eds), *Courts, Tribunals and New Approaches to Justice* (1994) ch. 5, 109. Non-official inquiries include the JUSTICE/All Souls Review published as *Administrative Justice: Some Necessary Reforms* (1988), witheringly criticized by C. Harlow, 'The JUSTICE/All Souls Review: Don Quixote to the Rescue?' (1990) 10 *Oxford Journal of Legal Studies* 85; the University of Bristol conference on administrative justice held in 1997, papers from which were published in M. Partington and M. Harris (eds), *Administrative Justice in the 21st Century* (1999); and M. Adler (ed.), *Administrative Justice in Context* (2010).

[12] The 'proportionate dispute resolution' agenda, discussed below, emerged from the DCA in 2004.

[13] Responsible in the past e.g. for the Citizen's Charter initiative and reform of ombudsmen.

[14] See e.g. the CLG 'empowerment' white paper *Communities in control: real people, real power*, Cm. 7427 (2008), which led to an independent review: *Getting it right, and righting the wrongs*, which led to the development of a 'practitioners' toolkit, available at www.communities.gov.uk/publications/communities/gettingitrighttoolkit.

[15] The Law Commission has worked on three inter-connected administrative justice projects in recent years: dispute resolution in housing; financial compensation for administrative wrongs; and (currently) reform of the public sector ombudsmen.

[16] In October 2010, the coalition government announced the proposed abolition of the AJTC as part of the 'bonfire of the quangos' to reduce public expenditure. The AJTC's most recent work has been to develop a set of principles, see *Principles for Administrative Justice: The AJTC's Approach* (March 2010).

be made more efficient.[17] The Legal Services Commission, responsible for ensuring access to justice and the public funding of litigation, also has an interest in the future shape of administrative justice.[18] The Local Government Ombudsman and, under the leadership of Ann Abrahams, the Parliamentary and Health Service Ombudsman have sought to influence strategic thinking and practice through a series of publications and initiatives. In addition, parliamentary select committees have investigated aspects of the administrative justice system.[19] The picture that emerges is of much activity and some collaborative working between some organizations. There is, however, an absence of the sort of political leadership that would be required to introduce coherent changes to the administrative justice system.

PROPORTIONATE DISPUTE RESOLUTION

In 2004, the Department for Constitutional Affairs (DCA) published a white paper, *Transforming Public Services; Complaints, Redress and Tribunals*.[20] This fell short of providing a comprehensive vision of administrative justice (little is said about judicial review or the constitutional context, for example) but it did go a long way towards explaining the then Labour government's diagnosis and prescription for a better system. The white paper coined the phrase 'proportionate dispute resolution' (PDR) to explain the idea that has guided reforms:[21]

> Our strategy turns on its head the Department's traditional emphasis first on courts, judges and court procedure, and second on legal aid to pay mainly for litigation lawyers. It starts instead with the real world problems people face. The aim is to develop a range of policies and services that, so far as possible, will help people to avoid problems and legal disputes in the first place; and where they cannot, provides tailored solutions to resolve the dispute as quickly and cost effectively as possible. It can be summed up as 'Proportionate Dispute Resolution'.[22]

[17] See e.g. the following reports by the Comptroller and Auditor General, *Citizen Redress: What citizens can do if things go wrong with public services*, HC 21 (2004–05); *Department for Work and Pensions: Handling Customer Complaints*, HC 995 (2007–08); *Feeding back? Learning from complaints in health and social care*, HC 853 (2007–08).

[18] See e.g. Legal Services Commission consultation paper *A New Focus for Civil Legal Aid* (2004), which dealt with ADR and judicial review.

[19] See e.g. Public Administration Select Committee, Fifth Report of Session 2007–08, *When Citizens Complain*, HC 409; Sixth Report of Session 2007–08, *User Involvement in Public Services*, HC 410; Session 2007–08, *Public Services: Putting People First*, HC 408.

[20] See DCA, above, n. 9.

[21] A 'ghastly slogan', as one minister acknowledged: Lord Filkin, 'New Routes to Justice', 14th Annual Denning Lecture, 9 June 2004; he explained that 'By PDR we really mean... you don't want to have a highly costly adversarial system dealing with issues that could be dealt with more quickly, simply and cheaply by means that are good enough for the disputees'.

[22] See DCA, above, n. 9, para. 2.2; see also DCA Strategy 2004–09, *Delivering Justice, Rights and Democracy* (2005) 55–61.

In practical terms, the broad strategy of PDR consists of a series of more specific reform initiatives.[23] These include:

(1) a commitment across central government to make the framework of law defining people's rights and responsibilities as 'fair, simple and clear as possible';

(2) to give people better information about their rights and responsibilities and where they can go for help when problems arise;

(3) to 'ensure that people have ready access to early and appropriate advice and assistance when they need it, so that problems can be solved and potential disputes nipped in the bud long before they escalate into formal legal proceedings';

(4) to 'promote the development of tailored dispute resolution services, so that different types of dispute can be resolved fairly quickly, efficiently and effectively without recourse to the expense and formality of courts and tribunals where this is not necessary';

(5) 'to deliver cost-effective court and tribunal services, that are better targeted on those cases where the hearing is the best option for resolving the dispute or enforcing the outcome'.

We will return to aspects of the reforms later.

The cross-party attraction to PDR can be explained in several different ways. One explanation is that it represents the triumph of the alternative dispute resolution (ADR) movement, a way of thinking about dispute resolution whose advocates have been hugely successful in bringing its philosophy and practices into mainstream policy making about court and tribunal reform in recent years.[24] The trend away from adjudication is apparent not only in the UK but in other countries;[25] and even international courts have seen the attractions of PDR as a way of controlling case-loads.[26] A different explanation may be that PDR fits into the practical priority of the government for citizen-centred service delivery: making access to dispute resolution services easier could be seen as part of this. Another explanation may be that governments are motivated by concerns about escalating public expenditure in this area, especially on legal aid. It should not be assumed, however, that redressing grievances outside courts and tribunal hearings will *necessarily* be cheaper.[27]

[23] See DCA, above, n. 9, para. 2.3.

[24] See S. Roberts and M. Palmer, *Dispute Processes: ADR and the Primary Forms of Decision-Making* (2nd edn, 2005).

[25] See S. Boyron, 'The Rise of Mediation in Administrative law Disputes: Experiences from England, France and Germany' [2006] *Public Law* 320.

[26] See Lord Woolf et al., *Review of the Working Methods of the European Court of Human Rights* (2005), available at www.echr.coe.int.

[27] For analysis of mediation in one context, see V. Bondy and L. Mulcahy, *Mediation and Judicial Review: an empirical research study* (2009) 86: 'There was little, if any, evidence to support the claims that mediation is quicker or cheaper than judicial review'.

CATEGORIES OF WRONGFULNESS

If, in a practical and straightforward way, administrative justice involves putting things right when a public authority goes wrong, we need to know what 'wrongful' means in this context. As the avenues of challenge to official decisions have expanded beyond the courts (ombudsmen from the 1960s onwards and an expansion in the number of tribunals matching the expansion of the welfare state from the 1940s), three broad categories of wrongfulness have come to be recognized.

The first is unlawfulness. Public officials must properly understand the scope of their legal powers, use fair procedures, avoid irrational or disproportionate use of powers and (since 1973) act in conformity with EC law and (since October 2000) the rights set out in the Human Rights Act 1998. In England and Wales it is typically the Administrative Court which is responsible for adjudicating on these alleged failures through claims for judicial review. Appeals to tribunals may also involve arguments about lawfulness.

The second is maladministration leading to injustice. This is typically investigated by the various public sector ombudsmen – which now include in relation to England and Wales: the Parliamentary Commissioner for Administration (more often referred to as 'The Parliamentary Ombudsman', dealing with complaints against central government departments and bodies); the Health Services Commissioner for England ('The Health Service Ombudsman', for complaints about the NHS); the Commission for Local Administration in England ('The Local Ombudsman', dealing with local authorities); Public Services Ombudsman for Wales; and, offering similar grievance-handling services, the Housing Ombudsman Service; the Independent Police Complaints Commission; Independent Review Service for the Social Fund; the Information Commissioner; Office of the Independent Adjudicator for Higher Education; and some of the work of the Office of Communications (Ofcom).[28]

Maladministration has not been given a statutory definition. Speaking when the Parliamentary Ombudsman was established in 1967, Richard Crossman MP, the minister responsible for the legislation, famously set out what has come to be known as the 'Crossman catalogue' of examples of maladministration: 'bias, neglect, inattention, delay, incompetence, ineptitude, perversity, turpitude, arbitrariness and so on' – 'a long and interesting list'.[29] In 1993, the then Parliamentary Ombudsman (Sir William Reid, a former senior civil servant) expanded the list:

> rudeness (though that is a matter of degree); unwillingness to treat the complainant as a person with rights; refusal to answer reasonable questions; neglecting to inform a complainant on request of his or her rights or entitlement; knowingly giving advice which is misleading or inadequate; ignoring valid advice or overruling considerations which would produce an

[28] Several ombudsman-type systems have been set up by statute to deal with complaints private sector enterprises (e.g. the Financial Services Ombudsman, the Office of the Immigration Services Commission, and the Pensions Ombudsman) and business sectors have also set up similar systems themselves (e.g. Telecommunications Ombudsman (Otelo) and the Press Complaints Commission).

[29] *Hansard*, HC, vol. 734, col. 51 (18 October 1966).

uncomfortable result for the overruler; offering no redress or manifestly disproportionate redress; showing bias whether because of colour, sex, or any other grounds; omission to notify those who thereby lose a right of appeal; refusal to inform adequately of the right of appeal; faulty procedures; failure by management to monitor compliance with adequate procedures; cavalier disregard of guidance which is intended to be followed in the interest of equitable treatment of those who use a service; partiality; and failure to mitigate the effects of rigid adherence to the letter of the law where that produces manifestly inequitable treatment.[30]

The third category of wrongfulness is that the original decision maker has gone wrong on the merits of the matter. Merits review is a process by which a person other than the original decision maker, reconsiders the facts, law or policy aspects of the initial decision, and determines what the correct or preferable decision ought to be. The process of review is often described as 'stepping into the shoes of the primary decision maker'. Merits review is typically the province of internal appeals or complaints systems (where a different, probably more senior official has a second look at a decision at the request of the citizen affected)[31] and of some tribunals appeals.

These three categories are increasingly beginning to overlap. For example, some of the grounds of judicial review – which are to do with lawfulness – are strikingly similar in scope to some aspects of maladministration, due to the expansion of judicial review. As Henry LJ put it:

What may not have been recognized back in 1974 [when the Local Government Ombudsman was set up] was the emergence of judicial review to the point where most if not almost all matters which could form the basis for a complaint of maladministration are matters for which the elastic qualities of judicial review might provide a remedy.[32]

An aggrieved person may therefore be faced with two options – judicial review and ombudsmen investigation. An illustration of this is the campaign against the way in which the Ministry of Defence set up a compensation scheme for civilians interned in the Far East during the Second World War. Eligibility criteria depended on the closeness of a British detainee's links with the UK (which had the effect of excluding British people who had been born and brought up in places such as India and Hong Kong). The Parliamentary Ombudsman issued a damning report on the scheme, finding that maladministration had caused injustice, less than a week after the High Court upheld the lawfulness of the scheme.[33] The boundaries between the ombudsman and court

[30] *1993 Annual Report of the Parliamentary Commissioner for Administration, Sir William Reid* (1993).

[31] See Cowan and Halliday, above, n. 2.

[32] *R* v. *Local Commissioner for Local Government for North and North East England ex parte Liverpool City Council* [2001] 1 All ER 462.

[33] See Parliamentary Commissioner, *A Debt of Honour: The ex gratia scheme for British groups interned by the Japanese during the Second World War*, HC 324 (2004–05); *R. (Association of British Civilian Internees: Far East Region)* v. *Secretary of State for Defence* [2002] EWCA Civ 473, [2003] QB 1397 (holding that the Secretary of State's decision to include birth in the UK as a factor was not as a matter of law irrational).

system are under conceptual strain, even if in practice both institutions seek to avoid taking jurisdictional points.[34]

There are other signs of the categories of wrongfulness overlapping. In the past it was anathema for the Administrative Court in hearing a judicial review claim to carry out 'merits review' and to seek to stand in the shoes of the original decision maker and form its own view of the underlying facts and the proper outcome.[35] The Human Rights Act 1998 and the developing case law of the European Court of Human Rights are requiring national courts to increase the intensity of review. What that means varies between different Convention rights. In relation to ECHR, Art. 5 (deprivation of liberty) judicial controls must, in the context of restrictions placed on people under the mental health legislation, be 'sufficiently intrusive to constitute an adequate examination of the *merits* of the relevant medical decisions'.[36] In relation to Art. 2 (right to life), the Court of Appeal has speculated that the best approach may be:

> for the court *to make its own judgment* as to whether there would be an interference with the right to life under Article 2, rather than making a judgment as to the reasonableness of the decision made by the Prison Service

albeit that:

> even were it to be the case that it is for the court to make that *primary judgement*, the reality is that the court would have to attach considerable weight to the assessment of risk made by those with professional involvement in the areas with which the case was concerned.[37]

It is not only the courts which are said to be straying into merits review: this accusation has also been levelled against the ombudsmen.[38]

Though in many respects far-reaching, the reforms discussed in this chapter do little to clarify these category confusions and uncertainties.

[34] The Parliamentary Ombudsman is barred from investigating 'any action in respect of which the person aggrieved has or had a remedy by way of proceedings in any court of law' subject to the proviso 'that the Commissioner may conduct an investigation notwithstanding that the person aggrieved has or had such a right or remedy if satisfied that in the particular circumstances it is not reasonable to expect him to resort or have resorted to it' (Parliamentary Commissioner Act 1967 s. 5(2)). Similar provisions apply to the Local Government Ombudsman.

[35] See e.g. *R.* v. *Somerset County Council ex parte Fewings* [1995] 1 All ER 515 (Laws J): '...the judicial review court is not concerned with the merits of the decision under review. The court does not ask itself the question, "Is this decision right or wrong?". Far less does the judge ask himself whether he would himself have arrived at the decision in question...The only question for the judge is whether the decision taken by the body under review was one which it was legally permitted to take in the way that it did'.

[36] *HL* v. *United Kingdom* (2005) 40 EHRR 32.

[37] *R. (on the application of Bloggs 61)* v. *Secretary of State for the Home Department* [2003] EWCA Civ 686, [2003] 1 WLR 2724 at [81]–[82] (Keene LJ).

[38] For an early example, see K. C. Wheare, *Maladministration and its Remedies* (1973) 153.

CONSTITUTIONALISM

Having introduced some aspects of administrative justice, we can now move on to look at the first trend within the reform strategy – the promotion of constitutionalism. This has a wide reach, extending beyond citizen and public authority disputes. The reforms to the judicial system brought about by the Constitutional Reform Act 2005 embrace all courts, not only those dealing with administrative adjudication. Tribunals, Courts and Enforcement Act 2007, Pt 1 affects tribunals (such as employment tribunals and the Lands Tribunal) that deal with citizen-citizen disputes as well as those concerned with grievances against public authorities. At a general level we can say that the aim of this revitalization of the judicial system and tribunals is to promote greater openness and transparency and to emphasize independence from government. These goals have an especial importance when a public authority is one of the parties.

THE CONSTITUTIONAL REFORM ACT 2005

In the summer of 2003, in a U-turn of policy, the Labour government embarked on a major programme of judiciary-related constitutional reform. A previous edition of this book considered the evidence for various explanations of the reasons for this change of view – pragmatic factors to do with changing roles of judges, external pressure from the Council of Europe, constitutional principles, and the specific personalities and events of that time.[39] Whatever may have been the immediate impulse for the timing of change, the reforms have now taken hold and have created a new set of constitutional relationships:

- The office of Lord Chancellor has been redefined. He is no longer head of the judiciary and does not sit as a judge (or as Speaker of the House of Lords). But although the Lord Chancellor is now a more 'mainstream' minister, he retains important constitutional responsibilities to defend the independence of the judiciary. He continues to have a role in judicial appointments (though less influence than before) and judicial discipline. Since 2003, the office of Lord Chancellor has been combined with that of Secretary of State for Constitutional Affairs (Secretary of State for Justice after May 2007).
- The Lord Chief Justice of England and Wales has become Head of the Judiciary in that jurisdiction.[40] The enlarged areas of responsibility attached to the role of the Lord Chief Justice have been accompanied by provision of new administrative support, including a Judicial Communications Office.
- The system for appointing judges in England and Wales has been reformed with the creation of a new Judicial Appointments Commission, the role of which is to

[39] A. Le Sueur, 'Judicial Power in the Changing Constitution', in J. Jowell and D. Oliver (eds), *The Changing Constitution* (5th edn, 2004) ch. 13.

[40] Constitutional Reform Act 2005, s. 7.

run selection exercises and make recommendations to the Lord Chancellor.[41] The Lord Chancellor has limited power to reject recommendations or to require the selection panel to reconsider the selection.

- In October 2009, the country's top-level court ceased to be the Appellate Committee of the House of Lords sitting in the Palace of Westminster (and, for devolution issues, the Judicial Committee of the Privy Council) when the new UK Supreme Court began to operate.
- The relationship between the judges and Parliament has changed. Those members of the senior judiciary who hold peerages (the Lords of Appeal in Ordinary, retired law lords, and some other senior figures such as the current Lord Chief Justice of England and Wales) have lost their right to take part in the scrutiny and legislative work of the House of Lords.[42] The Lord Chief Justice of England and Wales, the Lord Chief Justice of Northern Ireland and, in relation to the Scottish legal system, the Lord President of the Court of Session now have a right to make written representations to Parliament on matters that appear to them 'to be matters of importance relating to the judiciary, or otherwise to the administration of just-ice, in that part of the United Kingdom'.[43]

In these various ways, a new constitutional settlement has been established between the judiciary, Parliament, and government.[44]

TRIBUNALS, COURTS AND ENFORCEMENT ACT 2007

A second area in which the processes of constitutionalism can be seen is in reform of tribunals. Introducing the Tribunals, Courts and Enforcement Bill to the House of Lords in November 2006, the Lord Chancellor was clear about the aim:

> First and foremost, Chapter 1 of Part 1 puts it beyond doubt that the tribunal judiciary are independent from the Executive, and that the tribunals themselves are independent of the departments which make the decisions under review. It is right that this has happened and it strengthens our commitment to increasing public confidence in tribunals. It is a vital part of the Bill.[45]

Over the years, Acts of Parliament have attached tribunals to many administrative schemes run by central government, their agencies and local authorities. The main reasons for establishing tribunals have been to provide a less costly, more expert and informal alternative to the courts. Prior to the 2007 Act, there were more than 70 separate tribunals hearing appeals against decisions of these various public authorities. The largest 10 dealt with a total of over 133,000 cases a year. The Appeal Service

[41] Ibid., Pt 4.

[42] Ibid., s. 135.

[43] Ibid., s. 5.

[44] See House of Lords Constitution Committee, 6th Report of 2006–07, *Relations between the executive, the judiciary and Parliament*, HL 151.

[45] Lord Falconer, *Hansard*, HL, col. 761 (29 November 2006).

was by far the largest tribunal, hearing appeals in relation to welfare benefits. Other major tribunals dealt with mental health issues, immigration and asylum, income tax and value added tax, schools, and criminal injuries compensation.

Tribunals, Courts and Enforcement Act 2007, Pt 1 'creates a new, simplified statutory framework for tribunals which provides coherence and will enable future reform'.[46] The background to the Act was a review carried out by Sir Andrew Leggatt, a retired judge, into the tribunal system in England and Wales.[47] In a far-reaching report he lamented that the quality of the 70 or so tribunals (the case load of which varied from nil to hundreds of thousands) 'varies from excellent to adequate'.[48] There was a lack of coherence, with no unified administrative support for the various tribunals and widely differing procedural rules.

The report provided a blueprint for a new institutional structure. The DCA's white paper *Transforming Public Services* accepted the gist of the Leggatt recommendations, though not all aspects of the detail and in one important respect – the focus on ADR – it went much further.

The 2007 Act created two overarching or 'generic' tribunals, the First-tier Tribunal and the Upper Tribunal (the main role of which is to hear appeals from the First-tier), into which various existing tribunal jurisdictions are transferred. The First-tier and Upper Tribunals may be arranged into 'chambers' according to subject matter or geographical area, or both.[49] When a right of appeal to a tribunal is created by an Act of Parliament, it is no longer necessary to spell out the detail of the composition and procedure of that tribunal – jurisdiction will be conferred on the First-tier and Upper Tribunals. As before, panels hearing cases often consist of both legally qualified members (now called judges) and non-legally qualified members able to provide expertise (for instance people with a background in healthcare in cases dealing with disability benefits or mental health).

Administrative support to tribunals is provided by Her Majesty's Court and Tribunal Service, an executive agency of the Ministry of Justice. Initially, judicial leadership for the new tribunal system came in the form of a new office, that of the Senior President of Tribunals (the holder of which is Sir Robert Carnwath, a Lord Justice of Appeal); in September 2010 the government announced plans for the Lord Chief Justice of England and Wales (and his counterparts in Scotland and Northern Ireland) to take over this role to provide unified leadership of the judiciary in the courts and tribunals.

[46] Explanatory Notes to the Tribunals, Courts and Enforcement Bill, para. 5.

[47] Report of the Review of Tribunals by Sir Andrew Leggatt: *Tribunals for Users – One System, One Service* (2001), available at www.tribunals-review.org.uk. For discussion, see A. Bradley, 'The tribunals maze' [2002] *Public Law* 200, and R. Carnwath, 'Tribunal Justice – a New Start' [2009] *Public Law* 48.

[48] Report of the Review of Tribunals, ibid., p. 5.

[49] As of May 2011, the First-tier Tribunal was organised into six chambers: Social Entitlement; Health, Education and Social Care; War Pensions and Armed Forces Compensation; the General Regulatory Chamber; Immigration and Asylum; and Tax. The Upper Tribunal consisted of four chambers: Administrative Appeals; Tax and Chancery; Lands; and Immigration and Asylum.

The 2007 Act provides for a clearer and more flexible system for challenges to the lawfulness of tribunal decisions, allowing transfer of cases between the Administrative Court (to which a dissatisfied party may claim judicial review)[50] and the Upper Tribunal. The Upper Tribunal is given powers of 'judicial review' (the quotation marks are in the Act), enabling it to make all the remedial orders and apply the grounds of review previously confined to the Administrative Court on claims for judicial review.

The Upper Tribunal is a superior court of record, giving it a status similar to that of the High Court. A uniform right of appeal from the Upper Tribunal (subject to permission being granted) to the Court of Appeal in England and Wales is created, replacing the perplexing array of appeal routes that existed previously.

As well as seeking to create a clearer system, the Act seeks also to promote separation of powers between tribunals and government. The statutory guarantee of judicial independence, created by the Constitutional Reform Act 2005 in relation to the courts, is extended to tribunals. The function of making procedural rules for tribunals is transferred from the Lord Chancellor and other ministers to a new Tribunal Procedure Committee. A new public body, the Administrative Justice and Tribunals Council, was given the role of keeping the new tribunals and the whole administrative justice system under review.[51] The Senior President of Tribunals is required to publish his policy on the deployment of judges and members to the various chambers 'to ensure openness and transparency' and to seek the concurrence of the Lord Chancellor 'to ensure appropriate executive accountability to Parliament'.[52]

INFORMALITY

At the same time as pursing policies designed to promote values associated with constitutionalism through the creation of a more formal and transparent constitutional status for courts and tribunals, successive governments have been following a policy of informality in dispute resolution. This emphasis on informality can be seen in three main areas.

NIPPING DISPUTES IN THE BUD

First, the proportionate dispute resolution strategy announced by the DCA in 2004 seeks to encourage the resolution of disputes and complaints at an early a stage by the public authority against which the grievance has arisen. This can happen in several ways. At its most informal, this involves situations where the aggrieved citizen simply

[50] Or the Court of Session in Scotland.

[51] Replacing the Council on Tribunals. In 2010 the government announced proposals to abolish the AJTC (see above).

[52] Explanatory Notes to the Bill, above, n. 46. At the time of writing, the government is proposing to transfer all the functions of the Senior President of Tribunals to the Lord Chief Justice of England and Wales and heads of the judiciary in Scotland and Northern Ireland.

asks for a decision to be looked at again. In other circumstances, the internal processes for handling complaints are regulated by policies or legal frameworks. Examples of the latter are disputes about decision making to do with homeless persons. Housing Act 1996, Pt VII was an attempt to steer challenges in this context away from judicial review claims; the Act creates a right to request a review of the decision by an appropriately senior person in the authority (and, if the complainant is still dissatisfied, there is an appeal on a point of law to the county courts). The rationale for diverting homeless people's complaints away from judicial review was that they often turned on factual and judgement disputes (for example, whether the accommodation offered was suitable) rather than issues of law, and such disputes were best dealt with locally by the authority itself if possible, or failing that an ordinary court in easy reach of the claimant and local authority:

'Nipping disputes in the bud long before they escalate into formal legal proceedings'[53] has a commonsense attraction that is hard to resist. Clearly it is sensible to put things right as soon as possible and no one would suggest that lawyers or other third parties need to be involved in all cases. But while internal dispute resolution has many advantages it needs also to be acknowledged that – from the constitutional point of view – it does little to promote the rule of law or legal values.[54] Empirical evidence suggests that officials involved in dealing with internal complaints can have a very low opinion of lawyers – in one context, even expressing the cynical view that local solicitors got involved in homeless persons cases only when conveyancing work was slow and that lawyers lacked expertise of the law and system.[55] Commentators (writing in 1998) formed the view that 'we must come to the depressing conclusion that such systems have become a cheap way of denying justice'.[56]

When challenges to the lawfulness of attempts at internal dispute resolution have been brought to the courts, they have been wary of over-judicializing the process. The Court of Appeal has held that there is no apparent bias where a reviewing officer in a homeless persons unit looks at successive requests for review by the same person, a situation that arises in over 10 per cent of cases in some local authorities.[57] The House of Lords considered whether, in order to comply with the requirements of ECHR, Art. 6 (giving people a right to an independent and impartial tribunal whenever a 'civil right or obligation' is determined), a local authority deciding homelessness cases should have some mechanism for obtaining independent findings of fact (for example

[53] DCA, above, n. 9, para. 2.3.

[54] For a valuable analysis of the different 'normative modes' of administrative justice see M. Adler, 'A Socio-Legal Approach to Administrative Justice' (2003) 25 *Law & Policy* 323. On the rule of law as institutional morality, see Chapter 1 above.

[55] See D. Cowan and J. Fionda, 'Homelessness Internal Appeals Mechanisms: Serving the Administrative Process – Part One' (1998) 27 *Anglo-American Law Review* 66, 77. See also S. Halliday, 'Internal Review and Administrative Justice: some evidence and research questions from homelessness decision-making' (2001) 23 *Journal of Social Welfare and Family Law* 473, and J. Gulland, 'Independence in complaints procedures: lessons from community care' (2009) 31 *Journal of Social Welfare and Family Law* 59.

[56] Cowan and Fionda, above, n. 55, 185.

[57] *Feld* v. *Barnet LBC* [2004] EWCA Civ 1307, [2005] HLR 9.

contracting out that function to a third party), and held – contrary to the Court of Appeal – that no such requirement should be imposed;[58] and in a subsequent case the UK Supreme Court held that local authority decision making about entitlement to social housing was not a 'civil right' and so Art. 6 did not apply at all.[59] So while the actual decisions reached in internal review processes are subject to judicial control by judicial review claims (or in the case of homelessness decisions, by appeals to the county court), the law is slow to intervene to insist on legal controls of the processes beyond those spelt out in any legislative framework governing them.

THE TWILIGHT ZONE: NON-STATUTORY COMPLAINTS HANDLERS

A second manifestation of the values of informality is the range of non-statutory 'independent' grievance-handling bodies that have been established by public authorities to handle complaints at arm's length (see Table 10.1 below). The focus of these bodies is on maladministration, though as we have seen the boundaries between maladministration and issues of lawfulness are often hazy. For example a failure to follow published guidelines may be both bad administration and legally flawed as failing to give effect to a legitimate expectation.

While the values of informality promote the innovation of these bodies, and the ease of access to them for complainants, the values of constitutionalism prompt some probing questions. Although these bodies are keen to label themselves 'independent', that independence is of a different character from that enjoyed by judges in courts and tribunals (now protected by Constitutional Reform Act 2005, s. 3). The people making recommendations in these bodies have no security of tenure comparable to that of judges; their relationship with the public body whose decisions they examine is governed by contract. Their non-statutory nature means that Parliament has had no opportunity to check, debate and approve of their status and methods of operation. Scrutiny of their work by Parliament is rather haphazard and confined mainly to written answers by ministers to MPs' questions.

THE RISE AND RISE OF ADR

A third way in which we can see informality is in the seemingly inexorable rise of interest in the use of ADR associated with claims for judicial review, appeals to tribunals and ombudsmen. ADR includes resolution techniques such as:[60] arbitration; conciliation; early neutral evaluation; mediation; and negotiation. Interest in ADR is neither new nor confined to the administrative justice. The ADR movement has its origins in the 1960s and 1970s with the rejection of adversarialism and a loss of confidence in the

[58] *Runa Begum* v. *Tower Hamlets LBC* [2003] UKHL 5, [2003] 2 AC 430 at [40] (Lord Hoffmann), disapproving of *Adan* v. *Newham LBC* [2001] EWCA Civ 1916, [2002] 1 WLR 2120.

[59] *Birmingham City Council v Ali* [2010] UKSC 8, [2010] 2 WLR 471.

[60] DCA, above, n. 9, para. 2.11.

Table 10.1 Examples of Non-statutory Complaints Handlers

Body	Date set up	Departments, agencies, etc. from whom complaints arise	Case load in 2009–10 (or previous year if not available)	Head
Adjudicator's Office	1993	HM Revenue & Customs; Valuation Office Agency; Insolvency Service	1,837	Judy Clements since 2008; previously Dame Barbara Mills QC
Independent Case Examiners	1997	Child Support Agency (part of the Child Maintenance and Enforcement Commission); Debt Management; Pension, Disability and Carers Service; Financial Assistance Scheme; Jobcentre Plus; Child Maintenance and Enforcement Division (Northern Ireland); Northern Ireland Social Security Agency; Independent Living Fund	Child Maintenance: 610 resolved; 347 investigated Department for Work and Pensions: 130 resolved; 187 investigated	John Hanlon; previously Jodi Berg
Independent Complaints Adjudication Service for Ofsted	1998	Ofsted (Office for Standards in Education, Children's Services and Skills)	An annual report is not routinely published. It is thought that between 20 and 25 cases a year are received	The service has since 2009 been run by CEDR, the Centre for Effective Dispute Resolution; previously Elizabeth Derrington
Independent Complaints Reviewer	1998	Land Registry; Audit Commission; Charity Commission; Homes and Communities Agency; National Archives; Northern Ireland Youth Justice Agency; Children's Commissioner for Wales; Tenants' Services Authority	Land Registry, 64 Audit Commission, 1 Charity Commission: 20 (7 accepted for investigation)	Jodi Berg and Elizabeth Derrington

professionalism of lawyers. More recently, ADR has come into the mainstream. What may originally have been a desire to see the transformation of human relationships through new methods of dealing with disputes has become closely tied into the work of courts. In England and Wales ADR plays a growing role in ordinary civil litigation since the adoption of the Civil Procedure Rules (CPR) in 1999. The CPR reformed the procedural rules covering the conduct of litigation, increasing the role of judges as case managers and encouraging parties to settle cases at the earliest opportunity rather than at the door of the court.

What was new was the emphasis placed on ADR in the context of administrative justice. There remain doubts as to the applicability of ADR to public law matters. Government seems to have changed its mind about the extent to which ADR may be used in public law. The Ministry of Justice in its report, *The Annual Pledge Report 2008/09: Monitoring the Effectiveness of the Government's Commitment to using Alternative Dispute Resolution*, conceded that 'There may be cases that are not suitable for settlement through ADR, for example cases involving... abuse of power, public law, human rights'.[61] Today none of those categories is ruled out as intrinsically unsuited to ADR. To date, academic analysis of the scope for ADR in public law cases has been mixed – ranging from scepticism, through cautious welcome, to generally positive responses.[62] The white paper emphasized the fact that there are known unknowns in the context of tribunals: the use of ADR 'may mean a significant reduction in the number of cases which require a full judicial determination or they may turn out to be just another step in the process, adding cost and slowing things down'.[63]

ADR AND TRIBUNALS

The white paper *Transforming Public Services* made clear the government's policy for a transformation in how tribunals operate away from adjudication to refocus on an array of dispute resolution techniques:

> The organisation [the new tribunal system] will inherit existing jurisdictions and procedural rules but its overarching mission will be dispute resolution and we expect it, in conjunction with departments, users and representatives, to develop new ways of operating. We believe this to be possible even where the issue is one of entitlement rather than compensation. In many cases appellants succeed before tribunals because they bring new evidence, possibly as a result of advice, or because they are more articulate orally than on paper and the tribunal is the first opportunity they have had to explain their case. In other cases the tribunal

[61] See www.justice.gov.uk/about/docs/alternative-dispute-resolution-08-09.pdf.

[62] See: M. Adler,'Tribunal Reform: Proportionate Dispute Resolution and the Pursuit of Administrative Justice' (2006) 69 *Modern Law Review* 958; G. Richardson and H. Genn, 'Tribunals in Transition: Resolution or Adjudication?' [2007] *Public Law* 116; M. Supperstone, D. Stilitz and C. Sheldon, 'ADR and Public Law' [2006] *Public Law* 299, 319; V. Bondy and L. Mulcahy, *Mediation and Judicial Review: an empirical research study* (2009); and V. Bondy and M. Sunkin, *The Dynamics of Judicial Review Litigation: the resolution of public law challenges before final hearing* (2009).

[63] See DCA, above, n. 9, para. 6.22.

> accepts evidence which the original decision maker was not prepared to accept. These are benefits that flow from having a tribunal hearing but it is possible to imagine ways in which the same benefit could be achieved without the stress and formality of a hearing. And where it is clear to the tribunal that there is likely to be a particular outcome to a case it must be helpful to everyone if reconsideration can be prompted before a hearing takes place.[64]

The white paper suggested that civil servants or government lawyers employed by the Tribunal Service, not necessarily judges, will have key roles:

> Staff working on behalf of and with delegated powers from the judiciary could well have an important role to play in such a process. This will mean new skills for staff, different working arrangements for judiciary and staff and new powers for both.[65]

OMBUDSMEN AND ADR

The appetite for ADR is not confined to the new tribunal system. It is seen as having a role in relation to the work of the ombudsmen (whose role is to investigate maladministration leading to injustice rather than lawfulness). The relationship between the public sector ombudsmen and ADR is a curious one. On the one hand they are sometimes presented *as a form of ADR*. The white paper lists them as such.[66] The courts have also suggested from time to time that an ombudsman investigation would be a preferable route for a claimant than continuing with a claim for judicial review.[67] On the other hand, the ombudsmen are important grievance-handling organizations in their own right, which, like courts and tribunals, may wish to use *ADR techniques* in fulfilling their roles in addition to formal investigations and publishing reports.[68]

The legal powers of the ombudsmen are typically expressed in the following terms: to carry out investigations, to make formal reports, and to recommend action that ought to be taken by the public authority to rectify injustice where it is found to have occurred. No specific provision is made in the legislation for informal resolution of complaints, though this is often attempted by the ombudsmen before a formal, in-depth investigation is launched, using the evidence submitted by the citizen and telephone calls to the public authority. The Collcutt report into the ombudsmen system in England, commissioned by the Cabinet Office in 2000, called for a refocusing in the present arrangements: there should, the report recommended, be an express statutory requirement for the ombudsmen to try informal dispute resolution before a formal investigation, and the legislation should be amended to reflect this:[69]

[64] See DCA, above, n. 9, para. 6.20.

[65] See DCA, above, n. 9, para. 6.21.

[66] See DCA, above, n. 9, para. 2.11.

[67] See e.g. *R. (on the application of Anufrijeva)* v. *Southwark LBC* [2003] EWCA Civ 1406, [2004] QB 1124.

[68] For comment from the Parliamentary and Health Service Ombudsman herself, see A. Abrahams, 'The ombudsman and "paths to justice": a just alternative or just an alternative?' [2008] *Public Law* 1.

[69] *Review of the Public Sector Ombudsmen in England: A Report by the Cabinet Office* (2000) para. 6.36.

> Informal resolution... [is] used by the ombudsmen to get a 'quick fix' but their status under current legislation is rather uncertain. Any new legislation should be based around the concept of the ombudsman seeking resolution, by an agreed settlement if possible, with investigation and the ability to make recommendations as an option. The process should be sufficiently flexible to allow proportionate effort and any approach which is judged appropriate by the ombudsman.

The Regulatory Reform (Collaboration etc between Ombudsmen) Order 2007 gives the ombudsmen express statutory power to 'appoint and pay a mediator or other appropriate person' to assist in the conduct of an investigation. So far, however, the three main public sector ombudsmen seem to have made relatively little use of ADR in practice – though the Parliamentary and Health Service Ombudsman, Ann Abraham, has acknowledged that there may be cases where mediation is 'especially appropriate in enabling the parties to explore their differences with a trained facilitator, achieve insight and empowerment, and devise for themselves a way forward'.[70] The Local Government Ombudsman reported in March 2010 that they 'do not routinely offer mediation as a means to resolve complaints; although a small number of mediations are being carried out as part of a pilot scheme in operation in the Coventry office'.[71]

ADR AND JUDICIAL REVIEW

It remains unclear to what extent ADR will become important in relation to potential or actual claims for judicial review. For many years, the courts hearing judicial review claims have insisted that claimants use all other convenient redress routes before bringing the matter to court. A pre-action protocol requires that any internal complaints system be used before proceedings are started, or reasons for not doing so revealed to the court.[72] If a tribunal appeal exists, that must generally be used in preference to judicial review.[73]

The claim for judicial review procedure in the Administrative Court is a two-stage process: a claimant must first obtain the permission of the court, which is granted or withheld on the basis of the claimant's written case and any reply the defendant public authority chooses to submit to the court; if permission is granted, the claim proceeds to a full hearing. A large proportion of claimants are refused permission to proceed at the first stage, and of those that are granted permission a significant number are withdrawn before trial.[74] The permission stage has in effect evolved into a form of 'early neutral evaluation' (a type of ADR). Research suggests that some public authorities

[70] 'The ombudsman and "paths to justice": a just alternative or just an alternative?' [2008] *Public Law* 1, 4.

[71] See www.lgo.org.uk/guidance-inv/settling-complaints/mediation.

[72] www.dca.gov.uk/civil/procrules_fin/contents/protocols/prot_jrv.htm.

[73] *R.* v. *Secretary of State for the Home Department ex parte Swati* [1986] 1 WLR 772.

[74] See further V. Bondy and M. Sunkin, 'Settlement in Judicial Review Proceedings' [2009] *Public Law* 237.

show little inclination to negotiate with a claimant until after permission has been granted, and that the view of the court that there is an arguable case acts as an incentive to settle before trial.

A more explicit attempt to encourage the use of ADR was made by the Court of Appeal in 2001;[75] pronouncements were made about the need for litigants and their legal advisers to use ADR methods rather than judicial review. Mr Cowl and other residents challenged the lawfulness of the council's decision to close a residential care home. The scenario was sadly familiar: the council needed to prune almost £1 million from its social services budget but the residents of the home argued that promises of a 'home for life' had been made and that they accordingly had a legitimate expectation that the premises would remain open. Their claim for judicial review was refused by the Administrative Court, holding that there was insufficient evidence to establish a 'home for life' promise and that at the time of the closure decision it was not irrational for the council to proceed on the basis that there was no such promise. The Court of Appeal dismissed an appeal. The importance of the judgment lies in the general guidance issued by the court on the importance of ADR. Lord Woolf CJ complained that 'insufficient attention' has been paid 'to the paramount importance of avoiding litigation wherever possible' in disputes with public authorities. ADR was generally, he said, capable of meeting the needs of the parties and the public and saved time, expense and stress. The Court of Appeal said that the legal aid authorities should cooperate with the Administrative Court 'to scrutinise extremely carefully' claims for judicial review so as to ensure that parties tried 'to resolve the dispute with the minimum involvement of the courts'. Ample powers existed under the CPR for the Administrative Court to hold, on its own initiative, an *inter partes* hearing at which both sides could explain what steps they had taken to resolve the dispute without the courts' involvement using complaints procedures and other forms of ADR. The lawyers in the case were not criticized since they were 'merely following the unfortunate culture in such litigation of over-judicialising the processes which were involved'. Today, sufficient should be known about ADR 'to make the failure to adopt it, in particular when public money is involved, indefensible'. There is now a 'heavy obligation' to resort to litigation only if it is really unavoidable. If litigation is necessary, the courts should deter the parties from 'adopting an unnecessarily confrontational approach to the litigation'.

The impact of *Cowl* has remained modest. There are many unresolved questions as to which cases in principle are amenable to ADR, how ADR is to be funded, how the use of ADR relates to the strict and short time limits that apply in judicial review claims, who will carry out the ADR and where, and whether ADR on any large scale is needed given that so many judicial review claims are either dismissed at the permission stage or settled by the parties without recourse to mediation. According to one generally optimistic analysis (by members of the public law Bar who are trained

[75] *Cowl* v. *Plymouth CC* [2001] EWCA Civ 1935, [2002] 1 WLR 803.

mediators) 'the use of ADR in public law disputes is considerably less straightforward than it might be in many other areas of law'.[76]

A CLASH OF VALUES?

It remains too early to provide any sort of definitive assessment of the administrative justice reform agenda and its implementation. The institutional and structural changes brought about by the Constitutional Reform Act 2005 and Tribunals, Courts and Enforcement Act 2007, Pt 1 are still bedding down and changes are proposed (abolition of the AJTC and office of Senior President of Tribunals). The expansion of informal dispute resolution – in judicial review, tribunal hearings and in relation to the ombudsmen – has yet to be put into practice on a large scale. What can be attempted, however, is an assessment of the values that underlie the reforms. What is suggested in this chapter is that there are two trends – changes associated with the promotion of constitutionalism and changes designed to implement values associated with informality. It is paradoxical that just at a time when courts and tribunals, traditionally the arenas for adjudication by judges, are being put on new and firmer constitutional footings so – simultaneously – there are attempts to steer disputes away from them. If the 'informalization' project is as successful as its supporters hope, fewer cases will be decided by judges finding facts and applying the law, and more by civil servants and third-parties through negotiation, mediation, early neutral evaluation and so on. This final section of the chapter outlines two of the main constitutional risks in this and suggests that one way to help minimize these risks is to recognize that administrative justice is a constitutional right not merely a service to be delivered.

BEHIND CLOSED DOORS: MIND THE TRANSPARENCY GAP

Courts and tribunal hearings are normally open to the public and press and much of their legitimacy stems from the fact that carefully and fully reasoned justifications are given for findings (justice is not only done but seen to be done). A body of precedent is generated which elaborates standards of good administration and principles of law that in turn provide a guide for future action. ADR by contrast is almost always a private affair. While in citizen–citizen disputes that may be acceptable, it is open to question whether that is so where a public authority is one of the parties. In place of a reported and reasoned decision, the most that we get to know about ADR proceedings is usually at best a brief anonymized summary published by a public authority. For example:

[76] M. Supperstone, D. Stilitz and C. Sheldon, 'ADR and Public Law' [2006] *Public Law* 299, 319.

> The claimants brought an action for damages for unlawful detention, sex and race discrimination and negligence arising from the immigration detention. Significant and sensitive issues concerning policy and procedure in immigration were raised. The matter was successfully mediated.[77]

It needs to be recognized that the pursuit of informality risks creating a transparency gap. There is a public, not merely a private, interest in challenges brought by citizens against public authorities. Under the Tribunals, Courts and Enforcement Act 2007, the Administrative Justice and Tribunals Council (the successor to the Council on Tribunals) has duties to formulate a programme of work, to 'keep the administrative justice system under review' and make an annual report; it is imperative that internal complaints and appeals schemes and the deployment of ADR by public authorities, courts and tribunals do not fall beneath the radar and that adequate information about informal dispute resolution is included. However in 2010 the coalition government announced plans to abolish the AJTC as part of the cost cutting measures made in response to the economic crisis.

COMPULSION OR CHOICE?

In its traditional form in the public law context, the principle of access to justice means that citizens should not be impeded in their attempts to challenge the lawfulness of public authorities' decisions. The government's proportionate dispute resolution strategy starts from the assumption that for most people's disputes, achieving a ruling from an independent judge sitting in a court or tribunal is unnecessary; and that justice has a broader meaning and can be delivered in a variety of forms. In the rush towards informality what must not be overlooked however is the existence of a fundamental right to access to a court or tribunal.[78] Parliament and the courts generally decry attempts by government to oust the jurisdiction of the courts, as without formal hearings the constitutional principle of the rule of law cannot be given practical effect.[79] So long as ADR is offered as an option there is perhaps little risk that it will hinder access to an independent judge. But what if its use is to be made compulsory or refusal to use it made subject to sanctions? The white paper acknowledged this:

> Of course the rights of participants have to be safeguarded and in many cases a hearing will be unavoidable. None of these proposals is intended to result in any individual receiving less than the entitlement or remedy they would obtain from a full judicial determination, nor, conversely, is it intended to distort duties which a department owes to all its clients, the tax payer and the community.[80]

[77] DCA, *Annual Report 2005/06 Monitoring the Effectiveness of the Government's Commitment to using Alternative Dispute Resolution*, available at www.justice.gov.uk/docs/annual-pledge-report-2006-07.pdf.

[78] ECHR, Art. 6, discussed below.

[79] See Chapter 1 above.

[80] See DCA, above, n. 9, para. 6.23.

Such assurances are however no substitute for legal clarity. There may be signs that ministers may sometimes view formal justice as an inconvenience. In a letter to the House of Lords Constitution Committee, one minister said:

> In the tribunal context, I do not see 'ADR' as an 'adjunct' to formal proceedings. The tribunals have a duty to be accessible. Formal proceedings may well hamper that objective. I see 'ADR' not as an alternative but as potential ways of providing justice in a more practical and effective manner...[81]

When published in draft form,[82] before formal introduction to Parliament, the Tribunals, Courts and Enforcement Bill contained the following clause:

> A person exercising power to make Tribunal Procedure Rules or give practice directions must, when making provision in relation to mediation, have regard to the following principles –
>
> (a) mediation of matters in dispute between parties to proceedings is to take place only by agreement between those parties;
>
> (b) where parties to proceedings fail to mediate, or where mediation between parties to proceedings fails to resolve disputed matters, the failure is not to affect the outcome of the proceedings.

By the time the Bill was introduced to the House of Lords to begin its legislative process, the Government had decided to remove that clause. It was re-inserted only following a report of the Constitution Committee[83] and an amendment moved by a backbench peer.[84]

ECHR, Art. 6 guarantees that 'in the determination of his civil rights and obligations or any criminal charge against him, everyone is entitled to a *fair and public hearing* within a reasonable time by *an independent and impartial tribunal established by law*' and that 'judgment shall be *pronounced publicly*' (emphasis added). Thus the ECHR sets up the independent judicial body as the paradigm dispute-resolution mechanism: there is a fundamental right to formal adjudication and access to court. Many citizen–state disputes involve a 'civil right', though that category is notoriously difficult to define.[85] Where a Convention right (rather than a 'civil right') is in issue,

[81] Letter from Baroness Ashton of Upholland to the House of Lords Constitution Committee, November 2006.

[82] The DCA published the Bill in draft in July 2006, but undermined one of the main aims of draft Bills (to enable parliamentary scrutiny ahead of the formal legislative process) by doing so on the day that Parliament rose for its summer recess. The DCA later declined to make public the responses received to the draft Bill.

[83] Select Committee on the Constitution, 1st Report of Session 2006–07, HL 13.

[84] Lord Goodlad, *Hansard*, HL, col. 254 (31 January 2007). Lord Thomas of Gresford, the Liberal Democrat spokesman, said 'people should not be pushed into mediation. They should always have at the back of their mind that they are entitled to a hearing within the structure of the tribunal system and that an independent judge will decide. The problem with mediation is that you have the Government or a similar body on the one side and the individual on the other, and the bargaining power is not equal' (col. 258).

[85] Thus the European Court of Human Rights has held that the revocation of professional and trading licenses, disputes about planning permission and some social security disputes and state pensions are 'civil

Art. 13 provides comparable protection in relation to Convention rights.[86] A person with an arguable claim must have an 'effective remedy before a national authority', though that remedy does not have to be in the form of a judicial body. What *is* required however is that the body – whether a judicial body or otherwise – must have adequate powers of investigation and the capacity to make binding orders. The rights guaranteed by Arts 6 and 13 do not stand in the way of ADR, so long as ADR is offered or encouraged as an option to the aggrieved citizen rather than acting as a restriction on access to adjudication by a court. That should be recognized in UK legislation.

ADMINISTRATIVE JUSTICE AS A CONSTITUTIONAL RIGHT

It has been suggested in this chapter that where there is tension or conflict between the values of constitutionalism and informality, the former ought to prevail because this will better ensure that citizen's' rights are protected in an open and accountable manner. One way of helping achieve this would be to recognize that administrative justice is a constitutional principle, not merely a service to be delivered.

Some constitutional systems have expressly acknowledged the existence of a specific right to justice in relation to administrative action. For example, South African Constitution, s. 33 provides that 'Everyone has the right to administrative action that is lawful, reasonable and procedurally fair' and requires legislation to be enacted 'to provide for the review of administrative action by a court or, where appropriate, an independent and impartial tribunal'.

As we have seen, the ECHR, drafted in the 1950s before we were so attuned to the need for specific rights against the administrative state, makes no express reference to administrative justice. ECHR, Art. 6 guarantees a right to formal adjudication for any dispute that involves a 'civil right or obligation' but this fits uneasily in the context of decision-making by public authorities as not all administrative disputes involve such rights and obligations. Some other Convention rights require public authorities to act proportionately and with legal authority,[87] both aspects of administrative justice. Beyond the ECHR, the Council of Europe has developed a range of conventions, resolutions and recommendations that more explicitly engage with various aspects of administrative justice.[88] The European Union, in Charter of Fundamental Rights, Art. 41, recognizes a 'right to good administration'.

rights' for the purposes of Art. 6; but the following are not – disputes relating to elections, tax liability (*Ferrazzini* v. *Italy* [2001] STC 1314) and situations where there is a broad discretion rather a defined entitlement.

[86] ECHR, Art. 13 was not expressly incorporated into domestic law by the Human Rights Act 1998, but the duty on the courts under s. 2 of the Act to have regard to the case law of the European Court of Human Rights means that it has often had decisive influence on the courts' approach.

[87] E.g. Arts 8–11, where a public authority interfering with a right must do so only 'in accordance with the law' and so far as it is 'necessary in a democratic society', which involves a proportionality test.

[88] See www.coe.int/t/e/legal_affairs/legal_co-operation/Administrative_law_and_justice. For a useful overview, see R. Benitez, 'Administrative Justice in a World in Transition: Pan-European Values in Administrative Justice' (2001) 30 *Common Law World Review* 434. See further below.

How might a constitutional right to 'administrative justice' or 'good administration' be given effect in UK law? One option that may be on the horizon would be to include a right to administrative justice in any British Bill of Rights that may be adopted in years to come.

A different tack would be for English common law to recognize administrative justice as an aspect of the broader constitutional principle of the rule of law – one of the fundamental rights protected (subject to parliamentary sovereignty) by the courts.[89] In the English legal system, principles of administrative justice have developed in the form of the grounds of judicial review – illegality, irrationality, and procedural impropriety – to prevent arbitrary decision making by public authorities.[90] There are signs that an overarching right to good administration may be adopted. Laws LJ, in a judgment about legitimate expectations (the rule that where a person has been assured he will be treated in a particular way by a public authority, he must be so treated unless there is a pressing reason of the public interest to do otherwise), described:

> a requirement of good administration, by which public bodies ought to deal straightforwardly and consistently with the public. In my judgment, this is a legal standard which, although not found in terms in the European Convention on Human Rights, takes its place alongside such rights as fair trial, and no punishment without law. That being so there is every reason to articulate the limits of this requirement – to describe what may count as good reason to depart from it – as we have come to articulate the limits of other constitutional principles overtly found in the European Convention.[91]

What is the point of labelling something a 'constitutional right' in the UK? It means less than it does in other countries. In the absence of a codified constitution, any prescribed legislative process for constitutional legislation, or a specialized constitutional court, to say something is or ought to be regarded as 'constitutional' in the UK operates mainly as a warning that care needs to be taken in legislating or adjudicating on an issue.

Where legislation deals with a constitutional right, special attention needs to be paid to the express aims and also any unintended consequences of the government's proposals. This has been recognized by the fact that the House of Lords has a select committee on the constitution, which examines all Bills for their constitutional implications and draws to the attention of that House any matters of concern.[92] In the House of Commons, where a Bill is of 'first class' constitutional importance, the

[89] Others include e.g. the right of access to a court (*R.* v. *Lord Chancellor ex parte Witham* [1998] QB 575), freedom of expression (*Derbyshire CC* v. *Times Newspapers* [1993] AC 534), and prohibition on torture (*A* v. *Secretary of State for the Home Department* [2005] UKHL 71, [2006] 2 AC 221).

[90] See Chapter 1 above.

[91] *R. (on the application of Nadarajah)* v. *Secretary of State for the Home Department* [2005] EWCA Civ 1363 at [68].

[92] www.parliament.uk/hlconstitution.

normal procedure is altered, and such a Bill may have its clause-by-clause scrutiny in a committee of the whole House rather than in a standing (or Bill) committee. Robert Hazell has recently argued that a better constitutional protection would be for Bills of clear constitutional significance to be subject to proper consultation and pre-legislative parliamentary scrutiny (in which a committee considers a draft of the Bill before it begins its formal legislative process through Parliament).[93] If administrative justice is a constitutional matter we can expect and demand a greater degree of care in legislating about it.

A second area in which care is taken when constitutional rights are at stake is in the courtroom. If it is correct (as Laws LJ suggests) to say that there is a fundamental right to administrative justice recognized by the common law, the court's approach to adjudication may be modified in three important ways. First, the principle of legality will apply:

> A power conferred by Parliament in general terms is not to be taken to authorise the doing of acts by the donee of the power which adversely affect the legal rights of the citizen or the basic principles on which the law of the UK is based unless the statute conferring the power makes it clear that such was the intention of Parliament.[94]

This is a technique of statutory interpretation designed to protect constitutional rights from being circumscribed by implication. If Parliament (for which read 'the government') wishes to restrict, alter or otherwise affect the rights of citizens to seek justice in disputes with public authorities, the legislation attempting to do that must spell out the intended consequences in plain and blunt terms.

A second way in which a court may modify its method where a constitutional right (in the British sense) is in issue is where a claimant for judicial review argues that a public authority's decision is unlawful on the grounds that it is irrational (or unreasonable). Where this is so, the court adopts an 'anxious scrutiny' approach, meaning that to a considerable extent the burden is shifted away from the citizen having to demonstrate that the decision was unreasonable and onto the public authority to provide a cogent justification for its action.[95] And thirdly, if a legislative provision is classified as 'constitutional', it is immune from implied (and therefore possibly unintended) repeal.[96]

So for both Parliament and for the aggrieved citizen, labelling something 'constitutional' has practical benefits.

[93] R. Hazell, 'Time for a New Convention: Parliamentary Scrutiny of Constitutional Bills 1997–2005' [2006] *Public Law* 247.

[94] *R.* v. *Secretary of State for the Home Department ex parte Pierson* [1998] AC 539, 575 (Lord Browne-Wilkinson).

[95] A. Le Sueur, 'The Rise and Ruin of Unreasonableness' [2005] *Judicial Review* 32.

[96] *Thoburn* v. *Sunderland City Council* [2002] EWHC 195, [2003] QB 151.

FURTHER READING

ADLER, M. (ed.), *Administrative Justice in Context* (2010).

USEFUL WEBSITES

Local Government Ombudsman: **www.lgo.org.uk**
Ministry of Justice: **www.justice.gov.uk**
Parliamentary and Health Service Ombudsman: **www.ombudsman.org.uk**
Report of the Review of Tribunals by Sir Andrew Leggatt: **www.tribunals-review.org.uk**
Tribunals Service: **www.tribunals.gov.uk**

PART III

REGULATION AND THE CONSTITUTION

Editorial note

Regulation has become an increasingly important element in the UK's constitutional arrangements. This has been particularly the case in relation to the environment, privatized industries, public expenditure, access to official information, and standards of conduct in public life. Thus the regulation of power is the focus of this part of the book.

The environment provides a clear example of a web of constitutional connections between different branches of government and different levels of government and between other regulatory and non-governmental bodies. The environment also serves as an illustration of how one area of law, policy and public administration can engage practice and principle that themselves bring about changes to the overall constitutional structure. Chapter 11, through the lens of environmental law, therefore provides a case study of constitutional interaction and change.

Before the privatization of many industries in the 1980s and 1990s much regulation was internal to government: government itself regulated, often in an informal manner, the industries that were publicly owned. Since privatization regulation has been formalized, statutory, and external to those industries. Independent expert regulatory bodies have been created to take on these tasks. Chapter 12 examines the implications of this development. However, much of government activity remains largely internally regulated. The control of public expenditure (the focus of Chapter 13) is the paradigm example: the Treasury regulates government departments' spending in various ways. The National Audit Office and Parliament do so too, but Parliament's role is increasingly only formal.

Sunshine can be a powerful disinfectant, and the accountability of public bodies is enhanced by openness about their activities. Chapter 14 considers the impact of the Freedom of Information Act 2000, which provides for and regulates rights of access to information.

Finally in this part of the book, the regulation of standards of conduct in public life is considered in Chapter 15. As a result of a number of scandals in the 1990s and 2009 and a loss of trust in politicians and others in public life, standards of conduct have been increasingly subject to regulation. A range of techniques is discussed in this chapter, including self-regulation with or without independent elements, the adoption and publication of codes of conduct, even the criminalization of some breaches of rules relating to conduct and conflicts of interest. In 2010, in the wake of the MPs' expenses scandal, the Independent Parliamentary Standards Authority was established to set and pay MPs' expenses.

Overall, the chapters in this part show that the British constitution is becoming increasingly rule-bound, regulated, and juridified.

11

ENVIRONMENTAL REGULATION AS AN INSTRUMENT OF CONSTITUTIONAL CHANGE

Richard Macrory

SUMMARY

Less than a generation ago the Chief Scientist of the then Department of the Environment and Transport could argue, with some justification, that one of the defining characteristics of the British approach to environmental policy was a preference for voluntary arrangements between government and industry rather than legal compulsion.[1] Even in areas where there were explicit legal frameworks, the substantive legislation was often expressed in extremely broad terms, allowing regulators and the regulated to negotiate solutions without the intervention of legal process and the courts. To take one example, long familiar to British environmental lawyers, the core legal requirement concerning atmospheric emissions from major industrial processes was to use the 'best practicable means' to prevent or minimize emissions, a statutory expression that remained in force 100 years from 1875 until 1990 – despite the heavily open-textured language of that central duty, there is not a single reported case in the higher courts concerning its interpretation throughout that period. The translation of the legal obligation into practical reality was largely the result of a dialogue and negotiation between chemical engineers and other technically qualified staff working within the regulated industry and the national regulatory body, the Alkali Inspectorate and its successor, the Industrial Air Pollution Inspectorate. These distinctive characteristics of environmental regulation in this country no longer hold true. The last 40 years has seen an extraordinary expansion in the depth and scale of substantive legislation bringing about a fundamental change in the prevailing legal culture operating in this field.

This chapter, though, deals with environmental law not in order to analyze the reasons behind the massive expansion of the law in this area,[2] still less to consider in any detail the substance

[1] M. Holdgate, 'Environmental Policies in Britain and Mainland Europe', in R. Macrory (ed.), *Britain, Europe and the Environment* (1983) 6–18.

[2] See R. Macrory, 'Environmental Law: Shifting Discretions and the New Formalism', reproduced in R. Macrory *Regulation, Enforcement and Governance in Environmental Law* (2010).

of contemporary environmental regulation – rather, the subject serves as a useful illustration of two aspects of constitutional change. First, the environment provides a clear example of the web of complex constitutional connections between different branches of government and different levels of government (local, central, and the European Union) and between other regulatory and non-governmental bodies. Secondly, the environment serves as an illustration of how one area of law, policy and public administration can engage practice and principle that themselves bring about changes to the overall constitutional structure. This chapter should therefore be seen a case study of constitutional interaction and change. Indeed, I will argue that the real significance of the developments over the 30 years, and in hindsight the one with the most long-lasting impact, is the extent to which environmental law and regulation has proved to be at the forefront in articulating principles and precedents that are central to a contemporary constitutional settlement. Legal rights to public information and participation in decision making, access to justice, the accountability of regulatory authorities are issues that have a universality and help define the relationship between citizen and state. In all of these areas environmental law has played a key role in pioneering concepts and practice and continues to do so.

INTRODUCTION

Why should environmental law have proved a fruitful area for driving legal innovation concerning fundamental principles? The roots of contemporary environmental regulation can still be traced back to the 19th century, and the policy response to unacceptable side effects of the industrial revolution. The first non-governmental organizations concerned with environmental issues were formed in the latter half of that century, with specialized laws and regulatory agencies well developed by the post-War period. Yet it was the growth of modern environmental groups from the 1970s onwards that posed profound challenges to familiar ways of handling issues. Rather than dealing with environmental issues on a topic by topic basis typically reflected in the legislation of the time (air pollution, water, and so on), the new wave of organizations demanded a more holistic approach that looked at environmental impacts as a whole and pressed for more preventative solutions beyond the more immediate amelioration of pollution impacts. Concern at the urgency and enormity of the environmental challenges implied a rejection of the cautious gradualism which appeared to characterize policy development. More recently the concept of sustainable development became a familiar part of language of the policy debate but is equally subject to differing interpretations and competing visions.[3] A simple balancing of environmental, economic and social agendas is pitched against a vision that would argue that without a secure environmental basis, economic and social progress will prove unattainable. Others have promoted a more politically challenging vision of sustainable development incorporating ideas of greater economic and social justice both within and between generations,

[3] R. Macrory, 'The Environment and Constitutional Change', in R. Hazell (ed.), *Constitutional Futures: A History of the Next Ten Years* (1999) 178, 179.

and a revitalization of local and community identities.[4] It took some years before the environmental dimensions of the UK legal structure were seriously addressed in this debate – the UK Environmental Law Association, for example, was not formed until 1987. But the restless challenge to long established ways of thinking about and handling policy issues that have been such an integral part of the modern environmental movement provided a potent basis for treating environmental law as a significant engine for constitutional change. Regulatory practices and styles of policy making were subject to sustained scrutiny and critiques in a way not experienced before. Fundamental re-evaluations provide a powerful engine for innovation.

PUBLIC ACCESS TO INFORMATION AND PARTICIPATION

General rights of public access to information in the UK as enshrined in the Freedom of Information Act 2000 are now a familiar part of the constitutional landscape. But such broad rights were first enshrined in British law in the environmental field some eight years before, and these in turn found precedent in individual areas of environmental law from the 1970s, deriving from a lengthy period of intellectual and policy argument conducted in the environmental policy community. Registers of regulatory consents in fields such as water pollution had existed since the 1950s but they were open only to persons 'interested' in the register, interpreted narrowly to mean someone with a legal interest such as an owner of fishing rights in the waters concerned rather than a member of the general public. Industry in particular fought hard to restrict wider access on the grounds of confidentiality. The Royal Commission on Environmental Pollution, established in 1970, was the first official body to seriously raise the issue, which it did in its Second Report,[5] urging the Government 'to devise measures which will increase the availability and flow of information on the production and disposal of industrial effluents and wastes'.[6] Largely as a consequence, one of the first major environmental statutes of the time, the Control of Pollution Act 1974, mainly dealing with the regulation of waste, water pollution and noise, contained provisions concerning registers of applications for consents, consents, and monitoring results which were to be open to any member of the public. The Royal Commission demonstrated the value of being a standing commission by constantly returning to the subject of openness over the next 12 years in a number of different reports, and arguing consistently that a presumption of public access would lead to improved environmental protection. In its Tenth Report, published in 1984,[7] the Commission carried out an extensive analysis of the arguments

[4] T. O'Riordan and H. Voisey, *Sustainable Development in Western Europe: Coming to Terms with Agenda 21* (1988).

[5] Royal Commission on Environmental Pollution, *Three Issues in Industrial Pollution*, Cmnd 4894 (1972).

[6] Ibid., para. 9.

[7] Royal Commission on Environmental Pollution, *Tackling Pollution – Experience and Prospects*, Cmnd 9149 (1984).

for and against greater access to environmental information, and concluded that while some progress was being made in more recent individual laws, insufficient priority was being given to the principle. It concluded with a statement that could have formed the rallying-call for general freedom of information legislation:

> A guiding principle behind all legislative and administrative controls relating to environmental pollution should be a presumption in favour of unrestricted access for the public to information which the pollution control authorities obtain or receive by virtue of their statutory powers, with provision for secrecy only in those circumstances where a genuine case for it can be substantiated.[8]

The underlying principle of open access to environmental information was also beginning to gain momentum with the European Community and in 1990 the Community adopted a Directive on the subject, the first sector of Community policy where such a general right was granted.[9] The Directive was framed in the language of a human right, and gave broad rights to anyone, including non-governmental associations, to acquire environmental information held by public authorities and other bodies performing public functions. There was no precondition of holding a legal or other special interest in the matter concerned, a challenge to the administrative practice in many member states.[10]

Transposition of the Directive required the UK to move beyond its then practice of incorporating public registers in specific environmental laws to promoting legislation giving much broader rights in the form of the Environmental Information Regulations 1992.[11] Though containing various exemptions in line with the Directive, the regulations created a precedent in the concept of general access to information held by public authorities.[12] The Freedom of Information 2000 Act acknowledges the distinctive and independent nature of the environmental rights, essentially by providing that any information falling with the terms of the Directive and implementing regulations is treated as not covered by the Act as 'exempt' information.[13] Indeed, it is arguable that the scope of exemptions is narrower under the environmental information regulations than the Freedom of Information Act 2000,[14] and the EU dimension means that the European Court of Justice has jurisdiction in the area, and has already given a strongly progressive, liberal interpretation of the Directive.[15]

[8] Ibid., para. 2.77.

[9] Council Directive (EEC) 90/313 on Freedom of Access to Information on the Environment [1990] OJ L156/58, replaced by Council Directive (EC) 2003/4 on Public Access on Environmental Information [2003] OJ L41/26.

[10] L. Kramer, *EC Environmental Law* (6th edn, 2007) 150, and see generally R. Hallo (ed.), *Access to Environmental Information in Europe* (1997).

[11] SI 2000/227. Replaced by Environmental Information Regulations 2004 (SI 2004/3391).

[12] The first law granting general rights to information was in fact the Local Government (Access to Information) Act 1985 giving rights of access to agendas and background papers for meetings of local authorities.

[13] Freedom of Information Act 2000, s. 39.

[14] D. Hughes, *Environmental Law* (4th edn, 2002) 163.

[15] C-321/96, *Mecklenburg* v. *Kreis Pinneberg-Der Landrat* [1998] ECR I-3809.

The environmental field can also be seen to have developed important legal principles concerning rights of public participation in decision making though its contribution is perhaps somewhat more subtle. The UK had long established opportunities for public participation in certain fields, particularly in town and country planning where public inquiries were regularly held into planning appeals, and formed a familiar part of the administrative landscape.[16] Indeed, in the 1970s and 1980s it was the planning inquiry that was seen by many in the modern environmental movement as a unique forum where new ideas and ways of looking at development proposals could be articulated and raised, leading to a number of major inquiries involving the exploration of complex issues of public policy well beyond the narrow confines of land-use planning.[17] More specialized environmental legislation such as the Control of Pollution Act 1974 reflected a growing demand for participation rights by including provisions for rights of participation in various pollution consent procedures.[18] But as with rights of information, it was at European level that such rights were expressed in law with a more general application. The 1985 Directive on environmental assessment,[19] applying to consent procedures for numerous types of development proposals from transport and energy projects to waste disposal and deforestation, incorporated consultation with the general public as part of the assessment process. It was the first piece of EC environmental legislation to have incorporated such public participation rights, and indeed probably the first EC law in any field to have done so. It took some years before the British courts fully appreciated the significance of these participation rights as an integral and obligatory element of European style environmental assessment,[20] with Lord Hoffmann eventually declaring in *Berkeley* v. *Secretary of State for Environment, Transport and Regions*:[21]

> The directly enforceable right of the citizen which is accorded by the Directive is not merely a right to a fully informed decision on the substantive issue. It must have been adopted on an appropriate basis and that requires the inclusive and democratic procedure prescribed

[16] *Report of the Committee on Administrative Tribunals and Inquiries* (Franks Report) Cmnd 218 (1957). *The Report of the Committee on Public Participation in Planning: People and Planning* (The Skeffington Report) (1969) was a significant endorsement of the public policy value in engaging with the public in land use plan development.

[17] D. Pearce, L. Edwards and C. Bennet, *Decision-making for Energy Futures: A Case Study of the Windscale Inquiry* (1979); T. O'Riordan, R. Kemp and M. Purdue, *Sizewell B: An Anatomy of an Inquiry* (1988); J. Jowell, 'Policy, Inquiries, and the Courts', in R. Macrory (ed.), *Commercial Nuclear Power – Legal and Constitutional Issues* (1982).

[18] R. Macrory and B. Zaba, *Polluters Pay – The Control of Pollution Act Explained* (1978), an example of a citizen's guide to the new legal rights contained in the 1974 Act.

[19] Council Directive (EC) 85/337 on the Assessment of the Effects of Certain Public and Private Projects on the Environment [1985] OJ L175/40.

[20] The EC legislation had been inspired by the US legislation on environmental impact statements under National Environmental Policy Act 1970, s. 102, but while the US law focused on the production of a written assessment by public officials, the EC law was deliberately focused on procedural requirements, including participation.

[21] [2001] 2 AC 603.

by the Directive in which the public, however misguided or wrongheaded its views may be, is given an opportunity to express its opinion on the environmental issues.

The 1998 United Nations Economic Commission for Europe (UNECE) Aarhus Convention (the Convention)[22] developed the participation principle even further by containing a second pillar wholly devoted to participation, and requiring parties to the Convention to ensure that the general public had opportunities to participate in consent procedures for individual projects, plans and programmes relating to the environment, and environmental rule-making and legislative drafting.[23] Considerable discretion is left to the parties as to the precise form of participation that is offered, but the underlying principles are clear. The provisions in the Convention concerning access to justice, considered in the next section, are posing the most immediate challenge to current UK practice, but it would be rash for government to ignore the implications of the Convention's participation provisions, especially those concerning plans and rule making. *R. on the application of Greenpeace* v. *Secretary of State for Trade and Industry*[24] concerned a challenge to the government's consultation procedures on nuclear energy policy. The court found the government's own procedures to have been flawed, but it is significant that Sullivan J noted that even if the government had not committed itself to the widest possible consultation should the nuclear option be re-opened, it might have been obliged to do so because of its obligations under the Convention.

ACCESS TO JUSTICE

Disputes before the courts involving environmental issues have a long history, and Victorian law reports are littered with cases mainly involving conflicts between private rights such as the use of water or intrusive pollution, or testing the ambit of new public health legislation. It was not, however, until the 1980s that environmental organizations and affected individuals began to use the courts more regularly to explore issues of public law. Those bringing a claim for judicial review must demonstrate that they have 'sufficient interest' in the issue at hand,[25] a phrase that was once interpreted very restrictively by the courts, largely confining it to those with a defined legal interest at stake. Contemporary practice shows a far more liberal approach, and a number of the leading cases involving public interest groups involved questions of environmental law[26] reaching a sort of apotheosis in *R. (Edwards)* v. *Environment Agency*[27] where a

[22] Convention on Access to Information, Public Participation in Decision-Making and Access to Justice in Environmental Matters (the Convention) (25 June 1998).

[23] Convention, Arts 6–8.

[24] [2007] EWHC 311 (Admin).

[25] Supreme Court Act 1981, s. 31(3).

[26] E.g. *R* v. *HM Inspectorate of Pollution ex parte Greenpeace Ltd (No. 2)* [1994] 4 All ER 329 doubting the more restrictive earlier decision of *R* v. *Secretary of State for the Environment ex parte Rose Theatre Trust* [1990] 1 All ER 754, and *R* v. *Secretary of State for Trade and Industry ex parte Greenpeace* [1998] Env LR 415 where Laws J noted that this type of public interest litigation was now an 'accepted and greatly valued dimension of the judicial review jurisdiction'.

[27] [2004] Env LR 43.

homeless individual was still granted standing to challenge the legality of a permit for a local cement works because he breathed the potentially polluted air. Standing in the environmental field will rarely prove a hurdle in the contemporary judicial climate, and the debate has moved on to the question of the exposure to costs in public law cases where the general costs in the cause rule, developed in the context of disputes between private parties, is applied by the courts. Legal aid is increasingly constrained, and in any event is not available to a non-governmental organization.

In recent years the courts themselves have acknowledged that the loser pays principle developed in the context of private law disputes may not always be appropriate in the context of public law where it may be important in the general public interest that the law is tested. In a non-environmental case, the Court of Appeal in 2005[28] revived the more general use of protective costs orders (PCOs) under which a claimant in judicial review would in the early stages of litigation be limited as to the amount of costs they could be exposed to even if the case were lost. The *Corner House* principles were, however, only to be applied if five factors were present: '(i) the issues raised are of general importance; (ii) the public interest requires that those issues should be resolved; (iii) the claimant has no private interest in the outcome of the case; (iv) having regard to the financial resources of the claimant and the respondent(s) and to the amount of costs that are likely to be made it is fair and just to make the order (v) if the order is not made the claimant will probably discontinue the proceedings and will be acting reasonably in so doing'. Expressed as such, the principles were clearly seen as an exception to the general rule concerning costs, and PCOs were expected to be made in only a small number of cases each year.[29] Nevertheless, the general approach might have made a limited but valuable contribution towards reducing the freezing effect of costs exposure in public litigation, and one that would have been legally sound had it not been for developments in the environmental field, both internationally and at European level.

The origins of the Aarhus Convention can be traced back to the 1992 Rio Declaration on Environment and Development which was produced after the major UN Conference known as the Earth Summit. Principle 10 of the Declaration emphasized the importance of citizen participation in environmental issues, both in terms of access to information and active participation in decision making, but also included a tentative reference to access to judicial remedies and redress.[30] Three years later,

[28] *R (Corner House Research)* v. *Secretary of State for Trade and Industry* [2005] 1 WLR 2600.

[29] *R. (on the application of Bullmore)* v. *West Herts Hospital NHS Trust* [2007] LTL, 27 June 2007, and *River Thames Society* v. *First Secretary of State* [2006] EWHC 2829 (Admin).

[30] 'Environmental issues are best handled with the participation of all concerned citizens, at the relevant level. At the national level, each individual shall have appropriate access to information concerning the environment that is held by public authorities, including information on hazardous materials and activities in their communities, and the opportunity to participate in decision-making processes. States shall facilitate and encourage public awareness and participation by making information widely available. Effective access to judicial and administrative proceedings, including redress and remedy, shall be provided', available at www.unep.org/Documents.Multilingual/Default.asp?documentid=78&articleid=1163.

a Pan-European conference adopted the Sofia Guidelines which fleshed out some of the principles particularly in relation to access to information and participation, and this in turn led to the UNECE preparing a Convention on the subject, involving more than 40 countries though with the notable exceptions of the USA and Canada.[31] The proposed Convention was initially confined to provisions concerning access to information and public participation, and had this continued to be the case the provisions would probably have posed little in the way of challenge for the UK where generally such principles in the environmental field were by now well developed. Early on in the negotiations, however, it was agreed to include a so-called 'third pillar' relating to questions of access to justice, and Art. 9 of the Convention gives rights to members of the public and environmental non-governmental organization to challenge the legality of decisions by public authorities granting consent for a wide range of projects as well as other acts or omissions 'which are contrary to the provisions of national laws relating to the environment'. Again, the liberal approach to standing expressed in the Convention would pose little problem for a jurisdiction such as the UK, but Art. 9(4) requires that parties ensure that procedures for rights of access must 'provide adequate and effective remedies, including injunctive relief as appropriate and be fair, equitable, timely, and not prohibitively expensive'. The UK along with all other member states with the exception of Ireland duly signed and ratified the Convention, as did the European Community.

The legal commitment to ensure access to judicial procedures that are not 'prohibitively expensive' has subsequently come to drive the debate in the UK and prove a potent source of change which will spread well beyond the field of environmental law. It is still somewhat unclear why the UK found itself agreeing to a commitment containing such potentially unsettling implications. Given that nearly all the obligations in other parts of the Convention could be readily met and that in many ways the Convention was politically viewed at the time as a means of raising the standards of Eastern European countries to those of the West, it may have just been conveniently ignored. At the same time there was a view that the reference in Art. 9(4) referred only to court fees rather than any exposure or risk of exposure to litigation costs, and the official government line was that UK procedures met the obligations.[32] The restrictive interpretation of Art. 9(4) was given some support by the Irish High Court in 2007,[33] but it is increasingly a view that appears untenable. In 2004 the Court of Appeal had already noted the difficulties of the conventional costs principles in judicial reviews meeting up to the aspirations of the Convention, and clearly felt that Art. 9(4) was not confined to the court fees:

[31] J. Jendroska, 'Public Information and Participation in EC Environmental Law – Origins, Milestones and Trends', in R. Macrory (ed.), *Reflections on 30 Years of EU Environmental Law* (2006) 63, 69–71.

[32] 'Our administrative and judicial systems are fully compliant with the requirements for access to review'. Summary of Implementing Measures to achieve Aarhus Compliance with the UNECE Aarhus Convention, available at www.defra.gov.uk/environment/policy/international/aarhus.

[33] *Sweetman* v. *An Bord Pleanala and the Attorney General* [2007] IEHC 153.

> If the figures revealed in this case were in any sense typical of the costs reasonably incurred in litigating such cases up the highest level, very serious questions would be raised as to the possibility of ever living up to the Aarhus ideals within our present system[34]

If the Convention had retained the characteristics of a more conventional public law Convention, it may well have been the case that a national government could have resisted pressures for change even where breaches occurred. But this was not the case for a number of reasons.

First, a number of senior members of the judiciary made it increasingly clear that they were sensitive to the implications of the Convention, and expressed concerns both judicially and extra judicially that the UK might not be in compliance. The Court of Appeal, for example, doubted that the principles concerning PCOs developed in *Corner House* which excluded PCOs where a private interest was involved were applicable to environmental cases.[35] The Court reached a clear conclusion that it disagreed with the government's view that the Art. 9(4) obligation was confined to court fees.[36] Pressure continued to mount with a judicial-led initiative to establish a committee to suggest how the Convention principles could be implemented within current procedures. Chaired by a High Court judge and including representatives from environmental practitioners and non-governmental organizations, the resulting report[37] made a powerful case for improving procedures in judicial review cases, and extending the use of PCOs.

The second source of pressure was the enforcement procedures developed under the Convention itself. The Convention was, as with many international conventions, rather vague about compliance mechanisms but required parties to establish compliance arrangements that were of a 'non-confrontational, non-judicial, and consultative nature'.[38] The First Meeting of the Parties went on to establish a Compliance Committee with powers to hear complaints both from parties to the Convention and members of the public, described by one of the leading architects of the Convention as 'strong and unprecedented'.[39] In 2010 the Compliance Committee published draft findings in two cases from the UK which directly raised the compatibility of costs principles in judicial reviews with Art. 9(4) of the Convention, and in both found

[34] *R. (on the applications of Sonia Burkett)* v. *London Borough of Hammersmith and Fulham* [2004] EWCA Civ 1342 at [76], *per* Brooke LJ.

[35] *R. (on the application of England)* v. *Tower Hamlets* [2006] EWCA Civ 1742.

[36] *Morgan and another* v. *Hinton Organics (Wessex) Ltd. and others* [2009] EWCA Civ 107, 'The requirement of the Convention that costs should not be "prohibitively expensive" should be taken as applying to the total potential liability of claimants, including the threat of adverse costs orders', at [47], *per* Carnwath LJ.

[37] Working Party Group on Access to Environmental Justice (Chair Mr Justice Sullivan), *Ensuring Access to Environmental Justice in England and Wales* (2008). The Group issued a follow up report in 2010.

[38] Convention, Art. 15.

[39] J. Jendroska, 'Public Information and Participation in EC Environmental Law – Origins, Milestones and Trends', in R. Macrory (ed.), *Reflections on 30 Years of EU Environmental Law* (2006) 63, 72; V. Koester, 'Review of Compliance under the Aarhus Convention: a rather unique compliance mechanism' (2005) 2 *JEEPL* 31; V. Koester, 'The Compliance Committee of the Aarhus Convention – An Overview of Procedures and Jurisprudence' (2007) 37(2) *EPL* 83.

that British practice did not meet the requirements of costs not being prohibitively expensive.[40]

A finding by the Compliance Committee of a breach might well be politically embarrassing, but at the end of the day there are no formal sanctions available under the Convention. However, the final distinctive nature of the Art. 9 provisions was the fact that the European Community was party to the Convention and had implemented the provisions on access to justice by including the wording under amendments to two core environmental directives, the Directive on Environmental Assessment and the Directive on Integrated Pollution and Prevention Control.[41] Within the context of those Directives, the obligation that access to justice procedures are not prohibitively expensive is now one of EU law, bringing with it the implications of the distinctive enforcement procedures available to the European Commission, leading to potential action before the European Court of Justice and a financial sanction for failure to comply with its judgments. Already in relation to the Assessment Directive the European Commission commenced infringement procedures against the UK following a complaint from a coalition of environmental non-governmental organizations, and in 2010 issued a Reasoned Opinion, the last stage before action before the European Court of Justice.[42] In April 2011 the case was referred to the Court of Justice.[43]

It is difficult to see how this three-way pressure from the judiciary, the international convention, and the European Union will not lead to significant change, even at a time of restrictions on public expenditure. In its most recent decision on Aarhus,[44] the Court of Justice of the European Union has held that the Aarhus Convention now forms 'an integral part of the legal order of the European Union. As such it applies to all areas of environmental protection covered by EU environmental law, and in relation to access to justice, there was a duty on national courts 'to interpret, to the fullest extent possible, the procedural rules relating to the conditions to be met in order to bring

[40] Aarhus Compliance Committee Draft Findings ACCC/C/2008/27, and in particular ACCC/C/2008/33, para. 133: 'The Committee concludes that despite the various measures available to address prohibitive costs, taken together they do not ensure that the costs remain at a level which meets the requirements under the Convention. At this stage, the Committee considers that the considerable discretion of the courts of E&W in deciding the costs, without any clear legally binding direction from the legislature or judiciary to ensure costs are not prohibitively expensive, leads to considerable uncertainty regarding the costs to be faced where claimants are legitimately pursuing environmental concerns that involve the public interest'.

[41] Council Directive (EEC) 85/337 on the assessment of the effects of certain public and private projects on the environment [1985] OJ L175/40, and Council Directive (EC) 96/61/EC concerning integrated pollution prevention and control [1996] OJ L257/26 (now codified under Council Directive (EC) 2008/1 on integrated pollution prevention and control [2008] OJ L24/8.

[42] http://europa.eu/rapid/pressReleasesAction.do?reference=IP/10/312&type= en. European Environment Commissioner Janez Potonik said, 'When important decisions affecting the environment are taken, the public must be allowed to challenge them. This important principle is established in European law. But the law also requires that these challenges must be affordable. I urge the UK to address this problem quickly as ultimately the health and wellbeing of the public as a whole depends on these rights', Press Release, March 2010.

[43] European Commission press release 18/11/439, Brussels, 6 April 2011.

[44] *Lesoochranarske zoskupenie VLK* v. *Ministerstvo zivotneho prostredia Slovenskej republiky* (Case C-240/09 Court of Justice of the European Union, 8 March 2011).

administrative or judicial proceedings' in light with the objectives of the Convention. In the arguments concerning a specialist environmental court considered below one ground for resisting change was that it was inappropriate to make a special case for the environment compared with other fields of law. In the context of the Convention, the same argument has been made, but, because the legal obligation to implement within the environmental field is a reality, far from providing a ground for maintaining the *status quo*, it has had the reverse effect of creating pressure for change in all areas of judicial review. Both the difficulties of defining the boundaries of the Convention and the unfairness of confining its principles to one area of law have been acknowledged by the courts.[45] Jackson LJ's major review of Civil Litigation Costs published in 2010[46] recognized the significance of the Convention but similarly argued that any change in the costs principles should apply to all judicial reviews. He recommended a solution of 'qualified one way costs shifting' where essentially the defendant pays the claimant's costs if the claim is successful, but the claimant does not pay the defendant's costs if the claim is unsuccessful. Jackson was prepared to allow for exceptions giving considerable judicial discretion and taking in account financial resources of the parties and their conduct in connection with the proceedings. A follow up report of the Sullivan Working Party[47] welcomed the general thrust of the Jackson proposals but recommended a rule that involved less judicial discretion and uncertainty, 'An unsuccessful Claimant in a claim for judicial review shall not be ordered to pay the costs of any other party other than where the Claimant has acted unreasonably in bringing or conducting the proceedings'. The implication of the proposed shifts in approach is that the permission stage of judicial review will become more significant in weeding out unmeritorious claims rather than the potential exposure to costs acting as a surrogate filter to frivolous action. The fundamental reappraisal of costs principles in judicial review, initiated rather cautiously by the judiciary in *Corner House*, is now largely been driven by obligations and perspectives created within environmental law.

REFORMING REGULATORY SANCTIONS

Despite a long history of regulatory controls in the environmental field, the way in which they were actually enforced remained somewhat obscure until the early 1970s. Discretion and secrecy permeated the enforcement role of regulators, and specialized government agencies such as the Alkali Inspectorate regulating air emissions from key sectors of industry preferred a policy of gentle persuasion rather than aggressive legal

[45] *Compton* v. *Wiltshire Primary Care Trust* [2008] EWCA Civ 749 at [20]; *R. (Buglife – The Invertebrate Conservation Trust)* v. *Thurrock Thames Gateway Development Corporation* [2008] EWCA Civ 1209 at [17]; *Morgan* v. *Hinton Organics (Wessex) Ltd* [2009] EWCA Civ 107 at [33].

[46] www.judiciary.gov.uk/publications-and-reports/reports/civil/review-of-civil-litigation-costs.

[47] Working Group on Access to Justice (Chair Lord Justice Sullivan), *Ensuring Access to Environmental Justice in England and Wales – Follow Up Report* (2010).

action. Pressure from the new wave of non-governmental organizations in the 1970s began to shed light on how these bodies actually operated, and this was followed by a series of sophisticated socio-legal research studies designed to analyze how individual enforcement officers exercised their enforcement discretion in dealing with regulatory breaches.[48] Criminal law with offences mainly drafted in strict liability terms dominated the structure of environmental laws, but it was clear that whatever the strict letter of the law officers often exercised their own sense of judgement as to what constituted or did not constitute criminal behaviour before deciding whether to prosecute or not.

The creation of new national regulatory bodies in the 1990s such as the Environment Agency was motivated in part by the desire of industry in particular to see a more consistent approach to the implementation and enforcement of controls across the country. This desire for consistency was not confined to the setting of consents and licences but affected the strategy for enforcement as well, with the result that the Environment Agency became the first national regulatory body to publish a detailed Enforcement Policy setting out the core principles as to how it would respond to regulatory breaches and the circumstances in which it was likely to prosecute or not.

Nevertheless, the range of sanctions available to environmental regulators still remained fairly narrow – warning letters, a formal caution, or an actual prosecution. Many regulators possessed powers under different environmental laws to serve notices requiring the industry concerned to take the necessary steps to come back into compliance, but sanctions for breach of such notices remained equally narrow and in the last step were based on the criminal law. There was criticism both of the apparently small sentences, mostly fines, imposed by the lower criminal courts in dealing with environmental offences, and the opportunity that strict liability offences allowed lawyers to persuade lay magistrates to down-play the seriousness of offences[49] – a somewhat ironic development given that the strict liability offence had originally been developed in the nineteenth century expressly to make prosecution of industry and businesses simpler. This was coupled with critiques of the limited range of sanctions available and the heavy reliance on criminal law, especially compared with the practice in the field of environmental law in other jurisdictions such as Germany and Australia.[50]

In 2004 a report commissioned by the Department for Environment, Food and Rural Affairs[51] called for environmental regulators to be given the power to impose civil financial penalties as an additional form of sanction to criminal prosecution, and

[48] Examples include K. Hawkins, *Environment and Enforcement: Regulation and the Social Definition of Pollution* (1984); G. Richardson, A. Ogus and P. Burrows, *Policing Pollution: A Study of Regulation and Enforcement* (1982); B. M. Hutter, *The Reasonable Arm of the Law? The Law Enforcement Procedures of Environmental Health Officers* (1988).

[49] P. de Prez, 'Excuses, excuses: the ritual trivilization of environmental prosecutions' (2000) 12(1) *JEL* 65.

[50] J. Abbott, 'The Regulatory Enforcement of Pollution Control Laws: The Australian Experience' (2005) 17(2) *JEL* 161.

[51] M. Woods and R. Macrory, *Environmental Civil Penalties – A More Proportionate Response to Regulatory Breach* (2004).

most likely to be appropriate to the normally responsible operator who through carelessness or an oversight had caused a serious regulatory breach. Civil penalties of this sort were not unknown in British law and were extensively used in fields such a financial regulation and competition law, but would have been an innovation in more traditional areas of business regulation. Although well received, the report did not attract sufficient political support to justify change. Industry in particular was alarmed at the prospect of suddenly shifting from a familiar system of regulatory prosecution with criminal burdens of proof resting on the regulator to one where the regulator could impose large financial penalties on a civil standard of proof and by-pass the courts, leaving the burden on industry to raise any defence by appeal. Given that it was the more responsible end of industry which would most likely be at the receiving end of civil penalties with the criminal law reserved for the more egregious offenders, this seemed potentially doubly unfair. The report laid important groundwork but failed to address in sufficient detail these wider issues of regulatory governance which would be necessary to secure political purchase. More fundamentally, a convincing case had to made out for singling out the environment for special treatment compared to many other areas of regulation such as health and safety and trading standards that would appear to be susceptible to the same analysis.

The debate concerning environmental sanctions appeared to have ground to a halt, and the impetus for what would eventually prove the decisive shift came from a quite unexpected and unconnected government initiative. In 2004 the Treasury commissioned a wide-ranging review of the administrative burdens imposed on business by regulatory enforcement. The Hampton Review published in 2005[52] argued that too many regulators, especially at local government level, had adopted an excessively 'tick-box' mentality to enforcement, losing sight of the overall aims of regulation. Hampton called for a greater emphasis on a risk-based approach to regulatory enforcement, focusing resources on the clearly non-compliant, and adopting a more enlightened and cost-effective approach towards legitimate business. The Review acknowledged that that excessive reliance on the criminal law appeared inimical to a philosophy of a more nuanced relationship between regulators and the regulated, and recommended the government to initiate a special review of regulatory sanctions.

The subsequent Macrory Review on regulatory sanctions reported in 2006.[53] As with Hampton, the Review encompassed an enormous spectrum – some 61 national regulators as well as all local authorities, and covering areas such as health and safety, planning, trading standards, environment, and food standards. Despite very different sets of laws in such a disperse range of regulation, common patterns emerged, with the core formal sanction under nearly all areas being a criminal offence, usually drafted in strict or semi-strict terms. It was equally clear that there were very similar patterns of the range of non-compliant actors, whatever the field of regulation. At one end of the

[52] P. Hampton, *Reducing Administrative Burdens – Effective Inspection and Enforcement* (2005).

[53] R. Macrory, *Regulatory Justice: Making Sanctions Effective*, Final Report, Cabinet Office (2006).

spectrum, there were the truly egregious, individuals or companies who knew exactly what they were doing and were often making large sums of money out of breaking the law. At the other end were responsible businesses who through no intention committed a breach – an unexpected equipment breakdown, for example. The middle ground covered a range of different circumstances, involving carelessness or a failure to give sufficient priority to regulatory compliance but lacking direct intention or recklessness. British enforcement practice has never required the police or regulators to prosecute for every offence, and in many instances warnings or a more formal caution might be an effective response at least where responsible businesses were concerned. But even unintentional breaches might give rise to significant harm or the risk of such harm and in such circumstances a formal sanction would be appropriate and indeed expected by the public. But it was questionable whether the criminal law was appropriate and Macrory argued that the criminal law was in effect being made to do too much work within the regulatory system – indeed there was a danger that the criminal law itself was being devalued in the process.

The Macrory Review advocated six core penalty principles that should underline the design of any effective regulatory sanctions system. A sanction should: (i) aim to change the behaviour of the offender; (ii) aim to eliminate any financial gain or benefit from non-compliance; (iii) be responsive and consider what is appropriate for the particular offender and regulatory issue; (iv) be proportionate to the nature of the offence and the harm caused; (v) aim to reverse harm caused by regulatory compliance; and (vi) aim to deter future non-compliance.

The current system dominated by the criminal law was found wanting against these principles. The Review argued that regulators should have access to a much wider range of non-criminal sanctions including civil penalties, familiar in areas such as competition and economic regulation but far less common in other areas. Civil penalties allow a regulator to calculate and impose a financial sanction without the intervention of a court unless the offender decides to appeal.

For many these proposals could represent an unacceptable shift of discretionary powers to regulators and the Review addressed these issues in a rather more sophisticated way than in previous studies. First, regulators were to be given power to offer enforcement undertakings as an alternative to the imposition of a civil penalty. Here the business itself would in effect design its own self-imposed sanction which could then be accepted by the regulator. The Review was insistent that such undertakings were made available to the public to avoid the impression of secret deals between regulated and the regulated, but they offered an attractive form of sanction for the legitimate business that had made a one-off serious regulatory breach. Perhaps rather surprisingly there was very little evidence presented to the review that the criminal standard of proof presented a significant hurdle in detection and enforcement – the problem with the criminal law was more its inappropriateness for certain types of breaches, the slowness of procedures, and the frequent lack of knowledge amongst lay magistrates. The Review therefore recommended no change to the existing regulatory offences and that the same standard of proof – the criminal standard of beyond all reasonable doubt – should apply whether or nor a criminal or civil penalty was imposed. In practice regulators would continue to investigate to criminal standards and with all the procedural protections of the criminal law, and only then, assuming that a case could be proved and that a formal sanction necessary, determine whether a criminal or civil response was appropriate. This approach was intended to avoid problems that have plagued many other regulatory systems where there can be lack of coordination between different bodies responsible for criminal and civil investigation, or where a civil response may be considered to be reserved for weaker cases. In pure legal terms, this aspect of the proposed design was probably the most innovative element of the Review and offers the prospect of a truly integrated sanctions system not found in other jurisdictions. Finally, the Review contained recommendations designed to diminish the opportunities of abuse by regulators. These principles – termed 'characteristics' in the Review – provide something of a constitutional bedrock in the design of regulatory systems. Regulators who acquired the powers would be legally obliged to publish enforcement policies spelling out the circumstances in which they were likely to impose different sorts of sanction,[54] as well as guidance on how they proposed to calculate civil penalties. Regulators should regularly make public reports on both outputs (the number of enforcement actions taken and so on) and outcomes (the extent to which key policy goals are being secured). Internal practices and procedures that might inadvertently distort the choice of sanction route should be avoided, and in particular the regulator should never receive directly any income from civil penalties – the Review was well aware that the perception whether justified or not that regulators were financially interested in the enforcement of regulatory requirements had undermined public credibility in areas of regulation such as traffic parking or speeding.

Many of the arguments concerning the limitations of wholesale reliance on the criminal law as a regulatory sanction had already been rehearsed in the environmental field, but by looking at regulatory sanctions across such a wide spectrum, the Review did not have to make any special pleading for any particular field of law. Instead, it was able to articulate common principles that should be adopted in all areas, and largely as a result, all the recommendations in the Review were accepted by the government. Regulatory Enforcement and Sanctions Act 2008, Pt III provided the framework for the core powers concerning civil sanctions as well as the recommendations on regulatory governance. The Review did not advocate that all regulators should be obliged to acquire the new powers – it would be up to ministers to draw them down by regulations – and in 2010 two national regulators, the Environment Agency and Natural England were the first to acquire the new powers.[55] Since then the Environment Agency has published its proposed guidance on how to calculate civil penalties, and a revised enforcement policy incorporating the new powers with the first civil penalties are likely to be imposed in 2011.

[54] At the time of the Review, some regulator bodies including the Environment Agency, already published an enforcement policy, but only 17 out of 60 national regulators had a policy that was publicly available: Macrory, ibid., paras 5.7–5.17.

[55] The Environmental Civil Sanctions (England) Order 2010 (SI 2010/1157), and the Environmental Sanctions (Misc. Amendments) (England) Regulations 2010 (SI 2010/1159). Similar regulations have been made for Wales.

Other regulators have expressed interest but it is clear that it is in the environmental field that the first serious experience of the new regime will be tested and evaluated. It is too early to predict the real impact of these reforms but a significant shift in thinking about the design of regulatory sanctions in the UK has begun to take place. Regulators and their departmental sponsors are more than ever conscious of financial pressures on public resources, and a critical element in the eventual success of the reforms in likely to be their impact on cost-savings. The new system deliberately does not lighten the costs of investigation by regulatory bodies, but where a civil penalty is proposed it should make it simpler or faster to resolve the issue without the need for the involvement of a court or tribunal. But it is possible to envisage in practice regulators becoming over confident or ambitious in applying proposed civil sanctions, followed by protracted negotiations and arguments between regulators and the regulated, coupled with an extensive number of appeals. If that were to happen, regulators and their ministers might conclude that in pure economic terms the traditional criminal enforcement system was preferable, and the system would revert back to its familiar pattern of relying on the criminal law.[56]

This scenario is possible but unlikely, not least because the sanctions review has now set in train a substantial review of the use of criminal law in the regulatory system. The Review itself did not advocate the abandonment of criminal law, and made important recommendations concerning the improvement of the current system, including giving criminal judges a wider range of sanctions where a case had been proved. These include publicity orders, corporate rehabilitation orders, and orders that could speedily remove a financial gain made from non-compliance with regulatory requirements. Yet the Review also questioned the continued reliance on offences drafted in strict liability terms allowing companies to be held vicariously liable for acts they knew nothing of or had even prohibited.[57] It fell shy of making blanket recommendations concerning the future structure of the criminal law but recommended that the government initiated a review of the drafting and formulation of criminal offences relating the regulatory non-compliance. As a result, the Law Commission launched a study on the subject, and published an initial consultation paper in 2010.[58]

[56] There are also concerns within the Coalition Government as to whether regulators rather than the courts should have the power to impose financial sanctions: *Civil sanctions regime is 'intolerable' says Minister*, ENDS Report 7 April 2011.

[57] The combination of strict and vicarious liability was described by Glanville Williams as a 'tyrannous combination' and quoted by Simon Brown LJ in *National Rivers Authority* v. *Alfred McAlpine Homes East Ltd* [1994] 4 All ER 286.

[58] The Law Commission, *Criminal Liability in Regulatory Contexts*, Consultation Paper No. 195 (2010).

AN ENVIRONMENTAL COURT

Legal cases involving environmental issues have in the UK long been heard in the ordinary courts appropriate for the type of action brought. Environmental judicial reviews are handled by the Administrative Court, though clearly with some degree of specialization developing amongst the judges who are assigned particular cases. Similarly, the prosecution for criminal offences concerning the environment has taken place before the ordinary criminal courts, with private civil actions such as nuisance or negligence arising from pollution handled by the civil courts. But for over 20 years in the UK there has been intense debate on a possible role of a specialized environmental court or tribunal, though often the arguments have been dogged by very different visions of what the concept might entail in practice.

The first official recommendation for an environmental court appears to have been contained in a report by Sir Robert Carnwath, then a leading planning barrister and now a judge in the Court of Appeal and the Senior President of the new Tribunal System. The report was largely concerned with strengthening the enforcement mechanisms within the existing town and country planning system[59] but he made a cautious case for combining the jurisdictions of various courts and tribunals dealing with planning and environmental protection into a single judicial forum. Three years later, the then Lord Chief Justice, Lord Woolf, provided a broader vision.[60] He argued that a distinctive feature of environmental law was the possibility of a single pollution incident giving rise to many different types of legal action heard in different legal fora – a coroner's inquest (if deaths involved), criminal prosecution where regulatory offences had been committed, civil actions for compensation, and judicial review if public authorities are involved. He felt there was a strong case for a single environmental court which would handle all the legal consequences that arose from an environmental incident or problem. Lord Woolf's vision was for a body which was not just a court or existing tribunal under another name, but something quite radically different:

> It is a multi-faceted, multi-skilled body which would combine the services provided by the existing courts, tribunals, and inspectors in the environmental field. It would be a 'one-stop shop' which should lead to faster, cheaper, and more effective resolution of disputes in the environmental area.[61]

Largely as a result of Lord Woolf's lecture, the then Department of Environment and Transport and the Regions commissioned a major study examining the experience of specialized environmental courts in other jurisdictions, and considering possible models that could be adopted in the UK. The Grant report[62] considered six different

[59] R. Carnwath, *Enforcing Planning Control* (1989).

[60] H. Woolf, 'Are the Judiciary Environmental Myopic?' (1992) 4(1) *JEL* 1.

[61] Ibid., p. 14.

[62] M. Grant, *Environmental Court Project: Final Report* (2000). S. Tromans, 'Environmental Court Project' (2001) 13(3) *JEL* 423.

forms of court or tribunal that might be adopted, but in essence there were two main routes that could be followed – the so-called 'big bang' approach involving the creation of a major new environmental court probably as a division of the High Court, or strengthening existing judicial and quasi-judicial institutions from the bottom up to develop greater expertise in environmental law. The political appetite for institutional change was, however, not present at the time.[63]

Two years later, following a recommendation of the Royal Commission on Environmental Pollution,[64] the Department for Environment, Food and Rural Affairs commissioned a further study on the subject but one with a narrower focus. The Report[65] examined over 50 sets of environmental regulations to determine the extent to which they contained statutory rights of appeal and where these appeals were heard. The town and country planning system contained a well-established appeal system for developers with appeals heard by an executive agency of government, the Planning Inspectorate. Compared to this, the system for environmental appeals was far more muddled with a wide range of different bodies involved – the Secretary of State, the High Court, magistrates' courts and the Planning Inspectorate amongst others. The lack of coherence appeared to simply a matter of historical accident rather than a conscious decision by policy makers, and the Report recommended that an environmental tribunal be established to act as a single statutory appeals body.

But there were two particular challenges to the proposal. As with the initial debates on the use of civil penalties in environmental enforcement, the question that had to be addressed was whether the environment deserved special treatment. The report argued that there were a number of features that did indeed distinguish environmental law from many other legal fields – the extent to which technical and scientific questions were frequently intertwined with legal issues, the prevalence of EU environmental legislation, the emergence of core underlying legal principles such as the precautionary principle, the heavy involvement of public bodies exercising considerable discretion, the growing significance of international environmental treaties, and the developing concept of sustainable development as an underlying policy goal. Many of these features are to found individually in other areas of law such as workplace safety but it was the combination of all which appeared to place environmental law in a distinctive position and required a more specialized judicial approach. But not all found this argument convincing. The Scottish government, for example, rejected the argument:

> We acknowledge the special characteristics listed by Macrory and Woods and accept that they are features of environmental law. However, we are not persuaded that these features, or indeed this combination of features is unique to environmental law and it could be argued that similar

[63] Lord Brennan initiated a debate on the subject in the House of Lords. According to Lord Bach, the Minister, 'The Government welcome the opportunity to debate this issue. We are not persuaded of the need for an environmental court, certainly not on its possible shape', *Hansard*, HL, col. 100 (9 October 2000).

[64] Royal Commission on Environmental Pollution, *Environmental Planning*, Cm. 5459 (2002) para. 5.37.

[65] R. Macrory and M. Woods, *Modernizing Environmental Justice – Regulation and the Role of an Environmental Tribunal* (2003).

> statements could be made equally about other areas of law such as health, health & safety and employment none of which have specialist courts/jurisdiction.[66]

The second challenge related to the proposal's rather modest vision of an environmental tribunal. This may have been workable but at the time did not align with the approach being promoted by environmental non-governmental organizations and lawyers in a study also funded by the Department for Environment, Food and Rural Affairs. The Environmental Justice report[67] was particularly concerned with the costs and risk of exposure to costs involved in environmental litigation, and argued that a far more radical approach was needed in the form of a new division of the High Court with the power to hear all civil law claims with a significant environmental component. Faced with the environmental law community itself advocating very different models of a specialist environmental court or tribunal, it was a hardly surprisingly that the government felt unable to act, and the debate appeared to have ground to a halt.

This proved to be an over-pessimistic presumption. Two years later the Review of Regulatory Sanctions[68] had to consider the question of appeals against the imposition of the civil sanctions it was recommending. Under European Convention on Human Rights, Art. 6, there would in any event have to be a right of appeal to an independent court or tribunal, and even if this had not been the case, the Review would have recommended such a right as a matter of fairness and a check against regulatory abuse. Appeals could have gone back to the ordinary courts, but the Review took advantage of the fact that a new, more flexible tribunal system was being created,[69] and recommended that appeals against civil sanctions should go to a new regulatory tribunal. Once the regulator had decided that a civil sanction was the appropriate route, then all procedures should remain within the administrative system rather than become possibly confused by being heard within criminal courts. The government accepted the recommendation and the Regulatory Enforcement and Sanctions Act 2008 provided that appeals should go to the First-tier Tribunal, the first level of tribunals established under the new system,[70] unless a more specialized and appropriate tribunal already existed.

As discussed above, it is the national environmental regulators who in practice have been the first bodies to acquire the new civil sanction powers, and the Order provided for appeals to go to a Tribunal. The new tribunal system had divided the First-tier level into a number of chambers, grouping together jurisdictions dealing with similar work or requiring similar skills, and was decided that sanctions appeals best fell within the

[66] Environment and Rural Affairs Department, Scottish Government, *Strengthening and Streamlining: The Way Forward for the Enforcement of Environmental Law in Scotland* (2006) para. 2.99.

[67] Environmental Law Foundation, World Wildlife Fund and Leigh Day and Co *Environmental Justice* (2004).

[68] Macrory, above, n. 53.

[69] The system of tribunals was reformed under Tribunals, Court and Enforcement Act 2007 following the major review by Sir Andrew Leggatt, *Report of the Review of Tribunals: Tribunals for Users – One System One Service* (2001), available at www.tribunals-review.org.uk.

[70] Appeals go to the Upper Tribunal.

General Regulatory Chamber. Since the first appeals would fall within the field of environmental regulation, in April 2010 an internal administrative decision was taken to establish an environmental tribunal within the Regulatory Chamber. With remarkably little fanfare or fuss, England and Wales gained a specialist environmental judicial body after almost 20 years of debate. Admittedly, its jurisdiction is extremely limited compared to earlier visions of an environmental court or tribunal but the important institutional step had been taken, and in future its remit may well be extended to encompass a wider environmental remit.[71] From one perspective the creation of the environmental tribunal at this point was purely a matter of chance – if regulators in other fields had been the first movers to acquire civil sanctions the story might have been very different. Yet the initial focus on the environment was not wholly surprising. It was in the environmental field that the most substantial intellectual case for civil sanctions had been made for a number of years prior to the Regulatory Enforcement and Sanctions Act 2008, and it was in the same field of law that the arguments for a new specialist form of court or tribunal had already been extensively rehearsed. It remains to be seen what longer-term impact the presence of a specialist tribunal will make to the development of environmental law in this country but it is likely to be considerable.

THE FUTURE

Disputes involving environmental law issues often display inherent characteristics that in any event do not lend themselves to easy resolution by conventional legal institutional arrangements, and this has provided some of the impetus for innovation. Lord Woolf has noted how environmental litigation tends to display an unusual combination of technical and scientific complexities, challenging policy issues, and issues that cut across traditional divides between criminal and civil law, and public and private interests.[72] In addition, the fusion of environmental obligations developed under European Union environmental law and international public environmental law has now added a distinctive and powerful pressure to the national discourse, making it difficult for government to stone-wall legal and policy change. But perhaps more significantly the search for new legal ways of doing things reflects an unease with the capability of more traditional legal and regulatory techniques in contemporary environmental challenges. The British environmentalist Tom Burke has spoken of an 'old' and a 'new' environmental agenda.[73] The older agenda encompassed such subjects as water pollution and waste disposal where the problem was generally well understood, the science of cause and effect reasonably settled, and the policy maker is usually faced with situations where nearly all those affected by

[71] In 2010 Lord Justice Carnwath in his capacity as Senior President of Tribunals commissioned a study to re-examine the issue of consolidating administrative appeal, under enviromental regulations. The final report, R. Macrory, *Consistency and Effectiveness – Strengthening the New Environmental Tribunal* (2011) argued that most environmental appeals should now go to the First-tier Tribunal (Environment).

[72] Lord Woolf, 'Environmental Law and Sustainable Development', in H. Woolf, *The Pursuit of Justice* (2008) 391.

[73] R. Macrory, 'Maturity and Methodology – A Personal Reflection' (2009) 21(2) *JEL* 251, 254.

policy change will gain – the public will generally welcome tighter environmental controls, but equally legitimate industry will often support regulation in that it drives out the sub-standard. Legal techniques that are likely to be effective are often well established, and while there will always be problems in enforcement and implementation, the basic legal tool-kit is not called into question. The newer environmental agenda concerns issues such as transport, climate change, resource use and biodiversity, where the underlying knowledge and science may be far less certain, and the policy solutions by no means bring about immediate win–win situations. It is far less clear what sort of legal techniques are appropriate, or indeed what role law may play in their resolution. In this light it is hardly surprising that in recent years much of environmental legal development has shifted from prescribing clearly defined solutions to providing more open-ended approaches where the law provides a combination of legal rights and opportunities for more extensive citizen engagement and obligations and procedures designed to make the state more accountable for what it does. One test of an effective constitutional and legal system is its ability to handle and accommodate competing visions, and to adapt to new perceptions and understandings. From this perspective, environmental law has proved remarkably creative over the past quarter of a century and provided a laboratory and impetus for deeper changes in our legal and constitutional system.

FURTHER READING

MACRORY, R. and MAURICI, J., 'Rethinking regulatory sanctions – Regulatory Enforcement and Sanctions Act 2008 – an exchange of letters' (2009) 21(4) *Environmental Law and Management* 183–6.

MACRORY, R. and WOOD, M., *Modernizing Environmental Justice: Regulation and the Role of an Environmental Tribunal* (2003), reprinted in Macrory, R., *Regulation, Enforcement and Governance in Environmental Law* (2010).

Regulatory Justice: Making Sanctions Effective (Final Report of the Macrory Review on Regulatory Sanctions), reprinted in Macrory, R., *Regulation, Enforcement and Governance in Environmental Law* (2010).

WOOLF, H, 'Are the Judiciary Environmentally Myopic?' (1992) 4 *Journal of Environmental Law* 1–14.

USEFUL WEBSITES

Department for Business, Innvoation and Skills: **www.bis.gov.uk/policies/better-regulation/reviewing-regulation/improving-compliance-among-businesses**

Environment Agency: **www.environment-agency.gov.uk/business/regulation/default.aspx, especially under 'Business and industry'**

European Commission, Environment Directorate-General: **http://ec.europa.eu/environment/index_en.htm**

Tribunals Service, First-tier Tribunal (Environment): **www.tribunals.gov.uk/environment**

United Nations Economic Commission for Europe, Aarhus Convention on Access to Information, Public Participation in Decision-making and Access to Justice in Environmental Matters: **www.unece.org/env/pp**

12

REGULATION AND LEGITIMACY

Tony Prosser

SUMMARY

Although governments have to a large degree withdrawn from ownership of the economy, debate over public regulation has increased in recent years. This chapter examines the institutions and techniques used, including regulation of the public utilities such as telecommunications, energy, water, and rail but also referring to broader areas of regulation including healthcare and health and safety. It is suggested that regulation has a number of rationales, notably control of natural monopoly, creating and policing competitive markets, protecting basic rights, and promoting social solidarity through the provision of universal service. The arrangements adopted for regulating the public utilities after privatization have improved, especially as a result of reforms introduced since 2000, though the regulators' work has proved much more complex than originally thought. Other regulators have also engaged in procedural innovation. The means available for challenging regulatory decisions remain inconsistent and untidy, although the existence of the Competition Appeal Tribunal permits detailed scrutiny of competition decisions. There may also be a greater concern with matters of legal principle in regulation as a result of European developments.

INTRODUCTION

There is a widely accepted view that the 1980s and 1990s were the epoch of a withdrawal of the state in favour of the marketplace. Yet, paradoxically, there is also a perception that regulation has grown enormously during this period, so much that some writers now consider us to live in a 'regulatory state'.[1] Regulation is far more visible than in earlier times, its extent inspires considerable public debate, and

[1] See e.g. G. Majone, 'The Rise of the Regulatory State in Europe' (1994) 17 *West European Politics* 77–101; M. Moran, *The British Regulatory State: High Modernism and Hyper-Innovation* (2003).

regulatory authorities themselves have a much higher profile than when government took a greater role in delivering services. Regulation is central to economic life, for example through the role of competition law and the regulation of the public utilities of telecommunications, energy, water supply, and rail transport, and also in relation to social provision, both public and private, notably in the health and education sectors. The paradox is, however, apparent rather than real. Even where government has withdrawn from direct provision of services, markets cannot be seen simply as the products of non-intervention, for they must be actively created and policed by public authorities. A vivid illustration of this has been the financial crisis of 2008–09 which has been attributed to inadequate regulation and the failures of unregulated markets, though so far a clear vision of how such regulation might be improved has not appeared. Even where public provision retains a role, there has been a marked stress on consumer empowerment through setting standards and inspecting performance against them, and in many areas regulators still take decisions on social principles rather than facilitating markets. These roles all raise constitutional issues of the legitimacy of regulatory decisions, issues that have only recently been fully addressed in British constitutional scholarship, and which are central to this chapter.

I shall adopt an institutional approach, examining some of the key institutional forms used by public actors to replace, shape, or intervene in markets or to develop regulation based on non-market principles. This will mean the neglect of many important areas; in particular the crucial one of 'self-regulation' will not be considered.[2] Nor will it be possible to consider in detail the institutions implementing general competition policy, nor the work of advisory bodies. I hope that there will be compensation for this loss of scope through the advantages of a focus on institutional issues; after all, institutional design is one of the key concerns of constitutional lawyers.

RATIONALES FOR REGULATION

There are several different rationales for regulation; these in themselves raise constitutional issues relating to the balancing of different principles and to the best institutional arrangement for resolving conflicts between them. Some rationales for regulation are based on economic principle. The first of these seeks to prevent the profit maximization of natural monopolies from distorting the efficient distribution of goods; the second seeks to resolve the problems which arise when markets operate freely, such as so-called 'externalities' which occur when the unregulated price of a good does not fully reflect its true cost to society (for example, the cost of pollution caused in

[2] For good discussions of the complexity of self-regulation, see I. Ayres and J. Braithwaite, *Responsive Regulation* (1992); J. Black, 'Constitutionalizing Self-Regulation' (1996) 59 *MLR* 24, and 'Decentring Regulation: Understanding the Role of Regulation and Self Regulation in a "Post-Regulatory" World' (2001) 54 *Current Legal Problems* 103.

its manufacture).[3] A further rationale is that of regulating for competition, where the regulator does not limit the operation of markets but develops and encourages them. This may take the form of encouraging the creation of competitive markets in previously monopolistic areas; a notable example is that of energy supply. Just as important is the policing of markets after they have come into existence. This is of course primarily a task for general competition law, implemented both by the general competition authorities and by the sectoral utility regulators. It will also include the protection of consumers, now an essential task for the regulators of the public utilities and also of great importance in financial services regulation. In addition to the economic rationales, there is a quite different tradition of what is rather unhelpfully dubbed 'public interest regulation' based upon more general social or distributive principles. Thus some types of regulation, such as that of broadcasting, may be based on the protection of citizenship rights, for example to balanced news coverage; the protection of rights of patients including informed consent and quality of provision characterizes regulation in health and social care, and some regulation can be seen as promoting social solidarity, for example in providing universal access to services and contributing to sustainable development.[4]

Some of the most important regulatory innovations of recent years have been the arrangements adopted for the privatized utilities, notably telecommunications, gas and electricity, water, and railways. In the very limited official discussion available the original rationale seems to have been conceived as primarily economic, concentrating on the control of monopoly.[5] However, if one examines the legal sources for the regulators' powers, the privatization statutes, and the licences of the utilities in question, one finds that in every case a predominantly economic rationale limited to requiring regulators to maximize economic efficiency seemed to play only a secondary role and broader public interest considerations loomed large, for example ensuring that services were made available to meet all reasonable demands, including potentially unprofitable services, and that special consideration was given to the needs of vulnerable groups such as pensioners and the disabled.[6]

As mentioned above, regulation for competition has also played an increasing role, and primary duties to promote competition or to secure effective competition were included in later statutes relating to electricity and gas.[7] The Utilities Act 2000

[3] See e.g. S. Breyer, *Regulation and its Reform* (1982) 15–35; C. Foster, *Privatization, Public Ownership and the Regulation of Natural Monopoly* (1992), esp. ch. 9; A. Ogus, *Regulation* (1994) Pt I, and R. Baldwin and M. Cave, *Understanding Regulation* (1999) Pt I.

[4] See e.g. the citizenship duty applying to the Office of Communications in Communications Act 2003, s. 3(1)(a); see also T. Prosser, 'Regulation and Social Solidarity' (2006) *J. of Law and Society* 364.

[5] See the two official Littlechild reports: S. Littlechild, *Regulation of British Telecommunications' Profitability* (1984), and *Economic Regulation of Privatised Water Authorities* (1986).

[6] For further details, see T. Prosser, *Law and the Regulators* (1997) 15–24, and e.g. Telecommunications Act 1984, s. 3(1)(a). See also *R. (T-Mobile (UK) Ltd, Vodafone Ltd, Orange Personal Communication Services Ltd)* v. *The Competition Commission and the Director General of Telecommunications* [2003] EWHC 1566 (QBD).

[7] Electricity Act 1989, s. 3(1)(c); Gas Act 1995, s. 1, inserting a new s. 4(1)(c) into the Gas Act 1986.

was intended to replace the untidy mix of duties on the regulators by a new single competition-based primary duty, although it was at first only applied to the energy regulator. The new primary duty was to protect the interests of consumers, wherever possible by promoting effective competition; subsidiary duties in respect of the elderly, disabled, and chronically sick were also included, and the Secretary of State was given new powers to issue guidance on social and environmental objectives to which regulators will be required to have regard.[8] Similar provision is made for the water regulator in the Water Act 2003, and the Communications Act 2003 recasts the duties for regulation of telecommunications and broadcasting, including to further the interests of both consumers and citizens.[9] In the energy field, the regulator must have regard to the need to contributed to sustainable development, and recently the protection of consumers has been redefined to include reduction of carbon emissions and security of supply; the regulator must also consider whether means other than competition will best protect the interests of consumers.[10] Thus even in an area where economic regulation apparently predominates, there is in fact a mix of regulatory rationales, including social ones, making it particularly important to secure legitimacy for the resolution of conflicts between the different principles involved. In other areas, such as healthcare regulation, social rationales will clearly predominate. This means that institutional design is of considerable constitutional importance.

REGULATORY INSTITUTIONS

THE UTILITY REGULATORS

After the privatizations of the 1980s and 1990s, new regulatory agencies were established in relation to the public utility industries which seemed unlikely to operate in fully competitive markets; although they were by no means the first of the major UK regulatory bodies, they provide a useful introduction to the issues raised by regulatory institutions in general. The specialist agencies were the Office of Telecommunications (Oftel), the Office of Gas Supply (Ofgas), the Office of Electricity Regulation (Offer) (these latter two were later merged into the Office of Gas and Electricity Markets or Ofgem), the Office of Water Services (Ofwat), and the Office of the Rail Regulator (ORR). Each agency was headed by a director-general in whom the powers were vested personally; in this one sees a reflection of the highly personal style of UK government through ministers, and it was a key influence on the way in which these regulators operated in their early years. However, the agencies were deliberately distanced from ministerial responsibility through the adoption of the status of 'non-ministerial government department', a notion which seems curious given the centrality of ministerial responsibility in the UK constitution, but does seek to prevent accusations of political

[8] Utilities Act 2000, ss. 9, 10, 13 and 14.

[9] Communications Act 2003, s. 3(1).

[10] Energy Act 2008 s. 83; Energy Act 2010, ss. 16–17.

interference which could discredit the achievement of privatization. Most agency staff were seconded from the ordinary civil service for periods of about three years.

These arrangements underwent a process of reform, commencing with the Utilities Act 2000.[11] This established a new regulatory commission for the energy sector in the form of the Gas and Electricity Markets Authority.[12] A commission model was adopted also for postal services, and the telecommunications and broadcasting legislation created Ofcom in a commission form.[13] Provision was made to convert the Office of the Rail Regulator into a commission in the Railways and Transport Safety Act 2003, and the Water Act 2003 did the same for Ofwat. The commission model for regulation has now convincingly won in comparison to the older model of giving powers to an individual director-general. More recently, all the utility regulators have adopted a private-sector model of a board including executive and non-executive members; for example, the board of Ofgem consists of a chairman and four executive members, together with seven non-executive members

A further important change is that this model of regulation has been extended to some of the few enterprises which remain in public ownership. The most important example is that of the Post Office. Under the Postal Services Act 2000, its status was changed to that of a public limited company wholly owned by government. It is however regulated by an independent commission, the Postal Services Commission (Postcomm) which has responsibilities for price control, competition issues, and for ensuring the provision of a level of universal service defined by statute. In part this reform is due to European liberalization of postal services which requires, for example, definition of universal service and separation of regulation from operation.[14] However, it also reflects the use of independent regulation for privatized enterprises, as do the arrangements adopted for regulation of the publicly owned Scottish water industry under the Water Industry Act 1999 by the Water Industry Commission for Scotland.[15] Postcomm is now to be merged with Ofcom, reflecting changes in the market and also the coalition government's policy of reducing the number of arm's length bodies.

Finally, the effects of European liberalization have not been confined to postal services. Telecommunications regulation is now based on the 2002 regulatory package of directives, and part of the requirements of the directives is that national regulatory authorities be established independent of those providing electronic communications services; this does not necessarily prevent regulation by a government department,

[11] The background is the Labour government's review of utility regulation: Department of Trade and Industry, *A Fair Deal for Consumers: Modernising the Framework for Utility Regulation*, Cm. 3898 (1998), and *A Fair Deal for Consumers: The Response to Consultation* (1998).

[12] See Pt I and Sched. 1.

[13] Communications Act 2003, s. 1.

[14] See the Postal Services Directive (EC) 97/67 [1998] OJ L15/14; and the amending Council Directive (EC) 2002/39/ [2002] OJ L176/21.

[15] Water Industry Act 1999, ss 12–13 and Sched. 2; see also now Water Industry (Scotland) Act 2002, Pt I, the Water Services etc. (Scotland) Act 2005, and T. Prosser, 'Regulating Public Enterprises' [2001] *Public Law* 505, 514–20.

but if the government retains a presence in providing services there must be effective structural separation of the regulator from this.[16] The role of independent regulation is regularly supervised at a European level.[17] Similar provisions apply in the energy sector and have recently been strengthened to require greater regulatory independence.[18] Because of these developments, co-operation between the various regulatory authorities in Europe has become increasingly important, and it is these EC law requirements which are the most important for the spread of independent regulatory authorities beyond the UK, and for ensuring their guaranteed future.

It has always been the case that the government had the key role in shaping the environment in which the privatized enterprises operate. Ministers are responsible for important matters of general policy (for example, the broad mix of different sources of electricity generation). Apart from the fact that ministers appoint the regulators, it was ministers who initially possessed the major powers of deciding on the degree of competition which the enterprises would meet, through issuing licences (called authorizations in the case of gas and appointments in the case of water companies) necessary for the enterprises to do business; it was the conditions of these licences that determined the fundamental constraints in which the enterprises operate. The regulatory agencies were given the function of enforcing these conditions together with a number of other tasks, which include drawing up service standards (for example, relating to failure to maintain electricity supply or to meet agreed appointments with consumers) and monitoring performance by the utilities against them.[19]

This apparent division of labour was however made less neat by the fact that the regulatory agencies have functions relating to the modification of the licences, normally by agreement with the enterprise itself but, if this cannot be obtained, through a reference to the Competition Commission (formerly the Monopolies and Mergers Commission). The agencies thus have a role in setting the basic rules of the game as well as monitoring their implementation, and it is this which has probably aroused the greatest controversy. In addition, government continues to possess important residual powers, especially in the case of electricity where, for example, the minister was given a power of veto over licence modifications.[20] In gas and electricity, however, the power

[16] Council Directive (EC) 2002/21 on a common regulatory framework for electronic communications networks and services [2002] OJ L108/33, art. 3(2). See also now Council Directive (EC) 2009/140 amending Council Directive (EC) 2002/21 [2009] OJ L337/37.

[17] See e.g. Commission of the European Communities, *Progress Report on the Single European Electronic Communications Market (15th Report)*, COM(2010) 253.

[18] Council Directive (EC) 2009/72 concerning common rules for the internal market in electricity, [2009] OJ L211/55, art. 35(4); Council Directive (EC) 2009/73 concerning common rules for the internal market in natural gas [2009] OJ L211/94, art. 39(4).

[19] See the Competition and Service (Utilities) Act 1992.

[20] Electricity Act 1989, ss 11(4) and 12(5); a similar veto power was added for gas by the Gas Act 1995, Sched. 3 inserting new ss 23(5) and 24(4A) into the Gas Act 1986. For the ability of a minister to require licence modification in the special case of the use of a regulation under different statutory powers, see *Mercury Personal Communications* v. *Secretary of State for the Department of Trade and Industry* [2000] UK CLR 143.

to issue licences has been given to the regulators rather than the minister and in the case of telecommunications EC law has severely limited discretion in the licensing process through providing a general entitlement to provide electronic communications services without the need for individual licences but subject to general conditions drawn up by Ofcom.[21]

The powers of the regulators to modify licence conditions have been extremely important as these powers have enabled regulators to amend the basic rules under which regulated enterprises operate. For example, regulators periodically set new price controls that limit the amounts regulated enterprises can charge for important services. Thus, for example in the case of British Telecom, the initial control from 1984 was of RPI-3 which meant that controlled prices could rise by a figure three per cent below the rise in the retail price index measuring the prices of a range of products. This was subject to threats of tightening at least three times during the first five years; in 1989 it was amended to RPI-4.5 and extended to a broader range of services. Further revisions took place in 1991, 1993, 1997 and 2002; retail price control was finally abolished in 2006, although wholesale controls on prices charged to competitors remain. Licence conditions have also been used to require enterprises to trade fairly, and to meet social objectives such as avoiding disconnection of supply. Where such a licence modification is proposed by a regulator, the enterprise may choose to accept it or, if it refuses, the regulator may then refer the proposal to the Competition Commission which issues a report on the basis of which a licence modification may be imposed on the enterprise.

The duty to protect the interests of consumers is an important requirement for all the public utility regulators (except in rail, where this is primarily the responsibility of the Department for Transport), although the combination of roles as consumer champion and impartial arbiter between consumer and other interests is a potentially very difficult one. Part of the Labour government's early reforms was to create new, independent consumer bodies in energy, posts and water.[22] In communications, Ofcom is also obliged to establish a Consumer Panel.[23] However, the move to independent, sector-specific consumer representation was later reversed after considerable tension and adversarial relations between consumer bodies and the regulators, culminating in a judicial review claim brought by the consumer body in postal services against the regulator.[24] The specialist bodies in energy and posts were replaced with ombudsman schemes; consumer representation passed to the new general body Consumer Focus, which undertook a detailed review of the operation of the utility and other

[21] Gas Act 1995, s. 5; Utilities Act 2000, s. 30; Communications Act 2003, Pt 2, and Council Directive (EC) 2001/22 [2002] OJ L249/21.

[22] See Utilities Act 2000, s. 2 and Sched. 2; Postal Services Act 2000, s. 2 and Sched. 2, and Water Act 2003, s. 35 and Sched. 2. The new bodies adopted the titles Energy Watch, Postwatch, and CC Water.

[23] Communications Act 2003, s. 16.

[24] *R. (on the application of the Consumer Council for Postal Services)* v. *Postal Services Commission* [2007] EWCA Civ 167.

regulators.[25] However, Consumer Focus is itself to be abolished as part of the review of arm's length bodies, with its functions passing to Citizen's Advice Bureaux.

The key points about the regulatory institutions are thus that, while strongly distanced from governmental intervention in their ordinary operation, they work within a framework created by governmental decisions at the time of privatization, they have responsibilities determined by the privatization of particular industries rather than by a coherent sectoral approach (except in the case of electronic communications where the initiative has come from Brussels), and the original structure of individual directors-general reflected the personalized model characteristic of British government without as yet a clear procedural code. Nevertheless, we have seen some gradual moves towards a more coherent and consistent model since 2000, with the adoption of the commission model as standard and some clarification of the regulators' statutory duties, although uncertainty remains on the most appropriate means of consumer representation.

OTHER REGULATORY BODIES

The importance of the regulators of the public utilities in providing a regulatory model should not obscure the fact that there are many other types of regulation in the UK, some of which are date back further than the 1980s.[26] They exhibit a wide variety of institutional forms and functions. Some share the concern of the utility regulators with consumer protection; an important example was that of the Financial Services Authority, established under the Financial Services and Markets Act 2000 in the form of a private company limited by guarantee. This was given four regulatory objectives of market confidence, public awareness, the protection of consumers, and the reduction of financial crime, each defined more fully in subsequent sections of the statute.[27] Perhaps reflecting the inherently controversial natures of its decisions and the litigious nature of the businesses regulated, the Authority was made subject to more sophisticated procedural requirements for rule making and adjudication in individual cases than were other regulatory bodies.[28] However, with the financial crisis of 2008–09 the Authority was criticized as having failed properly to supervise effectively the rapidly changing developments which had undermined financial stability, and the new coalition government announced that it would be wound up, with general regulatory responsibility passing to the Bank of England and consumer protection being given

[25] Consumers, Estate Agents and Redress Act 2007, ss 30 and 42–52; S. Brooker and A. Taylor, *Rating Regulators* (2008).

[26] For pioneering discussion of earlier regulatory bodies, see R. Baldwin and C. McCrudden, *Regulation and Public Law* (1987).

[27] Financial Services and Markets Act 2000, ss 2(2) and 3–6.

[28] See e.g Financial Services and Markets Act 2000, ss 155, 387, 388, 394 and 395.

to a new Consumer Protection and Markets Authority.[29] In this case the effectiveness of regulatory supervision had been severely weakened by a number of factors. These included the range of different regulatory functions given to a single body, inadequate coordination due to complex institutional relationships with the Treasury and the Bank of England, the limited role of national regulators in global markets, and the adoption of a 'light touch' in regulation.[30]

In other areas of public policy, both regulatory form and regulatory functions vary dramatically. For example, some regulators such as the Food Standards Agency take the form of non-ministerial government departments; others, like the Care Quality Commission, are bodies corporate; many (like the latter Commission) do not have Crown status, whilst some do perform their functions on behalf of the Crown, notably the Food Standards Agency and the Health and Safety Executive. Some perform licensing functions through which they can regulate the performance of potentially controversial activities; a major example is that of the Human Fertilisation and Embryology Authority. This is responsible for licensing and inspecting clinics carrying out IVF and donor insemination treatment, and establishments undertaking human embryo research. Others are more in the nature of inspectorates applying standards drawn up by government departments, notably the Care Quality Commission which is responsible for monitoring and enforcing registration requirements set out in regulations made by the Secretary of State. The Health and Safety Executive also has as one of its major roles enforcing regulations made by the Secretary of State after a proposal from the Executive or after consulting it; the Executive also has a substantial policy role of its own.

It is thus very difficult to classify this wide range of regulatory bodies clearly by form or function. One common element is that the members of the regulatory bodies are appointed by ministers. However, even this conceals considerable variation; thus the Health and Safety Executive has a tripartite model in which employers, trade unions and government are represented, and arrangements for security of tenure also vary widely, though in most cases dismissal of a board member during the contracted term of service is only possible for misconduct or incapacity rather than because of policy disagreement with the minister.[31]

Similarly, relations with government may be extremely diverse, although it is fair to say that no regulator is entirely independent of ministers in all its activities. For example, the primary duty of the Environment Agency is to make a contribution towards attaining the objective of sustainable development; however, what this means is defined by ministerial guidance and the duty only comes into operation when the

[29] For details of these extraordinary events, see J. Black, 'The Credit Crisis and the Constitution', in D. Oliver, T. Prosser and R. Rawlings (eds), *The Regulatory State: Constitutional Implications* (2010). The reforms are set out in HM Treasury, *A New Approach to Financial Regulation: Judgement, Focus and Stability*, Cm. 7874 (2010).

[30] For further details, see Black, ibid.

[31] For more detailed coverage of a number of different regulatory bodies of this kind, see T. Prosser, *The Regulatory Enterprise* (2010).

guidance has been issued.[32] As mentioned above, some important regulatory bodies apply standards laid down by ministers through regulations; in many cases standards are also pervasively set by EU law. Thus it was estimated that by 2005 over 95 per cent of the legislation handled by the food standards agency originated from the European Union, whilst in the fields of health and safety at work and environmental protection most standards are also EU-based.[33] As a result it does not make sense to assess any regulatory body in isolation; what is much more important is to examine the network of institutions in which it operates and which must be held accountable as a whole. Nevertheless, something can be said about the accountability of regulators themselves, and it is to this that I shall now turn.

REGULATORY ACCOUNTABILITY

It is evident then that regulation involves difficult judgments based on a variety of factors, both social and economic. What are the procedures by which these judgements are made? The regulators are not elected nor are they subject to that most attenuated form of accountability, ministerial responsibility to Parliament. They therefore lack direct democratic legitimacy. Nor do they apply a coherent body of rules which have parliamentary approval; as we saw earlier their statutory duties are vague and often contradictory, and remain difficult to interpret even after the new single primary duty. Even where they apply standards developed through EU or ministerial processes, these typically leave considerable scope for autonomy in how they are applied by regulatory bodies themselves. Issues of regulatory accountability are thus of great constitutional importance.[34]

One way to achieve accountability may be, while accepting the inevitability of discretionary decisions, to design accountable decision-making procedures, as has been attempted in the USA.[35] It is argued that the legitimacy of the regulators' decisions would be increased through the requirement of open hearings involving the participation of affected interests, the giving of detailed reasons for decisions, and the availability of judicial review as a form of check on decision making. The underlying rationale is a kind of pluralist one; the truth (if indeed such a thing exists) best emerges through the open testing of as many different conceptions of it as possible.[36]

[32] Environment Act 1995, s. 4 and Department for Environment, Food and Rural Affairs, *The Environment Agency's Objectives and Contributions to Sustainable Development: Statutory Guidance* (2002).

[33] See B. Dean, *2005 Review of the Food Standards Agency* (2005) paras 2.4.2 and 6.9.1.

[34] For a particularly useful analysis of the accountability issues, see the House of Lords Constitution Committee, *The Regulatory State: Ensuring its Accountability*, HL 68 (2003–04).

[35] See e.g. Prosser, above, n. 6, pp. 277–86; S. Breyer and R. Stewart, *Administrative Law and Regulatory Policy* (6th edn, 2006); G. Palast et al., *Democracy and Regulation* (2003).

[36] For a detailed discussion of this argument, see R. Stewart, 'The Reformation of American Administrative Law' (1975) 88 *Harvard Law Review* 1669.

The US practice was not however taken seriously in the design of the British regulators; it is fair to say that it was seen as a threat which would straitjacket regulators in legal complexities.[37] Yet the other extreme, which was adopted, of a near-total absence of mandatory structured procedures in regulation, faced considerable criticism. A couple of caveats need to be made here. First, the creation of the regulators of the public utilities resulted in considerably greater openness than was the case under nationalization, through imposing a form of external supervision which did not exist previously. Secondly, individual regulators have been, by the standards of British public bodies, exceptionally open in reaching their decisions. Moreover, taking regulatory bodies as a whole, considerable progress has been made in developing innovative regulatory techniques.[38]

A particularly interesting example of the evolution of regulatory procedures was that of Oftel, Ofcom's predecessor in regulatory telecommunications. From the outset, the first Director General of Telecommunications promised an open approach, although he was criticized for failure to give proper reasons for fear of legal challenge.[39] During the directorship of Don Cruikshank during the mid-1990s further important steps were taken to ensure openness. An operating plan and work programme were published annually and the most important innovations concerned consultation procedures. It was already the practice to publish frequent consultation documents and to invite representations, but from March 1995 it was announced that all responses to consultations would be made public unless clearly marked confidential; the latter type of response might be given lesser weight by the regulator. Consultation would also incorporate a second stage; after representations had been received the Director General would be prepared to receive further comments on them for a period of 14 days, thus permitting review of submissions by others. Full explanations would be given for decisions, including references to the arguments of the parties consulted and a summary of views submitted.[40] In addition, public hearings would be employed as part of the consultative process. All these procedural innovations were used in decisions relating to price control, fair trading, and universal service. Regulation of telecommunications passed to Ofcom from the end of 2003; it has also made a commitment to consult widely before reaching decisions, and is subject to various procedural duties under the Communications Act 2003, for example to review regulatory burdens, to carry out impact assessments, to publish promptness standards, and to establish, and consult, a consumer panel.[41] It has consulted extensively on major issues including public service broadcasting and telecommunications markets.

[37] See e.g. Foster, above, n. 3, pp. 259–67.

[38] See Prosser, above, n. 31, pp. 233–4.

[39] See Oftel, *Annual Report 1985*, HC 461 (1985–86) para. 1.27.

[40] Oftel, *Consultation Procedures and Transparency* (1995).

[41] Communications Act 2003, ss 6–8, 12 and 16.

The other utility regulators also did much to open up their procedures, although it is fair to say that none went so far or developed such consistent procedures as Oftel.[42] More consistent arrangements were developed in the Utilities Act 2000 and in the later utilities statutes. Thus, for example, the energy regulator is required to develop a forward work programme annually after consultation and to give reasons for a wide range of decisions, including revocation and modification of licences and for enforcement action.[43] It is also under a duty to have regard to best regulatory practice, including accountability and proportionality.[44] Though divergencies are to some degree inevitable in substantive decisions made within any system of regulation which includes discretion, this is not necessarily the case in relation to procedures, where US experience shows that it is possible to adopt a reasonably standardized set through the Administrative Procedure Act.[45]

A key point is that the US legislation adopts different approaches to rule making and adjudication. Relatively formal procedures, normally involving hearings with cross-examination, are prescribed for adjudication. Rule making, while less formally prescribed, is also, however, subject to a number of structured procedural requirements, including as a minimum giving notice of the proposed rule and receiving comments on it, a minimum which has been supplemented in a variety of ways by agencies and courts.[46] In the UK, the Oftel model went a considerable way towards the US approach to rule making; another model is that of the Financial Services Authority which falls under a requirement to adopt a sophisticated procedure of consultation where it makes rules, including publishing cost–benefit analysis and its response to representations. In relation to more individualized decisions, legislation has also imposed duties to give reasons on the regulators in determining a number of types of individual disputes[47] and the exercise of administrative justice functions by the regulators falls under general review powers of the Administrative Justice and Tribunals Council, though this is itself to be abolished as a result of the review of arm's length bodies.[48] Moreover, many of the general administrative reforms of recent years will apply to the utility regulators; thus, as non-ministerial government departments they fall within the scope of the Freedom of Information Act 2000 and the jurisdiction of the Parliamentary Ombudsman; the Code of Practice on Consultation will also apply to them.[49]

We do appear to be moving towards a more coherent procedural regime for decisions by the utility regulators, although it has to be said that the forthcoming abolition of Consumer Focus and of the Administrative Justice and Tribunals Council will

[42] For details, see Prosser, above, n. 6, pp. 83–6, 113–15, 144–7, 177–8 and 198–9.

[43] Utilities Act 2000, ss 4, 42 and 87.

[44] Energy Act 2004, s. 178.

[45] See I. Harden and N. Lewis, *The Noble Lie* (1986) 302–10.

[46] See Harden and Lewis, ibid., and for an example of rule making on universal service under the US Telecommunications Act 1996, see Prosser, above, n. 6, pp. 281–6.

[47] See e.g. Competition and Service (Utilities) Act 1992, ss 11, 17, 23, 34 and 36.

[48] Tribunals, Courts and Enforcement Act 2007, Sched. 7, para. 13.

[49] Better Regulation Executive, *Code of Practice on Consultation* (2008).

remove key parts of this regime without adequate replacement. The position is more complex for other regulatory bodies. Here a wide range of different procedures has been adopted. An important one is the holding of the meetings of regulatory boards in public; this is the practice of a number of regulators, notably the Food Standards Agency, the Environment Agency, and the Health and Safety Executive, and has met with considerable success. In most cases private meetings will have to be held as well to deal with confidential matters, but the important point is that policy making takes place in public. In many cases open meetings are also required on the part of advisory committees, which are extensively used by some regulatory bodies. The tripartite nature of the board of the Health and Safety Executive, within which employers, the workforce and local and devolved governments are represented, means that affected interests are directly made part of the policy-making process. This also applies to the Executive's complex network of advisory committees. For example, detailed consultations take place in the preparation for the making of regulations; new construction regulations in 2007 went through a process of consideration by two working groups and a formal advisory committee before submission to ministers, and in all of these industry and workforce interests were represented. A discussion paper and consultation document were also published as part of the process. There was also a Parliamentary debate on the new regulations.[50]

A further example of procedural innovation is the establishment by the Food Standards Agency of a permanent Advisory Committee on Consumer Engagement to review its processes. Such is the diversity of practice outside the utility regulators that it would be difficult to rationalize it into a common model, although better means could be created for comparing different procedural innovations and learning best practice from them.

Finally, parliamentary scrutiny has played a more important role than was initially envisaged, especially in relation to the utility regulators.[51] Thus their work on particular subjects has been frequently examined by select committees; perhaps most importantly, the House of Lords Select Committee on the Constitution published a major report in 2004 on *The Regulatory State: Ensuring its Accountability*, followed three years later by an examination of *UK Economic Regulators* by a newly established Committee on the Regulators.[52] Detailed work on the regulators is also carried out by the National Audit Office and the Public Accounts Committee, examining both the work of individual regulators and the utility regulators as a group.[53] Alongside this is the extensive process of regulatory reform, through which regulatory bodies are subject to detailed review to minimize regulatory burdens and increase regulatory

[50] They became the Construction (Design and Management) Regulations 2007 (SI 2007/320).

[51] See D. Oliver, 'Regulation, Democracy and Democratic Oversight in the UK', in D. Oliver, T. Prosser and R. Rawlings (eds), *The Regulatory State: Constitutional Implications* (2010).

[52] HL 68 (2003–04); HL 1889 (2007–08).

[53] E.g. National Audit Office, *Pipes and Wires*, HC 723 (2001–02); Public Accounts Committee, *Pipes and Wires*, HC 831 (2002–03). For discussion, see E. Humpherson, 'Auditing Regulatory Reform', in D. Oliver, T. Prosser and R. Rawlings, *The Regulatory State: Constitutional Implications* (2010).

responsiveness.[54] An important recent initiative has been joint examination by the National Audit Office and the Better Regulation Executive of a number of regulators to assess to what extent they have implemented better regulation principles.

APPEALS AND JUDICIAL REVIEW

A further important element of accountability is the existence of opportunities to check the decisions of the regulators through appeal or judicial review; this is an area where there is considerable inconsistency at present.[55] In the case of some older regulators, enforcement was undertaken through use of the courts; this remains the case for the Health and Safety Executive, the Environment Agency and some other regulators. Here of course the normal appeal mechanisms in the judicial system will be available. However, there has been a growing trend to give direct enforcement powers to regulators themselves without the need to go to court; moreover, many decisions other than those involving direct enforcement of regulatory requirements will have important implications for those regulated and for others.

In the case of the utility regulators, an example of a form of review is through the role of the Competition Commission; where the regulatory body proposes a licence modification to which the company does not consent, there must be a reference to the Commission.[56] In one sense this could be seen to represent an appeal from a preliminary decision of the Director-General that such a modification is required. However, the main role of this procedure was in practice to put pressure on companies to agree to modifications so as to avoid such a reference and the resulting delay and heavy commitment of management time. There have been a number of high-profile references in other cases; indeed, such a reference was crucial to preparing the ground for the opening up of the gas market to competition. The threat of referral has great advantages as a sanction for the regulator. However, the ability of the regulated firm to veto a licence modification made without a Commission reference privileges that firm above others affected, such as competitors or consumers who have no such 'appeal' rights. Licence modification references continue to go to the Commission in its reporting function, not to the Competition Appeal Tribunal. This means that third party rights of appeal to the tribunal will not be available.[57]

Even considering only the utility regulators, a 'mish-mash' of different arrangements exists in relation to other decisions. The most important development has been in the case of telecommunications licensing, where a right of appeal on the merits to the Competition Appeal Tribunal is provided by the Communications Act 2003 for

[54] For a summary, see Prosser, above, n. 31, ch. 10.

[55] For a detailed analysis, see T. Prosser, 'The Place of Appeals in Regulation: Continuity and Change', in Centre for the Study of Regulated Industries, *Regulatory Review 2004/5* (2005).

[56] Telecommunications Act 1984, ss 12–15; Gas Act 1986, ss 22–7; Electricity Act 1989, ss 12–14; Water Industry Act 1991, ss 14–16.

[57] Competition Act 1998, s. 47.

any person affected by the decision; considerable use of this right has been made by regulated companies.[58] This full appeal is due to the special requirements of EC law in relation to the liberalization of telecommunications.[59] However, the government is now proposing that it be limited to grounds similar to those for judicial review, having decided that this is compatible with the EU law requirements.[60] There is a further appeal on a point of law for a party or anyone else with a sufficient interest to the Court of Appeal.[61] Where the regulators exercise their concurrent powers with the Office of Fair Trading to apply the Competition Act 1998, there is a right of appeal on the merits to the Competition Appeal Tribunal and on a point of law to the Court of Appeal; provision is also made for third party appeals by a person with a sufficient interest.[62] Such appeals have played an important role. Thus in one third party appeal, the Court of Appeal noted the breadth of the appeal right to the tribunal, permitting the latter, where it differs from the regulator on questions of law, fact or evidence, to remit a decision or substitute its own decision; it did not however have the power to instruct the regulator how to proceed if the case was remitted. The Tribunal and the Court of Appeal in this case also considered arguments based on the European Convention on Human Rights (ECHR), arguments which are likely to be increasingly important in relation to regulatory decisions.[63] In a number of cases, the Tribunal has had to consider in detail complex matters involving economic analysis.[64] Yet another different model applies where financial penalties are imposed by a regulator; here there is a right of appeal to the High Court against the penalties and their amount on grounds similar to judicial review.[65] Certain decisions of the energy regulator in relation to the organization of the wholesale markets may be appealed to the Competition Commission on specified grounds.[66]

A recent development has been of considerable importance in this context. The Macrory review of regulatory penalties recommended that regulatory bodies should be able to impose 'monetary administrative penalties' as an alternative to criminal prosecution; appeals would be heard by a Regulatory Tribunal rather than by the courts.[67] Implementation has taken place through the Regulatory Enforcement and

[58] Communications Act 2003, s. 192. Such an appeal also applies in competition-based broadcasting decisions: s. 317.

[59] Council Directive (EC) 2002/21 on a common regulatory framework for electronic communications networks and services [2002] OJ L108/33, art. 4(1).

[60] Department for Innovation, Business and Skills, *Implementing the Revised EU Electronic Communications Framework: Overall Approach and Consultation on Specific Issues* (2010).

[61] Communications Act 2003, s. 196.

[62] Competition Act 1998, ss 46–49, as amended by Enterprise Act 2002, s. 17.

[63] *Office of Communications* v. *Floe Telecom Ltd* [2006] EWCA Civ 768. On the scope of the Tribunal's powers, see also *Vodaphone Ltd.* v. *British Telecommunications plc* [2010] EWCA Civ 391.

[64] For a rehearing involving such detailed economic analysis, see *Albion Water Ltd* v. *Water Services Regulation Authority* [2006] CAT 23.

[65] Utilities Act 2000, ss 59 and 95; Postal Services Act 2000, ss 30–37; Transport Act 2000, s. 225; Water Act 2003, s. 48.

[66] Energy Act 2004, ss 173–177.

[67] R. Macrory, *Regulatory Justice: Making Sanctions Effective – Final Report* (2006).

Sanctions Act 2008 empowering ministers to authorize regulators to employ such sanctions; appeal will lie to the First-tier Tribunal created by the Tribunals, Courts and Enforcement Act 2007.[68] The power to impose such penalties is not applicable to all regulators, but the new General Regulatory Chamber of the Tribunal may provide the impetus for a more rational system of administrative appeals.

In other cases judicial review will be the only remedy against regulatory decisions, for example after a licence modification has been made.[69] Once more, the US experience has in the UK been seen as offering lessons as to what should be avoided, and so there has been a reluctance to accept that the courts should play a central role in establishing principles for the operation of the regulatory bodies. Experience so far suggests that there will not be automatic resort to judicial review by those disappointed by regulatory decisions, despite the willingness of the courts to accept such challenges not only by judicial review but, in certain cases where contracts are involved, by private law action.[70] This has not resulted in a flood of cases from those regulated despite initial fears that it might do so.

In the USA, over-enthusiastic judicial review of issues of substance rather than of procedure has been identified as a major cause of the 'ossification' of the rule-making process.[71] The UK courts have in general intervened in matters of procedure while not double-guessing regulators on matters of substance. In the first case of judicial review of a utility regulator, judicial review was sought of a refusal by the Director General of Gas Supply to order reconnection of gas to the applicant's home after allegations of meter tampering.[72] The application was successful on the ground of procedural impropriety because the applicants had been given no opportunity to comment on evidence obtained by the Director General from a meter reader, although all grounds alleging substantive illegality were rejected. The court stressed the broad discretion conferred on the Director General and his autonomy as regards questions of fact. A similar stress on the breadth of the substantive discretion of the regulator appeared in later cases attempting to challenge substantive decisions.[73] Thus, in the frequent situation of a conflict between different statutory duties of the regulator, 'he is given the choice how that conflict is to be resolved, and to decide priorities, and so long as he bears in mind the entirety of his duties, has a predisposition to fulfil all the duties so far as

[68] Regulatory Enforcement and Sanctions Act 2008, Part III.

[69] For a comprehensive account of the of the courts and related bodies here, see R. Rawlings, 'Changed Conditions, Old Truths: Judicial Review in a Regulatory Laboratory', in D. Oliver, T. Prosser and R. Rawlings, *The Regulatory State: Constitutional Implications* (2010).

[70] *Mercury Communications* v. *Director General of Telecommunications* [1996] 1 All ER 575 (HL); see also A. McHarg, 'Regulation as a Private Law Function?' [1995] *Public Law* 539.

[71] T. McGarity, 'Some Thoughts on "Deossifying" the Rulemaking Process' (1992) 41 *Duke LJ* 1385, 1400, 1410–28.

[72] *R.* v. *Director General of Gas Supply ex parte Smith*, CRO/1398/88 (QBD), 31 July 1989.

[73] *R.* v. *Director General of Telecommunications ex parte British Telecommunications plc*, CO/3596/96 (QBD), noted by C. Scott at (1997) 8 *Utilities LR* 120; *R.* v. *Director General of Telecommunications ex parte Cellcom Ltd.* [1999] ECC 314; *R. (T-Mobile (UK) Ltd, Vodafone Ltd., Orange Personal Communication Services Ltd.)* v. *Competition Commission and Director General of Telecommunications* [2003] EWHC 1566 (QBD).

this is practicable and with those duties in mind makes a decision which promotes one or other of the objectives specified (and is rational), his decision stands and is not open to challenge'.[74] In the context of rail, making a decision which had particularly important implications for the role of competition in the industry, the Administrative Court emphasized that given the regulator's expertise in a highly technical field, it would be 'very slow indeed' to impugn the regulatory decision, and that it was no part of the Court's function to substitute its own view on matters of economic judgment.[75] This approach is not limited to the utility regulators; for example, the House of Lords emphasized the width of discretion of the Human Fertilisation and Embryology Authority in a challenge to the grant of a licence to permit the creation and use of embryos for diagnosis in the context of saving a sibling child. Thus '[t]he Authority was specifically created to make ethical distinctions and, if Parliament should consider it to be failing in that task, it has in reserve its regulatory powers...'.[76]

In other cases the courts have taken a more interventionist approach, for example in a decision relating to the different treatment of two electricity licence holders.[77] Although it has correctly been criticized as misunderstanding the role of the (then) Monopolies and Mergers Commission in the licence modification process, the decision does at least appeal to a principle of equal treatment rather than simply reassessing the substantive merits of the regulatory decision.[78] A decision that the use of prepayment devices in water was unlawful is also best understood as preventing the by-passing of the rigorous procedural safeguards applying to the disconnection of water supply.[79] Thus these decisions are not simply examples of over-detailed judicial intervention in the substance of regulatory discretion. Indeed, it is the establishment of expert regulators with discretionary powers which has done most to prevent such 'ossification' of decision making.[80]

Increasing liberalization and the move towards competition law prohibitions more susceptible to judicial enforcement are, of course, likely to lead to increased litigation; however, this is largely to be conducted through appeal to the Competition Appeal Tribunal rather than through the use of judicial review. Similarly, rights under

[74] *Ex parte Cellcom*, ibid., at [25], *per* Lightman J.

[75] *Great North Eastern Railway Ltd v the Office of Rail Regulation* [2006] EWHC 1942.

[76] *R. (on the Application of Quintavalle)* v. *Human Fertilisation and Embryology Authority* [2005] UKHL 28, [2005] 2 AC 561 at [28], *per* Lord Hoffmann. The concluding reference is to the minister's power to make regulations on the subject of the litigation in question.

[77] *R.* v. *Director General of Electricity Supply ex parte Scottish Power*, noted at (1997) 8 *Utilities LR* 126. See also A. McHarg, 'A Duty to be Consistent? *R.* v. *Director General of Electricity Supply, ex parte Scottish Power*' (1998) 61 *MLR* 93.

[78] See McHarg, ibid.

[79] *R.* v. *Director of Water Services ex parte Lancashire County Council and Others*, *The Times*, 6 March 1998, noted by D. Legge, *sub nom R.* v. *Director of Water Services, ex parte Oldham Metropolitan Borough Council* [1998] 9 *Utilities LR* 123.

[80] For a grossly inappropriate judicial role in the substance of economic regulation in the absence of a regulator in New Zealand, see the decision of the Privy Council in *Telecom Corporation of New Zealand* v. *Clear Communications Ltd* [1995] 1 NZLR 385; cf. *Albion Water Ltd* v. *Water Services Regulation Authority* [2006] CAT 23 before the Competition Appeal Tribunal.

the ECHR may increasingly be claimed as a means of challenging regulatory decisions. For example, in *Marcic* a claim was brought against a sewage provider in nuisance and under the Human Rights Act 1998, claiming repeated foul flooding of the claimant's property breached both ECHR, Art. 8 providing the right to respect for one's home, and Art. 1 of the First Protocol, providing for the peaceful enjoyment of possessions.[81] The claim was rejected in the House of Lords on the ground that there was a statutory scheme of regulation which was the appropriate vehicle for prioritizing work taking account of the balance between the rights in question and the acceptable qualifications to them, in particular the interests of the community as a whole. The statutory scheme set an appropriate balance between Convention rights and interests limiting them; moreover the regulator 'is a public authority within the meaning of the 1998 Act and has a duty to act in accordance with convention rights'.[82] The implication is clearly that a regulator has a central role in deciding on the application of Convention rights and in balancing qualified rights in the environmental field against competing public interests. This should open up considerable scope for rights-based arguments addressed to the regulatory body itself, and for judicial review of the resulting decisions.

Other Convention rights may also found challenges; in the regulation of communications, the Art. 10 right to freedom of expression is of particular importance. In considering a challenge to a finding by Ofcom that generally accepted standards had not been complied with by the broadcaster of a radio interview, which had degenerated into a shouting match and contained highly offensive language, the High Court emphasized that the Court itself had to decide whether there was a disproportionate infringement of the right to freedom of expression. Although the political nature of the programme justified a high degree of protection of the right, the gratuitously offensive and abusive nature of the broadcast meant that Ofcom's finding was justified.[83]

A further issue of importance is the question of whether, in those areas where judicial review is the only remedy available against regulators, this is sufficient to comply with ECHR, Art. 6 giving the right to a determination of civil rights by an independent and impartial tribunal established by law. The attitude of the UK courts so far is that the current law, as developed after the Human Rights Act 1998 to permit more searching review, is adequate to do so, but the cases in which this has been determined may be distinguished either as concerning matters of policy where there is a legitimate role for a minister accountable to Parliament, or as not involving the determination of a freestanding Convention right.[84] By contrast, regulatory decisions do not necessarily involve matters of policy in this sense, and the right to peaceful enjoyment of possessions under Art. 1 of the First Protocol may be at issue, for example

[81] *Marcic v Thames Water Utilities Ltd.* [2003] UKHL 66, [2004] 2 AC 42.

[82] Ibid., at [71], *per* Lord Hoffmann.

[83] *Gaunt* v. *Ofcom* [2010] EWHC 1756 (QB).

[84] *R. (on the application of Alconbury Developments Ltd)* v. *Secretary of State for the Environment, Transport and the Regions* [2001] UKHL 23; *Runa Begum* v. *Tower Hamlets London Borough Council* [2003] UKHL 5.

where a regulatory decision affects freedom of an enterprise to trade. We are likely to see some interesting attempts to challenge regulatory decisions in the courts over the next few years; moreover, the background of a Convention right is likely to result in more searching review, notably on the basis of proportionality.[85] Meanwhile, the mess of different types of procedures for challenging decisions by the regulators needs urgently to be cleared up. A general appeal right to the Competition Appeal Tribunal from the economic regulators, with appeal to the General Regulatory Chamber of the First-tier Tribunal in other cases, is one solution which would avoid the possibility of successful challenge for breach of Art. 6. A similar appeal right was in fact proposed by the House of Lords Constitution Committee, but was one of its few recommendations to be rejected by the government; as mentioned above, the likelihood is that in electronic communications the scope of the appeal right will be narrowed.[86]

Another possibility is the use of private law actions, for example in misfeasance in public office, against regulators. Such a case was brought against the Bank of England in its former regulatory role in relation to the banking system, where statute explicitly provided immunity for anything done by the Bank in its regulatory role in the absence of bad faith. The case was discontinued on the direction of the court part way through with no liability being found on the part of the Bank; the hearing had by then run for 255 days, with opening speeches by counsel of 90 and 119 days, at a cost of £100 million (not including earlier hearings on points of law, which had resulted in the litigation overall lasting for a period of 12 years).[87] The heavy criticism by the judge of the conduct of the case may well deter such actions in the future.

CONCLUSIONS

Many of the problems described above result from the difficulty of fitting bodies such as regulators into the constitutional structure; accountability has traditionally been based almost exclusively on ministerial responsibility to Parliament and, despite the long history of regulatory boards not headed by ministers, other means for accountability have not been developed with any degree of sophistication. What was particularly striking on the establishment of the utility regulators was the personalized nature of regulation; the assumption seemed to be that appointing an acceptable personality as regulator would ensure a high-quality result. This in turn reflected the traditionally highly personalized traditions of constitutional government in the UK, once more based around ministerial responsibility rather than any stronger concept of

[85] See *Belfast City Council v Miss Behavin' Ltd* [2007] UKHL 19; cf. *R. (on the application of Pro-Life Alliance)* v. *BBC* [2003] UKHL 23.

[86] *The Regulatory State: Ensuring its Accountability*, above, n. 34, paras 219–32; *The Regulatory State: Ensuring its Accountability: The Government's Response*, HL 150 (2003–04) paras 60–73.

[87] *Three Rivers District Council* v. *The Governor and Company of the Bank of England* [2006] EWHC 816 (Comm).

the state and of administrative law.[88] The reforms undertaken since 2000 have moved away from the personalized model to regulatory boards and towards a more coherent system of procedural requirements for the regulatory process. However, as we have seen with the procedures for challenging regulatory decisions, considerable inconsistency remains, especially in relation to appeal rights. The absence of normative principle reflects a more general problems of constitutional thought in the UK,[89] and the absence of clearly applicable constitutional norms of due process has encouraged the highly pragmatic approach described, though again there are signs of a more coherent approach since 2000.

Any attempt to reform regulation more widely in order to create a more coherent system must recognize the sheer breadth of different types of regulation going beyond the economic sphere. Although the coalition government elected in 2010 has taken steps to cut the number of regulatory bodies, this has amounted more to reorganization and mergers rather than wholesale abolition. Thus in health, it is proposed that the functions of the Human Fertilisation and Embryology Authority will eventually be transferred to other organizations, whilst the powers of Monitor, the regulator of NHS foundation trusts, will be substantially increased.[90] Probably more important is the proposal to take general powers for ministers to abolish, merge or modify by order a number of arm's length bodies, though they do not include the regulators discussed here.[91] This is based on the belief that accountability is best secured by policy and discretionary decisions being taken within core government subject to ministerial responsibility to Parliament.

However, a rule-based system of regulation with only limited regulatory discretion, or the wholesale lifting of regulatory burdens, are unlikely to be effective given the impossibility of reducing the range of regulatory principles to a limited number of determinate rules. This would also have the effect of limiting severely the ability of regulators to respond to the rapidly changing environments in which they operate. Similarly, requiring that the decisions of regulators be based as far as possible on economic rather than social criteria do not reflect the range of different regulatory objectives and functions as defined by statute; if anything there has been a tendency for even the utility regulators to move towards accepting a greater role for social considerations in their decisions rather than the reverse and this is recognized both in the reforms since 2000 and in broader European developments. A further uncertainty is in relation to challenge in the courts and the role of the Human Rights Act 1998; although private law actions are less likely after the failure of that against the Bank of England over BCCI, it is possible that the use of judicial review will increase and

[88] See K. Dyson, *The State Tradition in Western Europe* (1980).

[89] See T. Daintith, 'Political Programmes and the Content of the Constitution', in W. Finnie, C. Himsworth, and N. Walker (eds), *Edinburgh Essays in Public Law* (1991) 41.

[90] See e.g. Department of Health, *Liberating the NHS: Regulating Healthcare Providers* (2010); *Liberating the NHS: Report of the Arm's-length Bodies Review* (2010).

[91] Public Bodies Bill, cll. 1–7.

that the Act will both encourage more searching judicial scrutiny and require further procedural development by the regulators themselves.

What is needed can perhaps be summarized as a greater concern with procedural and substantive principle. I have stressed that initially it was at the level of procedure that the regulatory arrangements seemed at their weakest as a matter of law, but here reforms since 1998, building on best practice of the regulators themselves, may be the beginning of moves towards a more principled system. Indeed, there has been increased concern within government itself about regulatory procedure and there have been attempts to develop more coherent procedural systems across regulation in general through the regulatory reform initiatives which have been of growing importance; one theme within them is to increase regulatory responsiveness.[92] The time is ripe for incorporating the lessons learned into a more general Regulatory Reform Act setting out standardized procedures for regulation, especially for consultation and for challenge of decisions.[93]

Secondly, we need to develop further substantive principles of regulation in place of the highly empirical approach taken so far. Unresolved questions include: What is regulation for? What is the relationship between economic and social goals? What rights to services are implied by constitutional requirements and particular statutory arrangements? Impetus to this approach may be given by the increasing amount of regulatory intervention in these areas at the European level, which may lead to a less pragmatic and more litigious approach to regulation in the future and so may force these issues to be more effectively confronted than has been the case in UK domestic law. Already utility liberalization has been accompanied by a clearer definition of concepts of universal service, notably in telecommunications but also in postal service where, for the first time, UK law has needed to provide such a definition. Indeed, it can be argued that this is the source of a growing body of public service law reflecting both continental traditions of public service and the necessary conditions to make market liberalization politically and socially legitimate.[94] It is also striking that it is through the implementation of European obligations that a more satisfactory appeal process is being provided in electronic communications. Similarly, European developments have led to a rationalization of the historically highly pragmatic arrangements for the policing of competition in the UK, and have also resulted in the creation of a specialist court in the form of the Competition Appeal Tribunal. As a result of these developments, we now have the foundations for undertaking a discussion of regulation in terms of constitutional principle, something not characteristic of previous UK debate. It is certainly much needed; the financial crisis may indeed have had the effect

[92] See Prosser, above, n. 31, pp. 214–18.

[93] Despite its title, the Legislative and Regulatory Reform Act 2006 performs the quite different function of facilitating the ministerial lifting of regulatory burdens, whilst also requiring some regulators to have regard to minimal principles of better regulation.

[94] See, T. Prosser, 'Public Service Law; Privatization's Unexpected Offspring' (2000) 63 *Law and Contemporary Problems* 63–82.

that '[t]hose who think the global market economy can be run without regulation or with self regulation or light-touch regulation have been entirely routed'.[95] However, the debates on the constitutional contribution to types of regulation which avoid the problems shown up in the crisis are only beginning.

FURTHER READING

Centre for the Study of Regulated Industries, *Regulatory Review 2006/2007* (2007, and published every two years).

House of Lords Select Committee on the Constitution, *The Regulatory State: Ensuring its Accountability*, HL 68 (2003–04).

Morgan, B. and Yeung, D., *An Introduction to Law and Regulation* (2007).

Oliver, D., Prosser, T. and Rawlings, R., *The Regulatory State: Constitutional Implications* (2010).

Prosser, T., *Law and the Regulators* (1997).

Prosser, T., *The Regulatory Enterprise* (2010).

USEFUL WEBSITES

Better Regulation Executive: **www.bis.gov.uk/bre**
Care Quality Commission: **www.cqc.org.uk**
Health and Safety Executive: **www.hse.gov.uk**
Human Fertilisation and Embryology Authority: **www.hfea.gov.uk**
Ofcom: **www.ofcom.org.uk**
Ofgem: **www.ofgem.gov.uk**
Ofwat: **www.ofwat.gov.uk**
Office of Rail Regulation: **www.rail-reg.gov.uk**
Postcomm, the Postal Services Commission: **www.psc.gov.uk**

[95] Ed Balls, MP, quoted in 'Ministers Accused of Regulatory Amnesia', *The Financial Times*, 23 September 2008.

13

PUBLIC EXPENDITURE AND THE CONTROL OF PUBLIC FINANCE

John McEldowney

SUMMARY

The control of public expenditure entered a critical period as the newly elected coalition government, from May 2010, embarked on major cuts in public spending to reduce the budget deficit. A budget deficit of 11.1 per cent of GDP set tough challenges for effective public expenditure controls. The financial crisis and political influences dominate the technical rules of financial reporting and control. This has significant constitutional ramifications and potential for tensions between political controls and parliamentary accountability over government spending. Political controls will dominate as government cuts intensify. Treasury influence in policy matters related to the economy and in controlling budgets has intensified. One innovation has been that its economic forecasts are subject to evaluation by the Office of Budget Responsibility, created after the 2010 election, audited by the National Audit Office (NAO) and answerable to Parliament through the Treasury Select Committee. The Bank of England will be given pre-eminent responsibility over banking regulation, a restoration of its historic role, with the abolition of the Financial Services Authority (FSA) in 2010. The NAO is increasingly called on to consider the implications of government policy under governance reforms through a newly created Board. The Audit Commission with responsibility over local government was abolished and local authority auditing will be gradually passed to private sector firms. Current and future Public Finance Initiative (PFI) projects are under intensive review with a likely shift to simple public procurement as an alternative. All quangos are being reviewed and, if thought unnecessary, culled. Every item of government spending over £25,000 is to be published. Political sensitivity continues over the Barnett formula for the allocation of funds to the devolved bodies in Scotland, Wales, and Northern Ireland and its reform remains. Parliament and its post-hoc review of public expenditure struggles to keep pace with fast changing events as the Treasury Select Committee attempts to act as watchdog over the financial crisis. The potential for parliamentary scrutiny has intensified: the

Fiscal Responsibility Act 2010 gives Parliament limited oversight over the amount of government borrowing; the Constitutional Reform and Governance Act 2010 provides improved transparency in financial reporting. The 2010 Budget Responsibility and National Audit Bill (HL) proposes reforms, including a Charter for Budget Responsibility for fiscal and debt management and proposes changes to the annual Financial Statement and Budget Report. The question is how to reconcile the provision of financial information to Parliament, including the systems of audit and accountability, with the coalition government's overarching policy of reducing the budget deficit and public borrowing. The use of public expenditure controls in such unprecedented budget cuts is likely to have a lasting impact on the systems of financial audit and control.

INTRODUCTION

The main focus of this chapter is on the management and control of central government funds available for the government's own use or for that of other parts of the public sector. Local government is not covered in this chapter. Controlling public expenditure involves: surveying public expenditure as a whole in relation to resources; improving management of the public sector through strict financial controls; and providing the opportunity for parliamentary control. The unprecedented growth in public spending of the 2000s, the financial crisis and support for the main clearing banks since 2008, aggressive use of quantitative easing of over £2000 billion all necessitated[1] the Treasury's Spending Review 2010 with a planned 40 per cent cut across all public spending.[2]

The management and control of central government expenditure is best understood on the basis of the chronology of budgetary operations. This involves a planning phase before expenditure is undertaken and an accountability phase thereafter. The planning phase is undertaken by the Treasury's Annual Public Expenditure Survey (PES) through Treasury-appointed Departmental Accounting Officers. A similar exercise is undertaken by the devolved administrations. In the case of trading funds[3] the Treasury appoints the Chief Executive as the Accounting Officer. The accountability phase is carried out through the audit of public funds under the NAO. The Treasury's financial data and economic forecasts are subject to regular review by the newly created Office for Budget Responsibility.

[1] Julia Black, *Managing the Financial Crisis – The Constitutional Dimension*, LSE Working Papers (12/2010), and 'The Credit Crisis and the Constitution', in D. Oliver, T. Prosser and R. Rawlings (eds), *The Regulatory State: Constitutional Implications* (2010).

[2] John Wanna, Lotte Jensen and Jouke de Vries, *Controlling Public Expenditure* (2003); Alex Brazier and Vidya Ram, *The Fiscal Maze* (2006).

[3] Trading Funds are established under Treasury supervision and might include executive agencies or related bodies. See HM Treasury, *A Guide to set up Trading Funds* (2006).

This chapter is structured as follows: first, the institutions relevant to the control of public expenditure and their roles in the process are surveyed.[4] Secondly, attention is given to the processes of planning public expenditure. Thirdly, the accountability phase through the audit of public expenditure is assessed. Finally, some conclusions are offered as to the adequacy of financial control in the context of the planned reductions in public expenditure.

GOVERNMENTAL INSTITUTIONS

Central government is the amalgam of departments, ministers, and civil servants found at the heart of policy making and the delivery of public services. Devolution to Scotland, Wales, and Northern Ireland has financial implications, such as the Barnett Formula, considered in outline below. The creation of various agencies falls under the responsibility of central government if they are in receipt of public funding which is authorized through a government department.

ACCOUNTING OFFICERS

Each government department has an Accounting Officer[5] appointed by the Treasury under the Government Resources and Accounts Act 2000, and directly responsible to the House of Commons for the authorization and control of departmental expenditure. If the permanent head of a department is appointed as an Accounting Officer, he is known as the Principal Accounting Officer and in large departments is supported by a Principal Finance Officer and the Principal Establishment Officer. Chief executives of agencies established under the Next Steps initiative may be designated Agency Accounting Officers. Accounting Officers appointed by the Treasury may be assigned to distinct revenue and expenditure arrangements involving public funds. Accounting Officers are obliged to undertake two functions: to ensure that resources in their department deliver departmental objectives 'in the most economic, efficient and effective way' taking account of regularity and propriety; to ensure that there is adequate internal audit conforming to the *Government Internal Audit Manual* and under the current version of *Managing Public Money*, ch.3 (a guidance manual for public accounting).[6]

Ministers may be held to account in matters of public expenditure by the departmental Accounting Officer acting on behalf of Parliament through various Committees of the House of Commons. Specifically, Accounting Officers may be asked to defend the performance of their wider responsibilities for the economy, effi-

[4] Local government expenditure is not considered in this chapter.

[5] See the Treasury guidance, *Managing Public Money* (updated annually) ch. 3.

[6] There are a variety of documents available from the Treasury on the work of the Accounting Officer, including Cabinet Office, *Best Practice Handbook*.

ciency, and effectiveness of departmental expenditure before the Public Accounts Committee (PAC). There is a presumption that the Accounting Officer will maintain, even in the face of ministerial resistance, the standards of strict financial propriety and regularity as well as 'prudent and economical administration, efficiency and effectiveness'.

The *Pergau Dam*[7] affair of 1995 showed how Treasury procedures operated when the minister overruled the Permanent Secretary of the Overseas Development Administration acting as Accounting Officer, who had reservations about the economy and efficiency of the grant in aid to Malaysia for the construction of a dam. Guidance for resolving disputes is contained in *Managing Public Money*, as is the 'template' for the use of what are termed 'Dear Accounting Officer Letters'.

Increases in Treasury statutory powers under the Banking Act 2009, ss 74 and 75, whereby the Treasury could make regulations over the fiscal consequences of any banking stabilization powers, led to expressions of concern by the House of Lords Delegated Powers and Regulation Reform Committee that the Treasury's powers lacked sufficient parliamentary scrutiny.[8] The retrospective nature of the powers was also criticized by the House of Lords Constitution Committee.[9] Despite the concerns the Treasury's powers remained in the Banking Act 2009.

THE TREASURY AND THE CHANCELLOR OF THE EXCHEQUER

The Treasury fulfils a dual function in being a government department and also holding government departments to account through a system of internal controls over public expenditure. These functions are combined through the requirement of Treasury authority for lawful expenditure, and Treasury supervision of expenditure undertaken by departments.[10]

The development of resource accounting and resource budgeting under the Government Resources and Accounts Act 2000, fully operational since 2003–04, is intended to gauge public expenditure more accurately than previously. Whole Government Accounts include accounts of bodies within central government,[11] trading funds and public corporations including NHS Trusts and Foundation Trusts.

The then government, in its green paper, *The Governance of Britain*[12] announced in July 2007 steps to simplify financial reporting to Parliament. The aim was to align

[7] *R. v. Secretary of State for Foreign Affairs ex parte World Development Movement Ltd* [1995] 1 All ER 611 (*Pergau Dam*). See F. White, I. Harden and K. Donnelly, 'Audit, Accounting Officers and Accountability: the Pergau Dam Affair' [1994] *Pub L* 526–34.

[8] House of Lords, *Delegated Powers and Regulatory Reform Committee Session 2008–09*, HL 12, paras 3–4.

[9] House of Lords, *Select Committee on the Constitution Banking Bill*, Third Report Session 2008–09, HL 19, and 11th report, HL 97.

[10] See *The Treasury Committee, Evidence on the Role of the Treasury*, HC 73 I–II (2000–01).

[11] This also includes local authority accounts that are linked to trading funds and central government accounts.

[12] Green paper, *The Governance of Britain*, Cm. 7170 (July 2007), also see the earlier white paper, *Modernising Government*, Cm. 4310 (March 1999).

the different bases on which financial information was reported to Parliament and ensure continuity between different formats. This builds on the principles laid before Parliament since 1998 in the Treasury's Code for Fiscal Stability, comprising transparency, stability, responsibility, and fairness and efficiency in the formulation of fiscal policy.[13] The Alignment (Clear Line of Sight Project) undertaken by the Treasury engages with the aims of greater transparence. The Fiscal Responsibility Act 2010 strengthened the Code and parliamentary scrutiny by requiring the Treasury to undertake a number of key measures:

- From 2011–16 the Treasury must ensure that the public sector borrowing as a percentage of GDP is reduced from the previous year;
- That overall by the end of the financial year 2014 The Treasury has a duty to ensure that borrowing is reduced by at least a half from the financial year 2010;
- To secure sound finances, the Treasury has duties to make good reductions in applying the fiscal stability principles to the public finances;
- The Treasury must make regular progress reports to Parliament to ensure that the strategy to provide reductions in borrowing and sound finances are secured in the relevant Economic and Fiscal Strategy Reports and Pre-Budget reports.

The Act provides Parliament with the power to vote on the government's medium-term fiscal plans including proposed borrowing and debt totals. The coalition government formed in 2010 must meet the borrowing expectations in the Act. The Office for Budgetary Responsibility[14] was set up after the coalition government took office after the election in May 2010. The 2010 Budget Responsibility and National Audit Bill is currently before Parliament and places the Office of Budgetary Responsibility on a statutory basis. The nature of any parliamentary scrutiny will be uncertain if the coalition government succeeds in its ambition to move to fixed-term five-year Parliaments. This is likely to make organizational changes in the conduct of the business of the House related to the length of the Parliament.

The Chancellor of the Exchequer presents the annual budget, containing a financial statement and review of taxation levels, to the House of Commons in the spring of each year. For a brief period from 1993 to 1996, the government adopted a 'unified budget' covering both the government's tax plans[15] for the coming year *and* the government's spending plans for the next three years. In July 1997 the Labour government reverted to spring budgets with a Pre-Budget Report announced in the autumn

[13] The 2010 Budget Responsibility and National Audit Bill (HL) envisages replacing the Code with a Charter for Budget Responsibility covering the coalition government's policy on fiscal and debt-management policy.

[14] Under the 2010 Budget Responsibility and National Audit Bill (HL) the Office for Budget Responsibility is put on a statutory basis and will produce official forecasts for the annual Budget based on independent evaluations and analysis of financial issues associated with fiscal projections.

[15] Tax Law Review Committee, *Making Tax Law*, TLRC Discussion Paper No. 3 (2003) advocating simplification of the tax system and reviewing parliamentary scrutiny of tax legislation.

of each year. In May 2010 there was an emergency budget after the coalition government took office, accompanied by a detailed breakdown of departmental spending.

The timetable for the financial year from April to March coincides with the announcements of taxation and spending plans. In addition to the oral Budget statement to the House of Commons the Financial Statement and Budget Report contains an analysis of financial strategy and proposed plans and developments. Treasury control of the purse will be at its most intense with the implementation of the Spending Review 2010 under the system of Whole Government Accounts.

The Treasury[16] was the central department responsible for regulating financial institutions as part of a Tripartite Agreement between the Treasury, the Bank of England, and the FSA under the revised Memorandum of Understanding 2002. The financial crisis provided the basis for innovative changes to this arrangement. For example, in December 2009, the Treasury established the Asset Protection Agency under a Framework Agreement for supervising government debts. The current Tripartite arrangements are set to end with the decision to abolish the FSA following new legislation planned for 2010–11.

THE BANK OF ENGLAND

The Bank of England, the UK's central bank, acts as a banker to the government, and with the other major banks is a member of the clearing system. Since 1997[17] the Bank of England has had operational responsibility for the setting of interest rates to meet the government's inflation target. The Bank of England Act 1998 provides a statutory framework for the Bank's role. There is a requirement, under s. 4, of annual reports to the Chancellor of the Exchequer which must be laid before Parliament. There is a Monetary Policy Committee of the Bank that meets on a monthly basis and sets interest rates. This removed interest rates from the political objectives of the government of the day. Membership of the Monetary Policy Committee is subject to confirmation hearings by the Treasury Select Committee who may question the proposed appointee.[18] The Treasury Select Committee holds regular sessions on policy with the Bank of England. The Chancellor of the Exchequer provides broad policy parameters for the Bank. The UK's decision not to enter the euro in 1998 is one example[19] of the powerful influence of Gordon Brown when Chancellor under Tony Blair's Premiership.[20] Accountability for the new arrangements is through a report to the Treasury Committee and to the House of Commons. The Bank issues a Quarterly Inflation

[16] The Treasury has considerable powers to freeze assets of individuals under the Crime and Security Act 2001.

[17] *Hansard*, HC, col. 508 (20 May 1997).

[18] *Hansard*, HC 520 (1999–2000). The Treasury Committee's views are not binding on the Treasury, and only in one instance was the nominee challenged by the committee.

[19] R. Ware, *EMU: The Constitutional Implications*, House of Commons Research Paper 98/78 (27 July 1998).

[20] For a full account, see A. Rawnsley, *The End of the Party* (2010) 188–97.

Report, a Quarterly Bulletin containing research and analysis, and an Annual Report and Accounts of its activities. The Bank also publishes the Financial Stability Report containing informed debate about financial stability. In extreme economic circumstances the government retains the right to override the Bank, but subject to ratification by the House of Commons.

The Bank of England's *Framework for Monetary Policy*[21] has twin objectives, to deliver price stability through the government's inflation target and to support the government's economic policy. The Bank's performance over the past years has been subject to public debate[22] especially since the banking crisis.[23]The setting of interest rates by the Bank and removed from overt political manipulation by the government of the day resulted in economic stability and low inflation prior to the financial crisis from 2008.[24] The UK economy is also scrutinized by external organizations such as the International Monetary Fund (IMF) and the Organisation for Economic Co-operation and Development (OECD),[25] providing the Bank with comparative analysis in making decisions about the UK economy.[26] The Bank's performance is regularly monitored by what was the House of Lords Select Committee on the Monetary Policy Committee of the Bank of England, now the House of Lords Economic Affairs Committee.

The financial crisis led to substantial criticism[27] of the Tripartite arrangements of banking regulation. Banking failures led to the whole or partial nationalization of four major banks and two building societies and the injection of capital sums into the banking sector amounting to nearly £117 billion by the end of December 2009. After the formation of the coalition government in May 2010 there followed the unexpected abolition of the FSA,[28] and the return of financial regulatory powers to the Bank of England. The transfer of many of the functions of the FSA to the Bank

[21] The accounts held in the Bank of England on the government's behalf are the Consolidated Fund and the National Loans Fund. Also held are the accounts of the Inland Revenue and Customs and Excise (the Revenue Departments), the National Debt Commissioners, and the Paymaster General. There are detailed internal rules for the various financial transactions carried out by central government departments including the use of credit cards, debit cards, and the handling of receipts and payments. The Monetary Policy Committee comprises four external members appointed by the government, the Governor of the Bank of England, two Deputy Governors, and two other senior officials of the Bank. Meetings are attended by a non-voting Treasury representative. The decision is frequently made by majority vote: see Bank of England Act 1998, Pt I. See Bank of England, *Framework for Monetary Policy* (21 October 1999).

[22] HM Treasury, *Reforming Britain's Economic and Financial Policy: Towards Greater Economic Stability* (E. Balls and G. O'Donnell (eds) (2002).

[23] John F. McEldowney, 'Managing Financial Risk: The Precautionary Principle and Protecting the Public Interest in the UK', in J. R. Labrosse, R. Olivares-Caminal and D. Singh (eds), *Risk and the Banking Crisis* (forthcoming 2011). J. F. McEldowney, 'Defining the Public Interest: Public Law Perspectives on Regulating the Financial Crisis', in J. R. Labrosse, R. Olivares-Caminal and D. Singh (eds), *Financial Crisis Management and Bank Resolution* (2009) 103–32.

[24] Members of the eurozone are subject to the Resolution of the European Council on the Stability and Growth Pact [1997] OJ C236/1.

[25] OECD, *OECD Economic Surveys: United Kingdom* (2005). There are also IMF country reports.

[26] The Bank has a useful working paper series that provides authoritative analysis of the economy.

[27] FSA, *The Turner Review: A regulatory response to the global banking crisis* (March 2009).

[28] Hector Sants of the FSA has agreed to coordinate and supervise the new transitional arrangements.

of England may leave the Bank vulnerable to coming under political influence and untested in its new role. A new Financial Policy Committee will be/has been created within the Bank of England with statutory responsibility for maintaining financial stability. A new Prudential Regulation Authority will be responsible, as a subsidiary of the Bank of England, for the prudential regulation of all deposit taking institutions with operational responsibility transferred from the FSA. Banking itself is likely to be restructured to reflect a new emphasis on protecting consumers and market integrity with the creation of a dedicated Consumer Protection and Markets Authority. New legislation on financial regulation is promised for mid-2011 with an ongoing public consultation from July 2010 following the publication of the white paper, *A new approach to financial regulation: judgement, focus and stability* on 26 July 2010. An independent Banking Commission will be chaired by Sir John Vickers. Its task will be to assess the arguments relating to whether a bank is 'too big to fail', namely the desirability of breaking up the large banks in the public interest. This will include the structure of UK banking, the state of banking competition and the issues of how customers and taxpayers are to receive the best deal. This should be seen in the general context of a bank levy and the settling of pay and bonuses in the financial sector. The new arrangements give a pivotal role to the Bank of England and seek to adopt a preventative stance to avoid and prevent another financial crisis. The new Banking Commission will make recommendations to guard against any undue financial risks taken by the banks.

PARLIAMENT

'Parliamentary control of the purse' is a basic principle of the constitution that has evolved since before the Bill of Rights 1689.[29] The authority of the Commons over these matters is based on its powers over expenditure and taxation.[30] *Managing Public Money*, the Treasury's code of expenditure rules, stipulates the protection afforded by the constitutional principle of the requirement of statutory authorization for the expenditure of public funds and for the raising of finance through taxation. The nature of the protection rests on three principles, namely that propriety and regularity require parliamentary approval for departmental activities and services; that the Treasury may exercise delegated approval for departmental expenditure subject to ultimate parliamentary authority; and finally, that parliamentary authority, while at times dependent on Treasury support for much of its control mechanisms, is nevertheless paramount.

[29] Bill of Rights 1689, Art. 4 requires parliamentary authority for the raising of taxation. See G. Reid, *The Politics of Financial Control* (1966); M. Wright, *Treasury Control of the Civil Service 1854–1874* (1969); D. W. Limon and W. R. McKay (eds), *Erskine May: Parliamentary Practice* (22nd edn, 1997) 732 (23rd edn, 2004, W. R. McKay (ed.)).

[30] See Parliament Acts 1911 and 1949.

The requirement of statutory authority instituted by Gladstone in the mid-19th century created a 'circle of control' based on an annual cycle of revenue and expenditure. The management of public revenue is carried out by the Crown. Strong party controls over the members of the House of Commons and the general influence of ministers where the government has a majority in the House of Commons reduce the House of Commons' powers of control in practice to the right to criticize.

The Constitutional Reform and Governance Act 2010, introduced by the previous government, takes forward the Line of Sight (Alignment) Project, instituted since 1997, to bring transparency to financial reporting to Parliament.[31] The inclusion of the public spending element of non-departmental bodies into financial reporting is an aid to transparency. The enhancement potential for Parliament is dependant on MPs being willing to include public finance in their scrutiny functions.

The centrality of government rather than backbench control over expenditure decisions is evidenced in Standing Orders of the House of Commons numbers 46 and 47, which provide the Crown with the initiative and sole responsibility for expenditure. Private members, including the opposition, are unable to propose increased charges on public funds or initiate legislation involving expenditure out of public funds without a financial resolution. The initiative is with the government as the Commons may not impose conditions on the grants authorized or the resources applied for without the demand by the government.

An Appropriation Act satisfies the requirement for statutory authority through the supply procedure of the House of Commons on an annual basis by means of the Consolidated Fund Acts and by an Appropriation Act. Revenue collection is largely undertaken through HM Revenue and Customs, and as part of the Budget and Public Finance Directorate of the Treasury.

SUPPLY PROCEDURE AND THE CONSOLIDATED FUND

The supply procedures required to enable the House of Commons to vote supply and provide the government with funds from the Consolidated Fund, are technical and formal. Little substantial scrutiny[32] is involved in such procedures. The policy objectives on which the money is spent are not determined by the Commons but by the government of the day. Policy objectives, however, underline the constitutional authority of Parliament and the internal controls exercised by the Treasury. It must be emphasized that presentation of the main estimates to Parliament does not provide sufficient authority for expenditure. Statutory authority in the Appropriation Act is required. The system is complicated by the fact that in any one parliamentary session

[31] Since 1997 this is subject to the NAO auditing the forecasts to ensure that Treasury assumptions are made transparent, though the system of making forecasts is not open to such scrutiny. See Fabrizio Balassone and Daniele Franco, 'Public investment, the stability Pact and the "golden rule"' (2000) 21(2) *Fiscal Studies* 207–9.

[32] William McKay and Charles W. Johnson, *Parliament and Congress* (2010) 254–61.

Parliament is asked to authorize not only estimates for the current year but also Votes on Account for future years and any excesses from the previous year.

Supply estimates provide the House of Commons with the information needed to provide the government with funds from the Consolidated Fund. Votes on Account and the Consolidated Fund Act must be approved by the date of the budget. Estimates of departmental expenditure are drawn up and must be approved by resolutions of the Commons for the necessary release of funds from the Consolidated Fund. The Treasury publishes a single volume entitled *Central Government Main Estimates* containing one estimate for each department. The estimates provide the major part – over 70 per cent – of annual public expenditure. The Treasury persuaded Parliament in 2001 to replace cash-based Appropriation Accounts with Simplified Estimates and Departmental Resource Accounts.[33]

An annual Appropriation Act, which is normally not subject to any debate, is enacted by July/August each year, authorizing the Bank of England to make payments to government from the Consolidated Fund. The Appropriation Act gives statutory authority for the distribution of money between votes, but this often follows the spending of some of the money, which needs only the Consolidated Fund Act (giving a total figure) for approval. The estimates must conform to Treasury format and approval and must not be altered unless Treasury authority has been granted.[34] There are two Appropriation Acts in each Parliamentary session, one in March for the previous financial year, the other in July for the current main estimates.[35] The audit carried out by the Comptroller and Auditor General (C & AG) discussed below is focused on the estimates which, when divided into heads of expenditure, appear as 'votes'.

Departments work on the supply estimates in the summer or early autumn of each financial year. On or about the time of the budget each year, the estimates are published. If a department's needs exceed the estimates, then a 'supplementary' may be passed subject to Treasury and parliamentary approval. The Standing Orders of the Commons provide the government with three opportunities to introduce supplementary estimates, with the benefit of a guillotine procedure ensuring their speedy passage. Supplementaries may be presented in June, in November, and in February. At other times of the year estimates may be submitted but without the benefit of the accelerated' guillotine' procedure. In 2004 the government introduced a change that gives select committees up to 14 days to consider supplementary estimates.

The Treasury takes very seriously the requirement for statutory authority for authorization of public expenditure which 'must be and can only be given year by year

[33] HM Treasury, *Central Government Supply Estimates 2002–3 for the year ending 31st March 2003: Main Supply Estimates*, HC 795 (2001–02).

[34] See HM Treasury, *Managing Resources – Full Implementation of Resources Accounting and Budgeting* (April 2001).

[35] The reform was the result of the work of the Liaison Committee, the PAC, The Treasury Committee, and the Procedure Committee. See Procedure Committee, *Estimates and Appropriation Procedure*, HC 393 (2003–4).

by means of votes and the Appropriation Act'.[36] A minister 'when exercising functions which may involve the expenditure of money may only do what he does if Parliament votes him the money'.[37] Since 1982, there have been three specific days to consider the Estimates. The Commons may only reduce the estimates, but even this is unlikely if the government of the day has an overall majority. In modern times the Commons has not rejected an estimate and the scrutiny function appears a limited one.

Over the years the presentation of the Estimates has become more readable. Today they contain economic information and are cross-referenced to the Departmental Report. Since an agreement in March 1995 between the PAC, the government, and the Treasury Committee to introduce a simplified format of the Estimates with effect from 1996–67, the estimates are published in a single volume divided into three parts and linked to overall government planning. There is a new requirement on departments to produce an Estimate Memorandum to their parliamentary select committee at the same time as Main or Supplementary Estimates are presented. Improvements in the presentation of financial reporting have been in place since 2009.

THE CONTINGENCIES FUND

An example of a lacuna in Commons control over expenditure is the Contingencies Fund which may be used to finance urgent expenditure. The fund is a reserve fund intended to meet unforeseen items of expenditure and where advances that are made are regarded as 'exceptional'. In technical terms it is used 'to meet payments for urgent services in anticipation of parliamentary provisions for those services becoming available'. Total advances outstanding from the fund should not exceed 2 per cent of the previous year's total estimates provision.[38] Money withdrawn from the Fund must be repaid. The Treasury may authorize payment out of the Fund subject to the limit of 2 per cent set under the Contingencies Fund Act 1974. The instructions contained in *Managing Public Money* and *Supply Estimates: A Guidance Manual* provide that the criterion is not convenience, but urgency in the public interest. If the amount of money involved, or the potentially contentious nature of the proposal is such as to

[36] Details of the rules relating to supply may be found in *Supply Procedure, Government Accounting* (2000, rev.) The Appropriation Act begins life as the Consolidated Fund (Appropriation) Bill. Estimate day debates may take place in July and at the time of the Appropriation Act; in November–December for the winter supplementary estimates followed by any debates and a Consolidated Fund Act; and in February–March for the spring supplementary estimates, followed by any debates on the Consolidated Fund Act. HM Treasury, *Supply and other Financial Procedure of the House of Commons* (1977) paras 47–49, now largely updated by *Supply Procedure, Government Accounting*, ibid. The PAC considered in 1932 the question whether the Appropriation Act is sufficient authority for the expenditure, whether there is or is not specific statutory authority for the service concerned. The Treasury accepted that provided the government of the day undertakes to ask Parliament for authorization, services under the Appropriation Act would come within the PAC Concordat. However, in the first instance, it is preferable to seek specific statutory authority. The Estimates indicate where proposed expenditure is to be met by the Appropriation Act as the sole authority.

[37] HM Treasury, ibid., paras 47–9.

[38] See *The Contingencies Fund Account 2009–10*, HC 373 (22 July 2010).

create difficulty in justifying anticipation of parliamentary approval, it may be necessary to present a Supplementary Estimate, outside the normal timetable, to be followed by a special Consolidated Fund Bill.

The Contingencies Fund is unusual in that the main scrutiny of the government's use of the Fund largely depends on effective Treasury rather than parliamentary control. Legislation giving authority for the expenditure involved must be introduced at the earliest possible time and ought never to be postponed. Guidance issued in 1992 makes clear that the government of the day must be prepared 'to take the responsibility of assuming that legislation being considered by parliament will pass into law'.[39]

The Contingencies Fund has been used for a variety of purposes. Historically, this includes relief of national disasters, the manufacture of the first atomic bomb, victory celebrations, and in time of war for financing urgent supplies. It funded the Pergau Dam project following the decision of the divisional court declaring the aid to be *ultra vires*.[40] In 2008–09 advances from the Fund to the Department of Transport amounted to £1.5 billion plus £0.6 billion to the Ministry of Defence for normal departmental spending. Significantly, the Contingencies Fund was used to support the making of payments in the banking crisis through the use of a Supplementary Estimate of over £42 billion for the banks recapitalization.[41] No amendment or debate occurred in the grant of this request though generally the financial crisis was the occasion for many questions and debates more generally. Concern about the use of the Contingencies Fund is focused on the question of parliamentary accountability. The total expenditure from the Fund is considerable, but there are no clear statutory conditions for expenditure from the Fund. Reliance is placed on the system of internal Treasury control and audit[42] by the C & AG. No select committee directly monitors the use of the Fund and there are no satisfactory means to inquire into the policy behind the government's use of the Fund prior to the Fund being used. Any *ex post facto* inquiry faces a corresponding difficulty as the money has already been spent. The fact that the money is to be repaid seems hardly an adequate safeguard when questions arise about the purpose for which the Fund has been used.

Doubts about the legality of the existence of the Fund in the past have given way to greater risk analysis of the use of the Fund and tighter Treasury oversight. Parliament has, in effect, through inactivity allowed an exception in the form of the Contingencies Fund to the principle that Parliament should vote money before expenditure is incurred. There is also tacit acceptance that Treasury control may be more effective in this instance than parliamentary scrutiny, especially as such internal controls include robust systems of risk assessment.

[39] See J. McEldowney 'The Contingencies Fund and the Parliamentary Scrutiny of Public Finance' [1988] *Pub L* 232–45.

[40] See discussion below.

[41] *Hansard*, HC, vol. 482, col. 952 (2007–08).

[42] See *Contingencies Fund 2004–05*, HC 755 (3 March 2006).

THE COURTS

The courts have, since the 16th century, accepted Parliament's role in the matter of financial control. There is limited opportunity for judicial oversight in matters of expenditure. Public finance issues that arise before the courts involve issues of taxation – the supply side. Central government cases include *Auckland Harbour Board* v. *The King*,[43] in which Viscount Haldane noted that payments out of the Consolidated Fund without parliamentary authority were illegal. In *Woolwich Building Society* v. *Inland Revenue Commissioner (No. 2)*[44] the House of Lords articulated the general principle that money paid to a public body pursuant to an *ultra vires* demand for tax should be repayable as of right. The *Woolwich* case arose out of an Inland Revenue demand for tax from the Woolwich Building Society. The demand was later declared by the courts to have no legal basis. It was accepted that although the money paid to the Revenue was not paid under any mistake of law on the part of the taxpayer, the Woolwich Building Society had no express statutory right to repayment of the money. The House of Lords held that money paid pursuant to an *ultra vires* demand was *prima facie* repayable as a common-law right of the subject. In the *Woolwich* case the payment of tax amounted to almost £57 million with interest and dividends, an illustration of the role of the courts in revenue matters which can have a substantial indirect effect on expenditure totals. The government has estimated that the total cost of repaying composite rate tax to all building societies which had overpaid amounted to £250 million. There is also the prospect of challenges due to the Human Rights Act 1998.[45] A challenge from 'tax-paying pacifists'[46] seeking to adopt the jurisprudence of the European Court of Human Rights on European Convention on Human Rights (ECHR), Art. 9 (freedom of thought and conscience) to challenge the use of taxation for military purposes was rejected by the Court of Appeal. This does not rule out the use of ECHR, Art. 9 arguments in the future, depending on how far the Strasbourg court is willing to develop its jurisprudence on human rights into this area.[47]

[43] [1925] AC 318, 326.

[44] [1992] 3 All ER 737, 764 D–E (see also Lord Slynn at 783E–G). J. Beatson, 'Restitution of Taxes, Levies and Other Imposts: Defining the Extent of the Woolwich Principle' [1993] 109 *Law Quarterly Review* 401. *Pepper* v. *Hart* [1993] 1 All ER 86 on the taxation of benefits in kind which may lead to £30 million in refundable taxes.

In *Metzger and others* v. *Department of Health and Social Security* [1977] 3 All ER 444 the duty of the Secretary of State for Social Services to carry out reviews of the rates of pension payable under the Social Security Act 1975 was considered and the cost of uprating pension benefits ascertained. The impact on public expenditure would have been large if the court had decided to grant a declaration. In the event it refused to do so.

[45] *R. (Wilkinson)* v. *IRC* [2005] UKHL 30, and *R. (Morgan Grenfell)* v. *Special Commissioner* [2002] STC 786.

[46] *R. (on the application of) Boughton* v. *Her Majesty's Treasury (The Peace Tax Seven Case)* [2005] EWHC 1914 (Admin), and [2006] EWCA Civ 504.

[47] See *R (Wilkinson)* v. *IRC* [2005] UKHL 30.

It is accepted that the role of the courts generally in decisions on taxation and public expenditure[48] has been slight, but there is scope for future development. In *Pergau Dam*[49] (see above), the applicant, an international pressure group, challenged the legality of aid granted by the Secretary of State for Foreign Affairs to fund the construction of the Pergau Dam in Malaysia. The pressure group relied on information obtained through an NAO Report and information gleaned from debates and evidence taken by the PAC and the Foreign Affairs Committee. The NAO and the PAC assumed the legality of the aid but criticized aspects of its value for money. However, it was revealed in various correspondences that the Accounting Officer had serious reservations about the project.

Despite such Accounting Officer reservations written ministerial instructions were given to proceed with the financial aid. The Pergau project was funded, purportedly under Overseas Development and Co-operation Act 1980, s. 1. The Divisional Court held that the provision of aid was *ultra vires* the 1980 Act. As a result of this decision, the C & AG qualified his opinion of the aid on the basis of irregularity. Despite this finding and the decision of the Divisional Court, the government found the necessary additional aid required to finance the dam from a repayable charge on the Contingency Fund. Eventually the money was found from the Reserve Fund. Questions of legality may also be raised when value for money is questioned or the use of public funds is thought not to be proportionate.

PLANNING AND CONTROLLING PUBLIC EXPENDITURE

THE TREASURY'S ANNUAL PUBLIC EXPENDITURE SURVEY

The Treasury's annual PES[50] is the central factor in planning and controlling public expenditure. Inside the Treasury the Budget and Public Finances Directorate sets the

[48] In 1975, in *Congreve* v. *Home Office* [1976] QB 629, the Court of Appeal held that it was unlawful for the Home Office to make use of its revocation powers under the Wireless Telegraphy Act 1949, to revoke TV licences to prevent licence holders benefiting from an overlapping licence purchased to avoid an increase in the licence fee. Congreve and about 20,000 other licence holders had purchased a second licence, while their existing licence was still valid in anticipation of an increase in the licence fee. Lord Denning claimed that the Bill of Rights 1689 had been infringed as a levying of money without grant of Parliament. There is some doubt on this interpretation as Congreve had sought avoidance of a tax through the purchase of a second licence, clearly not intended by the Wireless Telegraphy Act 1949. However, the case illustrates how the judges will use statutory interpretation to uphold the principle of authorization. In *Bowles* v. *Bank of England* [1913] 1 Ch 57 Bowles was successful in suing the Bank of England for declarations that income tax could not be deducted by virtue of a budget resolution alone, and until such tax had been imposed by Act of Parliament he was not required to pay it. The case provided the background for what is now the Provisional Collection of Taxes Act 1968 which gives statutory force for a limited time to resolutions of the House of Commons varying taxation levels pending the enactment in the Finance Act.

[49] Above, n. 7. See I. Harden, F. White and K. Hollingsworth, 'Value for Money and Administrative Law' [1996] *Pub L* 661, 674.

[50] It is over 40 years since the Plowden Report recommended that decisions on public expenditure should be taken 'in the light of surveys of public expenditure as a whole over a period of years, and in relation to prospective resources'.

agenda between different departmental demands for money. The Central Expenditure Policy group referees the bids between spending departments and reports through the Chief Secretary to the Treasury to the Cabinet in July on the likely outcome in expenditure totals. Between the end of the PES round in October and the autumn statement in November, winners and losers in the expenditure debate have to be settled. The Code for Fiscal Stability since 1998 (referred to earlier) provided an emphasis on principles of fiscal management such as transparency, stability, responsibility, fairness, and efficiency.

In September 1992, after the UK's withdrawal from the Exchange Rate Mechanism,[51] the government's Autumn Statement introduced changes to the system of public expenditure control through the introduction of a New Control Total. This replaced the planning total and excludes the main elements of cyclical social security expenditure and any privatization proceeds. It includes local authority self-financed expenditure. Totals for the control of public expenditure include both local and central government expenditure. Refinements have been made, such as, in 1998, the introduction of Total Managed Expenditure (TME) comprising the total of public sector current expenditure and public sector net investment. All expenditure under TME facilitates better management under Treasury scrutiny. In 1998 the introduction of a Comprehensive Spending Review (CSR) allowed departments to take a more radical look at across-the-board expenditure and resist the temptation to see expenditure planning only in terms of an annual review. It also allowed comparison between Departmental Expenditure Limits which set firm three-year spending limits (the limits for departmental spending within the public expenditure total) and Actually Managed Expenditure which covers items which are reviewed and set on an annual basis (the actual expenditure undertaken by the department).

PES continues to provide a politically expedient outcome which achieves consensus from ministers. PES underlines the Treasury's pre-eminence and the role of the Chief Secretary in the development of ministerial policy. PES supported by the CSR, and the *Code of Fiscal Stability* has the potential to transform the setting of public expenditure totals through greater transparency and openness in the planning process.

THE TREASURY AND DEPARTMENTAL CONTROLS OVER PUBLIC EXPENDITURE

The Bank of England's independence in respect of interest rates marked a shift from prime ministerial influence to direct Treasury control and through the Chancellor of the Exchequer limited oversight through the Chancellor's relationship with the Bank

[51] The Exchange Rate Mechanism was established to prepare the way for the introduction of the single European currency (euro) and revised in 1999 to take account of the setting up of the euro.

of England's Monetary Policy Committee. This shift is most marked in recent years and is well documented in accounts on the role of the Chancellor of the Exchequer.[52] The various rules that set out apparent controls on the discretion of the Treasury and Chancellor, such as fiscal rules that determine the amount of borrowing relative to the size of the economy, are Treasury-made rules. The Treasury is effectively empowered to self-regulate,[53] and through improvements in the economic instruments to manage the economy.

The pre-eminence afforded to the Treasury through PES is complementary to the overall role of the Treasury in managing and controlling public expenditure. Under the Banking Act 2009, the Treasury may make regulations over the use of stabilization powers for the banking sector.[54] It exercises internal and less visible systems of control as well as external and more visible techniques. Treasury control is much improved through the adoption of a variety of *a priori* techniques. It prepares, monitors, audits, and authorizes under parliamentary scrutiny according to set rules and procedures. The relevant conventions, practices, and statutory arrangements are codified in various manuals. The most detailed is *Managing Public Money*. Dating back to 1934, with a revision in 1977, there is also a *Treasury Handbook: Supply and other Financial Procedures of the House of Commons*. The *Code of Fiscal Stability* is important because of its statutory authority and amendments are made through affirmation by the House of Commons. In addition, the Treasury has a *Handbook on Regularity and Propriety*. The *Financial Reporting Manual 2009–10* sets out all the technical accounting and disclosure requirements for the annual report and accounts.

In preparing legislation, departments are required to keep the Treasury informed of any proposal with a financial implication. Consultation is expected at an early stage and the amendments to Bills should be included if they affect the financial arrangements. This represents a major influence over how departments consider spending public money. Since the late 1990s the Treasury has adopted a more strategic role with reorganization and regular contact with spending departments through annual spending reviews and targets setting inputs and outputs.

Treasury control may be exercised within government departments through the Accounting Officer (discussed above) appointed by the Treasury, whose responsibilities are contained in detailed Memoranda. Accounting Officers are in effect expected to combine their task of ensuring a high standard of financial management in their

[52] Robert Peston, *Brown's Britain* (2004) 76–7, and Rawnsley, above, n. 20, p. 65. The importance of removing unnecessary burdens is highlighted in the Hampton Review, *Reducing Administrative Burdens* (2005).The perception of increasing Treasury influence is apparent from the reconstruction of the old building into a newly designed set of offices for the 1,050 staff. The offices were designed by Norman Foster and opened in 2002. The Treasury has undoubtedly gained from its newly found self-esteem

[53] There is also the quality of the civil service and a list of distinguished outsiders including in the recent past Shriti Vadera from UBS, Nick Stern from the World Bank, and John Kingman from BP. Currently, Edward Leigh MP and John Pugh MP have been asked to advise on accountability mechanisms.

[54] See House of Commons Research Paper 05/92, *The Centre of Government – No. 10, The Cabinet and HM Treasury* (21 December 2005), C. Thain 'Treasury Rules OK? The Further Evolution of a British Institution' (2004) 6(1) *British Journal of Politics and International Relations* 123.

departments with their duty to serve their ministers. The Accounting Officer is given responsibility for signing accounts, and ensuring Treasury sanction is obtained for expenditure authorized by Parliament and appearing as the principal witness on behalf of the department before the PAC.

There is a specialized manual for government Internal Audit. This contains the basic standards for the Treasury's internal audit representing good practice. An internal audit is an independent appraisal within a department as a service to management in measuring and evaluating standards within the department. Through the system of internal audit the Accounting Officer may be assisted in his task. Internal audit is not however seen as a substitute for line management; it is a means to ensure that appraisal within a department is properly carried out. It is usual practice to carry out such appraisal by the appointment of a unit charged with responsibility to the Accounting Officer. As the Accounting Officer is usually the permanent head of the department this 'reflects the view that finance and policy cannot be considered separately'. Thus good management is the key to his function. He must ensure compliance with parliamentary requirements in the control of public expenditure. In his role he is to avoid waste and extravagance and to seek economy, efficiency, and effectiveness in the use of all the resources made available to the department. However the Accounting Officer is also expressly concerned with *policy*. He has responsibility to advise ministers on all 'matters of financial propriety and regularity', more broadly as to all 'considerations of prudent and economical administration, efficiency and effectiveness'. and to ensure that departmental expenditure is justified to the PAC. In matters where a minister may disagree he is free to set out his own advice and the overruling of it by the minister. He is free to point out to ministers the possibility of potential criticism by the PAC of ministerial decisions.[55]

This in effect was the procedure followed in the *Pergau Dam* affair, discussed above. Procedures exist for an Accounting Officer to notify the C & AG should his advice be overruled.

The adoption of resource accounting is consistent with a more managerial approach to budgeting. It is intended to match more closely resources used to meet departmental objectives. The Government Resources and Accounts Act 2000 provides for the adoption of resource accounting and budgeting[56] and the introduction of Whole of Government Accounts consistent within the UK. Generally the Accepted Practice regime[57] is to provide a more complete financial analysis alongside the Alignment ('Clear Line of Sight') Project to ensure effective financial reporting.

55 *Supply Procedure, Government Accounting*, above, n. 36, and amendment 4/05, s. 4.1.2, para. 15.

56 The Government Resources and Accounts Act 2000 amends the Exchequer and Audit Departments Acts 1866 and 1921.

57 D. A. Heald and G. Georgiou, 'Consolidation principles and practices for the UK government sector' (2000) 30 *Accounting and Business Research* 153. HM Treasury, *Whole of Government Accounts progress to December 2000*, Memorandum to the Committee of Public Accounts and the Treasury Select Committee (unpublished).

DEVOLUTION AND FUNDING THE SCOTTISH PARLIAMENT, NATIONAL ASSEMBLY FOR WALES, AND THE NORTHERN IRELAND ASSEMBLY

The creation of the Scottish Parliament, National Assembly for Wales, and Northern Ireland Assembly requires consideration of the financial relationship between the UK's financial system of control and the devolved administrations. The general principles are contained in *A Statement of Funding Policy* issued by the Treasury. These are: that responsibility for overall fiscal policy, and in the drawing up of budgets and public expenditure allocation is retained within the UK's Treasury; that the UK government funding of devolution will normally be determined through departmental spending reviews; and that devolved administrations will make decisions for programmes within the overall totals.

The UK Parliament will vote the relevant provision for the devolved administration by means of a grant. At the devolved level additional elements of the budget will come from locally financed expenditure, funds from the European Commission, and borrowing undertaken by local authorities. In the case of Scotland, additional funds may arise from tax raising powers under devolution through the Scottish Variable Rate of Income Tax (though these powers have not as yet been exercised) and also through non-domestic rates. These arrangements have given the Scottish Parliament and committees an opportunity to scrutinize the spending plans and priorities of the Scottish Executive. There is a three-stage process from April to June (Year 1) and September to December (Year 1) and January to February (Year 2). There are some striking innovations such as the Finance Committee that oversees the consultation process within Parliament and an annual evaluation report allowing strategic planning throughout each year of the spending review period. The Executive submits a provisional expenditure plan (an annual evaluation report) and this is considered by the Scottish Parliament, along with a report of the Finance Committee. The Executive prepares a draft budget in September including spending plans for the following financial year. Based on comments made and information received, it is possible for the Finance Committee to make out an alternative budget, but within spending limits set by the Executive. In December, the Finance Committee prepares a report which is debated in plenary session and this allows amendments to be made to the Executive's spending plans. There is an annual Budget and accompanying Bill presented in January by the Executive. This provides parliamentary authority for spending in the coming financial year. Once the Bill is introduced it is given a speedy passage as only members of the Executive are able to move amendments. The advantages of this system are that there is more transparency than is the case with the UK Parliament and an opportunity for fuller debate and reflection on spending plans; and that counter-proposals may be made through the Finance Committee.

It is clear that in respect of devolution, the UK government retains a number of techniques of overall financial control.[58] These include the right to make adjustments

[58] See Iain McLean and Alistair McMillan, 'The distribution of public expenditure across UK regions' (2003) 24(1) *Fiscal Studies* 45–71.

to the budgets to devolved administrations, and the assumption that devolved administrations will carry any additional or unforeseen financial burdens. The UK government retains responsibilities for the receipt and disbursement of funds from the European Union.

It is generally assumed that any changes in the budgets for devolved administrations funded from the UK's tax revenues or by borrowing will depend on the spending plans of the comparable departments of the UK. The requirement of apparent 'parity' is achieved in general through the Barnett formula.[59]

The Barnett Formula determines changes to expenditure within the assigned budgets of the devolved administrations. Under the Formula, Scotland, Wales, and Northern Ireland receive a population-based proportion of changes in planned spending on comparable UK government services in England, England and Wales or Great Britain as appropriate.[60] The formula works on the principle that changes to the planned spending of departments of the UK government are calculated and applied against a comparability percentage and against each country's population as a proportion of the UK's population. The Barnett formula is under scrutiny. The Welsh Assembly undertook an Independent Review chaired by an economist Gerald Holtham, and the Holtham Commission has recommended that the formula be replaced.[61] In the case of Scotland, the Calman Commission[62] has undertaken similar studies arguing for greater transparency in funding arrangements between the UK and Scotland with a needs assessment introduced across the UK as part of the formula. Northern Ireland is considering its options in the light of decisions about the Barnett formula in general. It is likely that the formula will continue because of the political issues that would arise if it were to change, although alternative models for funding have been proposed.[63]

[59] The Barnett formula was first adopted in the 1978 PES under Joel Barnett, then Chief Secretary to the Treasury. *Scotland's Parliament*, Cm. 3658; Scotland Act 1998; *Serving Scotland's Needs: Department of the Secretary of State for Scotland and the Forestry Commission: The Government's Expenditure Plans for 1999–2002*, Cm. 4215 (March 1999). *A Voice for Wales*, Cm. 3718; Government of Wales Act 1998; *The Government's Expenditure Plans 1999–2002*, Departmental Report by the Welsh Office, Cm. 4216 (March 1999). Belfast Agreement, 10 April 1998; Northern Ireland Act 1998; *Northern Ireland Expenditure Plans and Priorities – The Government's Expenditure Plans 1999–2002*, Cm. 4217 (March 1999). HM Treasury, *Funding the Scottish Parliament, National Assembly for Wales and Northern Ireland Assembly* (31 March 1999). In Scotland, Northern Ireland, and Wales local authorities may borrow within set limits to fund their capital expenditure. There are some exceptions to the Barnett formula, as where various categories of expenditure are the sole responsibility of the devolved administration. HM Treasury, *Funding the Scottish Parliament, National Assembly for Wales and Northern Ireland's Assembly* (31 March 1999) para. 3.3.

[60] See House of Lords, *Select Committee on the Barnett Formula*, 1st Report Session 2008–09, HL 139 (17 July 2009).

[61] Calman Commission, *Independent Commission for Funding and Finance for Wales* (2009). Holtham Commission, *Replacing Barnett with a needs-based formula* (June 2009).

[62] Commission on Scottish Devolution, *Serving Scotland Better: Scotland and the United Kingdom in the 21st Century Final Report* (The Calman Commission) (June 2009).

[63] Northern Ireland Assembly, *Funding the United Kingdom Devolved Administrations*, Paper 82/10 (20 June 2010).

There is an Auditor General for Scotland, and his office scrutinizes the departments that fall under the Scottish Executive, NHS trusts and health boards, further education colleges, Scottish Water, and various government agencies.[64] There is an Auditor General for Wales with a Wales Audit Office, replacing the Audit Commission and the NAO in Wales since 2005.[65]

PRIVATE FINANCE AND PUBLIC PROJECTS

Private financing[66] for public projects is intended to shift the burden that falls on the public purse onto the private sector.[67] In the current financial crisis all private financing is under intense review. The principle underlying private finance is that it may lead to better executed projects, provide close co-operation between private and public sectors, avoid government deficits, and bridge the gap between public spending and revenue income. The Private Finance Initiative (PFI) was launched in 1992. There have been a variety of PFI projects in the NHS, roads, prisons, tunnels, light railway systems, major equipment, and office accommodation.[68] PFI developed the twin objectives of encouraging value for money in public sector expenditure and placing the financial risks on the private sector. Arising out of PFI arrangements is the Public Private Partnerships Programme (PPP), introduced by the Labour government in 1997 and intended to encourage rationalization and upgrading of local authority property, to improve value for money, to encourage the use of joint ventures, and to remove unnecessary obstacles to partnership. It is also a means of 'off balance sheet' financing, a mechanism to help meet public spending targets.

[64] This amounts to about 200 public accounts. There are 25 Scottish Executive departments, 23 NHS boards and trusts, 32 councils, 40 police, fire and other bodies, 39 further education colleges, and 37 non-departmental public bodies.

[65] In the cases of Scotland and Wales, both Auditor Generals exercise similar functions to their English equivalent (see below). However, unlike England, both Auditor Generals are able to scrutinize local and central government. This encourages an interconnected approach to auditing the public sector. Taken together, accountability falls on the devolved administration, with the UK Treasury operating under the system of financial control.

[66] See Economic and Fiscal Strategy Report 1998, *Stability and Investment for the Long-term*, Cm. 3978 (June 1998).Until 1989 private capital could be advanced for the public sector only in strict accordance with the Ryrie rules, Treasury enforced restrictions on private-sector involvement in public projects. See Memorandum by Professor David Heald, 'Private Finance in the UK Public Sector: Escaping from the Dilemmas of the Ryrie Rules', Treasury and Civil Service Select Committee 1992–93, HC 508–1; M. Freedland, 'Public Law and Private Finance – Placing the Private Finance Initiative in a Public Law Frame' [1998] *Pub L* 288. See *PFI: Strengthening long-term partnerships* (2006).

[67] See Grahame Allen, *The Private Finance Initiative (PFI) Research Paper 03/79* (21 October 2003).

[68] For details, see *Hansard*, HC, col. 998 (12 November 1992); *Private Finance*, Treasury Release 20/93, 17 February 1993. NAO, *PFI Contract for the New Dartford and Gravesham Hospital*, HC 423 (1998–99); NAO, *Examining the Value for Money of Deals under the Private Finance Initiative*, HC 739 (1998–99). NAO, *PFI: The First Four Design, Build, Finance and Operate Road Contracts*, HC 476 (1997–98); NAO, *PFI Contract to Complete and Operate A74(M) M74 Motorway in Scotland*, HC 356 (1998–99). NAO, *PFI Contracts for Bridgend and Fazakerley Prisons*, HC 253 (1997–98). See NAO, *Examining the Value for Money of Deals under the Private Finance Initiative*, HC 739 (1998–99).

Risk taking is shared with the private sector but usually at a higher cost than traditional procurement. The Treasury is the key regulator in terms of assessing risk and ensuring standards of delivery and that cost-overrun risks are met by the private sector.

PFI has grown in scale since its introduction in 1992 and is currently estimated to be nearly 17 per cent of total public sector capital investment. The NAO[69] noted that by 2009–10 there were at least 900 PFI projects with a total value of over £66 billion over 20 different sectors. (This figure relates to England only as PFI is a devolved matter.) This means that the operation of PFI is one of the largest programmes in the world.[70] Assessing the value of PFI projects is controversial.[71] Criticism of PFI is longstanding and the lack of transparency over complex and technical details has added to the controversy surrounding many schemes. Accounting systems within the PFI are also complicated.[72] PFI arrangements provide capital assets to be recorded as off balance sheet accounts for the public sector and it appears that this might be common practice amongst private contractors. A further concern is that parliamentary scrutiny of PFI is *ad hoc*, and too narrowly focused on issues of impropriety. PFI gained a bad reputation over the failure of the London Underground Metronet PPP in June 2007, where large sums of public money were guaranteed. This was a £17 billion modernization programme for the London Underground to run 30 years that was at the centre of considerable political and management controversy.[73] Large losses accrued as weekly cash flow deficits failed to be met because of major shortfalls in revenue. The result was that Metronet went into administration and its business was transferred to two nominee companies of Transport for London[74] under long-term arrangements agreed with the Treasury. Lessons were learnt to the effect that too little regulation and public sector techniques to cap public money sat uneasily with market-led competitive contracts entered into by the main companies.

Despite the fact that the NAO has undertaken more than 72 studies of individual PFIs and published 12 reports on the Sales of Assets arising out of PFI, and claimed substantial savings of £750 million over six years, there is public concern that the capacity of the public sector to act as overseers of the PFI arrangements is limited. Improvements in the scrutiny of PFI include a dedicated Treasury office engaged in monitoring projects, shortening procurement times and overruns, strengthening

[69] National Audit Office, *Managing the relationship to secure a successful partnership in PFI projects*, HC 375 (2001–02). See *National Audit Office Annual Report 2006*.

[70] D. McKenzie, *PFI in the UK and PP in Europe* (2009), *Public Private Finance Yearbook* (2008).

[71] HM Treasury, *PFI: Strengthening Long-Term Partnerships* (March 2006).

[72] There are two systems of accounting relevant to PFI – government financial reporting based on a modified Generally Accepted Accounting Practice in the UK or UKGAAP (since 2009–10 IFRS), and the national accounts (European System of Accounts or ESA and supplemented since 2004 by Eurostat Guidance).

[73] See *R. (Transport for London)* v. *London Regional Transport*, 30 July 2001, unreported, a failed attempt by the then London Mayor Ken Livingstone to have the contract stopped by the courts.

[74] The local government body responsible for the management of the transport system in London including the implementation of the transport strategy under a Management Board appointed by the Mayor of London.

payment systems and avoiding fraud.[75] Longstanding concerns remain. Better value for money is not always capable of being judged at the time it has to be made. The whole life of the projects need to be used as a basis for assessment including an appraisal of privately financed arrangements as compared with traditionally procured projects. Departmental liabilities on PFI/PPP projects need to be included in Departmental balance sheets. The House of Lords Select Committee on Economic Affairs has recently reported that there is an institutional bias in favour of PFI and that such bias needs to be re-considered.[76] In many instances PFI projects are on time and on budget, with the NAO recently finding that 88 per cent of projects are completed within three months of the contracted date. Savings are not always shared with the public sector, though this will be redressed by new arrangements for gains to be credited to the public sector whenever appropriate. The future is hard to predict as public funds become more scarce and the trend to save public money may favour traditional public procurement. The case for any PFI is likely to need stricter risk assessment than in the past to avoid failures. Large and complex projects seem ill-suited to PFI arrangements. It may however prove to be necessary to risk continuing PFI strategies in the midst of public spending cuts. The NAO recommends that under a newly created Infrastructure Financing Unit, the Treasury should monitor each project and take steps to ensure adequate finance. This includes looking at different ways to finance projects. Current estimates are that between £500 million and £1 billion of higher costs are contractually binding within existing PFI projects and are difficult to reduce.[77]

AUDIT TECHNIQUES IN THE CONTROL OF PUBLIC EXPENDITURE

The adoption of audit strategies for the public sector infiltrates almost every form of decision making in a wide variety of institutions.

PARLIAMENT'S ROLE: THE PUBLIC ACCOUNTS COMMITTEE, THE NEW SELECT COMMITTEES, AND THE COMPTROLLER AND AUDITOR GENERAL

Once expenditure is settled the question of scrutiny and audit arises. Since 1861 the PAC acts on behalf of Parliament to examine and report on accounts and the regularity and propriety of expenditure, which are matters usually covered by the C & AG's

[75] Ibid.

[76] House of Lords Select Committee on Economic Affairs, 1st Report Session 2009–10, HL 63-I.

[77] NAO Report of the Comptroller and Auditor General, *HM Treasury: Financing PFI Projects in the credit crisis and the Treasury's response*, HC 287, Session 2010–11 (27 July 2010) 12.

certification audit. In more recent times value for money audit (VFM) examinations have become a major part of the work of the PAC. In that regard the PAC works with the assistance of the C & AG. Recently, the PAC has proposed changes to Standing Order No. 148 which will enable it to appoint specialist advisers, a facility available to other Committees. The constitutional importance of the PAC is beyond question and linked to efficiency in government. There is a case for a systematic rather than random follow up by the PAC of how its recommendations have been treated by the government. The PAC produces about 50 reports a year. Its 12th Report in 2010 on *Maintaining financial stability across the United Kingdom's banking system*[78] provided an analysis of the banking crisis where the PAC provided an important review of the Tripartite system of banking regulation. The specialist and technical nature of the work of the PAC makes it difficult to devolve its powers to other bodies. Nonetheless, the PAC may become more effective by linking its work into the work of other committees in a more coordinated way than is possible at present.[79]

The PAC's authority and remit[80] differ from those of other select committees in two ways. First is the non-party political approach it adopts to its task and the fact that it is chaired by a senior opposition MP and has no more than 15 members. Secondly, its inquiries are almost all audit-based and it receives expert assistance from the C & AG through the work of the NAO. In the case of VFM examinations, its reports to Parliament carry considerable weight. In November 2009 the PAC was critical of the Treasury's indemnity of £28 billion to the Bank of England and a further emergency liquidity assurance of £60 billion to the Royal Bank of Scotland and the Halifax Bank of Scotland (HBOS).[81] Parliament had not received any prior notification before the indemnity had been agreed by the Treasury.

Select committees generally exercise *ex post facto* control over public expenditure. The Treasury Committee has been particularly active in developing strategies to obtain more information on public expenditure and its more effective control. In the recent financial crisis involving banking regulation, the Treasury committee led the way. It undertook 41 evidence sessions and published nine reports relating to the crisis between 2007 and 2009 and has remained active in scrutiny.[82] It is accepted that much of the work of Committees is by its nature retrospective review.

The Scrutiny Unit established in November 2002 in the Committee Office of the House of Commons provides select committees of the House of Commons and joint committees of the two Houses with advice on expenditure matters but also on the impact

[78] Public Accounts Committee Reports, *12th Report on Maintaining financial stability across the United Kingdom's banking system*, HC 190 (9 February 2010).

[79] See Public Accounts Committee Reports, *63rd Report on Delivering high quality services for all*, HC 1530 (2006).

[80] See Public Accounts Committee Reports on the poor quality of higher education, HC 283 (2000–01), and on the C & AG's Reports, *The Millenium Dome*, HC 936 (1999–2000), and HC 989-I (2000–01).

[81] PAC Report, *Maintaining Financial Stability Across the UK Banking System*, 12th Report, HC 190 (2001–10) para 11.

[82] Black, above, n. 1, p. 31.

of draft Bills. The Scrutiny Unit undertakes research as well as policy impact. It also publishes a Review of Departmental Annual Reports, and provides training and support on Impact Assessments. It assists in the Treasury's Alignment Project set up in July 2007 to ensure that financial reporting and accounts are consistent and transparent.[83]

This provides a detailed and in-depth overview of how departments are performing in terms of Treasury guidance and output measurements. The primary function of the C & AG since the Exchequer and Audit Act 1866 has been the requirement to examine accounts on behalf of the House of Commons. The National Audit Act 1983 recognized the constitutional implications of this requirement, made the C & AG an Officer of the House of Commons, and provided for his appointment. As head of the NAO, which was created under the 1983 Act and replaced the Exchequer and Audit Department, the C & AG is independent from both politics and political influence of the government of the day. This independence allows the C & AG to qualify financial accounts when he is not satisfied with the financial arrangements. In November 2002 this occurred over the Strategic Rail Authority sponsored by the Department of Transport[84] until it was agreed that Network Rail should be consolidated. The NAO's activities[85] cover benchmarking, quality control, developing efficient and effective monitoring systems, and engaging in annual reporting functions over departmental spending involving the audit of more than 600 accounts covering over £800 billion of public expenditure.[86] Its annual net working resources are approximately £76 million with outsourcing costs of nearly 20 per cent and employing 900 staff. The remit of the NAO was established under the 1983 Act, which has been criticized for failing to give the C & AG the right to trace 'all public money'. The NAO has also undertaken a significant monitoring of the financial management of the European Union.[87] Excluded from the jurisdiction of the NAO in National Audit Act 1983, Sched. 4 is the audit of the remaining nationalized industries and other public authorities. Local authorities are separately audited by the about to be abolished Audit Commission which is itself subject to audit by the NAO. The NAO is funded out of moneys provided by Parliament but one-fifth of the NAO's budget comes from audit fees, including international clients. The NAO is subject to oversight by the Parliamentary Public Accounts Commission. The corporate governance arrangements of the NAO are under review following John Tiner's report in February 2008, the 14th Report of the Public Accounts Commission.[88] The recommendations included limiting the length of term

[83] See HM Treasury, *Alignment (Clear Line of Sight) Second Parliamentary Memorandum* (2009–10).

[84] Eleventh Report of the Public Accounts Commission, Session 2001–02, HC 1251 (2002).

[85] There is a Public Audit Forum providing a discussion for the audit agencies; the NAO, the Northern Ireland Audit Office, the Audit Commission for Local Authorities, and the National Health Service in England and Wales and Audit Scotland.

[86] National Audit Office, *Corporate Plan 2003–4 to 2005–6* (2005) contains details of the bodies audited.

[87] See Report by the Comptroller and Auditor General, *Financial Management of the European Union: A Progress Report*, HC 529 (2003–04).

[88] HC 328 (2007–08).

of the C & AG, the terms and conditions of service and remuneration. Also included were recommendations about the role of the NAO and its relationship with the C & AG. Following the Tiner review, the Public Accounts Commission considered the next steps to be taken and published a response on 4 March 2008.[89] Its response was also considered by the NAO and further consultations took place before the clauses[90] in the Constitutional Reform and Governance Bill were agreed by the government but were omitted in the final legislation.[91] Part 2 of the recently introduced 2010 Budget Responsibility and National Audit Bill (HL) re-introduces the main principles in the recommendations omitted in the final legislation. The new proposals are to separate the C & AG as an independent officer of Parliament from the NAO, with the NAO receiving a new corporate status, providing resources to the C & AG who will be its Chief executive but under an independent Board.[92]

Significantly, following the Gershon Review in 2004, the NAO has undertaken regular reviews of efficiency savings across government. Its current strategy, the Efficiency Framework of 2007 is estimated to help make savings of £35 billion planned over the coming year in terms of the administrative costs of running government departments.[93]

CERTIFICATION AUDIT

The NAO[94] undertakes two forms of auditing, Certification Audit and Value For Money Audit. In the case of certification audit, the C & AG carries out on behalf of the House of Commons the audit and certification of all government departments and a wide range of public-sector bodies. These include appropriation accounts of departments. The C & AG provides an audit certificate which states his opinion as to whether either: (a) the 'account properly presents' the expenditure and receipts of the vote and payments of the organization; or (b) the account presents a 'true and fair view' where accounts are prepared on an income and expenditure basis.

This form of audit is 'departmental-led', that is, focused on departments. Increasingly, the style of the audit seeks to ensure 'regularity and propriety' with the

[89] Public Accounts Commission, 16th Report, HC 1027 (2007–08) para. 16.

[90] HC 1027 (2007–08).

[91] See House of Commons Library Research Paper 09/73, *Constitutional Reform and Governance Bill* (6 October 2009). These include: the term of office of the C & AG with a new maximum of ten years; the remuneration package to be linked to a comparable office of similar status and include some restrictions on employment after leaving office. There is a new corporate entity for governance granted to the NAO and its relationship with the C & AG – the C & AG is through the chief executive. The C & AG is not an employee of the NAO. This is intended to provide a strategic approach to the NAO and how it operates

[92] Remuneration, terms of conditions of the C & AG and limitations on powers to require efficiency and cost-effectiveness in the exercise of his responsibilities. There are similar powers for Wales.

[93] Public Accounts Committee, *Progress with value for money savings and lessons for cost reduction programes*, HC 439-I (11 September 2010).

[94] Tom Ling, *The NAO and Parliamentary Scrutiny, a new audit for new times*, CfPs Policy Paper Series (2005).

addition that the custodians of public money have stewardship responsibilities. The link between the Treasury and the NAO is through the Departmental Accounting Officer and is one of partnership but based on independent actors with specific responsibilities. The C & AG may seek an explanation from the department concerned if he is dissatisfied with any aspect of the accounts and may qualify his certificate with his reservations. The primary focus of such an audit is to assess whether accounts are accurate or whether they may mislead someone relying on them. They must present a 'true and fair view', must be 'properly presented', and in the case of Agencies must follow the format of Treasury accounts. In particular, if there is expenditure which requires Treasury authority which has not been given, the matter is reported through a draft report in the first instance to the Accounting Officer and then to the PAC and Parliament.

Normally, the audit work involved in certification audit is confined to the proper presentation of receipts and expenditure. In common with most of the auditing work of the NAO it is scrutiny *ex post facto* with the implication that any past errors may provide lessons for the future. This is open to the criticism that an *a priori* examination might offer a means of avoiding mistakes and therefore save public money.[95] The NAO has claimed that in 2005–06, its work resulted in £555 million in savings as a result of auditing over 500 accounts covering £800 billion in expenditure.

VALUE FOR MONEY EXAMINATIONS

VFM examinations are potentially more far-reaching as a means of audit. The National Audit Act 1983, s. 6 provides a statutory basis for VFM examinations at the discretion of the C & AG. Included within this jurisdiction are government departments and other public bodies where the C & AG has statutory rights of inspection or where he is the statutory auditor. VFM audit is not extended to any of the nationalized industries.[96] The 1983 Act placed VFM examinations on a statutory basis and over 60 reports are produced on an annual basis. However, the Act makes an important proviso that VFM examination shall not be construed as entitling the C & AG to question the merits of the policy objectives of the department or body concerned.[97]

Evaluating efficiency and effectiveness has been a common theme in recent years in the development of government policy objectives.[98] The NAO is ambitious in developing VFM examinations through their efforts to identify and prevent waste. It has become commonplace that government borrows techniques, methods, and objectives

[95] Public Accounts Committee, *Managing Risks to Improve Public Services*, HC 444 (2004–05).

[96] *Government Accounting* (1989) para. 7.1.20 revised in 2003.

[97] See C. Beauchamp, 'National Audit Office: Its Role in Privatization' (1990) *Public Money and Management* 55–8, 57. For examples, see National Audit Office, Session 1995–96, *The Work of the Directors of Telecommunications, Gas Supply, Water Service and Electricity Supply*, HC 645. Compare the approach to the early comments made to the Fourth Report of the Public Accounts Committee (4 November 1988).

[98] See a critical analysis by the NAO over selling the National Air Traffic Control System, HC 1096 (2001–02).

from business or commerce. How to measure efficiency and effectiveness is the key issue, and evaluation may be as difficult as setting the objectives in the first place.

In 1981 the Treasury and Civil Service Committee in its *Report on Efficiency and Effectiveness*[99] set out some criteria for evaluating efficiency and effectiveness. The criteria include clarifying the intention of the programme, setting *objectives* which are quantified as targets. Objectives can be assessed in terms of *output*. An *efficient* programme is one where the target is achieved with the least use of resources and instruments for change. An *effective* programme is one where the intention of the programme is being achieved. This means that the intention is contained in operational objectives that are set as defined targets. Thus the output of the programme is equal to the target set. In this way an effective and efficient programme may be evaluated.

The NAO has developed VFM strategies[100] that emphasize the avoidance of waste, the setting of clearly defined policy objectives, and obtaining good value for the taxpayer. There is a duty on government departments to consider the NAO's reports and the PAC recommendations, and to provide replies to the House of Commons on matters raised in the reports. There is a strong parliamentary link with the PAC following up the recommendations made by the NAO.[101] This is consistent with the Gershon Report that argued strongly for making efficiency savings to redistribute funds for better use. The government's claim was that £4.7 billion savings might be so identified[102] but there is a considerable risk that a reduction in the quality of services might result if over-ambitious targets have to be met. There is the need for a cost–benefit analysis to be used to assess the amount of savings as against the quality of services.

VFM examinations seem to be a blend of conventional auditing skills with management consulting techniques. In the former they benefit from a degree of independence and objectivity and the ascertaining of facts through the skills of an auditor. The latter draws on the analytical skills of the management consultant. In comparison with ordinary certification auditing VFM takes the opportunity to understand the effects of policy and whether those effects relate to the intention behind the policy. The NAO's experience of VFM studies has been growing since 1983.[103] In 2005–06 the NAO provided Parliament with 61 major reports on VFM, representing a substantial part of the NAO's work.[104] In 2009–10 the NAO undertook 90 reports on VFM.

[99] Treasury and Civil Service Committee, *Efficiency and Effectiveness in the Civil Service*, HC 236. See also Cabinet Office Efficiency Unit, *Helping Managers Manage* (1984).

[100] National Audit Office, *Helping the Nation Spend Wisely Annual Report* (1999) 13. See National Audit Office, *A Framework for Value for Money Audits*, Cmnd 9755; Treasury Minute on the First Four Reports from the Committee of Public Accounts Session 1985/86, paras 21–3; Cmd. 8413, para. 87; A. Hopwood, 'Accounting and the Pursuit of Efficiency', in A. Hopwood and C. Tomkins, *Issues in Public Sector Accounting* (1984); J. Sizer, *An Insight into Management Accounting* (1989).

[101] Public Accounts Committee, *Achieving Value for Money in the Delivery of Public Services*, HC 742 (2005–06).

[102] National Audit Office, *Progress in Improving Government Efficiency*, HC 802 (2005–06).

[103] See J. McEldowney, 'Audit Cultures and Risk Aversion in Public Authorities: An Agenda for Public Lawyers', in R. Baldwin (ed.), *Law and Uncertainty Risks and Legal Processes* (1997) 185–210.

[104] National Audit Office, *Annual Report 2006*.

Particularly difficult is the distinction between the implementation of policy, a legitimate concern of VFM, and the merits of policy which we have already noted is outside the jurisdiction of the NAO. A criticism levelled at all public-sector VFM examinations is that the emphasis on economic criteria does not take account of political choices and policy making or whether the merits of the policy, outside the remit of the NAO, impacted on the efficiency of decision making. Given its present remit, it is clearly impossible for the NAO to move to assess the merits of policy even where this may be indicated by their examination. The *ex post facto* nature of VFM has the benefit of hindsight but this may make it difficult to evaluate all the pressures experienced by a sponsoring department.[105] The NAO published a critical analysis of the banking crisis and the problems caused by the failure of Northern Rock.[106]

Perversely, the very transparency encouraged by audit systems may inhibit initiative and creative risk taking in favour of a cautious approach over-reliant on audit advice. Placing trust in the audit process itself may be a worthy goal and achieves better control over-expenditure but it may encourage heavy reliance on monitoring techniques instead of a more fundamental assessment of priorities. The political agenda may also become heavily dependent on the audit trail to provide legitimacy and public confidence for policies. This may obscure the setting of priorities and lead to the adoption of short-term as opposed to long-term goals.

The independent status of the C & AG means that heavy reliance is placed on cooperation between the departments, their Accounting Officers, and the NAO.[107] This is indicative of the delicate balance between gaining access to information through cooperation and maintaining an independence.[108] Although the NAO has achieved international status as a public sector audit office of high reputation and quality, criticisms remain of its capacity to operate proactive or preventative strategies to ensure effective public spending.

CONCLUSION

The financial crisis marks a new stage in the development of systems and techniques for the control of public expenditure. Recent improvements in financial

[105] F. White and K. Hollingsworth, *Audit, Accountability and Government* (1999).

[106] National Audit Office, *The Financial Services Authority: A review under section 12 of the Financial Services and Markets Act 2000*, Session 2006–07, HC 500 (27 April, 2007) 49 noted that from 2001–02 there were an average of 200 cases each year dealing with money laundering and other breaches of the financial standards. At ibid., para. 4.63, 17 cases involving financial penalties totalling £17.4 million, £14 million of which was for one market protection case and £505,00 related specifically to financial crime.

[107] See the proposals contained in the Budget Responsibility and 2010 National Audit Bill (HL) to modernise the work of the NAO and its governance arrangements.

[108] Memorandum from Michael Power, Professor of Accounting, London School of Economics, HM Treasury Select Committee Evidence 173, p. 174.

information through the Constitutional Reform and Governance Act 2010 and the strengthening in the systems of accounting and auditing open up clear potential for greater parliamentary oversight.[109] The Fiscal Responsibility Act 2010 further offers the opportunity for parliamentary oversight of government debt and borrowing. However, in the midst of the financial crisis the balance of influence between parliamentary control and government spending has shifted markedly to the government's advantage. This is partly because of the need for rapid public spending cuts and partly because the systems of accountability are the main means of delivering and controlling public spending. The coalition government's setting up of the Interim Office for Budget Responsibility in May 2010 to make an independent assessment of the public finances is an attempt to provide transparency[110] but it remains to be seen whether this will form a substantial check on government accounting.

The government's expenditure objectives are more visible and transparent than before but, being driven by large fiscal deficits, parliamentary accountability is likely to be weak. Evaluation of the case for cuts and the proportion of savings, the role of accountability systems, has given way to a government-centered agenda for change.

Strengthening parliamentary scrutiny largely depends on the House of Commons in general or individual MPs regarding financial control as relevant in their overall role in the scrutiny of government.

The financial crisis has also revealed the limited extent of *ex post* select committee scrutiny; despite the fact that the crisis had a major impact on institutions that control and regulate public finance, little could be done at the time. An unfortunate aspect of the Banking Act 2009 was the restricted role it gives to Parliament's role: the Bank of England was given real powers to implement stabilization options that were not subject to parliamentary control[111] and the Treasury was granted even wider regulatory powers without the need for prior parliamentary approval. The work of the Treasury Select Committee, however, in actively reporting on aspects of the financial crisis[112] has proved important and the Lords Select Committee on the Constitution has also been vigilant.[113]

[109] Mark Sandford, *External Scrutiny: The Voice in the Crowded Room*, CfPs Policy Paper Series (2002).

[110] National Audit Office, *HM Treasury: Examination of the Forecasts prepared by the interim Office for Budget responsibility for the emergency Budget 2010*, Session 2010–11, HC 142 (22 June 2010).

[111] See Banking Act 2009, ss 5, 10 and 74. Section 74 gave the Treasury Henry VIII-type powers to make regulations to cover stabilization measures.

[112] HC Treasury Select Committee, *Too important to fail – too important to ignore*, Ninth Report Session 2009–10, HC 261-1, p. 3 Summary. HC Treasury Select Committee, *Banking Crisis: Dealing with the Failure of UK Banks*, Session 2008–09, HC 416, paras 203–29. Treasury Select Committee, *Reporting Contingent Liabilities to Parliament*, Session 2009–10, HC 181. Treasury and Civil Service Committee, *The Regulation of Financial Services in the UK*, Sixth Report, HC 332-I (1994–95).

[113] HL Select Committee on the Constitution Banking Bill, Session 2008–09, HL 19, and HL 97.

The work of financial scrutiny has permeated many of the departmental select committees which have begun to adopt public expenditure as a subject for scrutiny[114] aided by the establishment in 2002 of the Scrutiny Unit.[115] This also aids select committees in pre-legislative scrutiny. However, audit systems have a remarkable tendency to centralize control.

Constitutional lawyers have accepted that controls over public expenditure lie at the heart of Parliament's control over government. The plethora of controls such as internal Treasury rules and procedures, audit systems, parliamentary reports, and management systems are fashioned to serve the dual purpose of the economic needs of the government of the day, and the interests of Parliament. Inside the system of financial control the internal workings of government can be detected, often less visible and transparent than the workings of the external systems of parliamentary accountability in select committees and in the role of the courts. Financial control systems share many characteristics familiar in the development of the common law – continuity and certainty in developing rules with the potential for incremental change. But, equally incrementally, financial controls appear to have developed many of the qualities of a codified system – written manuals containing fundamental principles that have been improved, updated, and strengthened containing many years' experience. It is possible to see financial controls as a model of what can be achieved with systemic change over 40 years through the appropriate combination of external expertise in the form of the NAO and the internal scrutiny performed by select committees. Treasury dominance in its influence over public expenditure is most marked especially in borrowing and debt arrangements. The partial or whole nationalization of four major banks represents a major stake in terms of public finances. This is a systemic weakness at the heart of public expenditure control, namely that gaps left by parliamentary inertia are readily filled by executive controls driven by Treasury influence. The government's pre-eminence in the rules of procedure that allows it the initiative in public expenditure severely weakens the ability of individual MPs to play a role in financial matters. A modest reform that permits modest expenditure increases (within the remit of offsetting costs elsewhere) to MPs would make a substantial change. It would allow a greater emphasis to be given in parliamentary debate to the policies and decisions that inform, manage, and control public expenditure. At a time when audit systems are strengthened, Parliament's relevance faces further decline. The weaknesses and inertia in parliamentary control appear to reflect a decline in the standard and quality of our democracy today.[116] The coalition government's proposed five-year fixed-term Parliament is also likely to emphasis the realties of government power over the purse and its pre-eminence in setting the agenda for control.

[114] See Education and Skills Committee, *Public Expenditure on Education and Skills*, HC 2004–05, HC 168, The Home Affairs Committee, HC 2004–05, HC 280, the Northern Ireland Affairs Committee, 2004–05, Northern Ireland Departments' 2002–03 Resource Accounts, HC 173.

[115] Scrutiny Unit set up under the late Robin Cook, then Leader of the House of Commons.

[116] O. Gay and B. Winetrobe, *Parliamentary Audit: the Audit committee in Comparative Context* (2003).

FURTHER READING

Balls, E. and O'Donnell, G. (eds), *Reforming Britain's Economic and Financial Policy: Towards Greater Economic Stability* (2002).

Brazier, A. and Ram, V., *The Fiscal Maze* (2006).

Daintith, T. and Page, A., *The Executive in the Constitution: Structure, Autonomy and Internal Control* (1999).

Gay, O. and Winetrobe, B., *Parliamentary Audit: The Audit Committee in Comparative Context, Report to the Audit Committee of the Scottish Parliament* (2003).

Hansard Society, Commission on Parliamentary Scrutiny, *The Challenge for Parliament: Making Government Accountable* (2001).

Heald, D. and McLeod, A., *Public Expenditure, The Laws of Scotland: Stair Memorial Encyclopaedia* (2002).

McKay, W. R. (ed.), *Erskine May: Parliamentary Practice* (23rd edn, 2004).

McKay, William and Johnson, Charles W., *Parliament and Congress* (2010).

Sharman of Redlynch, Lord, *Holding to Account: The Review of Audit and Accountability for Central Government* (2001).

Thain, C. and Wright, M., *The Treasury and Whitehall: The Planning and Control of Public Expenditure 1976–1993* (1995).

USEFUL WEBSITES

Audit Commission: **www.audit-commission.gov.uk**
HM Treasury: **www.hm-treasury.gov.uk**
National Audit Office: **www.nao.gov.uk**
Public Audit Forum: **www.public-audit-forum.gov.uk**
UK National Statistics: **www.statistics.gov.uk**
UK Parliament: **www.parliament.uk**

14

REGULATING INFORMATION

Patrick Birkinshaw

SUMMARY

This chapter briefly examines the arguments in favour of, and against, greater access to government information, openness, and transparency. The traditions of secrecy in British government have given way to 'reform' of official secrecy legislation and legislation for the secret services since the 1980s. Before the Freedom of Information Act 2000 (FOIA 2000), the courts granted rights to disclosure and inspection of government documents to litigants. (Future government reforms may limit disclosures of intelligence information.) The FOIA 2000 places positive duties on public authorities covered by the Act to disclose information they hold upon request, though subject to exemptions. The Act amounts to the most important provision on access to government information, and thus on increased openness.

The state has become a massive repository of information concerning identifiable individuals. This raises alarms about the security of its data banks and the protection of personal privacy. The Data Protection Act 1998 (DPA 1998) provides some protection, but there is a need for further reforms.

Overall, the FOIA 2000 and DPA 1998 represent important steps in the right direction by giving public access to official information and protecting individuals against abuse of personal information. The system is not perfect and areas for reform are identified.

INTRODUCTION

There is nothing new about an information state. The state, or officialdom, has acquired information since responsibility was assumed for defence, security, taxation, census taking or whatever. While the emphasis in the UK in the 19th and 20th centuries was on protecting the information that the state had acquired, most famously by the use of Official Secrets legislation commencing in 1889, slowly, but inevitably, pressure mounted for disclosure to the public of information held by the state and public bodies. Today the emphasis has moved towards proactive access to information from the state, and towards the state and state institutions operating transparently and openly.[1] Transparency is much broader than access. It means opening up the processes of governance to scrutiny, investigation, monitoring, and explanation and that where people wish to participate meaningful opportunities should be provided. Open government means opening up the processes of government and government meetings to public view and scrutiny. This development has been accompanied by growing awareness of the need to secure information about individuals and to protect their privacy by more effective regulation.

The arguments in favour of openness, transparency, and access to information have been well rehearsed.[2] They include the desirability of giving information about the operation of public authorities exercising public power to those who are primarily affected by that power – the public. Openness concerns the right to know what government is doing on our behalf and under our sufferance and in our name. It concerns widespread democratic involvement in the exercise of power, accountability, explanation, and the sharing of knowledge. It involves a vision of governance in which citizens are treated as responsible individuals and not simply as subjects or *les administrés* – there to be told what to do but not to know why they should do it or upon what basis they should do it. A wider ranging objective of openness involves establishing a context in which people are better able to understand how government works and to allow them to participate more effectively in governance. To make them feel, in other words, like stakeholders and not that 'nanny knows best'.

In the UK, until 2000, provision of information directly to the public of state held information did not sit easily with the custom and conventions of constitutional practice and representative democracy. The primary recipient of official information was Parliament by way of ministers responding to Parliamentary Questions in fulfilment of their ministerial responsibility to Parliament. These practices of governance had been developed over centuries. To provide information directly to the public would undermine the authority and position of Parliament, it was constantly reiterated. Provision of information, it was argued, would lead to unnecessary expense, could undermine public security, individual privacy, and confidentiality. It could produce captiousness and querulousness. Removal of the mystery surrounding governance would undermine the trust in government. Enforced secrecy, however, did not enhance that trust.[3]

Official enquiries, official papers, and reports, including from the late 1960s those of the parliamentary ombudsman, and *Hansard*, all provided invaluable information to researchers, scholars, press, and media. Vital information might be published to

[1] See Constitutional Reform and Governance Act 2010, s. 28 and Pt 5.

[2] See Public Administration Select Committee, *Your Right to Know: the Government's proposals for a Freedom of Information Act*, Third Report, HC 398 (1997–98) vol. I , and the reports below, n. 32.

[3] See the Franks Report, *Departmental Committee on Section 2 of the Official Secrets Act 1911*, Cmnd 5104, Vol. 1 (1972), and P. Birkinshaw, *Freedom of Information: the Law, the Practice and the Ideal* (4th edn, 2010) chs 2, 3 and 9.

assist those intent on social or political reform. But publication of much of this information was under the *control* of government and on its terms. There was no legal concept of a right to official information. Freedom of information (FOI), as will be shown, means access to publicly held information as a presumptive right subject to exemptions: it does not mean complete *freedom* of information.

The Public Records Acts 1958 and 1967 opened up public records to the public after initially 50 years, reduced to 30, and now to 20 years under the Constitutional Reform and Governance Act 2010. These provisions cover papers transferred to the National Archives. Scotland and Northern Ireland have their own arrangements. Those not transferred are not so covered.[4] Some may be 'closed' and not published. The FOIA 2000, as amended, now governs the position on rights of access to such material. Closure may only be in accordance with a relevant exemption under the FOIA 2000. This legislation is dealt with below in relation to general access rights.

OFFICIAL SECRECY

Traditional methods for regulating or censoring information fell into desuetude in the 1980s given the increasing access to information data banks at the press of a button. Before cyberspace, an indication of the limits on court orders enforcing confidentiality or official secrecy in globalized connections came with the *Spycatcher* saga in the 1980s, when the limits of criminal law and the Official Secrets Act led the government to invoke the civil law of confidence to protect government information. It became apparent that it was impossible to prevent reports of what had become publicly available.[5] The porous quality of the digitised globe was exposed dramatically at the end of 2010 when the first tranches of 250,000 US diplomatic and security despatches were released without authorization by WikiLeaks.

The first significant concession by central government towards relaxation of official secrets laws came with the Official Secrets Act 1989. The measure was described by the Home Secretary as an 'essay in openness'. Reform had been mooted for 17 years. This Act repealed Official Secrets Act 1911, s. 2, a notoriously broad blunderbuss covering by the criminal law every unauthorized disclosure of official information – or so it was widely reported. Whatever the position, s. 2 was a disreputable and hopelessly broad piece of legislation. The government's hand was forced by the notorious acquittal by a jury of Clive Ponting, a senior civil servant. Ponting had been prosecuted for leaking defence documents to the chair of the Commons Defence Committee revealing that

[4] Public Records Act 1958, s. 3(4).

[5] *AG* v. *Guardian Newspapers Ltd (No. 2)* [1988] 3 All ER 545. *Spycatcher* had been written by a former MI5 agent who could not be indicted under the 1911 Act because he was outside the UK jurisdiction. The book had been published overseas but copies had become freely available in the UK. The courts basically ruled that the law of confidentiality could not be used to suppress publication of information that had become widely available. An injunction would only be awarded where there was a danger to the public interest in publication. See *Observer and Guardian* v. *UK* [1991] 14 EHRR 153. Also, *AG* v. *Blake* [2000] 4 All ER 385 (HL).

the government had been misrepresenting the circumstances leading to the sinking by HM Navy of the Argentinian battleship *General Belgrano* during hostilities leading to the re-taking of the Falklands in 1982.[6] Presumably the jury placed a higher premium on openness than compliance with the judge's direction on the law.

Under the Official Secrets Act 1989, information was to be protected against unauthorized disclosure by the criminal law only when it fell within one of six protected classes of information, covering security and intelligence, defence, international relations, prevention of crime, disclosure of information relating to special investigations by the security and intelligence services, and interceptions of communications.

The Act included provisions about unauthorized disclosure (see s. 7) by three groups of persons. First, those who are security and intelligence officials or 'notified persons'. Disclosure by them of security and intelligence information is prohibited. Although the prohibition is virtually 'absolute', offences in Official Secrets Act 1989, ss 1(1) and 4(3) (below), are subject to a very limited defence. In *Shayler*, the Law Lords ruled that offences under ss 1(1) and 4 did not breach European Convention on Human Rights (ECHR), Art. 10 protecting freedom of speech.[7] The Act provides no public interest defence.

The second group is other Crown servants and government contractors who make 'damaging' disclosures of information under ss 1–3, or who disclose information under s. 4, knowing that it is protected under ss 1–4.

The third group is others (for example editors, journalists) who make damaging disclosures of information communicated in breach of the Act knowing, or having reasonable cause to believe, the disclosure would be damaging. Disclosure of information under s. 4(3) about special investigation powers conducted by the security and intelligence services or of interception material (phone taps, email and communications interception) does not require proof of such knowledge. Knowledge of the protected status under ss 1–4 has to be established. Prosecutions under the Official Secrets Act 1989 occur fairly regularly.

There are 336 specific statutory prohibitions on disclosure of information, breaches of many of which are punishable by criminal sanctions.[8] Furthermore, there are disciplinary offences of disclosure of information which are punishable in administrative proceedings against civil servants and police, as set out in civil service/police codes. It is to be noted that internal classification of documents in UK law has no legal effect – unlike EU law. Such classification is an instruction as to the manner in which information should be treated and kept, i.e. do not read on trains/planes/buses or remove from the office or disclose to a person without necessary security clearance (but see OSA s. 1(4)(b)).

Throughout the public sector generally, breaches of confidentiality would be regarded as a serious matter justifying disciplinary action and possibly dismissal. The

[6] *R.* v. *Ponting* [1985] *Crim LR* 318, C. Ponting, *The Right to Know* (1985).

[7] *R.* v. *Shayler* [2002] UKHL 11.

[8] Department for Constitutional Affairs, *Review of Statutory Prohibitions on Disclosure* (2005).

Public Interest Disclosure Act 1998 amended the contractual employment relationship to allow qualifying disclosures – 'whistleblowing' – in the public interest, but the thrust of the Act is that disclosure should be made to higher administrative echelons or named and official recipients, i.e. internal reporting. Under very exacting conditions outside disclosures may be made. There must be no element of personal profit in disclosure. The Public Interest Disclosure Act 1998 does not apply to the secret services or where breaches of the Official Secrets Act occur.

THE SECRET SERVICES

The Official Secrets Act 1989 was introduced contemporaneously with the Security Service Act 1989, which placed the security service MI5 on a statutory basis instead of allowing it to operate under the medieval obscurity of the royal prerogative. Under the ECHR, a statutory framework was necessary for the exercise by the service of its special investigatory powers. Provision was made for the authorization of interference with property (trespass) to obtain information under ministerial warrant. A commissioner (senior judge) was established to oversee the exercise of powers under warrant and a tribunal could hear complaints by those who were 'surveiled'. Subsequently, the Intelligence Services Act 1994 introduced limited forms of parliamentary oversight over the security and intelligence services by the Intelligence and Security Committee. Its members are 'notified persons' under Official Secrets Act 1989, s.1 and are covered by that section (above). Statutory regulation involving oversight of, and provision for dealing with, complaints about the intelligence service's (MI6) investigations was introduced. Interception of communications had been placed onto a statutory basis in 1985. The statutory regulation of interception, surveillance, and the special powers of the services was either repealed or overhauled by the Regulation of Investigatory Powers Act 2000.

The so called 'war on terror', as the Americans describe it, brought a new prominence to MI5 and MI6, raising troubling questions about the secrecy surrounding their operations. Problems emerged in relation to secrecy in judicial proceedings, discussed below. Questions were raised about the ability of the Intelligence and Security Committee to conduct meaningful investigations into the activities of the secret services when it was revealed in litigation that important documents relevant to its enquiries had not been disclosed to the committee.[9] The committee has complained about not getting the information it requires. Information may be withheld by the services where 'sensitive', or after a Secretary of State's determination. Its reports are vetted by the Prime Minister before publication. Meaningful oversight in this area may mean giving fuller and more effective powers and independence to parliamentary oversight and investigation, including appointing an opposition MP as chair. The chair of the Intelligence and Security Committee is at present appointed by the Prime Minister, unlike chairs of select committees, who are elected by MPs.

[9] *Binyam Mohamed* v. *Secretary of State* [2009] EWHC 152 (Admin).

The services are excluded from the FOIA 2000 and information held by public authorities from the services or relating to them is given an absolute exemption from that Act (below).

COURTS, SECRECY, AND OPENNESS

The special demands of justice before courts have required inroads into government secrecy. Long before the UK Parliament passed the FOIA 2000, the judges had increasingly recognized that the demands of justice might necessitate access to documents in the possession of government (or private parties) by litigants, although they realized that it was not for the courts to create an FOI Act. Such a right, however, had to meet a competing public interest claim from government. This was originally expressed as Crown Privilege originating from the immunity of the Crown from suit in its own courts.[10] Although the Crown Proceedings Act 1947 subjected the Crown to legal suit in defined circumstances, the Crown could still resist disclosure of documents to a litigant either where the *existence* of the document should not be disclosed or where, although the existence of the documents was acknowledged, inspection of their class or contents would be contrary to the public interest. Public interest immunity as it came to be known often set a dramatic scene in which the competing public interests of state security or protection of informers on one part and the doing of justice on the other have to be balanced by courts, if necessary after judicial inspection of the documents in question.

The immunity became a matter of media and public debate in the trial of British businessmen for criminal offences involving breaches of export regulations when they exported dual use equipment to Iraq in the 1990s. The collapse of the *Matrix Churchill* trial after it was disclosed by a minister giving evidence that the government had known about the export of the equipment (one of the defendants had been assisting MI6) and that the export regulations had been changed without informing Parliament led to the Scott report on *The Export of Defence Equipment and Dual Use Goods to Iraq*.[11] What was of importance was that the dual use trial had seen the reliance by the government on public interest immunity certificates in a criminal trial. (The judge ruled against the certificates in several claims.) Their use in criminal trials, although pre-dating *Matrix Churchill*, was to become more widespread in criminal trials involving terrorists and serious crime and where the prosecution was anxious to protect information about techniques, methods and informers.[12] Eventually, a procedure was devised in cases involving suspected terrorists before the Special Immigration Appeals Commission challenging their detention before deportation on the grounds of national security

[10] *Duncan* v. *Cammell Laird Co Ltd* [1942] AC 624 originally accepted the decision of the minister as final but *Conway* v. *Rimmer* [1968] AC 910 paved the way for the modern law.

[11] HC 115 (1995–96).

[12] *R.* v. *H* [2004] UKHL 3. See Criminal Justice Act 2003, Pt 5 and related codes and guidelines. After the Scott report, the government undertook to make public interest immunity claims only on a contents and not a class basis.

and in judicial proceedings challenging control orders involving suspected terrorists. The procedure involved the use of special advocates who would meet the suspected terrorist before 'closed material' was disclosed to the special advocate, but who could not thereafter meet the suspect. The suspect would not see the closed evidence and proceedings were conducted in camera for closed evidence and judgments involving closed material were not published.

The shortcomings involved in using special advocates were well known to the courts.[13] The European Court of Human Rights ruled in *A* v. *United Kingdom* in 2009 that, notwithstanding the security sensitivity of evidence in such cases, the suspect had a right to a fair hearing, and information relevant to a suspect's defence must be shown to the suspect in order for them to instruct their counsel.[14] Denying this would be a breach of ECHR, Art. 6 and open and fair justice. In *Secretary of State for the Home Department* v. *AF*,[15] the Law Lords too held that denying access to such information would constitute a breach of Art. 6 and that a previous decision of the Law Lords was inconsistent with *A*.[16] The courts have also refused to allow the extension of the special advocate procedure to civil litigation, although the case is on appeal to the Supreme Court.[17]

The UK courts have become more sensitized to the general question of transparency and openness. In the special circumstances of terrorism the courts have ruled that public disclosure in an open judgment should be made of US intelligence information about the involvement of MI5 in torture. This was despite the protests of the US government that judicial disclosure would jeopardize the sharing of intelligence in the future. A crucial factor in the Court of Appeal's judgment was that disclosure had already been ordered in an American court.[18] But for that, disclosure would not have been made. In the High Court the open judgment disclosure was ordered (subject to appeal) before the US litigation and represents a high water mark in judicial second guessing on the interests of national security – an area which the courts have consistently ruled to fall within the exclusive zone of expertise of the executive[19] In announcing a judicial inquiry by the Secret Services Commissioner into the allegations of torture, in which intelligence would be dealt with in private session, Prime Minister Cameron indicated that proposals would likely be made to restrict disclosure of intelligence information by courts in the future.[20]

Moving away from terror-related matters, courts have developed tests for giving cogent and reliable reasons for decision making.[21] In a striking case in 2007, the High Court ruled that the government announcement of a nuclear new-build policy was unlawful because of inadequate consultation and inadequate information

[13] *Abu Rideh* [2008] EWHC 1993 (Admin).

[14] *A* v. *United Kingdom* [2009] ECHR 301.

[15] [2009] UKHL 28.

[16] *MB* [2007] UKHL 46.

[17] *Al Rawi* v. *Security Service* [2010] EWCA Civ 482. Cf. *Roberts* [2005] UKHL 45.

[18] *R. (Mohamed)* v. *Secretary of State* [2010] EWCA Civ 158.

[19] *Rehman* [2001] UKHL 47.

[20] *Hansard*, HC, cols 175–90 (6 July 2010). A National Security Council was estabilished by the coalition government as the main forum for dicussion of security.

[21] *R* v. *Secretary of State for the Home Department ex parte Doody* [1994] AC 531, *Stefan* v. *GMC* [1999] 1 WLR 1293 (PC).

on economics and nuclear waste. The government did not appeal.[22] The courts also became more conscious of the need to protect information relating to personal privacy by the application of ECHR, Art. 8 to the law of confidentiality. The emphasis moved from protection of commercial confidences to protection of personal information.[23] But commercial organizations and celebrities were not slow to realize that they too had a right to privacy protection which might involve use of measures to stop publicity of any information about their involvement in litigation or of the litigation itself. An unsuccessful attempt was made to prevent publication of reports of Parliamentary Questions about litigation involving tax evasion and toxic waste dumping.[24]

EU REQUIREMENTS

Our international commitments brought about by membership of the Council of Europe and the European Community (now Union) pressured the UK government to introduce reforms allowing individuals access to personal information or data held by what are known as data controllers. The law is now the DPA 1998, implementing Directive (EC) 95/46. The DPA 1998 is one of a number of information statutes accompanying the FOIA 2000 and subsequent legislation. The legislation includes the Environmental Information Regulations 2004 (EIR 2004) (implementing Directive (EC) 2003/4)[25] and the Re-use of Public Sector Information Regulations 2004 (implementing Directive (EC) 2003/98). (Government sits on a vast bank of information. Some of it needs to be protected for reasons of security, international relations, prevention of crime, protection of privacy. But much of it has the capacity to generate creation of wealth and development in the hands of those with the necessary skills. This was the objective behind the Re-use Regulations.)

'OPENING UP' GOVERNMENT INFORMATION AND IT

The world has increasingly been networked by the internet. To no surprise, governments have become prime users of networked information. In relation to e-government, the white paper *Putting the Frontline First: Smarter Government*[26] and the launch of **www.data.gov.uk** outline developments on information technology (IT) and public service. There are many policy statements on consultation[27] and numerous provisions concerning the wider public sector and regulated (formerly nationalized) industries and publication of information. The Dacre review of the Public Records Act stated in

[22] *R. (Greenpeace)* v. *Secretary of State for Trade and Industry* [2007] EWHC 311 (Admin).

[23] *Campbell* v. *MGN Ltd* [2002] UKHL 22. ECHR, Art. 8 protects private and family life.

[24] www.guardian.co.uk/media/2009/oct/13/guardian-gagged-parliamentary-question.

[25] The Directive was based on the United Nations Economic Commission for Europe Aarhus Convention: Convention on Access to Information, Public Participation in Decision-Making and Access to Justice in Environmental Matters (25 June 1998), available at www.unece.org/env/pp.

[26] Cm. 7753 (December 2009).

[27] www.berr.gov.uk/files/file47158.pdf.

relation to government's use of IT that there had been 'a significant increase in both volume and candour of official information made available during recent years'.[28]

Many public bodies have responsibilities in relation to official information. The National Archives (formerly Public Records Office) is responsible for national archives. (It has already been noted that Scotland, Northern Ireland and Wales have their own arrangements.) The Office of Public Sector Information (OPSI) is at the heart of information policy, setting standards, delivering access and encouraging the re-use of public sector information. OPSI provides a 'wide range of services to the public, information industry, government and the wider public sector relating to finding, using, sharing and trading information'.[29] The Office for National Statistics operates under the independent UK Statistics Authority which reports to Parliament directly.

TOWARDS FREEDOM OF INFORMATION LEGISLATION

Although the UK government was a late convert to FOI, efforts had been made to introduce greater openness into government operations involving Crown and non-Crown bodies. In local government an access to information act was enacted in 1985: local authorities are under duties to allow the public to attend meetings of the authority and executive and, subject to exemptions, to disclose information[30] Some other authorities are covered by open meetings laws, but this is not pervasive in the UK.

For the Crown, as well as the legislation outlined above, various non-legislative devices were introduced before the FOIA 2000, including John Major's 1994 Code on Openness. This imposed a non-statutory obligation on bodies covered by the Code (essentially those under the jurisdiction of the Parliamentary Ombudsman) to disclose information to requesters subject to exemptions. The Code was operational until 31 December 2004 (after which date the FOIA 2000 came into force) and was policed by the ombudsman (whose recommendations are non-enforceable).

The Freedom of Information Bill was published in 1999. The Bill was preceded by a white paper,[31] pre-legislative consultation and scrutiny by a House of Commons select committee as well as a special committee of the House of Lords.[32] The white paper claimed that experience revealed the importance of changing culture by a requirement of 'active' disclosure, so that public authorities would get used to making information publicly available in the normal course of their activities.[33] It was

[28] Dacre, *Review of 30 Year Rule* (2009) 14, available at www.30yearrulereview.org.uk.

[29] www.direct.gov.uk/en/Dl1/Directories/DG_10012002.

[30] Local Government (Access etc) Act 1985, and SI 2000/3272, SI 2002/716 and SI 2006/69. Statutes concerning the admission of the press to meetings of local authorities go back to 1908.

[31] *Your Right to Know: Freedom of Information*, Cm. 3818 (1997).

[32] HC 398 I and II (1997–98), HC 570 I and II (1998–99), and HL 97 (1998–99).

[33] Cm. 3818 (1997) paras 2.17–2.18.

one of several Bills to be introduced by the Blair government as part of a package on constitutional reform. The Bill and the eventual Act were less open than the white paper's proposals. The Bill received royal assent in November 2000. Rights of access came into effect on 1 January 2005. Over four years were spent preparing for a change in the culture of secrecy.

FOI was accompanied by grand claims. 'It is part of bringing our politics up to date, of letting politics catch up with the aspirations of people and delivering not just more open government but more effective, more efficient, government for the future'.[34] It would signal a new relationship between government and governed, one which sees 'the public as legitimate stakeholders in the running of the country and sees election to serve the public as being given on trust'.[35] 'Public information' said Gordon Brown, did not belong to the government. It 'belonged to the public'.[36]

In January 2009, the Dacre Review of the Public Records Act emphasized 'the presumption of openness [and] the enhanced culture of transparency' implied by FOI legislation. However, the 'UK government has not fully reconciled itself to the implications of its own act'.[37] The report also described how 'openness, transparency and accountability have been strengthened' by the Act.[38]

On coming to power in May 2010, the coalition government immediately announced a new emphasis on extra-statutory transparency in a series of pronouncements.[39] An initially non-statutory Independent Office for Budget Responsibility would report on public financial forecasting forming the basis of the budget. (The 'independence' of the body was soon questioned.) The announcements included financial details of all government expenditure and contracts of government and details of senior officials' salaries. Publication would help to give people the information they really required rather than that which government wanted them to see. The government accepted this material was complex new data rather than easily usable comparative data. A Public Sector Transparency Board would be established in the Cabinet Office applying public data transparency principles.[40]

Giving individuals information they really needed was also at the heart of the coalition plans for reforming the NHS. Information was to be provided on outcomes and results of treatment and not just on waiting lists.[41]

[34] Tony Blair, *Speech to the Campaign for FOI Awards Ceremony*, 25 March 1996. [35] Ibid.

[36] Gordon Brown, *Speech on Liberty*, London, 25 October 2007. [37] Dacre, above, n. 28, p. 13.

[38] Dacre, above, n. 28, p. 11.

[39] *The Coalition: our programme for government – Government Transparency*, available at www.cabinetoffice.gov.uk/news/coalition-documents. On the Office for Budget Responsibility, see http://budget-responsibility.independent.gov.uk. For the development of policy on transparency, see http://transparency.number10.gov.uk.

[40] http://data.gov.uk/blog/new-public-sector-transparency-board-and-public-data-transparency-principles.

[41] *Equity and Excellence: Liberating the NHS*, Cm. 7881 (July 2010).

Any implicit criticism of FOI, and the fact that the FOIA 2000 was supposed to give the public the information they wanted, was overborne by the fact that extensions to the legislation were announced in the coalition agreement in May 2010.[42]

THE LEGAL FRAMEWORK[43]

The main driving force behind greater official openness has been the FOIA 2000. Under this Act the body responsible for overseeing, promoting, and enforcing the Act is the Office of the Information Commissioner. That office is responsible for a variety of additional information rights covered by the DPA 1998, the EIR 2004, and the Privacy and Electronic Communications (EC Directive) Regulations 2003. The latter three measures implement EC Directives.

The FOIA 2000 seeks to give presumptive rights of individual access to information held by public authorities in the UK, subject to exemptions. The Information Tribunal, which may hear appeals against the Information Commissioner's decision, has stated that FOIA 2000, s.1 creates a 'new fundamental right to information'.[44] The Act also seeks to make information available proactively through publication schemes. These were revised in 2009 together with guidance on such schemes by the Information Commissioner. The objective is that such schemes will cover more and more information, thus reducing the necessity of making a request for information. Basically schemes have to publish information about:

- Who we are and what we do
- What we spend and how we spend it
- What our priorities are and how we are doing
- How we make decisions
- Our policies and procedures
- Lists and registers
- The services we offer

Authorities have to specify what additional information they are to publish including financial reports, means of access and charges. These are organized according to groups

[42] http://www.conservatives.com/News/News_stories/2010/05/Coalition_Agreement_published.aspx, see under 10 on civil liberties, and *The Coalition; our programme for government* (2010). The Protection of Freedoms Bill (2011) contains amendments to the FOIA.

[43] The sponsor department for the FOIA 2000 is the Ministry of Justice. For advice on the Act, see www.justice.gov.uk/requestinginformation.htm and www.justice.gov.uk/guidance.htm. The Act established the Information Tribunal (now First Tier Tribunal Information Rights) and the Information Commissioner, see www.informationtribunal.gov.uk and www.ico.gov.uk. The Information Commissioner's office is an FOI champion under its statutory remit and also has numerous sites for advice and assistance, see www.ico.gov.uk/what_we_cover/freedom_of_information.aspx. The Department for Environment, Food and Rural Affairs is the government sponsor for the EIR 2004 and it offers advice on the EIR 2004 and the environment, see www.defra.gov.uk/corporate/policy/opengov/index.htm.

[44] EA/2006/0006, *DfES* v. *IC and Evening Standard (AP)*, para. 61.

of public authorities: central government, local government, etc. The Commissioner has produced general formats for different groups of authorities which they may develop for their own needs. The Commissioner has to approve such schemes but cannot control content.

ACCESS RIGHTS

The right of access under FOIA 2000 is to information held by a public authority.[45] On an application, an authority must confirm or deny whether it holds the information. Authorities bound by the Act are listed in FOIA 2000, Sched. 1. If not listed, for example the Queen, royal family, secret services, the body is *excluded* from the FOIA 2000. The number of bodies covered by the FOIA 2000 is huge: between 100,000 and 115,000. It famously includes Parliament. Many nationalized concerns, especially banks, are excluded. Some bodies are partly under the FOIA 2000 but are excluded for some items: the Bank of England and BBC are examples here. The latter has featured in a large body of litigation on its exclusion from the FOIA 2000 for the purposes of information held relating to 'art, journalism or literature'.[46]

The Minister of Justice has the power to designate private bodies as public authorities for FOIA 2000 purposes. In July 2009, four bodies were chosen as candidates for designation – all four had a notable quality of officialdom about them and included the Association of Chief Police Officers. The Minister of Justice may designate as a public authority a body that is performing functions of a public authority under contract, or performing functions of a public nature. In contracts, the FOIA 2000 will cover the authority. Guidance exists on how authorities should deal with requests for information about the contract.[47] The request is made to the authority not the private contractor. Private utilities are not covered by FOIA 2000 but the regulators are – so a request may be made for information held by them. Utilities are under duties to provide information under their governing statutes such as the Utilities Act 2000. Network Rail and Northern Rock were identified as possible candidates for designation by the Conservatives in April 2010.

The EIR 2004 cover a wider range of bodies because of the way the regulations are phrased including those performing *functions* of *public administration* and bodies *controlled* by an authority.[48] All authorities have to determine under which legal regime the information requested falls. It is not the responsibility of the requester.

The DPA 1998 covers holders of 'personal data' whether in the public or private sector. In the case of public authorities, they are covered by DPA 1998 protection in a broader range of 'unstructured' data, but these data are not regulated under the DPA 1998 as is the case with 'personal data' in electronic or 'structured filing systems'. These

[45] Guidance is provided on 'held', see above, n. 43.

[46] P. Birkinshaw, *Freedom of Information* (4th edn, 2010) 6 and 142.

[47] www.ico.gov.uk/upload/documents/library/freedom_of_information/detailed_specialist_guides/awareness_guidance_5_annexe_-_public_sector_contracts.pdf.

[48] See EA/2006/0061-62, *Network Rail Ltd* v. *IC and NRI Ltd, FoE etc*, EA/2006/0083, *Port of London Authority* v. *IC & another* and *Smartsource* v. *IC* [2010] UKUT 415 (AAC).

terms have been subject to a narrow interpretation by the Court of Appeal[49] which has been criticized by the EC Article 29 Data Protection Working Party. Personal data should be given a 'wide and flexible' interpretation.[50] In DPA 1998 cases the Commissioner acts more like a negotiator although he can assess a data controller's processing of data at the request of a data subject to see whether there is compliance with the data protection principles which set out the standards of data protection.[51]

The FOIA 2000 covers UK bodies, Welsh and Northern Irish bodies, and English bodies as specified. Scotland has its own FOI Act, the Freedom of Information (Scotland) Act 2002 for Scottish authorities.[52] The Scottish act is based largely on the UK measure but with some crucial differences. There is no appeal against an FOI decision to a tribunal in Scotland.

Anyone, irrespective of motive, may make a written request under the FOIA 2000 for information. The right covers 'recorded' information in whatever form. No interest or *locus* has to be established. Where the rights of others are involved, the provision of safeguards is contained in a code under FOIA 2000, s. 45. This sets out good practice in relation to consultation with third parties. A third party has no rights of appeal under the Act and would have to commence a judicial review or private action preventing disclosure under the FOIA 2000. After disclosure, injuries to a third party would have to be compensable under private actions. Breaches of the FOIA 2000 itself create no rights of action, but negligence and confidentiality are common law actions, not breaches of the Act. Disclosures are privileged unless malice is present.

Under the FOIA 2000, authorities have 20 working days to respond (the National Archives have 30 working days). This period may be extended where an authority is relying upon a public interest not to disclose (below). A further 20 working days should suffice, the Commissioner has suggested. Some cases have gone on for more than two years. Delays occur because of complexity or lack of personnel (in either an authority or the Information Commissioner's Office).

The FOI right is a right to 'information' but records and files, subject to exemption, may be inspected *in situ*. A summary may be requested. The requester may state a preference and 'so far as possible' an authority shall respect that preference. Documents may be requested. The requester has to supply a name for correspondence and an address (including email). Fees may be requested. The requester may be asked to clarify a request and for further information to assist the authority. An authority must provide advice and assistance.

If it is anticipated that the fees involved will exceed the fees limit the requester may be asked to make payment of the estimated amount. Fees are waived for up to £600 (central government, armed forces, and Parliament), £450 all other authorities.

[49] *Durant* v. *FSA* [2003] EWCA Civ 1746. The court held that data should have a 'biographical' focus to be personal data.

[50] See the Information Commissioner's Office, www.ico.gov.uk/upload/documents/library/data_protection/detailed_specialist_guides/personal_data_flowchart_v1_with_preface001.pdf.

[51] DPA 1998, s. 42.

[52] www.england-legislation.hmso.gov.uk/legislation/scotland/acts2002/asp_20020013_en_1.

Labour is costed at £25 per hour. Requests involving fees in excess of these amounts may be refused or complied with if the requester agrees to pay the required amount. Fees for copying and postage (disbursements) may be charged.

An authority refusing a request must state under FOIA 2000, s.17 which exemption applies and the reasons why it applies (if not apparent) and, if relying on a public interest, must state the reasons why the public interest applies. The Commissioner and Tribunal have given rulings on the giving of reasons. A mere reiteration of statutory words is not enough. The reasons must properly explain the basis of the decision without compromising properly exempt information. Notice also has to be given in the statement of the rights of internal review and of appeal to the Commissioner.

If information is refused, a requester may ask for an internal review. The justification for the administrative review was to keep the process cheap and accessible. This was also the reason for introducing the Commissioner and Tribunal. The Commissioner and Tribunal do not charge fees and each party bears their own costs before the Tribunal – unless they behave vexatiously. The Tribunal is meant to operate informally so legal representation would not be required. Legal representation is however becoming increasingly common.

THE POWERS OF THE INFORMATION COMMISSIONER AND INFORMATION TRIBUNAL

If the Commissioner believes the authority is failing in its duties, he may issue an enforcement notice which the authority may appeal against (FOIA 2000, s.52). When the Commissioner determines whether access should be given or denied, he issues a decision notice. In addition, the Commissioner has power to issue information notices. Failing to comply with notices by providing the information may be treated as a contempt which is punishable by fine or (rarely) imprisonment. There was one prosecution until 2009, but the process was used successfully on a couple of occasions to make authorities compliant. On contempt, it should be noted that all decision notices end by spelling out this sanction.

False statements and alteration of documents (for example in response to a request), except where properly authorized *before* a request, are criminal offences. The Commissioner may issue a practice recommendation under FOIA 2000, s. 48 in relation to practices which do not meet the standards set out in the Code of Guidance under s. 45 or s. 46 (on management of public records). The Commissioner has full powers of entry and inspection after obtaining a judicial warrant. These are considerable powers.

The Commissioner's office is on an FOI budget of about £5.5 million (2009–10) plus fees. The total FOI cost across the public sector is estimated at £35 million (2006–07). The office received no increase in 2008–09 despite a 15 per cent increase in case load.[53] The Commissioner has been the subject of complaints of delay in dealing with requests especially from the media. There are widespread complaints about inadequate resourcing and delays. Such complaints are likely to increase.

[53] *Annual Report 2008-09*, HC 619 (2008–09). Grant in aid remained at £5.5 million for 2009–10.

EXEMPTIONS

FOI regimes are always accompanied by exemptions. Most exemptions under the FOIA 2000 are qualified and subject to a public interest test which is measured first of all by the authority to which a request is made. Published guidance and case law explain the approaches that authorities should adopt.[54] It is then subject to the judgement of the Commissioner and on appeal covering fact, law or merits to the Tribunal. The onus of establishing an exemption, or public interest in non disclosure, lies on the authority, not the requester. Decisions of the Commissioner and Tribunal on the public interest ordering disclosure are subject to a ministerial veto (below). Whether information is intended for future publication, whether requests are repetitive or vexatious, whether information is available elsewhere – all grounds for denying access – are all appealable to the Upper Tribunal and the Court of Appeal. They can only hear appeals on a point of law from the Tribunal, i.e. not on the merits, so they cannot intervene in a judgement call unless it involves a legal error. To maintain secrecy, the balance in favour of secrecy has to outweigh that in favour of disclosure. In other words, where the interests are equal in weight, disclosure prevails.

Some exemptions under the Act are 'absolute', meaning there is no public interest override in favour of disclosure.

Some FOIA 2000 exemptions are class exemptions, i.e. if information falls within that class it is exempt. In other cases, the majority, exemptions are only allowed where damage or harm would be caused, or would be likely to be caused, by disclosure. Unless the exemption is absolute, a public interest test applies (above). Some authorities have tried to argue that intellectual property rights are a de facto FOIA 2000 exemption. They are not: they have to fall within an existing exemption, for example commercial interests, trade secrets, confidentiality.[55]

The exemptions are set out in FOIA 2000, ss 21–44. These define the protected interests. In the case of national security (s. 24, and also the secret services s. 23), a minister may enter a certificate to this effect which the Upper Tribunal may review but in a very limited way. Otherwise the exemption is reviewable by the Commissioner, i.e. the Commissioner may establish whether the exemption is made out or not. If it is established, then the Commissioner determines the public interest in disclosure or non-disclosure where the authority has decided not to disclose.

The numerous exemptions cover: information accessible to applicant by other means [absolute]; information intended for future publication; information supplied by, or relating to, bodies dealing with security matters [absolute]; national security (above); defence; international relations; relations within the UK; the economy; investigations and proceedings conducted by public authorities; law enforcement; court records [absolute]; audit functions; parliamentary privilege [absolute]: formulation of government policy, etc; prejudice to effective conduct of public affairs [absolute in relation to Parliament]; communications with the sovereign, etc. and honours.

[54] Above, n. 43.

[55] Under the EIR 2004, see *R. (Ofcom)* v. *IC* [2009] EWCA Civ 90.

Section 37 was amended by Constitutional Reform and Governance Act 2010, s. 46 and Sched. 7 so that communications by authorities with the sovereign and heir and second in line of succession to the throne are absolutely exempt as are communications with those who subsequently become sovereign, etc. Communications with other members of the royal family and royal household are subject to an ordinary exemption except where communication is with the sovereign, etc.

Exemptions continue with health and safety; environmental information (but dealt with under the environmental regulations); personal information [absolute – dealt with under the DPA 1998]; information provided in confidence [absolute]; legal professional privilege; commercial interests; and other legal prohibitions on disclosure [absolute].

In the case of all absolute exemptions apart from s. 23 and the new additions to s. 37, the exemption is absolute because there are other regimes dealing with access or there are legal prohibitions on disclosure which are binding on the authority. Superficially, it appears that there are 23 exemptions. In fact, there are more than this because some sections confer multiple exemptions. The wide number of exemptions has led to a great deal of criticism.

THE VETO

The FOIA 2000 allows a cabinet minister (Justice Secretary) to issue a veto which overrides the decision of the Commissioner or Tribunal to allow disclosure or to rule that the Neither Confirm Nor Deny provision (NCND) is not applicable (FOIA 2000, s. 53). The NCDC applies to most exemptions and allows an authority to override the duty to confirm or deny whether it holds documents upon request where such confirmation or denial would involve the disclosure of exempt information. The veto is final, subject to a judicial review. If the veto were exercised regularly, government would be heavily criticized by the Parliament, the media and press, and the public. It would seriously undermine the claims for the FOIA 2000.

There have been two vetoes to date (January 2011) both in 2009, and both referring to disclosure of cabinet minutes concerning discussion of the Attorney General's legal advice on invading Iraq, and on devolution.[56] In both cases the Justice Secretary emphasized the overriding need for collective responsibility and confidentiality of cabinet discussions. In the first case the veto was issued after the Tribunal upheld the Commissioner's decision notice ordering disclosure. In the second case the veto was issued after the Commissioner's decision to order disclosure. Although legally the decision on a veto is that of the Justice Secretary, an undertaking was given in 2004 that cabinet colleagues would be consulted. In the case of the Iraq veto, it was widely

[56] See Information Commissioner's Office, HC 622 (2008–09); Ministry of Justice, *Exercise of the executive override under s.53 FOIA* (2009), and Information Commissioner's Office, HC 218 (2009–10) on veto and devolution. See EA/2010/0031, *Cabinet Office* v. *IC*, below, text at n. 73.

felt that the veto was issued not to protect sensitive information but to prevent the public seeing how little meaningful discussion on such a fateful decision took place.

POLICY MAKING AND INTERNAL PROCESSES OF DECISION MAKING: SOME EXAMPLES

It is not possible to examine all the FOIA 2000 exemptions here, but particularly important issues have arisen in relation to policy making, internal processes of decision making, and privacy protection.

FOIA 2000, s. 35 protects among other things: government policy-making processes, collective responsibility of government, and advice of the law officers, and s. 36 the effective working of government and other authorities. They are both very broadly drafted. Provision is made under s. 35 for the release of statistical and factual information once a decision is taken and under s. 36 for statistical information. Section 35 is class-based; s. 36 is contents-based – where the reasonable opinion of a qualified person believes that prejudice or inhibition would be caused by disclosure.

DfES v. *IC and Evening Standard (AP)*[57] saw s. 35(1)(a) invoked. Information about setting of school budgets in England was requested; in particular the minutes of a policy committee. The formulation and development of policy had to be distinguished from implementation of policy and its analysis, the Tribunal reasoned. The Tribunal identified the dangers of 'sofa government' by use of specialist advisers. The words 'relates to formulation and development of policy' in s. 35 are to be construed broadly. There was no need to prevent disclosure of officials' identities. The status of 'minutes' does not automatically exempt documents even though they apply to the 'most senior of officials'. 'To treat such status as automatically conferring exemption would be tantamount to intervening within s.35(1) a class of absolutely exempt information for which the subsection gives no warrant...'.[58] The case set out the arguments in favour of disclosure and the application of the public interest test under s. 35(1).

The guiding principles are as follows. The content of particular information is relevant. No status is automatically exempt. The protection is against compromise or unjust public opprobrium of civil servants *not* ministers. Timing of a request is paramount. What is highly relevant in June 2010 may carry little weight by January 2012. A parliamentary statement announcing the policy 'will normally mark the end of the process of policy formulation'. Facts must be viewed carefully, however, and a public interest in exemption may not disappear on announcement. Fortitude and neutrality are expected of civil servants. But there may be good reason to withhold the names of more junior civil servants.

The Tribunal proceeded on the basis that ministers will behave fairly and responsibly to civil servants who may be associated with unpopular advice. There must be a *specific reason* justifying non-disclosure of a civil servant's identity – a blanket policy

57 EA/2006/0006, *DfES* v. *IC and Evening Standard (AP)*.

58 Ibid., at [69].

cannot be justified. There is a general public interest in transparency and a better understanding of how the government tackles important policy problems. The 'funding crisis' in schools was of great public concern. The information may not prove to be significant in any public debate but the public interest favoured disclosure.

R. Evans v. *IC and MoD*[59] concerned meetings of a minister and an arms lobbying company. Sections 36(2)(b)(i) and 35(1) were invoked. The case ruled that the public interest is that at the time of a request. That interest was not advanced by disclosing informal 'notes' of the meeting. As a general rule the public interest in maintaining an exemption diminishes over time. The witnesses were not able to show evidence of inhibitory effects of disclosure of formal notes. 'Where the information is in a raw unconsidered form the public interest in maintaining the exemption is likely to diminish more slowly than where the information is in a finished considered form.'[60] A fear of the inhibiting effect of disclosure on lobbyists was overstated. In relation to *notes* of meetings and telephone conversations the exemptions were maintained on public interest grounds because these were unfinished and incomplete. In relation to 'finished' background notes – there was no such inhibition and the public interest favoured disclosure. In a subsequent ruling the tribunal decided that s. 40 (personal data) protected the information (below).

The Commissioner and Tribunal have made some important decisions and have not been easily impressed by official pleas of damage to civil service impartiality, neutrality or effectiveness in using the public interest override to disclose advice to ministers. Civil service neutrality is a core feature in the UK constitution because the civil service is 'permanent' serving different governments independently and disinterestedly. Disclosure was nonetheless ordered and the alleged danger of a 'chilling effect' has not materialized. Where policy remains unresolved information has not been released.

The Commissioner and Tribunal have stated that there is an assumption built into the FOIA 2000 that disclosure of information by public authorities in response to a request is in the public interest in order to promote *transparency* and *accountability* in relation to the activities of public authorities. 'The public interest factors in favour of disclosure...can take into account the general public interests in the promotion of *transparency, accountability, public understanding* and *involvement* in the democratic process'.[61]

A general statement on the public interest was made in the FS50126011 Decision Notice[62] which contains helpful statements about assessing that interest under s. 35(1) (a) and (b). A request was made for information concerning Cabinet Office papers in relation to an Asylum and Immigration working group. The papers covered the approach to registration of workers from 2004 EU accession states. The Cabinet Office

[59] EA/2006/0064, *R. Evans* v. *IC and MoD*. [60] Ibid., at [41].

[61] EA/2007/0055, *Dr John Pugh MP* v. *IC* (emphasis added).

[62] FS50126011, Freedom of Information Act 2000 (Section 50) Decision Notice (5 August 2008).

claimed s. 35 was operative and the public interest favoured non-disclosure. The factors were set out:

'In favour of disclosure:

i. Promoting public understanding behind decisions taken.
ii. Public participation and debate in policy issues, especially where the subject matter is controversial.
iii. Accountability for decisions taken.
iv. Transparency in decision making.
v. Information contained within the papers which is already in the public domain.

Against disclosure

i. The short period of time that had elapsed between the meeting in question and the complainant's request, and that the policy in question continues to be kept under review.
ii. Effects on the principle of collective responsibility for decisions by revealing interdepartmental considerations which may reveal disagreements between Ministers and departments.
iii. Revealing the policy options presented to Ministers for collective discussion and decision-making could undermine the process of collective government and inhibit Ministers' from having a frank and fully-informed discussion in order to reach informed decisions.
iv. Effects on the comprehensiveness of information provided for consideration in policy making.'[63]

The balance lay in favour of disclosure.

The Tribunal has noted the 'default setting' of the Act favours disclosure; there are generic 'good governance' arguments for transparency; the specific content and circumstances must be established on a case by case basis and the lapse of time of request is paramount – is the issue still live?[64]

THE CATCH-ALL PROVISION

University of Central Lancashire v. *IC and David Colquhoun*[65] deals with the notorious 'catch-all' provision in s.36(2) where disclosure 'would otherwise prejudice, or would be likely otherwise to prejudice, the effective conduct of public affairs'. A professor made a request for copies of the course materials for another university's BSc degree in homeopathy. The issue of homeopathy training was the subject of significant

[63] Ibid., at [19].

[64] www.informationtribunal.gov.uk/DBFiles/Decision/i202/Scotland%20Office%20v%20ICO%20(EA-2007-0070)%20-%20Decision%2008-08-08%20+%20Annexes%20A&B.pdf.

[65] EA/2009/0034, *University of Central Lancashire* v. *IC and David Colquhoun*.

academic and public debate. The professor thought that the materials might inform that debate. The university refused, originally citing FOIA 2000, s. 43(2) – that its commercial interests would be damaged. This was unsuccessful. During the course of the Commissioner's investigations the university's Vice-Chancellor issued a certificate under FOIA 2000, s. 36(2)(c), claiming that disclosure would or would be likely to prejudice the effective conduct of public affairs, namely the administration of the university.

The s. 36 exemption was not made out because there was no evidence that it was a 'reasonable opinion reasonably arrived at' which is a requirement of s. 36. The university claimed that there would be disruption and consequent expense resulting from a flood of similar claims prompted by disclosure of the information; the Tribunal thought that this conclusion was tenuous. The evidence put forward to support a reasonable procedure for gathering the opinion was also inadequate; it consisted of a short email which tacitly acknowledged that the claim was speculative. Disclosure was ordered.

PERSONAL INFORMATION

One interesting development has been on the FOIA 2000/DPA 1998 interface. Data protection was widely invoked to attempt to prevent access to documents which contained the names of individuals, usually officials but sometimes lobbyists and government interlocutors. There was a fear that a coach and horses would be driven through the FOIA 2000. In numerous cases the Commissioner and Tribunal have ruled that under DPA 1998, Sched. 2, the legitimate interests of the requester may allow disclosure depending on the facts. There has been a willingness to protect the identity of junior officials. Furthermore, FOIA 2000, s. 41 exempts information protected by confidentiality and it is an absolute exemption. The law of confidentiality itself provides a defence against actions for breaches of confidentiality if disclosures are made in the public interest. There is no confidence in an iniquity. Unlike the FOIA 2000 and establishing the public interest in qualified exemptions, the onus on proving the public interest under confidentiality lies upon the requester. The development of protection of personal information by the application of ECHR, Art. 8 to the common law of confidentiality has been noted above. Documents may be redacted to allow non-confidential/private items to be disclosed.

Neither the FOIA 2000 nor the DPA 1998 protects 'privacy' as such. But protection of personal information traverses both statutes. By virtue of FOIA 2000, s.40, access to one's own data is provided for by the DPA 1998. Access to data involving another is made under the FOIA 2000 but subject to the Data Protection Principles. In essence, in most cases, contravention of these principles makes access to another's personal data an absolute exemption.

The Commissioner and Tribunal have made important decisions allowing access to documents with the names of persons on them where the requester has a legitimate interest in knowing that data.

For example, in the FS50088016 Decision Notice[66] the complainant requested a copy of the winning tender proposal for a particular consultancy post along with details of the scores awarded to all of the tenders which the Department for International Development received. While the department provided the complainant with the overall score awarded to the winning tender and the average score awarded to his tender (the complainant's tender was unsuccessful), the department refused to disclose the winning tender proposal (including CV and price bid) on the basis of ss 40(2) (personal data) and 43(2). The Commissioner ruled that the data was personal data, as it contained biographical information. However, disclosure would not breach the first data protection principle. The Commissioner reasoned that any tenderer should have realized that certain details about their bid may have been disclosed. Such tenders are open to public scrutiny. The Commissioner distinguished between information about the tenderer's professional and personal lives, and found that whilst the two were intertwined in places, the details were overwhelmingly about his professional life.[67] In applying DPA 1998, Sched. 2, the Commissioner thought that there was a necessary legitimate interest in ensuring openness, transparency and accountability, and that disclosure would impose no unwarranted interference (the tenderer's commercial interests were not taken into account). As regards the scores for tenderers, the Commissioner found that s. 40(2) exempted disclosure. The information constituted personal data and because of the department's policy of not giving tenderers their own cards back, it would have been reasonably assumed that they would not be disclosed to anyone else.

THE FOIA 2000 IN ACTION: SOME EXAMPLES

- The most significant case concerned the MPs' expenses saga where MPs had abused the system for claiming accommodation and other expenses (EA/2007/0061, 0122-23, 0131). The High Court judgment resulted in wider disclosure than the Commissioner had originally ordered.[68] Two ministers resigned and the Speaker of the House of Commons resigned because of severe criticism – the first time this had occurred since 1695. The expenses system was subject to a statutory overhaul under the Parliamentary Standards Act 2009.
- There was disclosure on negotiated terms of the Attorney General's advice on the legality of the war in Iraq after leaks.
- Disclosure was allowed by the Labour government of the so-called 'Black Wednesday' papers concerning a Conservative government and the financial catastrophe of 1992 when the UK had to leave the EC Exchange Rate Mechanism. Disclosure occurred shortly before the 2005 UK general election prompting allegations of party political influence on FOI.

[66] FS50088016, Freedom of Information Act 2000 (Section 50) Decision Notice (27 November 2008).

[67] See Case C-28/08 P, *Bavarian Lager*, 29 June 2010, ECJ.

[68] *Corporate Officer of the HC* v. *IC* [2008] EWHC 1084 (Admin).

- There were disclosures over a period of four years relating to the Iraq weapons of mass destruction dossier.[69]
- Disclosures have been made relating to government contracts and commercial interests of bodies dealing with public authorities.[70]
- Cabinet minutes have been the subject of vetoes as explained and in several other cabinet cases the Commissioner has ruled against disclosure.[71] In the FS50088735 Decision Notice,[72] the Commissioner ordered disclosure of the minutes of the cabinet meeting discussing the Westland helicopter episode in 1986 when there was a major dispute in policy between Mrs Thatcher and Mr Heseltine. The government objected to disclosure but the tribunal upheld the Commissioner's decision notice on appeal[73] and no veto was issued by the coalition government.
- Information on lobbyists' meetings with government has been disclosed and was not protected under s. 36(2)(b)(i) on public interest grounds but on the facts was protected under s. 40.[74]
- Refusals to disclose Prince Charles' correspondence with ministers have been upheld and are subject to appeal to the tribunal.[75]
- A very high profile case concerned research reports by scientists at the University of East Anglia on global warming just before the 2009 Copenhagen summit. There had been damaging leaks of emails between the scientists following FOIA 2000 and environmental regulations' requests and UK universities have received many FOI requests. They have frequently shown themselves to be over-defensive.
- There have been disclosures of restaurant inspection reports, EU subsidies paid to every farm, heart surgery survival rates by hospital, safety of nuclear plants, best and worst performing schools, local authority pension investments in hedge funds, Ryanair's airport contract with Derry council, reviews of Identity cards, items within the 1911 Census and the implications of 1997 tax changes for pension funds.

There is nothing in their record since the FOIA 2000 came into operation to suggest timidity on the part of the Commissioner or Tribunal. Many decisions on the public interest have been more robust than government would like and have incurred vetoes under s. 35. Civil service advisers must accept that they now operate in an FOI culture

[69] www.ico.gov.uk/global/search.aspx?collection=ico&keywords=Iraq+weapons+of+mass+destruction.

[70] See *Derry City Council* v. *IC* EA/2006/0014 and *Office of Government Commerce* v. *IC* EA/2006/0068 and 0080 and [2008] EWHC 737 (Admin). The High Court allowed an appeal because of procedural errors in the latter case and a re-hearing by the tribunal was ordered. The re-hearing ordered disclosure of important reports.

[71] EA/2008/0090, *D. Bowden* v. *IC*.

[72] FS50088735, Freedom of Information Act 2000 (Section 50) Decision Notice (22 December 2009).

[73] EA/2010/0031, *Cabinet Office* v. *IC*.

[74] EA/2006/0064, *R. Evans* v. *IC and Ministry of Defence*.

[75] On refusals to disclose the prince's correspondence to public authorities, see www.ico.gov.uk/global/search.aspx?collection=ico&keywords=Correspondence+from+Prince+Charles.

with greater openness and transparency accompanying their advice, although timing is crucial the Commissioner and Tribunal have ruled. National security and international and diplomatic relations have been respected although there have been public interest disclosures in the latter. The High Court has taken a very different line on the exclusion of the BBC for the purposes of 'journalism, art or literature', disapproving an interpretation of the Commissioner and Tribunal that subjected the BBC to disclosures.[76]

REVIEWS OF AND REPORTS ON FREEDOM OF INFORMATION

Major objectives associated with FOI have been identified from official publications by Hazell and colleagues[77] The study found that while openness and transparency in government had increased other objectives such as improving decision making, public understanding of government and its decision making, and increasing trust and participation in government had not increased, or not significantly. The claims by the promoters of the law were exaggerated, the authors found. Claims by government for one of its reforms are always likely to be subject to exaggeration. Furthermore, a study based on four and a half years of operation of a major reform is working on limited data. Cultures take years to change. Hundreds of years of non encouragement of wide public involvement in government will not be overcome in a short space of time. At the root of FOIA 2000 is basic principle: information affecting us and our welfare is not the preserve of government.

Reports from the Commissioner and Tribunal show that some bodies respond badly to the FOIA 2000 in terms of delay, detailed questions and so on.[78] Whether this is inefficiency or obstinacy it is not known. Cutbacks in expenditure may cause increasing delays, but there is very little evidence of deliberate obstruction.

The Information Commissioner's Office produces annual reports and other reports on all their work.[79] These are detailed and informative documents. The Commons Justice Committee has published reports on the work of the Commissioner.[80] The Ministry of Justice publishes quarterly statistics on FOI requests and an annual report. These contain detailed figures but only cover central government (departments and monitored authorities – 42 in all). Most of the 100,000–115,000 or so bodies are not covered. The Ministry of Justice reported in 2010[81] that monitored bodies received 40,548 FOI requests: 82 per cent were met within the 20-day period; 5 per cent were subject to a public interest extension; 58 per cent of resolvable requests were met in

[76] *BBC* v. *Sugar and IC* [2009] EWHC 2349 (Admin), upheld in [2010] EWCA Civ 715.

[77] Hazell *et al.*, *Does FOI work?* (2010).

[78] Information Commissioner's Office, *Annual Report 2008–09*, HC 619 (2008–09).

[79] www.ico.gov.uk/about_us/what_we_do/corporate_information/annual_reports.aspx.

[80] HC 146 (2008–09).

[81] Ministry of Justice, *Freedom of Information Act 2000*, Fifth Annual Report (April 2010).

full; 23 per cent resulted in information being withheld. Fees were levied in 3 per cent of cases and 99 per cent of these were in the National Archives. A total of 1,502 internal reviews were conducted across all monitored bodies and 206 appeals were made to the Commissioner. The report has details on exemptions claimed and other matters.

The Commissioner[82] received 3,734 complaints in 2009–10 (2008–09: 3,100); 49 per cent were closed in 30 days or less (2008–09: 47 per cent); 66 per cent were closed in 90 days or less (2008–09: 62 per cent); 24 per cent took longer than a year to close – ie come to a conclusion (2008–09: 33 per cent). Eleven cases were still ongoing after two years (2008–09: 118). Of closed cases in 2009–10, 52 per cent were informally resolved (2008–09: 49 per cent); 15 per cent were ineligible (2008–09: 24 per cent); in 17 per cent a decision notice was issued (2008–09: 10 per cent); in 5 per cent no internal review was carried out by the authority (2008–09: 9 per cent); 9 per cent were re-opened (2008–09: 6 per cent); in 2 per cent, cases were withdrawn or the Commissioner required no action (2008–09: 2 per cent). In 2009–10, 628 decision notices were served (2008–09: 296); the outcome was complaint upheld in 142 cases (23 per cent) (2008–09: 105: 35 per cent); complaint partially upheld in 198 cases (31 per cent) (2008–09: 153: 52 per cent); complaint not upheld 288 (46 per cent) (2008–09: 38: 13 per cent). On appeals to the Tribunal between 2005 and 2009 (322), the Commissioner's decision was upheld in 54 per cent of cases; the decision was overturned or varied in 30 per cent; and 15 per cent were withdrawn. There is no systematic collection of all requests and figures concerning requests covering all authorities. An estimate from the Commissioner was that in the first four and a half years of operation (May 2009) there had been a half million FOI requests, 11,500 complaints to the Commissioner, 1,225 Decision Notices, and 415 appeals to the Information Tribunal.[83] The appeals to the High Court (now to the Upper Tribunal) would number no more than 30 (approximation).

There was a detailed review of FOIA 2000 in 2006 by a private body think tank, Frontier Economics.[84] It was commissioned by government. However, this was written with a view to reforming the FOIA 2000 by the government, which had become somewhat annoyed by the operation of FOI and led to proposals for controversial measures which were subsequently abandoned by government

The Dacre review, noted above, led to reforms in relation to the Public Records Acts, but no reforms followed in respect of making cabinet minutes and documents absolute exemptions.

Overall, the surveys show increased support for FOI by the press and public and increased popularity of the measure. Press and media have come to have a high regard for the FOIA 2000. The Conservative Party in its manifesto of 2010 expressed support for the Act and even extending its ambit. A *volte face* on the FOIA 2000 would be disastrous public relations for government.

[82] Information Commissioner's Office, *Annual Report (2009–10)*, HC 220 (2010–11). The 2008–09 figures in brackets are from Information Commissioner's Office, *Annual Report 2008–09*, HC 619 (2008–09).

[83] *Private Data, Open Government: Questions of Information*, QEII Centre, 13 May 2009.

[84] *Review of the Impact of the FOIA* (2006).

THE DATA PROTECTION ACT 1998, SURVEILLANCE, AND PRIVACY

It was pointed out at the beginning of this chapter that the movement to greater collection, disclosure and access to information was accompanied by growing demands for privacy protection. The Commissioner has described how we are walking into a surveillance society in which privacy is inadequately protected.[85] Although the Identity Cards scheme seems doomed, the capacity of the state as well as entities such as Facebook to harness IT to store and disclose personal information is well known. CCTV cameras are everywhere. Regulation of Investigatory Powers Act provisions on surveillance are notoriously broad and some are used to cover relatively innocuous activities. National and international data banks exist for numerous subject areas and the DPA 1998 has shown itself to be inadequate to guarantee data security. A national government communications data bank was ruled out by the Home Secretary in 2009.[86] Recommendations for regulating transfer of data between holders and greater transparency and accountability for surveillance practices have been recommended by the House of Lords Constitution Committee[87] and in a Ministry of Justice review by Thomas and Walport.[88] Some of their proposals have found their way onto the statute book. The Criminal Justice and Immigration Act 2008 introduced custodial sentences for unlawful obtaining, buying, and selling of personal data and provided powers for the Commissioner to impose monetary penalties for serious breaches of the Data Protection Principles which occur 'knowingly' or 'recklessly'.[89] In addition, the Coroners and Justice Act 2009, Pt 8 provides powers for the Commissioner to inspect the processing of personal information. However, this only covers the public sector and not the private sector unless designated. The Commissioner must also prepare a code of practice on assessments and a code which contains practical guidance in relation to the sharing of personal data in accordance with the requirements of the DPA 1998. This is subject to approval by the Secretary of State and Parliament.

There have been a number of cases under the DPA 1998. The Court of Appeal in 2009 overruled the Commissioner and Tribunal, both of which had decided that minor convictions committed by young persons many years previously should be erased from the data held by police forces. Convictions may become 'spent' but there are numerous exceptions to this where information is required for specific purposes including employment. In the cases in question, the Court ruled that keeping the data

[85] http://news.bbc.co.uk/1/shared/bsp/hi/pdfs/02_11_06_surveillance.pdf, and Surveillance Studies Network, *A Report on the Surveillance Society* (2006).

[86] The current provision regulating data communications retention is SI 2009/859 implementing Council Directive (EC) 2006/24. The German constitutional court ruled the federal measure implementing the Directive was unconstitutional, see www.bverfg.de/pressemitteilungen/bvg10-011en.html.

[87] HL 18 (2008–09), and Cm. 7616 (2010).

[88] *Data Sharing Review* (2009), available at www.justice.gov.uk/reviews/datasharing-intro.htm.

[89] SI 2010/31 and SI 2010/910.

for a period of 25 years was not overlong or excessive and would therefore be subject to disclosure provisions in relation to the Criminal Records Bureau and prospective employers. A conviction or reprimand for common assault or minor acts of shoplifting by a teenager could jeopardize employment prospects for life where information is retained and disclosable for very long periods.[90]

In 2008 the UK was found to be in breach of ECHR, Art. 8 in relation to the indefinite retention of DNA data by the police including that of unconvicted suspects.[91] Since then the Crime and Security Act 2010 has been passed and provides a statutory framework for the retention and destruction of biometric materials, including DNA samples, DNA profiles and fingerprints that have been taken from an individual as part of the investigation of a recordable offence.[92] Destruction of DNA samples is required once they have been profiled and loaded satisfactorily onto the national database. All samples are required to be destroyed within six months of their being taken, but data will be retained. The retention periods for the various categories of data depend on a number of factors including the age of the individual concerned, the seriousness of the offence or alleged offence, whether the individual has been convicted, and if so whether it is a first conviction. The categories can be summarized as follows:

adult – convicted: indefinite retention of fingerprints, impressions of footwear and DNA profile;

adult – unconvicted: for six years;

under 18 years old – convicted of serious offence or more than one minor offence: indefinite retention;

under 18 years old – convicted of single minor offence: 5 years;

under 18 years old – unconvicted: may be retained for six or three years depending on seriousness.[93]

The coalition government's Protection of Freedoms Bill (2011) will remove or reduce most of these periods of retention. Special provision is made for national security and a Commissioner for retention and use of biometric material in such cases is to be appointed to review determinations and a code will be issued. The Bill also contains provisions for a Surveillance Camera Commissioner to monitor a secretary of state's code on surveillance.

[90] *Humberside Chief Constable of Police etc* v. *Information Commissioner* [2009] EWCA Civ 1079; see *R (L)* v. *MP Commissioner* [2009] UKSC 3 and *R (Wright)* v. *Secretary of State for Health* [2009] UKHL 3.

[91] *S and Marper* v. *United Kingdom* [2008] ECHR 1581, European Court of Human Rights.

[92] See *Keeping the Right People on the DNA Database* May 2009.

[93] Crime and Security Act 2010, ss 14–23 give additional powers to the police to take fingerprints and DNA samples from people who have been arrested, charged or convicted in the UK, and from those convicted overseas of serious sexual and violent offences.

REFLECTIONS AND CONCLUSION

FOIA 2000 is of assistance in meeting its identified objectives – openness, transparency, and access to information – but other procedures and opportunities need to be developed. Participation requires vehicles of participation and our open meeting laws are of limited application. We still have a long way to go in this respect. But in terms of access, we have travelled far. The ministerial veto under FOIA 2000, s. 53 is a problem but it has only been used twice in five years. Many systems have vetoes or something similar to give government the last word on sensitive issues.[94]

In some aspects, the UK does not do well on some internationally agreed criteria for an FOI regime[95] – the virtually absolute nature of some offences under the Official Secrets Act, the existence of the FOIA 2000 veto and absolute exemptions and the breadth of some exemptions. On the other hand, I would add that the enforcement machinery, cost-free provision, coverage, and effectiveness of the legislation together with the existence of an independent champion make the UK legislation leaders in world practice.

The saga of abuse of MPs of the expenses regime has been the most high profile FOI investigation. The disclosures ordered by the Commissioner were extended by the Tribunal and the High Court.[96] The episode led to a wide ranging ongoing reform of parliamentary standards.[97] Delay is a problem in a significant number of cases. This is true even when taken up by the Commissioner. There are few examples of outright defiance – the penalties are too severe. But resources to fund FOI are, and will continue to be, a problem. FOI is not likely to be considered a front-line service.

As far as the future of FOI is concerned, three points are particularly prominent. First, the exclusion and absolute exemption covering the security and intelligence services and GCHQ and the Serious Organised Crime Agency. Is there a case for making the absolute exemption a qualified one?

The second relates to the extension of FOI to cover the private sector where private organizations are acting on behalf of the state or engaging in delivery of public service. The government of 2010 has expressed a desire to extend the reach of FOI. Privatization of public service will increase pressure for FOI extension.

The third point concerns elevation of FOI to the lexicon of human rights. Slowly, but gradually, this is being brought to fruition[98] International analogues of ECHR, Art. 10 (freedom of speech) have been interpreted as providing a right to information

[94] Cf. Freedom of Information (Removal of Conclusive Certificates and Other Measures) Act 2009 (Australia).

[95] Atlanta Declaration, available at www.cartercenter.org/documents/Atlanta%20Declaration%20and%20Plan%20of%20Action.pdf.

[96] *Corporate Officer HC* v. *IC* [2008] EWHC 1084 (Admin).

[97] See discussion in Chapter 15 below.

[98] P. Birkinshaw, 'Freedom of Information and Openness: Fundamental Human Rights?' (2006) 58 *Administrative LR* 177.

as well as free speech.[99] The European Court of Human Rights has not travelled as far but recent rulings have advanced beyond the denial of Art. 10 as a free standing FOI provision,[100] so that where access to state-held information is necessary to realize the Art. 10 right, a right to information was thereby entailed.[101]

Much of what exists in the public sector is currently subject to fundamental review. The benefits and disadvantages of having such a law will undoubtedly be raised. Some FOI requests and investigations have taken an inordinate length of time and more funding is unlikely to go the Commissioner's office. Indeed cuts are likely.

The FOIA 2000 has its critics.[102] The pursuit of transparency has simply led to masses of largely useless information as a defensive mechanism, it is argued. FOI does not guarantee accurate information; it confers a right of access to information that is held. Government use of statistics has been criticized because of their unreliability and their 'colouring' by government. The point is, without a right of access to information, we have no means of establishing how reliable information is.

My belief is that FOI has become an unremoveable part of the constitution. Of the 70 or so countries that have such laws, none to my knowledge has repealed its FOI Act. There have been amendments making legislation less or more open; in Australia reforms have led to a removal of the veto and a strengthening of the law.[103]

In relation to data protection, many problems have emerged about information security and information privacy and effective protection for individuals. Scandals about sale of data to blacklist employees, long-term retention of data, wide exemptions, security of holding data all raise the spectre of 'big brother' gone amok. The Identity Cards Act 2006 is to be repealed. The coalition government has promised a freedom Bill to restore liberties and freedoms. In relation to data protection and surveillance, the whole area should be reviewed in the light of numerous studies, reviews and reports with a view to bringing forward legislation to make the law comprehensible, workable and effective in its balance of security and liberty.

A valuable addition to a bill of rights would be a fundamental right of access to information. The Human Rights Act 1998 may need to be built on.

One thing is certain: holding, disclosing, and regulating information have been transformed in the UK in little over a decade. Much of this regulation has a direct bearing on government and government–citizen relationships. Information and its regulation are a dramatic illustration of the changing constitution.

[99] *Cheyes* v. *Chile*, case 12.108 (2003), and American Human Rights Convention, Art. 13.

[100] Article 8 has been interpreted as providing a right to information as have Arts 2, 6 and 3.

[101] Application No 37374/05, *Tarsasag etc* v. *Hungary* (2009); App No 19101/03, *Jihoceske Matky* v. *Czech Republic*, 10 July 2006. See *A* v. *Independent News Media Ltd* [2010] EWCA Civ 343.

[102] C. Hood and D. Heald (eds), *Transparency: the Key to Better Governance* (2006).

[103] See above, n. 94.

FURTHER READING

Birkinshaw, P., *Freedom of Information: the Law, the Practice and the Ideal* (4th edn, 2010).

Hazell, R., Worthy, B. and Glover, M., *The Impact of the Freedom of Information Act on Central Government in the UK: Does FOI Work?* (2010).

McDonald, J. *et al.* (eds), *The Law of Freedom of Information* (2nd edn, 2009).

USEFUL WEBSITES

Information Commissioner's Office: **www.ico.gov.uk**

The website of the Information Commissioner's Office has detailed information on the FOIA 2000 and DPA 1998, case law, guidance, etc.

Ministry of Justice, Freedom of Information policy: **www.justice.gov.uk/about/freedom-of-information.htm**

The Campaign for Freedom of Information: **www.cfoi.org.uk**

15

STANDARDS OF CONDUCT IN PUBLIC LIFE

Patricia Leopold

SUMMARY

Since 1995 there have been a variety of reforms aimed at encouraging ethical behaviour by those in public life. This has resulted in new legislation, the introduction of soft-law codes, the creation of new regulators, and the establishment of new procedures. The aim is to provide systems that are sufficiently robust to satisfy an increasingly distrustful public. The challenge has been to provide clear, transparent, and fair schemes that retain elements of self-regulation but include an independent or external element or both. The Westminster Parliament and government have been the most reluctant of all the public bodies to take adequate account of these requirements, only doing so in response to events. This can be compared with the very different approach, partly imposed by Westminster that applies to the devolved institutions. Reforms in 2003 to the scheme regulating conduct at Westminster appeared to reassure MPs but, even before the expenses crisis of 2009, the package of reforms was not sufficient to improve public confidence in the honesty of public office holders,[1] a reflection perhaps of additional concerns about party funding, buying and selling honours, and the planned activities of retiring MPs and ministers. The 2009 parliamentary expenses crisis marked a low point in public confidence in politicians. It also suggested that self-regulation was not working properly and that some of the underlying ethical principles of the post-1995 reforms were neither adequately understood nor applied by those at Westminster. It remains to be seen how successful a new wave of reforms, hurriedly introduced in 2009–10, will be in satisfying politicians and reassuring the public. The initial impressions are not encouraging.

[1] National surveys on public attitudes towards conduct in public life were prepared for the Committee on Standards in Public Life in 2004, 2006 and 2008.

INTRODUCTION

The evolution of arrangements for regulating standards of conduct in public life in the UK reflects the way the constitution has developed over the centuries. Ad hoc and informal arrangements, in response to particular events, were the norm until very recently. Since 1995 there has been an incremental shift to a more principled approach, albeit one in response to events. An independent advisory Committee on Standards in Public Life (CSPL) was established in 1994 and there began a process of elucidation of much political activity,[2] that is the codification in writing of standards which had been assumed (wrongly in many cases) to be commonly understood. These changes can be seen with respect to many aspects regulating the conduct of those in public life, but are most marked with respect to the Westminster Parliament.

The frequent changes that have occurred to the regulation of conduct cannot be divorced from the wider issue of public distrust in politicians and in the integrity of Parliament. It was no surprise that press and public reaction to the publication of details of expenses claimed by MPs and peers in 2009–10 resulted in a decline in the standing of politicians.[3] However, given that for many years the reputation of politicians has not been high, it is unlikely that reforms to the enforcement of standards of conduct will in themselves make much difference. This is recognized by additional proposals for reform, for example to how Parliament and its members work, the electoral system and the composition of the House of Lords.[4] It remains to be seen whether a package of reforms increases public trust in politicians.

Allegations of poor standards of conduct in public life are not new. Several financial scandals featured in the period 1860 to 1930, the most notable of which were the Marconi affair,[5] which involved allegations of corrupt financial speculation by members of the government, and the sale of political honours by the Lloyd George coalition government.[6] Reforms consequent upon those scandals, such as the establishment of a statutory power to set up an inquiry[7] and the requirement that candidates for higher honours should be vetted,[8] are still in operation. The scandals of the late 1950s and 1960s were mainly of a sexual nature. It was not until the 1970s that cases of major financial impropriety arose again, in particular with respect to the architect John Poulson bribing civil servants, local councillors, and MPs to assist him to secure official contracts. One consequence of the Poulson affair was the introduction in 1974 of

[2] Dawn Oliver, *Constitution Reform in the UK* (2003).

[3] Hansard Society for Parliamentary Government, *Annual Audit of Political Engagement 7, the 2010 Report* (March 2010).

[4] See Chapter 7 above. [5] See HC 152 and 217 (1913).

[6] See the Royal Commission on Honours, Cmd 1789 (1922), and the Honours (Prevention of Abuses) Act 1925.

[7] Now regulated by the Inquiries Act 2005.

[8] Now undertaken by a non-statutory body, the House of Lords Appointments Commission.

a register of members' interests for the Commons. However, it was another 20 years before a series of scandals resulted in more widespread reforms. Although many of the allegations of misconduct in the mid-1990s were of sexual misbehaviour, it was the allegations of financial impropriety and abuse of governmental power that caused most concern. These included: the taking by MPs of cash for asking parliamentary questions;[9] the relationship of MPs with lobbying companies and multi-client consultants – 'MPs for hire';[10] the acceptance by MPs, ministers, and civil servants of gifts, favours, or hospitality from businessmen.[11] A range of reforms since 1995, including the establishment of a standing body, the CSPL, resulted in an initial reduction in allegations of serious financial misconduct in Parliament. The concerns raised in the early part of this century were mainly with respect to the funding of political parties, ministerial conflicts of interest and the resurrection of allegations of 'cash for honours'.

However, between 2006 and 2009 a new wave of serious allegations of misbehaviour came to light. With respect to the Commons the most serious was that some MPs were misusing the expenses and allowances available to them.[12] There were also allegations that some ministers and MPs planning to retire from the Commons were willing in the future to accept payment to provide access to government. For the Lords the allegations were not only with respect to allowances and expenses, but also that some peers were willing to accept money in return for influencing the content of legislation – 'cash for amendments'.

In January 2005 the Freedom of Information Act 2000 (FOIA 2000)[13] came into force and journalists unsuccessfully sought from Parliament more information on MPs' expenses than that provided by the Commons statutory publication scheme. The journalists complained to the Information Commissioner who ruled in favour of the journalists, a decision upheld on appeal by the Information Tribunal and the High Court.[14] While the legal proceedings were progressing, specific allegations on the misuse of expenses were considered by the Committee for Standards and Privileges and the Parliamentary Commissioner for Standards (PCS).[15] The unexpected consequence of the FOIA 2000 for Parliament was to open up and make transparent a 'deeply flawed system'[16] that it would have preferred to have remained hidden. The Commons agreed

[9] See HC 226 (1996–97).

[10] See the First Report of the CSPL, Cm. 2850-I (1995), paras 22–59 (the Nolan Report).

[11] See Ridley, F. F. and Doig, A. (eds) '"Sleaze": Politics, Private Interests and Public Reaction' (1995) 48 *Parliamentary Affairs* 551–749 (special edition).

[12] In this chapter the term 'expenses' will be used to cover both expenses and allowances. This follows the view taken by the CSPL that the sums involved did not represent entitlements 'rather amounts which have to be justified as necessary expenditure incurred wholly and exclusively in the performance of parliamentary duties', Cm. 7724 (2009) para. 1.29.

[13] See Chapter 14 above.

[14] *Corporate Officer of the House of Commons v Information Commissioner* [2008] EWHC 1084, [2009] 3 All ER 403.

[15] The reports can be found on the Committee for Standards and Privileges section of Parliament's website.

[16] Above, n. 14, at [44].

that the information requested would be published, but with some material concealed or 'redacted' for reasons of privacy and security. Before this could happen, in May 2009, *The Daily Telegraph* published the details in an unredacted form, and the full scale of the abuse of parliamentary expenses became clear. The seriousness of some of the allegations of misconduct was compounded by criminal investigations and prosecutions.[17] The revelations about the completely internal scheme under which MPs (and peers) claimed and were paid their various expenses suggested numerous failings: the rules were unclear and some appeared out of line with the Nolan principles;[18] the scheme was not transparent; there was poor oversight of both how the scheme worked and the items being claimed as expenses; the culture tolerated non-compliance with the rules; there was a more limited external audit than that found in other public bodies resulting in minimal accountability. The situation was summed up by the CSPL as a 'major systemic failure (by the Commons) in an area where the public had the right to expect the highest standards of integrity'.[19] In July 2009, with all party support, the Parliamentary Standards Act 2009 (PSA 2009) was passed. This created the Independent Parliamentary Standards Authority (IPSA) to set and pay MPs' expenses. Given the speed with which this legislation was passed, and the controversy surrounding its passage, it is not surprising that it was significantly amended by the Constitutional Reform and Governance Act 2010. The changes included giving IPSA responsibility for MPs' pay and pensions.

The discussion of the regulation of standards of conduct in this chapter will primarily be with respect to both Houses of Parliament, ministers, and the devolved institutions.

THE COMMITTEE ON STANDARDS IN PUBLIC LIFE

The CSPL was established in 1995 to examine concerns about the standards of conduct of all holders of public office, including arrangements relating to financial and commercial activities, and to make recommendations designed to ensure the highest standards of propriety in public life.[20] The work of the CSPL has been central to the post-1995 approach to the regulation of standards of conduct. Its First Report,[21] which provided the basis for much of the initial reforms, identified seven generally applicable principles of public life (the Nolan principles). These were: selflessness, integrity, objectivity, accountability, openness, honesty, and leadership. To further implement and apply these principles it made three broad recommendations: the establishment

[17] Below, n. 27, and text.

[18] Above, n. 10, and below, text at n. 21.

[19] Twelfth Report, Cm. 7724, para. 1.4.

[20] *Hansard*, HC, col. 758 (25 October 1994). 'Public life' and 'holders of public office' include ministers, civil servants and advisers, MPs and MEPs, non-ministerial office holders, members and senior officers of various other bodies discharging public-funded functions, and elected members and senior officers of local authorities.

[21] Above, n. 10.

of codes of conduct reiterating the Nolan principles throughout the public sector; that the internal systems of scrutinizing and monitoring the behaviour of those in public life should be supported by independent scrutiny; education and training should be used to inculcate high ethical standards.

The first of these recommendations was central to the establishment of a new ethical landscape. Although such codes were expected to encompass common values, the promotion of ethical behaviour was encouraged by the assumption that each public body would produce its own code of conduct. The codes were also expected to include rules on the disclosure of interests which could prohibit holders of public office from undertaking certain activities or from holding certain interests and, where appropriate, require other interests to be publicly registered and declared before certain activities are undertaken. There are three main reasons why outside interests should be disclosed: to provide information about those in public life that might be thought by others to influence their actions or conduct; to demonstrate an individual's particular expertise in a matter; and to promote a culture among those active in public life which supports and sustains ethical behaviour.

The CSPL is free to choose its subjects of inquiry (after consultation with the Cabinet Secretary) and since 1994 it has issued 12 reports. In addition to examining arrangements in most areas of the public sector, the CSPL monitors the ethical environment, reviews the implementation of its recommendations, considers and responds to issues of concern about standards, tracks public perception, and publically promotes ethical behaviour in public life.

PARLIAMENTARY PRIVILEGE

The rules on standards of conduct in Parliament have to be seen in the context of a number of ancient and undoubted rights and privileges regarded as essential for parliamentary independence. A different approach to parliamentary privilege in the devolution legislation has meant that these privilege issues do not arise in Scotland, Wales, and Northern Ireland.[22]

The most important privilege is freedom of speech. The Bill of Rights 1689, Art. 9 provides that 'the freedom of speech and debates or proceedings in Parliament ought not be impeached or questioned in any court or place out of Parliament'. An aspect of this privilege relevant to regulating conduct is that members should be free from undue influence from financial and other interests outside Parliament and that they should not use their position as a means to gain personal financial advantage. The parliamentary enforcement and regulation of this privilege has been possible by a further privilege, 'exclusive cognizance', which means that Parliament has exclusive jurisdiction over its own affairs, the concept of self-regulation. Historically, this has allowed both

[22] Below, n. 91, and text.

Houses to decide how to regulate their affairs without interference from outside bodies. For example, each House could decide how to regulate the conduct of its members and the content and administration of its system of expenses. Parliament's rules on these, and other internal matters, are usually found in its resolutions and standing orders. Allegations of breaches of these rules are for Parliament to investigate and, where appropriate, impose sanctions. Parliament's reluctance to regulate its affairs by statute, or to introduce an external element into its proceedings, has been based on a fear that to do so would enable the courts to intervene in its procedures and activities.[23]

Although the regulation of standards of conduct has left intact the principles of parliamentary privilege, there have been several encroachments on self-regulation with the establishment of commissioners for standards in 1995 for the Commons and in 2010 for the Lords, the creation of the Electoral Commission in 2000 (which checks that loans and donations to MPs are properly recorded) and the appointment of Sir Thomas Legg to review and report on MPs' claims for expenses since 2004.[24] However, the most significant dent in 300 years of self-regulation was the establishment in 2009 of the IPSA.[25] No longer will the determination or the administration of the schemes for MPs' expenses, salary, and pensions be subject to the authority of the Commons or any of its officers.[26]

Parliamentary privilege does not give members of either House general immunity from the civil or criminal law, as was confirmed by the Court of Appeal in *R* v. *Chaytor and others*[27] the case of three former MPs and a peer facing charges of false accounting with respect to expenses claims. However, no liability will lie if the alleged activity, or the evidence with respect to it, was done or said in the course of 'proceedings in Parliament'. In *R* v. *Chaytor and others* the Supreme Court agreed with the Court of Appeal and rejected the defence argument that to submit an expenses claim was to take part in a proceeding in Parliament within the ambit of Art. 9. The Supreme Court, in a unanimous opinion, held that neither Art. 9 nor the exclusive jurisdiction of the House of Commons posed any bar to the jurisdiction of the Crown Court to try the defendants.[28] However, parliamentary privilege could prevent criminal investigations or prosecutions against MPs or peers because of the difficulty of obtaining and adducing evidence which could be regarded as questioning proceedings in Parliament. This was part of the police explanation for not opening an investigation into the 'cash for amendments' allegations against four peers.[29] The deployment of evidence which could be regarded as questioning proceedings in Parliament could still occur in the prosecutions of MPs and peers. In these circumstances, as the Court of Appeal recognized, the admissibility of the evidence will have to be decided as and when it arises

[23] This would not necessarily be the case, see *Hamilton* v. *Al Fayed* [2001] 1 AC 395.

[24] HC 348 (2009–10).

[25] Above, n. 51, and text.

[26] The responsibility for pay and pensions will not take effect until April 2012.

[27] [2010] EWCA Crim 1910 (CA), and [2010] UK SC 52 (SC). Both decisions give a summary of the history of the law on parliamentary privilege, and the relationship between the courts and parliament. See also HC 523 (2007–08) for details of the relationship between the Commons' complains system and the criminal law.

[28] [2010] UK SC 52 at [69]–[71] and [81]–[83].

[29] Below, n. 85, and text.

in the trial.[30] The position whereby a prosecution has to be stayed because either the Crown or a defendant MP or peer seeks to adduce evidence which questions proceedings in Parliament, can only be altered by legislation. This is likely to be achieved by new legislation on parliamentary privilege rather than piecemeal in a variety of different statutes.[31] A draft bill on reforming parliamentary privilege was proposed in the 2010 Queen's Speech.

THE HOUSE OF COMMONS

It would be inaccurate to suggest that until 1995 Parliament had neither rules on conduct nor a code of conduct. Resolutions, reports from committees and decisions of each House, together with the standing orders, provided rules and a type of code of conduct. Although the various rules and resolutions could be found in *Erskine May*[32] – the standard text on Parliamentary procedure – updated editions of *Erskine May* are relatively infrequent, and it is a weighty tome. There was no accessible and comprehensive account of the ethical standards expected of members. Before 1995 Commons resolutions passed to regulate standards of conduct were reactions to events, not proactive, principled decisions to improve behaviour.

The earliest attempt to regulate the conduct of members of the House of Commons was in 1695 when it was resolved that the acceptance of a bribe by a member of either House to influence him in his conduct as a member was a contempt of Parliament. To understand the other resolutions of the House of Commons on standards of conduct it should be remembered that it is only since 1911 that MPs who are not ministers have received a salary.[33] It had always been accepted that they could take paid employment outside the House, practise in their professions, own land and property. However, as the resolutions attempted to make clear, payments for such activities should not be connected with the parliamentary actions of MPs. Members were not to place themselves under any financial or other obligation to those outside Parliament that could interfere with or inhibit the exercise of their right to freedom of speech. An 1858 resolution prohibited professional advocacy for fee or reward and a 1947 resolution confirmed a longstanding convention prohibiting members from entering into contractual agreements with any body that would control or limit their complete independence and freedom of action in Parliament. It was 1974 before a resolution confirmed the convention that members were both prohibited from voting upon a matter in which they had direct pecuniary interests

[30] [2010] EWCA Crim 1910 at [36].

[31] For example, a clause in the 2002–03 draft Bribery Bill which allowed Art. 9 to be waived to enable words or conduct of an MP or peer to be admissible in a prosecution for bribery, was not included in the Bribery Act 2010.

[32] W. R. MacKay (ed.), *Erskine May: Parliamentary Practice* (23rd edn, 2004).

[33] A consequence of the decision of the House of Lords in *Amalgamated Society of Railway Servants* v. *Osborne* [1910] AC 87, which prevented trade unions from paying salaries to Labour MPs.

and in certain parliamentary proceedings were expected to declare such interests. In 1975 a non-mandatory register of members' interests was established in which members were expected to register, under several specified categories, pecuniary or other material benefits that might reasonably be thought by others to influence their parliamentary activities. This was a paper recording exercise with no attempt by the Commons to establish or codify the ethical standards expected of members in their outside activities.

In its First Report[34] the CSPL identified shortcomings with the regulation of standards of conduct in the House of Commons and made four main recommendations: a new code of conduct for MPs; an improved register of members' interests; the establishment of an independent PCS and a strengthened Committee on Standards and Privileges. The recommendations were designed to establish effective machinery to ensure high standards of conduct which both preserved Parliament's control over its own affairs and introduced an independent element. The recommendations were broadly implemented and a new regime governing the registration and declaration of interests and the investigation of complaints took effect in 1995–96. Although in the period from 1996 to 2009 this regime was refined and amended, the core principles remained the same. The 2009 expenses crises resulted in changes to some of these principles.

THE CODE OF CONDUCT AND GUIDE TO THE RULES RELATING TO THE CONDUCT OF MEMBERS

The first House of Commons *Code of Conduct and a Guide to the Rules relating to the Conduct of MPs* came into effect in 1996 following resolutions of the House. Both have been revised several times and the most recent version was approved by the Commons in February 2009.[35] The code is a short document based on the Nolan Principles, and its stated purpose is to provide: 'guidance on the standards of conduct expected of Members in discharging their parliamentary duties and in so doing (to provide) the openness and accountability necessary to reinforce public confidence in the way in which Members perform those duties'. The code applies to members in all aspects of their public life but does not regulate what they do in their private and personal lives. It provides both broad principles of conduct – such as the obligation of members to the monarch, the law, and Parliament – and more specific obligations such as basing their conduct on a consideration of the public interest, avoiding conflicts of interests, not accepting bribes, registering and declaring interests, and not acting as paid advocates. There have been additional rules and duties added from time to time in reaction to events. For example, in 2005 the rule on payments and allowances was clarified and expanded to require MPs to ensure that their use of expenses, allowances, and

[34] Above, n. 10.

[35] HC 735 (2009–10). The code is the 2005 version, but there are several changes to the guide.

facilities was in accordance with the rules of the House. At the same time a duty to co-operate with any investigation into their conduct by or under the authority of the House was added to the rules.

The code was designed to guide members as to how to behave, as was the *Green Book*[36] which guided MPs through the system of expenses and which specifically referred to the Nolan principles, reminding MPs that they were 'responsible for ensuring that their use of allowances is above reproach'. But none of this prevented abuses of the internally administered expenses scheme. The original version of the PSA 2009 sought to address a perceived weakness in the force of the code of conduct by giving IPSA responsibility for producing and enforcing a new statutory code on financial issues which would replace the non-statutory code of conduct. The CSPL was critical of these provisions on two main grounds. First, the code of conduct on financial interests, as opposed to the payment of expenses, was a standards issue relating to how MPs behave as members of the House 'including whether they have financial or other interests which might affect their judgments or conduct as legislators or in holding the Executive to account. This is potentially a privilege issue'.[37] Secondly, reiterating the first CSPL Report,[38] it considered it vital that the House 'buys into the standards of conduct and behaviour it considers acceptable in relation to financial and other standards issues... To be robust and effective standards and values have to be developed from within'.[39] Parliament accepted these criticisms and the relevant parts of the PSA 2009 were repealed by the Constitutional Reform and Renewal Act 2010, enabling the Commons to retain responsibility for its code.

The guide seeks to assist members in discharging the duties found in the code. It has always been more detailed than the code, with sections explaining and amplifying the rules on the registration and declaration of financial interests, lobbying for reward or consideration, and the complaints procedure. The guidance is not intended to provide for all circumstances, and members are encouraged to seek advice where necessary from the PCS or the Registrar of Members' Financial Interests (the Registrar). The early versions of the guide caused more controversies than the code, with several significant alterations which reflected both ambiguities and lacunae in the rules.

The purpose of the registration of financial interests[40] is openness; registration does not imply any wrongdoing. The rules require the registration of 12 categories of financial interests. These include: directorships, remunerated employment and profession, gifts and hospitality, financial sponsorship, overseas visits, land and property, shareholdings, related undertakings, sponsorship, gifts, heritable property, interests in shares. Changes to the rules on the registration of interests since 1996 have included: the introduction of thresholds for the registration of gifts, benefits, and services; the inclusion of partners as well as spouses in a number of categories; and a new rule requiring the registration of family members employed and remunerated through

[36] *The Green Book: A Guide to Members' Allowances.*

[37] Above, n. 12, para. 13.19. [38] Above, n. 10. [39] Above, n. 12, paras 13.22–13.23.

[40] The term 'financial' was added to the word 'interests' in 2009.

parliamentary allowances.[41] Since 2009 members are required to register the exact amount of payment, the hours worked and the name of the source of the payment for any extra-parliamentary work related to their membership of the House. This change, seen as a further move towards openness and transparency, was not universally welcomed by MPs. It could also lead to a move towards restricting the number of hours MPs can spend on other activities, or even prohibiting them from having second jobs, illustrating how rules on standards of conduct can have wider implications.

A complicated and irksome aspect of registration was an overlap with the Electoral Commission rules on the registration of political donations. This was resolved in 2009 following an amendment to the Political Parties, Elections and Referendums Act 2000.[42] New rules only require MPs to register on the financial register the details required by the Electoral Commission on gifts, donations, and 'regulated transactions' (for example loans and credit facilities), etc. The Electoral Commission extracts the information required for its statutory publication obligations.

The Register of Members' Financial Interests is compiled by the Registrar afresh at the start of every Parliament and is regularly updated and available electronically. In debates or other proceedings, members are required to declare not only relevant interests currently on the register, but also interests held in the recent past or expected in the future. The rules on the declaration of interests go beyond the rules on registration of financial interests. MPs are expected to declare relevant indirect interests and non-financial interests where these might be thought by others to influence his or her actions.

The rules on the declaration or registration of interests appear in recent years to have caused few problems. In 2009–10 only 2 per cent of complaints resolved by the PCS were concerned with the registration of interests.[43] A marked rise in complaints in recent years has been caused by concerns on the use by MPs of their expenses.

ENFORCEMENT AND SANCTIONS

Until 2009, with the establishment of the IPSA, enforcement procedures were internal to the House, implemented by the PCS, the Committee on Standards and Privileges, and the House itself. They were in effect disciplinary powers. The 1996 system for enforcing standards of conduct in the House of Commons proved more controversial than either the code or the guide. Perceived problems with the procedures originally established were addressed in 2003.[44] A lack of accessible information and guidance for either MPs or the public as to how the rules and procedures worked was addressed by the PCS by a series of publically available guidance notes. The fallout from the

[41] The CSPL has proposed that MPs should no longer be allowed to use public money to pay family members they wish to employ; above, n. 12, para. 6.

[42] As amended by Electoral Administration Act 2006, s. 59.

[43] See HC 418 (2009–10) para. 3.18; the previous year the figure was 12 per cent, HC 608 (2008–09) para. 3.7.

[44] See HC 403 (2002–03) for details.

expenses crisis has resulted in changes in aspects of the enforcement procedures and the imposition of sanctions but only with respect to expenses.[45]

THE PARLIAMENTARY COMMISSIONER FOR STANDARDS

The PCS was the independent element in the 1996 scheme for regulating standards in the Commons. The Commons has resisted any suggestion to put the PCS on a statutory basis partly because of the risk that this could expose the PCS's activities and decisions to judicial review. Following reforms in 2003 the PCS is appointed for a five-year non-renewable period and can only be dismissed by the House after receipt of a reasoned adverse report from the Standards and Privileges Committee (the Committee). To enable accountability and transparency the PCS makes an annual report to the Commons. The roles of the PSC are to: maintain the four registers of interests;[46] advise MPs on registration requirements; advise the Committee on the interpretation of the code; monitor the operation of the code and make recommendations thereon to the Committee; receive and investigate specific complaints about the conduct of MPs.

In carrying out the first two of these roles the PCS has the assistance of the Registrar who is the first port of call for members who require advice. In this way the PCS avoids conflicts between these roles and his investigatory role. To ensure that MPs are aware of their registration obligations, major briefing sessions are held after a general election or as necessary or as requested by groups of MPs. Evidence, in the form of few complaints to the PCS on breaches of the rules on financial registration, suggests that this approach has been successful.

It was the investigative role of the PCS that caused the greatest controversy in the early days. At present the PCS can only act on receipt a complaint. Provided it is within the terms of reference,[47] the complaint is investigated and a report made to the Committee with a finding of fact and an opinion on whether there has been a breach of the code. The Committee does not have to accept the conclusion of the PCS that the facts as found amount to a breach of the code, but can conduct its own investigation, reach its own conclusion, and issue a report to the House. Should there be a disagreement between the Committee and the PCS, or a dispute as to the facts, or where the consequences of an adverse decision and the subsequent imposition of a substantial penalty could have a detrimental effect on the career of the MP concerned, an investigatory panel can be established to assist in establishing the facts. This facility has never been used. Although the PCS has no independent powers to summon persons or to require the production of papers or records, this does not appear to have caused any problems.

[45] Above, n. 12, and text.

[46] In addition to the Register of Financial Interests there are registers of Members' Staff, Journalists and All Party Groups.

[47] Figures in PCS annual reports show that the majority of complaints fall outside the terms of reference.

Frivolous or vexatious complaints have not been an issue since the PCS issued a guidance note in 2003. A rectification procedure also introduced in 2003 has been successful in dealing with minor or inadvertent failings. In 2005, following the inclusion in the code of a provision on the misuse of allowances, facilities or services, a similar rectification procedure was introduced to cover those who made a reimbursement within a reasonable time.

THE COMMITTEE ON STANDARDS AND PRIVILEGES

The Commons Select Committee on Standards and Privileges oversees the work of the PCS and is at the heart of the self-regulatory process acting as a quasi-judicial body. An issue has been whether the Committee is sufficiently independent and impartial. To address this the Committee, unlike other select committees, has equal numbers of government and opposition members. The CSPL has agreed with a suggestion by the Committee that it should also include two lay members to be recruited through the official public appointments process and who would have full voting rights on the Committee. If this proposal is accepted then it would go towards enhancing the robustness and independence of the disciplinary process in the Commons. The details have still to be agreed and a procedure established to address issues of parliamentary privilege.[48]

The Committee, not the PCS, recommends what punishment, if any, should be imposed on an MP. These range from a reprimand, suspension from the House with loss of salary, loss of salary without suspension, to expulsion and imprisonment.[49] In 2009 it was agreed that a MP who was not standing for re-election and who had been found to have committed a particularly serious breach of the rules on parliamentary expenses, could have part of his resettlement grant withheld. The final decision on sanctions is for the House, which (being made up of politicians who may be influenced by consideration of whether the MP in question is a member of their party and of the political consequences of a decision) is not of course an impartial body. It may decide to reject the Committee's report, or not to accept the recommended punishment. It is questionable whether this final decision by the House can be properly regarded as providing an appeal mechanism for MPs dissatisfied with the Committee's recommendation. The Commons has consistently rejected any suggestion of an appellate tribunal, as it would break the principle of self-regulation.

Between 2007 and 2009 an increasing number of complaints about the misuse of expenses and allowances were investigated under the above procedures.[50] However, the decisions made on some of these complaints, coupled with the publication of details of all expenses claims and information on the rules for such claims, raised wider concerns on how MPs' expenses were set, regulated and enforced. There was

[48] HC 67 (2009–10) paras 3–9.

[49] The threat of imprisonment is more theoretical than real.

[50] See a variety of reports from the Committee on Standards and Privileges.

a feeling that MPs were not being sufficiently called to account for their misbehaviour and that those who had misbehaved were being let off lightly by their peers. This gave rise to support both within and outside Parliament for a new scheme giving the administration and policing of expenses to an independent body – an acceptance that the Commons should no longer be the sole body responsible for deciding on the acceptability of the conduct of its members.

THE INDEPENDENT PARLIAMENTARY STANDARDS AUTHORITY

The PSA 2009 created an independent external regulator, the IPSA. The Act originally provided that IPSA would: draw up, maintain, administer and enforce the expenses scheme for MPs; maintain the register of financial interests and establish a statutory code on financial interests; and appoint a new Commissioner for Parliamentary Investigations to investigate both breaches of the code on financial interests and alleged wrongly or misclaimed expenses. Following a report from the CSPL[51] changes were made to the IPSA and its responsibilities were both reduced, by removing responsibility for the financial register and code and increased by adding responsibility for pay and pensions. Its first task, after the consultation exercise required by the PSA 2009 and in the light of recommendations from the CSPL, was to produce a new scheme for MPs' expenses designed to be fair, workable and transparent. This scheme, to be administered by IPSA staff, was produced in time for the start of the new Parliament in May 2010. Not unexpectedly, given the haste with which this reform was introduced, the new scheme and its administration have had quite extensive teething problems, with both MPs and the IPSA publically voicing claims and counter-claims on how it is working.[52] In March 2011 IPSA published a package of adjustments to the scheme.

Investigations of allegations of breaches of the rules on expenses will be carried out by an independent Compliance Officer (CO) whose powers are more extensive that those of the PSC. For example, the CO can conduct an investigation on his own initiative, as well as at the request of the IPSA, a MP or following a complaint from an individual. Both the IPSA and the MP are required to provide any information requested by the CO who will prepare a provisional finding to which the parties concerned can respond, and in certain circumstances this may be the end of the investigation.[53] If this is not the case then, after considering the responses, the CO will make a statement with his definitive findings. Since the IPSA is a move away from parliamentary self-regulation it was possible to provide an appeal procedure. If the IPSA refuses an MP's expenses claim then an appeal can be made to the CO and from there to First-tier Tribunal. A variety of enforcement powers and sanctions are available: the IPSA can recover overpaid expenses by making deductions from pay; the CO can serve a

[51] Above, n. 11, and text.

[52] A Westminster Hall debate on 16 June 2010 raised many issues about the IPSA, see *Hansard*, HC, cols 137WH–60WH (16 June 2010). The IPSA issued a detailed response on its website.

[53] PSA 2009, s. 9 as amended.

penalty notice for up to £1000 or make a repayment direction which may include the payment of interest; it is a criminal offence to provide false or misleading claims for expenses.[54] MPs may appeal to the Tribunal against sanctions imposed by the CO. The investigatory and enforcement powers of the IPSA are specifically stated in PSA 2009, s. 10A not to affect the disciplinary powers of the Commons, enabling it to impose its own sanctions on a MP who has been dealt with by the CO. The enforcement powers of the IPSA have still to be tested.

Further changes to the IPSA can not be ruled out. Not all of the CSPL recommendations have been implemented, and the IPSA has yet to commence work on salary and pensions. There are concerns as to its actual independence since the approval of its budget is subject to the approval of the Speaker's Committee – an example of a regulator being controlled by the regulated.

THE HOUSE OF LORDS

The House of Lords was slower than the Commons formally to regulate standards of conduct. Like the Commons it was a long-established practice that a member of the House of Lords should not advocate, promote, or oppose any legislation in the House if he was, or had been, acting in connection with it for any fee or reward. If a peer had a direct pecuniary interest in a subject being debated, he could take part in the debate but was expected first to declare the interest. In 1995 reforms following an internal review[55] postponed an investigation by the CSPL. These included an amendment of its rules on the declaration of interests and the establishment of a register of interests, but registration was mandatory only with respect to two of the categories of interest. Guidance on the registration of interests was provided by an official, the Lords' Registrar, and a sub-committee of the Lords Committee on Privileges which investigated any allegations of a failure to register. The requirements were both vague and undemanding and from 1995 until 2000 there were no allegations of failures to register or to declare interests.

In 2001, with some reluctance, the Lords accepted the recommendation from the CSPL[56] that all members of the House of Lords in receipt of a writ of summons and not on leave of absence should be required to register all 'relevant interests' and adopt a code of conduct. The 2002 code of conduct included the seven Nolan Principles,[57] provided rules on the registration and declaration of financial and other interests, and for the enforcement of the rules. It was a 'light touch' approach which appeared to work well with few complaints in the period 2002–06, and as a consequence a planned review of the working of the code was postponed.[58] However, a rising trend in complaints coupled with media stories alleging misconduct by peers persuaded the Lords

[54] PSA 2009, Sched. 4 as amended.

[55] HL 90 (1994–95).

[56] Cm. 4903 (2001); see also the Williams Report, HL 68 (2000–01).

[57] See above, text at n. 21.

[58] See HL 69 (2003–04).

of the need to review its rules and procedures to ensure that they met 'public expectations of clarity, transparency and integrity'. Following a report by the Eames group[59] a new *Code of Conduct and Guide to the Rules* came into force at the start of the 2010 Parliament. In addition, and in response to the allegations of misconduct, an external review of Lords allowances was held by the Senior Salaries Review Body (SSRB)[60] which led to changes in the scheme of financial support for members of the Lords with effect from the start of the new Parliament in 2010.[61]

THE CODE OF CONDUCT AND GUIDE TO THE RULES

One of the main changes in 2010 was to follow the Commons and have a short code setting out the principles of conduct and the main duties of peers, and a more detailed guide explaining in more detail the rules and principles with a particular focus on registering and declaring interests. Many of the changes to the code and the rules found in the guide are in response to events in the period prior to the Eames report. Although there are broad similarities with the Commons' code, such as the requirement to observe the Nolan principles, there are differences which reflect the differences in the two Houses.

The 2010 Code is a significant departure from its predecessor. It seeks to place the rules on conduct within the context of the role of the House in the governance of the country. It also has a more prominent moral dimension, as perhaps might be expected as a consequence of a review chaired by a Lord Spiritual. To encourage peers to make a positive commitment to the values embodied in the code, it provides that they are required to sign a formal undertaking to abide by the code both when being first introduced into the Lords and at the start of each new Parliament. The Eames Report stated that it sought to establish a balance with 'a Code which focuses on general moral principles and duties to which members are required to make active and regular commitment, and on the other hand detailed guidance on the practical implementation of the rules'.[62] There is an expectation that in future the political groups and the House administration will back up the formal undertaking by peers by focusing on standards and not just on political or practical matters. An important aspect of self-regulation in the Lords is the longstanding principle that members should act on their personal honour and reference to this was included in both the 2002 and 2010 codes. The Eames Report endorsed a decision by the Committee of Privileges that this required more than a technical compliance with the code,[63] and this is reflected in rule 7 of the code which requires members 'not only to obey the letter of the rules, but to act in accordance with the spirit of those rules and the sense of the House'. This should also be read in the context of a positive duty to act in the public interest stated to be one of the

[59] Eames Report, HL 171 (2008–09); HL 81 (2009–10).

[60] Cm. 7746 (November 2009).

[61] HL 89 (2009–10); some of the SSRB proposals have yet to be implemented.

[62] Above, n. 59, para. 34.

[63] HL 88-I (2008–09) 12.

overarching principles underlying the code. The code also makes it clearer than its predecessor that the Nolan principles underpin the code as a whole and set the ethical context against which members' conduct will be judged.

Peers, with a few exceptions, are not salaried. Those who attend the House may submit a claim for attendance and a variety of other expenses.[64] One of the justifications for an appointed second chamber is the expertise that can be brought to the House by having members with a wide range of outside interests and careers; something alluded to in the code. These are factors which have greater significance for the regulation of conduct in the Lords than the Commons. An important change of substance in the code and explained in some detail in the guide is an outright ban on parliamentary consultancies, that is the acceptance of payment in return for either parliamentary services or advice on how to lobby Parliament. This change was a response to the allegations that there were 'peers for hire' and the uncertainties and ambiguities in the previous rules as illustrated by recent Committee of Privileges reports.[65] There is no attempt to curtail the outside interests or careers of peers provided that a clear distinction is made between their outside interests and their parliamentary work. A particular source of uncertainty in the previous code was the 'no advocacy rule', which the Eames Report said was hard to enforce since it invited analysis not of actions or facts but of motivation.[66] A new definition, modelled on the Commons' code, provides that a member 'must not seek by parliamentary means to confer exclusive benefit on an outside body or person from which he or she receives payment or reward'.[67] This means that there is no need to show that a payment was made in return for a benefit; it is sufficient that a payment was made. This rule does not prohibit peers from speaking on matters where they have relevant interests, provided those interests are declared and 'caution is exercised'. The code and the rules in the guide together provide details on what interests have to be registered and declared. These do not differ greatly from the previous code but, unlike the rules in the Commons, they are subject to thresholds. The compilation and maintenance of the Register is by the Registrar of Lords' Interests, and the Sub-Committee on Lords' Conduct keeps the code and the guide under review.

COMPLIANCE AND SANCTIONS

The House of Lords has few formal rules or sanctions and is said to thrive on self-discipline, which until recently was the justification for a light touch with respect to the enforcement of the code. Breaches of the code were investigated by a sub-committee of the Committee of Privileges with an appeal to the full Committee and a final decision by the House – a completely internal procedure. Investigations into the misuse of expenses were also conducted internally, by the Clerk of the Parliaments, a

[64] See the House of Lords website for details.

[65] See e.g. above, n. 63.

[66] Above, n. 59, paras 63–64, and see above, n. 63.

[67] Code 8 (c).

senior member of the House Administration. The most significant of the 2010 reforms was the appointment of an independent Commissioner for Standards to investigate alleged breaches of the code, the rules governing members' expenses and their use of parliamentary facilities. Bringing complaints on expenses into the scope of the code enables these rules to be enforced in the context of the underlying principles of the code and gives members whose claims are investigated, significant guarantees of procedural fairness.[68] The procedure for investigating complaints although similar to the Commons has some significant differences.[69] If the Commissioner becomes aware of evidence sufficient to establish a *prima facie* case that the code has been breached then, unlike the PCS, he may start an investigation without a complaint. If, following an investigation into the facts, the Commissioner finds a breach of the code or rules on expenses he will make a report to the sub-committee on Lords' Conduct. The sub-committee reviews this report and where appropriate recommends a disciplinary sanction to the full Committee.[70] Unlike the Commons, there is also the opportunity for a member to appeal directly to the Committee against both the Commissioner's findings and any sanction recommended by the sub-committee. The Committee, having if necessary heard an appeal, reports its conclusions and findings to the House which will take the final decision. The code provides that all stages of an investigation have to be in accordance with the principles of natural justice and fairness. One objection to the imposition of a mandatory register of interests was that the Lords had no real sanction to deal with those found in breach of the rules, other than 'naming and shaming', which the CSPL had accepted was a real and effective sanction. In theory, the Lords has a power to imprison and to fine, but neither has been used for over a hundred years. In 2009 the House accepted, contrary to the advice of the then Attorney General, that it could suspend members for a definite period not longer than the remainder of a current Parliament.[71] The 2010 Constitutional Reform and Governance Bill contained clauses to provide for the resignation, suspension and expulsion of peers, but these clauses were lost in the 'wash-up' at the end of the 2009–10 Parliament.

GOVERNMENT MINISTERS

Ministers, as members of one or other House, are bound by the relevant code of conduct. They are also required to comply with the *Ministerial Code*, the rule book on

[68] It may also enable the Lords to avoid becoming subject to a statutory body such as the IPSA.

[69] The rules also include guidance on procedure, rectification and frivolous complaints; see HL 205 (2007–08).

[70] Now called the Committee for Privileges and Conduct.

[71] But in accordance with the advice given by Lord Mackay, a former Lord Chancellor, HL 87 (2008–09). Two peers found to have breached the code were suspended until the end of the session. In October 2010 a further three peers, found to have wrongly claimed expenses, were suspended; see HL 37, 38, 39 (2009–10).

ministerial conduct which is issued afresh (and revised) by a Prime Minister on taking office.[72] Only in 1992 was the predecessor of this code publicly published, and since 1997 it includes a foreword by the Prime Minister. It was substantially revised, shortened and refocused in 2007 in order to establish a code which was more clearly based around the principles of ministerial conduct and as such would be simpler for ministers to use and simpler for Parliament and the public to judge their conduct.[73] The code includes the Nolan principles and provides guidance on matters such as Ministers and Civil Servants, Ministers and Parliament and Ministers' Private Interests. The executive responsibilities of ministers requires the rules on private interests to be more detailed and demanding than the rules found in Parliament's codes of conduct. The rules are designed to ensure that 'no conflict arises, or could reasonably be perceived to arise between their public duties and their private interests, financial or otherwise'.[74] On taking office ministers are required to provide their permanent secretaries with written details of all interests which might be thought to give rise to a conflict of interest. In 2009 the first annual statement setting out ministers' interests relevant to their ministerial responsibilities was published, a move towards greater transparency.

An important change to the administration and enforcement of the code made in 2006 was the appointment of an Independent Adviser on Ministers' Interest (the Adviser), who has two roles. First, he advises the Prime Minister on revisions to the code, and ministers on how best to avoid conflicts between their private interests and ministerial responsibilities. Secondly, after a request by the Prime Minister, the Adviser will investigate allegations of a breach of any aspect of the code – not just the section on private interests. Despite the Adviser having the second of these roles, the Public Administration Select Committee (PASC) did not regard the post as sufficiently independent and impartial to enable 'fair, defined accountability for ministerial conduct'.[75] The PASC aired several concerns: the absence of a discretion to investigate allegations of misconduct; the method of appointment and lack of job security for the holder of the post; the level of reliance on the Cabinet Office; the absence of any sanction for a breach of the code other than resignation and the lack of public visibility for the post.[76] The government responded that as the Prime Minister had ultimate responsibility to account to Parliament for his decisions and actions in relation to the appointment of ministers, it was right that the Adviser should only conduct an investigation at his request.[77] To date, the Adviser has only had one alleged case of misconduct referred to him, and his report was published in full.

[72] The text of the 2010 code can be found at www.cabinetoffice.gov.uk.

[73] The changes were explained in the green paper, *The Governance of Britain*, Cm. 7170 (2007). The 2010 code is very similar to its predecessor.

[74] Code, s. 7.1. [75] HC 381 (2007–08) para. 34.

[76] Until May 2009 the Adviser had a website.

[77] HC 664 (2007–08).

A continuing concern is the activities of former ministers.[78] The 2010 code prohibits ministers from lobbying government for two years after leaving office, and requires them to seek and abide[79] by advice from the independent Advisory Committee on Business Appointments (ACoBA) about any appointments or employment they wish to take up on leaving office. The ACoBA applies government guidelines on the acceptance of appointments by former ministers, guidelines which in 2009 it suggested were inconsistent with the ministerial code[80] and which the PASC has asserted allowed former ministers to 'use with impunity the contacts they build up as public servants to further a private interest'.[81] This assertion was denied by the government.[82] New guidelines were published in autumn 2010. The only sanction if a former minister does not comply with the ACoBA advice is transparency – it publishes its decisions. This has greatest strength when a former minister remains in Parliament as then political pressure can be brought to bear.

THE AWARD OF HONOURS AND PEERAGES

Concerns about the propriety of award of honours and peerages are not new.[83] The issue for regulating standards of conduct is the appropriateness of peerages and honours being awarded for political service. In 2005 there were two reports which formed the basis of reforms to the awarding of honours and peerages whether for political service are otherwise.[84] Both reports raised the lack of transparency in the system, and the PASC report specifically discussed the potential of using peerages and honours to reward those who were party donors or in some other way provided a service to a political party. The matter came to a head in late 2005 with media allegations concerning the sale of peerages and honours.[85] It was also reported that the House of Lords Appointments Commission (HoLAC) had advised against several party nominated 'working peers' on the ground of impropriety – allegedly for making undeclared 'loans' to a political party. This corresponded with a report from the Electoral Commission that political parties were asking supporters for loans rather than donations, in order to avoid the reporting requirements of the Political Parties Elections and Referendums Act 2000 (PPERA 2000).[86] Subsequent police investigations into breaches of either the Honours (Prevention of Abuses) Act of 1925, which makes it an offence to take money as an 'inducement or reward' for procuring an honour for

[78] See e.g. Channel 4 Dispatches, *Politicians For Hire*, 22 March 2010.

[79] The 2010 code states that ministers *must* abide by the advice, the 2007 code stated that they were *expected* to do so.

[80] 10th Report (2008–09). [81] HC 36-I (2008–09) para. 46. [82] HC 1058 (2008–09) para. 47.

[83] Above, n. 6, and text.

[84] The Phillips Review of the Honours System and the PASC report HC 212 (2003–04); government response Cm. 6479 (2005).

[85] See HC 153 (2007–08) for details.

[86] This was rectified by amendments to PPERA 2000 by the Electoral Administration Act 2006, and the Political Parties and Elections Act 2009.

someone, or the PPERA 2000 concluded with no prosecutions, on the ground that there was not a realistic prospect of a conviction for any offence.

Changes to the system of awarding honours and peerages have been made to encourage greater transparency.[87] It is accepted that donations to a political party or political activity should not be a bar to being honoured, but it should be neither an advantage nor a disadvantage. The HoLSC assesses non-political nominations for a peerage on the grounds of both suitability and propriety, but political nominations solely on grounds of propriety; the suitability of political nominees is for the political parties to ascertain. This led the PASC to conclude that 'the rules for entry to the House of Lords are far too ad hoc'.[88] The controversy over political honours spills over into other areas of constitutional concern: the funding of political parties and the system of appointment to the House of Lords,[89] particularly after the next stage in reform.

SCOTLAND, WALES, AND NORTHERN IRELAND

A study of the regulation of standards of conduct in Scotland, Wales, and Northern Ireland demonstrates how standards of conduct can be regulated by legislation, enforced by the criminal law and supervised by the courts.[90] The lack of an historical context and the experience at Westminster before devolution, allowed certain requirements on standards of conduct and their enforcement to be legislatively imposed from the outset. Unlike the position at Westminster the devolved institutions derive what rights and privileges they have from the devolution legislation.

Each devolved institution was required to: establish and publish a register of members' interests; provide rules on the declaration of interests; and prohibit paid advocacy by members, either directly or through another member. A breach of these rules may be a criminal offence. As at Westminster, there have been changes and reforms, both actual and proposed, to all three standards of conduct regimes. Although there are certain similarities in the procedural and institutional provisions in each of the three institutions, there are also elements that reflect the particular circumstances of each country. All have standards committees[91] to supervise standards of conduct, and all have appointed standards commissioners.

CODES OF CONDUCT, REGISTERS OF MEMBERS' INTERESTS

All three institutions have adopted codes of conduct which, although similar to the Westminster code and based on the Nolan principles, are tailored to their respective

[87] See www.direct.gov.uk/en/Governmentcitizensandrights/UKgovernment/Honoursawardsandmedals/TheUKHonourssystem/index.htm.

[88] HC 153 (2007–08) para. 135. [89] See Chapter 7 above.

[90] See *Whaley* v. *Lord Watson of Invergowrie* 2000 SLT 475.

[91] In Scotland it is the Standards, Procedures and Public Appointments Committee, in Wales the Committee on Standards of Conduct, and in Northern Ireland the Committee on Standards and Privileges.

circumstances or background.[92] For example, in Northern Ireland the code additionally requires members to promote equality of opportunity and good relations, show respect and considerations for others and to work responsibly with each other. An interesting provision in Scotland is the requirement that members should be accessible to constituents and should conscientiously serve and represent their constituents' interests. This provision, which in effect polices the quality of service offered by members, has caused disquiet and the most recent edition of the guide includes explanations of what would be regarded as unreasonable behavior or demands by constituents. Investigations of a breach of this part of the code are undertaken by the Presiding Officer not the Standards Commissioner.

In all three institutions the rules on members' interests require the registration and declaration of various types of financial or remunerated interests, enforced by criminal sanctions. Only in Scotland are these rules found in legislation, the Interests of Members of the Scottish Parliament Act 2006. The categories for registrable financial interests in all three institutions are similar to those at Westminster and have caused few problems. Following developments at Westminster, both Wales and Northern Ireland require registration to include the exact details of the amount earned outside the Parliament/Assembly; in Scotland, remuneration is still permitted to be in 'bands'. The rules on the interests of members' families have been changed in Northern Ireland bringing them closer to the more stringent indirect interest registration requirements introduced in Wales in 2002. The registration rules for the Welsh Assembly are closer to those that apply to members of local authorities than is the case in the other devolved bodies. This can be explained in the context of the executive functions of the Welsh Assembly, which are similar to some of the functions possessed by local authorities, for example with respect to planning appeals. In Wales and Northern Ireland, the Assemblies were required to make provision for the registration and declaration of a range of non-financial interests also enforced by criminal sanctions. The Scottish Parliament decided not to include non-financial interest in its statutory registration scheme, although members may chose to register membership of charities, trade unions, etc. Scotland continues to have the least onerous requirements with respect both to non-financial interests and to the interests of partners and dependent children.

Unlike the position at Westminster it is the Clerk to each of the standards committees, not the Commissioner, who is responsible for compiling the register of members' interests and giving advice to members. The rationale for this is to keep separate the giving of advice and the receipt and initial investigation of complaints.

STANDARDS COMMISSIONERS AND THE INVESTIGATION OF COMPLAINTS

Each devolved institution quite quickly created a standards commissioner to provide an independent element in investigations. The next stage, making this Commissioner

[92] The current codes for Scotland and Northern Ireland are from 2009, for Wales it is 2006, but it is due for review, see SOC (3)-01-11: Paper 1.

a statutory position, caused little controversy. Scotland did so in 2002,[93] Wales in 2009, and Northern Ireland in 2011.[94] In June 2010 the Northern Ireland Assembly agreed to introduce the necessary legislation.[95] The reasons for creating statutory commissioners are similar in all three institutions. These include: strengthening public confidence in the governing of the conduct of members; ensuring the independence of the office and providing powers to call for witnesses and papers backed up by criminal sanctions. There are similarities including guidelines on dismissal and appointment, and reporting requirements. However there are some differences. For example, the investigation of complaints on the initiative of the Commissioner, that is without first receiving a complaint, is possible in Wales and Northern Ireland. The Scottish Commissioner does not have to take directions from Parliament or the relevant committee on how to conduct an investigation, but he has to comply with other types of directions. In contrast, although the Welsh Commissioner must attend before the committee at its request, he is not subject to the direction or control of the committee or Assembly. The position in Northern Ireland is similar to Scotland.

In all cases the Commissioner undertakes an initial investigation similar to that undertaken by the PCS, and passes his report to the committee, which may accept it or conduct its own investigation. The initial decision on sanctions is for the committee. It is for the Parliament/Assembly to decide whether to approve the committee's report and its recommendations. In this way the devolved institutions have an element of self-regulation. In Scotland, as in the Commons and Northern Ireland, the final decision by the Parliament is seen as constituting an appeal by a member dissatisfied with the committee's decision. In Wales, the Presiding Officer can in certain circumstances, set up a panel which includes an independently qualified legal person who is not connected with the Assembly, to hear an appeal before the matter is considered by the Assembly. Wales is unusual as, since 2006, its standards committee has only four members and as such it is not party balanced, although all parties are represented. At present none of the committees has lay members but this, and a reduction in the size of the committee, is one of the options being considered in Northern Ireland.

SANCTIONS

Unlike the Commons, none of the devolved institutions has the power to expel a member. Members may have their rights and privileges withdrawn or may be excluded from the Parliament or Assembly for a period with or without salary. There may be a criminal investigation and prosecution in respect to several types of breaches of the

[93] Scottish Parliamentary Standards Commissioner Act 2002; from April 2011 the Scottish Parliamentary Commissions and Commissioners etc Act 2010 will merge several different commissioners, including the Standards Commissioner, into a new office: the Public Standards Commissioner for Scotland.

[94] National Assembly for Wales Commissioner for Standards Measure 2009.

[95] See Assembly Members (Independent Financial Review and Standards) Act 2011.

codes of conduct, including a failure to attend as a witness or answer questions. To date no prosecutions have been brought for any of the possible offences.[96]

CONCLUSION

The expenses crisis has dominated the discussion of standards of conduct in public life since early in 2009, but this should not be allowed to detract from the fact that there is a now widespread acceptance of the need to have and enforce high ethical standards in public life, something that did not exist before 1995. Significant as the expenses affair has been, there have been other recent developments and plans for reforms which should not be overlooked. Whereas Westminster has increased the number of ethical regulators, Scotland has decided to amalgamate and reduce the number, a change brought about by concerns that a plethora of regulators had resulted in gaps in accountability and legislative ambiguities.[97] Northern Ireland, on the other hand, proposes to appoint a new Commissioner for Standards and discontinue the previous practice of using the ombudsman. In 2008, Scotland introduced a panel of independent advisers to assist the First Minister in guiding him on the application of the ministerial code; there is no equivalent in Northern Ireland, nor any plan to change this situation. Scotland was ahead of Westminster in routinely publishing receipts for MSP expenses in 2006 and, although expenses are internally administered, this has not undermined public confidence in the scheme.[98] Although there have been significant changes to how the ministerial code at Westminster is enforced with greater transparency as regards the approval of outside appointments for former ministers, further reforms are likely to be sought. The standards framework for local government is set to change with a proposal in the 2010 Queen's Speech to abolish Standards for England, the standards board for local authorities. What will replace this will no doubt be considered by the CSPL. The Constitutional Reform and Governance Act 2010 puts the Civil Service Commissioners on a statutory footing and enshrines in statute the core civil service values of integrity, honesty, objectivity, and impartiality, something recommended by the CSPL in 2003.[99] A potentially controversial proposal for reform is to allow MPs who are guilty of 'serious wrongdoing' to be subject to a 'recall' by constituents. Will a decision that there has been serious wrongdoing have first to be taken by the IPSA and/or the Committee on Standards and Privileges? One of the most significant reforms awaited is on lobbying, since there is concern about the assistance both ministers and former ministers can give to lobbyists. The existing approach has been to have rules and guidance on the targets of lobbying such as ministers, while

[96] Andy Kerr MSP was reported by the Commissioner to the Procurator Fiscal who decided on a direct measure, an alternative to prosecution where it is considered to be in the public interest to take action but that prosecution may not be appropriate.

[97] See SAPICe Briefing 10/20, 17 March 2010, and above, n. 93.

[98] CSPL, *Annual Review and Report 2009–10*, para. 14.

[99] Cm. 5775.

allowing lobbyists to be self-regulating. To improve transparency there is now widespread support for the introduction of a statutory register of lobbyists,[100] although this was not included in the 2010 Queen's Speech. The ethical landscape will continue to expand, but as the CSPL remarked in the context of the lobbying proposals 'it remains the case that the ultimate protection... is the determination of public office holders to behave with integrity'.[101]

The CSPL has suggested that 'revelations about the expenses regime in the House of Commons has been the single most damaging issue for public trust in politicians since... (1995)'.[102] What these revelations illustrated was that having a system regulating conduct based on the Nolan principles was not sufficient to prevent abuses. The question is, will the recent reforms will be more successful? For this to be the case there has to be a change in culture and leadership at Westminster from what went before. It is not enough to provide new and detailed rules on expenses independently administered. Somehow, as the CSPL has suggested, the Nolan principles have to become 'embedded into the culture of our public service organizations and translated into personal values, reinforced in everyday behaviour and by systems and processes'.[103] The House of Lords appears to be addressing this by making it clear that the Nolan principles underpin the new code of conduct, and by its willingness (albeit belatedly) to accept the need for better and more effective governance. The Commons, having accepted with alacrity the establishment of the IPSA, now appears to doubt the wisdom of its own creation. To make the IPSA work will require effective leadership in the House and by the political parties, something that will not necessarily be popular with all MPs. It will also require more than a grudging acceptance by MPs that they have had to join other professionals in a move away from self-regulation. A significant move towards helping MPs to accept the new regime will be to develop a dialogue between the IPSA and MPs. This is likely to be achieved by the establishment of a liaison group where problems and their possible solutions can be discussed and trust and understanding can be established. It is important for the credibility of the IPSA that this type of initiative is taken as Constitutional Reform and Governance Act 2010, s. 28 requires it to 'have regard to the principle that members of the House of Commons should be supported in efficiently, cost-effectively and transparently carrying out their Parliamentary functions'.

Although the IPSA only has responsibility for setting and paying MPs' salary and expenses, it appears that it could become a major player in deciding how MPs work and what they do; a quite considerable move away from being a regulator. The creation of the IPSA brought an end to the position whereby expenses became a backdoor way of supplementing pay, but by giving it the additional responsibility for setting salary levels it is recognized that salary and expenses are a package that has to be looked at as a whole. However, as Sir Ian Kennedy, IPSA Chair, has acknowledged, any scheme that the IPSA comes up with can not be divorced from how the Commons works and

[100] HC 36 (2008–09); HC 1058 (2008–09).

[101] Above, n. 98, para. 26.

[102] *Annual Review and Report 2008–09*, para. 50.

[103] Ibid., p. 4.

how MPs spend their time. For example, a consequence of MPs choosing to work idiosyncratic hours is that they require additional expenses for travel and food, and as a result 'ways of working…become directly a matter of value for money'.[104] The big 'exam question' posed by Sir Ian is: 'what does a modern 21st century legislator need from the public purse to do the job s/he was elected to do?'[105] The IPSA intends to consult widely on this question to discover what the electorate wants and what MPs think is right. The answer, he suggests, has implications for expenses and assessing the appropriate level of salary.[106] It will be interesting to see if the IPSA's answer is awarded a 'first' by either the public or MPs.

FURTHER READING

Allington, Nigel F. B. and Peel, Gillian, 'Moats, Duck Houses and Bath Plugs: Members of Parliament, the Expenses Scandal and the Use of Web Sites' (2010) 63 *Parliamentary Affairs* 385–406.

Bradley, A. and Ewing, K., *Constitutional and Administrative Law* (15th edn, 2010) ch. 11.

Gay, O. and Leopold, P. (eds), *Conduct Unbecoming* (2004).

Joint Committee on Parliamentary Privilege Report (1998–99), HL 43/HC 214 (the Nicholls Report).

Leopold, P., 'The application of the civil and criminal law to members of Parliament and parliamentary proceedings', in D. Oliver and G. Drewry (eds), *The Law and Parliament* (1998) ch. V.

Oliver, D., 'Regulating the Conduct of MPs. The British Experience of Combating Corruption', in P. Heywood (ed.), *Political Corruptions* (1997).

Riddell, Peter, 'In Defence of Politicians: In Spite of Themselves' (2010) 63 *Parliamentary Affairs* 545–57.

Ryle, M., 'The law relating to members' conduct', in D. Oliver and G. Drewry (eds), *The Law and Parliament* (1998) ch. VII.

Ten Years After Nolan (2006) 59(3) *Parliamentary Affairs*, special edition.

USEFUL WEBSITES

Advisory Committee on Business Appointments: **http://acoba.independent.gov.uk/about_us.aspx**

Cabinet Office: **www.cabinetoffice.gov.uk**

Committee on Standards in Public Life: **www.public-standards.gov.uk**

Independent Parliamentary Standards Authority: **www.parliamentarystandards.org.uk**

Parliamentary Commissioner for Standards: **www.parliament.uk/mps-lords-and-offices/standards-and-interests/pcfs**

UK Parliament: **www.parliament.uk**

[104] Lecture to the Hansard Society, 22 March 2010.

[105] Lecture to the Institute for Government, 22 July 2010.

[106] Ibid.

INDEX